PSYCHOLOGY: THE SCIENCE OF MENTAL LIFE

PSYCHOLOGY: THE SCIENCE OF MENTAL LIFE

SECOND EDITION

George A. Miller
Robert Buckhout

HARPER & ROW, PUBLISHERS, INC.
New York, Evanston, San Francisco, London

DEDICATED TO OUR CHILDREN

Illustrations by Patrick Korch

PSYCHOLOGY: THE SCIENCE OF MENTAL LIFE, Second Edition

Copyright © 1973 by George A. Miller and Robert Buckhout

Appendix D copyright © 1973 by Harper & Row, Publishers, Inc.

Standard Book Number: 06-044478-9

Library of Congress Catalog Card Number: 72-11494

Contents

Preface

The first edition of *Psychology: The Science of Mental Life*
was dedicated appropriately to Edwin G. Boring. To psychologists who have endured graduate training, the presentation of
the history of psychology through the eyes of this remarkable
man is a familiar and unforgettable experience. The hallmark of
Boring's analysis was the fitting of the events in the history of
psychology into the context of the evolution of western
thought. The edition was aptly described as an attempt to
present basic introductory psychology as it grew in the minds
of some of the great men and women who made its history. By
examining the biographies and the social and cultural contexts
in which these people developed their ideas, we hope to convey
the importance of personal insight to the student. While we
have updated the material and expanded the coverage, the
spirit of the original volume and much of the text remains.

Although the two authors could easily be described as
quite different in any number of ways, we share special feelings
about the psychological profession that influence the coverage
of material. We feel that the modern interest in relevance can
be met by looking to history as well as to the media. Many of
the people we biographed spoke from the depths of their
culture—a trait that is often marked by both excitement and
relevance. We also are convinced that psychology has produced
some findings that will endure beyond tomorrow's headlines.
Finally, we note the political and social nature of the science of
mental life—acknowledging that psychology, like the physical
and biological sciences, is the highly fallible product of human
beings. As such, we encourage in the nonpsychologist the development of critical and skeptical attitudes toward anything
that is said about human behavior. Psychology—more than any
other science—is still evolving very rapidly.

We are grateful to Caryl Sutton for her contributions on
the bibliographic, editorial, and skeptical sides of book writing.
Patrick Korch is a young artist from Palo Alto, California,
whose illustrations resulted from extensive talks and reading in
the area of psychology. I feel that he has done some beautiful
interpretations of the various chapters, contributing the sensitive talents of gifted artist to enhance our discussion of a
science.

We are delighted to be continuing our association with

Harper & Row, who provided us not only with a free hand to do our work, but the able assistance of a very talented team—Sandra Turner, production, Jared Pratt, design, and Judy Kahn, whose copyediting added much to the book's coherence. We are also grateful to George Middendorf, executive editor, who as a friend of ours, brought the two authors together for this project. I felt very privileged to have the chance to collaborate with George Miller. We hope that you enjoy reading a book that we found a great deal of pleasure in writing.

R. B.
Brooklyn College

. . . what a real living human being is made of seems to be less understood today than at any time before, and men—each one of whom represents a unique and valuable experiment on the part of nature—are therefore shot wholesale nowadays. If we were not something more than unique human beings, if each one of us could really be done away with once and for all by a single bullet, story-telling would lose all purpose. But every man is more than just himself; he also represents the unique, the very special and always significant and remarkable point at which the world's phenomena intersect, only once in this way and never again. That is why every man's story is important, eternal, sacred; that is why every man, as long as he lives and fulfills the will of nature, is wondrous, and worthy of every consideration.

. . . Few people nowadays know what man is. Many sense this ignorance and die the more easily because of it, the same way that I will die more easily once I have completed this story.

I do not consider myself less ignorant than most people. I have been and still am a seeker, but I have ceased to question stars and books; I have begun to listen to the teachings my blood whispers to me. My story is not a pleasant one; it is neither sweet nor harmonious, as invented stories are; it has the taste of nonsense and chaos, of madness and dreams—like the lives of all men who stop deceiving themselves.

Each man's life represents a road toward himself, an attempt at such a road, the intimation of a path. No man has ever been entirely and completely himself. Yet each one strives to become that—one in an awkward, the other in a more intelligent way, each as best he can. Each man carries the vestiges of his birth—the slime and eggshells of his primeval past—with him to the end of his days. Some never become human, remaining frog, lizard, ant. Some are human above the waist, fish below. Each represents a gamble on the part of nature in creation of the human. We all share the same origin, our mothers; all of us come in at the same door. But each of us—experiments of the depths—strives toward his own destiny. We can understand one another; but each of us is able to interpret himself to himself alone.

—Hermann Hesse, Abridgement of "Prologue" to Demian. *(Copyright 1925 by S. Fischer Verlag. Copyright © 1965 by Harper & Row, Publishers, Inc. Reprinted by permission of Harper & Row, Publishers, Inc.)*

ONE

Introduction: Of Images and Men

Man is basically evil!
Man is basically good!
Man is predictable!
Man is a free agent!
Homilies such as these seem at first glance to be divisive
and banal oversimplifications, yet they express dichotomies that shape the dialogue of all men, including
behavioral and social scientists. The very brevity of these
expressions suggests that some common process underlies
our search for causes, our search for reasons, our
search for truth. We seldom defend the truth of our views
with lengthy written documents, so the briefer a slogan
is the better we like it. Indeed, these brief expressions
may be abbreviated even further; such symbols as the
mandala, the swastika, or the cross are expressions of
timeless themes in literature, religion, and the arts.

Scientists also value simplicity. The scientific
method aims not only at explanation, but also at parsimony.
When a scientist tries to explain a phenomenon, he is
usually seeking *invariance*, that is, a reduction in the variability of measurement and observation. The manipulation
of one variable should produce predictable sequences of
measureable changes in the other. Science seems complicated only because many simple truths must work together
in scientific models of most natural processes.

The scientist believes in a fundamental underlying
order to the universe. His experiments and theories are
directed toward discovering the laws that govern that order
so that it is possible to understand, predict, and in some
cases, control natural events. Philosophers of science have
tried to formulate rules by which this search should be
conducted. For example, it is customary for scientists to test
their theories against reality; clear counterevidence should
require the revision or total rejection of a theory. In fact,
however, scientists often engage in nonscientific behavior
and hold on to their theories even after they have been
proved inadequate or downright wrong. As we shall point
out, relatively few rules are followed in the game of science.

1

But is psychology a science? On this point you can argue with physicists, biologists, philosophers, poets, romantics, and your intuitive neighbor next door. It takes a certain amount of presumption to claim the exalted title of "science" for something all mankind is a party to. The effort to study the behavior of man according to the rules of science is only a little over a hundred years old, although his nature and condition has been the subject of philosophical exploration and common sense for centuries. The decision to study man scientifically represented an extraordinary act of faith in the principle of determinism that most scientists share. As the late E. G. Boring expressed it,

> Determinism is a paradigm which science has long accepted. Laplace held that if you could know absolutely all about the universe at some instant, then you could causally extrapolate to all its past and all its future. . . . In general, science asserts that causality and thus determinism are essentials of the orderliness of nature.[1]

The adoption of this faith by psychologists was followed by an imitation of the processes and institutional characteristics of the "senior sciences" of physics and chemistry. Surely, the use of the term *psychophysics* by nineteenth-century researchers to describe their studies of sensation and perception was not an accident. The history of psychology is well decorated with models and paradigms from the physical sciences applied to human behavior. Psychology and the senior sciences followed parallel trends toward more sophisticated technology, increasing specialization, and a search for basic elements and causal relations among them—a trend that is sometimes called reductionism.[2]

The publication of such books as Thomas Kuhn's *The Structure of Scientific Revolutions* and J. D. Watson's *The Double Helix* has done much to demystify the process of science.[3] Kuhn presents a dialectical analysis of science as an establishment challenged by revolutionary anomalies in thinking; successful revolutions ultimately replace the old establishment with a new one. The shared language of the members of a scientific establishment is an explanatory paradigm. The paradigm is a set of presuppositions and pragmatic ground rules and beliefs governing the practice of "normal science" which is held by leading figures of the scientific community at a particular time. The paradigm also includes criteria for the selection of admissible problems which can be assumed to have solutions providing that "correct" standards and methods are used. Problems that cannot be accounted for may be regarded as "metaphysical" or the concern of other disciplines.

Kuhn documents the challenges to the prevailing paradigms of physics posed by the discoveries of Lavoisier, Copernicus, Galileo, and Einstein. Revolutions such as these develop when the old paradigm is found to be contradictory to fact or overly complicated with correction factors and vagueness. New thinking about admissible problems or awareness of the need to consider new problems to correct or simplify established theories forces the need for a paradigm shift—a possibility that predictably meets with resistance.

> The invention of other new theories regularly, and appropriately, evokes the same response from some of the specialists on whose area of special competence they impinge. For these men the new theory implies a change in the rules governing the prior practice of normal science. Inevitably, therefore, it reflects upon much scientific work they have already successfully completed. That is why a new theory . . . is seldom or never just an increment to what is already known. Its assimilation requires the reconstruction of prior theory and the re-evaluation of prior fact, an intrinsically revolutionary process that is seldom completed by a single man and never overnight.[4]

The process marking the assimilation of revolutionary ideas is hardly smooth. Innovators have been fired or put on trial. The gatekeepers of the scientific establishment often refuse to admit the new ideas. They may refuse to publish "heresy" in the journals they control or may use their prestige with the lay public to discredit the advocates they disagree with. Scientific consideration of revolutionary ideas may be resisted for years, throughout the lifetime of the revolutionary advocate, so that honors for a theoretical triumph come posthumously—a fact that once caused Max Planck to observe that ". . . a new scientific truth does not triumph by convincing its opponents and making them see the light, but rather because its opponents eventually die, and a new generation grows up that is familiar with it."[5]

Kuhn and others have pointed out that many textbooks present an oversimplified, falsely linear view of the history of scientific advances bespeaking an orderliness that does not exist in fact. Since texts are intended to recruit and impress people with the then prevailing paradigm, the picture they draw is often narrow, orthodox, muted, and, above all, congenial to most of the important people in the given science. Such training tools are not designed to produce people who will discover fresh approaches; they train people who will be able to carry out efficiently the burgeoning chores of normal science. However, in Kuhn's view, this rigidity provides the scientific community with a necessary and sensitive indicator that something has really gone wrong when some anomaly in the paradigm does occur. Some philosophers have claimed that in making this point Kuhn is, in effect, skillfully defending conservatism and the status quo in science.

Compare this picture of science with the irreverant look at the race for the Nobel Prize described by Watson in *The Double Helix*.

Watson and his colleagues come across as brilliant, eccentric dilettantes who shifted out of their scientific specialty to engage in a highly competitive race to be the first to describe the structure of the DNA molecule. This race was marked by distraction, theft of data, a kind of espionage, withholding of data, and interminable gossip and backbiting directed at their colleagues.[6]

But how does this look at the nature of the scientific world affect our original question, "Is psychology a science?" If this closer inspection of "science" has revealed it as a pragmatic and terribly human enterprise, then the nature of the question changes. Psychology certainly looks like a science, but perhaps we should wonder what stage of development it is in. Kuhn writes about a paradigm-sorting process that can be observed in the preparadigm period of a science—a period in which there is a basic disagreement about first principles—and a stage to which the science returns when shaken by a revolutionary paradigm shift. The confusion of the preparadigm period seems to characterize the state of psychology today. There is disagreement over first principles—for example, over the basic nature of man. Psychologists continue to structure their thought on paradigms borrowed from the physical sciences, possessing relatively few of their own. They are afflicted by dichotomies, the most fundamental of which is the conflict between freedom and control (see the Rogers-Skinner debate in Appendix A). Psychology is one of the largest academic disciplines calling itself a science, but it is fragmented into hundreds of subspecialties in both research-oriented and applied fields. The fragments share the professional name, but not the same aims.

The confusion is obvious. Nobody is likely to overlook it. Psychologists certainly do not have to wait for a Nobel Prize winner to leak the contents of his diary in order to notice how characteristically human the science of psychology is. As workers in a science that is not characterized by paradigm consensus, therefore, psychologists must place their faith in one or another of the currently competing views. These views can be classified according to three operating traditions of inquiry: the "hard-nosed" or deterministic position, the "soft" or phenomenological position, and an intermediate position sometimes described as subjective behaviorism.

The hard-nosed tradition has dominated the psychology establishment as it has most other sciences; its followers, by and large, have thought of themselves as determinists. The sweep of this tradition can be traced in western science from Aristotle through Locke's concept of the mind as a tabula rasa on which experience writes to B. F. Skinner's thesis of a rather empty-headed man whose behavior is shaped by his environment. The hard-nosed psychologist will appear in later chapters under such labels as materialist, empiricist, logical positivist, reductionist, behaviorist, Skinnerian.

4

Despite the complexity of some of the theories, they tend to follow a similar basic pattern. A hard-nosed psychologist looks to the environment as the causal agent for behavior, tries to describe the stimuli, questions the extent of the role heredity plays in behavior, rejects supernatural and other unobservable influences on behavior (as his predecessors rejected the soul), seriously questions the role of volition or "free" will in behavior, and is convinced that behavior is orderly, predictable, and ultimately controllable. In its most uncompromising form (rarely found), the hard-nosed image of man is a living machine whose output (behavior, which includes thought) is determined entirely by input (environmental forces). Man does not exercise free will and is therefore not responsible for his actions; that is, the outcome of each apparent exercise of volition has, in fact, already been predetermined by all prior environmental influences, including the individual's prior behavior.

The second tradition is called soft by the hard-nosed psychologists. Since early hard-nosed thinkers in western countries had to battle the ecclesiastical authorities in terms of their faith in God and their control of political institutions, there has been a tendency to identify all critics of the hard-nosed approach as fuzzy thinkers who have not seen the flaws of religious mysticism and so are basically unscientific. The soft thinkers, in turn, tend to characterize the hard-nosed theorists as people who produce mechanistic models which diminish man; models which, though "convenient fictions," have tended to become ends in themselves. In the nineteenth century the soft theorists were the *phenomenologists* who believed in the description of immediate experience with as little scientific bias as possible. They appear in later chapters as gestalt psychologists, nativists, structuralists, wholists, mentalists, personality theorists, existentialists, and humanistic psychologists.

Soft theorists are a more diverse group, but they certainly are scientists in the sense that they search for causes and explanations. For them, however, the search must cover not only the environment, but man himself—his history, his genetic heritage, his subjective experience, his volition (for some), and numerous other unobservables. By questioning the basic assumption of determinism, the soft theorist questions the traditional limits of science, raising the possibility that man may be something more than the sum of his observable parts. Although their images of man differ, most soft thinkers believe that man is free or capable of intentional action—he is responsible for what he does. To the extent that man is self-determined, he is always in the state of *becoming*, as the humanistic psychologists argue.

Subjective behaviorists, attempting to build on the past record of genuine but hard-nosed accomplishments, have tried to upgrade and make more definitive the early models of behaviorism. In any number of highly polarized disputes, the subjective behaviorists have taken the middle ground as interactionists, believers to some extent still in an image of man as rational and somewhat predictable. For example, in the old question of inherited versus environmental causes of behavior, a subjective behaviorist might defend the role of both nature and nurture, speaking tolerantly of the contribution from both sides. This intermediate position, just a little soft, is rejected by proponents of both the hard and soft extremes. Subjective behaviorists, who we believe to represent the largest paradigm group in psychology, are dismissed by the dean of hard-nosed psychologists, B. F. Skinner, as muddled mentalists, dissipating their polished hard-nosed skills in a futile search for internal constructs in the mind or self, constructs that are unobservable and probably do not exist anyway. The soft theorists see the subjective behaviorists as pitiful remnants of the old behaviorist tradition trying to save a sinking ship as they cling to the perquisites of power with an historic but false view of the nature of man.

This classification is, of course, an oversimplification. Many psychologists overlap these descriptions or experience changes in faith throughout their careers. Some observers would argue for still a fourth category to include those who have an image of man as a seething vessel of inherited instincts—love (eros), death-wish (thanatos), aggression—which is modulated only by the effects of learning and civilization. With certain exceptions, we would place most of these thinkers, including Freudians, in the camp of the subjective behaviorists at the present time.

To the extent that these categories are valid, they are useful for spotting the different basic assumptions and paradigms underlying our several images of what man is. Each has its own schools, journals, heroes, and even its own establishment. Any student of the social sciences will find himself pulled between the three traditions and will ultimately have to choose for himself where he stands.

Critics from outside of the social sciences frequently pick the hard-nosed school as their favorite straw man to attack. An example can be found in the writing of Arthur Koestler, a skilled polemicist whose attacks on behaviorism have caused many a psychologist to wince.

> [Psychology] lives on specious analogies derived from the bar-pressing activities of rats. . . . The record of fifty years of ratomorphic psychology is comparable in its sterile pendantry to that of scholasticism in its period of decline, when it had fallen to counting angels on pinheads. . . .[7]

Rats are a part of research in psychology, but not a dominant part. Rat research was probably overemphasized in the laboratory because of a belief that psychological laws discovered at one level of the phylogenetic scale could be generalized to higher levels. Many psychologists now recognize that rat learning has limited relevance to human learning, but research on species closer on the phylogenetic scale, such as the chimpanzee, can add to what we know about similar learning processes in humans—with the added advantage of permitting research that would be impossible or unethical with human subjects.[8] Indeed, Koestler's target has become rather small in recent years as the most extreme forms of hard-nosed behaviorism attract fewer adherents, while membership in the soft and subjective-behaviorist traditions has been on the increase. Still, the three traditions coexist as paradigms to the amazement of many observers who wonder whether psychology will ever settle into some agreement over which image of man is the *true* one.

But there is the problem—truth!

The three traditions can be thought of as three myths—three convenient fictions—which enable thinking and useful research to go on, even though an ultimate answer may never be possible. Discovery of *the* objective, true picture of the nature of man is not possible as long as men can change and the observer of man is man himself, for men create themselves in the images men hold of man.

Even physicists have had to face this dilemma since the great revolution of Einstein's relativity theory. The impact of this theory—which is still to be realized fully—demolished the old comfortable picture of an observer witnessing a true reality, in spite of the fact that such a picture works remarkably well in ordinary life on earth. Our view of the skyline of the city of New York is reasonably stable here on earth, because we can assume a fixed position relative to an object which appears not to move. (Of course, its molecular elements are in constant motion.) Bertrand Russell has expressed the convenient concept of space.

> The idea of place is due to the fortunate immobility of most of the large objects on the earth's surface . . . everything in the heavens is moving relatively to everything else. When you travel from place to place on earth, you say the train moves and not the stations . . . but in astronomy it is arbitrary which you call the train and which you call the station: the question is to be decided purely by the *convenience* [italics added] and as a matter of convention.[9]

It would be impossible to review relativity theory here, but concepts in common use in the natural sciences, such as time, force, atoms, and particles, turn out to be the useful inventions of observers, mere theories, which help to explain nature, but which cannot be proven to exist as a fact of nature in any generic sense.

The closer we get to the elementary building blocks of nature, the more the very process of observation causes major disturbances in the things we observe. We can no longer talk about "particles" without including the process of observation. The question of whether a thermometer measures the temperature of the water or the temperature of the water *plus* the thermometer illustrates what has come to be called the uncertainty principle. In atomic physics a naïve belief in determinism is confounded by the case in which one tries to know all the facts possible about a particle in order to predict its path, velocity, and location. It is impossible to observe both the position and the velocity of a particle simultaneously with unlimited precision. There is a fundamental uncertainty in our most precise observations, an uncertainty that leaves determinism itself a convenient but fictional concept.

Werner Heisenberg sums up the impact of the revolutions in twentieth-century physics in the following way.

> The new situation becomes most obvious to us in science, in which it turns out . . . that we can no longer view "in themselves" the building blocks of matter which were originally thought of as the last objective reality; that they refuse to be fixed in any way in space and time; and that basically we can only make our knowledge of these particles the object of science. The aim of research is thus no longer knowledge of the atoms and their motion "in themselves" separated from our experimental questioning; rather, right from the beginning, we stand in the center of the confrontation between nature and man, of which science, of course, is only a part. The familiar classification of the world into subject and object, inner and outer world, body and soul, somehow no longer quite applies, and indeed leads to difficulties. In science, also, the object of research is no longer nature in itself but nature exposed to man's questioning, and to this extent man here also meets himself.[10]

The impact of these developments is that convenient theories (such as Newtonian mechanics) continue to be used for the problems that they solve (for example, missile firings), but they coexist with other paradigms (such as quantum mechanics). Fortunately, this confusion with respect to ultimate "true" answers is not too bothersome to our ever-pragmatic scientist.[11]

Instead of being disturbed by a wealth of paradigms about the nature of man, in these early stages of the development of psychology we should perhaps welcome the "confusion" and encourage more alternate theories, in search of the myth that seems not only the best predictor, but the one that is most agreeable to man who must make a choice. A model of man expresses an ideal, a belief, or a hope that motivates men, including psychologists, to do what they do. The limits of science, expressed in some psychological version of the uncertainty principle, may turn out to be the most certain thing we can know about the nature of man.

NOTES

1. E. G. Boring, "Cognitive Dissonance; Its Use in Science," *Science* 145 (1964): 680–685.

2. Reductionism is more likely to be used pejoratively in light of attacks by wholistic scientists and other critics.

3. T. S. Kuhn, *The Structure of Scientific Revolutions* (Chicago: University of Chicago Press, 1962); J. D. Watson, *The Double Helix* (New York: Atheneum, 1968).

4. Kuhn, *The Structure of Scientific Revolutions.*

5. M. Planck, *Scientific Autobiography and Other Papers* (New York: Philosophical Library, 1949), p. 33. Kuhn goes on to point out that it is unrealistic to expect a scientist to admit publicly that he was wrong (anymore than we would expect any president of the U.S. to admit that he had made a mistake on Vietnam).

6. The wheel of progress moves on—the brilliant work of Watson and his colleagues is enshrined in some basic biology texts as the Watson-Crick *Dogma*, the root paradigm for the molecular biology establishment.

7. A. Koestler, *The Ghost in the Machine* (New York: Macmillan, 1967), quoted by D. Krech, "Assault on the Citadel" (Review of A. Koestler, *The Ghost in the Machine*), *Science* 160 (1968): 649–650.

8. R. B. Lockard, "Reflections on the Rise and Fall of Comparative Psychology," *American Psychologist* 26, no. 2 (1971): 168–179.

9. B. Russell, *The ABC of Relativity* (New York: Harper, 1925).

10. W. Heisenberg, "The Representation of Nature in Contemporary Physics," in *Symbolism in Religion and Literature*, ed. R. May (New York: Braziller, 1960), pp. 215–232.

11. F. S. Kessel, "The Philosophy of Science as Proclaimed and Science as Practiced: Identity or Dualism," *American Psychologist* 24, no. 11 (1969): 999–1005.

TWO

Psychology, Science, and Man

Several years ago a professor who teaches psychology at a large university had to ask his assistant, a young man of great intelligence but little experience, to take over the introductory psychology course for a short time. The assistant was challenged by the opportunity and planned an ambitious series of lectures. But he made a mistake. He decided to open with a short definition of his subject. When the professor got back to his classroom two weeks later, he found his conscientious assistant still struggling to define psychology.

An alternative approach is to assume at the outset that everybody knows, more or less, what psychology is all about. "Psychology," said William James in the first sentence of his classic text, "is the science of mental life." Although this definition no longer means what it did when James wrote *The Principles of Psychology* in 1890, it is relatively familiar and mercifully short. We can use it to launch our discussion of psychology without prolonged introductions.

Psychology is the science of mental life. The key words here are *science* and *mental*.

Our conception of what a science of mental life should be has changed considerably since James's time. In 1890 mental life seemed to be a well-defined thing. No one doubted that a mind was there waiting for scientists to study it. But today, after decades of trying to study it scientifically, we are less certain. No longer is it self-evident what a psychologist means when he says that he studies mental life. The modern mind seems to be concealed from view, a mental iceberg floating nine-tenths hidden in a vague, unconscious sea; even its owner can do little more than guess which way it will drift next. At the time James wrote, scientific psychology was very young and the mental life that psychologists had been able to study was largely limited to the *conscious* mental life of *sane, well-educated, adult, western European, human* beings. Today, every one of the restrictions implied by those adjectives has been removed. As the science of mental life developed, its base broadened to

include children, animals, preliterate peoples, the mentally retarded, the insane. It is not obvious that all these newcomers share anything we could call a mental life, in the sense understood during the nineteenth century.

At the time James wrote, his claim that psychology was a science was little more than an expression of hope and enthusiasm. In 1890 scientific psychology was still a possible future development. A few men had begun to ask what they might do to make this branch of philosophy more empirical in its methods and conceptions. A few small laboratories had been founded, a few methods of measurement had been adopted, a few preliminary results had been reported. Whipped together with physiology, philosophy, and great common sense in the delightful Jamesian prose, the result was engaging and full of promise, but still a good deal less than a true science of the mind.

Scientific methods, however, are notoriously successful. Since James wrote his *Principles* there has been a remarkable growth in both the quantity and the quality of scientific research on psychological problems. Today when we say that psychology is a science we support the claim with several impressive accomplishments. Indeed, the rapid development of this young science has disrupted the daily pattern of our lives in scores of ways.

Scientific accomplishments usually affect us on at least two levels. On the one hand, scientific knowledge provides a foundation for technological advances, for the solution of practical problems that arise in the daily affairs of ordinary people. In this aspect, science is something that we exploit, just as we would exploit a natural resource. Many people think that this is all there is to science; they are confused by distinctions between scientists and engineers, between science and technology. But in its essence, science is something more than a useful art. Science has understanding, as well as control, as one of its aims. Thus science affects us at a deeper level by changing the way we understand the world we live in. Scientific advances mold our vision of reality, our fundamental and often unspoken set of assumptions about how the world *really* runs and what people are *really* like. Such effects of science are less tangible than the technological ones, but it is perilous to assume they are less important. Like all sciences, psychology has influenced our lives on both levels. It has given us technical tricks and it has changed our conception of human nature.

When new fields of scientific activity first take form they begin, almost necessarily, with things and ideas that are part of the common experience of all men. During this early period of growth the science is widely intelligible, and the discoveries it makes can be understood, argued, resisted, supported, or ridiculed by millions of people. At a later stage the science may become more precise, may achieve deeper insight or soar to greater heights of intellectual virtuosity, but it will never again have quite the same impact on the average man's view of himself and the world around him. At this later stage the science may be supported for the technical miracles it mysteriously provides, but it is no longer a living reality to more than a handful of specialists. As its technological impact on society tends to increase, its impact on the common understanding often fades into the background.

Psychology is still passing through its initial stage. It is still intelligible to most people. It is not unusual to hear a layman say, "I'm something of a psychologist myself, and I think . . ." What he thinks is often subtle and interesting and would not embarrass a more professional practitioner. In order to stay alive among our fellow men, we must all be psychologists. Of course, survival requires us to be mathematicians, physicists, chemists, and biologists, too, but there the distance has grown too great; no layman claims brotherhood without a prolonged initiation ritual conducted at some accredited university. It was not always so. There was a time when Everyman was a physicist, when Shakespeare would interrupt a play to argue against the heliocentric theory of the universe, just as a modern playwright may digress to illustrate or to oppose some new psychological theory today. It is in this initial stage of development that a science is most visible, most controversial, and most likely to change our vision of reality.

In spite of psychology's youth, however, the little knowledge it has painfully gained has fed a thousand different human needs. In some quarters demand has so far outrun supply that many psychologists fear their science has been oversold to an overwilling public. Yet even when we try to be conservative in our appraisal, it is plain that the new psychotechnology has already changed the way we live.

Consider our public schools. Everyone in the United States has felt the influence of modern psychology through its effects on our educational system. Indeed, there was a time when our schools seemed little more than a vast laboratory to test the psychological theories of John Dewey. Today, the schools appear to be a laboratory to test the practical behavioral control notions of B. F. Skinner as schools rush to try out teaching machines and "programed teachers" who administer reinforcements (rewards) in accordance with schedules not unlike those developed for use in training animals in the Skinner Box.[1] The recent fascination with behavioral control has led to the ill-advised use of drugs to improve the "focus" of elementary school children on their studies. Most potentially promising is the research being conducted on computer-assisted instruction with its focus on the individualization of instruction and assessment of student performance.[2]

The modern teacher has tried to use psychology—he has thumbed many a textbook ragged in search of the psychological principles underlying good teaching. Frequently the answer he seeks is not to be found, and the educator's pressing responsibilities to the young force him to extrapolate far beyond the established facts of scientific psychology; he hopes his guesses will be more intelligent if he tries to use psychology. Psychologists have tried to find answers for him. They have carefully explored a variety of conditions that affect how quickly a child can learn. They have painstakingly charted the stages of mental and social development. They have developed better techniques for measuring the progress of the child and the effectiveness of the teaching. They have provided counseling and guidance services outside the classroom. Yet all this is far too little, for the teacher's needs are great and vitally important.

One of the largest areas of psychotechnology is the mental testing business. It has been estimated that in 1969 over 250 million standardized tests of ability were given to our school children.

Mental tests, like the airplane, are part of our heritage from World War I. Before that time the tests were given individually to school children, and they tested nothing but intelligence. During the war, however, psychologists in the U.S. Army developed a pencil-and-paper test of adult intelligence that could be given to thousands of draftees—the famous Army Alpha Test—and so the large-scale testing procedures became firmly established in the public's consciousness. After that the testers began to branch out. They began to test aptitudes, to classify interests, to evaluate achievements. Now they can pigeonhole your personality and assess your emotional stability, masculinity, imagination, executive potential, chances of marital bliss, conformity to an employer's stereotype, or ability to operate a turret lathe. Whatever you plan to do, there seems to be a psychological test you should take first. Citizens who resent the many hours spent answering pointless questions are apparently in the minority, since enterprising newspapers and magazines have found that they can boost sales by providing daily or weekly questionnaires for their readers to answer. The flood of tests that has poured out across the nation has included many frauds—tests that are poorly conceived, confusingly phrased, completely unstandardized, and never validated. Psychologists have maintained reasonable professional standards among themselves, but it is not always easy to restrain the amateurs—it is as if everyone who bought a knife became a surgeon.

The uncritical acceptance of ability, personality, and intelligence testing has led to some profound social changes in which the actuality of a meritocracy can be seen everywhere. (Meritocracy is a term used to describe societies in which the greatest power goes to the cleverest people. Those who argue in favor of meritocracy usually assume that progress is our most important problem—too important to be left to any but the most intelligent men.) From the time of his entry into the school system, an American student is tested in comparative, competitive exams to determine whether he is qualified to pass on to the next level. In what seems like a satire based on self-fulfilling prophecies, Holtzman describes an all-too-familiar scenario.

> The rapid growth of higher education and the greatly increased number of students per course have forced more and more instructors to employ multiple-choice objective examinations for grading students. . . . [t]he relevance of scholastic aptitude tests for prediction of academic grades has increased rather than decreased. . . .

> Tests that are designed for normative use . . . discriminate against those who are culturally different from the majority.[3]

Attacks on the mental testing business were one small part of the social turmoil of the 1960s. Although the form of the attacks reached antiintellectual depths, they were justified in substance by psychologists' failure to assess the social consequences of their inventions.[4] One of the best reasoned attacks on testing can be found in Alan Westin's book, *Privacy and Freedom.*[5] Westin, a lawyer, demonstrates how an efficient testing technology creates the danger of an invasion of the privacy of the individual. He documents the misuse of polygraph (so-called "lie-detector") tests in police interrogations and in government agencies, the abuse of personality tests to enforce a conformity to company norms of behavior "adjustment," and the implicit danger to individuals rising from the growth of computerized data banks. In light of the serious danger presented by this technology, we envision a race between concerned psychologists trying to develop ethical standards for the use of potentially valuable tests and concerned legislators who may settle the issue by banning testing altogether.

In the area of intelligence testing, this controversy has become a full-fledged battle, partially as a result of the writing of Arthur Jensen, who equates the known poorer performance of blacks on intelligence tests to the hypothesis of innate genetic inferiority of certain races.[6] We shall examine this issue in more detail in Chapters 10 and 11.

Other areas of psychotechnology were also stimulated by the military. Once the Army saw how useful psychologists could be in the assessment of men, it began to discover other problems of a similar nature. Soon the psychologist became a familiar member of the military team. For example, during World War II much highly technical military equipment was developed that had never existed before. In the developmental stages it often seemed that no one less gifted than Superman would be able to operate the equipment. The task of making the equipment fit the man was tackled by psychologists, who were able to contribute their knowledge of what a human eye could see or a human ear could hear, how far and how fast a human hand could move, how much interference and distraction a human mind could overcome. A new profession called "human engineering" emerged from this work. Psychologists can help to design trainers and simulators, to plan training programs, to select men who are likely to succeed in each type of job. Moreover, in addition to man–machine problems, the military services have a vast range of psychological problems in the area known as mental health, where psychologists work together with psychiatrists to maintain morale and to heal the mentally wounded. A military branch is a small society unto itself—each application of psychology in our larger society has its parallel in this more limited world of warriors.

Psychologists have been involved in the manned space program since its inception, helping to select and train the astronauts and designing the ground-based simulators and training devices which necessarily abstracted the harsh environmental conditions of space. Psychologists with backgrounds in human engineering are now turning to problems of environmental and city planning, functional design of working environments, mass transit, school design, and other areas of general social concern.

One large and active sector of psychotechnology goes under the trade name of industrial psychology. Many of industry's concerns are similar to the Army's—how to select men who will be successful at different types of jobs, how to train workers to do their jobs better. Industrial psychologists have worked on the problem of fatigue: how should intervals of rest and work be alternated to give the greatest output with the least fatigue for the worker? The discovery that an employer often got less for his money from a laborer who worked a ten-hour day than from the one who worked an eight-hour day helped to change management's attitude toward many of labor's demands. Questions of fatigue lead quickly into questions of morale; industrial psychologists have worried mightily over this important factor. And morale, in turn, leads into questions of emotional adjustment. Clinical psychologists and psychiatrists have found their niche in the industrial scene, with a consequent reduction, so it is claimed, in illness, absenteeism, and accidents. Even the executives have succumbed to the psychologist's charms, and many a firm's management has been overhauled on the recommendation of a psychological consultant. There are people who feel that if the traditionally hard-headed American businessman is enough convinced of the usefulness of psychology to spend his own dollars on it, then there must be something to it after all!

A possible reason why some businessmen are willing to tolerate a psychologist underfoot is that they may have made a good profit by following his advice about advertising and selling the company's product. The psychologist has been keenly interested in techniques of persuasion, and his discoveries have colored our advertising, propaganda, politics, and entertainment as these are distributed broadside through our mass media of communication. And by probing around in the consumer's unconscious, a psychologist may turn up some useful information for the advertising agency. Just how far one can go in shaping the public mind with a television screen is debatable. But it is apparent that there are both good and bad ways to advertise; psychologists can often help distinguish between them in advance.

Business is not the only place where careful attention is paid to surveys of public opinion. Government agencies have used polls for years to guide our public policies; politicians are particularly sensitive to fluctuations in their popularity with the voters. And feedback from the grass roots is just one of several ways that social psychology is involved in the processes of government. For example, in 1954 psychological evidence was used in the United States Supreme Court decisions against racial segregation in the public schools, where it was held that separate but equal facilities for both races were impossible because the psychological consequences of segregation were too great a handicap for the minority group. The Court's decision rested as much on a point of psychology as on a point of law.

This recital could be extended for several pages. Psychological dogma influences the way we discipline our children, manage our businesses, and run our marriages. Studies of abnormal behavior modify our conception and treatment of mental illness, incompetence, perversion, criminality, and delinquency. The priest and the rabbi agree in their use of psychological techniques to guide their flocks to salvation. Novels, plays, and movies now feature psychological themes as one of their standard formulas. Psychological drugs have already changed the situation in our mental hospitals, and more are yet to come. Wherever people are involved, psychology can be useful—and that is almost everywhere. Whether we like it or not, the practical application of psychology to our daily affairs is already in an advanced stage.

It must be admitted, however, that not every application of psychology is firmly grounded in scientific evidence. Those who apply psychology to the dynamic processes of an evolving society often jump to conclusions that make their laboratory colleagues tremble and turn pale. But when decisions must be made here and now, they must be made in the light of the evidence at hand, no matter how fragmentary and inconclusive that may be. In the past the same decisions had to be made with even less help; today the man who must take the responsibility can at least console himself that he tried to be intelligent, that his guess was informed by whatever evidence existed. The sun will not stand still while he discovers and verifies every fact he needs to know. He works by guess and hunch and intuitive feel, searching always for what will work, for what will meet the present needs. By a shrewd mixture of intelligence, science, and salesmanship, the applied psychologists have given us better answers to hundreds of practical questions. And they will improve those answers just as fast as our growth in basic, scientific psychology permits.

But, if those are some of the practical consequences of scientific psychology, what are some of the impractical ones? What subtler influences has psychology had upon our contemporary attitudes toward life and the universe? Those subtler effects are not easily converted into 8 percent investments, yet there is a sense in which they are more deeply significant than any merely technological advances.

Scientific psychology educates public psychology. It informs and enriches the picture of man that we all share and that guides so much of our daily conduct. It modifies the public image that is taken for granted in our literature, in our schools, in our theatres, in art and music, in religion and government. It has been said that if human nature ever changes, it is because we learn to see ourselves in a new way. Our feeling for right and wrong, our sense of what is comic and what is tragic, our judgment of what will perish and what will survive are shaped and reshaped by our silently assumed psychology.

Consider, for example, the shadow that our implicit psychology casts on our conception of power, of how human behavior is controlled, of how man is governed. In every age the standards by which laws are written and enforced, goals are set, promises are kept or broken, actions are judged, and rewards are given derive from a loose consensus about human nature, about the gap between what is humanly desirable and what is humanly possible. Change man's image of himself and you send a jar reverberating through the foundations of his society. Those who sit in positions of power are particularly sensitive to tremors in the structure that supports them. They will not let man move from the center of the universe or evolve from a monkey without protest. And their protest can be passionate and merciless.

The extent to which the political system of a country can affect the kind of psychology carried on there is eloquent testimony to the investment that our rulers have in our public image of human nature. Psychologists in the United States during World War II were appalled to see their colleagues in Germany twist psychology to support the Nazi's fantastic claims of racial superiority. The history of Russian psychology also illustrates this danger. The leaders of the revolution were slow at first to recognize the importance of psychology; but by 1923 it was clear that Russian psychology, if it wanted to survive, would have to base its theories on materialistic philosophy. For a brief period, therefore, the official image of Soviet man was that of a physiological robot. When a government decides to impose its preconceived views, science, which is never easy, can become virtually impossible.

Our concern here, however, is not with direct interactions between psychology and government, but with the indirect influence psychology can exert by modifying slowly the opinions that every man holds of himself and his neighbors. What are these influences? A citizen should find it in his own interest to learn which way he is being pushed. Where does scientific psychology seem to lead? What image of man is the psychologist trying to promote? Unfortunately—or, perhaps, fortunately—no simple answer will suffice, for there are many psychologists and many different images.

There is a general scientific ethos shared by most psychologists.

They expect to base their image of man on empirical knowledge, not upon political dogma or traditional opinion or divine revelation or esthetic appeal. Once this much is said, however, it is difficult to continue until we know which psychologist we are talking about. There are many ways to be scientific, there are many different psychological problems to be studied, and there are innumerable ways to fit our scraps of evidence together into an image of man. It is not easy to see just which part of this complicated enterprise we should take hold of first.

One approach to scientific psychology is through its history; we can go back to the nineteenth century and try to recapture some of the enthusiasm and confidence with which scientific methods were first applied to the human mind. Everyone recognizes, of course, that the analytical methods of science can work miracles when applied to non-living systems. With living systems, however, scientific successes have been more modest. And with man, the most complicated of all living systems, it was not immediately obvious to everyone that the methods could be applied at all.

The modern psychologist's faith that scientific methods can be applied to the mental life of human beings is inherited from the nineteenth century, a time when science looked bigger than the universe itself.

NOTES

1. The "Skinner Box," described in more detail in Chapter 16, is the programed animal environment in which rewards are presented to an animal when he emits behavior which the program deems satisfactory.
2. W. H. Holtzman, "The Changing World of Mental Measurement and Its Social Significance," *American Psychologist* 26, no. 6 (1971): 546–553.
3. Ibid., p 553.
4. G. A. Miller, "Assessment of Psychotechnology," *American Psychologist* 25, no. 11 (1970): 991–1001.
5. A. Westin, *Privacy and Freedom* (New York: Atheneum, 1967).
6. A. Jensen, "How Much Can We Boost IQ and Scholastic Achievement?" *Harvard Educational Review* 39, no. 1 (1969): 1–123.

THREE
Wilhelm Wundt, Psychologist

EMPIRICISM AND THE DEVELOPMENT OF SCIENTIFIC PSYCHOLOGY

Psychology became an experimental science during the closing decades of the nineteenth century, at a time when European thought was dominated by *positivism*. In its narrowest sense positivism was the philosophy of Auguste Comte, who invented the term as a name for his ambitious work, *The Positive Philosophy*. Comte's aim was to provide a systematic survey of all knowledge. In order to cope with so large an enterprise, he had to limit himself strictly to facts whose truth was unquestionable, whose validity was insured by the recognized methods of science. Some men would have regretted this limitation, but Comte considered it one of the great merits of his work. It was acceptance of these limitations to which he gave the name, positivism. Once invented, however, the term came to be used rather loosely to describe any discussion of human beings phrased in the language of natural science. That is the broader sense intended here.

Positivism is positive in a polemical sense, meaning that it is not metaphysical. Any speculation about transcendental powers, hidden essences, or ultimate causes is dismissed as sophistry and illusion. The worst insult a positivist can give is to call someone a metaphysician. A positive philosophy accepts as real only those things that can be known. Everything that is mere conjecture, unsupportable by argument or observation, must be rejected. Philosophy must be based squarely on knowledge. A theory that cannot be tested by an appeal to facts is mere humbug. In particular, if nothing recommends a hypothesis except the satisfaction and comfort it can provide, commit it to the flames! This attitude inevitably gives offense to those who cherish their religious beliefs.

The men who tried to maintain this hardheaded, no-nonsense philosophy in every situation discovered that certain other philosophical ideas were particularly appealing. On the one hand, the positivists were powerfully attracted to the *empiricists*, who believed that the only source of true knowledge about the universe is sensory experience—what can

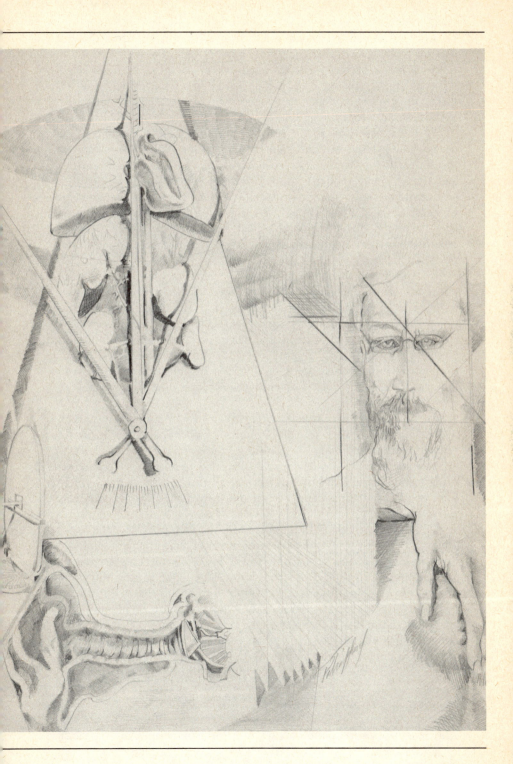

be seen, heard, felt, tasted, or smelled, or what can be inferred about the relations between, or invariances among, such sensory facts. Thus, when a positivist said that he based his philosophy on knowledge, what he usually meant was that he based it on the evidence of his senses, the kind of evidence that had proved so spectacularly successful in the natural sciences.

Positivists also found strong support—sometimes more than they wanted—from the *materialists*, who believed that everything in the universe can be understood in terms of the properties of matter and energy, and reduced to descriptions expressed in centimeters, grams, and seconds. Materialists usually believe that all the phenomena of consciousness will eventually be explained by the laws of physics and chemistry. Thus in psychological arguments they tend to focus attention on the anatomy and physiology—the structure and function—of the brain.

And in still another direction, the positivists, especially Comtean positivists, had a close tie with the *evolutionists*. Comte's theory assumed an evolutionary concept of society, which held that civilization evolves through three stages—the theological, the metaphysical, and the positive. It is not surprising, therefore, that Comte's followers were among the first to support Darwin's theory of biological evolution when it appeared in 1859. They, with Herbert Spencer and Thomas Huxley, grafted Darwin's theory onto the positive philosophy.

Thus positivism found strong allies. Empiricism, materialism, and evolutionism were the philosophical foundations of a scientific revolution that was rapidly changing nineteenth-century man's conception of himself and his world. Because psychology became an experimental science during this period, all three of these great traditions contributed to it, nourished it, and helped to define its problems and its methods.

Of these three traditions, empiricism was probably the most important during the initial development of scientific psychology. Empiricism has played a dual role in the history of psychology, for it provides both a method to increase knowledge and a theory about the growth of the mind. As a method empiricism means that we learn by making observations, by having new experiences, by conducting experiments. As a psychological theory empiricism means that a child's mind at birth is a blank slate upon which experience will write. It is possible, of course, to apply the empirical method without subscribing to an empiricist theory of the mind, but the historical fact is that men who subscribed to one often believed the other as well. If you hold an empiricist theory about the growth of the mind, you are likely to see the empirical method as the only possible way for anyone to acquire knowledge—scientist, philosopher, child, or plain man. An empiricist theory of the mind is particularly useful to support and explain the success of empirical methods in modern science.

Empirical methods are sometimes contrasted with rational methods of acquiring knowledge. In this context, the empirical method is said to be inductive, whereas the rational method is deductive. The empiricist theory, on the other hand, has generally been contrasted with a *nativist* theory of the mind; the empiricist says that a child must learn everything through experience, and the nativist replies that some things are inherited and must be present at birth.

Although it is possible to find clear anticipations of empiricism—it was Aristotle, after all, who coined the famous metaphor of the infant's mind being a blank slate—its greatest thrust was felt in the writings of the seventeenth-century British philosopher John Locke. Locke deeply admired Isaac Newton and tried to develop a philosophy based, like Newton's science, on observable things and events.

In his great *An Essay Concerning Human Understanding* (1690), Locke defended the premise that all ideas originate in experience.

> Let us then suppose the mind to be, as we say, white paper void of all characters, without any ideas:—How comes it to be furnished? Whence comes it by that vast store which the busy and boundless fancy of man has painted on it with an almost endless variety? Whence has it all the *materials* of reason and knowledge? To this I answer, in one word, from EXPERIENCE. In that all our knowledge is founded; and from that it ultimately derives itself. Our observation, employed either about external sensible objects, or about the internal operations of our minds, perceived and reflected on by ourselves, is that which supplies our understandings with all the *materials* of thinking. These two are the fountains of knowledge, from whence all the ideas we have, or can naturally have, do spring.[1]

A newborn infant must acquire his ideas of this world by observing what goes on around him; the limits of his understanding are set by the limits of his senses and his reason.

Locke's argument was immediately successful, and empiricism rapidly became the dominant philosophy of the eighteenth century. Its influence extended into every intellectual nook and cranny; into education, into social, political, and economic theory. Its effect on psychology was only one aspect of this broad and influential movement.

We can summarize briefly the major implications for psychology. First, of course, empiricism places enormous emphasis upon the processes of *sensation*, for the senses are the doors to the mind through which all knowledge of the world must pass. The British—the most loyal adherents to an empiricist position—have always baffled their continental friends by their faith in perception as the cornerstone of all philosophical truth. Second, empiricism usually leads to *analysis into elements*, analysis of conscious experience into the simple ideas that are the basic building blocks of the mind. The simple ideas—blueness, loudness, saltiness, the odor of turpentine—are sensory elements into which the more complicated ideas can eventually be analyzed. Third, empirical analysis into elements creates a need for a corresponding conception of empirical synthesis into compounds—a theory of *association* whereby simple elements can combine to form more complicated elements. As the empiricists developed their doctrine, the importance of associative processes became more and more obvious; there was much debate over rival sets of laws describing how associations are formed. Fourth, empiricism emphasizes the importance of *conscious* processes in knowledge—of perceptions and images—and neglects the possibility that mental processes might not always be immediately apparent to their host. Fifth, it is a theory about the *individual* mind; social implications are not considered. All minds are created free and equal. An individual mind is a private, personal thing, completely independent of all other private, personal minds and free to enter into any contracts or agreements with others that suit its own purposes.

Even in its youth empiricism made easy alliances with materialism. A worthy precursor of positivistic thinking about the human mind was provided by a British physician, David Hartley, who in 1749 explained in his *Observations on Man* how our ideas become associated with one another. It is simply a matter of resonance. According to Hartley, an idea is a vibration in the nerves. By resonance, one vibration sets off another. Thus he explained how one idea can lead to another, and so proposed a material basis for the empiricist theory of the mind.

By the second half of the nineteenth century, of course, physiological theories had advanced well beyond Hartley's mechanical vibrations in the nerves; by then it was clear that chemical and electrical processes were involved. But the general purpose of the endeavor did not change. Materialists are never satisfied that they understand something until they can explain it in terms of the properties of material substances. Their task is to find a materialistic basis for everything, including thought, that takes place in the human body. This was the program for physiology during the nineteenth century, and by 1870 the doctrine that all human acts can be explained by physicochemical principles had completely captured the thinking of physiologists and physicians.

Sensory physiology developed quite rapidly during the nineteenth century. Physiologists who studied the nervous system scored some of their earliest successes with the receptor organs and with the sensory nerves leading from the receptors to the brain. The bulk of this work was done in Germany—G. T. Fechner, Hermann Ludwig von Helmholtz, Ewald Hering were among the leaders—but the work bore an interesting relation to the empiricist philosophy of England. The Germans knew how the receptors worked; the British knew why they were important. Given the positivistic spirit of the times it was inevitable that the two lines of thought should converge. When this happened, psychology became an experimental science.

WUNDT AND THE ESTABLISHMENT OF SCIENTIFIC PSYCHOLOGY

Wilhelm Wundt, the son of a Lutheran pastor, was born in 1832 in Neckarau, a suburb of Mannheim, in the German state of Baden.[2] His childhood was solemn and studious. When he was 8 years old, his schooling became the responsibility of the vicar who was his father's assistant. The boy formed a deep attachment to his mentor and gave to him the affection normally reserved for parents. When the vicar was called to a neighboring town, Wilhelm went with him. There is no record of any other boyhood friends, no foolish pranks or young adventures, no boisterous laughter or silly giggles—only study, reading, work, and more study. As far as one can tell, he was a humorless, indefatigable scholar from the day of his birth.

The Wundts were not a wealthy family, and Wilhelm had to consider how he would support himself. He decided to become a physician, because that profession would enable him to earn a living and to study science simultaneously. At Heidelberg he studied anatomy, physiology, physics, chemistry, and medicine, but slowly discovered that the medical profession was not for him. He had, instead, the luckiest of gifts, a calling, something he loved to do, and he determined to answer it by becoming an academician. The fact that his subject was physiology was accidental, and almost incidental. His real goal was to satisfy a lifelong lust for scholarship. He took his doctorate in medicine at Heidelberg in 1856 and was then habilitated as *Privatdozent* in physiology.

In 1858 Hermann Ludwig von Helmholtz, soon to become the greatest physiologist in the world, moved to Heidelberg. Young Wundt received an appointment as his assistant. But it was dreary work; Wundt was responsible for drilling the sudden influx of new students in their laboratory fundamentals. After a few years of this routine he resigned in order to resume his former position. The years spent in the same laboratory with Helmholtz did not inspire him to novel achievements in physiology. Indeed, it was during this period that he lost interest in pure physiology and began to question the positivistic philosophy. He was finding himself intellectually, deciding his position, and laying out the program of work that would occupy him for the rest of his life. For six decades, long after he had left Heidelberg to become the famous professor at Leipzig, Wundt followed this program with persistence and unremitting energy.

What Wundt did was to look at the psychological problems posed by the British philosophers with the eyes of a man trained in the traditions of German physiology. The notion that psychology could become a science of observation and experiment had been stated clearly and explicitly by the British philosopher John Stuart Mill in his *Logic* as early as 1843, but it required a person who really knew how observation and experiments are made to bring it off. Wundt was that person.

It would be wrong, however, to think of Wundtian psychology as a simple union of British empiricist philosophy and German materialist physiology. Wundt was not willing to reduce the mind to a physical process in the brain, nor was he willing to abandon metaphysics as empty nonsense. Thus, even though positivism had created an intellectual atmosphere in which it seemed reasonable to be scientific about everything, even consciousness, the founder of this new science thought of himself as in revolt against the positivistic spirit of his day. In this respect Wundt anticipated some aspects of the upheaval of the 1890s when a great flood of genius—Weber, Durkheim, Sorel, Pareto, Freud, James, Dewey, Croce, Bergson—broke free at last from the constrictions positivism had placed on social and psychological thought.

The program to which Wundt devoted his life was first published in the introduction to his book, *Contributions to the Theory of Sensory Perception*, in 1862. The body of the book—a summary of the medical psychology of perception—is of little value a century later, but the introduction is interesting. It sets forth three projects that the young physiologist invented: to create an experimental psychology, to create a scientific metaphysics, and to create a social psychology. He then set to work with what may have been the most tireless pen in the whole history of German scholarship. By 1920, some fifty thousand pages later, his projects were complete and he could permit himself to die.

The sheer bulk of his writing made Wundt almost immune to criticism. A critic would be outwritten, evaded by qualifications, and buried under mountains of detail. Wundt's theories were more like classification schemes than like systems of functional relations; they tended to be loosely knit and almost impossible either to prove or to disprove. There was no vital center to his thought where an opponent could slay him with a single blow. "Cut him up like a worm," said William James, "and each fragment crawls." The same quality makes it impossible to summarize his work or reduce it to a simple formula.

For Wundt, psychology involved the analysis of consciousness into elements, the determination of the manner in which these elements are connected, and the determination of the laws of connection. This conception he borrowed from the British empiricists. Just as chemists had analyzed matter into atoms and anatomists had analyzed living systems into cells, psychologists, he decided, must analyze mind into the elementary sensations and feelings that make it up. Wundt once summarized this thesis in a ponderous, German way.

> All the contents of psychical experience are of a composite character. It follows, therefore, that *psychical elements*, or the absolutely simple and irreducible components of psychical phenomena, are the products of analysis and abstraction. . . . As a result of psychical analysis, we find that there are *psychical elements of two kinds*. . . . The elements of the objective contents we call *sensational elements*, or simply *sensations:* such are a tone, or a particular sensation of heat, cold, or light, if in each case we neglect for the moment all the connections of these sensations with others, and also their spatial and temporal relations. The subjective elements, on the other hand, are designed as *affective elements*, or *simple feelings*. . . . The actual contents of psychical experience always consist of various combinations of sensational and affective elements, so that the specific character of a given psychical process depends for the most part, not on the nature of its elements, so much as on the union of these elements into a composite psychical compound.[3]

Since the contents of psychical experience at any given instant are likely to be rather complex, the variety of ways to analyze them into elements, to classify and relate those elements to one another provided material for almost endless subtleties and fine distinctions—a realm in which the patient, scholarly, encyclopedic Wundt was grand master.

Yet his purpose was as straightforward as his arguments were complicated. His first goal was to establish psychology as a science. By 1874, the year he moved to Leipzig as professor of philosophy, the hard-working Wundt was well along toward his goal. That year the first edition of his *Physiological Psychology* was published. In the preface he said, "The work which I here present to the public is an attempt to mark out a new domain of science." This book, which he rewrote and expanded five times, was Wundt's masterpiece. It firmly established psychology as a laboratory science with its own problems and its own experimental methods. This scientific version became known as "the new psychology," in order to distinguish it from "the old psychology," which had been produced in the philosopher's armchair.

When a living system is studied from the outside, it is physiology. According to Wundt, when we study a living system from the inside, it is psychology. The only way we can study a living system from within is by self-observation or *introspection*. Of course, the most remarkable thing about introspection is that we can do it at all, but Wundt could shed no more light on that accomplishment than we can today. So he accepted it as given and went on to ask what could be learned from it.

We learn little about our minds from casual, haphazard self-observation, just as we learned little about mechanics from centuries of casual, uncontrolled observation of falling bodies. It is essential that observations be made by trained observers under carefully specified conditions for the purpose of answering well-defined questions. To Wundt, "scientific" meant "experimental"; if psychology was to become a science, it would have to use its introspective approach in an experimental situation in a laboratory where all conditions could be precisely controlled and repeated. Only in the special environment of a laboratory could the elusive elements of conscious experience be analyzed accurately.

At Leipzig Wundt presented the odd spectacle of a professor of philosophy who gave scientific demonstrations during his lectures. How else could an ex-physiologist make his point? These demonstrations became such an important part of his thinking that in 1879 he started his own laboratory, the world's first formal laboratory of psychology. As he began to train young philosophers to use the scientific method, it became necessary to find some place to publish their results. In 1881 he started a magazine called the *Philosophische Studien*, the first effective journal for experimental psychology. With a handbook, a laboratory, and a scholarly journal, the new psychology was well under way.

In his prime, *Herr Geheimrat* Professor Doctor Wilhelm Wundt was tall, thin, slightly stooped, with a large head, a pleasant face, and a full beard. He wore thick, dark glasses and could use only part of the vision of one eye during the last half of his life. In spite of this handicap, he worked with unflagging zeal. He seems to have had no capacity for boredom. In the morning he worked at home on the many books that remain his monument, read student theses, and edited his journal. In the afternoon he took a walk and attended examinations or visited his laboratory. On his arrival at the laboratory, he went directly to his private room, where he held conferences. Some days he toured the laboratory and inspected the experiments. His lectures were given at four o'clock, well after dark during the winter months. As a professor he enjoyed a high social standing and easy financial circumstances, a position of privilege granted all German professors before World War I. His security and his family made life seem both cheerful and productive.

Wundt was the most popular lecturer at Leipzig; the largest lecture hall was never large enough to hold all those who wanted to hear him. One of his most famous students, E. B. Titchener—who later disseminated Wundtian psychology to America from his professorial chair at Cornell University—recalled vividly the great man's classroom manner. Wundt would appear at exactly the correct minute—punctuality was essential—dressed all in black and carrying a small sheaf of lecture notes. He clattered up the side aisle to the platform with an awkward shuffle and a sound as if his soles were made of wood. On the platform was a long desk where demonstrations were performed. He made a few gestures—a forefinger across his forehead, a rearrangement of his chalk—then faced the audience and placed his elbows on the bookrest. His voice was weak at first, then gained in strength and emphasis. As he talked his arms and hands moved up and down, pointing and waving, in some mysterious way illustrative. His head and body were rigid, and only the hands played back and forth. He seldom referred to the few jotted notes. As the clock struck the end of the hour he stopped and, stooping a little, clattered out as he had clattered in.

The work done in his new laboratory and published in his new journal extended in several directions. Most of it, of course, concerned sensation and perception, particularly vision and hearing; perception was the problem considered fundamental in Wundt's empirical philosophy. In these experiments Wundt was able to exploit the methods of measurement devised by that eccentric genius, Gustav Theodor Fechner, and he had the famous Fechner Law to guide him.[4] In every respect, the analysis of perceptual processes into their elements was the simplest and most profitable line to follow in the new psychology. Next most popular were the studies of reaction time, for these seemed to provide a way to measure the speed of thought.

Psychology cannot be constructed entirely in terms of elementary sensations and their modes and levels of integration. The field of consciousness, said Wundt, has a small, bright area at its center; he directed some of his students into research on the problems of attention. Other students attempted to study association and memory. Still others introspected on their feelings and emotions. The six rooms of his little laboratory buzzed with the discoveries and arguments of the students as they applied analytic introspection to one problem after another.

One series of experiments on attention used a metronome, an instrument for marking exact time in music. As all music students know, a metronome produces clearly audible clicks at regular intervals; the rate of the clicks can be adjusted to suit the tempo of the music. Wundt's listeners were asked to form rhythmic groupings of the clicks and to report their conscious experiences. The introspective method used in such experiments is simple to describe, but it requires considerable training and self-discipline to use. Stimuli—in this case the sequence of clicks—are presented while the subject pays careful attention to all that he notices. When stimulation ends, the subject gives a full verbal report. In an experiment on attention, the subject may be interested in whether a particular pattern of clicks can be held in consciousness as a unitary whole. However, exactly the same source of stimulation can be used to investigate other aspects of conscious experience.

Consider how he worked: Wundt reported from his own introspections that at the end of a rhythmic row of beats he had the impression of an agreeable whole. That is, some rhythmic patterns are more pleasant, more agreeable than others. He concluded from this self-observation that part of the experience of any pattern of beats is a subjective feeling of pleasure or displeasure, a feeling that can be located somewhere along a continuum ranging from the agreeable to the disagreeable. While he listened to the clicks, however, he detected another kind of feeling about them. As he expectantly awaited each successive click he felt a slight tension; after the anticipated click occurred he felt relief. This alternation between tension and relief was clearest when the clicks came at a slow rate. In addition to a pleasure-displeasure continuum, therefore, his feelings seemed to have a tension-relief dimension. But that was not all. When the rate of the clicks was increased, he said, he felt mildly excited; when the rate slowed, he had a quieting feeling. In this way, by patiently varying the speed of the metronome and carefully noting his subjective experience—his sensations and feelings—Wundt teased out three distinct and independent dimensions: agreeableness-disagreeableness, strain-relaxation, excitement-calm. Every conscious feeling, he said, can be located somewhere in three-dimensional space (see Figure 3.1).

This was the kind of introspective evidence on which he based

FIGURE 3.1

Wundt's tridimensional theory of feeling. Every feeling is supposed to be located somewhere in this space.

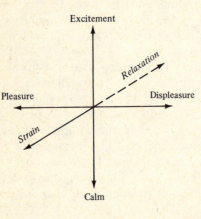

his hotly disputed tri-dimensional theory of feeling. Emotions, he argued, are complex combinations or patterns of these elementary conscious feelings, and each elementary feeling can be completely described by stating its position along each one of three dimensions. History has dealt harshly with his effort to reduce emotions to conscious contents of the mind: emotions may involve feelings, people may be able to make judgments based on those feelings, but it is not possible to say that emotions are *nothing but* feelings. Wundt's analysis ignored the meaning of the situation in which the emotion is experienced.

Nevertheless, Wundt's introspections held a great fascination for his students. Who would have guessed that anything as familiar as one's own mind could harbor all these shadowy and unexpected elements? Who could guess what other pumpkins might turn into coaches when examined with the marvelous inner eye? Wundt's talent for making the perfectly familiar seem completely novel and mysterious—by stripping off its meaning and cutting it up in pieces—was the source of both his strength and his weakness as a psychologist.

Note how hard it is to disprove his claims. If your own introspections give you a different result, how can you decide who is right? Perhaps you misunderstood his description of his experience; perhaps you paid attention to the wrong things; perhaps you do not know how to introspect properly; perhaps you and Wundt are not made the same way; and so on. His experiments, unlike experiments elsewhere in science, do not ensure agreement among all those who witness them. Introspective observation is essentially private, and disagreements cannot be settled by repeated observations.

But scientific psychology had to start somewhere. It was not obvious in advance that a direct attack on the mind would not be the best approach. And there was always the hope that introspective reports would parallel the physiological indicators.

In spite of his eccentric experimentalism, however, Wundt was a professor of philosophy. With scientific psychology flourishing, therefore, he began next to record his philosophical convictions. In 1880 he produced a *Logic*, in 1886 an *Ethic*, and in 1889 the crown of his work, a *System of Philosophy*. Today these massive monuments to Wundt's tireless scholarship hold little interest for psychologists and even less for philosophers. But that he could argue against the prevailing positivism and in favor of a greater emphasis on metaphysical problems in philosophy shows how far he had outgrown his student days. His conception of scientific metaphysics was simply a contradiction in terms to any good positivist.

It was during this time—his "philosophical decade"—that the first of a long string of students from America began to appear in Leipzig. Upon arrival they found themselves apprenticed to the perfect model of a German professor. At their first conference he would appear holding a list of research topics. Taking the students in the order in which they stood—there was no question of their being seated—he assigned one topic to each. He supervised their work on these topics most carefully; when the thesis was completed he held complete power of acceptance or rejection. If part of the work failed to support his theories, it might be instantly deleted. German scientific dogmatism was no myth, and it flourished undisguised in the little laboratory at Leipzig.

The last of Wundt's three lifetime projects was to create social psychology. This he did with characteristic industry in the ten volumes of his *Elements of Folk Psychology* which appeared during the last twenty years of his life. The concept of *Volk* which had gradually emerged during Germany's struggle for political unification now seemed ripe for psychological exploitation. Thus he moved even further away from positivism; in his view, the collective, social, folk mind transcended the individual minds that composed it. The folk mind manifested itself in languages, art, myths, social customs, law, and morals—cultural works that an individual never makes in isolation.

This opinion had an important implication, for it divided his science of psychology into two parts, the experimental and the social. According to Wundt, the simpler mental functions—sensation, perception, memory, simple feelings—can be studied by laboratory experiments on the minds of individuals. But the higher mental processes involved in human thinking are so strongly conditioned by linguistic habits, moral ideas, and ideological convictions that scientific experiments are impossible. Human thinking, he said, can be explored only by the nonexperimental methods of anthropology, sociology, and social psychology. Thinking cannot be understood through the analysis of logic, for it is too often illogical; and it is too complicated to be studied by simple introspection on the mental events that accompany it. Only by studying the *products* of thought as these have accumulated during man's history can we hope to understand thinking.

Wundt had for many years maintained an active interest in the emerging science of linguistics and, when he turned his attention to social psychology, language played a central role in his theories. The psychological problem he saw was to explain the relation between the "outer" phenomena of speech and the "inner" structure of thought. A spoken sentence was both a sequential and a simultaneous thing— sequential in its utterance, but simultaneous in consciousness. In his attempts to explain how the inner thought was transformed into an outer utterance, Wundt anticipated many ideas that were rediscovered and refined by linguists and psychologists more than fifty years later.[5]

In these later works Wundt departed even further from the empiricist philosophy of the day. Perhaps that explains why his surprisingly modern ideas about the psychology of language were so long overlooked. Wundt's major interpreter on the American scene was Titchener, an Englishman steeped in the empiricist tradition of his native land. Titchener and his students had little sympathy for or understanding of Wundt's opposition to positivism. All that most Americans heard the aging Wundt say was that complicated mental processes cannot be studied experimentally, and that was a conclusion they rejected. Given the enthusiasm and the positivistic frame of mind of Wundt's disciples, they would accept no limits to the applicability of experimental science.

Because his social psychology and his acute analysis of the mental processes involved in language were not appreciated, Wundt's influence on the science he founded derived almost entirely from the three fat volumes of his experimental psychology. Where Mill only talked about doing psychological experiments, Wundt did them. He conducted them in a laboratory that he designed for the purpose, published them in his own journal, and tried to incorporate them into a systematic theory of the human mind. And he trained his students well. They founded more laboratories and continued to experiment. As a direct result of his labors, psychology was provided with all the trappings of a modern science. For that service, all psychologists, even those who bitterly opposed his theories, are permanently indebted to the indefatigable Wilhelm Wundt.

NOTES

1. John Locke, *An Essay Concerning Human Understanding*, bk. II, chap. 1, para. 2.
2. Edwin G. Boring, *A History of Experimental Psychology*, 2d ed. (New York: Appleton-Century-Crofts, 1950), see chap. 16 and references cited therein.
3. Wilhelm Wundt, *Outlines of Psychology*, trans. C. H. Judd (Leipzig: Englemann, 1907), pp. 31–32.
4. Fechner's Law says that the subjective magnitude of a sensation is a logarithmic function of the magnitude of the physical stimulus that produces it (see Chapter 7).
5. Arthur L. Blumenthal, *Language and Psychology: Historical Aspects of Psycholinguistics* (New York: Wiley, 1970).

FOUR
Levels
of Awareness

A revolution is taking place presently in the study of awareness. This revolution embraces two of the major trends in contemporary psychology—subjective behaviorism and humanistic psychology. Coming on the heels of the increasingly widespread use of hallucinogenic drugs and a technological explosion in the physiological laboratories, the researchers are paying attention to an area of human behavior that is of major concern to the counterculture in America.[1] Thus, the behavioral scientists' work dovetails with the turn to subjective experience occurring in all strata of American life. Our sources for understanding this revolution will necessarily embrace the humanities, the arts, and the sciences.

We will focus on consciousness—its existence, its permanence, its alterability, and its measurability. The bridge from the historical past to present conceptions of consciousness will be found to be structurally sound. The search for consciousness did not begin in 1970, *The Greening of America*[2] notwithstanding. Consciousness is a word worn smooth by a million tongues. Depending upon the figure of speech chosen it is a state of being, a substance, a process, a place, an epiphenomenon, an emergent aspect of matter, or the only true reality. Maybe we should ban the word for a decade or two until we can develop more precise terms for the several uses that "consciousness" now obscures. Despite all its faults, however, the term would be sorely missed; it refers to something immediately obvious and familiar to anyone capable of understanding a ban against it. Of course, some of our problems may arise from the fact that we must use consciousness to understand consciousness. Turning a tool on itself may be as futile as trying to soar off the ground by a tug at one's bootstraps. Perhaps we become confused because whenever we are thinking about consciousness, we are surrounded by it and can imagine only what consciousness is *not*. The fish, someone has said, will be the last to discover water.

A psychologist's difficulties in formulating a definition for consciousness are similar to a biologist's difficulties in defining life. Although biology is the science of life, most biologists confess they do not know what life is. They are sure life is not a substance—not a material thing—but a process, or group of processes, that occurs in some things and not in others. And biologists agree with one another rather well about which things are alive and which are not. The defining properties of the system are the clue. There must be a steady turnover of materials and energy, a process called metabolism; the system must be capable of reproducing itself; it must be capable of growing; and it must be capable of responding to energies in the world around it. Whenever all these properties are present, a biologist can be confident the system is living. On this planet, at least.

But, it may be asked, is life nothing more than a list of properties? Isn't something missing? On this question biologists disagree. There is nothing more, some may say, for life is a process that emerges whenever a sufficiently complex chunk of matter is organized in a certain way. If one criticizes this use of the concept of emergence because it seems to sneak unscientific notions in through the back door, the biologist may argue that emergence is not something new and mysterious that he has just invented. Your lap emerges when you sit down; stand up and it goes away. The emergence of life in a system of properly organized molecules (which are not themselves alive) is no more mysterious than the emergence of a bridge game in a group of four properly idle people. According to this theory, one of the biologist's tasks is to study the conditions that must be satisfied before a physical system will exhibit this property and come to life.

But there are people who cannot accept such a theory of life. To them life is something more than a physicochemical equation. What that something more may be, however, is itself a problem that provokes disagreement. Some say that life exists, just as matter exists, but it transcends any physical methods of isolation or examination. One could know everything there is to know about physics and chemistry, it is argued, and yet never suspect that life existed.

There are biologists who dislike a physicochemical theory of life because it seems to reduce biology to a branch of physics. Other biologists wish to leave room for new discoveries whose nature cannot at present be imagined; only a fool claims to know everything. Some of those who object to an emergent materialism do so because they believe in the divine origin of life. And some of the nicest people object to materialism because it offends their personal dignity as living organisms. So crass a doctrine destroys all the poetic beauty of living things. What is missing from the scientific definition of life is life itself. But, of course, how many potential chemists have lost interest when they discovered that the formula for water was not wet?

A biologist's discussion of life can be compared to a psychologist's discussion of consciousness. Most psychologists confess they do not know what consciousness is. They are sure it is not a substance—

not a material thing—but a process, or group of processes, that occurs in some objects and not in others. And they can sometimes agree, though not nearly as well as the biologists, about which things are conscious and which are not. Their approach is to define the properties the system must have to qualify, and to search for them. But admittedly there is no consensus as to the defining characteristics.

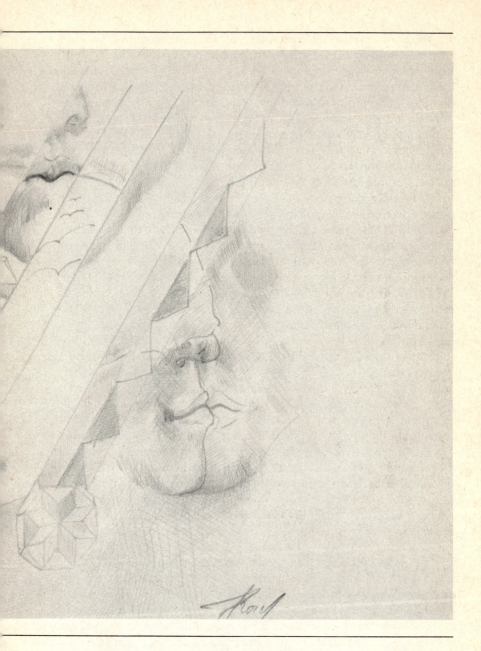

What properties might be included? Should we require that a conscious system be able to perceive, to remember, to feel emotions, to think? These are excellent psychological processes, but they lead us directly to the question; what *use* do we expect to make of the list? Do we, for instance, expect to stand in front of a tree or a computing machine or a boulder and ask if it is conscious? If so, we will have to ask about its perceptions, memories, feelings, and thoughts. To question these properties will raise more problems than it settles. If a poet believes that a river is conscious because it perceives a path downhill, because it remembers how to reach the sea, because it becomes angry during the spring floods and thinks long, solemn, majestic thoughts in summer, do you see any argument to dissuade him? How can we distinguish a metaphorical from a literal use of such words as perception, thought, feeling? And if we cannot foresee perfect agreement about so obvious a matter as the consciousness of a river, imagine the quarrel that will arise over the doubtful cases.

Possibly there are other properties easier to agree upon. For instance, should we insist that a system be alive before we will say it is conscious? That decision alone would settle many puzzling problems. It would, for instance, deny the existence of any divine Consciousness to watch over us. And, passing from the sublime to the ridiculous, a decision that only living organisms can be conscious would settle once and for all whether any computing machine, however clever, could be conscious. And we could say definitely that social groups have no collective consciousness. Indeed, if we took this step, we should then go on to the next and limit the domain of consciousness to living animals. It is unlikely that the study of botany would be impeded by a decision that all plants were lacking in consciousness. Consciousness seems to go along with mobility in living systems.

Further criteria could be considered. For instance, we might insist that a conscious system be one capable of reacting to its own reactions. A stone can react: kick it and it moves. But it does not make this movement the occasion for another reaction. A human being will do something and talk about it; his speech is a reaction to his own earlier behavior, and one usually accepts what he says as evidence that he was conscious of what he was doing. Of course, engineers can build clever electromechanical devices, called servomechanisms, that also respond to their own responses, so we should probably not make this our only criterion.

Another property that a conscious system should probably have is an ability to profit from experience, that is, to learn and to remember. This requirement does not eliminate many members of the animal kingdom, however; so far as we know they all can modify their behavior to some extent as a result of experience. And here, again, modern technology can produce many inorganic devices that remember. A magnetic tape recorder, for example, can remember the acoustic waves it hears far better than any human listener can.

We could continue in this way to accumulate recognizable properties to use in testing for the presence of consciousness. But notice something odd about them. Each seems to come back to processes or functions that can also be performed in various mechanical, electrical, or chemical ways.[3] As in the biological case, this argument seems to move toward a definition of consciousness in terms of an emergent property of sufficiently complex physicochemical systems. It is all too easy to foresee the complaints that will arise—indeed, have already arisen repeatedly—when an intelligent layman is told that his consciousness is merely the side effect of a chemical reaction going on in his brain.

It should be plain, however, that psychologists are not as far along with consciousness as biologists are with life. We are still not sure whether we should say that an earthworm or a cockroach or a catfish or a robin or a cat or a monkey is conscious. One feels intuitively that a paramecium is not conscious and that a chimpanzee probably is. But where along the branching experiments of evolution does consciousness intrude? The more one struggles with this question, the more clearly one recognizes that there is an important difference between a definition of life and a definition of consciousness.

A biologist can say that a system is alive or not alive. It is a form of hangman's humor to joke about being only a little bit dead. The case is not so open-and-shut when we talk about consciousness. It is more natural to admit to degrees of consciousness. A man is more conscious than a cat, perhaps, but the cat is more conscious than a frog, and so on. The proposition is not completely clear, but neither is it completely senseless.

THE MEASUREMENT OF CONSCIOUSNESS

Although a meaningful way to determine which of two animals is the more conscious is not yet at hand, considerable progress has been made in determining degrees of consciousness within a single individual from one moment to the next. Begin with the familiar fact that man, like many other animals, follows a daily cycle of sleeping and waking. Within every span of twenty-four hours we expect to find his state change from highly conscious to deeply unconscious. The sleep cycle is the most obvious change in behavior that we could ever hope to find. The sleep–waking cycle is but one of many measurable biological changes called circadian rhythms which can be measured through changes in such indices as heart rate (HR), skin resistance (electrodermal response or EDR), skin temperature, breathing rate, gastrointestinal movements or motility, muscle action potentials (MAP), and brain wave activity (electroencephalogram or EEG). We can measure these changes on sophisticated polygraph machines and relate the obtained quantities to the person's verbal report in order to gauge the degree of consciousness at any given moment.[4]

One simple way to gauge the depth of sleep is to produce a sound that grows progressively louder until it wakes the sleeper. The intensity needed to awaken him is then a measure of how deeply he slept. (The difference between normal sleep and a drugged state is that the person in normal sleep can always be roused by sufficiently intense stimulation.) With this technique it is a simple matter to show that the depth of sleep fluctuates considerably during the night.

A more complicated technique is to take an electroencephalogram, a recording of the electrical activity in the brain. Fortunately, it is not necessary to make a hole in the sleeper's skull to accomplish this purpose. Electrodes placed on the scalp can pick up enough, with the help of special amplifiers, to record what is going on inside. These records of brain waves were first investigated by Hans Berger in 1929; since then thousands of technical papers have been published on the subject.[5]

Brain waves show periodic oscillations at various frequencies ranging from 1 cycle per second (1 Hertz) or even lower (the so-called delta waves) up to 45 or 50 Hertz (Hz). These rhythmic waves tend to change in various ways according to what the person is doing. If a person relaxes with his eyes closed and lets his attention wander vacantly, alpha waves will usually occur—electrical fluctuations of about 0.00005 volts at a frequency around 10 Hz. But give him a problem to think about, or let him open his eyes, and the alpha waves disappear to be replaced by the smaller, faster beta waves, which oscillate at 20 to 25 Hz. This is illustrated in Figure 4.1.

There are several theories about the source of brain waves. One line of speculation goes like this. In order to give waves large enough to be measured through the skull, a large portion of the brain must be linked together so that it is all active and inactive simultaneously. This synchrony occurs only when the brain is not disturbed by signals coming to it from the sense organs. Thus, when the level of consciousness is low, as in resting or in sleep, we should find large, slow brain waves—as if the brain cells were marking time, waiting to be used. At higher levels of awareness, this pattern would break up, different parts of the brain would become involved in various activities with different characteristic rhythms, and the result would be smaller, faster brain waves. This line of argument seems to account for some of the gross phenomena that have been observed.[6]

As a person falls asleep, his level of awareness goes through several successive stages; these can usually be recognized from an examination of the brain waves. As he becomes drowsy and his thoughts tend to drift, his brain waves begin to get slower. As he begins to doze lightly, "sleep spindles" appear, short bursts of periodic wave-form. As he sinks into deep sleep, his brain produces large and slow delta waves. These various levels are illustrated in Figure 4.2.

Sleep research is currently one of the most active research areas

FIGURE 4.1

*Brain waves show the shift from alpha waves (about 10 per second)
when the person is resting, to smaller, faster beta waves (A) when the
eyes are open, (B) when solving a problem in mental arithmetic, or (C)
when responding to other sensory stimuli. (From "The Physiology of
Imagination," by John C. Eccles, September 1958. Copyright © 1958
Scientific American, Inc. All rights reserved.)*

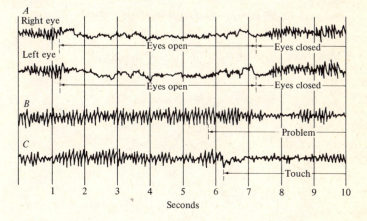

in laboratories around the world, with data and complexity mounting
annually. Fine-grained analysis of EEG records has led to recent
classifications of human sleep into five stages; to some observers this
suggests five stages of consciousness, a gradient that is continuous with
the waking state.[7] Some scientists prefer to view sleep as having but
two stages: dreaming and deep sleep during which dreaming presumably does not take place.

Dreaming is a particularly interesting phenomenon to study
with these techniques. Is a person conscious or unconscious when he
dreams? Common sense says that he is somewhere in between, conscious of the dream but unconscious of the world around him, and the
evidence from brain waves tends to support this opinion. In the course
of a night's sleep a person falls rapidly into a very sound sleep that lasts
for about an hour, then gradually becomes more active as the brain
waves get more rapid. The sleeper will come close to waking and then
slip back again into deeper sleep. These fluctuations in the depth of
sleep take about 90 minutes, and they continue throughout the night
(see Figure 4.3). It is during periods of light sleep, when a person is
most easily roused, that dreams occur.

The occurrence of dreams can be detected easily by an observer.[8] A faint light on a dreamer's eyes will show that his eyeballs
are moving rapidly to and fro, as though he were watching some scene

41

FIGURE 4.2

Brain waves characteristic of the different stages along the continuum from excitement to deep sleep. (From H. H. Jasper, "Electroencephalography," in Epilepsy and Cerebral Localization, *ed. W. Penfield and T. C. Erikson, 1941. Courtesy of Charles C. Thomas, Publisher, Springfield, Illinois.)*

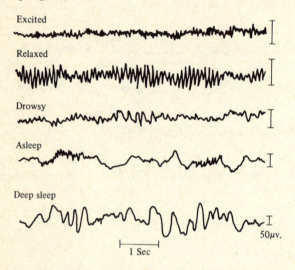

Excited

Relaxed

Drowsy

Asleep

Deep sleep

50μν.

|— 1 Sec —|

that he "sees" projected on the inside of his eyelids. (These eye movements also can be detected and recorded with the same kind of electronic equipment used to record brain waves.) They are called rapid eye movements (REM), and the stage of sleep where dreaming is assumed to take place is called REM sleep. Deep sleep is referred to as NREM for obvious reasons.[9]

If the sleeper dreams of a tennis match, his eyes move back and forth from left to right. If he dreams that he is picking up basketballs and throwing them through a hoop over his head, his eyes move up and down. If he is watching some action nearby, his eyes make large, irregular movements. At the same time that the eyes start to move, the pattern of the brain waves usually indicates lighter sleep; moreover, the sleeper's heart may begin to pound and he may begin to breathe more rapidly—common symptoms of an emotional experience.[10] A person awakened during one of these REM periods is likely to have a dream to report; if he is awakened at other times, during NREM sleep, he does not. When awakened from NREM sleep, he is often bewildered. He may have any of a variety of emotions to report. He may be sure that he had been dreaming, but not be able to recall the dream. Or he may feel that he was not asleep at all. But he seldom reports dreams and those few that he does report are probably remembered from

FIGURE 4.3

Episodes of dreaming alternate with periods of deeper sleep. This hypothetical function shows the depth of sleep as a function of the number of hours the person had been sleeping. On the average, episodes of dreaming last longer as the night wears on.

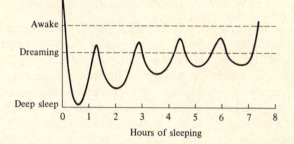

Hours of sleeping

periods of dreaming earlier in the night. According to the objective evidence, everyone is a dreamer, but not everyone can recall his dreams. It has been observed that if a person's REM sleep is repeatedly interrupted for several days, he becomes progressively more irritable, and, when left undisturbed, will show a marked increase in the percentage of REM sleep. This suggests that he may be making up for a deprivation of the opportunity to dream; apparently, dreaming is in the same category with other biological needs.

Considerations such as these encourage psychologists to think of consciousness as more-or-less rather than all-or-none. There is a gradual change of psychological state that runs from the deepest sleep up through dream states, quiet resting, perceptual awareness, symbolic manipulation, and finally to states of strong emotion. Corresponding to these psychological changes is a sequence of physiological changes that seems to correspond to increasing arousal, or activation, as shown by brain waves, muscular tension, hormonal activity, and other physiological indices.[11]

Neurophysiologists who study the brain have located centers deep in the oldest part of it where sleep and wakefulness seem to be regulated.[12] This part has been called the ascending reticular activating system. When this system is functioning, the brain waves become desynchronized, just as they do during states of conscious activity and attention. When the activating system is not functioning, however, information from the sense organs does not get relayed on to the higher centers in the cortex of the brain, and a state of sleep results. Exactly how the activating system works is a very complicated matter, but it is obviously important for controlling the level of activity everywhere in the nervous system. Beginning in the 1950s the discovery and exploration of these control systems quickly became one of the most exciting areas of research on the brain. Even the banal references to "cough control centers" on television commercials has some grounding in our newly acquired scientific facts.

THE BASES FOR CHANGING CONSCIOUSNESS

One of the historical legacies that blocked progress in our understanding of the physiological basis of consciousness was a convenient paradigm that divided the nervous system into two parts. One part was a voluntary system in which the evolutionarily newer cerebrum controlled skeletal motor activity. The other part was an autonomic nervous system in which the "primitive" areas of the brain controlled the allegedly "nonconscious" activities such as breathing, heart rate regulation, circadian rhythms, and visceral activities. However, recent research by Neal Miller and his colleagues, show clearly that the autonomic nervous system can be conditioned by external stimuli and that learning can take place in these areas.[13]

The impact of this research *should* mean the formal abandonment of the paradigm that includes the autonomic nervous system, but

CITATION ACCOMPANYING THE DISTINGUISHED SCIENTIFIC
CONTRIBUTION AWARD PRESENTED BY THE AMERICAN PSYCHOLOGICAL
ASSOCIATION, 1959

"For his sustained and imaginative research on the basic principles of learning. Through brilliantly conceived and skillfully executed experiments, he and his students have served as a major spearhead in the current breakthrough in the area of motivation and learning. The importance of his research in extending knowledge is matched by its importance in stimulating the research of others. His influence has been greatly enhanced by his clear reports and reviews, in which he is never afraid to point out the broad implications of his results. In every respect, he is a fortunate model to set before budding young psychologists."

NEAL ELGAR MILLER

we do not expect to see that happen. The new paradigm, extended to human beings, asserts that all behavior, including visceral, is subject to conscious, voluntary control; and recent research with humans has confirmed this. The public acceptance of the significance of this research has spawned speculative writing hauntingly reminiscent of the journalism surrounding heart transplants, as the scientific ability to control our consciousness seems within reach.[14]

If we assume that some of the observed individual differences in visceral and emotional behavior are learned (over and above known inherited tendencies), it is a natural step to try to retrain the viscera or the brain to newer, better, or at least healthier levels of functioning. The key element in this causal chain is feedback—now dubbed "biofeedback"—which can be actuated by visceral changes using special purpose computers to provide more intelligible knowledge to the conscious person as to just what state his heart, stomach, brain, or intestine is in. One scientist, working with Miller's basic design, has successfully conditioned heart patients with dangerous arrhythmic heart beats to speed, slow down, and regulate their heart rates with mental effort alone. After sufficient training, the patient can withdraw from the artificial feedback (red lights, etc.) and control his heart rate in the interests of his health. How the patient does this is unknown, as few subjects can verbalize what they do to control their heart rate.[15]

ALTERED STATES OF CONSCIOUSNESS

A route to "blowing one's mind" by enjoying two fads at once was offered in 1971 in a Berkeley, California, head shop where one could try out both a water bed and a cheap ($250) set of earphones that provided biofeedback for the conditioning of alpha rhythms. One might also talk with a confident practitioner of transcendental meditation who could knowingly cite journal articles that gave scientific credence to his chosen pathway to Nirvana. These diverse trends parallel the extension of Miller's autonomic instrumental conditioning to the conditioning of various EEG components, spawning a research paradigm that is now called the autoregulation of consciousness.

Joe Kamiya, a cautious and yet uninhibited scientist, performed the key experiments, using apparatus costing far more than $250.[16] EEG recordings are filtered to pass the alpha frequency band into apparatus that controls a tone that is sounded for the subject. Subjects are instructed to make the tone come on (or go off) in any way that they can, while the researcher checks the EEG record for alpha. After a few hours of chance performance most subjects are able to keep the tone on for about 80 percent of the time and later they are able to bring on alpha on command. But, once again, they are unable to tell

45

how they do it; often the query of "how?" is met with hostility as subjects seem unwilling to explain their private perceptions. This is a profound problem for the philosopher of science, who has seen psychology, like most sciences, built on a foundation of the consensus of observations, having previously classified introspection as being too unreliable. The few reports that exist refer to alpha as pleasant, associated with relaxation of the mind and a tuning out of external stimuli except for the feedback tone. There is a tendency for people with experience in Zen, Yoga, or other contemplative disciplines to learn alpha control more rapidly. Investigators report a general decrease in metabolism (lower oxygen consumption, heart rate, breathing, skin conductance, etc.) as well as a high incidence of alpha in transcendental meditation.[17] Various claims are being made for the mental and physical curative powers of meditation and "being in alpha," but they remain unproven.[18]

The relation of this work to altering consciousness with drugs is fairly obvious, a point that has not been lost on those who see psychedelic drugs as the ultimate means of voluntarily controlling one's consciousness. In fact, an unusual and possibly productive merger of the hard-nosed laboratory scientist with the seeker of mystic experience and expanded awareness is taking place, the effects of which on psychology may be quite revolutionary. As Neal Miller has observed, "We must re-examine a lot of phenomena we may have dismissed as fakery before." It is sobering indeed to consider that the new subjective behaviorists are looking once again at ESP, private events, magic, rituals, hypnosis, and other phenomena with a more open mind.

Research on the effects of various drugs, spurred by an aroused and worried community, has produced few laboratory findings that have not been contradicted within a short period of time.[19] Laboratory research, dictated by medical and ethical considerations, produces some hard physiological data on the effects of marihuana and lysergic acid (LSD), but attempts to correlate these data with pooled estimates of the subjects' conscious experience are frustrated by the private nature of the experience and the artificiality of the laboratory setting, which distorts the rituals, the informality, the "vibes," and other unknowns that "heads" feel but cannot express. The laboratory scientist may well have lost sight of the fact that his tools were not designed to be useful in all behavioral settings and that the new (to him) frontier of voluntarily controlled private experience may require a very different research paradigm.

Those who had hoped that research would confirm a bleak picture of the consequences of drug use or of drug users as depraved psychopaths have received little support from recent published research.[20] Clearly, marihuana, like any intoxicant such as alcohol, has effects on cognitive functioning, driving skills (though not as strong as alcohol), verbal fluency, and other behavior, but there is no support for the contention that it or hallucinogenic drugs provoke psychosis or violence. In fact, personality assessment of marihuana users indicates that they show evidence of an openness to experience, creativity, a lower degree of authoritarianism, more social poise, more impulsive behavior, more rebellious and pleasure-seeking behavior; while non-users appear to be more rule abiding, inflexible, conventional, and less successful academically.[21]

The collection of anecdotal information from drug users is a predictably unreliable method; the usual problems associated with introspective reports are complicated in the area of drugs by a tendency of drug users to make reports that conform to what they have heard from others, frequent false testimony, evidence from users who unwittingly purchased adulterated acid or a camel dung substitute for hashish, and confusion over the difference between testimony from addicted narcotic users rather than from serious users of hallucinogenic drugs. The most useful and dramatic testimony has come from articulate writers who experienced altered consciousness in experimenting with LSD, peyote, mescaline, and other hallucinogenic drugs. One remarkable book of this type is *The Teachings of Don Juan* by Carlos Castaneda, a student of anthropology, who observed and then participated in the psychedelic world of Don Juan, a Yaqui Indian medicine man (brujo). Castaneda's research paradigm involved his becoming an apprentice to Don Juan, being fully initiated into the rituals, the context, the ecology, and the growth in personal awareness that accompanied the very disciplined use of peyote, datura, and mushrooms as a means of becoming "a man of knowledge."

Castaneda's first encounter with peyote yielded the following description.

> . . . My field of vision had diminished to a circular area in front of my eyes. . . . I had the sensation of intense convulsions and in a matter of instants a tunnel formed around me, very low and narrow and strangely cold. . . . Every memory came back to me at once and suddenly all was clear in my mind. . . . I could not distinguish anyone or anything. All I was capable of seeing was the dog becoming iridescent; an intense light radiated from his body. I saw again the water flowing through him, kindling him like a bonfire. I got to the water, sank my face in the pan, and drank with him. My hands were in front of me on the ground and, as I drank, I saw the fluid running through my veins setting up hues of red, yellow and green. . . . I drank until the fluid went out of my body through each pore, and projected out like fibers of silk, and I too acquired a long, lustrous, iridescent mane. . . . A supreme happiness filled my

whole body. . . . We played and wrestled until I knew his wishes and he knew mine. . . . The euphoria that possessed me was indescribable. . . . I laughed until it was almost impossible to breathe. . . . The passage from my normal state had taken place almost without my realizing it: I was aware; my thoughts and feelings were a corollary of that awareness; and the passing was smooth and clear. But this second change, the awakening to serious, sober consciousness, was genuinely shocking. I had forgotten I was a man! The sadness of such an irreconcilable situation was so intense that I wept.[22]

In subsequent episodes, Castaneda is led through other psychedelic experiences, which include divination and the appearance of *mescalito* (the personification of the power of the drug), all of which conflict with his sense of ordinary reality. Don Juan, as the teacher, is repeatedly exasperated by Castaneda's western style of analytical thinking, which prevents him from adopting the special sense of reality needed to appreciate what he is experiencing. After a trip during which Castaneda turns into a crow, he keeps asking Don Juan if his body really flew, despite his clear recollection of flying.

"You always ask me questions I cannot answer. You flew. . . . What you want to know makes no sense. Birds fly like birds and a man who has taken the devil's weed flies as such."

". . . Then I didn't really fly. . . . Where was my body?"

"In the bushes. . . . The trouble with you is that you understand things in only one way. You don't think a man flies; and yet a brujo can move a thousand miles in one second to see what is going on . . . So, does he or doesn't he fly?"

This is a strange world into which we are led by that strangest of all philosophers of science—a medicine man. But Castaneda now and Timothy Leary, Aldous Huxley, and Alan Watts before him point up the value of direct participation in the exploration of one's own inner space; a lesson that William James, who wrote about consciousness changes due to nitrous oxide, would greatly appreciate.[23]

MAINTAINING CONSCIOUSNESS

Those of us who begin each day with a cup of coffee to "get us going" are already making use of biofeedback and manipulating the state of our awareness. We may assume that for any given individual there is an optimum definition of states of consciousness ranging from deep sleep, through resting, general alertness, to high anxiety. The basic meaning of the previously described research is that the individual differences possible in nervous system functioning amount to physiological styles as idiosyncratic as what we have come to call personality.

Recent research by psychophysiologists has been directed toward the understanding of the behavior of people who quite clearly go to great lengths to adjust and change their conscious levels—smokers, alcoholics, drug users, early and late risers, people who fly over time zones. Presumably, such people are interfering with and modifying those basic circadian rhythms with varying degrees of success. It is worth noting some of the earlier work on these basic cycles in human beings.

In the maintenance of the state of sleep, most of us find that it is easier for us to sleep in a dark, quiet place. This condition allows little excitation of the sense organs and thus reduces the amount of nervous activity affecting the lower centers in the brain, producing the relative quiescence we have since childhood associated with falling asleep. When the activity of the lower centers is decreased and they no longer support the activity of the higher centers, the brain falls into the slow, rhythmic activity that is characteristic of brain waves during sleep. In order to remain awake and alert, therefore, it would seem that we need to have a great many things going on around us affecting our perceptions in striking ways.

If we are going to stay alert, our environment must keep surprising us. The surprises may be small, but something at least mildly unexpected is needed to keep us on our toes. It is not enough merely to have energy falling on our eyes, ears, skin, or other receptors; the critical feature is that the pattern of those energies must keep changing in unforeseen ways. If one makes continuous physiological measurements of the brain waves, the pulse, the electrical resistance of the skin, and the like, it is possible to follow the fluctuations as a person drifts into lower levels of awareness or is suddenly jolted to attention. Physiological indicators show increasing habituation whenever the person can formulate some kind of expectation, some internal model for what is going on around him; arousal occurs when his internal model disagrees with external reality and, in general, the larger the disagreement, the larger the arousal.

E. N. Sokolov, a Russian scientist, has contributed a research paradigm—the orienting reflex—that has helped to structure the psychophysiological research on this pattern of arousal.[24] The orienting reflex can be measured as a change in electrodermal or EEG activity that occurs when a novel stimulus is presented, for example, in the common experience we all have of turning our head when we hear a strange sound.

At McGill University in Montreal, a group of psychologists under the leadership of D. O. Hebb tried to discover what would happen to people deprived of a normally varying sensory input.[25] The investigators paid college students to stay in a quiet cubicle on a comfortable bed for twenty-four hours a day. The students wore goggles that admitted light, but the light was diffused and they could not recognize any patterns. They wore cardboard cuffs, extending beyond the fingertips, which permitted free movements of their joints but little tactual perception. Their plight is pictured in Figure 4.4. Students would stay for periods of two to six days before they quit and demanded to be let out. At regular intervals the psychologists would ask some questions over an intercommunication system and would give simple psychological tests.

Different persons reacted in different ways, of course, but nobody really enjoyed being isolated. After a student had caught up on his sleep and thought (or tried to think) about some of his personal problems, the isolation became extremely boring.

The tests showed that as time wore on problems became harder to solve; the students reported that they were unable to concentrate. The most striking result was the occurrence of hallucinations. At first the symptoms were rather slight; when they closed their eyes, they noticed that their visual field was light, not dark. After staying in the cubicle longer, they began to see dots of light, lines, or simple geometrical patterns. Still later these developed into something like wallpaper patterns. Then came isolated objects, without backgrounds. And finally, for a few persons, there were integrated scenes usually containing dreamlike distortions. In general, the students were surprised by the hallucinations, which were a new experience for them. Then they were amused or interested to discover what they would see next. Later some of them complained that the vividness interfered with sleep. Auditory and bodily hallucinations also occurred, but were less frequent. When the students finally left the cubicle they were apt to be mildly confused and their intelligence test scores were temporarily lower.

It should be noted that some of the problems encountered in sensory deprivation research are much like those reported in drug research. The nature of the subject's expectancy or set may affect the verbal responses he gives. For example, in certain military research laboratories, the reporting of hallucinations became the socially expected thing to do—a self-fulfilling process, which was further confounded by the failure of the experimenters to run proper control groups.

The studies of the effects of reduced stimulation emphasize the dual role of sensory events. Our senses not only give us specific information about our environment, but also have a nonspecific function in maintaining the normal, waking organization of the brain. If we do not use our sensory systems for a period of time, they do not work as efficiently as they normally would. It is as though perception is a skill which begins to decline when not exercised.

The same changes in the brain waves which we have described

FIGURE 4.4

Experimental cubicle constructed to study the effects of perceptual isolation. The subject wears a plastic visor to limit his vision, cotton gloves and cardboard cuffs to restrict what he can touch, and hears only the noise of a fan and an air conditioner above him. Wires attached to his scalp make it possible to record his brain waves. Communication between the subject and the experimenter is possible over a system of microphones and loudspeakers. The room is always lighted and, except for brief intermissions to eat or go to the toilet, the subject lies on the bed twenty-four hours a day until he can stand it no longer. (From "The Pathology of Boredom," by Woodburn Heren, January 1957. Copyright © 1957 Scientific American, Inc. All rights reserved.)

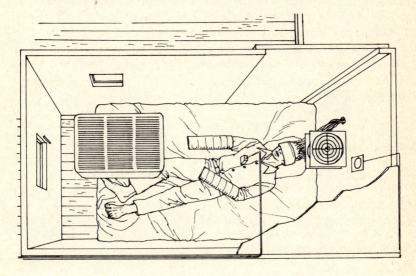

for man have been found in other animals. In fact, it is probably easier to tell from a record of the brain waves whether an animal is awake or asleep than it is to tell whether it is a man or a monkey. One assumes that if the monkey's behavior and his bodily processes show the same pattern as man's, then the monkey also must go through the same daily cycles of sleep and waking, of consciousness and unconsciousness. We cannot be certain, for the monkey will not talk. On the other hand, so long as he does not talk, he will not contradict us. Since neither proof nor disproof is possible, one must appeal to other criteria, such as simplicity and consistency, to support the view that consciousness is not a uniquely human characteristic.

It may someday be possible to say something intelligible about the degree of consciousness achieved by different animals. Already there is much we can say about variations in the level of awareness in man. But even with the most delicate scientific instruments our observations are woefully coarse and indirect. We have been using the term "conscious" to describe a general state of an organism. A description of the consciousness of an alert human being that tells us no more than we can read from his brain waves must seem to an intelligent layman to be a rather poor joke. We know vastly more about our conscious minds than any electric meter can show. Recall the exquisite sensitivity with which Virginia Woolf or James Joyce display a human mind and you will appreciate the gap that exists. Even for our more limited scientific needs, however, the faithful description of a human consciousness requires techniques far more sophisticated than any we are likely to find in a physiological laboratory. We shall want to say, for example, that even when we are most highly conscious there is much going on in our minds that we are not directly aware of. In some sense not yet defined we are both conscious and unconscious at the same time. The oldest meter in the world cannot measure such a contradiction! Before we can understand these higher levels of consciousness, therefore, we will have to come at the problem again from a different direction.

NOTES

1. T. Roszak, *The Making of a Counter Culture* (New York: Doubleday, 1969).
2. C. Reich, *The Greening of America* (New York: Random House, 1970).
3. A. M. Turing, "Can a Machine Think?" in *The World of Mathematics*, ed. J. R. Newman (New York: Simon and Schuster, 1956), vol. 4.
4. The polygraph, notorious for it's questionable use in so-called "lie-detection" work, is a basic tool of the *psychophysiologist* (a recently coined word which reflects the movement of psychology into yet another area). Polygraphs with high-gain amplifiers capable of measuring in the microvolt range, when coupled with on-line digital computers, have made a direct study of the physiology of living human beings possible.
5. W. G. Walter, "Intrinsic Rhythms of the Brain," in *Handbook of Physiology*, Sec. I: Neurophysiology, ed. J. Field, H. W. Mogoun, and V. E. Hall (Washington: American Physiological Society, 1959), vol. 1, chap. 2, pp. 279–298.
6. More elaborate theories have been proposed, a characteristic of research on organs which are complex and inaccessible to direct manipulation. One of the most interesting concerns a homeostatic model in which a cortical tonus is maintained between dreaming and nondreaming (deep sleep) where deprivation of one state causes the brain to make up the deficit by compensating with an increase in the time spent in that state when the opportunity presents itself. See H. S. Ephron and P. Carrington, "Rapid Eye Movement Sleep and Cortical Homeostasis," *Psychological Review* 73, no. 6 (1966): 500–526.
7. L. C. Johnson, "A Psychophysiology for All States," *Psychophysiology*

6, no. 5 (1970): 501–516. An excellent review of the state of the art of sleep research can be found in this article.

8. W. Dement and N. Kleitman, "The Relation of Eye Movements During Sleep to Dream Activity: An Objective Method for the Study of Dreaming," *Journal of Experimental Psychology* 53 (1957): 339–346; N. Kleitman, "Patterns of Dreaming," *Scientific American*, November 1960, pp. 82–88.

9. Before we get too comfortable with this neat distinction, we must take note of a dissenting voice. A group of researchers, taking the trouble to monitor EEG and REM over 24-hour periods, report seeing REM throughout the waking as well as the sleeping periods. They believe that REM is part of an overall cyclic pattern in the cortex, not necessarily related to sleep versus dreaming, the significance of which is unknown. See E. Othmer, H. P. Hayden, and R. Segalbaum, "Encephalic Cycles During Sleep and Wakefulness in Humans: a 24 Hr. Pattern," *Science* 164 (1969): 447–449.

10. This so-called "autonomic storm" is a phenomenon which also occurs in deep (NREM) periods for reasons which are not clear. A major problem for researchers results from the fact that different indices may have entirely different time histories and mathematical properties. The various central nervous system and peripheral nervous systems measures may or may not be related to consciousness.

11. D. B. Lindsley, "Attention, Consciousness, Sleep and Wakefulness," in *Handbook of Physiology*, ed. Field, Magoun, and Hall, vol. 3, chap. 64, pp. 15–63.

12. J. D. French, "The Reticular Formation," *Scientific American*, May 1957, pp. 1–8.

13. N. E. Miller, "Learning of Visceral and Glandular Responses," *Science* 163 (1969): 434–445.

14. B. L. Collier, "Brain Power: the Case for Bio-feedback Training," *Saturday Review*, 12 April 1971, pp. 10–58.

15. Investigators report similar vagueness in the subjects who successfully control the alpha waves of the EEG. But imagine the vagueness of any researcher when you ask him what an EEG really is!

16. J. Kamiya, "Operant Control of the EEG Alpha Rhythm and Some of Its Reported Effects on Consciousness," in *Altered States of Consciousness*, ed. C. T. Tart (New York: Wiley, 1969), pp. 507–517.

17. E. R. Hilgard, "Altered States of Awareness," *Journal of Nervous and Mental Disease* 149, no. 1 (1969): 68–69.

18. R. K. Wallace, "Physiological Effects of Transcendental Meditation," *Science* 167 (1970): 1751–1754.

19. L. Grinspoon, "Marihuana," *Scientific American*, June 1969, pp. 17–25.

20. F. Barron, M. E. Jarvik, and S. Bunnell, "*The Hallucinogenic Drugs*," *Scientific American*, April 1964.

21. J. C. Grossman, R. Goldstein, and R. Eisenman, "Openness to Experience and Marijuana Use: an Initial Investigation," *Proceedings of the 79th Annual APA Convention* 6 (1971): 335–336.

22. C. Castaneda, *The Teachings of Don Juan: A Yaqui Way of Knowledge* (New York: Ballantine, 1968), pp. 33–35.

23. The literature on drug usage and its meaning for consciousness is enormous and growing. See T. Leary, "The Politics, Ethics and Meaning of Marijuana" and A. Watts, "Psychedelics and Religious Experience," in *Toward Social Change: A Handbook for Those Who Will*, ed. R. Buckhout et al. (New York: Harper & Row, 1971).
24. E. N. Sokolov, "Neuronal Models and the Orienting Reflex," in *The Central Nervous System and Behavior*, ed. M. A. B. Brazier, Transactions of the Third Conference (New York: Josiah Macy, Jr., Foundation, 1960).
25. W. Heron, "The Pathology of Boredom," *Scientific American*, January 1957. See also P. Solomon et al. eds., *Sensory Deprivation* (Cambridge: Harvard University Press, 1961).

FIVE

The Selective Function of Consciousness

Are there any obvious facts about consciousness, any propositions that every educated adult in our culture would have to accept?

A few, perhaps. No doubt everyone agrees that consciousness is filled with well-organized objects, events, and symbols; consciousness refers to things that exist outside itself. Everyone agrees that the content of consciousness changes from one moment to the next. And we all must agree that we cannot think about everything at once. Everyone would probably agree that changes in consciousness are continuous; there is no succession of discrete photographs, but a stream that flows from one state of consciousness to the next. Probably we would agree also that consciousness is filled with relations; we continually judge the good-or-bad, the more-or-less, the before-or-after of one particular conscious object in terms of, or relative to, other objects.

Such statements merely list things that intelligent people already understand. However, of all these simple statements, and many others that might be added, there is one that stands out as being central to the psychologist's task: *consciousness is selective*. We are constantly swimming through oceans of information, far more than we could ever notice and understand; without some effective way to select what is important, we would surely drown.

No one has described the selective function of consciousness more eloquently than William James in his famous chapter on "The Stream of Thought." The following summary paragraph is still worth careful reading.

Looking back, then, over this review, we see that the mind is at every stage a theatre of simultaneous possibilities. Consciousness consists in the comparison of these with each other, the selection of some, and the suppression of the rest by the reinforcing and inhibiting agency of attention. The highest and most elaborated mental products are filtered from the data chosen by the faculty next beneath, out of the mass offered by the faculty below that, which mass in turn was sifted from a still larger amount of yet simpler material, and so on. The mind, in short, works on the data it receives very much as a sculptor works on his block of stone. In a sense the statue stood there from eternity. But there were a thousand different ones beside it, and the sculptor alone is to thank for having extricated this one from the rest. Just so the world of each of us, howsoever different our several views of it may be, all lay embedded in the primordial chaos of sensations, which gave the mere *matter* to the thought of all of us indifferently. We may, if we like, by our reasonings unwind things back to that black and jointless continuity of space and moving clouds of swarming atoms which science calls the only real world. But all the while the world *we* feel and live in will be that which our ancestors and we, by slowly cumulative strokes of choice, have extricated out of this, like sculptors, by simply rejecting certain portions of the given stuff. Other sculptors, other statues from the same stone! Other minds, other worlds from the same monotonous and inexpressive chaos! My world is but one in a million alike embedded, alike real to those who may abstract them. How different must be the worlds in the consciousness of ant, cuttlefish, or crab![1]

Phrases such as these should roll forward majestically into a lecture hall of thousands of upturned faces, hushed and waiting. They are too large in their conception for a scientist's laboratory, too spacious in their style for a scholar's study. How could anyone more forcefully express his conviction that consciousness is at all times primarily a *selecting* agency? It selects not only what we do, but how we see, as well. Could a listener doubt he had heard the Truth?

Of course, there are always cynics—suspicious people who charge that eloquence flourishes where the evidence is weakest. If you select one world and your friend selects another, they say, there must be some meaningful consequence; you must bump into each other, or have violent arguments, or be mutually invisible, or *something*. How do we get a scientific grip on James's ideas and force them to lead us toward some outcome, some measurement?

To critics who will settle for nothing short of proof, there is little to say. But for those willing to consider examples, there are many at hand. The dots in Figure 5.1 will group and regroup themselves, shifting as we move our eyes about from point to point. Or look up at the stars on a clear night and try to imagine how men came to see there Aries the Ram, Taurus the Bull, Gemini the Twins, and all the other zodiacal constellations that encircle the sky; try to imagine how many alternative organizations might have been selected from the same "monotonous and inexpressive chaos." Or drop ink onto paper haphazardly, then fold the paper to produce a symmetrical design. You will recognize many familiar objects in the ink blot, and your friends will recognize different ones. Twenty years after James wrote about the selective nature of consciousness, the Swiss psychiatrist Herman

FIGURE 5.1

A regular grid of dots can show a variety of patterns.

Rorschach recognized that the choices people make when they recognize things in such patterns reflect significant aspects of personality; the result was his famous ink-blot test.[2] It is an example of a *projective test*, so-called because the person unwittingly projects himself into his perception of the environment. James said that all perceptions are, at some stage in our development, similarly selected from an assortment of alternative perceptions we might have had instead.

Rhythm provides an illustration of James's thesis. Some of the earliest scientific observations reported from the first laboratory of experimental psychology—the laboratory founded by Wundt at the University of Leipzig—concerned the perception of rhythmic patterns.[3] In order to reproduce those early experiments we require an accurate metronome. If the metronome is constructed correctly, every click will be the same as every other click, and every interval between clicks will be the same duration as every other interval.

A metronome generates a steady train of clicks, yet no one hears it as a steady train; the listener imposes a rhythmic pattern of his own choosing, in common time, triple time, or whatever he prefers. Two different listeners can be exposed to exactly the same steady train of acoustic pulses, yet hear them in entirely different patterns. The consequence of imposing a rhythmic organization is to make some clicks sound louder than others and to make some intervals sound longer than others, although we know such impressions are illusory. In William James's metaphor, a rhythmic pattern is the psychological sculpture that we carve as we will from the indifferent clicks of the clock.

We can make several different observations of our conscious selection of a pattern for these clicks, but we need a collaborator. One person should control the metronome (he is the *experimenter*), and

FIGURE 5.2

An inkblot of the sort used by Rorschach.

the other person should be free to concentrate on his perception of the clicks (he is the *subject* in the experiment). With two persons, try the following test. The experimenter sets the metronome going at a medium rate, say, one click a second or a little slower, and lets it run for, say, exactly ten separate clicks. Then after a short pause he lets it run again for exactly the same number of clicks, or for one more or one less. A subject who listens attentively to these two strings of clicks will recognize immediately whether they were the same. It is not a matter of counting the clicks as they occur; the recognition of the pattern is direct and immediate. It is similar to the visual difference between a triangle and a square; the distinction can be drawn immediately, without counting the sides. Or, to put the point differently, the two strings of clicks are perceived as complete wholes, and one whole is compared with the other. (It should be noted, however, that the rate is important. If the metronome is too slow, the pattern falls apart. If it is too fast, no rhythm is perceived.)

The space we call "here" and the time we call "now" are not infinitesimal, like mathematical points. They have extension, they cover a span in space and in time. The size of that span is an important feature of consciousness. How much we include in here-now is not a question we can refer to experts on physical space and time; it is determined by the way our minds work, by the limitations of our own consciousness. The psychologist must find his own method to measure the size of the clear focus of consciousness that we call our attention.

We can use a metronome to estimate the temporal duration of here-now. Phrase the matter in terms of clicks: How many clicks of a metronome can a subject hold together in consciousness? The answer depends on the speed of the clicks and also on the way the clicks are rhythmically grouped. The early German psychologists (who tried it with clicks coming about once a second) found that when they grouped the clicks by pairs

click-click—*click*-click—*click*-click—*click*-click

the maximum number they could hold in mind at once was sixteen, or eight pairs of clicks. However, if they adopted a more complicated rhythmic pattern

CLICK-click—*click*-click—*CLICK*-click—*click*-click

they could appreciate a total of forty clicks at one time before the pattern broke apart. With the complicated pattern, one rhythmic chunk consists of eight clicks, and five of these chunks can be grasped in consciousness at once. The additional span—forty instead of sixteen—is attributable to the more complicated rhythm, which in turn was achieved by having four intensities of emphasis. (A curious fact reported by Wundt and his students was that they were unable to differentiate more than four grades of emphasis.)

Other exercises are possible with a metronome, but we have seen enough to demonstrate the point. Consciousness is free, within limits, to select whatever pattern you like. While one is listening to waltz time, a neighbor can hear the same clicks in march time. This depends on what one selects through the "reinforcing and inhibiting agency of attention."

William James was not thinking merely of rhythmic patterns. Clicks are just one way to illustrate the selections we must make in order to maintain a conscious organization of the world around us. As a matter of fact, James disliked this example, since the clicks of a metronome are so discrete and independent. He preferred to describe consciousness as a stream that flows continuously, not as a succession of discrete ideas or sensations. Even so, the clicks exemplify James's thesis that everything in your consciousness must have a pattern and a meaning that are peculiarly your own. In William James's theory, the selection of that pattern is the central task of consciousness.

We introduced the metronome in order to conciliate the cautious critics who felt that if James was talking about anything real, this reality must make an observable difference in the way the world runs. If we have saved James from their wrath, however, we have done it by offering an even better target. Any self-respecting cynic should now be eager to attack, not James, but Wundt! "How in the name of science can anyone refer to such shenanigans as an *experiment!*" The critic is red in the face; suppose we listen to his complaints.

"In the first place," he assails Professor Wundt, "how can you say that eight pairs, or five octuplets, or any other aggregates set a limit to consciousness? When I listen I am uncertain as to the exact instant my conscious whole breaks down; it doesn't break so much as crumble and fade away. Perhaps you were counting unconsciously. Am I supposed to accept your work just because you are a famous professor? Suppose I summon up all the prestige I can muster and use it to tell the next subject that his limit will be just half of what you claim. Will he dare to contradict me? Is your result so clear and inevitable that we can rule out any possible distortions caused by the suggestibility of the subject? There is no way to check on the subject, to decide whether he is fooling us, and himself as well. If you admit his subjective reports as if they were scientific evidence, you will have no criterion left whereby to exclude prejudice, authority, or revelation. You would undermine the very foundations of modern science!"

Our critic is here launching into a familiar argument, so we need not record his hoarse shouts in every indignant detail. At the heart of the problem lies the privacy of the experience that Wundt reports; the experience is something to which he claims special, immediate, personal, privileged access. But no one has yet built much of anything scientific out of private experience. Science has achieved its remarkable success only because it has insisted inflexibly that it must be public, impersonal, explicit, symbolic. Reports of private, subjective experiences—even when carefully controlled in the manner prescribed by Wundt—provide no basis for sure agreement. The clicks of the metronome are relatively innocent, but in more interesting and only slightly more complex situations the introspective reports obtained from subjects in different laboratories simply do not agree. Introspectors have a notorious talent for finding in their minds almost anything they look for. Even Wundt's own students, all trained to introspect in the same way in the same laboratory, frequently disagreed with each other and with the master.

This situation became so disturbing, as a matter of fact, that such men as I. P. Pavlov in Russia and J. B. Watson in the United States attracted much favorable attention and support when they claimed that consciousness does not exist; that if it does exist, one cannot make a science out of it; and that if one could, it would have to be a science of behavior, not of consciousness. The persistence of such mentalistic confusion is due, they said, to the lack of an adequate physiology of the brain. The assault upon Wundt's introspective method was so successful that even today, half a century later, some psychologists feel slightly sinful when they permit themselves to refer to the mind, consciousness, attention, sensation, etc. Consciousness may exist, in some metaphorical sense of existence, yet it has no effect upon the physiological processes in the body. Can a shadow carry stones?

But this is only one line our critic can take. There are others.

He might ask Professor Wundt, "What about differences among people? Surely you cannot believe that everyone will give the same report. What of those people—most Africans, musicians generally, and tympanists in particular—who spend years of loving study on beautifully intricate and complex rhythmic patterns? Or, at the other extreme, what about young children or animals? Are they not different from a dignified and elderly *Gelehrter?* How elastic are the limits? How does the ability to organize rhythmic patterns vary as a function of other things?" One doubts whether Wundt considered these questions; if so, they did not interest him. It remained for Francis Galton in England, James McKeen Cattell in the United States, Alfred Binet in France, and many other psychologists all over the world to discover and develop the importance of individual differences.

Finally, a critic always has recourse to the devastating question, "So what? Suppose all you say is true. Even suppose it is true for everybody, everywhere. What then? What of poetry and work, of love and death and beauty? What of everything that really matters? The dust on your metronome, *Herr Professor,* is six feet deep. While we yearn to understand the deep, throbbing forces that drive us headlong through our modern jungles, you sit at your metronome counting clicks. It is better to count the leaves on trees, for then at least you get fresh air and exercise for your pains."

Critics who reject the significance of Wundt's observations may reject psychology completely—at best, they turn from Wundt to seek a psychology more directly relevant to their own lives. They may be curious about the phenomena of their personal consciousness, yet feel that to reduce those phenomena to the status of metronome clicks is a preposterous distortion. These were the rebels who found Henri Bergson in France, Sigmund Freud in Austria, and Carl Jung in Switzerland such a welcome relief.

These criticisms of Wundt suggest some of the directions taken by modern psychologists. For the moment, however, it is important to establish that, in spite of all the objections, the observations reported by Wundt were essentially correct.

Attention is not some superstitious fiction; its effects can be demonstrated by physiological techniques every bit as objective and scientific as any used by Pavlov or Watson. For example, it is possible to record the electrical activity of the auditory nerve of a cat. If one presents repeated clicks to a relaxed and drowsy cat, one can record repeated pulses of neural activity in the cat's ear. But now distract the cat's attention. Let the cat smell the odor of fish, or let it glimpse mice constrained in a glass beaker. Once the cat begins to pay active attention to what its nose or its eyes are reporting, the neural pulses from its ear almost completely disappear. When the acoustic clicks become irrelevant the cat seems not to respond to them in any way. The central mechanism of attention is so powerful and effective that when one kind of information has been selected, the other receptor organs are simply turned off.[4]

Moreover, rhythmic grouping is a universal fact about people; all cultures have some form of rhythmic performance such as music or dancing. Of course, there are individual differences, but for the average adult in our culture, the numerical values given by Wundt for the conscious span are approximately correct. There are several ways to measure such spans, some more objective than others, but all give similar results. As a matter of fact, Wundt was aware of other possible methods; he himself cites them in support of his studies with the metronome.

Consider some of the possible methods. Suppose we ask subjects to sit in a darkened room where they can watch a projection screen. On the screen we flash briefly a picture of round, black dots against a white background. The number of dots can vary from two or three up to a hundred or more. The pattern of the dots is always different, always haphazard. The exposure time for the random pattern of dots will be of the order of a tenth of a second, long enough for a clear view of the pattern but too short for subjects to move their eyes to a second fixation point in the pattern. (The device used for producing these brief exposures is called a tachistoscope.) On the basis of one short glance a subject must guess how many dots there were in the pattern.

Up to five dots, perhaps six, subjects are never in doubt and almost never wrong. They do not need to count the separate dots; they see the number directly. For seven or more dots, however, subjects begin to make mistakes; the larger the number of dots, the bigger their errors are likely to be. There is a sharp break in their performance, a break that occurs in the neighborhood of six dots.[5] This value, six, can be taken as a measure of the span of attention. It should be compared with the five to eight rhythmic chunks Wundt reported when listening to clicks of a metronome. It can also be compared with the six positions for the points that are used in Braille printing for the blind. Six points are as many as the blind person can recognize accurately by touch. Since the values for visual dots, auditory clicks, and tactual points are all so similar, one argues that it is not the sense organs—eye, ear, or skin—that set the limit. Instead, the limitation is imposed centrally, at a point in the nervous system where all the different senses converge to pass through the same bottleneck. It is, so the argument goes, our attention, not our sense organs, that is limited.

Another way to measure the momentary capacity of consciousness is to ask a subject to repeat something he has just heard or just read. This task is frequently included on tests of intelligence. The tester says, "Listen to the following numbers, and when I am through

Cartoon of POGO, by Walt Kelly.

repeat them back in the same order." He then gives two numbers. If the subject repeats them both, in the right order, the examiner goes on to three, then to four, to five, and so on, until the subject begins to make mistakes. The number of digits he can, on the average, repeat perfectly after one presentation is his span of immediate memory. The test is not diagnostic for superior adults; a very long span of immediate memory is not a reliable indication of superior intelligence. However, an unusually short span, two or three digits only, is a fairly reliable indication of mental deficit. As a rough figure, people of average intelligence can repeat six or seven digits without error. Note that this value is once more in the range we have learned to expect.

The span of immediate memory is not greatly affected by the kind of symbols we use to test it. If we ask a subject to repeat letters of the alphabet, we again find that he makes mistakes when there are more than about six or seven. Indeed, if we use short words taken at random from the dictionary, his span will be about five. This last result is particularly interesting, since the five words will be composed of some fifteen or twenty letters. That is to say, when the letters do not spell anything, but are chosen at random and so must be recalled individually, we can hold six or seven in mind at once, but if the letters spell words, we can recall three times as many. The situation is analogous to the rhythmic groups of the metronome, where the number of clicks that could be held together varied from sixteen to forty depending upon the way they were grouped.

How grouping helps to increase the amount of information that we can keep in mind at any instant can be explored as follows. Ask a generous and cooperative friend to let you test his span of immediate memory. First test him with ordinary digits, as above. Then test him with haphazard sequences of two words, "yes" and "no." The span for the average person is about eight or nine of these binary items. For example,

> no, no, no, yes, no, yes, yes, no, no

is as far as most people can go before they become confused and fail to remember accurately.

Now teach your friend the following code:

no-no-no	= 0	yes-no-no	= 4
no-no-yes	= 1	yes-no-yes	= 5
no-yes-no	= 2	yes-yes-no	= 6
no-yes-yes	= 3	yes-yes-yes	= 7

Make him practice it for thirty minutes. When he can snap it out quite automatically, test his span again. This time, however, instruct him to group the words into triplets as he listens to them, to recode the triplets as numbers, and to remember the number. When the time comes to recite he should simply translate back again from numbers into words. This new procedure, which requires the subject to group the items, turns the sample sequence given above into "no-no-no," "yes-no-yes," and "yes-no-no," which in turn is recorded as 054. The number 054 is easily remembered. In fact, we already know how many digits he can remember, and since each digit is worth three "yes" answers or "no" answers, we can predict how long a sequence of "yes" answers and "no" answers he will now be able to reproduce. A typical result is to increase his span from eight or nine up to twenty-one or twenty-four binary items.[6]

This trick of recoding one set of symbols into another is used by computing engineers. They must examine long rows of small lights which may be on or off according to the internal state of the computing machine. It is difficult to remember a pattern of lights if each light is regarded as a separate item of information. Therefore, people who work around the machines quickly memorize a little code, similar to the one given here, which enables them to group the lights and so to remember many more of them at one time.

Grouping clicks of the metronome into rhythmic feet, grouping letters of the alphabet into words, grouping rows of lights into coded triplets, share the feature that they enable us to make better use of our span of consciousness, to hold more information in mind at one time. This same economy works in our favor when we express our experiences in words and then remember the words, rather than the raw experience itself. We insulate ourselves from the world around us by a curtain of language. The reward is a greater efficiency in dealing with patterns, with organized parts of the world. It is the language we speak more than anything else we do, that represents the particular sculpture we have carved out of "the primordial chaos of sensations."

Notice that the selective function of consciousness and the limited span of attention are complementary ways of talking about the same thing. If there were no limits on the variety of information that we could contemplate simultaneously, there would be little cause to talk about selectivity. The fact that our minds are limited, critically limited to a minuscule allotment of seven psychological units at a time, forces us to use each symbol as effectively as possible. When a problem is too complex to fit into a man's consciousness, various elements of the problem must convene and elect symbols to represent them. And if there are still too many component parts, the elected symbols must themselves group together and elect more symbols to represent them at a still higher level in the hierarchy. Because consciousness is limited, we must consolidate and symbolize. How we choose to consolidate and symbolize is our style of selection, our way of comprehending this segment of our universe.

One hypothesis that has emerged from research on linguistics is the linguistic-relativity hypothesis, sometimes called the Whorf hypothesis in honor of the man who formulated it, Benjamin Lee Whorf. In essence, this hypothesis asserts that our language influences the way in which we perceive the world, it serves as a culturally built-in filter of our experiences, thus determining the selectivity of consciousness. As Whorf himself expresses it,

> The background linguistic system (in other words, the grammar) of each language is not merely a reproducing instrument for voicing ideas but rather is itself the shaper of ideas, the program and guide for the individual's mental activity, for his analysis of impressions, for his synthesis of his mental stock in trade. . . . We dissect nature along lines laid down by our native languages. . . . the world is presented in kaleidoscopic flux of impressions which has to be organized by our minds—and this means largely by the linguistic systems in our minds. We cut nature up, organize it into concepts, and ascribe significances as we do, largely because we are parties to an agreement to organize it in this way—an agreement that holds through our speech community and is codified in the patterns of our language.[7]

65

Anthropologists have reported on tribal languages that have, for example, words for only two color categories in the spectrum of colors, as opposed to the multitude of color categories in English. Presumably, the people who speak those languages would see a two-color rainbow—that is, would differentiate only two color categories—while we would see our customary seven colors (or would we?). This and other anecdotal examples have led to the Whorf hypothesis becoming a bit of a cliché, but it should be noted that there are dissenters who point to recent research on the semantic structure of different languages that stresses the great amount of *similarity* between languages. In related research, on the coding abilities of bilinguals, Kolers found that while a bilingual person may perform specific mental operations in the language that he first learned the operation in, he is able to understand the problem and give the answer in either language. Comprehension and perception in these highly sophisticated people appeared to be independent of language.[8]

However, the Whorf hypothesis remains compelling. Perhaps it cannot be thoroughly tested with educated people whose linguistic influences and shared communication tend to make their experiences rather homogeneous. It seems more likely that the answers will come from the study of people with unique experiences as well as a different language.

We have discussed some aspects of auditory selectivity. Now let us consider an example of visual attention. When we look at a picture of an unfamiliar landscape or a group of people we usually feel that we grasp it in consciousness as a whole, as a unified experience. Yet when we must answer questions about it, we are chagrined to discover that we did not see much after all. If we have only a single, brief glance, we will not be able to name more than about five or ten things that were in the picture. We may, for example, correctly recall that there was a horse in the picture, yet have no notion whether it was facing to the right or to the left.

But what if we have a prolonged look and can move our eyes over the entire scene? As we scan the picture our eyes do not glide smoothly along, but jump rapidly from one fixed position to the next. Sudden changes in the point of fixation can be recorded by special cameras, and it has been found that we make about three or four fixations per second when viewing a complex picture. A finite period of time is required in order to stop paying attention to one part of a picture and to start paying attention to another.

Some interesting records of eye movements have been made by Russian psychologists; two examples are shown in Figure 5.3. A. L. Yarbus recorded a person's eye movements while looking at pictures. Yarbus made the records by reflecting a beam of light from one eyeball onto sensitized paper; since the eyeball is not a perfect sphere, each movement altered the angle of reflection. His records show that normal eye movements tend to trace out the outlines of the scene being viewed. The picture of the young girl is almost redrawn by the viewer's eyes; the major details of the forest scene are clearly revealed. Each discontinuity in the recorded trace indicates a place where the person's eyes paused briefly to inspect the picture. The continuous lines show the very swift movements between resting points. Russian psychologists have used such records to diagnose effects of brain injuries; unlike the normal records shown here, the records produced by patients with brain damage may be irregular and show little relation to the contours of the picture.

Records of eye movements show clearly that the unified, integrated experience we get when we look at a scene is something we must actively construct out of dozens of short, quick snapshots aimed at different parts of it. Our attention shifts rapidly from one point to another until gradually we become familiar with all the parts and the relations among them.

William James, in the passage that has guided our discussion of consciousness and attention, pointed out that attention both selects and suppresses; attention is both a reinforcing and an inhibiting agency. If you choose one line of thought, you necessarily reject others. If you remember one episode, you are not remembering other episodes. The collection of symbols and feelings that are potentially available to consciousness, but that are temporarily unconscious, form part of what is usually called the preconscious mind. These momentarily rejected but potentially conscious ideas prove that we cannot identify mind with consciousness. The contents of the preconscious system are both mental and nonconscious, so we are forced to recognize that there is more to the mind than meets the inner eye.

The attentional filter hypothesis, a mechanistic model proposed by Broadbent, has served as a useful paradigm in research on attention.[9] The model schematizes a person who controls which one of two information channels he is going to attend to by shutting off the information processing in the other channel, much as the cat did in the previously described experiment. Such a filter can be thought of as a part of consciousness that functions on the basis of will, a person's attitudes and biases, the limits of his biological makeup, and other factors that determine selection in an individual. While no single part of the brain could be assumed to play the role of filter, our understanding of the ascending reticular activating system suggests that it plays some role in altering the general state of awareness of the cortex. But, even if a fine-grained filtering mechanism were found, the information that is momentarily blocked from attention must go somewhere.

A crude example, recommended only by its simplicity, is provided by our friend who learned to group and recode sequences of "yes" and "no." In the particular sequence given as an example, he would be conscious that the three triplets, "no-no-no," "yes-no-yes,"

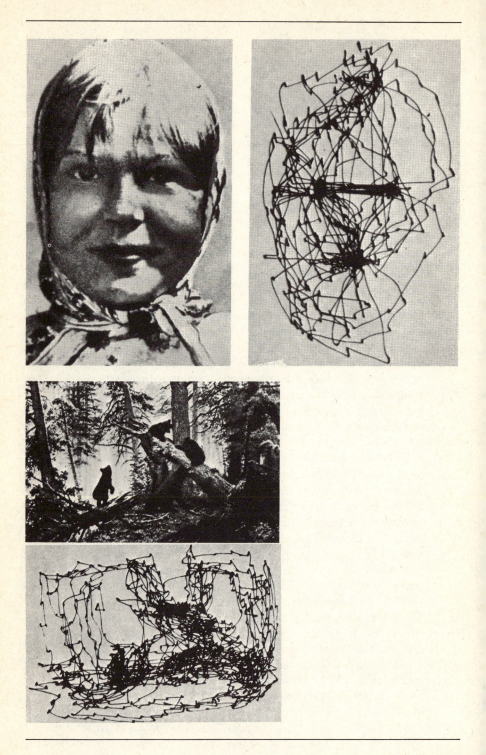

and "yes-no-no" occurred. But he would not be aware that "no-no-yes" also occurred. When he recalls the sequence correctly, of course, he will necessarily say "no, no, yes," as part of it, but if we ask him whether or not he said "no, no, yes," he cannot be certain until he has repeated the sequence with a new orientation toward it. Until he has done this, he is not aware of what he said. We should not make a mystery of the phenomenon; the particular triplet occurs out of step with the grouping he used. He was not thinking about the grouping in these terms.

One can say, with James and many other psychologists, that the ideas and the organizations that a person chooses will actively *suppress* his awareness of other ideas and other organizations. But we should remember that this is a figure of speech. We are not required to conjure up some vigilant demon who actively shoves things downward out of sight. Suppression is accomplished more subtly, as a necessary consequence of the fact that attention is limited and selective. When repressive demons seem to be at work, we have passed beyond the normal processes of preconscious thought into the darker regions of the unconscious mind.

Processes of preconscious organization and selection are critically important in creative thinking. Somehow, by free association or by the confluence of many simultaneous streams of thought, preconscious processes enable us to leap to intuitive conclusions that we are able to verify or disprove consciously only after slow, tedious, step-by-step argument and deduction. "Preconscious mentation," a psychiatrist has said, "is the Seven-league Boot of intuitive creative functions."[10]

What determines how the preconscious will work, what contents and patterns it will present to consciousness, how much freedom or constraint it will enjoy? Rigorous answers cannot be given. One supposes that what we pay attention to—the middle-sized things that populate the center of our minds—are in large measure determined by the way we are built, both genetically and habitually. We pay attention to sudden noises or unexpected flashes of light because we are born with reflex reactions to such stimuli; we group the sounds of speech in certain ways because we have learned to speak and understand the language they represent. But over and beyond those relatively stable patterns of selection and organization there still remains, even in the sophisticated adult, an area of freedom where personal needs, interests, motivations are allowed to act.

An advertising man, after spending more than a billion dollars

---

◄——— FIGURE 5.3

Records of eye movements show which parts of a picture receive the most attention. (*From* The New York Times, *24 April 1960.*)

69

of his client's money to find out what makes people notice something, concluded that we allocate our attention to different categories of information according to how important we judge them to be. There is a limit to what we are willing to notice and remember about tires, tobacco, or toothpaste; advertisers compete for their share of the very small amount we care to know about their type of product. The advertising man developed this view of an average consumer: "It is as though he carries a small box in his head for a given product category. The box is limited either by his inability to remember or his lack of interest. It is filled with miscellaneous data, and, when a new campaign forces in more, some data are forced out, and the box spills over."[11] An effective advertisement may increase an advertiser's share of the box, but it will not increase the size of the box itself. The size of each box is a basic parameter of the preconscious system, one not likely to be much affected by bright colors and catchy tunes.

It is probably worth making a distinction between preconscious *contents*—symbols and feelings that could be conscious but momentarily are not—and preconscious *processes*—operations and transformations that seem to be necessarily unconscious. Thinking is a good example of a preconscious process. The fact that the process of thinking has no possible access into consciousness may seem surprising at first, but it can be verified quite simply. At this moment, as you are now reading, try to think of your mother's maiden name.

What happened? What was your conscious awareness of the process that produced the name? Most persons report they had feelings of tension, of strain unrelated to the task, and then suddenly the answer was there in full consciousness. There may have been a fleeting image or two, but they were irrelevant. Consciousness gives no clue as to where the answer comes from; the processes that produce it are unconscious. It is *result* of thinking, not the process of thinking, that appears spontaneously in consciousness.[12]

Look across the room at a chair.

Did you see it as a chair? Or did you see it as a mosaic of isolated sensations that had to be consciously welded into a coherent perception?

The fact that the perceptual object was so immediately present in consciousness implies that the many operations you had to perform upon the visual information were all unconscious. Helmholtz noticed this more than a century ago when he spoke of the unconscious inferences or unconscious conclusions that are always involved in perception. Of course, the average person ordinarily remains ignorant of all the work he does when he recognizes a chair. In order to convince him, we must ask him to describe a machine that would recognize objects the same way he does. Then he begins to appreciate what a complicated process must be operating.

What is true of thinking and of perceiving is true in general. We can state it as a general rule: no activity of mind is ever conscious. In particular, the mental activities involved in our desires and emotions are never conscious. Only the end products of these motivational processes ever become known to us directly. The impulses behind our actions can only be inferred from their conscious and behavioral consequences.

Take dreams as an example. Dreams can provide a highly imaginative, sometimes truly creative synthesis of the events of the day, of remembered episodes, personal associations, desires, passions. The synthesis is often cleverly contrived, as you will discover if you attempt to decipher some of your own dreams. In order to interpret them, the basic assumption you must make is that nothing in your dreams occurs accidentally. Everything can be explained in terms of your personal history. Often—but not always—the events and people that occur in your dreams do not mean what they seem to mean on the surface, but turn out on closer analysis to stand as symbols for something else, usually something less pleasant for you to contemplate. Whether the dream symbols are introduced to disguise a disturbing idea or whether they represent the same kind of psychological processes involved in slang or figures of speech is still a matter for argument. But the point is that dream episodes are fabricated by a kind of thinking whose end product appears spontaneously, surprisingly, during sleep. "The interpretation of dreams," said Sigmund Freud, "is the royal road to a knowledge of the unconscious activities of mind."

Then there is hypnosis. Under hypnosis a subject temporarily allows another person, the hypnotist or operator, to plan for him, to manage his thoughts and images. During this period the operator may tell the subject that after he returns to normal he will do something without remembering why. The commonist demonstration is posthypnotic amnesia; a subject is told that he will remember nothing that went on during the time he was hypnotized. Thereafter, the subject's unwillingness to explore this part of his memory is similar to the avoidance of unpleasant, painful facts by normal, unhypnotized persons. These avoided ideas are kept out of consciousness. But they can return when the proper signal is given or when the proper occasion occurs for them to take effect. Thus, a hypnotist may tell the subject to trip and stumble accidentally against the first bald man he sees after he awakens. The awakened subject has no reportable memory of this instruction, he behaves quite naturally in every way; but when the signal—the bald man—appears, the subject stumbles against him, apologizes, and goes on unaware that his stumbling was not accidental.

Hypnotists should always make clear to a subject when the suggestion will be completed. Even if it is not acted upon, the hypnotist cannot assume that it was ignored. In any case, he must cancel it, terminate it. The sort of difficulties that can arise are illustrated in this story.[13] A hypnotist attempted to produce a blister on the right forearm of a young woman by suggesting to her that he was applying a piece of red-hot metal to it. The suggestion apparently had no effect, and the hypnotist went on to other things, forgetting to cancel the blister-producing idea. The patient went home, but returned several days later suffering from a burn on her right forearm where a blister had formed on the very spot previously chosen by the hypnotist. The patient had no memory of the suggestion. She had "accidentally" spilled scalding water on her arm when lifting a pot with her left hand to make coffee. The accident finally terminated a suggestion that the hypnotist thought had been completely ineffectual. Similar stories can be adduced by any experienced hypnotist.

A theoretical argument with practical consequences continues over the question of whether hypnosis produces a genuine altered state of consciousness.[14] One side argues that a person under hypnosis is merely role-playing, that is, voluntarily submitting to suggestion; his consciousness in this state differs from the waking state only in such a way as to be more open to suggestion. Defenders of hypnosis as an altered state see the trance state as one in which the person has surrendered control and is no longer able to control his behavior. This dichotomy of opinion played a part in the trial of Sirhan-Sirhan, the convicted slayer of Senator Robert Kennedy. Sirhan's attorneys claimed that he practiced self-hypnosis in accord with the beliefs of the Rosicrucian movement, and that since his plan to kill Senator Kennedy came during the trances, he was not responsible for his behavior. As expert witnesses from both sides testified in this trial, the research dilemma became a public matter, with the jury eventually accepting the argument that Sirhan could not be excused. Neither the researchers nor the courts have closed the debate over whether a person can be held responsible for his actions when he is in an allegedly altered state of consciousness.

Still another source of evidence that the processes of the mind are not conscious is the fact that life is full of accidents that can not possibly be wholly accidental, but seem to be determined by causes unknown to the actor. The posthypnotic accidents just mentioned illustrate the mechanism whereby such events can occur, but hypnotism is not a necessary precondition. Sigmund Freud filled a book, *The Psychopathology of Everyday Life*, with examples of the forgotten name, the mispronounced word, the inadvertently broken promise, the misplaced wedding ring, the unexpectedly favorable (but unfortunately inaccurate) balance in the bank account, and so on—all normal occurrences with definite and discoverable causes that the person did not consciously recognize. The motives often revealed by these little slips are so widely recognized today that the "Freudian slip" has become an established fact even in lay psychology. Not every slip requires a Freudian explanation, but many do.

These are but a few of the reasons for believing that a person cannot be conscious of all his mental processes. Many other reasons can be cited. Drugs are known that relax some people and put them into a state in which they can recall emotionally disturbing episodes that they cannot recall under normal circumstances. Physiological measurements reveal the occurrence of emotional responses to particular events, emotions that have no representation in the person's conscious experience. And so on and on.

We have described these mental operations as preconscious; they influence conscious contents and reflect the person's efforts to cope with his environment. Medical psychologists, however, recognize another kind of nonconscious process, more rigid, more compulsive, more maladaptive. These are unconscious mechanisms. They manifest themselves most clearly in the abnormal behavior of neurotic and psychotic patients—unfortunate persons no longer able to lead productive lives. Difficulty with the selective and organizing functions of consciousness is a common symptom of neurosis. Sometimes emotionally disturbing ideas are stubbornly rejected; at other times they break through and interrupt every effort at concentration. Thus the neurotic unconscious seems to block the normal flow of preconscious processes. Unconscious processes typically have their own dynamism, independent of the situation in which the person finds himself; they are wounds that never healed, losses never mitigated, remnants of the ancient battles of childhood. These are realms explored by psychoanalysis.

It was not very long ago—less than a century—that mind and consciousness were regarded as one and the same. As soon as one begins to examine consciousness, however, one realizes that it is selective, that there is a preconscious system of rejected options. But only in the twentieth century have we begun to appreciate how vast this nonconscious region is, how much we rely on the intuitive leaps of preconscious thought, how crippled we can be by the scars of unconscious wounds.

Our ideas about nonconscious mental activities are still open for debate and revision. Some psychologists split the questions up one way, some another. But most psychologists who have tried to peer beyond consciousness know well that they can find in this elastic concept almost anything they want. The preconscious and the unconscious are repositories for all the processes that psychologists assume *must* exist to explain what people do. Some psychologists assume that the nonconscious contains a seething mass of passion and desire. Or it is full of instincts or habits or all the tacit mental functions that are performable, not knowable. But, whatever else may be hidden in these dark recesses, one can be sure there will always be room left for the psychologist's theories. For it is only through theory, never through direct awareness, that one discovers the nonconscious mind.

Two passengers leaned against the ship's rail and stared at the sea. "There sure is a lot of water in the ocean," said one. "Yes," answered his friend, "and we've only seen the top of it."

NOTES

1. William James, *The Principles of Psychology* (New York: Holt, 1890), vol. 1, pp. 288–289.
2. For a critical review, see S. B. Sarason, *The Clinical Interaction, with Special Reference to the Rorschach* (New York: Harper, 1954).
3. W. Wundt, *An Introduction to Psychology*, trans. R. Pinter (London: Allen, 1912).
4. R. Hernandez-Peon, H. Scherrer, and M. Jouvet, "Modification of Electrical Activity in Cochlear Nucleus During 'Attention' in Unanesthetized Cats," *Science* 123 (1956): 331–332.
5. E. L. Kaufman, M. W. Lord, T. W. Reese, and John Volkmann, "The Discrimination of Visual Number," *American Journal of Psychology*, 62 (1949): 498–525.
6. G. A. Miller, "The magical number Seven, Plus or minus Two," *Psychological Review* 63 (1956): 81–97.
7. B. L. Whorf, *Language Thought and Reality: Selected Writings*, ed. J. B. Carroll (Cambridge, Mass.: Technology Press of MIT, 1956), pp. 212–213.
8. P. A. Kolers, "Reading and Talking Bilingually," *American Journal of Psychology* 79 (1966): 357–376.
9. D. E. Broadbent, *Perception and Communication* (London: Pergamon, 1958) and *Decision and Stress* (New York: Academic Press, 1971).
10. L. S. Kubie, *Neurotic Distortion of the Creative Process* (Lawrence: University of Kansas Press, 1958).
11. R. Reeves, *Reality in Advertising* (New York: Knopf, 1961).
12. K. S. Lashley, "Cerebral Organization and Behavior," in *The Brain and Human Behavior*, Proceedings of the Association for Research on Nervous and Mental Disease (Baltimore: Williams & Wilkins, 1958).
13. Recounted by Andre M. Weitzenhoffer, *General Techniques of Hypnotism* (New York: Grune and Stratton, 1957), p. 83.
14. E. R. Hilgard, "Altered States of Awareness," *The Journal of Nervous and Mental Disease* 149, no. 1 (1969): 68–79.

SIX

William James, Philosopher

AMERICAN PRAGMATISM

"The modern movement known as pragmatism," wrote Ralph Barton Perry, "is largely the result of James's misunderstanding of Peirce." It is one of the rare passages in his distinguished biography, *The Thought and Character of William James*, where Perry seems less than fair to his hero. James understood quite well how his lifelong friend, Charles S. Peirce, defined pragmatism. But James imposed a personal stamp on his friend's invention. A more accurate summation, perhaps, is that Peirce provided a tool that James used in ways Peirce could not accept. And so it happened that pragmatism, the most characteristic philosophic expression of the American mind, was born with two heads.

Three, really, if we count John Dewey's. According to Morton White, "Peirce is the pragmatic philosopher of science, James the pragmatic philosopher of religion, and Dewey the pragmatic philosopher of morals." But White adds a warning that, "It is not always the same pragmatism that they apply to these different problems."[1] What the three philosophers had in common was not so much a specific set of doctrines as an attitude of mind, a general way of defining and attacking problems. In details they could hardly be expected to agree—three more different personalities than the eccentric, creative, sometimes deliberately obscure Peirce, the urbane, eloquent, almost evangelistic James, and the systematic, discursive, democratic, but often dull Dewey can scarcely be imagined. That they could tolerate one another was a tribute to their common vocation.

The name and the doctrine of pragmatism first saw light in the early 1870s when Peirce explained his ideas to "The Metaphysical Club," a group that included Peirce, James, Wendell Holmes, Chauncey Wright, and several other defiant young intellectuals around Harvard at the time. Peirce published his argument in 1878 in one of his least obscure papers, "How to Make Our Ideas Clear." His original, careful but cumbrous statement of the pragmatic rule for attaining clarity was: "Consider what effects, which might

conceivably have practical bearings, we conceive the object of our conception to have. Then, our conception of these effects is the whole of our conception of the object." "Practical bearings" are the crucial words. What, for example, is electricity? According to Peirce, our whole conception of electricity is our conception of the practical effects of electricity.

As Peirce formulated pragmatism, it was a method of getting at the meanings of our ideas. To discover the meaning of a statement, one must translate it into a hypothesis to the effect that if such-and-such an operation is performed, such-and-such experiences will ensue. The meaning of the statement, "John is 6 feet tall," becomes clear when we translate it into the hypothesis, "If you count the number of times a foot rule can be placed end-to-end between the floor and the top of his head when he is standing erect, you will find that the result is six."

Peirce's approach to meaning contrasts sharply with the traditional approach of British empiricists. In the eighteenth century Bishop Berkeley, for example, held that the meaning of any statement is the mental image we form of it. The meaning of "John" is the image of John. The meaning of "John is 6 feet tall" is the image of John tucked into an image of the 6-foot span. The image theory of meaning involved British empiricists in absurd difficulties. For example, what is the meaning of triangle? It is your mental image of a triangle. But your image must be an image of a particular triangle—isosceles, equilateral, scalene, right-angled, obtuse—whereas the meaning of triangle in general is all and none of these simultaneously. Therefore, said Berkeley, it is impossible to have an abstract idea! It was this sort of nonsense Peirce explicitly and emphatically denied. The meaning of triangle is contained in the hypothesis, "If one examines the sides one discovers there are three, intersecting, straight lines," and in the hypothesis, "If one counts the number of angles, one sees that there are three," and in the hypothesis, "If one adds up the number of degrees in the angles, one sees that there are 180 degrees," and so forth. Whether or not an abstract image can be found in the furniture of the mind is entirely irrelevant, said the pragmatic Peirce, to the meaningfulness of the concept. In 1878 the mind was still being analyzed into elementary sensations, images, and feelings by Berkeley's intellectual descendents; Peirce's contribution to logic was therefore potentially of considerable significance for psychology.

Without William James, however, it is unlikely that Peirce's pragmatism could have affected psychology for another fifty years or so. It would probably have remained, like so many of Peirce's creative insights, buried in obscurity, awaiting exhumation by the patient editors who compiled and published many of his papers in 1930, sixteen years after his death. But James appreciated Peirce's concept, transformed it, assimilated it into his own thinking, and made it part of the large and motley assortment of ideas he accepted in his philosophic vision of a pluralistic universe. Where Peirce was often obscure—sometimes even deliberately obscure—James was brilliantly clear and interesting, with a gift of apt metaphor seldom equalled in science or literature. And so the pragmatic thesis was spread abroad in the most persuasive manner possible. It was so persuasive, in fact, that Peirce scarcely recognized that James's version derived from his own. To make the distinction explicit, Peirce renamed his own views "pragmaticism," which he hoped would be "ugly enough to be safe from kidnapers."

In 1907 James, in a book entitled *Pragmatism*, applied Peirce's maxim to the concept of truth. What is the meaning of a statement such as " 'John is 6 feet tall' is true"? Does it mean anything more than "John is 6 feet tall"? Following Peirce's advice, one tries to translate the statement into a hypothesis: If one performs such-and-such operations, such-and-such experiences will ensue. But how can this translation be made? There seem to be no reasonable operations that one can perform to test whether "*P* is true" is meaningful. Does that mean that "true" is meaningless by pragmatic standards? James argued that it was necessary to generalize the notion of an operation; not merely physical operations, but psychological operations must be permitted. To tell someone "*P* is true" is to tell him that he can believe it. Still, this is only half the hypothesis: "If you believe *P*, then . . ." Then what? What experiences should result from believing *P* if *P* is indeed true? Surely nothing evil or unfortunate can result from believing the truth. The complete hypothesis, therefore, must be "*P* is true" means "If you believe *P*, the effects will be satisfactory to you."

So long as the proposition *P* involved "John is 6 feet tall" or other correspondingly testable propositions, little harm could come from translating "*P* is true" in the way James advocated. But what if *P* were some such proposition as "There is a God"? This was exactly the class of statements James was most interested in, and his pragmatic formulation of truth enabled him to reintroduce into philosophy problems that the positivistic and materialistic thinkers of the nineteenth century had long since rejected. James argued that "There is a God" is true if, when one believes it, the results are satisfactory. Although he made the argument in erudite and subtle terms, the message that came through to the philosophically unsophisticated public who heard him was: "Anything is true if it works." To European ears this sounded as if the raw, backwoods Americans were trying to rationalize their preoccupation with material objects and financial profits or, at best, as if a new form of antiintellectualism had taken root in the United States. A major trouble with James's theory of truth—a difficulty Peirce recognized immediately—was that the operation of believing and the consequence of satisfaction are personal, subjective, individualistic, whereas the customary definition of truth is public. James insisted that the truth he was talking about was a truth for the individual. Peirce insisted that the truth science requires is interpersonal. A scientific proposition is not simultaneously true for those who believe it and false for those who do not—it is either true or false, and one group or the other must be wrong. Of course, Peirce was not in favor of an idealistic Absolute Truth; but James's alternative was so completely relative that it seemed to Peirce a fatal mistake.

If Peirce invented pragmatism and James popularized it, John Dewey applied it—that is, he applied pragmatism to social problems in general and to education in particular. In Dewey's hands the new philosophy emphasized experimental approaches to all problems, logical and ethical as well as scientific. He began with a biological conception of man, the conception of an organism trying to adapt to, or come to terms with, its environment. When difficulties are encountered it becomes necessary for the organism to stop and think. An emphasis on the instrumental nature of thought was one of Dewey's most characteristic contributions to the pragmatic tradition; his own version of pragmatism he called instrumentalism. In this biological orientation Dewey remained close to the views James expressed in *The Principles of Psychology*. In his pragmatism, however, Dewey seemed to favor Peirce. Dewey's interest in social processes, for example, made him agree with Peirce that truth must be publicly, socially determined, not set by the whim of an individual.

Whereas Peirce had said that operational thinking is necessary to discover the meaning of any scientific conception, Dewey argued that operational thinking is necessary to judge the *value* of any thing or activity. A thing is not valuable merely because one happens to enjoy it; in order to assign value to it, one must conduct carefully controlled experiments, just as a scientist would conduct experiments, to determine its meaning. Evaluations are a form of empirical knowledge, not essentially different from other forms of knowledge, which must be constructed by operational and experimental techniques.

Dewey's pragmatic theory of value made him a philosopher of morals—and it was this interest in moral issues that spurred him to lead the growing movement to reform the American school system.[2] The schools Dewey had known as a boy were kept, not taught, by untrained appointees of the local politicians. Discipline was maintained by physical force. Children sat silently with their hands folded on top of their desks and listened to teacher. Occasionally they would be called to recite a lesson by rote, but no questions were tolerated. No one knew what subjects could or should be taught. The only principle that guided the choice of topics was the implicit assumption that they must

79

not be related to the child's world outside of the schoolroom—the purpose of education was to make a child appreciate a set of cultural products entirely alien to his own life.

Dewey began his attack on this principle from an urgent conviction that what is most important in education is its moral purpose. Discipline, natural development, culture, social efficiency are moral traits—marks of a person who is a worthy member of the society that education is designed to further. Dewey wanted the schools to instill in children the best of American ideals. Unfortunately, the American ideal of the good mixer somehow became dominant over the American ideal of individualism; intellectual excellence became second in importance to life adjustment. In Dewey's own lifetime "Learning by doing" had degenerated into an empty slogan and progressive education passed into scornful disrepute.

From 1896, when he opened his first experimental school at the University of Chicago, until his death in 1952, John Dewey was the foremost spokesman for progressive education; he saw it as a race between intelligence and catastrophe. Although he has often been criticized irresponsibly by people who have not read his books or understood his ideas, we should remember that it was John Dewey more than any other single individual who gave the United States a public school system intelligently planned to support a democratic government. If progressive education was a failure, the fault was not one of conception, but of execution.

The significance of these philosophical innovations for the development of psychology in America appeared first in the formation of the Chicago school of philosophy and psychology. As philosophers, the members of the Chicago school were known as pragmatists; as psychologists, they were *functionalists*. Although James through his writings provided much of the inspiration, it was Dewey who directly instigated the work of the functional psychologists. On the psychological scene at that time their principal competitor was the Wundtian experimental psychology imported from Leipzig. Whereas the Wundtians attempted to analyze the structure of the mind, the American psychologists, under the influence of evolutionism and pragmatism, directed most of their attention to its functions.

Dewey's instrumentalism asserted that the function of the mind is to guide behavior. While structuralists focused exclusively on the mind as the proper subject of psychological study, functionalists permitted the mind to share the spotlight with its "practical effect," with the behavior that resulted from mental processes.

The consequences of this shift in emphasis were important. One consequence was that functionalism could readily absorb studies of animal behavior as a part of psychology; the studies of cats in a puzzle box that E. L. Thorndike (1898) conducted at Columbia, the studies at

Johns Hopkins by H. S. Jennings (1897) on adaptive processes in protozoa, R. M. Yerkes's (1907) investigations at Harvard of the dancing mouse, W. S. Small's (1900) studies of the rat in a maze at Clark, J. B. Watson's (1907) work at Chicago on the somesthetic cues in maze learning by rats—these were but a few of many experimental studies of animal behavior that accorded with functionalism, but were of little interest to psychologists who, following Wundt, had made introspection the indispensable tool of their science.

By broadening the definition of psychology, the American functionalists were able to incorporate studies of animals, of children, of the mentally retarded and the insane, and of primitive, preliterate peoples. And they were able to supplement introspection by other methods of collecting data; physiological experiments, mental tests, questionnaires, and descriptions of behavior all became legitimate sources of information in the study of psychological processes. By the time of Wundt's death in 1920 the purely introspective, experimental science he had founded in Leipzig was merely a small part of, and had been overshadowed by, the larger and more pragmatic American science of psychology. Ten years later the victory of the functional psychologists was complete. In the United States today functional psychology *is* psychology (a claim that will not continue undisputed).

The liberating effects of enlarging the science of mental life to include a science of behavior were so striking that some workers tried to jettison the mind entirely and to define psychology as the study of behavior, pure and simple. This possibility had been latent for several years before John B. Watson opened his campaign for *behaviorism* in 1913. If Watson had not been so inept as a philosopher, he might have offered behaviorism as a pragmatic theory of mind, comparable to Peirce's pragmatic theory of meaning, James's pragmatic theory of truth, and Dewey's pragmatic theory of value. The mind—the other chap's mind, at any rate—is something whose existence is inferred entirely from the behavior we observe. "John is conscious" must be translated into the hypothesis "If I call to John, he will answer" or "If I stand in John's way, he will detour around me" and so on. In short, if I present him with such-and-such stimuli, he will make such-and-such responses. To paraphrase Peirce, "Consider what effects, which might conceivably have practical bearings, we conceive the mind to have. Then, our conception of these effects is the whole of our conception of the mind."

Watson did not put his argument in these terms; what he said, instead, is that the aim of behavioristic psychology is to be able, given the stimulus, to predict the response; or, to put it another way, to be able on seeing the reaction take place, to define the stimulus that produced the reaction. Thus he emphasized the simple fact that everything we do consists ultimately of the motion of material objects from one place to another. No introspective inferences about any mysterious mind-stuff were required. Mental phenomena were reduced to the behavioral evidence from which they were inferred: sensation and perception were reduced to discriminative responses; learning and memory to conditioning and maintaining stimulus-response connections; thinking to talking and problem solving; motivation and value to choice behavior; emotion to activity of the autonomic nervous system, glands, and smooth muscles. Everything intangible was simply replaced by its most tangible manifestation. During the 1920s behaviorism became one of the major influences on psychological thought in the United States.

Behaviorism was not James's idea of psychology, and it is ironic that his pragmatic philosophy proved so hospitable to these materialistic ideas. Of course, James often spoke of behavior in a very modern sense, especially when he wrote about education and the formation of habits, but his outstanding gift as a psychologist lay in a very different realm. His sensitivity to the subtle nuances of his own conscious life and his ability to communicate what he experienced through electric metaphors in beautiful prose are unrivaled among scientific psychologists. A psychology without consciousness is a psychology without need for James's greatest talent.

JAMES–PHILOSOPHICAL PSYCHOLOGY

William James was born in 1842 in New York, the first of five children. Second born was Henry, the novelist; third, Garth Wilkinson; fourth, Robertson; and last, Alice, who was only six years younger than William.

Their father, Henry James, Sr., was wealthy enough to live on his income, which left him the leisure to write tracts on Swedenborg and to be a devoted parent. He organized his family into one of the most high-spirited and exclusive debating clubs in all history; the atmosphere he created for them was vividly recalled by Edward Emerson.

> "The adipose and affectionate Wilkie," as his father called him, would say something and be instantly corrected or disputed by the little cock-sparrow Bob, the youngest, but good-naturedly defend his statement, and then, Henry (Junior) would emerge from his silence in defence of Wilkie. Then Bob would be more impertinently insistent, and Mr. James would advance as moderator, and William, the eldest, join in. The voice of the moderator presently would be drowned by the combatants and he soon came down vigorously into the arena, and when, in the excited argument, the dinner knives might not be absent from eagerly gesticulating hands, dear Mrs. James, more conventional, but bright as well as motherly, would look at me, laughingly reassuring, saying, "Don't be disturbed,

Edward; they won't stab each other. This is usual when the boys come home."[3]

It would be difficult to devise a better way to learn to think for oneself, or to learn that intellectual combat need not interfere with personal affection. Even when the children grew up their debate continued. Throughout their lives they wrote frequent, voluminous, fascinating letters that—fortunately for the many biographers attracted to this amazing family—they were wise enough to preserve for posterity.[4] Few families remain so close so long.

The schooling of this precocious brood seems to have been a series of accidents. Until he was nine William passed from one governess to another; then he started school, but after he had tried several, his parents decided that American schools were not good enough, and in 1855 the family set off for Europe. For five years they traveled like a pack of intellectual gypsies through England, Switzerland, France, and Germany while the children absorbed the languages and any other aspects of European culture that took their fancy. Whatever else might be said for it, this unconventional program of studies left William anything but the backwoods American barbarian that his critics later assumed him to be. William James was literally a man of the world, and throughout his life he was, through reading, correspondence, and frequent journeys abroad, in constant contact with the best that England and the continent could offer. The overseas voyages were in large part the result of a unique Jamesian formula; when someone in the family became ill he was sent not to a hospital, but to Europe. Since their health was seldom good, the Jameses all became great travelers.

In 1860 William announced that he was going to be an artist. His father was not a little grieved, for he had always counted on a scientific career for Willy. But he believed in liberty, so he agreed to take his family back to America and to William Morris Hunt. As the younger Henry expressed it, "We went home to learn to paint."

Fortunately, the vocational experiment was a complete success, and the autumn of 1861 found William a student of chemistry in the Lawrence Scientific School at Harvard. His teacher was Professor Charles William Eliot, who a few years later was to become Harvard's president. In later years Eliot recalled William as a very interesting and agreeable pupil, but not wholly devoted to the study of chemistry. He was inclined toward "unsystematic excursions" in unpredictable directions—his personal notebooks during those years ranged over the whole field of literature, history, science, and philosophy. After two years of chemistry, he decided that his interests lay more in the direction of natural history, and so, with the notion of coupling this with a possible medical career, he entered the Harvard Medical School.

Except for his work under the saintly Jeffries Wyman, medical

A pencil-drawn self-portrait by William James, about 1866.

studies did not please William James. His first impressions were that there is a great deal of humbug in the practice of medicine. "With the exception of surgery, in which something positive is sometimes accomplished," he commented in a letter to his cousin, "a doctor does more by the moral effect of his presence on the patient and family, than by anything else. He also extracts money from them."

He kept at it, however, until the spring of 1865, when he took a year off to join the Thayer Expedition to Brazil. He saw the expedition up the Amazon as an opportunity to work with the famous Swiss-American zoologist, Agassiz, and to try out yet another possible career, biology. Once again the vocational experiment was instructive, and long before the expedition was over he knew that a life filled with careful collecting and orderly classifying was not for him. Somewhat reluctantly, he resumed medical studies. The subject was no more attractive to him than when he began it—indeed, he rather dreaded the prospect of becoming a doctor—but until he discovered something else that really would attract him as a career, there seemed no alternative to the medical school. His next choice would have to be the right one; his two previous mistakes were already more than he felt he should allow himself.

Not all choices are deliberate, however. James's future was shaped by ill health. Insomnia, digestive disorders, eye troubles, a weak back, and deep depressions combined to produce a new interruption of his medical studies. It was obvious to everyone that he was suffering from America; Europe was the only cure. In 1867 he went to Dresden and Berlin, where he took baths for his back, read widely in German and other literature, toyed with thoughts of suicide, displayed his loneliness and homesickness by the tremendous volume of his correspondence, and remained just as miserable as he had been at home. After a sojourn of almost two years he returned to Cambridge, took up his medical courses once again, and in the spring of 1869 received his degree. His M.D. was the only academic degree he ever acquired by passing the necessary examinations.

His spirits continued their steady decline, and the spring of 1870 found him in the deepest melancholy. His will to live was at its lowest ebb. He was in a fundamental spiritual crisis, paralyzed by a sense of moral impotence, soul-sick (as he realized) for lack of a philosophy to live by. By now positivism repelled him. It was in these dark months that he began to build his philosophy, not as an intellectual exercise, but as a desperate measure he could not avoid if he wanted to stay alive.

The turning point came when he discovered a number of essays on free will by Charles Renouvier. Renouvier convinced him that the activities of the mind have causal effects on the body—a possibility that the materialistic physiology of the day wholly rejected—and that these activities can be controlled by deliberate choice. "My first act of free will," he recorded in his diary at the time he first read Renouvier, "shall be to believe in free will." From then on James's philosophy was identified with his personal convictions. And his first conviction was that he must believe in the efficacy of the will, believe that by sheer belief he could cure himself.

His gospel of belief was a cheerful success. No one knows what cures mental illness; approximately two out of every three cases recover regardless of the therapy, or even, as in his case, without therapy. But whatever the reason, he was convinced that his personal difficulties had been relieved by philosophic insight, and the insight involved a new conception of freedom. Renouvier was perhaps the greatest individual influence on the development of James's thought, and with that help he slowly fought his way back to health and full activity once more.

By 1872 he was well enough to accept Eliot's offer of a teaching position—he agreed to teach physiology to the undergraduates in Harvard College. He proved to be a satisfactory teacher and having a job to do turned him away from further morbid self-examination. In 1875–1876 he offered a course on "The Relations between Physiology and Psychology" which marked the first American introduction of the new, experimental psychology. The undergraduate version of that course, offered in the following year, was known as the "new Spencer elective," since it used as a text the 1200-page *Synthetic Philosophy* of Herbert Spencer. He was able to extract $300 from the Harvard Treasurer for use in purchasing laboratory and demonstrational equipment for the course, a munificence bestowed during the same year that Wundt established in informal demonstrational laboratory in Leipzig.

James had moved from pure physiology and anatomy into physiological psychology and, because psychology was at that time the responsibility of the Department of Philosophy, James's professorship was in philosophy, rather than physiology. Thus he continued his slow but inevitable migration away from medicine through physiology and psychology to philosophy.

In 1878, the year of his marriage, James agreed to write a text on psychology for Henry Holt & Co. He felt he could finish it in two years but, as a matter of fact, the composition of the book took twelve—and Holt waited. The manuscript grew in close connection with the author's classroom instruction, and an animated, polemical style was a natural result. The chapter on "Habit" is an excellent example, one that has been reprinted repeatedly in anthologies. It is, in fact, a lay sermon.

—Habit simplifies the movements required to achieve a given result, makes them more accurate and diminishes fatigue.

—Habit is the enormous flywheel of society, its most precious conservative agent. It alone is what keeps us all within the bounds of ordinance, and saves the children of fortune from the envious uprisings of the poor.

—In most of us, by the age of thirty, the character has set like plaster, and will never soften again.

—The great thing, in all education, is to make our nervous system our ally instead of our enemy. We must make automatic and habitual, as early as possible, as many useful actions as we can.

—In the acquisition of a new habit, or the leaving off of an old one, we must take care to launch ourselves with as strong and decided an initiative as possible. Never suffer an exception to occur until the new habit is securely rooted in your life.

—Seize the very first possible opportunity to act on every resolution you make, and on every emotional prompting you may experience in the direction of the habits you aspire to gain.

—Keep the faculty of effort alive in you by a little gratuitous exercise every day.

The chapter is full of wise advice to the young student. Of course, one might ask what manner of science this is. On what experiments did he base his generalizations? What scientifically controlled observations did he make? What laboratory procedures did he use to test his hypotheses? The answer would be, none whatsoever. James's psychology, at its best, came from his own sharp observations of the life around him. He approved of experimentation, he studied it and fostered it, but he did not do it himself. Yet in spite of its personal origins in his own experience, the chapter on habit is still read with profit by every new generation of students—although today it is assigned more often for courses in literature than in psychology.

In 1882, within a span of ten months, he lost both of his parents. In a family group so closely knit their deaths were profoundly felt, and it might have been expected that William would not easily withstand the emotional strain. Although his letters express his personal feelings, one searches through his work almost in vain for the effects of his bereavement. He had learned how to live with his feelings, how to rise above grief as well as depression, but one can speculate that it was not easy. In 1884 he published an article, "What Is an Emotion?" that must have been conceived during his deepest grief and prepared for publication in the following year. It gives us some hint of the device he had discovered. "There is," he wrote, "no more valuable precept in moral education than this, as all who have experience know: if we wish to conquer undesirable emotional tendencies in ourselves, we must assiduously, and in the first instance cold-bloodedly, go through the *outward motions* of those contrary dispositions we prefer to cultivate."[5] If we act cheerful and kindly, those emotions will replace the depressions and sullenness we wish to be rid of. It is an application of the principle he had learned from Renouvier; we can will to believe what we should believe.

When the *Principles* appeared in 1890, the chapter on "The Emotions" continued this same line of thought. He had discovered in the meanwhile an article by the Danish physiologist C. Lange which agreed with his own views, and the theory has been known ever since as the *James-Lange theory of emotion*. The essence of it is captured in the following famous paragraph.

> Our natural way of thinking about these coarser emotions is that the mental perception of some fact excites the mental affection called the emotion, and that this latter state of mind gives rise to the bodily expression. My theory, on the contrary, is that *the bodily changes follow directly the perception of the exciting fact, and that our feeling of the same changes as they occur* is *the emotion.* Common-sense says, we lose our fortune, are sorry and weep; we meet a bear, are frightened and run; we are insulted by a rival, are angry and strike. The hypothesis here to be defended says that this order of sequence is incorrect, that the one mental state is not immediately induced by the other, that the bodily manifestations must first be interposed between, and that the more rational statement is that we feel sorry because we cry, angry because we strike, afraid because we tremble.[6]

In meeting his personal problem, he believed he could control his emotions by voluntarily initiating the bodily manifestations appropriate to them. For the scientific problem, the point was that he had proposed a physiological process associated with emotion, a proposal that could be tested experimentally in the laboratory. It was almost forty years before anyone proposed a better theory.

Even more deeply involved in the development of James's thinking, however, was a chapter in the *Principles* entitled "The Stream of Thought." That, too, started life as an article, "On Some Omissions of Introspective Psychology," published in the same journal and during the same year as the article on emotion.[7] The use of the term "omissions" in the title of the article indicates that James had found something in his own consciousness that his less observant predecessors had overlooked; the use of the term "stream" in the later title of the chapter indicates that the omission he had detected was of the fluid, fleeting, transient phases of consciousness that serve to link successive states in an on-going flow.

British empiricists usually described their minds as if their consciousness were filled by a sequence of discrete, independent pictures flashed on some inner screen, each still and motionless, each connected to the next by some mechanical trick of association. Nothing could have seemed more artificial to James, who likened consciousness to a bird's life, made of an alternation of flights and perchings. This was his famous distinction between substantive and transitive parts of the stream of thought. The resting places are occupied by sensory images; the path of flight is filled with relations between the matters contemplated during the periods of rest. Previous introspective psychologists had failed to respect the transitive states—this was the omission he charged them with, the implications of which he went on to develop in detail.

His persistent concern with relations among conscious elements led him directly to the puzzling psychological question of the *self*. In every person's stream of consciousness there is a dichotomy between the *me* and the *not-me;* at the same time it is *I* who am aware of this dichotomy. With characteristic sensitivity to his inner life, James divided the self into *I* the knower and *me* the known. The *me* is simply an object like any object we might be conscious of, although it is obviously of supreme interest. It is the *I*, the active sense of personal identity, that poses the real puzzle. In associationistic psychology the self was somehow compounded of ideas, each separate, each ignorant of its mates, but sticking together and calling each other up according to certain laws. Such an account might suffice to explain the empirical *me*, but it was obviously inadequate to the judging *I*. The *I* that knows its own ideas cannot itself be one of those ideas. In addition to the ideas that are known, therefore, there must be an active ego that knows them, relates them in the stream of consciousness, and is the source of whatever unity and organization they possess.

His attempt to expand the contents of consciousness to include more than had hitherto been suspected—to include the relations among the elements and, therefore, the self as the necessary source of those relations—was in many ways characteristic of him. For one thing, it indicates the importance he set on experience as the source of our knowledge; he was above all an empiricist, a philosopher of experience, even though he did not fall into the narrower empiricism of his British predecessors. For another, it shows how he was able to open up, enlarge, and enrich the content of psychology; he was forever expecting to find something more, something new and unexpected, and he tried to leave his theories open toward the future and the abundance it would bring. It demonstrates his sensitivity to mental subtleties and his ability to capture experience *sui generis* and to communicate it to another person. And it exhibits once again his eloquence, unfettered by pedestrian facts from the laboratory.

In 1904 James, by then a full-time philosopher, developed his empiricism one step further. "Everything real," he wrote, "must be experienceable somewhere, and every kind of thing experienced must somewhere be real."[8] In this "radical empiricism" he tried to redefine experience in a way that made it even broader than conscious experience, tried to categorize subjectivity in the mental sense and objectivity in the physical sense as particular modes of experience in his pure, phenomenal sense. His final philosophic step, in his pluralistic universe, was to identify experience with metaphysical reality. These philosophical adventures, although more important to his thinking than, say, his pragmatism, have not had the same degree of influence on subsequent generations of psychologists. But they are indicative of his continual effort to broaden the scope of his empiricism, to leave room for more than he could clearly see a need for at the moment. It was this attitude that made his psychology an ideal vehicle for a growing science that sought to include more and more phenomena within its scope.

After the fourteen hundred pages of the *Principles* had been published in 1890 he felt he had said all he knew about psychology and that he would turn to philosophy. He wanted someone else to take on the responsibility for psychology at Harvard. Harvard brought Hugo Münsterberg from Germany to teach the courses in psychology, and freed James for his work as a philosopher.

In 1892 James revised the two volumes of the *Principles* into the profitable "Briefer Version"—known to several generations of students as "Jimmy"—and he wrote some articles and reviews, but his major contributions to psychology seemed to have been made. His notes during the next few years were not without considerable interest, however. For example, in 1894 he was the first American to call attention to the work of Breuer and Freud.[9] But, to every psychologist's regret, it appeared that psychology was merely a bridge over which

James intended to pass from medicine to philosophy, and that the *Principles* was to be his only payment for the privilege of passage.

But then in 1902 he published *The Varieties of Religious Experience*. It was a magnificent reentry into the psychological arena—this time into a part of it that later psychologists were to call clinical psychology. *The Varieties* was written for his Gifford Lectures delivered in Edinburgh in 1901–1902. It was in part an act of filial piety—he wanted to understand a little more the value and meaning of religion in the sense his father had experienced it. And it was in part a working out of his own experiences; his crisis of 1870 was used to illustrate the state of the sick soul, and his personal "salvation" gave him a conception of the religious experience of being reborn. But in the main it was an expression of the psychological interests he had continued to pursue during the 1890s; interests in the exceptional mental states that characterize psychic experiences, mob violence, hypnosis, psychopathology. He was convinced that the real backbone of the world's religious life was not the carefully argued systems of theology, but a mass of concrete experience—voices, visions, responses to prayer, conversations with the unseen, changes of heart, deliverances from fear. And he was convinced that religion is something more primordial than reason but of equal authority, something intellectuals could omit from their theories of psychology only by distorting their conception of the nature of man.

Although psychiatrists and clinical psychologists have continued to be interested in the morbid mental states that he described in *The Varieties*, they have not made much use of his suggestion that faith can operate as a healing agent. A conversion experience can be a kind of cure, a source of change in the personality structure of the individual. The records of miracle cures attributed to religious faith are well documented. Every doctor has seen patients cured by placebos —sugar pills whose only healing powers derive from the patient's faith in the doctor and the science he represents.[10] Such cures are usually dismissed as the product of suggestibility, the implication being either that the patient was not really sick to begin with, or that he is not really cured after all, or that if he was sick and is cured, then some hocus-pocus occurred.

Although James continued to carry on a full load of lecturing and writing, his health was never good. *The Varieties of Religious Experience* was largely written in bed, where he was recovering from a grim, thirteen-hour scramble, when he was lost in the Adirondack Mountains. The ordeal aggravated a valvular lesion of his heart, and recovery was slow and not complete. The condition grew progressively more serious during the succeeding years and was eventually responsible for his death in 1910.

It is much easier to appreciate William James than to evaluate him. If one points to the thousands of students who read his books, to the inspiration he provided for Dewey and the functional psychologists at Chicago and Columbia, to the sensitivity with which he exposed to view a rich world of inner experience, to the intelligence of his arguments and the beauty of his prose, it is obvious that he was, and still is, the foremost American psychologist.

Yet there is another side, and many psychologists have pointed to it. James was really more of an artist than a scientist, a man who would not enter the laboratory and who disliked the paraphernalia of the careful experimenter. He paid no attention to the embryonic development of mental testing or to the early uses of statistical techniques in analyzing psychological data; he was far too much of an individualist ever to summarize a person by an integer. He had no interest in many of the developments that his own work made possible, and even his clinical pursuits were cast in a strangely unscientific context of religious belief. He is an immortal, a classic, a literary psychologist, a dim figure from the dusty past—yet, according to his critics, he is no longer a moving force on the current scene.

Perhaps the critics are right, but they are not wholly convincing. There are still those who read James for pleasure, who derive strength from him, and find in him still an impulse toward greater freedom. "Neither the whole of truth nor the whole of good is revealed to any single observer," he once said, "although each observer gains a partial superiority of insight from the peculiar position in which he stands." A partial superiority of insight is all he would have claimed for himself.

Fortunately, the final evaluation of William James as a scientist can wait for a time—his value as a wise and profoundly human being should suffice to keep his memory fresh for many years to come.

NOTES

1. M. White, *The Age of Analysis* (Boston: Houghton Mifflin, 1955).
2. L. A. Cremin, *The Transformation of the School: Progressivism in American Education* (New York: Knopf, 1961).
3. R. B. Perry, *The Thought and Character of William James* (Boston: Little, Brown, 1935), vol. I, pp. 171–172. For a brief introduction to James's life and works, see Margaret Knight, *William James* (London: Penguin, 1950).
4. See, for example, William James, *Letters*, ed. Henry James (Boston: Little, Brown, 1926).
5. William James, "What Is an Emotion?" *Mind* 9 (1884). See also Saul Rosenzweig, "The Jameses' Stream of Consciousness," *Contemporary Psychology* 3 (1958): 250–257.

6. W. James, *The Principles of Psychology* (New York: Dover, 1950), vol. 2, pp. 449–450.
7. William James, "On some Omissions of Introspective Psychology," *Mind* 9 (1884): 1–26. See also R. B. Perry, *In the Spirit of William James* (New Haven: Yale University Press, 1938), chap. 3, pp. 75–123.
8. W. James, *Essays in Radical Empiricism*, ed. Ralph Barton Perry (London: Longmans, Green, 1912), p. 160.
9. W. James, "Reviews of Janet, Breuer and Freud, and Whipple," *Psychological Review* 1 (1894): 195–200.
10. Jerome D. Frank, "The Dynamics of the Psychotherapeutic Relationship," *Psychiatry* 22 (1959): 17–39.

SEVEN
Subjective Yardsticks

A great scientist, Lord Kelvin, once said, "When you cannot measure . . . your knowledge is of a meager and unsatisfactory kind." He was, of course, a physicist. You can be sure he was not a mathematician; mathematics is often regarded as a science, even as the Queen of the Sciences, yet it demands no skill for making measurements. Nor could he have been a logician, a botanist, a linguist, a psychoanalyst—there is a long list of creditable sciences that do not rely on measurements. But in physics the art of measurement is both elegant and essential. It would be difficult to imagine physical science shorn of clocks, balances, and meter sticks.

It is a bit ironic that Kelvin's proclamation is better known among social scientists than among natural scientists. Social science has always been a little defensive about its status, a little sensitive about its claim to be scientific. So when a great physicist announces that measurement is the key to scientific knowledge, he is apt to receive more attention than he deserves. In truth, a good case could be made that if your knowledge is meager and unsatisfactory, the last thing in the world you should do is to make measurements. The chance is negligible that you will measure the right things accidentally. Nevertheless, many social and behavioral scientists, assured that measurement is the touchstone of scientific respectability, have rushed out to seek numbers before they knew what the numbers would mean.

Psychologists are by now reasonably well recovered from such feelings of professional inferiority, but there are still a few who believe that good measurement is the highest mark of good science, that deeper understanding lies always in the direction of greater precision. One can still find psychologists making extravagantly precise and elaborate measurements just to demonstrate how throroughly scientific a psychologist can be. Some people will not admit that if a thing is hardly worth doing, it is hardly worth doing well.

The worship of measurement for its own sake is not, to be sure, a majority view. More common, but equally wrongheaded, is the opposite opinion that measurement violates the dignity of man, that numbers bruise the human spirit. At this extreme there seems to be a fear that the paraphernalia of science will block our view of one another and clutter our channels of direct, intuitive understanding.

Wisdom, as usual, lies somewhere between compulsion and revulsion. The first sensible step is to acknowledge that measurement is a means, not an end in itself.

Precise measurement is an indispensable part of the larger enterprise of understanding ourselves and our universe. The knowledge so acquired is not a useless ornament of the educated mind; it sets policy, guides action, and supports decision in every realm it touches. But not all measurements are equally valuable. Measurements made without a supporting context of theory or practical application seldom justify the time and money spent on them. To make measurements without knowing why is like buying gasoline without owning a car. A blind faith that measurement is necessarily a good thing, that someday somebody will provide a theory to explain every conceivable measurement we might make, completely ignores the delicate play between observation and analysis. Outside of a supporting framework of problems, facts, and theories measurement is empty; inside such a framework it may unlock the secrets of the universe.

We should also be aware of the arbitrary nature of any particular system of measurement. In the United States, the cumbersome English system of measurement has left the country out of step with the rest of the world which, for the most part, employs the metric system. Since conversion to the metric system appears to be inevitable, it is interesting to note that the National Bureau of Standards is recommending a ten-year period in which to complete the conversion program at an estimated cost of from $10–40 billion.[1] Beyond the problems of revising scales, tools, and books, there is the intangible problem of language usage, which is very much tied up with our perception of the world around us. Whether it is the vital statistics of beauty contestants or the marking off of football fields, a matter of running a mile or our inability to hit something with a 10-foot pole, the changeover will require a resocialization of all citizens accustomed to the old system—whose comfort in expressing distance in inches cannot be simply dismissed by a revelation of the fact that the inch was originally defined as the length of three barleycorns laid end to end. How one measures or the units arbitrarily chosen through language and social convention has little to do with the contribution measurement makes in our attempts to explore and understand our world.

The great virtue of measurement is that it enables us to bring mathematics to bear on our problems. Once we have replaced the objects or events we want to understand by numerical symbols, we can proceed to operate on those symbols according to the rules of mathematics, rules developed and elaborated by the most brilliant minds in history. We can borrow temporarily the intelligence of Archimedes, Newton, or Gauss. It is not the numbers themselves that we prize so highly; it is what the numbers enable us to do. And what we can do with them is intimately related to the extent to which the rules of measurement we use exploit all the properties of the number system.

What is measurement? In its broadest definition, it means assigning numbers to things according to explicit rules.[2]

The level of refinement can vary tremendously. There are at least two ways to make more refined measurements. One is to reduce the errors, to be sure one assigns the right number to the thing measured. Another is to make the rules more specific. Everyone recognizes the virtues of precision, but the importance of the rules is not as widely appreciated. Consider some of the different rules that can be applied.

In the broadest sense of our definition the assignment of numbers to the jerseys of football players can be called a form of measurement. In this case the rule for assigning numbers to things is very simple: no two players on the same team can have the same number. The rule is a little more complicated than that, as all football fans know, for low numbers are usually given to players in the backfield and each position in the line has its special decade. Even with this embellishment, however, the numbers serve only to identify the players. One would not ordinarily think of the numbers as measuring anything, in spite of the fact that they satisfy the weak conditions imposed by the definition. In this sense it could be said that even a botanist makes measurements, because the names he assigns to different plants serve much the same purpose as the numbers worn by football players. We can think of the names as numbers written with a system of twenty-six, rather than ten digits. In this broadest possible sense of measurement numbers serve merely as names; we say we have a *nominal scale* of measurement.

Usually, however, we expect our measurements to exploit the ordered character of the number system. We expect something to increase or decrease as the numbers increase or decrease. The assignment of numbers to houses on a street is an example. As in the case of football players, no two objects—no two houses on the same street—can receive the same number. The numbers therefore serve all the purposes served by a nominal scale. But that is not all. The rule for assigning house numbers is more explicit: the farther one goes along the street, the larger (or the smaller) the numbers become. If you are given two addresses on the same street, you discover in an instant in what order you will come upon them as you walk along. This more elaborate rule is a clear improvement over the football example, but it is still far short of what Kelvin had in mind. If you are given two addresses on the same street, you cannot tell whether the houses are side by side or three miles apart. All you know is their order. We call this an *ordinal scale* of measurement. Many kinds of psychological measurements are as crude as this: for example, our statements of preference among a set of objects or events.

Greater refinement is possible if, in addition to identifying and ordering the objects, the numbers also indicate the sizes of the intervals between objects. To have an *interval scale* one must be able somehow to determine whether the differences between objects are equal. Here at last is a form of measurement that is quantitative in the ordinary sense of the word. An interval scale must have a standard unit of measurement, a unit interval. The assignment of numbers to days by a calendar is an example of this kind of measurement. Every day has its separate name, thus all the properties of a nominal scale are preserved. The order of the numbers corresponds to the order of the days; accordingly, ordinal properties are preserved, too. Moreover, given any two dates, one can calculate directly how many days intervened between them.

Psychologists often try to create scales with equal intervals, but there is still much disagreement about acceptable methods. It is not possible to lay psychological phenomena end to end or to put them into a scale pan—to add them in the familiar sense that lengths or weights can be added. Therefore, it is necessary to invent new procedures that differ from, but are logically equivalent to, the operations of physical measurement. But even if it were impossible for psychologists to construct interval scales (and it is not), measurement of the more primitive kinds would still be possible. And often the more primitive measures are sufficient for the decisions and inferences that concern us.

There is yet another stage of refinement possible in the measurement process. In addition to operations for determining identity, order, and a unit interval, operations are available for the determination of the equality of ratios. This sophistication presupposes a scale with a natural value that corresponds to zero. Physical scales—length, mass, density, voltage, etc.—frequently have such natural zero points. Psychological scales are seldom so well behaved. When it is possible to fix an appropriate zero point on an interval scale, it is called a *ratio scale*.

The social and behavioral sciences are sometimes criticized for not being able so to formulate their variables that they can be encompassed by ratio scales of measurement. The criticism unfortunately is true. However, much can be accomplished with the cruder varieties of scales. And as our understanding becomes less meager and unsatisfactory, we may be able to discover better methods than we have now.

Suppose we consider an example that will highlight some of the difficulties of psychological measurement. How is one to measure the psychological phenomenon of anxiety? Everyone knows the cruel bite of this emotion, everyone recognizes that it varies in intensity from moment to moment and from person to person. In principle, therefore, one should be able to use numbers to indicate how anxious a person is. But how to find the numbers?

One method exploits a reaction that physiologists discovered many years ago. When a normal person experiences a strong emotion, there is usually a decrease in the resistance to the passage of a weak electric current through his skin. All one has to do therefore is apply electrodes to his skin and measure its resistance (the EDR).[3] This is simple and convenient; many psychological experiments have relied on exactly this technique to measure emotional responses. There are things about it, however, that must be clearly understood. It is not a kind of *psychological* measurement; the quantity involved is electrical, the resistance measured in ohms. Anxiety, however, is not to be measured in ohms. S. S. Stevens has suggested that the measurement in ohms might better be called an *indicant*, rather than a measure of anxiety. An indicant is something that presumably correlates closely with what one would like to measure, and so can be substituted for a measure when the more direct approach is impossible. But it is necessary to assume that the indicant is valid, whereas a measure is valid by definition. There are many circumstances where psychologists have settled for indicants, but hope some day to find scales of measurement.

If we wish to be certain that our indicant of anxiety is valid, how should we proceed? A direct approach is to ask people to introspect on their anxiety, to report verbally how much anxiety they are feeling. These observations through the inner eye could then be used to check the electrical measurements on the polygraph. Now, it is perfectly easy to get verbal reports from persons who are exposed to different kinds of threatening situations, but certain difficulties appear. For example, when a particular situation occurs and the person's skin resistance takes a sudden drop, his introspections may reveal nothing at all. His skin says one thing, his words another. Which are we to believe? We may not call the subject a liar. Psychologists have sometimes argued that the feeling of anxiety is so intolerable that the mind has subtle tricks for avoiding it. If so, the EDR may be reflecting a perfectly valid emotional reaction that is not directly accessible to consciousness. It would seem that we have encountered a problem where direct introspective report does not give us a true measure. Until someone thinks of some better procedure, therefore, we must measure anxiety in terms of skin resistance, breathing rate, heart beat, and so on, all indicants, rather than direct measurements of emotion. Perhaps the problem will not be resolved by finding a true measure of emotion, but by redefining what we mean by emotion as a psychological phenomenon.

Professor Richard Lazarus and his colleagues have made a

creative use of measurement and experimental design in their studies of anxiety responses to a highly stressful film.[4] Lazarus showed a film of primitive operations on the genitals to a group of uninstructed students. The students showed extremely large EDR's and related verbal indices of anxiety. A second group of students viewed the film, but with a sound track that intellectualized the nature of the primitive operations. A group of executives heard a sound track that emphasized denial. Both the second group of students and the executives showed much smaller EDR's than those observed in the uninstructed group. These measurements lead to the speculation that the anxiety inferred from the changing skin resistance patterns was modifiable depending upon the frame of mind (or set) of the observer. Thus, this index of anxiety changed in ways that could be predicted from theories of emotion, giving some justification for starting out with a rather simple index of electrical activity in the skin.

Measurement in psychology is not always as difficult as the example of measuring anxiety may suggest. There are subjective phenomena that submit with docility to a psychologist's yardsticks. Suppose, for example, that we apply our general ideas to the measurement of sensations. The intrinsic qualities of sensation—sourness, redness, middle C—can only be described and named. But certain aspects of sensations are variable, and the magnitude of those variations can be measured. Lights grow and fade in brightness, sounds swell and recede in loudness. How can these changes be measured? According to our definition, the problem is to assign numbers to sensations according to certain rules. This form of psychological measurement is the oldest, the most elaborately developed, the most precise, and, in the opinion of many generations of students, the dullest kind of measurement that psychologists perform.

Historically, sensation was the first problem of psychological measurement to be attacked in a systematic way; the results formed a major piece of evidence that psychology might someday develop into a real science. The problem was given particular emphasis because Wundt, following the British empiricists, considered sensations to be fundamental building blocks of the mind. If one could measure sensations, one could then measure any other perceptual phenomenon by analyzing it into these elementary, measurable components of experience.

The procedures used to measure sensations were developed during the nineteenth century by Weber, Fechner, Helmholtz, Wundt, Galton, and many others. They were so successful that it was many years before anyone suspected there might be something more to the study of perception than the straightforward task of measuring sensations. Even today the field of sensory psychology is a tidy little kingdom unto itself, a subscience concerned with physical aspects of the stimulus, with neurophysiological processes in the receptors and the sensory nerves, and with the experience or behavior of the stimulated organism. These sensory processes can be studied intensively by scientists who have little interest in the remainder of psychology and who would prefer to avoid anything that seems vague or intangible by comparison with the rigorous standards they maintain for the measurement of sensations.

The principal tool a sensory psychologist uses is a hypothetical entity called the threshold. A threshold is a boundary separating what we can experience from what we cannot. If a light is too dim to see, we say it is below the visual threshold; if a sound is too faint to hear, it is below the auditory threshold. Conversely, if the light energy or the sound energy is intense enough to trigger off some response, then it is above the threshold. Sometimes the threshold is referred to as the *limen;* stimuli that cannot be detected are subliminal, those that can be, supraliminal. But, whatever one calls it, the underlying idea is that our sense organs are not infinitely delicate, that there is a point separating physical energies that are adequate to excite the sense organs from those that are not. Because of this intimate relation implied between the physical and the psychological magnitudes, the techniques of measurement used by sensory psychologists are usually referred to as *psychophysical methods.*

Psychologists often speak as if the threshold were a hard and fixed value, as if stimuli greater than the threshold were always detected and stimuli less than the threshold were never detected. When we examine the matter more carefully, we are forced to recognize that a threshold is a statistical concept. A given level of physical energy may be perceived at one instant and not perceived a few moments later. Because of this characteristic unpredictability and uncertainty, one speaks of the *probability* of detecting a stimulus.

There are dozens of sources of this uncertainty: fluctuations in the metabolic processes that feed the sense organs, tiny mechanical differences in the orientation of the receptor, spontaneous activity in the nervous system, lapses of attention, the attitude of the observer, coincidence of the stimulus with the thud of a heartbeat or the blink of an eyelid. How can one foresee which of these will work in favor of detection, which will oppose it at a given instant? It is a question of competing probabilities. When we measure a threshold, therefore, we look for the stimulus value that is missed as often as it is detected, that is, where the probability of detection is 0.50.

As a light gets dimmer and dimmer, the probability that one can see a short flash gradually diminishes. The task is to measure the probability at each stimulus intensity. A hypothetical example is graphed in Figure 7.1; as the stimulus value goes up, the proportion of times it is detected also increases. The stimulus value at which one can

FIGURE 7.1

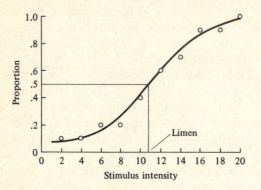

The proportion of stimuli detected by the subject is plotted as a function of the stimulus intensity. The 50 percent point is usually defined as the limen.

see the light half of the occasions it flashes, i.e., the point at which the probability is .5, is usually taken as the statistical definition of the threshold.

We occasionally detect subliminal stimuli and miss supraliminal ones. Thus, for example, a subliminal advertisement is one that can be perceived less than half the times it is presented. Although there has been some irrational fear of what advertisers might do to us with subliminal tricks, it is probably fair to say that the public should be grateful for the relief such advertising provides. The more subliminal the advertising gets, the better most of us will like it. Perhaps someone will invent a subliminal billboard.

In order to measure the amount of stimulus energy required to reach the threshold, it is necessary to use physical equipment that presents energies—lights, sounds, tastes, and so on—in known amount to the receptor organs of the person or animal being tested. And it is necessary that the equipment should be able to vary the amount of energy over a range of values running from well below to far above threshold. The design, construction, maintenance, and operation of equipment having the necessary sensitivity and accuracy usually requires considerable scientific and engineering skill. Once the equipment is assembled and calibrated, a person—the subject—is brought into the situation and asked to report when he detects the presence of a stimulus. He may be instructed to report vocally or to punch a key that signals when he has detected the stimulus. The specific instructions are quite important; if he is encouraged to be conservative in his judgments, he may appear to be rather insensitive, whereas if he is encouraged to guess, he may report many stimuli that were not really there. The way a subject balances his misses against his false reports can make a significant difference in the measured value of his threshold. Considerable training is often necessary before a subject can reliably maintain a fixed criterion of judgment in a psychophysical experiment.

Given a properly trained and carefully instructed subject, the threshold measurement can begin. In one of the standard procedures the experimenter presents a particular intensity of the stimulus, a value selected in advance, and records whether or not the subject responds to it. He then presents another value, also selected in advance in random fashion, and again notes the subject's response. This sequence is repeated again and again, each time with different values. In a typical experiment the investigator may select in advance eight or ten different intensities all in the region where he expects the threshold to lie. He continues the procedure until he has presented the subject with, say, 100 stimuli at each of the preselected intensities; 100 are needed at each intensity to get reliable estimates of the probabilities of detection. In all, therefore, 800 or 1000 stimuli may be presented in the course of measuring a single threshold for a single subject. The proportion that the subject detects at each intensity is plotted, a curve is fitted to the points, and the threshold is estimated as in Figure 7.1. And this procedure must be repeated with other subjects until the investigator can be sure the value obtained is not attributable to the idiosyncrasies of a particular subject. Shortcuts are possible and are necessarily adopted for clinical tests—few patients are as amenable and uncomplaining as an experimental subject—but the laboratory measurement of a threshold value frequently requires several hours.

One reward for such painstaking labors, however, has been the discovery of man's amazing sensitivity to certain forms of energy. In the case of vision, for example, under optimal conditions a visual sensation will result if only five or ten quanta of blue light reach the layer

TABLE 7.1

Some Approximate Detection Threshold Values	
Sense modality	*Detection threshold*
Light	A candle flame seen at 30 miles on a dark, clear night (ca. 10 quanta).
Sound	The tick of a watch under quiet conditions at 20 feet (ca. 0.0002 dynes/cm²).
Taste	One teaspoon of sugar in 2 gallons of water.
Smell	One drop of perfume diffused into the entire volume of a 3-room apartment.
Touch	The wing of a bee falling on your cheek from a distance of 1 cm.

From *New Directions in Psychology* by Roger Brown, Eugene Galanter, Eckhard H. Hess, and George Mandler. Copyright © 1962 by Holt, Rinehart and Winston, Inc. Reprinted by permission of Holt, Rinehart and Winston, Inc.

101

of sensitive receptor cells in the retina. Since light quanta are the smallest possible packages of radiant energy, and since it is highly improbable that more than one of the five or ten packages fall on any single receptor cell, this result seems to imply that one light quantum is sufficient to activate one visual receptor cell! It is physically impossible to be more sensitive than this. And the ear is almost as good as the eye. A tone of 2000 Hz can be heard when the movement of the air particles against the eardrum is smaller than the diameter of a hydrogen molecule. In olfaction, one part of mercaptan in fifty billion parts of air produces a detectable odor. It seems likely that our sense organs are, for some stimuli, as sensitive as is compatible with the conditions and requirements of life. If these organs were more sensitive, they would begin to respond to the random dance of molecules in the air and in the receptors themselves.

The measurement of threshold values has practical as well as theoretical application. Designers of buildings, work spaces, vehicles, etc. can use the data to construct environments suited to the behavioral potential of the people who must use them. Because the organs are easily accessible, we have more knowledge of vision and audition than we do of taste, smell, touch, kinesthetic, or vestibular senses.

Although it is sometimes convenient to think of sensation as the uncluttered response of sensory nerves to fixed quantities of incoming stimulus energy, psychophysicists have never been willing to ignore the statistical nature of perception—a fact that becomes most pronounced when we ask people to identify extremely small amounts or small changes in stimulus energy. Indeed, most published threshold data result from extrapolations downward since it is impossible to actually present exactly one quanta of light to exactly one cell in one person. In the late 1950s a number of researchers contributed to the development of a model of the perceiving organism that has come to be known as the *statistical decision model*[5] or signal detection theory.

Experienced researchers had for some time been concerned with "calibrating" the observer so that his responses would be based on actual stimulus changes rather than on guesswork or trying to please the researcher. In this attempt to approach having an "ideal observer" the experimenter would employ a "catch trial" in which no stimulus is presented in order to catch the observer in a lapse of attention or faking. Investigators Swets, Tanner, and Birdsall conceive of the observer as a person faced with a psychophysical choice based on the magnitude of the stimulus, the likelihood that the stimulus or signal has occurred, the rewards due to him if he is correct, and the penalty if he is incorrect. We might imagine an experiment in which the signal, a tone, comes on 50 percent of the time, while on 50 percent of the trials there is no tone, a condition that communication specialists refer to as "noise." The ideal observer for this situation is one who responds

TABLE 7.2

Statistical Decision Model		
Presence	*Observer's detection response*	
of signal	*"Yes"*	*"No"*
On	Hit	Miss
Off	False alarm	Correct rejection

"yes" 50 percent and "no" 50 percent of the time. The performance of the actual observer is usually calculated by dividing his percentage of false alarms by his percentage of hits. (Correct rejections and misses have the same ratio.) If the ratio is equal to 1.0, he would be performing as well as the desired or ideal observer. If his performance deviates from the ideal, researchers have found that they can sharpen an observer's performance by various motivational techniques, for example, providing money for hits and deducting money for false alarms.

In the world outside the laboratory there are a number of situations that approximate this experimental paradigm. As an example, military personnel who man radar scopes searching for signals of an imminent attack work in an environment where noise is frequent and the threatening signal is (it is hoped) rare. An observer in such a situation is under great pressure to keep his false alarms to a minimum and to be right if a true threatening signal occurs. Because the tangible feedback of getting a hit is rare, we approach the point at which the stimulus input could be called deprived, and it is frequently found that radar observers become bored, fall asleep, or miss signals. The only feedback is usually negative, where there is hell to pay if he dares turn in a false alarm. As a result, frequent drills are scheduled to keep the radar operators on the alert. There is a story from the early days of radar that radar operators saw the threatening signals of the planes approaching Pearl Harbor but hesitated to give warning for fear of being accused of "crying wolf." The tragic consequences of errors in using subjective yardsticks are a part of history.

To summarize the impact of signal detection, we must refer back to our earlier discussion of the uncertainty principle and relativity. On closer inspection through the eyes of the signal detection enthusiasts, we find that the concept of the threshold, which relates discrete changes in matter with discrete changes in nervous tissue activity, is merely another convenient fiction—a product of the way in which man observes nature.

However, measuring minimum detectable amounts of energy occupies only a small part of a sensory psychologist's time and effort. Of even greater interest to him is the measurement of *difference thresholds*—the smallest difference between two stimuli that can be detected. For example, two different intensities of light may be displayed side by side; if the viewer can detect a contour where one field stops and the other starts, he reports which side is brighter. Or two tones may be sounded, one after the other; a listener reports whether the second was louder or fainter than the first. Quite frequently the results of these experimental measurements of differential sensitivity—measurements of the fineness of resolution of our sensory equipment—can be interpreted more or less directly in terms of the anatomy and physiology of the receptors themselves. Psychophysics is a close relative of biophysics.

A wide variety of sensory differences has been subjected to this kind of testing. The results are contained in hundreds of different professional journals and are summarized in scores of handbooks.[6] The measurement can be represented best if we use symbols: let M represent the magnitude of the weaker stimulus, and let $M + D$ represent the magnitude of the stronger stimulus. Thus D is the difference between the two intensities of stimulation, and it is D that the subject is trying to detect. As D gets smaller and smaller, approaching zero, the likelihood that a subject will detect it gets less and less; the threshold value of D can be estimated from such data. Let us use D' to designate the particular value of D that corresponds to the threshold. Then the results of thousands of measurements of difference thresholds can be summarized in a simple rule noted first by Ernst Heinrich Weber in 1834. In its details the rule is wrong, but it is so simple and so nearly true over such a wide range of conditions that it is still remembered and referred to as Weber's Law. The rule says that D', the size of D necessary for detection, increases as a direct function of the size of M. The stronger the stimulus, the larger the increment required. For example, if you strike a match in a room where a single candle is burning, the increment in illumination is quite obvious, but the same increment of light in a room where a thousand candles are burning is scarcely noticeable.

More precisely, Weber stated that the ratio D'/M is a constant for all values of M, the value of the constant varying from one sense modality to another. Today it is known that the ratio D'/M may change when M is extremely small or extremely large, but within the normal ranges of stimulation Weber's Law is usually a reliable guide. Thus it can be said, for example, that the Weber fraction is approximately 1/100 for the just noticeable difference in the brightness of a light and is approximately 1/10 for the just noticeable difference in the intensity of a tone. The size of D', in absolute or in fractional terms, has been measured and tabulated for an amazing variety of situations, far more than we could survey here; the information exists and can be found in a good psychological library.

Now suppose we stand back a few paces from these meticulous measurements and try to understand why psychologists—and not only physiologists, doctors, or engineers—must be concerned with such things. Is it merely historical accident? British philosophers of empiricism long ago pointed to the senses as the source of all our knowledge about the universe; "Nothing is in the mind," they said, "that is not first in the senses." And, in the materialist tradition, physiologists long ago developed techniques for measuring what the sense organs can do. Wundt adopted these two lines of thought as the foundation for his new science. Problems of sensory psychology have been handed down ever since from one generation of psychologists to the next. But some people feel that modern psychology has outgrown this problem and that from now on it should be left to physiologists.

Certainly the measurement of sensations no longer occupies the central position in psychology it once did. But it still provides essential information about important psychological concepts. It is, for example, absolutely fundamental to our understanding of the crucially important psychological concept of *similarity*. Similarity is the basis of our ability to recognize objects and group them in classes—chairs, books, ship, shoes, and sealing wax—each member of a class being related to, and therefore a symbol of, the others. This skill enables man to profit from experience, to recognize a new situation as similar to an old one. It would be impossible to give any coherent account of how people behave without somehow including the fact that they tend to generalize on the basis of similarity.

One important kind of similarity might be called sensory similarity. Sensory similarity is what we mean when we say that blue is more like green than red, or that a flute sounds more like a clarinet than like a trombone, or that tuna tastes more like chicken than like apple pie, and so on. If we can find a reasonable way to talk about these sensory similarities, perhaps we can generalize our ideas, extend them to more complex structural and semantic similarities.

What does a person mean when he says two sensations are similar? When he says that blue is more like green than like red, he may merely be repeating what he was taught to say. Perhaps his parents or his teachers told him that blue and green are similar; we cannot know what our subjects were taught about colors before they came to the laboratory. Perhaps this is all that similarity amounts to.

If we are convinced, however, that there is some other definition of similarity—a specific sense in which blue and green are *really* similar—we might approach the matter in the following way. Suppose one defines similar stimuli to be stimuli to which people tend to respond in the same way. Then the matter can be explored experimentally. A person can be instructed to make some response—raise his hand, call out, push a button—every time a blue light goes on. Then the investigator surprises the subject with lights of other colors. The response should occur more frequently—and more quickly and intensely—when green is unexpectedly substituted for blue than when red is. On performing this experiment, we discover, in truth, that the probability of response decreases as the similarity between the original and the test stimulus decreases. This measurement is generally referred to as determining a gradient of *stimulus generalization*.

Another convenient technique for measuring similarity is to ask people to name the colors that are shown them, and then to make the conditions of judgment so difficult that they are sure to make mistakes. To force the subjects to make mistakes the colors can be presented at low illuminations or for very short periods of time or at a rapid rate. Confusions will occur; we expect discrimination to fail first between blue and green, indicating that they are somehow closer together, or more alike, than blue and red.

In other words, the trick is to make *failure of discrimination* a measure of similarity. We will examine this trick in detail. Notice, however, that this equation between confusability and similarity is a definition, not a discovery.

The use of confusability to measure similarity goes back at least as far as 1860 when G. T. Fechner proposed to use the difference threshold—the just noticeable difference or jnd—as a unit with which to measure the subjective magnitude of a sensation.

Fechner's argument went something like this. Suppose one wishes to measure how bright a particular sensation of light is for the person who experiences it. Obviously, one cannot use physical measurements of intensity to measure how it *looks;* the problem is to develop an independent measure of the psychological intensity of the sensation. This can be done as follows. First, measure how much the physical intensity of the light must be decreased before the subject is barely able to detect the difference. Then change the intensity of the light to this new, lower value and again measure the size of the difference threshold. Since both changes were just barely noticeable, Fechner assumed that they were subjectively equal. Now decrease the intensity again by a just noticeable amount. This process is repeated until finally the light is entirely invisible. Since every decrement was subjectively equal to every other decrement, the number of times one had to decrease the intensity of the light—the number of just noticeable differences in intensity—can be used as a measure of the subjective magnitude of the sensation.

Of course, the measure is not limited to this particular situation. Once one accepts Fechner's assumption that the just noticeable difference, the jnd, can be used as a standard unit of subjective measurement, one can count the number of jnd's between any two stimuli and use this number as a measure of their discriminability. The smaller the number of jnd's, the greater their similarity must be. In this way Fechner used confusability to measure similarity.

It should be apparent that the actual experimental operations involved in carrying out this measurement—measuring one difference limen after another until the absolute threshold is reached—are far too tedious to carry out every time a sensory magnitude is to be measured. Some short cuts are needed, and here, at last, mathematics can be useful. By certain relatively simple calculations many hours of tedious measurement can be avoided. Fechner assumed that Weber's Law was true, so that

$$\frac{\Delta M}{M} = \text{constant}$$

where now ΔM $(= D')$ indicates the size of the increment in the stimulus magnitude M that is necessary to make the increment just detectable. Since Fechner assumed that all jnd's are subjectively equal, he could write

$$\Delta S = k \frac{\Delta M}{M}$$

where ΔS denotes the amount of change in the psychological magnitude of the sensation that results when the physical magnitude of the stimulus is changed by ΔM, and k is a constant of proportionality that depends upon the particular units of measurement one adopts. Now he could rewrite the equation as

$$\frac{\Delta S}{\Delta M} = \frac{k}{M}$$

which he then proceeded to solve by assuming that it was really a differential equation,

$$\frac{dS}{dM} = \frac{k}{M}$$

As students of the calculus know, the solution of this equation is

$$S = k \log_e M + c$$

where c is the constant of integration and e the base of the natural logarithms. In this way he derived *Fechner's Law*, which states that (if we ignore the irrelevant constants) the subjective magnitude of a sensation is measured by the logarithm of the physical magnitude of its stimulus.

The reader should now be much impressed by how scientific all this sounds. Even if one does not understand the calculus, it is still a solemn thing to see it used. In the nineteenth century it seemed even more impressive; Wundt's new psychology could scarcely have achieved scientific recognition as quickly as it did without this fundamental and ingenious contribution from Fechner.

What kind of man was Gustav Theodore Fechner? In his fine history of experimental psychology, E. G. Boring says of him:

He first acquired modest fame as professor of physics at Leipzig, but in later life he was a physicist only as the spirit of the *Naturforscher* penetrated all his work. In intention and ambition he was a philosopher, especially in his last forty years of life, but he was never famous, or even successful, in this fundamental effort that is, nevertheless, the key to his other activities. He was a humanist, a satirist, a poet in his incidental writings and an estheticist during one decade of activity. He is famous, however, for his psychophysics, and this fame was rather forced upon him. He did not wish his name to go down to posterity as a psychophysicist. He did not, like Wundt, seek to found experimental psychology. He might have been content to let experimental psychology as an independent science remain in the womb of time, could he but have established his spiritualistic *Tagesansicht* as a substitute for the current materialistic *Nachtansicht* of the universe. The world, however, chose for him; it seized upon the psychophysical experiments, which Fechner meant as contributory to his philosophy, and made them into an experimental psychology.[7]

Fechner tells us that it was on the morning of October 22, 1850, while he was lying late in bed thinking about how he might combat the materialistic tendencies of his times, that the general outline of his idea occurred to him and he saw how he could use physical magnitudes of stimulation to measure subjective magnitudes of sensation. Thus October 22 is sometimes celebrated by psychologists—only half in jest—as the birthday of their science.

The irony of Fechner's achievement, however, was that he succeeded so well that what he was most interested in—sensation, mind, the subjective view of reality—became excess baggage. Instead of proving by empirical evidence that sensations were real because they could be measured in physical units, he provided a way to talk about them that was completely materialistic. A later generation would adopt his insight as part of a larger conviction that it is *discrimination*, not sensation, that must be measured. The psychology, at least in the spiritual sense Fechner meant the term, could be left out entirely. Perceptual similarity, so the argument runs, can always be reduced to objective questions of discrimination and confusability.

Today a psychologist tries to predict behavior generally. He does not limit himself to the subjective experience that a conscious, human adult is able to judge and to talk about. In this broader context the study of discrimination has largely displaced the older study of sensation. Obviously, discrimination is an indispensable feature of intelligent behavior. Insofar as our receptors provide the information that guides our behavior, it is important for us to understand their capacities and their limitations. This broader perspective has, in general, had a refreshing effect on this branch of the psychological enterprise.

Consider briefly how the psychophysical methods have been generalized and extended far beyond the realms of sensory psychology. Late in the 1920s L. L. Thurstone, who taught psychophysics at the University of Chicago, became bored with what he was teaching. He admitted that psychophysics offered the satisfaction of clean and quantitative logic, a rare satisfaction for a psychologist to enjoy, but he could not convince himself that the sensations he was measuring so precisely were worth all the time and trouble he lavished on them. He decided to change what he was teaching and to use the same methods to measure something worthwhile.

> Instead of asking a person which of two cylinders is the heavier, we might as well ask something interesting, such as, "Which of these two nationalities do you in general prefer to associate with?" or "Which of these two offenses do you consider to be in general the more serious?" or "Which of these two pictures or colored designs do you like better?" Questions of this sort of discrimination might be multiplied indefinitely, and if they could be handled with some sort of psychophysical logic, it is clear that we should have here the possibilities of objective description of more psychological significance than the sensory limen.[8]

And so Thurstone put the study of attitudes on a quantitative basis.

Thurstone's transfer of psychophysical logic from sensations to attitudes was an important generalization, one that breathed new life into an old and often doddering subject. However, there are ways to measure similarity other than the one Fechner invented and Thurstone generalized; there are units of subjective measurement other than the jnd. Some of the other methods are much simpler, and they do not assume that you can get red by adding up various shades of pink.

Suppose we ask a subject to make direct, numerical estimates of the magnitudes of his sensations. One technique is to give a person a standard stimulus and tell him, "I want you to imagine that the magnitude of this is 100. Now, if this is 100, what number would you assign to the following stimuli?" A series of intensities are then presented and his numerical estimates are recorded and averaged with the estimates obtained from other subjects. The assumption that a subject is capable of making valid numerical estimates seems justified by the repeatability of his replies, by the agreement among different judges, and most of all by the internal consistency of the results obtained.

It is often the case that when some aspect of sensation has been measured both according to Fechner's method of jnd's and by some more direct assignment of numbers to magnitudes, the results obtained are not the same. Or, to put the best foot forward, sometimes the results of these two different methods of measurement are the same. When the two methods agree we feel that all is well and that our assumptions about an observer's ability to make direct numerical estimates must have been essentially correct.[9] But what can we say when the two disagree? And disagree systematically? Whereas the Fechnerian argument makes sensory magnitude a logarithmic function of the stimulus magnitude, the newer methods of direct estimation indicate that it should be a power function

$$S = kM^n$$

where k and n are constants for any particular sense modality.

Professor S. Smith Stevens argues that this relationship finally reduces the amount of error common in the use of the Weber and Fechner ratios so that it should be understood as a natural law, the so-called *power law*.[10] In his paper "The Surprising Simplicity of Sensory Metrics" Stevens presents an impressive array of experimental data to support his contention that the power law applies to all sensory modalities. As the data in Figure 7.2 illustrate, all sensory modalities yield straight-line power functions when plotted on log-log paper; only the slope of the line differs, with sharper slopes for electric shock

---

CITATION ACCOMPANYING THE DISTINGUISHED SCIENTIFIC CONTRIBUTION AWARD PRESENTED BY THE AMERICAN PSYCHOLOGICAL ASSOCIATION, 1960

"For his researches in psychophysics and the measurement of sensation, and for his contributions to the theory of scaling and the philosophy of measurement. He has made clear the distinction between scales of just noticeable differences, category scales, and ratio scales, and has shown, in a dozen instances and mostly by his own research, how equal stimulus ratios beget equal ratios of sensory magnitudes, thus establishing the power function as a modern substitute for Fechner's logarithmic law. He stands out as the pioneer in a new psychophysics a wise man in the theory of measurement, and a keen experimenter who extracts his theories from nature by judiciously controlled observation."

STANLEY SMITH STEVENS

FIGURE 7.2

Equal-sensation functions obtained by matching force of handgrip to various criterion stimuli. Each point stands for the median force exerted by ten or more observers to match the apparent intensity of the criterion stimulus. The relative position of a function along the abscissa is arbitrary. The dashed line shows a slope of 1.0 in these coordinates. (From S. S. Stevens, "The Surprising Simplicity of Sensory Metrics," American Psychologist 2, no. 1 (1962): 29. Copyright 1962 by the American Psychological Association and reproduced by permission.)

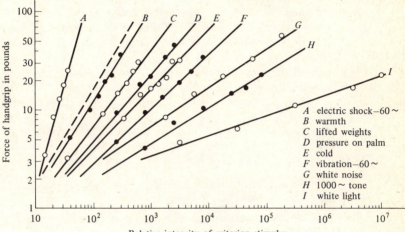

than for sound or light. But in its most concise expression, the power law states that equal stimulus ratios produce equal sensation ratios. In a more recent paper Stevens reports some success in localizing power functions in sensory nerve cells studied with microelectrodes.[11]

Psychologists who work on these problems are far from unanimous about the proper way to resolve discrepancies among different methods of measurement. At times their arguments become violent, proof enough for anyone who needed it that precise measurements do not always suffice to settle scientific disagreements. It is clear, however, that an old and venerable problem is still exciting interest, still leading us toward new concepts and methods of measurement that will eventually enrich many different fields of psychology.

NOTES

1. C. Holden, "NBS Urges 10-Year Metric Conversion Plan," *Science* 173 (1970): 613.

2. S. S. Stevens, ed., *Handbook of Experimental Psychology* (New York: Wiley, 1951), pp. 23–30.

3. The old term is the galvanic skin response or GSR. It is now called the electrodermal response or EDR. It is usually measured on a polygraph, similar to the way EEG is recorded.

4. R. S. Lazarus, *Psychological Stress and the Coping Process* (New York: McGraw-Hill, 1966).

5. J. A. Swets, W. P. Tanner, and J. G. Birdsall, "Decision Processes in Perception," *Psychological Review* 68, no. 5 (1961): 301–340.

6. An introduction to sensory psychology providing references leading into the extensive literature on the subject is F. A. Geldard, *The Human Senses* (New York: Wiley, 1953). For a more advanced discussion see W. Rosenblith, ed., *Sensory Communication* (New York: The M.I.T. Press and John Wiley, 1961) and J. F. Corso, *The Experimental Psychology of Sensory Behavior* (New York: Holt, Rinehart & Winston, 1967).

7. E. G. Boring, *A History of Experimental Psychology*, 2d ed. (New York: Appleton-Century-Crofts, 1950), pp. 275–276.

8. L. L. Thurstone, *The Measurement of Values* (Chicago: University of Chicago Press, 1959).

9. For a discussion of two classes of sensory scales of measurement, see S. S. Stevens and E. H. Galanter, "Ratio Scales and Category Scales for a Dozen Perceptual Continua," *Journal of Experimental Psychology* 54 (1957): 377–411.

10. S. S. Stevens, "The Surprising Simplicity of Sensory Metrics," *American Psychologist* 17, no. 1 (1962): 29–39.

11. S. S. Stevens, "Neural Events and the Psychophysical Law," *Science* 170 (1970): 1043–1050.

EIGHT
The Analysis of Perceptions

When the junior author was visiting in a remote Indonesian village in July, 1969, portable television sets were brought in by the government so that villagers, who had no electricity, could witness the first Apollo landing on the moon. The question that ran through the minds of many of the villagers was this: why hadn't the astronauts waited until the moon was full before attempting to land on it.

If this anecdote seems to support the virtues of education over ignorance, we wish to point out that the question of the perception of the moon is, despite the overwhelming television coverage, not a simple matter of perceiving what is real. As the many psychologists who have conjectured over the cause of the moon illusion realize, we see the moon near the horizon as bigger, in spite of our knowledge that it is an illusion. You may have experienced already the disappointment of many a photographer who thought he had placed that big, beautiful moon in his picture of the skyline. Many psychologists have tried to explain it in terms of terrain, angle of view, proximity of other objects, or a variety of other factors, but the mystery of the moon illusion remains; so persistent is the phenomenon that it is possible to demonstrate it in your own room.

Simply cut out two equal circles of paper and tack one to the ceiling and one to a wall. Take the time to observe both objects and stand back from the wall so that the paper "moon" on the wall appears to be the same size as the one on the ceiling. Checking the vertical and horizontal distances with a tape measure will invariably show that the horizontal distance is greater, illustrating the fact that it appears to be larger. Some investigators point to this demonstration as evidence for an innate mechanism involving the vestibular mechanism and the direction of gravity. It can also be shown to work in reverse by viewing the horizontal object by bending over and looking at it from between your legs. The "moon" will then appear to be smaller!

Moving to an area that we know more about, we suggest another experiment. You have three basins of water. In one the water is cold, in the second it is tepid, in the third

hot. Put one hand into the cold water and the other into the hot. After you leave them immersed a minute or two you will discover that the difference in warmth disappears. When your two hands seem to be approximately the same neutral warmth, remove them both and plunge them into the remaining basin, the one containing the lukewarm water. Now the water here seems to have two temperatures at the same time, warm to one hand and cool to the other. But you *know* that the water must have a single temperature! It is not reasonable to say that the same water is both warm and cool simultaneously, even though it feels that way. Something has gone wrong with the usually reliable machinery for finding out about the world we live in.

The dilemma of the three basins was used by John Locke in 1690 as part of his argument that the apparent qualities of objects—warmth, for example—are not in the objects themselves, but in the minds of the persons who perceive the objects. The object is not warm, said Locke; it merely possesses the capacity of arousing the idea of warmth in us. If the warmth we perceive were truly in the object itself, as it appears to be, it would be impossible for us to perceive two different warmths in one object at the same time. Thus, Locke used the three basins to drive the wedge of his argument between the objective and the subjective views of reality.

In revisiting this ancient landmark today, however, we have a somewhat different purpose in mind. Our present interest in it derives from its usefulness as an example of why many psychologists persist in using two different terms, sensation and perception, to describe the way we are affected by events going on in the world around us.

When you first hear a strange language spoken, it is merely a rapid flow of sound. The voice is recognizable as human, but that is about all you get from it. When you have learned the language, however, the jumble of auditory sensations sort themselves out into phonemes, syllables, words, and phrases. Now you perceive the patterns that underlie and organize the flow of sounds. But there is still a third level that emerges when you learn the language, a conceptual level of meaning and reference. You not only learn to perceive what the sounds are, you learn to understand what they signify.

Are these three levels—sensation, perception, conception—really distinct modes of functioning? Do they appear in all our efforts to cope with reality? Are percepts and concepts always the result of learning? These are some of the basic questions we face when we try to analyze the processes of perception.

The gaps between sensation, perception, and conception have puzzled men at least since the time of Socrates. How can we discover the permanent, stable, reliable, true conception of ourselves and our world? How do we identify the solid, substantial reality that lies behind the shifting, deceptive, changing, fallible appearances presented to our senses? How do we build our image of the universe out of the conglomeration of stimuli that affect our sense organs? To build a world-that-is out of a world-that-seems-to-be is one of the great triumphs of childhood.

Some psychologists like to think of sensations as the basic data reported by the sense organs, data stripped as far as possible of all inference about their cause or their meaning. In the case of the three basins, our sensations are the feelings of cold, cool, warm, and hot wetness. Perceptions, on the other hand, may be affected by what we know of our environment from our past, as well as our present, experience with it. We perceive the water, not just the wetness. Ordinarily, we perceive the water to *be* warm, not merely to *feel* warm, though in the dilemma of the three basins our perception becomes confused and we seem to perceive two contradictory things at the same time.

Notice that there is nothing confusing about our sensations: one hand feels warm and the other feels cool. The sensations are simple enough and quite straightforward, so the temptation is strong to begin with them when we try to explain what happens with the three basins. If we concentrate on our sensations and ignore perceptual and conceptual problems for the moment, the dilemma can be understood and explained quite simply. It is a typical example of a very general phenomenon, called *adaptation*. The fundamental fact is that if you wait long enough, and if the temperature is not too extreme, the skin tends to adapt to the temperature of its environment. When you sit

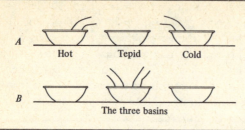

A — Hot   Tepid   Cold

B

The three basins

down in a hot tub, at first you may think you have been scalded, but after a minute or two it seems comfortably warm and may even come to feel neutral in temperature. When you go swimming in a cold pool, you feel at first that you will surely freeze, but if you keep going it may become bearable, even neutral, in its apparent temperature. Once your skin has adapted to the environmental temperature, your judgment of warm or cool is relative to that adaptation level. That is to say, when the skin has become adapted to a particular temperature, any higher temperature will feel warm and any lower temperature will feel cool. The dilemma of the three basins is simply a clever trick to illustrate the phenomenon of adaptation in a striking manner.

When we take this approach to the problem, we are concerned only with the sensations of warm and cool, not with an inference about the real temperature of the water. We say only that the same sensations can be produced by different temperatures, depending upon what our skin has become accustomed to. Of course, once the process of sensory adaptation has been identified, it becomes an interesting problem in its own right. Many questions remain to be answered. For example, what are the limits within which complete adaptation can occur? (Below about 65° F. and above about 105° F. the water does not come to feel neutral even after long exposures.) How rapidly does adaptation take place? (If it is not complete in two or three minutes, it probably will never feel neutral.) Will a change of five degrees from the neutral point feel like an equal change in warmth regardless of what the neutral temperature was? (No. A 5° F. change in the middle of the range, say, at 85° F., is equivalent to an 8° F. change at the extremes.) Is adaptation a function of the size of the skin area that is exposed? (Yes. It takes longer for a larger area to adapt.) And so the questions about adaptation can be posed and answered by careful psychophysical experiments in the laboratory.[1] The fact remains, however, that these are questions about how the water feels, not about the actual physical temperature of the water. Calling the process adaptation does not resolve the underlying problem of the three basins.

If one takes this approach to the study of perception, one is likely to give special weight to sensations as the primitive elements out of which more complicated perceptions can be built, and on the basis of which inferences can be drawn about reality. Thus sensory processes are seen as simple and primary, whereas perceptual processes are complex and derivative. Wilhelm Wundt is a famous example of a psychologist who adopted this view. But it is a difficult view to defend. The trouble is that most people feel intuitively that the things and events are primary and, in some sense, simple. Sensations are, to them, the result of analyzing one's perceptions in a highly artificial way, and so are considered to be complex, derivative phenomena. Gestalt psychologists provide an excellent example of a view exactly opposite to Wundt's.[2]

The argument as to which comes first, sensation or perception, has consumed more time and attention than it deserves. However, the position a psychologist takes will affect the kind of research he does, and affect the development of the science.

For example, consider a traditional attitude toward the study of hearing. It was pointed out quite early by G. S. Ohm—who is usually remembered today for his studies of electricity—that the ear acts as an acoustic analyzer. That is to say, when two different frequencies of a vibration affect the ear simultaneously we hear them both at the same time and do not (as in color vision) perceive some synthetic compromise halfway between the two of them. Moreover, it was known that all complex sounds—noise, music, speech—can be analyzed into the sum of many simple sounds by means of techniques based on concepts developed by the nineteenth-century French mathematician J. B. J. Fourier. Since a complicated sound is the sum of several simple sounds, the sensation produced by a complicated sound must be the sum of the sensations produced by the several simple sounds. Therefore, the argument went, it is not necessary to study the perception of complex sounds. Consequently, nearly all the pioneer work on audition was focused on the study of pure, simple tones, for they were considered to be the sensory atoms out of which everything auditory is built. It was not until the development of the telephone that practical considerations overrode theoretical biases and a group of engineers at the Bell Telephone Laboratories began to study the perception of speech directly.[3] Acoustic analysis of the speech waves into simple components gave only a first approximation to what listeners could understand. Intelligibility is also a function of many psychological variables. Alertness, familiarity with the language, the meaning of the message, and the listener's expectations, all influence what is heard.

By way of contrast with a theory that builds up compound perceptions out of the simpler atoms of sensation, the gestalt psychologists ask us to consider the perception of melodies. We listen to a melody played in one key. Then it is repeated, but in a new key. We have no difficulty in recognizing it as the same melody; some of us may even be unaware that the pitch was different the second time through. Clearly, then, something besides our particular sensations of pitch must be involved when we recognize a tune. We cannot learn anything about a melody by studying its several notes in isolation. The search for conditions that determine our recognition of patterns, relations, and configurations represents a very different approach to the problem of perception.

The gestalt psychologists—Max Wertheimer, Wolfgang Köhler, Kurt Koffka, Kurt Lewin, Karl Duncker and many others— forced their colleagues to admit that a complex perception cannot be explained as a linear sum of the sensations that its parts arouse. The gestalt slogan, which has become a battle cry of all soft theories of psychology, states that "the whole is greater than the sum of the parts." Figure 8.1 shows an example of the kind of objections they raised.[4] A wheel rolls slowly across a room that is totally dark. A light attached to the rim of the wheel traces out the cycloid path in *a*. A light attached to the hub produces a simple horizontal line, as in *b*. But if we now attach lights to both the hub and the rim, we do not get a simple sum of the two lines, as in *c*. Instead, the motions of the two lights are related to one another to give the unified pattern suggested in *d* where one light is now seen to revolve around the other; the cycloid path vanishes completely. This is but one of a large variety of examples that show how difficult it is to analyze perceptions into their sensory elements.

An alternative view of the matter is that perception and sensation are not essentially different processes. The difference lies not in what we experience but rather in the way we describe what we experience. Sensation and perception correspond to two languages people have for talking about their experience, about the information their sense organs are providing. When they talk about their sensations, they speak cautiously and try to say how their experience would appear to someone who had no conception of its true source or meaning. When they talk about their perceptions, they speak more freely without trying to distinguish what they sense from what they know must be the case. Of course, questions about how things *really* are are shot through with metaphysical pitfalls that could take many volumes to explore in detail; such scholarship will not detain us here.

The American psychologist J. J. Gibson has called the cautious, attentive approach *literal* perception, and the casual, familiar approach *schematic* perception. "In the course of practical behavior," he says, "perception is no more literal with respect to color, size, shape, and sequence than is necessary, since literal perception takes time and effort. The percept is reduced to a cue for action. But perception can become literal whenever the observer needs to discriminate. Under favorable conditions it can be surprisingly exact, as the experiments of

FIGURE 8.1

In pitch darkness a wheel with lights on the rim A or the hub B rolls slowly along a table. When both lights are on, the perception is not the simple sum of the perception of each light alone: A + B does not equal C. The cycloid motion is lost and one light seems to rotate around the other, as in D. (From D. Krech and R. S. Crutchfield, Elements of Psychology *[New York: Knopf, 1958].)*

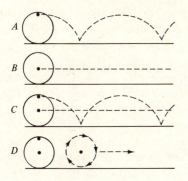

the laboratory demonstrate. One can always look at a thing carefully if there is a reason to do so."[5] Thus an observer exercises control over the amount of detail he will take in, just as an artist might control the amount of detail he will include in a drawing. The smallest, most literal details are neither the first nor the easiest for us to appreciate.

Schematic perceptions are not merely less detailed; they are usually more meaningful, too. When an observer becomes cautious and attentive, he tries to jettison these meaningful aspects first. This is not always possible, but he tries anyhow. Coleridge said that esthetic appreciation demands a "willing suspension of disbelief." So does perception. If you become too suspicious, if you try to eliminate all your interpretations and expectations, your perceptual world will crumble into meaningless fragments.

Imagine that you are visiting a psychological laboratory—probably around 1915. As you walk in, a psychologist comes over and, without waiting for introductions, asks what you see on the table.

"A book."

"Yes, of course, it is a book," he agrees, "but what do you *really* see?"

"What do you mean, 'What do I *really* see'?" you ask, puzzled. "I told you that I see a book. It is a small book with a red cover."

The psychologist is persistent. "What is your perception *really*?" he insists. "Describe it to me as precisely as you can."

"You mean it isn't a book? What is this, some kind of trick?"

There is a hint of impatience. "Yes, it is a book. There is no trickery involved. I just want you to describe to me *exactly* what you can see, no more and no less."

You are growing very suspicious now. "Well," you say, "from this angle the cover of the book looks like a dark red parallelogram."

"Yes," he says, pleased. "Yes, you see a patch of dark red in the shape of a parallelogram. What else?"

"There is a grayish white edge below it and another thin line of the same dark red below that. Under it I see the table—" He winces. "Around it I see a somewhat mottled brown with wavering streaks of lighter brown running roughly parallel to one another."

"Fine, fine." He thanks you for your cooperation.

As you stand there looking at the book on the table you are a little embarrassed that this persistent fellow was able to drive you to such an analysis. He made you so cautious that you were not sure any longer what you really saw and what you only thought you saw. You were, in fact, as suspicious as the New England farmer who would admit only that, "It looks like a cow on this side." In your caution you began talking about what you saw in terms of sensations, where just a moment earlier you were quite certain that you perceived a book on a table.

Your reverie is interrupted suddenly by the appearance of a psychologist who looks vaguely like Wilhelm Wundt. "Thank you, for helping to confirm once more my theory of perception. You have proved," he says, "that the book you see is nothing but a compound of elementary sensations. When you were trying to be precise and say accurately what it was you really saw, you had to speak in terms of color patches, not objects. It is the color sensations that are primary, and every visual object is reducible to them. Your perception of the book is constructed from sensations just as a molecule is constructed from atoms."

This little speech is apparently a signal for battle to begin. "Nonsense!" shouts a voice from the opposite end of the hall. "Nonsense! Any fool knows that the *book* is the primary, immediate, direct, compelling, perceptual fact!" The psychologist who charges down upon you now bears a faint resemblance to William James, but he seems to have a German accent, and his face is so flushed with anger that you cannot be sure. "This reduction of a perception into sensations that you keep talking about is nothing but an intellectual game. An object is not just a bundle of sensations. Any man who goes about seeing patches of dark redness where he ought to see books is sick!"

As the fight begins to gather momentum you close the door softly and slip away. You have what you came for, an illustration that there are two different attitudes, two different ways to talk about the information that our senses provide.

The notion that perceptions are built from sensations the way a wall is built of bricks is now generally recognized to be unsatisfactory. Ordinarily, the perception of an object is possible only because we are willing to go far beyond the sensory information we are given.[6] We are usually unaware how far we leap to reach a perceptual conclusion. The leap itself is, of course, unconscious. All such processes are unconscious; only their end product appears in consciousness and is accessible for introspective analysis. But even though our conscious experience is much the same, the way we describe it need not be. When we talk about our sensations, we are trying to talk about the information we must have had *before* we made the leap; when we talk about our perceptions, we are trying to talk about the same information *after* we have made the leap. The question as to which way of talking is truer, which more natural or more immediate, is an interesting one, but it is not essential that we decide it before we can proceed with our study of perception.

The leap that carries perception beyond sensation is often called, after Helmholtz, an unconscious inference, and the perception itself an unconscious conclusion. Inferences and conclusions sound very intellectual, and some people object to this way of talking about perception. We should clearly recognize that the inferences of perception are not the articulate, deductive inferences of a trained logician; they are more the tacit, inductive inferences of a gullible child.

Hermann von Helmholtz, a pioneer researcher in visual and auditory perception, battled the soft theorists constantly, proposing the idea of an unconscious inference to help explain three-dimensional perception, which is derived from separate, disparate images that are transmitted to anatomically separate parts of the occipital or visual cortex. To many gestaltists the unconscious inference seemed like a "fudge factor," invented in a desperate attempt to deny their assertions that complex perceptions are innate. History and research have shown that both arguments had substance. The unconscious inference was the basis for later statistical perception theories that stress decision-making. In turn, the classic neurophysiological research of Hubel and Weisel on the occipital cortex of the cat showed that groups of cells respond to curves, boundary, and shading of visual forms, providing those complex bits of information that can be integrated into an inference.[7]

Two processes, one that tries to test hypotheses, another that tries to integrate details, must cooperate for veridical perception. And each process, if given full sway, carries its own style and attitude with it. In the cautious, literal attitude we remain open to many hypotheses; we welcome evidence that will narrow the field. In the confident, schematic attitude we have already adopted our hypothesis, and we take all the evidence as consonant with it.

What does it mean to say that perception ordinarily goes beyond the information that the senses actually provide? Some examples are needed.

An interesting class of perceptual problems arises from the fact that the retina—the light-sensitive surface in the back of the eyeball where the optical image is projected—is a two-dimensional surface. The world we move around in has three dimensions. How are we able to perceive a three-dimensional world with a two-dimensional retina? It is easy to play tricks on such a device. For example, a small object nearby can cast exactly the same image onto the retina as a larger object farther away; this is a simple fact of projective geometry. In principle, therefore, it should be impossible to decide whether anything is a small object nearby or a large object in the distance. In fact, we manage to make these judgments of distance with considerable accuracy. How do we do it? The clues we use have been studied in great detail. For one thing, our two eyes give us slightly different images of the object, a fact that can be easily verified—what child has not spent hours fascinated by the discovery?—by covering first one eye and then the other. The nearer an object is, the larger will be the difference in its image in the two eyes. Thus the amount of difference between the eyes provides information useful for judging distance. A much simpler kind of information is provided by the fact that near

---

FIGURE 8.2

If two playing cards, both of standard size but separated from a subject by different distances, as in A, are viewed with one eye against a dark background, they will cast different optical images on the retina of the eye. The smaller image will be judged to be farther away; relative size is a cue for the perception of distance. This judgment will be confirmed if the nearer card blocks the view of a corner of the distant card; interposition is another cue for the perception of distance. However, if a corner of the nearer card is carefully cut away, as in B, the distant card will now appear to be in front of the closer card, but will seem much smaller in size, as in C. In this case interposition is a more compelling cue than relative size. (From D. Krech and R. S. Crutchfield, Elements of Psychology *[New York: 1958].)*

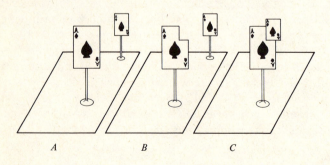

A   B   C

objects will block distant objects from view. Moreover, a distant object is likely to appear hazy, to move more slowly, to have less intense colors, to have finer surface texture, and so on and on.

In addition to all these sensory clues, however, we make considerable use of our prior knowledge of the object we are looking at. We know, for example, approximately how large shoes are. When we see a shoe, therefore, we can judge its distance in terms of its assumed size. It is possible, to be sure, that an energetic psychologist might construct a shoe 6 feet long. If he does, he can easily fool people about its distance, for no one normally expects to see shoes that size. In short, it is a part of our tacit assumption about the world that shoes—and people, trees, cigarettes, cars, and the like—regularly come in certain familiar sizes. When we judge distance, we use our knowledge of these sizes to infer the distance that would be appropriate.

Figure 8.3 makes the point. How far away you think the ball is depends on whether you think of the ball as a marble, a Ping-Pong ball, a billiard ball, or a large beach ball. Your *perception* changes directly as a function of your *conception* of the scene you are viewing.[8] In Chapter 9 we will pursue this topic further.

Our previous familiarity with the visual environment has such an important effect on what we see that many psychologists have used this familiarity as the basis for defending a distinction between sensation and perception. Sensations are unlearned, they say, but perceptions are the meanings we learn to attach to the patterns of sensation. The assumption that we have no unlearned perceptions is probably too strong, but it is certainly true that learning can account for many of the perceptual schemata we use. In the example of the three basins, our sensations of warmth and coolness are unaffected by previous learning; but there would be no perceptual illusion if we had not previously learned that a given volume of water must have a relatively uniform temperature. Many other perceptual phenomena can be accounted for by arguments similarly phrased in the language of learning.

FIGURE 8.3

Where you see the ball will depend on what kind of ball you assume it is.

But let us consider some more examples. Distance is not the only perceptual judgment one can study. For example, how bright is a particular surface? Your estimate depends not only upon the color you assign to the surface, but also upon the kind of light you think is falling on it. If you are misled in your estimate of the illumination, you will make an incorrect judgment of the brightness of the surface. The importance of a viewer's assumptions about the ambient illumination can be demonstrated by an amusing trick. Take two discs and paint one white, the other black. Hang them by black threads about a foot apart. Take a spotlight and focus it carefully on the black disc. Now dim the lights in the rest of the room until the black disc under the spotlight seems as bright as the white disc that has no special illumination. Put a screen up so that the spotlight is out of sight. The experimental situation is diagramed in Figure 8.4. Now you are ready to test your friends. Call them into the room and ask them to judge which of the two discs is brighter. After they have looked and decided, you can reveal the source of illumination to them. One way to reveal it is to light a cigarette and blow smoke into the beam of the spotlight. Or move the screen. Or accidentally put your hand into the beam. The viewer will almost certainly have an "Oh, no!" reaction as the highly

---

FIGURE 8.4

Concealed illumination experiment. The person who does not know about the spotlight will judge the black and white discs to have equal brightness. A small piece of paper thrust into the light beam, however, makes it obvious that the left disc is black.

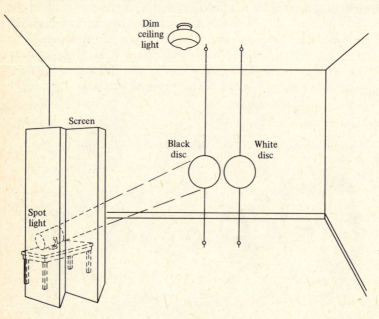

illuminated, apparently white disc is suddenly seen for what it is—a *black* surface! There is no change in the sensations aroused by the two discs, but the change in perception is like going from day to night. In this case no amount of meticulous introspection will enable us to isolate our sensations from their perceptual matrix.

And, incidentally, when the objects are withdrawn from the light beam, the disc returns immediately to its original appearance. Simply knowing that the spotlight is there is not enough; we must see the illumination. So apparently our percepts are not completely at the mercy of our conceptual knowledge.

Nevertheless, these examples of perceptual inference should suffice to make the point that our tacit assumptions about the nature of the perceived object can play an important role in determining what we see. The point can be made to look paradoxical, for it seems to imply that we must know what we are seeing before we can know what we see. But there is really no paradox. We often know partially, in advance, what we do not know completely. We know what kinds of things to expect in different situations, what actions or events are the most probable in a given place at a given time in the company of given people. We try to interpret any new experiences we have in such a way as to be consistent with our previous experience. Of course, when a strange psychologist takes you into the House of Unknown Horrors that he calls his laboratory and asks you to sit quietly in a dark room until you see or hear something, you are not likely to do much perceiving. It is doubtful that you could recognize your own face in such a context. In the strange and unpredictable world of the laboratory you may indeed try to retreat to the literal description of your sensations in order to communicate your experiences. Perhaps that is why psychologists who spend most of their time studying people in a laboratory environment often forget how much inference is involved in the perceptions that occur in more familiar settings, and how much aid a little advance information can furnish.

But no matter how cautious one tries to be, one cannot give a completely literal description of one's experience in the language of pure sensation. Some inferences about the nature of our world will always slip in to spoil the game. For example, it is difficult, probably impossible, to describe visual experience in terms of local patches of different colors and brightnesses without saying anything about the fact that these patches have boundaries, that there are relatively sharp discontinuities, contours, in the visual field, where one surface appears to stop and another begins. But these are not pure sensations. As the gestalt psychologists like to point out, these are *relations* among the parts of the whole visual field. The contour exists by virtue of a relation between two adjacent patches of colored surface. Instead of the relatively simple appreciation of color, one must make the more complicated judgment of a difference between two spatially distinct regions of color. That there is a space in which these colors exist, that there is a thing whose extent can be defined by its boundaries, are assumptions about the nature of the world we live in. The fact that they are assumptions whose validity we believe completely, and without which we would be unable to function, does not alter the fact that they are assumptions.

Contours define shapes, and shapes are much harder to describe than simple sensations. If the contours are three straight lines that bound a surface of relatively uniform color, one sees a triangle. But one does not speak about a sensation of triangularity in the same way one speaks about a sensation of redness. The difference between them is that the discussion of triangles must involve relational aspects of the total situation that can be ignored when one speaks of colors. For one thing, one speaks about the triangle as a unit, as a whole, as a thing. And for another, the perceived triangle stands out from the surrounding area; it forms a figure against a background. This figure-ground relation is so spontaneous and natural that one usually ignores it entirely. One way to appreciate its importance is to have the relation suddenly change. For example, in the upper half of Figure 8.5 you can

FIGURE 8.5

Figure and ground can often be organized in various ways: A, B, C, and D indicate four different organizations that we might expect to find if we could get a cross-section view. The easiest configuration to see is probably A, which represents a white triangle seen lying on top of a square black card that seems in turn to lie on top of the white page. However, figure and ground can also be organized as B, a square black card with a triangular hole lying on top of the page, or as C, a square hole cut in the white page to reveal a black background underneath it. The hardest to see is probably D, which is supposed to represent the "real" situation—black ink and white paper all in the same plane.

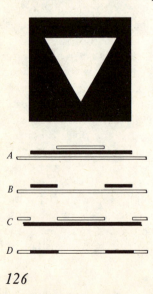

see a white triangle against a black background; or you can see a black template lying on a white page, in which case the black area becomes the figure against a white ground, and so on. Four different ways of organizing this arrangement are indicated schematically in the lower half of the figure. As you stare at the figure, the figure-ground relations can switch back and forth almost, but not quite, at will. (Another example is shown in Figure 8.6 and left as an exercise for the reader.)

We see things and not the holes between them; this simple fact cannot be explained in a language of pure sensations. These configurational aspects of experience have been emphasized most strongly by gestalt psychologists. They argue that the perceptual field at any moment is highly organized, highly structured. If this statement has any meaning, it is that what we experience in one part of the perceptual field is related to what we experience in other parts. To talk about sensations as if they exist in isolation or can be moved from one part of the field to another without changing, is, therefore, extremely artificial. As soon as a sensation takes its place as part of a perceptual whole, its character is changed by the other parts of the configuration.

Now we have considered principally examples of spatial configurations; but temporal configurations are equally interesting and important. For instance, motion is an example of organization in both time and space. We can obtain an impression of movement, of course, when nothing has moved, which is the basis for the motion picture; a sequence of still pictures is presented rapidly enough to produce the illusion of continuity. We can study the illusion more simply in the laboratory with two lights that go on briefly one after the other. If the lights are placed side by side, there will appear to be movement from one to the other. The effect has been called the phi phenomenon. A person who does not know how the lights are arranged may be convinced that a light went on in one spot, and then moved through the intervening space and stopped in the second spot, where it vanished. In other words, the observer reports light coming from the space between the two sources. It is not possible to speak about this transient light as emanating from nowhere, as if it were an independent atom of sensation, for it derives its existence entirely from the pattern or configuration of the two lights in space and time.

The first and only psychologist to win a Nobel prize (and that

---

FIGURE 8.6

What is this?

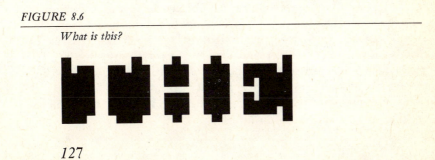

CITATION ACCOMPANYING THE NOBEL PRIZE IN PHYSIOLOGY AND MEDICINE, 1961

"For his discoveries concerning the physical mechanisms of stimulation within the cochlea."
(*From T. L. Sourkes,* Nobel Prize Winners in Medicine and Physiology, 1901–1965 [*New York: Abelard-Schuman, 1967*] *pp. 390–396.*)

GEORG VON BÉKÉSY

in physiology) was Georg von Békésy, whose importance in the history of perception research has not always been fully recognized.[9] It is impossible to summarize briefly the lifetime work of a creative scientist, but for this discussion we will focus on his contributions to the understanding of how the ear transforms acoustical energy into meaningfully coded signals in the nervous system. Békésy was committed to the use of mechanical analogies and to the belief that somehow a theory that adequately explains one sensory process should be congruent with theories in the other senses. Central to his thinking is the selective function of attention, that remarkable ability to filter incoming information to prevent overload and permit adaptive responding. Arguing that sensory *inhibition* is as important as sensory excitation, he believed that sensations result from patterns of summed excitations of some nerve cells plus inhibition of others.

In his auditory research, Békésy followed the lead of Helmholtz who proposed the place theory of hearing, based on the physical similarity between the stretched out floor of the inner ear (the basilar membrane of the cochlea) and standard musical instruments. The place theory assumed that the fibers of this membrane are plucked in the way a stringed instrument is plucked—the shorter fibers for high notes and the longer fibers for low notes. However, physiological research had shown that these fibers are not under tension in the lateral direction, thus breaking down a neat physical analogy. Von Békésy worked for many years with mechanical models of the inner ear; he made actual observations through a microscope of inner ears from deceased hospital patients (floating crystals in the fluid so that he could see how sound waves were propagated), did histological studies of the underlying patterns of nerves, and studied how people perceived vibrations on their skin. He saw that a sound transmitted into the fluid medium of the inner ear produces a traveling wave of considerable complexity, but the maximum energy (shown by crystal deposits) gathers at one point, which varies in location with the frequency or pitch of the tone. At this point the skin is depressed and maximum excitation occurs with inhibition of the surrounding nerves to create a funneling action that contributes to sharp localization of the stimulus (see Figure 8.7). Thus the place theory remains valid but for a different reason.

Von Békésy built a plastic tube that simulates, on the arm, the action of the inner ear. Sounds are introduced into the tube while a subject rests his arm. Trained subjects are easily able to locate the point of maximum stimulation, which varies with the frequency of the tone. Von Békésy extended his research to the sense of taste in his quest for a single theory to explain how the nervous system transforms physical energy into excitatory and inhibitory patterns.[10]

Most psychologists no longer try to reduce the perceptual world to sensory elements, nor assume that they can learn about complicated experiences by studying only the simple ones. More and more, psychologists who study perception are shifting away from their old question, "How can I analyze this perception into its basic atoms?" and are beginning to ask a different question, "How can I discover the transformations that a perceiver can impose upon the information he takes in?" And with each new step forward in understanding the trans-

FIGURE 8.7

The area of sensation produced by a local stimulus and its surrounding area of inhibition. (*From* Journal of the Acoustical Society of America 87.)

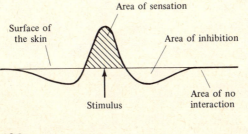

formations, one gains increased respect for both the complexity and the beauty of our perceptual machinery.

NOTES

1. R. S. Woodworth and H. Schlosberg, *Experimental Psychology*, rev. ed. (New York: Holt, 1954), pp. 286–293.
2. Gestalt is a German word that can be translated approximately as "pattern or configuration." Probably the most readable introduction to gestalt psychology is Wolfgang Köhler's *Gestalt Psychology* (New York: Liveright, 1929).
3. H. Fletcher, *Speech and Hearing in Communication*, 2d ed. (New York: Van Nostrand, 1953).
4. E. Oppenheimer, "Optische Versuche Uber Ruhe and Bewegung," *Psychologische Forschung* 20 (1935): 1–46.
5. J. J. Gibson, *The Perception of the Visual World* (Boston: Houghton Mifflin, 1950), p. 211.
6. J. S. Bruner, "Going Beyond the Information Given," in *Contemporary Approaches to Cognition* (Cambridge: Harvard University Press, 1957), pp. 41–69.
7. D. H. Hubel and T. N. Wiesel, "Receptive Fields and Functional Architecture in Two Non-striate Visual Areas (18 and 19) of the Cat," *Journal of Neurophysiology* 28, no. 2 (1965): 229–289.
8. A. H. Hastorf, "Influence of Suggestion on Size and Distance," *Journal of Psychology* 29 (1950): 195–217.
9. Georg von Békésy, *Sensory Inhibition* (Princeton: Princeton University Press, 1967).
10. Georg von Békésy, "Similarities of Inhibition in the Different Sense Organs," *American Psychologist* 24, no. 8 (1969): 707–719.

NINE
Space

The world consists of more-or-less solid objects arranged irregularly in familiar, stationary, three-dimensional space. This organization of things in space seems common, natural, and inevitable. We all take it for granted; it is too banal for comment. When we stop to analyze it, however, this altogether familiar organization becomes a rich source of insight into the way our minds work.

Consider space. One does not literally *see* space, the way one sees surfaces, colors, contours, shadows; one *infers* it, either perceptually, conceptually, or both. Space is one of the abstract schemata we impose on our world in order to make experience more coherent and meaningful.

A spatial schema can take several different forms. Space can be flat, as in a child's drawing; with two-dimensional retinas in our eyes the wonder is that we so seldom see a flat world. Or space can be positional; this is probably the schema most used whenever we are interested in specifying the location of one thing relative to another. Or space can be the great container of all objects; that is the infinite system of absolute coordinates so valuable for classical physics.[1]

Which of these schemata is the true one? Prior to the time of Newton space was generally defined as a relation between objects. Empty space was thought to be meaningless, because space and place could be understood only in terms of the objects involved. But Newton boldly introduced the framework of absolute space and stated his laws of mechanics in terms of spatial coordinates that extend to infinity in all directions. Today we find Newton's system so natural and obvious that we are surprised to learn how bitterly his contemporaries objected to this metaphysical assumption that space, like God, was infinite. But no one could then find a way to deal with the inertia principle in terms of a relative schema. Not until Einstein's theory of relativity was it possible for physicists to give up the container concept and return to a simpler positional schema. Fortunately, however, we do not have to decide which schema is correct in order to get ahead with our studies of psychological space.

Psychologically, there are two related, but roughly distinguishable ways one can impose spatial schemata on ordinary affairs. There is, first, *perceptual space*, which provides a frame of reference for everything we see, hear, or touch as we go about our daily business. Perceptual space is the indispensable guide for all our movements and manipulations. But there is also a second schema, which can be called *conceptual space*. This includes the space that physicists and astronomers talk about, but also something much more familiar to a layman. Our psychological worlds do not end with the furthest reach of the senses. Behind that wall there is a room full of familiar things, and beyond that a yard, also familiar, and the whole is embedded in the matrix of a town, which in turn fits into a region located on a continent that is part of a sphere that rotates around the sun. This extended image of space is built up slowly by experience, by fitting smaller regions together into larger ones, by asking questions, by studying maps. It is never perceived directly, however, as a face, a room, or a doorway can be perceived. People can tell us about it, can even draw pictures of it, but they are conceptual, not perceptual pictures.

But the trouble with this distinction is that so much of conceptual space keeps intruding into perceptual space. It is almost impossible to keep them separate. As soon as one begins to consider even the simplest problems, one discovers that space perception is riddled with inferences, hypotheses, assumptions, meanings, expectations, that derive from conceptual space. Figures 8.2 and 8.3 provide two simple examples of a conceptual influence on perception. The great puzzle is why our conceptual space seems to affect some perceptions and not others.

Perceptually, an amazing thing about space is its immobility. Look at some object. Now look to the right of it. Now to the left. The object does not move, but sits solidly still in one place while you move your eyes or your head. You perceive a stationary object—a truly marvelous accomplishment. You do not find this strange?

Recall what happens to optical images in your eyes. Patterns of light and shadow must flash rapidly across your field of vision every time you shift your eyes. Your sensations are in kaleidoscopic flux, yet your perception of the world around you remains quite stable. When your eyes move to the right, the effect on your visual sensations should be exactly the same as if your eyes remained fixed while the entire scene swung to the left. In principle you should be able to perceive it either way: with you fixed and the world moving or with the world fixed and you moving.

You see the world as fixed because this is your tacit theory of space—if "theory" can be used so loosely. In order to believe in your theory, you have to learn a very precise and delicate relation between the movements of your eyes and the changes in your visual experience. If you doubt the fragility of your apparently fixed, stable objects, do this. Take a pair of binoculars and once more scan back and forth across some object. Now you will find—unless you have used the binoculars a great deal—that the object moves as you change your angle of regard. The magnification provided by the binoculars alters the customary ratio of movements to visual changes. With this delicate perceptual-motor system out of balance, you can move mountains by turning your head. Perceptual mountains, that is. Your conceptual mountains remain stationary even while your eyes report they are moving.

Binoculars are not the only way to put the perceptual-motor system out of adjustment. Try the following illusion. Take a strip of paper about 2 inches wide and 8 inches long and fold it three times as shown in Figure 9.1. Place it on the table resting on the two folds, with the outside flanges sticking up. Now close one eye. Imagine that the two corners labeled *x* in Figure 9.1 are not down on the table, but are actually standing up above it, as if they were on the top edge of a standing screen. (A similar reversal is more easily achieved while looking at the two-dimensional drawing in Figure 9.1, but with a little persistence you can also reverse the three-dimensional object.) When you have succeeded in getting the reversal to occur, slowly move your head to the left and right. If your perception of the paper is reversed, you will see it tilt and twist in a surprising way.[2] Once again, moving your head moves the world.

This phenomenon can be made to seem even more dramatic if you will hold the paper, one end in each hand. Now, with the figure reversed, rotate your hands toward your body. The paper almost feels alive as it twists in the opposite direction!

Anyone who argues that all percepts must be familiar and meaningful has trouble understanding illusions like this one. Where could we have learned to see such improbable motions? Nowhere, of course. In this case it is not the percept itself that is learned and probable and familiar; what we have learned is a way to process the incoming information. Whatever it is that we do when we see three-

FIGURE 9.1

The Mach-Eden illusion. Fold a strip of paper as shown and examine it with one eye. Imagine that the corners X, which in fact lie on the supporting surface, are on the top edge of a standing screen and that the illumination comes from the opposite side. While the three-dimensional figure is reversed, head movements produce apparent movement in the object itself.

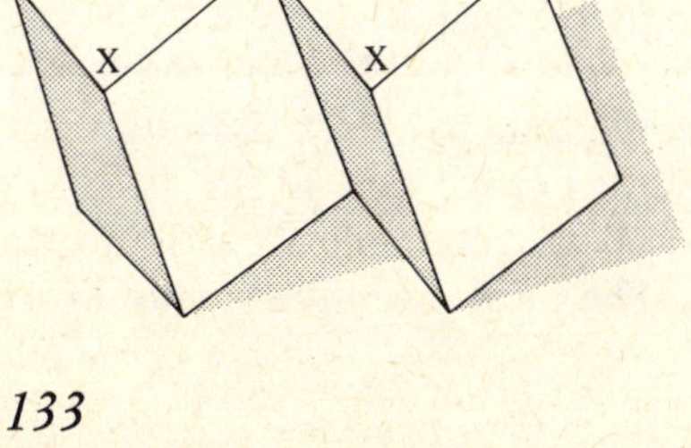

dimensional objects, whether it is learned or inborn, we persist in doing even when the outcome is surprising and unfamiliar. Any learning that is involved in space perception has to do with the operations we perform; we do not simply memorize new connections between visual stimuli and motor responses. We learn to make the transformations which are usually most successful in reducing the gap between our perceptual and our conceptual space.

The fact that the apparatus by which we learn about the world is itself in part a product of learning is demonstrated by our ability to relearn according to new rules. If the outcome of our perceptual transformations persists for a long enough time in looking strange and unusual, we may eventually come to terms with it. The remarkable extent of human plasticity was demonstrated by G. M. Stratton as early as 1896.[3] Stratton constructed an optical headgear that rotated the visual field 180 degrees; not only was the world turned upside down, but left and right were reversed. It was a clumsy thing consisting of a tube 8 inches long mounted in a plaster cast, but he wore it for 87 hours over a period of 8 days, replacing it by a blindfold while he slept. His right eye could see through the tube, although the inverted field was greatly reduced in size; his left eye remained covered by the plaster cast. In spite of the inconveniences of this gadget, Stratton was able to make some instructive observations.

On his first day in topsy-turvy land he was thoroughly disoriented. His feet were above his head; he had to search for them when he wanted to see if he could walk without kicking things. His hands entered and left his field of view from above instead of from below. When he moved his head, his visual field swung rapidly in the same direction. He could not easily recognize familiar surroundings. He made inappropriate movements and could scarcely feed himself. In spite of nausea and depression he kept going and gradually he began to get accustomed to his rig. By the second day his movements had grown less laborious. By the third he was beginning to feel at home in his new environment. By the fifth day the world had stopped swinging when he moved his head; he was thinking about his body in terms of new images and was often able to avoid bumping into objects without thinking about them first. Most of his world was still upside down, but this didn't bother him much any more. Stratton commented that he did not modify his old conception of space; he simply suppressed it and learned a whole new set of visual-motor relations. His old, familiar conception of the world was no help to him. In fact, the conflict between the old and the new was the major obstacle he had to overcome. When the experiment was finished and he took the lenses out of the tube, he was again disoriented and bewildered for several hours before he became accustomed to the normal view of things.

Stratton's experiment has been repeated; there is no doubting the validity of his observations. The most extensive studies of this type have been reported by Ivo Kohler, who used either left-right or up-down reversals, but not both at the same time.[4] The up-down reversal is easier to adapt to, but in both cases a person learns to make correct movements days or even weeks before he begins to perceive a scene as if it were normally oriented. Even then there are puzzling effects when one part of the scene looks normal but another part looks reversed; perceptual adaptation becomes complete only after many weeks of wearing the lenses.

These experiments demonstrate that a completely new relation between the visual world and the world of muscular movements can be learned in a relatively short period of time. The visual-motor relation we are accustomed to is not inviolate. It is simply something we have learned to live with.

The importance of movement can be emphasized by a short detour into fantasy. Imagine a special tree that through some kind of druidical magic is half animal and half plant. This wonderful tree has sense organs—receptors sensitive to light, sound, odor, taste, touch, static position—connected by sensory nerves to a large and elaborate brain. The tree has everything that an animal has, except that it lacks a motor output. There are no motor nerves, no muscles, no glands. In short, the tree cannot *do* anything about the information it picks up. It must stand rooted in one spot, as trees have always done, moving only with the wind.

Here is the question: Would this strange tree have any advantages over an ordinary tree?

Any knowledge the imaginary tree might acquire would, of course, be useless. What good would it do the tree to see lumberjacks coming? What advantage can it gain from knowing the forest is on fire if it can do no more than feel pain? Without muscles, the tree cannot speak; it has no way to communicate its knowledge to other trees or to share in their experiences.

But to discuss the tree in these terms seems to imply that a motionless tree can accumulate knowledge. The implication may go too far. A tree that cannot move can know almost nothing, even though it has all the marvelous equipment of receptors, nerves, and brain. A basic difficulty the magical tree can never overcome is that it cannot move its sense organs. Animals can move, not only to approach the things they want and to avoid the things they fear, but also to change the location of their eyes and ears. This simple fact has a tremendous influence on the way they must organize their experience.

A tree with eyes might see a house nearby, but the tree could never suspect that the house had another side concealed from view. To discover the thickness of reality it is necessary to move around in it. We must be able to walk around the house and then, somehow, to construct a single object that accounts for all the different views we had of it. A tree with eyes but unable to move would not need an explanation for such diversity as movement generates; it would never see deeper than the flat surface of appearances. The tree's world would have the same flatness a child sees when it looks at the stars as tiny holes in the great black dome of the night.

Moreover, our tree would not be able to distinguish size from distance. When things approached the tree they would be seen as expanding in size. The tree would have no way to learn that it takes a long time to move through a long distance. And without motions through distances, the tree would have no use for time, and hence no way to date its memories. In place of three dimensions of space and one of time, the motionless tree would have but two dimensions of space. In fact, if the tree's eyes were exactly like ours, it might see nothing but movements: when a visual image is completely stabilized on our retinas so that it continues to stimulate the same visual receptor cells in spite of our eye-movements, the image will disappear entirely in twenty or thirty seconds.[5] It is another case of sensory adaptation. For our visual system to work at all, it must experience continuous change in the images that fall on it. This change comes automatically when we move about.

A sentient but immobile intelligence would not develop anything resembling the state of consciousness that men, and probably other mammals as well, take for granted. Only an active being can possess knowledge of an objective reality as something distinguishable from its own private pains and joys.

Our conception of space and time is reserved for creatures who can move about in space and time, who need space and time to reduce and simplify the confusion of appearances reported by their moving sense organs. To attain the conception of a stable environment of objects when the only evidence we have is a haphazard flow of energies into our receptors is one of the great triumphs of childhood. Yet we scarcely notice that it happens. Space and time were always there, as far back as we can remember. In the words of the great German philosopher, Immanuel Kant, space and time are a priori categories of experience, given by the nature of the mind itself. But of course! Before we had the concepts of space and time as a coordinate system to organize our experience, we had no intelligible cognitive structure. Of course we cannot remember or imagine what it was like not to have such a frame of reference. But that does not mean there was never a time in childhood before we had discovered these majestic coordinates of the adult mind.

Sensitive trees are pure fantasy. Nothing of the kind could ever exist. Or could it?

Before we move on too quickly, we should pause to consider the frog. Oddly enough, in the visual modality, at least, there is a crude resemblance between a frog and a tree with eyes.

A frog's head and eyes do not move to notice events or to

search for objects or to look where it is going. They move, but only to compensate for movements of its body, for instance, when a wave rocks its lily pad. The frog's eyes are actively stabilized. It has, at least to a first approximation, the kind of immobile visual apparatus that the magical tree would have. It is true, of course, that frogs can move and trees cannot, but on land frogs move by sudden jumps. Since they are equally at home on land or in water, they do not care where they come down. What a frog sees during its jumps we will never know, but we can probably assume that on land most of the frog's looking is done while it is stationary. The resemblance is imperfect but a frog is enough like the imaginary tree to make the comparison interesting.

What does a frog see? The most striking thing about its vision is that the frog never responds to stationary objects. It will automatically try to eat any buglike object that is about the right size and moves. But the frog would starve to death in the midst of plenty if its prey were motionless. It does not see color. The lens of its eye is the fixed-focus type and leaves the wretch nearsighted on land, farsighted under water. Its visual acuity must be very poor; it cannot see details the way we do. In short, the frog, like our tree, has a very limited kind of vision. All the evidence says that frogs have not the faintest inkling of the elaborate spatio-temporal world we humans inhabit.

It is possible to get some idea of what a frog can see by recording electrical potentials from its visual nervous system. With a microelectrode properly placed in the optic nerve, the experimenter can vary the pattern of light entering the frog's eye until he discovers what it takes to stimulate a particular nerve fiber. With this technique it has been found that there are four different groups of fibers.[6] Each group is activated by a different kind of stimulation in the eye. Apparently, therefore, there are four separate operations on the image in a frog's eye; the outcome of each different operation is transmitted to the brain by a different group of fibers.

One operation detects the occurrence of any sharp edge separating light from dark. If such an edge moves into the field of vision and stops, one group of fibers starts to fire nerve impulses up to the brain. A second operation detects small, moving spots; this is the bug-detector. Another operation detects the presence of a moving edge. A fourth detects the onset of darkness in any large area of the visual field. These four operations comprise the total vocabulary of visual forms and events in a frog's world. Obviously, anyone who insists on talking about perception as a compound made up of many elementary color patches will find little to say about a frog.

These studies prove that it is possible to get some use out of a stationary eye after all. Granted, it is nothing at all like our own visual experience, but notice how the stationary eye is used. It waits inert until one of four things happens and then it responds appropriately. To everything else a frog is blind. In other words, a frog has four a priori categories of experience; certainly its visual experience is not constructed by some kind of Wundtian association of simple sensations. The frog is on the side of Immanuel Kant and against the British empiricists.

Before we conclude that frogs are hopelessly special and unique, we should recall that there is a long, largely German, tradition in philosophical psychology according to which perception is to be considered in terms of the operations of testing and sorting, rather than in terms of associating elementary sensations. Perhaps a frog is not an unusual, but an unusually simple, case.

If a frog's eye can perform four separate operations, presumably a mammalian eye can perform many more. Can one specify what they might be?

Perhaps a few of them can be illustrated. For example, operations on the image in the human eye probably should include the rules of grouping discovered by gestalt psychologists. The gestalt psychologists have not generally talked about their work in this context, however, so we must interrupt our argument briefly to illustrate the sort of puzzles they like to study.

An important question for gestalt psychology is to understand why some parts of the visual world hang together as unitary configurations and other parts do not. Located irregularly in space, denser below the natural plane of our eyes, are middle-sized clumps of stuff that resist our pushes, that go all together when they do move, that have colors and textures and shapes that persist in time. We usually see these clumps as figures which stand out against their backgrounds. Gestalt psychologists have listed a number of factors that affect the passively perceived patterns.[7]

Proximity. The smaller the interval between them, in space or time, the greater is the tendency to group two things together as a unit. The effect of proximity is illustrated in Figure 9.2.

FIGURE 9.2

Proximity causes us to group the dots into three pairs of vertical columns.

FIGURE 9.3

Similarity causes us to see vertical, rather than horizontal, lines of dots.

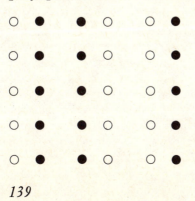

Similarity. If two things are similar, we tend to perceive them as belonging together. The effect of similarity is illustrated in Figure 9.3.

It is a simple matter to put the different factors in competition with each other. For example, in Figure 9.4 the columns of similar dots are farther apart, or, if you prefer, the columns that are closest together consist of dissimilar dots. Such patterns are fickle; they shift easily whichever way they get the most attention.

Common fate. If things move together, at the same time in the same direction, we group them together as a unit.

Set (Einstellung). An observer who has seen things grouped in one manner will remain set to see them that way even when the conditions are slowly changed until the original grouping is no longer appropriate.

Direction. If one pattern continues in the same direction as another, the two patterns will be grouped together (as, for example, when two lines intersect to form four line segments).

FIGURE 9.4

Proximity and similarity are here put in opposition. The resulting grouping is unstable.

Closure. Things will be grouped together if this produces a closed, stable, balanced, symmetric, "good" figure.

Habit. Things will be grouped together if they are familiar in that grouping. For example,

NOONNOONNOONNOONNOON

would, according to the factor of similarity, be seen as pairs of N's alternating with pairs of O's, but reading habits enable us to see this configuration either as an alternation of NO and ON, or as a sequence of NOON's. In this example, habit and similarity conflict, but we can tip the scales in either direction by allying proximity with one or the other.

N OO NN OO NN OO NN OO NN OO N

or

NO ON NO ON NO ON NO ON NO ON

or

NOON NOON NOON NOON NOON

All of these factors are purely sensory—no movements by the observer are required. Our intelligent tree might be able to notice such clusterings and groupings in its environment on the basis of these gestalt factors.[8] But it would have little reason to suspect the existence of objects and no real use for the objective hypothesis even if it did suspect. Many other factors become effective, many other perceptual operations are required, as soon as we begin to move about and to obtain simultaneously varying information about an object from two or three sense modalities at the same time. Then we must, if only for the economy in our cognitive bookkeeping, reduce all our many different impressions to a single object that is the source of those impressions. We can summarize a great variety of stimulations by a single conception of an object and so simplify our idea of the world we live in. We need not memorize separately all its different aspects, distances, illuminations, motions, warmths, and so on in order to remember an object and to recognize it when we see it later.

These gestalt factors describe some of the ways we transform our perceptual experience. They indicate some of the operations we use to impose structure, coherence, and organization on our perceptual flux. The same can undeniably be said of a frog. In a sense, therefore, we can imagine a certain functional similarity between a frog's perception of space and our own. But the differences far outweigh the similarities. We have greater acuity, a wider variety of operations, a way to cope with moving sense organs. We have color perception, depth perception, stereoscopic perception. And most important of all, a human eye is backed up by the vast resources of a human brain. This marvelous organ enables us to learn or invent new operations, and new ways of combining the results of old operations. Whereas a frog is forever limited to its four, we can devise new operations, new tests, new categories.

Instead of worrying about magical trees, therefore, it might be much more to the point to wonder how a child experiences space and how he acquires, combines, and builds his vocabulary of perceptual skills. Unfortunately, children cannot say and adults cannot remember how a child's conception of space differs from an adult's. The most we can do is to patch together various scraps of evidence is as plausible a guess as we can formulate.

Some psychologists have tried to infer the child's world from his drawings. To anyone who objects that a child is too poor a draftsman to show us what he really sees, they reply that it is not lack of skill that makes the child's drawings what they are. A right-handed adult who draws with his left hand can produce unskilled drawings, but they are totally different from a child's. There is a lack of differentiation in a child's drawings that cannot be explained as mere clumsiness. The child seems to have something very different in mind.

Rudolf Arnheim has summarized the development of drawings as a succession of stages.[9] At first the child gestures, scrawling with motions that make his feelings visible. Then, says Arnheim, he discovers the circle, the closed contour that isolates the space inside from the space outside. These circular scribbles have the character of objects, and a child will use them to represent all objects, indiscriminately. At this stage, for example, one circle may represent both head and body, as though the two were not yet clearly differentiated for the child.

Next he begins to combine circles and straight lines, but his first serious experimentation with linearity is usually confined to the horizontal and vertical directions. Only later does the child add oblique angles. Eventually he begins to fuse several units into a continuous,

FIGURE 9.5
_____

Do children really see people this way?

141

more differentiated contour. By this time a fairly advanced level of perceptual-motor skill has been attained.

At first a child draws everything the same size; a house, a man, a cow will all be equal in height. Any child who lived in such an elastic space would never be able to find his way around, but when he draws pictures he seems to tell us that all objects are equal, that they are all isolated from each other by a standard distance and never overlap, that they all present their most typical and familiar aspect toward the artist's eye, that the child can even see through the surface to the parts inside.

It is impossible to believe that such pictures faithfully represent what a child perceives; indeed, many children spontaneously express dismay that their pictures look so strange. Instead of perceptions they are loaded with conceptions, only slightly less stylized than the pictograms that must have served as the earliest kind of writing. It is as if the child drew up a verbal list of all the objects he wanted to include in a finished picture, then drew each independently, according to his own conception of the object. Adult notions of perspective, of light and shadow, of foreshortening, of interposition of a near object in front of a distant one—which are part of the repertory of the adult draftsman—are completely missing from children's drawings. It is not that the child wants it this way, but unequipped with this repertory, the child cannot conceal the underlying conceptual nature of his drawing.

With these drawings we seem, therefore, to have passed beyond the realm of space perception, beyond the tacit and immediate proc-

---

FIGURE 9.6

Of course, some things are exactly as they appear. (From Allen Neil, The Worm Runner's Digest [The Planarian Press, University of Michigan].)

Neil Illusion 1

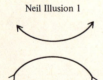

Note that the lines do not appear parallel.

Neil Illusion 2

Note how one line appears longer.

Neil Illusion 3

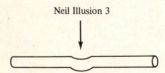

Note how the pipe appears bent under the arrow.

Neil Illusion 6

Note how quickly the figure disappears when you look directly at it.

esses that guide us through three dimensions, and into a realm of purely conceptual space, a synthetic realm filled with isolated, equal-sized, stereotyped, almost Platonic objects.

The two realms must be related, yet distinct; compatible, yet self-sufficient. If it ever becomes absolutely necessary to draw a sharp line between them, we will be in serious trouble. Like so many of the terms psychologists use, the distinction is meaningful but vague. Exactly how these crude notions of perceptual and conceptual space should be replaced by scientific terms more precisely defined is one of the thorny questions facing psychologists of the future.

NOTES

1. M. Jammer, *Concepts of Space* (Cambridge: Harvard University Press, 1954).
2. This illusion was brought to our attention by Murray Eden. Ernst Mach, the famous Viennese physicist and philosopher, studied it as early as 1866, but he was interested principally in the apparent brightnesses and shadows on the surfaces when they were reversed, and did not notice the effects of movement. See Ernst Mach, *The Analysis of Sensations*, trans. C. M. Williams (New York: Dover, 1959), pp. 209–210.
3. G. M. Stratton, "Some Preliminary Experiments on Vision Without Inversion of the Retinal Image," *Psychological Review* 3 (1896): 611–617; "Vision Without Inversion of the Retinal Image," *Psychological Review* 4 (1897): 341–360, 463–481.
4. I. Kohler, "Rehabituation in Perspective," *Die Pyramide*, nos. 5–7 (1953).
5. R. W. Dichburn and B. L. Ginsborg, "Vision with a Stabilized Retinal Image," *Nature* 170 (1952): 36–38; L. A. Riggs, F. R. Ratliff, J. C. Cornsweet, and T. N. Cornsweet, "The Disappearance of Steadily Fixated Test-Objects," *Journal of the Optical Society of America* 43 (1953): 495–501.
6. J. Y. Lettvin, H. R. Maturana, W. S. McCulloch, and W. H. Pitts, "What the Frog's Eye Tells the Frog's Brain," *Proceedings of the IRE* 47 (1959): 1940–1951.
7. The best introduction to the gestalt theory of the formation and segregation of wholes (by immobile organisms) is "Laws of Organization in Perceptual Forms," by Max Wertheimer, abstracted and translated in W. D. Ellis, *A Source Book of Gestalt Psychology* (London: Routledge & Kegan Paul, 1938), pp. 71–88.
8. Perhaps this overestimates once more what the tree could achieve since it has no eye muscles and could not change the direction in which it is looking. The stabilized image would tend to disappear; and it could not move its eyes along a contour, which some psychologists regard as an essential step in our learning to recognize different shapes.
9. Rudolf Arnheim, *Art and Visual Perception* (Berkeley and Los Angeles: University of California Press, 1954).

TEN

Francis Galton, Anthropologist

Are people the result of their genetic heritage, their experience, or some exotic combination of both? When the question is posed in this manner, the obvious multiple choice answer is the more reasonable combination of factors—an interactionist position, which is sometimes augmented by a reference to development time. However, the division between behavioral scientists on what we cryptically call the nature-nurture dichotomy can not easily be dismissed as a mere academic exercise. The nature-nurture debate is producing contemporary social strife, with bewildered citizens turning to one side or the other to collect "expert" support for basic policy and proposals for social change, the direction of which depends on answers science has never been able to give with any degree of finality. For many years the behavioral sciences in general and psychology in particular could be described as predominately interested in nurture, focusing on the effects of the environment and experience on behavior, consistent with the hard-nosed philosophy of the behaviorists. But in the past few years controversy has exploded with the publication of several treatises that stress the nature side of the question of causality. Whether this controversy signals a time of paradigm shift is perhaps less important than the effects of this debate on our society. We live in a world where paradigm battles can no longer be relegated to obscure journals read only by knowledgeable scientists. This debate, already brought out into the open by skilled polemicists on both sides, has tragic life or death meaning to millions of our citizens, especially those who are not a part of the white majority. We may be at a threshold of history—a period of cultural change that will greatly affect our future—similar to the period in the nineteenth century described in this chapter. We will first re-create the context in which the most articulate spokesman of the nature side of the question lived—Francis Galton.

THE AGE OF DARWIN

One of the most important books in the history of western thought is Charles Darwin's *The Origin of Species by Means*

144

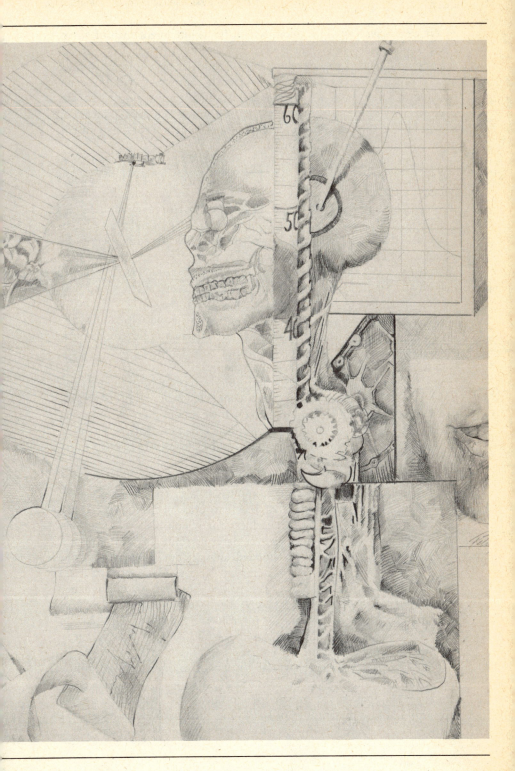

of Natural Selection. This book, which freed intelligent men of an ancient superstition and signalized the scientific maturity of the life sciences, influenced the development of modern psychology as much as any other single event in the nineteenth century. It would be impossible to understand what psychologists today are trying to accomplish or why they go about it as they do unless one first understood something of the importance of evolutionary theory for our contemporary vision of man and his destiny.

The appearance of Darwin's book in 1859 set off controversy of the most intense and exciting kind. Within a year of its publication a debate at Oxford between Thomas Henry Huxley—who fought for science, Darwin, evolution—and Bishop Wilberforce—who defended the Book of Genesis—caused a public sensation in England. Wilberforce asked Huxley whether it was through his grandmother or his grandfather that he claimed descent from an ape, thus phrasing the central issue in terms every person could understand. Huxley replied that an ape would be preferable to the Bishop as an ancestor, and with that the battle began. Science and religion were at it again.

Although we tend to think of biological evolution as Darwin's theory, its origins are quite ancient. Its systematic development in modern times is often said to have begun with George Louis Leclerc, Comte de Buffon, whose forty-four volumes of *Natural History* published in France between 1749 and 1804 attempted to tie together isolated facts and observations into a connected story. Buffon's highly readable style did much to popularize nature studies, but he is usually remembered as a poor scientist. Nevertheless, he saw that the historical development had to be accounted for and that an Aristotelian argument in terms of final causes would not suffice.

It was Erasmus Darwin who, toward the end of the eighteenth century, considered almost every important idea that has since been put forward as an explanation of the way one species can be transformed into another, including the ideas for which his two grandsons, Charles Darwin and Francis Galton, later became famous. Erasmus Darwin's belief that all warm-blooded animals developed from "one living filament" endowed with animality by the Creator deserved a better reputation than it gained. Perhaps his Victorian grandsons failed to mention him because they were embarrassed by his penchant for irregular romantic adventures, but more likely the reason was that his name became linked in the public mind with an evolutionary theory put forward by the Chevalier de Lamarck.

Lamarck's was a behavioral theory of evolution. The giraffe reached up for the highest branches until, after many generations, he stretched his neck to its present odd proportions. The crane got its long legs through generations of stretching them while standing in the water, and the snake lost its legs entirely after generations of retracting them in order to move through the grass without being detected. The behavior of one generation affects its bodily structures; these small changes are then passed on to its offspring. This process continues generation after generation until the cumulative effect is sufficient to create a recognizably new species. The doctrine is usually referred to as "the inheritance of acquired characteristics," and its best-known recent advocate is the Russian, Trofim Denisovich Lysenko. Unfortunately, Lamarck's examples made the theory of evolution sound slightly ridiculous and when the famous French naturalist Baron Cuvier refused to entertain an evolutionary hypothesis because the evidence was so inadequate the theory seemed to have suffered a mortal blow.[1]

Although evolution was not scientifically respectable during the first half of the nineteenth century, people persisted in talking about it. Auguste Comte advanced an evolutionary hypothesis for social development. Herbert Spencer accepted Lamarck's ideas and searched for a philosophic justification for the concept of progress. Charles Darwin set about collecting the evidence that would be needed to convince such men as Cuvier. Patrick Mathew and Edward Blyth developed the idea of natural (as opposed to artificial) selection. Just a year before *The Origin of Species* was published Alfred Russell Wallace sent Darwin a paper setting forth a theory of man's origins based, like Darwin's theory, on natural selection. Respectable scientists tried to keep the lid on, but inside the evolutionary kettle pressure was slowly building up. Darwin's book in 1859, with its mass of detailed evidence and argument collected throughout a quarter of a century, was the explosion that at last forced man to revise his conception of himself. Prior to 1859 biological evolution had been a controversial speculation; after 1859 it was a controversial fact.

Important as they were, however, Darwin's ideas would not concern us here had they not influenced the young science of psychology so strongly during its formative years. Consider some of the more obvious lines of influence.

The most direct consequence of seeing man in the framework of an evolutionary theory was the emphasis it placed upon his relation to other animals, especially to the great apes. Darwin, foreseeing the violence that would result from applying the theory to man, concentrated his argument in *The Origin of Species* on the lower animals almost entirely. The evasion fooled no one. Finally, in *The Descent of Man* (1871), Darwin applied his argument to the most interesting animal of all—and showed him to be merely another temporary phase in the story of life. The process of biological evolution is going on now as it always has, and it affects man as it affects all animals.

To most psychologists it was immediately obvious that the techniques they used to study the most highly evolved animal would now have to be generalized and extended to other animals as well. The available evidence for the continuity from animals to man was largely anatomical, but one could dream of showing similar continuities in the development of behavior and even in the development of the mind itself. One effect of evolutionism on psychology, therefore, was the introduction of a new universe of subjects into the psychological laboratory. And so animal psychology was born.

A second consequence of evolutionary thinking was a shift in emphasis, a change in what psychologists considered their goal to be. Whereas the introspective psychologists considered their major task to be the analysis of the contents of consciousness and relating them, where possible, to physiological processes, Darwin's theories were phrased in terms of the struggle for survival. After Darwin, the question, "What *functions* does consciousness serve?" seemed much more fundamental than the question, "What *elements* does consciousness contain?" The very fact that an animal had evolved through thousands of generations implied that the changes were adaptive, that the modified animal was better prepared than its ancestors to fight the battles of life in the present environment. The adaptation of an organism to its environment became a central concern of all the life sciences, psychology as well as biology, and the inner contemplation of mental images began to lose its appeal. The behaviorist J. F. Dashiell later constructed a paradigm that pictured an animal, a barrier, and a goal to facilitate the study of the elaboration of purposive (adaptive) behavior related to the goal (survival), which includes learning (such as solving the problem of the maze, or whatever barrier is interposed) and changing drive states (to inhibit behavior not directed at overcoming the barrier).[2]

A third, rather unfortunate consequence of Darwin's book was the growth of a philosophy that has since been called social Darwinism. In his discussion of evolution Darwin emphasized the competition among different animals—each would tend to increase its number in a geometric progression if it were not held in check by the competition for food. In this struggle the weak would perish and leave the strong to continue the species. This Malthusian emphasis on struggle, coupled with a belief that acquired characteristics can be inherited, caught the public fancy. It was interpreted to mean, for example, that capitalistic competition was the source of all social progress. In America social Darwinism as preached by Herbert Spencer ("Survival of the fittest") and William Graham Sumner ("Millionaires are a product of natural selection") provided the newly rich industrialists with scientific proof that their great wealth was fair payment for their superior talents.[3] But they were badly misled by the language Darwin and Spencer used. "Survival of the fittest" carries a suggestion that the strong, healthy, aggressive organisms will always survive, whereas the truth seems to be that usually the most fertile, not the strongest, are most likely to escape extinction.

Another important effect of evolutionism on modern psychology was the emphasis it put on variation, on individual differences. Clearly, if every offspring is identical with its parents, evolution will not occur. There are, however, several sources of variation. In the first place, the offspring are different from their parents because they have had different experiences. Darwin and his contemporaries thought the effects of these experiences were inherited, but genetic research has since discarded this possibility. A second reason offspring are different from their parents is that they receive a random combination of the genes from each parent—and this kind of random variation *is* inherited. Moreover, a third reason the offspring are different from their parents is that unpredictable mutations occur in the genes themselves; the mutations are also inheritable. The important point is this: any hereditary variation that gives its possessor an advantage in fertility, that increases the probability his offspring will live to reach sexual maturity, will automatically increase the fraction of animals possessing that variation.

Variation is an essential component of any evolutionary theory. Thus, where Wundt searched for the general, universal principles governing all minds, psychologists interested in evolution began to catalogue all the ways minds could differ from one another.

Evolutionism gave a statistical flavor to psychological thinking that has increased with every succeeding generation of psychologists. When one goes beyond the question, "What is the average value?" and begins to ask about the range of variation that can occur, to ask how one kind of variation is related to another, to ask whether an observed variation should be attributed to chance, and so on, the need for sophisticated tools of statistical analysis quickly becomes apparent.

No one better represents an evolutionary attitude toward psychology than Galton. Evolutionary ideas were not quite what Wundt had had in mind for his new psychology. But if the psychology of Wilhelm Wundt offered little room for questions growing out of evolutionism, then it simply had to be loosened up until room was found. And the person who showed most clearly how this could be done was the ingenious Englishman, Sir Francis Galton.

GALTON AND THE EVOLUTIONARY ATTITUDE TOWARD PSYCHOLOGY

Francis Galton, the last of nine children, was born in 1822 at the Larches, near Sparkbrook, Birmingham, England. His father was a successful and prosperous banker.

Young Frank was extremely intelligent. If we can believe the records of his boyhood achievements, his IQ must have been nearly 200—which places him in a class with some of the most intelligent men who ever lived.[4] His father decided that the boy should become a doctor, should have a profession that would enable him to earn his own living if that became necessary. At 16, therefore, Galton became a House Pupil at the Birmingham General Hospital. At this tender age he walked rounds with the doctors, dispensed to outpatients, read medical books, set broken bones, amputated fingers, kept hospital records, vaccinated children, pulled teeth, and read Horace and Homer on alternate days. But a hospital is not a pleasant way of life, and only his father's determination kept him at it.

After a year of hospital horrors he went to King's College, London, where he attended medical lectures, absorbed the scientific atmosphere, and confirmed his opinion that doctors, like parsons, are far too positive. He moved on to Trinity College, Cambridge, where he put a plaster bust of Newton opposite the fireplace and studied mathematics. The standard program at Cambridge consisted of hard work and competitive examinations; the standard consequence was bad health and mental depression, with degrees for those strong enough to survive. Galton, undoubtedly one of the most intelligent men of his time, managed to graduate, but not with honors. Once more he returned to the study of medicine, but his father's death released him from a profession he had come to hate.

After a tour of Egypt and Syria—the Mohammedans impressed him—he made a serious attempt to settle down. For a time he was in danger of following his elder brothers into the life of an English country gentleman. But his wanderlust, a romantic, Victorian interest in distant and exotic things, defeated him. Six fallow years ended in 1850, when he invented a teletype printer and set off to explore Africa. He filled a book with his adventures, and won a medal from the Royal Geographic Society.

In the 1850s he was a geographer. His own explorations were terminated by marriage and bad health, but he served on countless committees, wrote a book for explorers called *The Art of Travelling*, organized expeditions for others, and read countless reports until at last his restless attention began to wander once more. From geography to meteorology was a short step. He designed instruments to plot weather data (mechanical inventions of every description were a lifelong hobby), made the first serious attempt to chart the weather over large areas, and his charts led him to discover and name the anticyclone (a remarkable theoretical insight based on the crudest kind of data).

He read relatively little and then only what was necessary for the problem at hand, but when his cousin, another nonacademic scientist, published *The Origin of Species*, Galton read it and became immediately a strong supporter of the new theory.

As an ex-doctor and ex-biologist, Galton was at first interested in the biological details. The genetic hypothesis Darwin advanced was that the organs of the body secrete gemmules, little vestiges of themselves, into the blood. The blood, he hypothesized carried the gemmules to the sex glands. The sex glands use the gemmules to build sex cells. Therefore, the sex cells contain a master plan for building another organism just like the parent. Darwin used his gemmule hypothesis to explain the inheritance of acquired characteristics. If the organs of the body are changed by events during the life of the parent, the changes must appear in the gemmules, then in the sex cells, and finally in the offspring. This was the theory whose validity Galton questioned.

He was not convinced that acquired characteristics can be inherited. To test Darwin's theory, he transfused blood between black rabbits and white rabbits and found that the transfusions have no effect on the color of the offspring. Therefore, the imaginary gemmules could not be an explanation of the mechanism of heredity. In spite of these results, however, both Darwin and Galton continued to look to the blood for an explanation. Gregor Mendel might have helped them, but his work went unappreciated for thirty-five years. And Darwin had explicitly rejected the early experiments of the Frenchman Charles Naudin which had shown the parent strains blending in the first generation but reappearing again in the second, experiments which were less elegant but which anticipated Mendel's results. Blood was too much a part of the everyday language of kinship for anyone to assume it was completely irrelevant to the hereditary mechanism.

The genetic side of Darwin's theory did not detain Galton for long; it was the social implication that really fired his imagination. In his travels he had seen many different societies of men. He knew something of the variation in human physical characteristics and he suspected the differences in mentality were even greater. "It is in the most unqualified manner," he wrote, "that I object to pretensions of natural equality."[5] It seemed obvious to him that the great variation among men—physical, mental, and moral—must be inherited. And it was equally obvious that the human strain can be improved, just as livestock is improved, by artificial selection. It was necessary merely to decide what characteristics one wished to establish, to develop techniques for measuring the extent to which an individual possessed them, and to control breeding in the light of the results of the measurements.

---

*I have no patience with the hypothesis occasionally expressed,
and often implied, especially in tales written to teach children
to be good, that babies are born pretty much alike, and that
the sole agencies in creating differences between boy and boy,
and man and man, are steady application and moral effort. It is*

*in the most unqualified manner that I object to pretensions of
natural equality. The experiences of the nursery, the school, the
University, and of professional careers, are a chain of proofs
to the contrary. I acknowledge freely the great power of education and social influences in developing the active powers of the
mind, just as I acknowledge the effect of use in developing the
muscles of a blacksmith's arm, and no further. Let the blacksmith
labour as he will, he will find there are certain feats beyond his
power that are well within the strength of a man of herculean
make, even although the latter may have led a sedentary life. . . .*

*Everybody who has trained himself to physical exercises
discovers the extent of his muscular powers to a nicety. When
he begins to walk, to row, to use the dumb bells, or to run, he
finds to his great delight that his thews strengthen, and his en-
durance of fatigue increases day after day. So long as he is a
novice, he perhaps flatters himself there is hardly an assignable
limit to the education of his muscles; but the daily gain is soon
discovered to diminish, and at last it vanishes altogether. His
maximum performance becomes a rigidly determinate quantity.
He learns to an inch, how high or how far he can jump, when he
has attained the highest state of training. . . .*

*This is precisely analogous to the experience that every student
has had of the working of his mental powers. The eager boy,
when he first goes to school and confronts intellectual difficulties,
is astonished at his progress. He glories in his newly-developed
mental grip and growing capacity for application, and, it may
be, fondly believes it to be within his reach to become one of the
heroes who have left their mark upon the history of the world.
The years go by; he competes in the examinations of school and
college, over and over again with his fellows, and soon finds his
place among them. He knows he can beat such and such of his
competitors; that there are some with whom he runs on equal
terms, and others whose intellectual feats he cannot even approach.
. . . Opportunities occur—they occur to every man—and he
finds himself incapable of grasping them. He tries, and is tried
in many things. In a few years more, unless he is incurably
blinded by self-conceit, he learns precisely of what performances
he is capable, and what other enterprises lie beyond his compass.
When he reaches mature life, he is confident only within certain
limits, and knows, or ought to know, himself just as he is probably judged of by the world, with all his unmistakable weakness
and all his undeniable strength. He is no longer tormented into
hopeless efforts by the fallacious promptings of overweening
vanity, but he limits his undertakings to matters below the level
of his reach, and finds true moral repose in an honest conviction
that he is engaged in as much good work as his nature has
rendered him capable of performing.*

—*Francis Galton*
From Hereditary Genius

To achieve this end he officially founded the science of human eugenics and contributed to the eugenic dream of a superman. By selecting men and women for rare and similar talents and mating them together generation after generation, an extraordinarily gifted race would evolve. Even moral and religious sentiments could be improved by rigid selection.

The evidence he gathered—for he was not one to sit quietly by when there were observations to be made—was presented in four important books on the inheritance of mental traits in man, books calculated to support his eugenic creed with scientific facts: *Hereditary Genius* (1869), *English Men of Science* (1874), *Human Faculty* (1883), and *Natural Inheritance* (1889).

The purpose of *Hereditary Genius* was to show that eminence follows family lines far too frequently to explain it on the basis of environmental influences. In tackling this question he assumed implicitly that eminent men are naturally superior and that superior men are naturally eminent—no mute, inglorious Miltons worried him. His quaint and optimistic identification of talent with success was illustrated when he wrote: "If a man is gifted with vast intellectual ability, eagerness to work, and power of working, I cannot comprehend how such a man should be repressed."[6] Once the Great Man is born he must inevitably realize his genius for the profit of all mankind. The only difficulty, as Galton saw it, was to get him born. Thus breeding better men was the central task for social progress.

Such theories were not uncommon in the elite class in which Galton lived; nor were they uncommon in England, then the greatest colonial empire in history. The "white man's burden," later immortalized by Kipling, was an ethos that guided many colonial administrators in dealing with emergent natives.

To test the eugenic thesis, he necessarily became entangled in problems of measurement. And, after measurement, statistics. In *Hereditary Genius* he relied upon his own subjective estimates of eminence as his method of measurement, and he stated his conclusions in statistical form: great men have a higher probability of producing great sons than do average men. There were forty-eight eminent sons for every one hundred eminent fathers, a figure so high that he considered giving some of the credit to the mothers, but not high enough to make him consider seriously the advantages of environment, education, and opportunity that such sons might enjoy. His own education, for example, he regarded as largely a waste of time. For Galton, the Great Man provided a hereditary nucleus around which ability clustered with a closeness that rapidly diminished as the distance of kinship from its center increased, as the bloodline thinned out.

The *Inquiries into Human Faculty and its Development*, published in 1883, established Galton as the pioneer of scientific psychology in England. The book is a collection of miscellaneous essays loosely connected by their preoccupation with psychological subjects. He approached psychology with the attitude of a physical anthropologist. He wanted the same kind of data about the dimensions of a man's mind as anthropologists were already collecting about man's anatomy. And he fully expected to find that the mental measurements, when they could be made, would turn out to be closely related to the body measurements. He realized that if they were to provide a complete description of a man, anthropometric measures of stature, weight, skin color, etc., would have to be supplemented by psychometric measures of the senses, the memory, the imagination. But to the day he died he was unwilling to admit that the size of a man's skull had no value as a measure of his intelligence. Of course, neither the skull nor any other anatomical feature has ever been shown to be related to intelligence.

His task, therefore, was to develop a set of psychological measurements that could be made quickly and accurately on thousands of people. This gave him an excuse to be an inventor again, and with great enthusiasm and ingenuity he set about devising instruments to measure the senses. He invented a whistle (the length of a closed pipe was varied by a threaded plug in the end of it, and calibrated to a tenth of a turn) to measure the highest frequencies of acoustic vibration that men can hear. He invented a simple photometer to test how accurately people can match two spots of color. He used a calibrated pendulum to measure how quickly people can respond to lights and sounds. He selected a series of weights and measured kinesthetic sensitivity by having people arrange them in order from lightest to heaviest. He invented a bar with a variable distance scale that he could use to test people's ability to estimate visual extensions. He used a rotating disc to test the capacity for estimating the perpendicular. He invented a device—not entirely successful—to measure the velocity of movement attained when a person strikes a blow. He tested smell by having people arrange in order bottles containing material with the same odor but of different intensity. All his tests were simple and relatively inexpensive. They were to be used by anthropologists, as they used scales and measuring tapes, to gather data from large numbers of persons.

Galton's study of psychology was not limited to these sensory phenomena. His next interest was in mental imagery. He became one of the first persons to use the form of persecution known today as the psychological questionnaire. He asked his victims to imagine their breakfast table. Was the image dim or clear? Bright or dark? Extended or clear only in spots? Colored or not colored? His first subjects were scientific acquaintances, since he thought they would be competent to give the most accurate answers. He was astonished to learn that most of them had no clear imagery, and some considered it fanciful when others spoke as if they did. But when he turned from scientists and academicians to ordinary people leading ordinary lives, he found they had perfectly distinct images, full of detail and color. Women and children were especially emphatic in their reports of concrete, detailed imagery. Perhaps, he speculated, imagery is antagonistic to the kind of abstract thought that scientists practice; the ability to form clear images may atrophy from disuse.

He noted that there were large differences in the flexibility of images among persons who reported having them. Some respondents said that their first image was the clearest and that further images would blur and confuse the details. Others claimed to have complete mastery over their images, to be able to call up the face of a friend at will and to modify it in any manner that occurred to them. Following Galton's description of the tremendous variations among individuals in the clarity and flexibility of their mental imagery, it was a rash philosopher indeed who would persist in supposing that anything universally valid could be said about such a general faculty as Imagination, or that there existed a typical Mind that all human minds resembled.

Galton also tackled the problem of measuring the association of ideas; his motto was, "Whenever you can, count." His first attempt consisted of walking 450 yards down Pall Mall, fixing his attention on every successive object that caught his eye until it suggested one or two thoughts to him. The first time he did this he was amazed to notice that samples of his whole life had occurred to him; many incidents he thought long forgotten were fleetingly represented in his associations. Several days later he repeated the walk. His admiration for the teeming activity of his mind was seriously diminished when he discovered that his associations were in large measure repetitions of the associations he had had during his first attempt.

To get a better grip on these fleeting ideas he devised a scheme that involved writing words on small slips of paper. Later, after he had forgotten the particular words, he laid one of the slips partly under the edge of a book. Then he leaned forward until he could read the word he had written. In one hand he held a watch to time his reactions and with the other he wrote quickly the first two ideas that the word suggested. And this was how he invented the word association test—the first attempt to subject associationism to experiment. Wundt quickly adopted the experiment, improved it by limiting the response to a single word, and made it a part of the methodological equipment of his laboratory in Leipzig.

In summarizing his studies of associations, Galton wrote:

Perhaps the strongest of the impressions left by the experiments regards the multifariousness of the work done by the mind in a state of half-unconsciousness, and the valid reason they afford for believing in the existence of still deeper strata of mental operations, sunk wholly below the level of consciousness, which may account for such mental phenomena as cannot otherwise be explained.[7]

Which was a surprising thing to say in an age when many psychologists considered an unconscious mind to be a logical contradiction. He spoke of the ideas in full consciousness as being in the "presence-chamber" of his mind; nearby was the "antechamber of consciousness" full of related ideas waiting to be summoned into the presence-chamber.

Galton was never satisfied with a problem until he discovered something to count, some proportions to calculate, or some averages to compare. The recourse to statistical analysis was a persistent feature of his work on psychological questions. In this respect he continued and expanded the ideas of the Belgian, Adolph Quetelet. Quetelet analyzed data on the stature of ten thousand people and drew a chart showing the number found at each height. A few persons were very short, a few very tall, but the majority in his sample clustered around the middle of the range. Thus, his curve had the shape of a bell, as shown in Figure 10.1, an example of the normal probability curve. Such a result, Quetelet argued, was to be expected if all men were cast in the same mold, but emerged with purely accidental differences. Galton accepted the argument as a basic principle of anthropometry and assumed it must hold true for mental as well as physical traits. Since the shape of the curve was relatively simple and remarkably stable from one trait to another, the entire distribution of measurements could be summarized by two numbers: one representing the average value, the other the range of variation or dispersion around the central

FIGURE 10.1

Measurement of height was made on 8585 English-born men. The number of men of each height is indicated by a vertical bar on the graph. The data of the graph are replotted as a frequency curve to emphasize its bell shape.

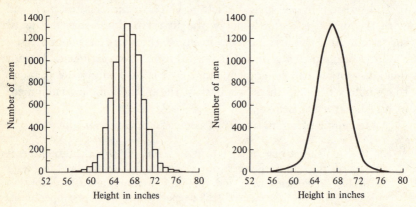

value. The problem of measurement, therefore, was to collect a large enough sample from which to plot the curve, and obtain from it reliable estimates of the average and of the variance around the average.

In order to collect the data he needed from large numbers of people, Galton in 1884 put together his Anthropometric Laboratory as a demonstration for the International Health Exhibition in London. For 3*d*. one gained entry to a long, narrow room where an attendant supervised instruments for measuring height, weight, span, breathing power, strength of pull and squeeze, quickness of blow, hearing, seeing, color sense, and other personal data. One passed along the line watching his data card fill with numbers, then departed with a good, clean feeling of having contributed to science by being measured accurately in many surprising ways.

The little laboratory attracted much interest and manufactured large quantities of data; the question was what to do with all the numbers that had accumulated on all the cards. As a first step, Galton charted the data as Quetelet had done and found the usual bell-shaped probability curves; the shape was the same for psychological as for anatomical measurements. The curves were interesting and instructive, but even after they had all been plotted it was obvious that there was a great deal more information on the data cards than he knew how to extract. Every person who had passed through the laboratory had contributed several different measures. What were the relations among them? Given two sets of measurements, how could one represent the fact that persons who scored high on one test tended to score high on the other? For example, tall people tend to weigh more than short people; how should the strength of the tendency be measured?

The problem of relating two sets of measurements also arose in a most critical fashion in his studies of inheritance. In these studies, he had two probability curves, one based on measurements of the parents, the other on measurements of their offspring. To establish the fact of inheritance, he had to demonstrate that there is a relation between the parents' measurements and their children's measurements. For example, tall parents tend to have tall children; how should the strength of this tendency be measured?

Galton had data on the heights of all the members of several families. He cast these up in the form of a table, with the possible heights of the parents (the average of each set of two parents represented a fictional "mid-parent") along the side, and the possible heights of the children along the top of the table. In the cells of the table he entered the actual number of children whose height was given by the column heading and whose "mid-parent's" height was given by the row heading. He carried this table with him everywhere he went; when he had a few moments free he would try to discover the reason for the paradox he saw there.

The puzzle is this: If two tall persons marry and have children, the children will usually not be as tall as the parents. The children will usually be taller than the average height of the general population, but they will be nearer to the average than their parents. The corresponding statement is also true of short families; two short parents will usually have short children, but the children will tend to be nearer the population average than are their parents. At first it seemed to Galton that the entire population must be converging slowly toward an average height; after a few more generations of this sort of regression toward the average everyone would be of equal stature, and all variation would have disappeared. But this, as he soon realized, is nonsense. If it were going to happen at all, it would have happened long ago. Is there some biological process that holds variation in check, that drags the offspring back toward mediocrity? Or was there something faulty in the mathematical analysis of the data that was leading him to look for natural forces that do not exist?

One morning he was studying his table while he waited in a railway station. Suddenly he recognized a pattern in the crude data. If he took the average of each *row*, and plotted it on a graph, the succession of points formed an approximately straight line. But if he took the averages, in the same way, of the successive *columns* in the table, the points also formed a straight line. The two lines were different, but they intersected at the average value for the entire population. (This situation is illustrated in Figure 10.2 for four tables of hypothetical data.) Moreover, he saw that the variation in the different columns, but the row and column variances were less than the over-all variance of the entire population. In short, he saw for the first time what now is called a "normal correlation surface." After this amazing insight it was only necessary to express the relations mathematically; the task was accomplished later by Galton's student, Karl Pearson.[8] The puzzling regression toward the average turned out to have a mathematical, not a biological origin.

The situation Galton was struggling with can perhaps be visualized more easily if one imagines an ellipse that surrounds the data. If the ellipse is long and thin, as it would be in the lower right corner of Figure 10.2, the correlation between the two variables is quite close. If the ellipse is a perfect circle, as in the upper left corner of Figure 10.2, there is no correlation between the variables; they are independent, and one cannot be used to predict the other. If the ellipse is of intermediate width, there is some correlation, but not perfect predictability. The correlation, if it exists, may be either direct or inverse, positive or negative. All these possibilities were captured by Karl Pearson in a single number, the "Pearson product-moment correlation coefficient," which varies from $+1$ when the correlation is direct and perfect, through 0 when there is no correlation, to -1 when the corre-

FIGURE 10.2

Hypothetical data are used to illustrate how the two regression lines change. In the upper left the two variables are independent (knowing the value of one variable does not help you guess the value of the other), the correlation coefficient is R = 0, and the regression lines are at right angles, on top of the coordinate axes. In the lower right the two variables are closely related, the correlation coefficient is R = 0.92, and the two regression lines are very close together. (After H. M. Walker, Elementary Statistical Methods [*New York: Holt, 1943*].)

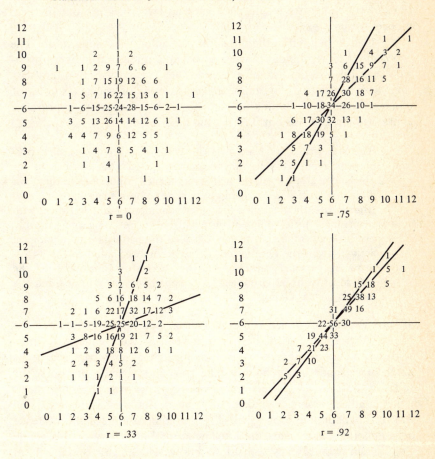

lation is inverse and perfect. The correlation coefficient *r* is given for all four examples in Figure 10.2.

Galton's insight led to the development of a measure of correlation, a measure that has since become one of the most important tools in the entire field of applied mathematics. Covariation is a central concept, not only for genetics and psychology, but for all scientific inquiry. A scientist searches for the causes of events; all he ever finds are correlations between antecedent and consequent conditions. To have a simple measure of correlation that can be used to test one's theoretical deductions has enormously facilitated the extension of scientific research into areas where perfect, one-to-one, causal relations are almost never noted, but where degrees of correlation may give some clue to the causal processes that are at work. Galton's insight has been, and continues to be, essential for vast stretches of modern social and behavioral science, and is useful in countless ways to engineers and natural scientists as well. Many of the statistical tools that later generations of psychologists would need grew in large measure out of these pioneer studies.

Galton pointed in the direction psychology was soon to go. The problems that psychologists were to become interested in were problems posed in the context of evolution—adaptation, variation, covariation, heredity versus environment, comparisons of species, studies of children. And so Wundt's science began to change its appearance almost as soon as it was born. As Boring describes it:

> The Americans travelled to Leipzig to learn about the new psychology from Wundt; they came back fired with enthusiasm for physiological psychology and experimental laboratories; they got their universities to let them give the new courses and have the new laboratories; they extolled their German importation; and then, with surprisingly little comment on what they were doing and probably but little awareness of it, they changed the pattern of psychological activity from the description of the generalized mind to the assessment of personal capacities in the successful adjustment of the individual to his environment. The apparatus was Wundt's, but the inspiration was Galton's.[9]

Where Wundt preserved the past, Galton built a foundation for the future. Although he spent only fifteen years actively engaged in pursuits we would recognize as psychological, Galton is the source of much more modern psychology than is Wundt. Partly, of course, he rode on the crest of the evolutionary wave that was changing men's vision in all the biological and social sciences. But what is more impressive to the modern eye, and probably more important for his influence on psychology, is the amazing intelligence and creativity of this gentle Englishman who always seemed to know which way to set out in search of the truth.

THE POST-GALTON ERA

As impressive as Galton's contributions were, his willingness to go beyond the data, beyond the correlations, to find support for his ideological commitment to eugenics is a part of the very human habit of panacea hunting. In approaching a problem like human ability, intelligence, disease, or crime, there is a tendency to ignore multiple causation and to argue that to solve the problem one must act or intervene in terms of a single factor. The eugenicist says *breed;* the environmentalist says *educate.*

To take a recent example of the rush to judgment, consider the finding of a supposedly excessive frequency of XYY chromosomes (a rare genetic anomaly) in the tissue samples taken from prison inmates, coupled with the finding of this anomaly in the cells of a notorious mass murderer. Tons of newsprint flowed with words of genetic crime control, the ethics of early incarceration, and so on. The debate was abruptly halted when geneticists pointed out that their normative data—the knowledge of the frequency of XYY in "normal" people—was so skimpy that the prison data proved nothing. But why did the data arouse such strong popular interest? Do we seriously believe in a theory of "bad seed" transmitted genetically? Apparently there is some popular support for such beliefs, despite their evident absurdity, because an identifiable genetic cell would be such a simple solution to a problem that seems now to have no solution. Even Galton in his day contributed to a prison study whose influence can be found to this day in comic strips, literature, and popular thinking.

In an attempt to classify human individual differences, the physiognomists, who flourished in the nineteenth century, attempted to draw pictures of the typical physiognomy of specific personality types. Although they drew pictures of typical "good" members of society, their depictions of various "criminal" types studied in prisons has had the most profound influence on popular thought. Pictures of "typical" murderers, stereotyped sex fiends, etc., flooded police departments for years, and were burned into the public imagination for decades. Clearly the physiognomists made an error of sampling by taking drawings of faces that could have been hardened into meanness by the harsh prison environment—regardless of the genetic background of the men.

Other genetically based "solutions" to man's problems were yet to come. The Jukes family history is one example; crime, bastardy, immorality, laziness were the epithets applied in 1875 to 507 of 709 members of this family on the biased and unverified assertions of one Richard L. Dugdale.[10] In view of the unavailability of records, Dugdale's obvious personal bias, and the fact that Dugdale did not even take into consideration the large percentage of genes from unknown sources due to illegitimacy among the Jukes descendents, critics dismissed the report as folklore. His genetic argument was dead wrong. Yet the Jukes story lived on for decades in popular media and in most introductory psychology textbooks, as have similar shoddy reports on inherited schizophrenia and other aberrant but unexplained conditions.[11]

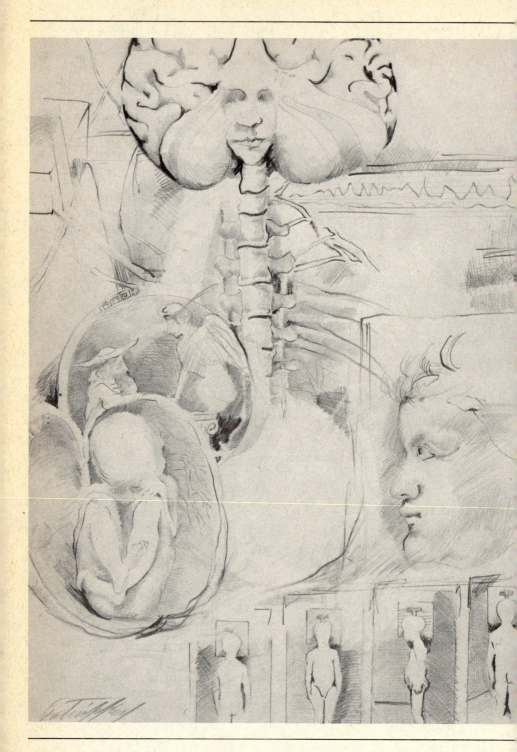

The problem in all of these cases is a knotty one—since heredity and environment are inextricably bound together, a definitive experiment observing the role of one, independent of the other, is impossible. Yet the evidence that pathology or greatness runs in families seems so compelling that people are ever ready to grasp for the first bit of proof. Similarly we can say the environmentalists, too, posture in ways that make them appear to ignore heredity. Certainly the father of behaviorism—John Watson—contributed to this image with his assertion that, given total control of the environment, he could create any type of human being. This specious argument of infinite plasticity reflects a real neglect by psychologists of research on genetic factors affecting behavior.

Utopias—or perhaps we should call them dystopias—have been written to describe both extreme views. Huxley's *Brave New World* forecasts a meritocratic society based on eugenics combined with test-tube breeding of quotas of citizens engineered for their place in the status quo. Skinner's *Walden II* envisions the environmentalist's totally controlled world with a uniform if benign level of existence for all and with a glaring failure to deal with either innate or cultural sources of individual differences. It is no wonder that we have today a polarized public consciousness, which responds explosively to what leading psychologists say about the nature of man. Existing governments are themselves social experiments that rely on theories put forward by social scientists. We will examine here the impact of the thesis of Arthur Jensen on the nature of racial differences in intelligence. (The environmentalists' leading spokesman will be dealt with in Chapter 16.)

GALTON'S GHOST—ARTHUR JENSEN

Jensen has the data; "The environmentalists have found a worthy adversary at last." Such were the milder reactions of some psychologists to Arthur Jensen's paper that said essentially that racial differences in IQ are genuine, that IQ is determined primarily by heredity (80 percent) rather than environment (20 percent), and that the massive efforts to give compensatory education to minority people (and the poor) had failed, as it must, because the largely black recipients do not have the IQ to profit from extra education.[12] Because Jensen's paper is long and unread even by his critics, we will summarize it briefly in his editor's words, and urge that it be read in the original.

> Arthur Jensen argues that the failure of recent compensatory education efforts to produce lasting effects on children's IQ and achievement suggests that the premises on which these efforts have been based should be reexamined.

163

He begins by questioning a central notion upon which these and other educational programs have recently been based: that IQ differences are almost entirely a result of environmental differences and the cultural bias of IQ tests. Jensen carefully defines the concept of IQ, pointing out that it appears as a common factor in all tests that have been devised thus far to tap higher mental processes.

Having defined the concept of intelligence and related it to other forms of mental ability, Jensen employs an analysis of variance model to explain how IQ can be separated into genetic and environmental components. He then discusses the concept of "heritability," a statistical tool for assessing the degree to which individual differences in a trait like intelligence can be accounted for by genetic factors. He analyzes several lines of evidence which suggest that the heritability of intelligence is quite high (i.e., *genetic factors are much more important than environmental factors in producing IQ differences*).

After arguing that environmental factors are not nearly as important in determining IQ as are genetic factors, Jensen proceeds to analyze the environmental influences which may be most critical in determining IQ. He concludes that *prenatal influences may well contribute the largest environmental influence on IQ*. He then discusses evidence which suggests that social class and racial variations in intelligence cannot be accounted for by differences in environment but must be attributed partially to genetic differences.

After he has discussed the influence of the distribution of IQ in a society on its functioning, Jensen examines in detail the results of educational programs for young children, and finds that the changes in IQ produced by these programs are generally small. A basic conclusion of Jensen's discussion of the influence of environment on IQ is that *environment acts as a "threshold variable."* Extreme environmental deprivation can keep the child from performing up to his genetic potential, but *an enriched educational program cannot push the child above that potential.* The average difference in mean IQ between blacks and whites is 15 points. The American Indian, who Jensen argues has even more environmental deprivation, has a higher mean IQ than blacks.

Finally, Jensen examines other mental abilities that might be capitalized on in an educational program, discussing recent findings on diverse patterns of mental abilities between ethnic groups and his own studies of associative learning abilities that are independent of social class. He concludes that educational attempts to boost IQ have been misdirected and that the educational process should focus on teaching much more specific skills. He argues that this will be accomplished most effectively if educational methods are developed which are based on other mental abilities besides IQ.

The article produced a flood of criticism, much of which appeared in a special issue of the journal in which Jensen first published. The criticism has ranged from the technical (which Jensen blithely evades) to the almost hysterical cries of racism, which has been embarrassing to many professionals, and an excuse for Jensen to indulge in some well-founded righteous indignation at attacks by students and colleagues on his right to speak. But the political and ideological consequences of Jensen's thesis cannot be ignored. He and his critics have gone to the open forum of the mass media.

That the nature-nurture question brings out the political orientation of scientists has been shown by Pastore who assessed the sociopolitical beliefs of twelve environmentalists and twelve hereditarians.[13] He found that the environmentalists tended toward liberalism, while hereditarians tended toward conservatism. Thus Jensen's vision of society (and Skinner's at the other extreme) should be considered in a thorough examination of the theoretical content of his work. Jensen's sincere advocacy of his beliefs is perceived as a threat by minority people, who have every reason to believe that if Jensen is believed, we could see a major reversal in efforts for social change, from reshaping society to reshaping the individual. In fairness to Jensen, he sees himself not as a eugenicist, but as one who faces facts about genetic reality. Indeed, the length of his articles is due in part to his feeling that evidence of genetic contributions to intelligence have been ignored in the literature, so he has resorted to a kind of "we shall overwhelm" style of writing which keeps his critics off balance and the controversy alive. In addition, Jensen has aligned himself publically with William Shockley, a hip-shooting, Nobel prize-winning physicist turned eugenicist, with a well-earned reputation as one of the most irresponsible scientist-polemicists in public life today. Both Jensen and Shockley toss simplified statistical assertions around in public and then claim persecution when all hell breaks loose.

Shockley extrapolates from some Army preinduction IQ test data (which are known to be biased in favor of whites and are sloppily collected anyway) to an argument that "each 1% of Caucasian ancestry raises average I.Q. by one point."[14] Jensen, a much more responsible scientist, nonetheless goes around saying that the proof of dysgenic (breeding inadequacy) factors in the black population is to be found in the fact that 16 percent of black children as compared to less than 2 percent of white children are classified as mentally retarded (IQ = 70). He relates this to higher birth rates among less able and poor blacks. But, as critics have pointed out, this simply isn't true, since a lot of low IQ women have *no* children.[15] When we compare birth rates with this correction, it is the high IQ women who have higher reproduction rates.

Another more disturbing fact of environmental life is that the testing and classification of the mentally retarded minority children may be biased and utterly false. In California 25 percent of all chicano children in some districts were placed in classes for the mentally retarded after IQ testing in the English language by white examiners.[16] Retesting in Spanish showed that at least 45 percent had been misclassified and that the group average IQ was 17 points too low. The school districts refused to reclassify the students until ordered to do so by the court, because they stood to lose a subsidy of $550 per child given for educating the mentally retarded. This is a depressing story of how bias, the incentives of society, and inadequate data combine to destroy the lives of minority people. Similar stories, which have led to a ban on IQ testing in some areas, suggest caution or disbelief in accepting any intelligence test data on nonwhite racial groups. To base eugenic policies or the reduction of education of disadvantaged citizens on data collected so far would be highly irresponsible in our opinion. We will examine the problems of intelligence testing in more detail in Chapter 11, but we should establish that IQ tests, like all tests, were developed by and for the white middle class as an attempt to determine efficiently the place of all citizens in society.

Since most states can assign a child the label of mental retardate and place him in a class for the mentally retarded on the basis of a low IQ score (70–79) we must ask whether this one score is a sufficient basis for evaluating human adequacy. Sociologist Jane Mercer points out that most experts agree that mental deficiency consists of both below average intellectual performance and impairment in adaptive behavior.[17] In her large sample survey study which included white, black, and chicanos, she measured adaptive behavior—the ability to play more complex roles in a wide circle of social systems—as well as IQ, asking how many mental retardates would be found in a community using IQ tests alone compared to the combined use of IQ and adaptation score. She found that the number of mental retardates found was 54.7 percent fewer when both IQ and adaptability were considered than when the more traditional definition of an IQ test score of 70 was used alone. Sixty percent of the chicanos and 90.9 percent of the blacks with IQs below 70 passed the adaptability test, while whites were more consistent on both measures. Thus, Mercer argues that blacks and chicanos fail IQ tests because they have not had the opportunity to acquire the cognitive skills needed to pass them; but, they are not incompetent in their ability to cope with the problems such as working, shopping, reading, voting, recreation, and others that go into the definition of adaptation to real life in the community.

In a follow-up study Mercer demonstrated that the IQ tests now in use are anglocentric, measuring the extent to which an individual's background is similar to the typical sociocultural pattern in American society. This pattern includes such factors as white-collar job, skilled or professional work, five or fewer in the family, intact family, ownership of the home, and urban upbringing of head of household. In a complex study relating IQ and these sociocultural

FIGURE 10.3

*Convergence of the average IQ test scores of black children when the
standard norms as sociocultural factors are increasingly controlled. The
heavy curve represents the white sample group and the lighter curve
represents the black sample group. (Reprinted from* Psychology Today
Magazine, *September 1972,* © *Communications/Research/Machines, Inc.)*

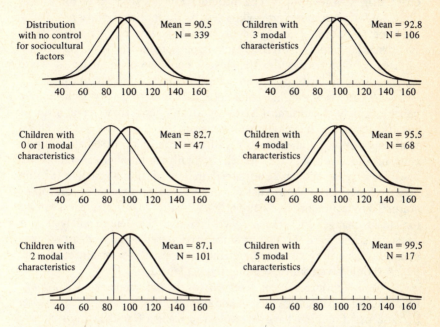

factors Mercer found that the more the family of the black and
chicano children is like the typical sociocultural pattern found in the
community (which is also typically white), the higher the IQ of the
child. As Figure 10.3 shows, when the social background is held constant, there is *no* difference between the measured IQ of black,
chicano, and white children.

E. L. Thorndike once stated: "In the actual race of life, which is
not to get ahead, but to get ahead of somebody, the chief determining
factor is heredity." This statement could be a credo for western
civilization's drive toward a single standard toward which every
institution is aimed and toward which most citizens are socialized. For
it to be valid, we would have to assume that every citizen has an
equivalent cultural background. But such an assumption would be
naïve, since in fact our society has discriminated not only against
blacks, but even against southern Europeans (who also show lower
IQ's than the dominant northern Europeans). The white majority
cultural leaders, whether environmentalists or hereditarians, tend to see
blacks and all minority groups as merely deficient or pathological
versions of mainstream American culture. Charles Valentine has at-

tacked this notion in a brilliant paper in which he debunks the notion of a single black culture—which exists only in the stereotype-seeking eyes of the white beholder (and probably the white IQ tester as well).[18] Valentine sees a fatal error in assuming that blacks are so deprived or different from white society that they "are more to be pitied than scorned. . . ." This provides excuses for failure for everybody, and a corresponding willingness to prescribe quick, large, panacea-type solutions. The theme of the *Moynihan Report* some years ago, with its criticism of the black family structure, was reduced by some spokesmen to the idea that blacks could be brought up to white middle-class standards, if they somehow acquired a Jewish mother!

In fact, as Valentine points out, blacks have a very rich, unique culture, partly bicultural (Afro-American), but they have little, if any, power in the mainstream of America. Further, white researchers, white institutions, and white testers have little or no first-hand knowledge of the black culture. Jensen is totally unfamiliar, as far as we know, with the ecology and social milieu of the black (or of the Native American). With shaky genetics and ignorance of the black cultural environment, he is nonetheless ready to offer a prescription for social change. In summary, we feel that the Jensen analysis is a welcome stimulus to discussion, since it triggered some healthy controversy, but as a prescription for change it is pseudo-scientific nonsense, which should be strongly, if benignly, neglected.

Our skepticism is not reserved for Jensen, since there is a more fundamental problem which Galton and others helped to create. Because psychologists have oversold the using of tests, a meritocratic society has based the fate of its people on the scores from those tests. Our society has become something of a worshiper of the normal curve, a dangerously self-fulfilling prophecy. In many ways we have taken a fiction that was convenient in sorting out human individual differences in simple biological traits and converted it into a fact of life. We have all sought one numerical standard and suffered dehumanization and oversimplification of man in the process. If we have learned anything from the foregoing analysis it is that there cannot be a single, universal standard of excellence, intelligence, success, or normality. As long as bias and discrimination affect the collection of IQ data, we recall the computer operators dictum: "Garbage in—garbage out."

The struggle of our black citizens has been admirably stated in this context by Marvin Bressler.[19]

> The Negro struggle for equal opportunity does not require proof that identical proportions of Negroes and whites occupy specified points on a curve of intelligence, but only that some Negroes are equal or superior to some whites. [This has been shown.] Since the second of these contentions is virtually tantamount to saying that a Negro is human, it asserts the most basic and incontrovertible of

scientific facts. And men are not required to submit their biological credentials to earn the freedom to participate in the amenities of a civilized society.

NOTES

1. Until recently the Lysenko theory was officially required to be acknowledged in Russian scientific writing—as the government found it politically useful.
2. Personal communication from Delos D. Wickens, a student of Dashiell.
3. Richard Hofstadter, *Social Darwinism in American Thought*, rev. ed. (Boston: Beacon, 1955).
4. Lewis M. Terman, "The Intelligence Quotient of Francis Galton in Childhood," *American Journal of Psychology* 28 (1917): 209–215. Terman's retrospective techniques of estimating intelligence provided the basis for a more comprehensive study of the childhood of great men by Catherine M. Cox, *The Early Mental Traits of Three Hundred Childhood Geniuses* (Stanford, Calif.: Stanford University Press, 1926). The present biography by Karl Pearson, *Life, Letters and Labors of Francis Galton* (London: 1914–1930).
5. Francis Galton, *Hereditary Genius* (New York: Macmillan, 1914), p. 14.
6. Ibid., p. 39.
7. Francis Galton, *Inquiries into Human Faculty and Its Development* (London: Macmillan, 1883), pp. 202–203.
8. Galton's discussion of regression toward the mean can be found in *Natural Inheritance* (London: Macmillan, 1889), pp. 95–110. For a general history of the development of statistical methods, see Helen M. Walker, *Studies in the History of Statistical Method* (Baltimore: Williams & Wilkins, 1929). See the Statistical supplement in Appendix D for a detailed description of how to compute the statistics used in this and later chapters.
9. E. G. Boring, *A History of Experimental Psychology*, 2d ed. (New York: Appleton-Century-Crofts, 1950), p. 507.
10. See N. H. Pronko, *Panorama of Psychology* (Belmont, Calif.: Brooks/ Cole, 1969), pp. 98–101.
11. Ibid., pp. 101–105.
12. A. Jensen, "How Much Can We Boost I.Q. and Scholastic Achievement," *Harvard Educational Review* 39, no. 1 (1969): 1–123. The summary in the text was written by the issue editor, pp. 1–2.
13. N. Pastore, *The Nature-Nurture Controversy* (New York: King's Crown Press, 1949).
14. W. Shockley, "Dysgenics—a Social Problem Reality Evaded by the Illusion of Infinite Plasticity of Human Intelligence" (Paper presented at the American Psychological Association Convention, Washington, D.C., September 7, 1971).
15. R. C. Lewontin, "Race and Intelligence," *Bulletin of the Atomic Scien-*

tists 26, no. 3 (1970): 2–26. Also contains a rejoinder by Jensen and a reply by Lewontin.

16. "Wrong Results from I.Q. Tests" (Editorial), *San Francisco Chronicle*, 27 January 1970.

17. J. R. Mercer, "Pluralistic Diagnosis in the Evaluation of Black and Chicano Children: A Procedure for Taking Sociocultural Variables into Account in Clinical Assessment" (Paper presented at the American Psychological Association Convention, Washington, D.C., September 3–7, 1971).

18. C. A. Valentine, "It's Either Brain Damage or No Father," in *Toward Social Change: A Handbook for Those Who Will*, eds. R. Buckhout et al. (New York: Harper & Row, 1971), pp. 126–133.

19. M. Bressler, "Sociology, Biology and Ideology," *American Scholar*.

ELEVEN
Alfred Binet, Psychologist

THE PSYCHOGENIC THEORIES OF CHARCOT AND JANET

During the early years of the French Revolution a remarkable man named Philippe Pinel became chief physician at a Paris hospital filled with madmen. As a beginning Pinel proposed to take off their chains. When the President of the Commune heard this reckless proposal he came in person to reassure himself. The lunatics greeted him with shouts, curses, and the clanking of chains.

"Citizen," he shouted to Pinel above the din, "are you mad yourself that you would unchain such beasts?"

"I am convinced," said Pinel, "that these mentally ill are intractable only because they are deprived of fresh air and their liberty."[1]

It speaks volumes for Gallic intelligence that Pinel was allowed to conduct his experiment. For the first time the insane were treated, not as criminals, not as if they were possessed by demons, but with the restraint and kindness that sickness requires. Pinel's reforms turned a madhouse into a mental hospital and laid new foundations for the psychiatry of the future, based on the medical model.

If insanity is a sickness, it would seem to be a sickness of the brain. In order to cure it, therefore, one must understand how the brain works. This line of reasoning, as old as Hippocrates, but especially appealing to positivistic thinkers in the nineteenth century, led to many important discoveries about the psychological effects of organic injuries and diseases in the nervous system. Psychiatrists who worked in this tradition found their major ally was the neurologist, and their favorite theories of insanity were theories of neural damage.

In spite of noteworthy successes, however, not all mental disorders could be traced directly to organic causes. The difficulties with a purely organic theory first became obvious, not in the study of psychosis, but in the study of neurosis. (As a rough and ready rule: if cognitive disorders predominate, it is usually psychosis; if emotional disorders predominate, it is usually neurosis; if moral disorders predominate, it is usually psychopathy.)

171

Once again a Frenchman led the way. The particular kind of neurosis that was to prove so very instructive was called *hysteria*. A patient with hysterical symptoms seems to have a great and senseless variety of bodily ailments. Parts of his body may be paralyzed so that he cannot move them or cannot feel anything in them, his vision and hearing may be impaired, his memory may be faulty, and the like. Hysteria was once considered a woman's disease, but this theory was discredited when the neurologist Jean Martin Charcot discovered male patients suffering from all the classical symptoms. For many years Charcot shared with his fellow neurologists the assumption that hysteria was a disease of the nervous system. There seemed little reason to doubt it—all the symptoms appeared to be organic in nature.

But then the neurologists learned about hypnosis. Some of Charcot's assistants at the famous neurological clinic he had created at the Salpêtrière in Paris became interested in hypnotism; they began to try it on one another and on the patients. They discovered that they could produce all the symptoms of hysteria in a normal person and then could cure him instantaneously, first by hypnotizing him and telling him he could not move or could not feel or could not see, then by awakening him from the hypnotic state. Even the great Charcot was unable to tell the difference between simulated, hyponotic symptoms and true, hysterical symptoms.

The possibility of psychological involvement in these apparently organic ailments put the whole problem of hysteria in a new light. Charcot began to examine hysterical symptoms in great detail; he soon discovered convincing evidence that they are not due to peripheral organic injury. For example, a neurologist knows from his study of anatomy which parts of the body are served by which nerves. In particular, he knows which areas of the skin will become insensitive if a particular nerve branch is damaged. When a patient complains that he cannot feel anything in his hand, a neurologist can usually diagnose which nerve must have been damaged, by carefully mapping out the insensitive area. If the area of anesthesia does not make anatomical sense—if it follows the pattern of a glove, say, rather than the true pattern of the nerve endings in the skin—the complaint cannot be attributed to organic damage to the peripheral nerves in the arm. Charcot discovered that hysterical symptoms usually made this kind of neurological nonsense, and that the same nonsense could be produced by hypnosis. In certain cases, apparently, it was even possible to relieve hysterical symptoms by hypnotizing the patient and telling him his symptom would vanish. The older view that mental illness is caused by damage to the nervous system clearly needed to be revised to include psychological causes. How that revision was to be phrased, however, remained obscure.

Pierre Janet, a student of Charcot, saw clearly that the emphasis should be shifted from the hysterical patient's symptoms to his state of mind. After observing many hysterical patients, Janet concluded that they suffered from mental dissociation. An emotional system of ideas becomes isolated from the rest of his mental life and presumably takes control of part of his body or part of his memory. These insulated subsystems were thought not to be controlled voluntarily by the patient. Today it seems obvious that Janet's descriptions of hysterical patients moved the problem of accounting for this neurosis from neurology into psychology. But Janet, paralyzed by the positivistic spirit of nineteenth-century medicine, hesitated to give a frankly psychological explanation. Perhaps, he thought, hysterics have an hereditary inability to integrate their experience. He saw the emotional struggles and conflicts that his patients were going through and he described the dissociation that existed in their mental life, but he could not accept the conflicts as the *cause* of the dissociation. That step was left for another student of Charcot—Sigmund Freud.

In spite of their reluctance to accept a purely psychological explanation of mental disorders, Charcot and Janet created in Paris an environment where psychogenic and somatogenic theories could compete, where the precise measurements of the laboratory and the rough-and-ready methods of the clinic could be used side by side. It was in this environment that Alfred Binet learned his psychology and adopted the catholic attitude that he carried into all of his later research. This proved to be perfect preparation for the work he was to perform.

BINET AND THE CLINICAL APPROACH TO THE MIND

Alfred Binet was born in Nice in 1857.[2] His mother, a talented painter, took him to Paris while he was still a boy; there he received his education at the center of French cultural and intellectual life. After taking his baccalaureate degree from the Lycée Saint-Louis he embarked upon the study of law. He enjoyed life as a law student and often talked about it in later years, but he discovered that his interest in law was only marginal. Instead of devoting himself single-mindedly to his law books, he found himself being pulled in several different directions at once. Paris was then as now an enormously stimulating place for a young intellectual, and Binet's energy could scarcely be contained by any single field of study. In particular, he could not suppress his interest in the natural sciences and especially in medicine. His fascination with medicine was a family affair—his father and his grandfather were both physicians.

Binet was never socially ambitious, but he did form many friendships with fellow students and collaborators, and much of his later research was published with coauthors. Among his friends at the Lycée was Babinski, later to become a famous neurologist; it was probably Babinski who introduced Binet to Charles Féré, an enthusiastic disciple of Charcot. Féré and Binet began to collaborate actively in research on abnormal psychology and hypnotism at Charcot's clinic in the Salpêtrière. At the same time he was absorbing the medical psychology of Charcot's clinic, Binet was also studying under the direction of his father-in-law, the histologist Balbiani, for his degree in science from the Sorbonne. It is characteristic of Binet's omnivorous intellectual appetite that in 1878, the same year he received his license as a lawyer, he published a scientific article on the psychic life of microorganisms.

During these years Binet's interests shifted more and more toward psychological problems. The shift was stimulated principally by his work with Féré in Charcot's clinic, but his newly awakened curiosity was not confined solely to the psychological problems of the clinical practitioner. He began to devour the British empiricist philosophers. His special interest was in the process of association and, like all of Binet's interests, it was quickly reflected in print. As early as 1880 he published a short paper on the fusion of images, a subject he was led to directly by reading about the association of ideas.

Although Binet is remembered today principally for his way of testing the intelligence of children, his contributions to psychology were much broader than that. It is the case of a mountain dwarfing some very respectable hills nearby. Binet's first book, *The Psychology of Reasoning* (1886), had as its subtitle, *Experimental Studies of Hypnotism;* it was the result of combining British associationism with French hypnotism. His knowledge of hypnotism derived from the work with Féré; his knowledge of associationism came from reading, not the German Wilhelm Wundt, but the British John Stuart Mill. Binet had no formal instructor in psychology, no one to teach him either the old, philosophical version or the new, experimental kind. What he knew of it he picked up by reading a few books: Ribot, Taine, Hamilton, and others, especially Mill. His training as an experimental investigator was obtained through his studies in biology and medicine and through his experience in the neurological clinic. He admired British psychology and in later years was probably nearer to Galton than to Charcot in his sympathies. But most of his psychological ideas came from his own thinking and his own observations, a fact which gave his work a freshness and originality that were characteristically his own. Of all his work his first book was the most heavily dependent upon traditional views. As he grew older he came to rely more and more upon his own intuition and experience.

In 1887, with Féré as coauthor, he published his second book, *Animal Magnetism. On Double Consciousness* appeared in an English edition in 1889 and *Personality Deviations*, his fourth book in six years, in 1892. All were written from a clinical, psychiatric view of psychology, but they indicate a period of transition in Binet's life, when his interests were moving from the abnormal to the normal. In spite of the speed with which they appeared, these books were both original and readable. Binet had enormous energy for hard work and a capacity to write about it rapidly in clear and flowing prose. Work cost him no effort. "I work quite naturally," he once said, "as a hen lays eggs."

In the summer of 1892 Binet was on his way to a little beach at Saint-Valery, where he spent his vacations with his family, when he happened to meet the physiologist H. Beaunis on the platform of the railroad station at Rouen. Beaunis was director of the laboratory of physiological psychology that had been created at the Sorbonne in 1889. The two men fell into a friendly argument about hypnosis and in the course of it Binet asked if he might do some work in the laboratory. Beaunis was glad to have this energetic young man as a collaborator, so a decision was made that fixed the future direction of Binet's career. He joined the four-room laboratory first as Beaunis's assistant, then became associate director and finally director when Beaunis retired in 1894. The directorship carried no specific responsibilities and, since he had an independent income, it left him completely free to pursue his own research.

The year 1894 was eventful for Binet. Not only did he become director of a laboratory, he also completed his doctorate in science with a thesis on the nervous system of insects. He published two more books: *The Psychology of Great Calculators and Chess Players*, a minor work, with Henneguy, and *Introduction to Experimental Psychology*, which reviewed both the standard methods of measuring sensation, reaction time, and memory, and the newer methods that used questionnaires. This latter part of the *Introduction* anticipated the methods which he was soon to use so effectively in his studies of children. It was in 1894 also that he founded his own journal, *L'Année Psychologique*.

Binet remained the editor and a major contributor to *L'Année* through fourteen volumes until his death in 1911. During those years he wrote a large book on *Suggestibility* (1900) which summarized his work on hypnosis, contributed *The Soul and the Body* (1906) to a traditional philosophical debate, and averaged about ten articles a year in his own and other journals.

Binet worked frequently with collaborators—although his dominating energy frequently antagonized them—but he was not a professor and he did no teaching. Students would have got in his way. He seldom appeared in public, being too busy with research and writing. His only deviation from complete loyalty to psychology seems to have been his tendency to write plays that were successfully produced in Paris. But even his plays usually had a psychological theme.

Binet performed experiments on adult subjects, but he preferred to work with children. There is one advantage (along with many disadvantages) in using the schoolroom for psychological experiments: young subjects are available in large numbers and are accustomed to following instructions. A long series of studies of children during the 1890s provided the necessary background for Binet's most famous work—the Binet-Simon scale for measuring the intelligence of school children.

A mark of a good idea is that it makes one forget how confusing things were before it was invented. Today the Binet-Simon scale seems such a simple and obvious way to measure intelligence that it is hard to believe how many brilliant men were unable to think of it. Francis Galton, for example, wanted to measure intelligence. He developed a collection of tests, and he contributed the statistical tools necessary to analyze the results. But Galton's tests were aimed at psychological processes fashionable in his day. He measured visual and auditory acuity and observed that, "The more perceptive the senses are of differences, the larger is the field upon which our judgment and intelligence can act."[3] It was a good idea, but it didn't work.

James McKeen Cattell was similarly hobbled by the empiricist tradition in the psychology of his day. Cattell, student of Wundt and friend of Galton, was one of the brightest lights in American psychology at the turn of the century. Yet look at the list of tests he proposed to measure intelligence.

1. *Dynamometer pressure*. How tightly can the hand squeeze?
2. *Rate of movement*. How quickly can the hand be moved through a distance of 50 cm.?
3. *Sensation-areas*. How far apart must two points be on the skin to be recognized as two rather than one?
4. *Pressure causing pain*. How much pressure on the forehead is necessary to cause pain?
5. *Least noticeable difference in weight*. How large must the difference be between two weights before it is reliably detected?
6. *Reaction-time for sound*. How quickly can the hand be moved at the onset of an auditory signal?
7. *Time for naming colors*. How long does it take to name a strip of ten colored papers?
8. *Bisection of a 50-cm line*. How accurately can one point to the center of an ebony rule?
9. *Judgment of 10-sec time*. How accurately can an interval of 10 seconds be judged?
10. *Number of letters remembered on one hearing*. How many letters, ordered at random, can be repeated exactly after one presentation?[4]

Cattell described these tests as beginning with bodily measures, then proceeding through psychophysical to mental measures. If indeed there is any continuum of measurements running from bodily to mental, Galton and Cattell explored only the bodily end of it. Today we know that of all Cattell's tests only the last, measurement of memory span, provides any indication of a person's intelligence, and even this measurement is of limited value.

The Frenchmen Binet, Henri, and Simon took up where Galton, Cattell, and others had left off. They pushed boldly along the imaginary continuum toward the higher mental processes, into measures of memory, imagination, attention, comprehension; it was at that end of the continuum that they began to get results. But it took someone with clinical attitudes to attempt such measures; the laboratory scientists knew intuitively that the higher mental processes were too complicated to permit valid measurement.

In a series of articles in *L'Année Psychologique* from 1894 to 1898 Binet and his assistant Victor Henri described their attempts to measure higher mental processes in children and adults. They were quite clear that sensory and motor measurements were easier to make and less variable when repeated, but, for all their virtues, such tests did not seem to distinguish sufficiently among different people. Binet wanted to measure mental functions that different people performed in different ways, with different degrees of skill. Since memory is an important component of intelligence, everyone agreed that it should be included. But Binet thought it might be possible to make similar measurements on many other psychological functions. For example, why not measure the vividness of imagery or the kind of imagery that a person has? Why not test his attention, both its scope and its duration? Why not test comprehension of sentences or synonyms or ask the person to find logical errors in a text? Many tests of suggestibility were available from the studies of hypnosis; could suggestibility be related to intelligence? Even esthetic judgments could be obtained and scored against the esthetic judgments of experts. Why not ask people to make moral judgments or judge emotions from pictures of facial expression? Why not study their will by asking them to withstand pain or fatigue? Why not measure the speed with which they could acquire a motor skill?

Why not, indeed? Who could say that all those higher mental functions were not involved in intelligence? No one had ever measured those functions in a large number of different people in order to relate the results to intelligence. The reasons for this neglect were unclear except for the fact that the inquiry did not seem tidy. In the minds of such academic psychologists as Wundt, psychology should begin with the simplest measures of the simplest mental elements. Wundt flatly denied that psychology could study thinking. Even those who were more optimistic felt that psychology could build up toward these more complicated kinds of measures only slowly. Psychology wasn't ready

177

to jump into the middle of the mind without any notion of what might be encountered.

Such a jump is what one might expect from a psychologist trained in the clinic. Because no two patients ever suffer from exactly the same complaints, a clinician is seldom able to repeat his observations precisely; if he is not to lose his way, he must inure himself to the complexities and variabilities that his patients exhibit, and learn to discover order in the most untidy and abnormal kinds of behavior. But the complexities a clinician must learn to live with frequently serve only to convince experimentalists that clinical data are worse than useless.

In 1904 the Minister of Public Instruction in Paris assembled a commission to consider the problem of subnormal children in the public schools. If the children who were likely to fail could be placed in special schools, they might be helped; Binet, whose studies of child psychology were well known, was a member of the commission. As early as 1894 he had begun to try his tests on school children; in 1903 he had reported an intensive study of the intellectual development of his own two daughters.

Binet quickly became disturbed because the discussions of the commission were so vague that everything they tried to do seemed confused and pointless. He took it upon himself, therefore, to provide clear definitions for the terms that were being used to describe subnormal children. He devoted his research thereafter to the pboblem of finding a scientific basis for a medical classification that would be more useful to educators. His principal collaborator in this attempt was Dr. Simon, a young physician in an asylum for backward children. From 1905 until Binet's death in 1911 at least twenty-eight articles and one book were written by Binet and Simon together.[5]

In 1905, primarily to facilitate the work of the commission, Binet and Simon published their first results. They used a large battery of different mental tests, some hard, some easy. Binet collected tests from everywhere, and his own mind bubbled over with ideas for others. To discover which tests were useful, he and Simon spent endless hours in the schools with the children, watching, asking, testing, recording. Each proposed test had to be given to a large number of children. If a test did not distinguish the brighter from the duller, or the older from the younger, it was abandoned. Note that the judgment of who was bright came from other criteria—usually teacher ratings of performance.

Tests that worked were retained, even though they often failed to conform with the theoretical principles Binet and Henri had announced ten years earlier. The memory tests worked. And the tests of comprehension worked—comprehension of words, of statements, of concepts, of pictures. Binet did not retain the tests on the basis of a theory; he watched the children and let their behavior decide which tests were good and which were irrelevant. The 1905 version of the "Metrical Scale of Intelligence" simply arranged all the tests that Binet had selected in an order of increasing difficulty. Each child passed as many tests as he could until they became too difficult for him. How far the child got down the list of tests could then be compared with how far other children of the same age usually got.

In 1908 a revised version was published. The tests were grouped according to the age at which 50 to 75 percent of a large sample of children passed them, from age 3 up to age 13. In 1911, the year of Binet's death, there was still another revision that extended the age up to 15 years.

According to the 1911 scale an average 3-year-old French child should pass half of these tests: he should be able to point to his nose, eyes, and mouth; repeat two digits; enumerate objects in a picture; give his family name; and repeat a sentence of six syllables. By age 7 the child should pass half of these tests: be able to show his right hand and left ear; describe a picture; execute three commands given simultaneously; count the value of six sous, three of which are double; and name four cardinal colors. By 15 the youngster should be able to repeat seven digits; find three rhymes for a given word in one minute; repeat a sentence of twenty-six syllables; interpret pictures; and interpret given facts.

These should give the flavor of Binet's tests to anyone who (though it is hard to imagine how) might have been sheltered from them heretofore. The age group of tests that a child could pass half the time defined his mental age, regardless of what his chronological age might be.

Binet used as the measure of retardation simply the difference between the child's mental age and chronological age. Thus a child who was 6 years old but passed only the items on the 4-year age group would have a mental age of 4, and so would be retarded two years in mental development. Binet regarded two years as a serious deficiency. Other psychologists decided later that it was better to use the ratio, rather than the difference between the two ages. Mental age divided by chronological age gives a mental quotient. If the two ages are the same, then the child is average for his age and the quotient is unity. If the child is retarded, the mental is less than the chronological age, and the quotient is less than unity. If he is advanced, the quotient will be greater than unity. When this quotient is multiplied by 100, the result is usually referred to as the intelligence quotient, or IQ. The various confusing arguments about whether the IQ is constant throughout life, or whether it can be raised or lowered with special circumstances, came later and cannot be blamed on Binet. His contribution was a simple, reliable method for determining a child's mental age.

One of Binet's advantages in solving this problem may have been that, although he read English fluently, he did not know a word of German. Some such insulation from Fechner, Helmholtz, and Wundt was probably necessary. If he had known more about what happened east of the Rhine, he might have been more willing to stop short with the study of sensations and reaction times. Fortunately, he was not overly concerned with scientific purity; he had a practical problem he urgently wanted to solve, and he did whatever seemed necessary to solve it. The solution did not come through an elegant experiment conceived in an armchair and conducted in a laboratory. It came through tedious hours spent testing children in the schools of Paris.

Instead of experiments, Binet conducted interviews—in the best tradition of the clinical interview. "For the all-round clinical appraisal of a subject's intellectual level," wrote Lewis M. Terman many years later, "the Binet type of scale has no serious rival. It is not merely an intelligence test; it is a method of standardized interview which is highly interesting to the subject and calls forth his natural responses to an extraordinary variety of situations."[6]

Within ten years of Binet's death in 1911, translations and revisions of the Binet-Simon scale were in use all over the world. The immediate, international enthusiasm demonstrated how great the need for such a measuring device had been. Oddly enough, the scale gained little fame in France. In his old age Simon recalled that it was not until the early 1920s that a French social worker, having visited clinics in the United States, found the Binet-Simon scale frequently mentioned there. On her return to France the social worker was instrumental in reintroducing the test to the land of its birth.[7] During World War II the test became very fashionable in France but under the names of Terman and Merrill, the Americans who revised it for use in the United States!

Binet was not a great man. He was a competent, hard-working psychologist whose career ended abruptly when he was still in his prime and still had much left to do. He trained no students, he wrote no immortal books, and his memory has been little honored by his countrymen. But even though he was not great, he was important—made important by subsequent events.

Over the years the demand for mental tests has steadily grown. The individual differences explored by psychological testing now include innumerable varieties, and the statistical methods of analyzing test data have grown in power and sophistication. The vein that Binet opened up is still being mined today.

IQ TESTING IN THE UNITED STATES

We reiterate how IQ tests are derived. They are made up of subtests of skills, tests that differentiate between a normally good performer in school and a poor one. The choice of tests include not only those that work in terms of predicting performance, but those that are representative of the skills that children in school are learning and can already perform at their age level. The children in school when these tests were developed in both France and the United States were all white and mostly from the middle or upper class, so that the tests were representative not only of performance and skills, but also of the social strata in which the children lived. Test makers will reject a test that fails to discriminate between bright and dull children.

Because of the implicit assumption that intelligence is inherited and should, like many other inherited traits, be normally distributed, test makers have always tended to search for tests that yield a normal curve. Even though geneticists warn that there are distributions with other shapes, test makers have kept the normal-curve faith and have extended it into that other area of testing, *ability* testing. For example, the graduate record exams (GRE) are designed to have a mean of 500 at the center of a normal distribution, but to keep the faith requires effort because each year the observed mean for all graduate record exam takers goes up (perhaps reflecting better education or improved test-taking skills). To keep up, the test makers change the test and make it more difficult to keep ahead. But the spiral continues.

Similar problems plague the IQ testing program, which now affects the place in school of virtually every child in the United States. The IQ tests used most widely are the 1937 Stanford-Binet (a revision in English of the original Binet test), the Wechsler Adult Intelligence Scale (WAIS), and its form for children, the Wechsler Intelligence Scale for Children (WISC). The tests have been standardized against the performance of "typical" (white, middle-class) Americans, and are highly regarded by professional educators since they are good predictors of how well students will do in school. Since verbal skills are important, the tests must be revised every now and then as word and concept usage changes in the culture, or again, as the children become test wise.

Do IQ tests really measure the inherited capacity to learn we call intelligence? Testing advocates think so, but argue that even if they don't, IQ as measured is genuinely important as a basis for predicting where a person belongs in a meritoocracy. High IQ is related not only to school performance but to socioeconomic status as well. Johnson has shown that professionals have an average IQ of 120, while day laborers average only 95.[8] Herrnstein, writing in a popular maga-

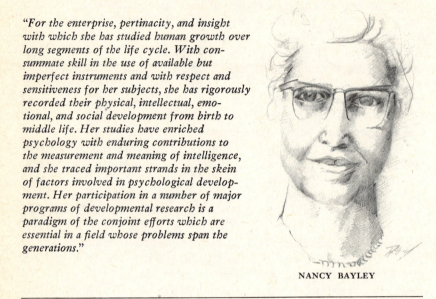

*"For the enterprise, pertinacity, and insight
with which she has studied human growth over
long segments of the life cycle. With con-
summate skill in the use of available but
imperfect instruments and with respect and
sensitiveness for her subjects, she has rigorously
recorded their physical, intellectual, emotional, and social development from birth to
middle life. Her studies have enriched
psychology with enduring contributions to
the measurement and meaning of intelligence,
and she traced important strands in the skein
of factors involved in psychological development. Her participation in a number of major
programs of developmental research is a
paradigm of the conjoint efforts which are
essential in a field whose problems span the
generations."*

NANCY BAYLEY

zine, argues that if we assume IQ to be primarily inherited, the
equilization of environmental and learning opportunity in the United
States will lead to a meritocracy based solely on heredity.

> As the wealth and complexity of human society grow, there will be
> precipitated out of the mass of humanity a low capacity . . . residue
> that may be unable to master the common occupations [increasingly
> professional], cannot compete for success and achievement and are
> most likely to be born to parents who have similarly failed . . . our
> society may be sorting itself willy nilly into inherited castes . . .
> the tendency to be unemployed may run in the genes of the family
> about as certainly as bad teeth do now.[9]

Thus Herrnstein envisions a destiny determined by inherited
IQ, and joins with Jensen in advocating a simplistic analysis based on
an inordinate amount of faith in the validity of IQ tests and an uncritical acceptance of a static model of meritocracy in the United States.

As should be clear from our argument here and in the previous
chapter, the assumption of a static number representing a person's
intelligence or the assumption of a static definition of society are
matters that we profoundly disagree with.

At the risk of biting the hand that feeds many a psychologist, we believe that the time has come to abandon the use of a single test to measure intelligence or the single standard of performance, especially at the early stages of a person's life. In part, this stand is based on the damage already done to millions of our citizens by having their careers and education channeled by their scores on tests that both discriminate against some people and oversimplify what it is to be human. But going deeper, we feel that the IQ test, in the hands of people in education (and the testing industry) who have a large stake in the shaky assumptions behind the test, is a dangerous weapon whose use should be curtailed.

The IQ test is now used as a hurdle through which a person must pass (with a high score) at a very early age to be eligible for access to the opportunities for social mobility in the meritocracy. In many school systems the early IQ test tags an individual with an IQ label that will specify the educational track (or rut) that person will remain in for life (unless the records are lost). It is hardly surprising that IQ tests *predict* performance, since it is obvious that the tests *determine* what a person will be allowed to perform. Studies of students in "track" systems in schools suggest that they quickly label themselves (if in the low track) as marginal, believing that IQ is destiny.

If the students don't talk themselves into poor performance, teachers do. Rosenthal has shown experimentally that when teachers were told that they had twenty "spurters" with high IQs in their class, the children (who actually had normal IQs) showed dramatic improvements in school work and even increased their IQs.[10] While the study had some statistical errors, it nonetheless confirmed the fact that teachers' expectations can affect the motivation, self-concept, and performance of school children. One wonders if such false information given on minority children generally wouldn't result in the reversal of the obvious inference: that teachers' *negative* expectations about alleged genetic or social inferiority of minority children serves to *depress* their performance on tests and in school. It should at least be recognized that tests contribute to their own validity ratings through the mechanism of such self-fulfilling prophecies.

The Human Side of the IQ Debate*

The complexity of the IQ debate causes us to forget sometimes how deeply the meanings of the argument may strike the feelings of the people affected. Shortly after the publication of Professor Herrnstein's article on IQ in The Atlantic, *a young white*

* Excerpted from T. J. Cottle, "The edge of the I.Q. Storm," *Saturday Review,* 15 April 1972, pp. 50–53.

*girl from Appalachia reacted to the article to a professor friend—
from a perspective which was not familiar to the scientist.
Despite the professor's disagreement with Herrnstein, he couldn't
calm the girl's feelings:*

> But it's true. He wouldn't lie. He's a Harvard professor . . . He
> can't lie . . . He's at Harvard. That means everything and he knows . . .
> You're smarter. You all are smarter . . . Professor Herrnstein is just
> not afraid to say it right out . . . Pretty soon . . . some other
> Harvard professor . . . will come to West Virginia or Kentucky
> . . . and start to give those tests to the school children back there . . .
> They'll find we're dumb too . . . I went to school with black children
> and we're dumber than they are. Much dumber . . . they can't even
> read the instructions . . . They are born dumb . . . they'll all score
> two and four and ten and they'll never let us come out. They'll lock us
> in those hills . . . just like they lock black people in the ghettos of
> every city. And they'll tell us we can't come out until we can read
> and do arithmetic and be intelligent like you . . . We're hillbillies!
> Born dumb hillbillies, and we're the next to be tested . . . Maybe
> they'll get the Indians first, but you can be sure that we'll be next.

Finally we offer a critique by the developmental psychologists (more in Chapter 21) who share our skepticism about assigning one number to intelligence. Gilbert Voyat argues that

> We cannot assign to intelligence a specific, static definition, in terms of properties, for this directly contradicts the idea of development itself. Any static definition reduces intelligence either to exclusively environmental factors or to almost exclusively genetic factors without implying the necessary *equilibrated* interaction between them.[11]

Voyat and Piaget see intelligence as a dynamic *process*, in which a maturing nervous system becomes capable of ever increasingly sophisticated stages of understanding information in the environment —a process that continues throughout life. The Piaget view avoids conceiving of IQ as a fixed quantity which is unmodifiable, rather he sees intellectual growth as a series of developmental stages with critical periods of transition. That the age at which a developmental stage is reached can vary across different cultures is obvious, just as the *importance* of certain stages can vary.

The impact of the critique is that since IQ tests have been designed by whites for western culture, they can never be fair to those outside the cultural mainstream. Testing of any kind should be based on relativity not absolutism. We feel that the fine work of Alfred Binet, which opened up an understanding of intelligence, has been distorted into a panacea tool for processing people by means of a simplistic numbering system into membership in a meritocracy. If society is to evolve into an organization that welcomes the diversity of its different cultures and permits individuals to actualize whatever native talents they have, we can perhaps take one small step by throwing out the IQ test, which has proven, in everyday use, to be racist, unfair, and inaccurate.

POSTSCRIPT

If you are white, we invite you to try your hand at a few items from an underground test that is culturally based on the verbal milieu of the black community. Like the Stanford-Binet test, we will not give you the answers; we encourage you to ask your black friends. *Res ipsa loquitor.*

The Chitlin' Test

Section 1. Chitlin' Intelligence Test

1. A "gas head" is a person who has a

   a. fast moving car
   b. a stable of "lace"
   c. "process"
   d. a habit of stealing cars
   e. long jail record for arson

2. If you threw the dice and "7" showed up on top, what was facing down?

   a. seven
   b. snake eyes
   c. boxcars
   d. little jees
   e. eleven

3. Jazz pianist Ahmad Jamal took an Arabic name after becoming really famous. Previously he had some fame with what he called his slave name. What *was* his previous name?

   a. Willie Lee Jackson
   b. LeRoi Jones
   c. Wilbur McDougal
   d. Fritz Jones
   e. Andy Johnson

4. In "C. C. Rider," what does "C. C." stand for?

   a. civil service
   b. church council
   c. country circuit, preacher, or an old-time rambler
   d. country club
   e. "Cheatin' Charlie" (the boxcar Gunsel)

5. "Down home" (the south) today, for the average "Soul Brother" who is picking cotton (in season from sunup to sundown), what is the average earning (take home) for one full day?

   a. $0.75
   b. $1.65
   c. $3.50
   d. $5.00
   e. $12.00

6. Hattie May Johnson is on the County. She has four children and her husband is now in jail for nonsupport, as he was unemployed and was not able to give her money. Her welfare check is now $286.000 per

month. Last night she went out with the biggest player in town. If she gets pregnant, then nine months from now, how much more will her welfare check be?

a. $80
b. $2
c. $35
d. $150
e. $100

7. And Jesus said, "Walk together children . . ."

a. Don't get weary. There's a great camp meeting.
b. for we shall overcome.
c. for the family that walks together talks together.
d. By your patience you will win your souls (Luke 21:19).
e. Find the things that are above, not the things that are on Earth (Col. 3:3).

Section II. The Nitty-Gritty Sentence Section

Tell what is being said in these sentences:

A. Did you check Adam's hog? The dude had a white on white in white with white. Ain't he foul. I talk to the cat but he was just too cool, he tried to high-sign me.

B. Did you make it to Paul's last night? It was outasight. They had goop-gobbs of bitches and they were all fine back. You know I backed on in, maintaining all the time.

C. Saturday, while I was standing on "the Ave," this player sheened by in his outasight hog with a bad skypiece and uptight threads with some too much gators. It's obvious he has his game together. He told this cat to lay dead or he was going to get his hat brought to him. The dude was bold. He kept fat-moufin' (fat-mouthin'); trying to style in front of the fellows. Everybody knew his front was weak.

NOTES

1. R. W. White, *The Abnormal Personality*, 2d ed. (New York: Ronald, 1956), p. 9.
2. F. L. Bertrand, *Alfred Binet et Son Oeuvre* (Paris: Alcan, 1930).
3. Francis Galton, *Inquiries into Human Faculty and Its Development* (London: Macmillan, 1883), p. 27.
4. J. M. Cattell, "Mental Tests and Measurements," *Mind* 15 (1890): 373–380.
5. T. H. Wolf, "An Individual Who Made a Difference," *American Psychologist* 16 (1961): 245–248.
6. L. M. Terman and M. A. Merrill, *Measuring Intelligence* (New York: Houghton Mifflin), 1957.
7. Wolf, "An Individual Who Made a Difference."
8. D. M. Johnson, "Application of the Standard Score I.Q. to Social Statistics," *Journal of Social Psychology* 27 (1948): 217–227.

9. R. Herrnstein, "I.Q.," *The Atlantic*, September 1971, pp. 43–64.
10. R. Rosenthal and L. F. Jacobsen, *Pygmalion in the Classroom* (New York: Holt, Rinehart & Winston, 1968).
11. G. Voyat, "I.Q.: God-Given or Man-Made," *Saturday Review*, 17 May 1969.

TWELVE

Recognizing and Identifying

Recognition seems so simple, direct, immediate. The skillful processing of information that must be involved is not itself apparent, for the object seems familiar as soon as the eyes encounter it.

In part, recognition seems so immediate because we spend most of our time in familiar surroundings. We work in the same rooms, see the same people, walk the same streets, live in the same houses for long periods of time. The perceptual information we receive each ordinary day is usually repetitious and redundant. We come to know the things we will encounter even before we encounter them.

Put us on unfamiliar ground, and we are much slower to realize what an object is. We hesitate, look several times, and make mistakes. For an adult it is impossible to imagine any environment that would be completely new and foreign to everything he has ever seen before, that would mislead him with respect to every assumption he made. Even a foreign language is not so completely foreign as that. But a little novelty makes us much more keenly aware of the hypotheses we hold and the inferences we make. As long as they work, we do not notice that we make them. It is when they fail that we become puzzled and search for reasons. After a few failures, we are in a much better frame of mind to accept the proposition that recognizing objects is an elaborate and delicate skill, even though we acquire the skill too long ago to recall how we did it.

When we encounter a common object—a hat, say—we either recognize that it is a hat, equivalent to millions of other hats, or we may recognize that it is Arthur's hat, a particular hat with its own identity, a hat we have seen many times before. To recognize that an object is a hat is to assign it to a class. To recognize Arthur's hat is to recognize an individual object. The class of all hats contains Arthur's hat as a member.

Classes of individual objects can be created in many different ways; putting things into their proper niches in a cognitive filing system is one of the most common of human activities. In general terms, a well-defined class exists if there is a *test* for inclusion. When the test is passed, the object under scrutiny is admitted to the class; when the test is failed, the object is rejected. The simplest tests involve a single perceptual attribute. For example, given normal color vision, we can create the class of blue objects by simply looking at them or, in special cases, comparing them side by side with samples known to be blue. But complicated tests involving many attributes are also useful.

The clearest way to conceive of the psychological processes of recognition and identification is in terms of such tests. One can imagine that the sensory input is matched, simultaneously and successively, against many remembered images or schemata. When the present input and the stored simulacrum match, the test is passed, and the object is included in the class of all objects that meet the test. The analysis of classes is more a task for logic than for psychology; many subtle and difficult problems are involved. Yet the psychologist cannot abdicate completely, for classification is too pervasive a psychological operation. As William James remarked, "Every new experience must be disposed of under *some* old head. The great point is to find the head which has to be least altered to take it in."

Experiments can be done to see how people learn the appropriate tests that determine class membership. One can, for instance, take a set of geometric shapes varying in several aspects—size, contour, color—and define a new concept in terms of a simple subset of the shapes. Figure 12.1 is an example. The geometric figures are shown to a subject one at a time; he is told about each one whether or not it is, say, a member of the "droomy" subset. Typically there is a period, after he has seen a few examples, when he is able to recognize the

---

FIGURE 12.1

> These nonsense figures—with a nonsense name—might be used to study how people discover the attributes that define a class of objects. Given enough instances and counterinstances, people can eventually say that "terrachos" have large surrounds and unfilled centers: the shapes and the locations of the centers are not relevant.

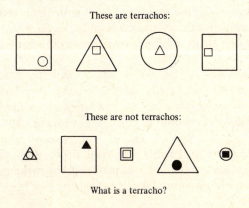

These are terrachos:

These are not terrachos:

What is a terracho?

droomy figures, but he cannot give any explicit verbal rules for what he is doing. If he persists in his effort to formulate a definition, he will eventually be able to say, "All the large green ones are droomy." In ordinary affairs, however, we are often content to leave the definition tacit.[1]

A most important class of objects is the class of all the things one has seen before, the class of familiar things. Psychologists have studied this class with special care. A person is shown a set of objects— geometric figures, for example—and then the ones he has seen before are mixed in with a large number of similar objects that he has not seen. His task is to identify the familiar ones. If the strange objects are very close in appearance to ahe familiar objects, the subjects may do poorly. Usually the best condition for experimentation is at an inter- mediate level of difficulty; the investigator selects objects strange enough to induce mistakes in identification, but not so indistinguish- able from the prototype as to produce utter confusion. One learns little about the way the subject is performing if he is always right, or if he responds entirely at random.

People are characteristically able to recognize a figure as famil- iar even though they have forgotten it—forgotten it in the sense that they would not have been able to name or draw it if they had been asked to recall or reproduce all the figures they had been shown. Thus, *recognition* is generally considered to be an easier test of memory than either *recall* or *reproduction*.

An almost universal reaction to the task of remembering figures is to give them descriptive names. The figure will be called "the large green triangle," and it is often difficult to tell whether it is the percep- tion, the description, or both that a subject remembers. Even with nonsense figures he will search for verbal descriptions: "square with one of its sides gone" or "Z backwards" and so forth. These verbal tags may either aid or interfere with recall and reproduction of the figure, but they seem to have relatively little effect upon recognition.[2] In Figure 12.2, for example, if a person describes the left figure as a picture frame, he will draw what he sees differently than if he merely describes it as two carpenter's squares placed together. His ability to recognize it when he sees it again, however, may be little affected by the way he described it.[3]

If a subject's task is not deliberately made difficult by forcing him to recognize nonsense figures briefly seen when they are hidden among many similar nonsense figures, but instead he is given familiar objects or pictures, we find that people have a truly amazing capacity to create and remember a rather special class of objects-seen-recently. Colored pictures clipped from magazines and mail order catalogues, when pasted on cards, provide a suitable set of materials for making the test. Show a person several hundred of them at a regular but leisurely

FIGURE 12.2

What we remember may depend on what we call it.

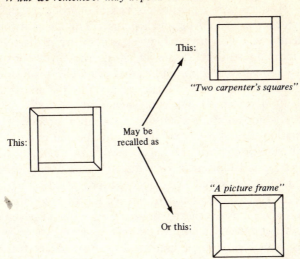

This:

"Two carpenter's squares"

This: May be recalled as

"A picture frame"

Or this:

rate, asking him to name each one as he sees it. Then select, say, twenty of those he has seen and mix them haphazardly with another set of twenty pictures that he has not seen. The subject's task is to sort them into two piles, those he has already seen and those that are new. He will make almost no errors.[4] Apparently, people have a remarkable capacity for keeping a set of visual impressions alive and accessible. An informal way to demonstrate this fact to yourself is to purchase two similar magazines from a newsstand, thumb idly through the pages of one, then the other, and ask yourself how many of the advertisements in the second magazine were also in the first. You will find that you make almost no mistakes. Observations such as these make some psychologists feel that storing things away in memory must be very simple and easy; the major source of errors and failures must lie in the processes of retrieval.

One of the most difficult problems facing judges and court officers in criminal trials is the problem of eye-witness identification. A person who witnesses an alleged crime views the situation under conditions that act to subvert his later attempt to recall events. Often his glimpse of the incident was brief; he may have been surprised, which rules out the positive effects of expectancy on recognition; the lighting may have been poor; he may have reacted with understandable anxiety or stress; and finally the interval from the incident to the trial may be months or years. It is at this time that lawyers ask that fateful question: "Do you see that woman anywhere in this courtroom?" With the exception of trickery of the sort employed by Perry Mason, it is no surprise that the witness rarely fails to identify the accused, who is sitting in the accustomed place for the defendant. Of course, if the witness were asked to draw a picture or even to describe the person in detail, his performance would be much poorer. This phenomenon has often been demonstrated in psychology classrooms by professors who stage an incident: a student rushes in, steals the professor's notes, throws a glass of water at him, and rushes out. The professor then passes out questionnaires asking students to describe the assailant. The results are usually quite varied, but seldom accurate.

Memory is not the only place that recognition processes can go astray. Expectations can also mislead us; the unexpected is always hard to perceive clearly. Sometimes we fail to recognize an object because we did not get a good look at it, or we saw it under conditions that camouflaged it, or it appeared in an incongruous place at a time we least expected it. It may even happen that we fail to recognize a perfectly common and familiar object whose name we would never otherwise forget, when it appears in an alien context.

Suppose a tachistoscope is used to display an object for a very brief period of time, so brief that the watcher fails to recognize it. Start with a very short exposure time, in which the watcher sees almost nothing, and then lengthen the time on successive exposures until he finally recognizes the object. Tachistoscopic exposures can force the person to make mistakes, and from his mistakes one can infer some of the factors that operate to determine his responses. And from the duration of exposure required for veridical perception of the object the difficulty of the recognition task can be inferred.

Now, suppose playing cards are shown in the tachistoscope. The experimenter measures how long a person must see an ordinary card to identify it correctly. Then, without warning, an unusual card is slipped in, say, a *red five of clubs*. The exposure duration becomes longer and longer until finally, at a very long exposure duration, the person realizes what it is. When he does recognize it, there is apt to be a strong emotional response, swearing, expressions of amazement, accusations that the experimenter has changed the card, and so on. Someone who had identified it as, say, an ordinary five of clubs when the exposure was quite short will stick with this identification as the successive exposures get longer and longer. He is set to see a black five of clubs; he persists in seeing what he expects to see long after he should recognize it for what it really is. He is trapped and misled by his own expectations.[5]

It is not difficult to trick and mislead people in various ways, but the real purpose of such experiments is to demonstrate that people have very definite expectations about what is going to happen. In most situations our expectations work excellently and save us a tremendous amount of time and effort. For example, suppose the objects being presented are monosyllabic English words. A listener who knows in advance that the word he will hear must be one of two particular words will be able to recognize it correctly at very faint intensities. The same listener, however, when told that the word will be one of a group of one thousand alternative words, will be completely unable to recognize the word correctly at this same intensity level.[6] The physical stimulation to which he is exposed is the same in both cases; the only difference is what he expects. What he can recognize clearly when it is one of two possibilities is completely obscured when it is one of a thousand. It is not enough therefore to state the physical magnitude of the acoustic waves; if we wish to predict whether a person will recognize the word accurately, we must also specify what it is that he *expects* to hear. This problem is similar to the signal detection situation (discussed in Chapter 7) where we must know the operating characteristics of the observer.

The size of the set of alternative objects (or, equivalently, the probabilities of the alternative objects) that are exposed is, therefore, an important attribute of a recognition task. What will be recognized depends on what might have been, as well as what actually is. The number of alternatives that any system can handle is, in general, a basic measure of the *information capacity* of the system.[7] This measure was applied first to machines and later adopted by psychologists to describe people. It was developed for communication engineering. A communication system must be designed to transmit a variety of different messages. The larger the number of alternative messages that it can transmit in a given interval of time, the larger the information capacity of the system and the more expensive it will be to build and maintain.

In the simplest examples, if a system can handle N alternative signals in one unit of time, it can handle $N \times N = N^2$ in two units of time, N^3 in three units of time, and, generally, N^m alternatives in m units of time. One feels intuitively that a measure of the total amount of information transmitted by the channel should increase linearly as a function of the time. Whereas N^m (the number of alternative messages) increases exponentially as m (the length of the message), the logarithm increases linearly. Therefore, it is convenient to use the logarithm of the number of alternatives as the measure of amount of information per unit time. In m units of time, the channel could transmit $\log N^m = m \log N$ units of information. If logarithms are taken to the base two, the unit of measurement is the *bit*. When it is said that the capacity of a communication channel is H bits per second, this means that it is capable of transmitting any one of 2^H alternative messages every second. This unit for measuring information is universally used by engineers who work with communication and computing systems.

It is possible to ask a person to serve as a communication

channel and to study how many alternative messages—how many bits of information—he can transmit.[8] The input to the channel then consists of the objects that the experimenter presents; the output is the subject's response when he identifies the objects. The better the correlation between the input and the output, the more information the subject transmits. This application of information theory to the test is somewhat irregular, since one usually imagines persons sitting at either end of the system—source and destination—with the electronic equipment between them. In the psychological laboratory, however, the stimulating and recording equipment are at either end, with a person serving as the channel between them. Logically, however, the mathematics that describes the former can also describe the latter situation.

Estimates of the largest amounts of information an average person can transmit per unit time, run around 25 to 35 bits per second.[9] In an absolute sense 2^{30} is a very large number, and we can feel proud of ourselves for doing so well. But when we remember that telephone and radio channels send tens of thousands of bits per second and that the capacity of television channels runs into the millions, we begin to suspect that man evolved under pressures other than acting as a communication channel.

The information-processing bottleneck in a human being may mean simply that he is not able to respond fast enough to report all the information that his receptors are taking in. One can test this possibility by presenting a single object to be recognized, drawn from a large set of alternative objects, then giving the subject all the time he needs to report as accurately as he can what it is that he saw. When this experiment is done, the amount of information he can process is still sharply limited; the exact amount transmitted, however, depends upon the way the various alternatives are presented.

If the alternative stimuli are all exactly the same except for differences in a single sensory aspect—size, brightness, and the like—the subject will have a difficult time recognizing which stimulus he is looking at. When a single aspect is varied, therefore, a subject typically gives back about 3 bits of information, that is, he can distinguish without error which of $2^3 = 8$ different values is being presented. If he is asked to distinguish between more than eight values, he will try, but he will make enough mistakes so that the net result will still be, effectively, eight distinguishable values. This limit is not specific for visual recognition; similar informational capacities characterize other sense modalities, if the stimuli to be identified differ in only a single aspect. Apparently we have encountered a rather general bottleneck in human information processing capacity.[10]

Clearly there is a discrepancy. It is known that a person can recognize which of many thousands of different pictures he has seen before; in this circumstance he is certainly not limited to seven or eight alternatives. How can these apparently contradictory observations be reconciled?

A person is limited, as has been noted, in his ability to recognize objects that differ from one another with respect to a single aspect. The pictures that he can recognize so easily, however, differ from one another in many aspects. Here perhaps is the source of the discrepancy. If so, it can be studied quite simply by adding more aspects, one at a time, to distinguish the objects the subject must identify.

For example, if the subject is asked to identify simple tones, it turns out that he can reliably distinguish among about four different loudnesses when the intensity is varied, or he can reliably distinguish among about five different pitches when the frequency of vibration is varied. But suppose one varies both aspects at once, intensity and frequency. We might expect to find that the four loudnesses could still be distinguished at each of the five pitches, which means $4 \times 5 = 20$ recognizably different auditory objects. This would be a significant increase in recognition ability—an improvement due directly to the introduction of additional aspects to distinguish the stimuli. In fact, however, the gain is not quite as great as it might theoretically be; instead of twenty there are only ten or twelve recognizable tones when two aspects are varied. In other words, when the subject has to judge two aspects at once, he may not do quite as well on either of them as he could if he judged them separately; nevertheless, the number of recognizably different objects is increased.

The same thing happens if one adds a third and a fourth aspect with respect to which the objects can differ. The amount of information contained in the subject's responses goes up, but not as rapidly as it might. By the time one gets to objects that differ with respect to half a dozen aspects, the accuracy of judgment drops for each separate aspect to just about the equivalent of a binary choice. Thus, when pitch is all that a person must judge, he may be able to recognize any one of five or six different values; but when he must judge variations in half a dozen aspects simultaneously, he may be able to recognize only one of two pitches, either high or low. Nevertheless, with six of these binary decisions the person is able to distinguish $2^6 = 64$ different objects, a tenfold improvement over his performance for variations in a single aspect.[11]

If we examine the information transmission rate of some performers, for example, piano players, it becomes clear that an enormous amount of information is being sent in complex units which do not require active, conscious organization of bits at the time. The piano player who plays chords or strings of chords is using a process that information theorist refer to as *chunking*.

These studies of our ability to recognize and identify auditory objects are not completely academic. They relate quite intimately to the way we communicate with one another. In our natural speech we generate phonemes that differ from one another with respect to at least nine or ten aspects—some linguists call them distinctive features—and the differences are usually binary or, at most, ternary. Thus, for example, in English there is a binary distinction between vowels and consonants. Among the consonants a binary distinction exists between stops and continuants. Among the stop consonants we have a binary distinction between voiced and voiceless. Among the voiced stop consonants, a ternary distinction between front, middle, and back. And so we eventually come to /b/, the initial phoneme in the word "boy," which is a front voiced stop consonant. All the other phonemes, of which English has about thirty or forty, can be classified in a similar manner. When we recognize one of these acoustic objects, therefore, it means that we have made several rough, binary decisions about the nine or ten distinctive features involved in the system of English phonemes.

Considerations such as these suggest that our perceptual equipment is designed to make many measurements simultaneously, but to do a fairly crude job on each one. This contrasts with the kind of scientific measuring equipment that measures one thing at a time, but measures it with great precision. The complementarity is scarcely surprising—scientists develop their measuring devices in order to study things that are not immediately obvious to ordinary observation. Meters must make the discriminations that the unaided senses cannot.

It also seems reasonable that higher organisms should be open to a wide variety of events. If a compromise is necessary, it seems far wiser to make rough decisions about everything than to make very acute distinctions as to a few aspects while ignoring completely the information provided by others. We do have some ability to trade breadth for accuracy, of course. This trading relation is a part of the subjective phenomenon called attention.

Psychological measurements of information demonstrate that there is an enormous reduction in the amount of information when it passes through a human nervous system. A television channel sends us millions of bits of information in picture and sound, yet all we can take in is a fraction of a fraction of 1 percent. There is a tremendous opportunity for selection by the perceiver of the information that he needs. This selection is not, of course, random or fortuitous. What information the viewer gets from all the dancing dots of lights on his picture tube will be determined by the way his perceptual mechanisms work. For example, the gestalt principles underlying the formation and segregation of wholes in the visual field can, when applied to this situation, be regarded as principles whereby the vast flood of transmitted information is reduced to the few drops of psychological information that a person can absorb. Suppose we reconsider some of the gestalt factors with this in mind.

The first thing to note about a television picture is that much of the information in it is highly redundant. A man stands, for example, near the center of the screen and talks to us. The background is completely stationary for many seconds. Successive frames of the picture are almost completely identical with preceding frames. One wonders why it should be necessary to send a picture of the same background over and over, frame after frame. Why not send it once and forget it until something happens to justify change? Or, if a contour is approximately straight, why not simply transmit a straight line, which can be represented by its two end points, thus dispensing with the necessity of transmitting the information along the contour. The economy of rectilinear contours is illustrated in Figure 12.3.

Such economical systems are conceivable, but it would take a great deal more information-processing in the television transmitter and in the home receiver than is presently necessary. It seems simpler to send tremendous quantities of redundant information than to do the elaborate processing that would be required to remove the redundancy.

One modern example of how redundancy can get in the way of recognition was an investigation of a curious star by astronomers at the Lick Observatory. Working on a hunch, the researchers made television tapes and played them back in slow motion. What emerged was two pulsar stars whose combined alternate pulsing had exceeded the normal flicker rate at which an image appears to be fused to the human observer; thus one star became two pulsars.

FIGURE 12.3

> The contours of a sleeping cat are efficiently preserved by a few points with straight lines between them. When a contour is relatively straight, the information it conveys is predictable and redundant. The most important information required to identify such a visual object is associated with the points where its contour changes direction. (From F. Attneave, "Some Informational Aspects of Visual Perception," Psychological Review 61 (1954): 183–193.)

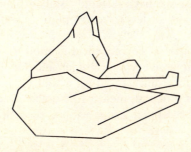

But suppose we now imagine the gestalt laws to be descriptions of how we take advantage of this redundancy when we look at the picture. For a simplified example, imagine that the spatial distribution of a set of points has to be described in such a manner that the description can be transmitted and the points placed in their correct positions at the receiving station. If the points are located in clusters, it may be more efficient to transmit first the location of a cluster and then the position of the points in that cluster.[12] Within any one cluster the number of alternative positions the points could occupy is less than the number of alternative positions they might occupy within the total display; hence, the amount of information transmitted could be reduced. But notice the principle whereby the economy was achieved: the points had to be grouped on the basis of proximity. And proximity is one of the gestalt factors.

Take another example. If some of the points are one shape and some another, it will be efficient to transmit first the positions of all points of one shape, then the positions of all the points of the other shape. In that way it is not necessary to send the shape description along with the location of every point; the shape description is sent just once for an entire group. But notice the gestalt principle involved: grouping by similarity.

From this point of view, gestalt factors describe the ways we eliminate redundant information, the ways we encode visual information more efficiently. In short, they simplify our cognitive bookkeeping. The kaleidoscopic flux of our experience is laced through with the correlations we call objects, and it is the task of our perceptual system to discover and identify the correlations, dependencies, and redundancies that signal an object's appearance. In the process of accomplishing this task it seems that the amount of information we are able to handle must be quite small. Because we are limited, the small amount of information that we can handle must be carefully refined to represent just those aspects that are significant for guiding our behavior.

A television set may process millions of bits of information per second, but is it not capable of *recognizing* anything. Before a television system could decide between third base and a package of cigarettes, it would need to be a great deal more complicated than it is. It would, in fact, need exactly what we have—a highly skilled brain for processing sensory information in order to extract the significant features.

The effect of personal values on correct identification has been investigated in a number of imaginative ways. Bruner and Goodman gave 10-year-old children the opportunity to adjust a spot of light to estimate the size of coins such as a penny, nickel, half-dollar. Demonstrating a phenomenon called perceptual accentuation, the children overestimated coin size as the value of the coin increased. A later study with relatively wealthy and relatively poor children showed that the poor children overestimated coin size more than the rich—a product of either placing more value on the coins or unfamiliarity with coins. One investigator, following this line of research, has shown that children's drawings of witches increase in size as the date for Halloween approaches, relating this phenomenon to increasing fear.

One of the most controversial set of findings in this area was reported by McGinnies who presented brief exposures of neutral and so-called taboo words (bitch, penis, etc.); observers needed much longer exposures to identify the taboo words than the neutral words. The results were explained at first in terms of a theory of *perceptual defense* which hypothesizes a brain mechanism that blocks recognition of emotionally threatening stimuli, filtering the words, but not allowing certain stimuli to pass up to higher levels of awareness. Supporting this interpretation were findings from a number of experiments in which emotional indices of anxiety (such as the electrodermal response) were much higher when taboo words were presented than when neutral words were presented.

A more prosaic explanation was offered by those who theorized that people don't recognize the taboo words because of their unfamiliarity with the words, which have a lower frequency of occurrence in printed media. This so-called *response-bias* effect could also be operating if the person recognized the taboo word and was too embarrassed or fearful of error to report it to the experimenter. Support for this latter interpretation comes from experiments in which the person is tested for recall of the words he originally learned to identify. Neutral words seem to follow the usual rules for memorization—people forget the words. The taboo words, on the other hand, tend to be recalled with increasing frequency in subsequent tests. Presumably, the person may become more at ease with the experimenter and be ready to admit to his knowledge of "dirty" words. But, since thousands of studies have been performed in an attempt to solve this controversy, we expect that no real agreement will be reached, since the limits of scientific probing of the person may have been reached. The uncertainty principle appears to be operating, since in order to learn whether the person is aware of the hard to identify words, we must ask him—a process that itself may make him aware. Generally, we would take the person's word for telling what he sees, but if perceptual defense is operating, we may expect that he would deny it. Or he might be ashamed to admit it. Or . . . ?

If the world around us were completely unpredictable, if what happened at one time and place had no correlation with what happened at any other time and place, we would not be able to develop our conception of a stable environment filled with solid, reliable objects. The objects provide the correlation, the redundancy, the predictability we must have before we can introduce order and structure into our conception of the world and of ourselves. In order to discover those correlations we must have sense organs and a nervous system that are constructed in certain ways not yet understood to perform certain functions now only dimly conceived. But somehow those functions must include more than a passive sensing of the input; only an active, moving, remembering organism would perform those functions in the way we do.

And we must practice. From the first day we open our eyes we must practice the skills needed to keep the world organized in space and time, the skills that extract critical information from the intricate flux of energy that activates our ever-moving receptors. Anyone who reflects upon the complexity and beauty of these processes which support all our cognitive life will surely find his wonder and amazement growing as rapidly as his knowledge and understanding.

NOTES

1. These experiments are reviewed in George Humphrey, *Thinking, An Introduction to Its Experimental Psychology* (London: Methuen, 1951), chap. 9. See also J. S. Bruner, J. J. Goodnow, and G. A. Austin, *A Study of Thinking* (New York: Wiley, 1956).
2. J. J. Gibson, "The Reproduction of Visually Perceived Forms," *Journal of Experimental Psychology* 12 (1929): 1–39.
3. W. C. H. Prentice, "Visual Recognition of Verbally Labeled Figures," *American Journal of Psychology* 57 (1954): 315–320.
4. Cf. R. N. Shepard and M. Teghtsoonian, "Retention of Information under Conditions Approaching a Steady State," *Journal of Experimental Psychology* 62 (1961): 302–309.
5. J. S. Bruner and L. Postman, "On the Perception of Incongruity: A Paradigm," *Journal of Personality* 18 (1949): 206–223.
6. Cf. G. A. Miller, G. A. Heise, and W. Lichten, "The Intelligibility of Speech As a Function of the Test Materials," *Journal of Experimental Psychology* 41 (1951): 329–335.
7. C. E. Shannon, "A Mathematical Theory of Communication," *Bell System Technical Journal* 27 (1948): 379–423.
8. Fred Attneave, *Applications of Information Theory to Psychology* (New York: Holt, 1959).
9. Henry Quastler, ed., *Information Theory in Psychology* (Glencoe, Ill.: Free Press, 1955).
10. G. A. Miller, "The Magical Number Seven, Plus or Minus Two: Some Limits on Our Capacity for Processing Information," *Psychological Review* 63 (1956): 81–97.
11. Irwin Pollack and Lawrence Ficks, "Information of Elementary Multi-

dimensional Auditory Displays," *Journal of the Acoustical Society of America* 26 (1954): 155–158.

12. Fred Attneave, "Some Informational Aspects of Visual Perception," *Psychological Review* 61 (1954): 183–193.

13. L. Postman, *History of Psychology in the Making* (New York: Knopf, 1962), see chap. 5.

THIRTEEN
Memory

She sent out for one of those short, plump little cakes called "petites madeleines," which look as though they had been moulded in the fluted scallop of a pilgrim's shell. And soon, mechanically, weary with the prospect of a depressing morrow, I raised to my lips a spoonful of the tea in which I had soaked a morsel of the cake. No sooner had the warm liquid, and the crumbs in it, touched my palate than a shudder ran through my whole body, and I stopped, intent upon the extraordinary changes that were taking place. An exquisite pleasure had invaded my senses, but individual, detached, with no suggestion of its origin.

The incident of the madeleine surrounds Marcel Proust's famous work, *Remembrance of Things Past*, as a frame surrounds a painting. Proust asks himself what this unremembered state could have been; he tastes the tea again and again, trying to stir the image, the visual memory linked to that taste. Suddenly the memory returns, a scene from his childhood, long forgotten but now vividly remembered, and with it his story begins. Seven volumes later he returns to the incident to explain its real significance.

Perhaps nowhere in literature has more talent been lavished on the description of a memory. And nowhere else can a contrast be drawn so clearly between an artistic and a scientific approach to mental events. Proust's little cake set off a psychological accident, so unique, personal, unexpected, and unexplained as to seem the complete antithesis of all we have learned to call scientific. The contrast does not concern the truth of Proust's account—one can grant that there is a sense in which it is true even though it may never have occurred. The contrast is in his method of displaying the truth.

Consider the difficulties that would face any scientist who wanted to study such mental phenomena. His first difficulty would be that he has no way to capture the thing he wishes to study. He can only sit and wait, hoping for the improbable. "There is," comments Proust, "a large element of hazard in these matters, and a second hazard, that of our own death, often prevents us from awaiting for any length of time the favors of the first." But even if he should live long enough, a scientist would still be in trouble because he would still have to contend with the privacy of his own experience. Once he has produced his specimen he must examine it alone. No one can help him, no one can verify the accuracy of his observations, no one can repeat his experiment. Indeed, no one can prove he ever had the experience he claims to remember. And, finally, the event must be described and communicated by language; how many scientists have sufficient skill to capture the subtle shades of their subjective states?

These elusive phenomena seem to be essentially unscientific. A prudent psychologist might well decide to leave such fragile flowers to Proust and his fellow artists. A scientist would do better to study the workaday memory that guides our plans, feeds our inferences, answers promptly when it is called, and stands still long enough to be measured. Proust recognized the importance of workaday memory, too, but he insisted that there was something special, something tremendously significant for the artist in the kind of memory stirred by his taste of the little cake. He seemed to warn psychologists that they ignore or deny these intimate memories at their peril, for they are closely integrated with the set of memories that we refer to as our personal identity.

There is a kind of double awareness that sometimes accompanies a vivid recollection of the past. As Proust says,

> During the instant that they last these resurrections of the past are so complete that they do not merely oblige our eyes to become oblivious to the room before them and contemplate instead the rising tide or the railway track edged with trees; they also force our nostrils to inhale the air of places which are far remote, constrain our will to choose between the various views they lay before us, compel our entire being to believe itself surrounded by them, or at least to vacillate between them and the present scenes, bewildered by an uncertainty similar to that which one sometimes experiences before an ineffable vision at the moment of losing consciousness in sleep.

Should this kind of experience be dismissed because it is so difficult to study? As Proust suggests, it is similar to a dream, a psychological phenomenon whose importance Freud has made overwhelmingly clear. In its most intense reality, such an experience is called an hallucination; it is common in cases of epilepsy, and can be produced under hypnosis. One of the most startling instances, however, was Wilder Penfield's demonstration that weak electrical stimulation of the surface of the brain, in the temporal lobes, can sometimes cause a previous experience of the person to intrude into his field of awareness. In Penfield's words,

> The "double consciousness," the going "back to all that occurred in my childhood," is an hallucination in which the patient re-experiences some period of time from his own past while still retaining his hold on the present. . . . During it a patient may hear music, for example. But, if so, he hears a single playing of the music,

orchestra, or piano, or voices; and he may be aware of himself as present in the room or hall. He may hear voices, the voices of friends or of strangers. If they seemed familiar to him during the interval of time now being recalled, they are familiar to him now. If they were strange then, they are strange now. He may see the people who were speaking and the piano being played by the man who played it then. He may, on the other hand, see things that he saw in an earlier period without being aware of sound. If he felt fright then, he feels fright now. If he felt a pleasurable admiration then, he feels it now.[1]

Apparently it is possible, under appropriate conditions, to see ourselves participating in past and present events simultaneously. The experience is surprising because the re-creation of the past is real, complete, and detailed. It is difficult to believe that we can remember so much so vividly, as though a permanent record of our stream of consciousness had been stored away somewhere. Compared with the inadequacy of the memory that serves our daily rounds, this total recall of a past episode is startlingly different. It makes us suspect that we have a great deal more brain power than we are using; one's first wish is to master this mental record and bend it to his service. Why can we not use this wonderful storage device to recall telephone numbers when we want them? Or to memorize speeches or to remember a friend's birthday? Why must complete recollection be so useless, involuntary, and unpredictable?

Penfield's observation suggests that we might be able to gain control of these personal memories if we knew more about their biological basis. Thanks to the work on the DNA molecule by Watson and his colleagues, our knowledge of the chromosomes, genes, and proteins of the human cell has increased to the point that research on the biochemical basis of the memory process has become a very big enterprise. Some researchers speculate that riboneucleic acid (RNA), the messenger chemical, is a coding agent for an organism's experiences and memories.[2] We know that brain cells have an abundance of RNA and that changes occur in RNA levels when an animal has learned a complex task. The controversial research employing the RNA hypothesis has been documented in, among other places, an irreverent periodical known as *The Worm-Runner's Digest*.[3]

The widely publicized research on learning in the flatworm (the planarian) has been prompted by the simplicity of the nervous system of the animal and its ability to regenerate a new head or tail when it has been cut in half. In some experiments worms are trained to contract at a flash of light and then they are cut in half. After regeneration the worms with new heads are retrained and are found to learn faster than untrained animals. Worms who are treated with a chemical that destroys RNA are unable to learn or remember. Further, when trained worms were fed to "cannibal" worms, the cannibals learned faster than comparable unfed worms; presumably, a function of the generalized effect of RNA changes during learning. These results have been repeated in substance by experiments in which chemicals extracted from the brains of trained rats and injected into other rats led to faster learning by the untrained rats.

Despite some newspaper stories, a "memory pill" does not appear too likely on the basis of this research. The experiments, despite their elegance, involve relatively heavy handed manipulation of variables with animals. There is also a great deal of skepticism among some scientists who have been unable to repeat the basic experiments. But the basic findings have been accepted generally, and research on the molecular basis of memory holds exciting promise for the future.

One of the limitations of the molecular approach is the fact that memory storage at the cellular level must eventually be squared with what we know about the interactions of cells across the synapses which must play an essential role in information storage. Concerning this possibility the vast neurological literature is amazingly unhelpful. It is known that considerable damage can be done to the tissues of the brain without producing any measurable impairment of memory and that particular memories do not seem to be stored in particular places. Moreover, it is known that nerve cells can be made to excite each other in cycles: neuron A excites neuron B, which in turn excites C, which may return and excite A again. But these cycles can last, at best, only a few seconds. They are not the kind of thing that might last a lifetime, that could persist through sleep and waking, through electric shocks, surgical insult, and the interference of other activity in adjacent neurons.

In the absence of evidence, therefore, the most anyone can offer is speculation. One plausible theory currently available says that when activity passes repeatedly over a particular synapse—the boundary between one neuron and the next—the resistance to conduction over that synapse is lowered. In the future, therefore, the same stimuli will be more likely to pass again over the same synapses and so will lead again to the same subjective experience and to the same objective behavior. But the theory of lowered synaptic resistance faces certain objections. A synapse is only a micron or so in size; a change at the synapse must be a change in a thin layer of protein molecules. The tissues of the body are being constantly renewed and rebuilt; it is hard to believe that delicate adjustments of synaptic resistance could long survive the processes of metabolism.

The famous psychologist and neurologist Karl Lashley spent more than thirty years in search of the engram, the permanent impression that experience is supposed to leave somewhere in the nervous system.[4] He began with a widely shared impression that the engram must be a path through the brain that connects sensory organs to muscles and glands—the memory of each particular sensory-motor association would be represented by an anatomically distinct path through the brain. Lashley tried to study these hypothetical paths by interrupting them surgically at different places in the brain. Human beings are naturally reluctant to serve as subjects in such experiments; Lashley practiced his brain surgery on lower animals. He began with rats, but the results were so surprising that he repeated his studies later with monkeys and chimpanzees. He trained his animals in various tasks ranging in difficulty from simple sensory-motor associations to the solution of difficult sequential problems. Then he cut, destroyed, or removed a portion of the animal's brain. After recovery from the operation, he tested the animal's memory for what it had learned.

Lashley experimented on all parts of the brain. He placed his lesions in the part of the brain that controls motor performance and so managed to produce paralysis, but he did not destroy the engram. He took out large amounts of tissue from the so-called association areas, but memory was not impaired. He cut all the connections between the sensory and the motor areas of the brain, but again the engram remained intact. A brain operation can affect an animal's behavior in many ways, but it does not seem possible to destroy particular memories by injuring the brain in particular places. The best he could do was to show a gross correlation between the total amount of brain tissue destroyed and a general impairment in the animal's performance. But *where* the tissue was destroyed was relatively unimportant. In summarizing his work Lashley said, "This series of experiments has yielded a good bit of information about what and where the memory trace is not. It has discovered nothing directly of the real nature of the engram." And then he added, wistfully, "I sometimes feel, in reviewing the evidence on the localization of the memory trace, that the necessary conclusion is that learning just is not possible."

Not all workers in this corner of psychology are as discouraged about the possibilities as Lashley was, but his experiments do seem to have ruled out most of the simpler explanations which might be proposed as a biological basis of personal memory. Either large parts of the brain work together in complex patterns during recall, or memories are multiply represented in several different regions of the cortex, or individual neurons may be capable of far more precise differentiations than are now understood, or biochemical processes of still unspecified nature take place somewhere scientists have not yet thought to look. But perhaps the simplest way to summarize the situation is to admit with Lashley that we know almost nothing at all about the underlying processes whereby the nervous system stores and maintains such large quantities of relatively precise information.

If we cannot evoke memories when we want to study them, if

we are completely ignorant of the place and nature of the biophysical processes that support them, what is left for a psychologist to study? Does this mean that we cannot proceed with our psychological studies? Not at all. Research into human memory is one of the oldest and most active branches of experimental psychology.[5]

By sheer chance Proust tasted his madeleine and so revived a system of memories long since abandoned. An electric current happened to release an otherwise inaccessible pattern of neural activity. It is as if the memory had continued to hold a full record of things past, but had become isolated. It was not so much forgotten as misplaced, until by a lucky accident a part of the memory system was pulled into consciousness and the rest trailed after.

Perhaps the difficulties we have in remembering things are not concerned so much with getting them into our memories as with getting them back out again later. In this respect our personal memory would seem to confirm a simple relation that usually holds for other storage systems, namely, retrieval is more difficult than storage. If one thinks of memory as a place where things can be stored, one should expect retrieval to be the major problem. It is simple to put documents into a filing case, furniture into a warehouse, information into a notebook, articles into a scientific journal, or books into a library. If we never expect to see the things again, it is easy enough to dump them like junk into a junk box. The problem appears only later when we try to find them.

When we organize a storage place according to rules and make records of where everything went, we are attempting by a little effort now to forestall an enormous effort later, when the time comes to retrieve something. Because this organizing and record-keeping must go on at the same time the thing is being stored, we seem to have trouble getting it into storage. When we are unable to remember something that happened to us, it may be either because we did not store it carefully, or because it has disappeared from where we put it, or because we have lost the records of where it went. Thinking of memory in terms of these analogies to other storage problems may make the process seem overly concrete, but it helps us to understand many of the characteristics of learning and forgetting.

When one takes the time and trouble to anticipate the retrieval problem, one passes out of the domain of accidental but often vivid recollections and into the world of workaday memory—a kind of memory that is less dramatic, but considerably more reliable.

How does our workaday memory function? Ordinarily we do not take our experience neat, but work it over before we try to store it away. Vivid, detailed, photographic resurrection of the past is not the most efficient way to remember. Everyday remembering is more like a syllogism than a photograph: we usually follow a sequence of steps to the past; only rarely do we conjure it up in an instantaneous panorama. An adult uses symbols—usually verbal symbols—to organize his memory so that he can find what he wants in it. We constantly translate our experience into symbols, store them in our memory, and retrieve the symbols instead of the experience itself. When the time comes for recall, we try to reconstruct the experience from the remembered symbols.

Frequently, what we store away so painfully in our workaday memory is a rule that will enable us later to construct, or to reconstruct, what we want to know. To illustrate the efficiency of these rules, consider a highly oversimplified way to test your memory. Imagine you are a subject in a psychological experiment. The experimenter says, "I am going to give you some numbers. For each one I say to you, say a number back to me. Use any numbers you like. Only please be consistent. Whenever I give you the same number again, give me back the number you said before. Is that clear?"

"No."

"I will give you a number, for example, 73. Then you give me a number, for instance, 528, or whatever you like. But I want you to remember what you say so that if I ever give you 73 again, you will give me 528 again."

With a task like this you would never give the experimenter 528 as a response to 73. It is far better to pick some simple number, such as 1. Make that your reply to everything, thereby lightening the load on your memory tremendously. You may expect the psychologist to complain.

"Look," he may say, "I want to test your memory. This is no test at all. You must give me a different number every time I give you a different number."

Humor him. Take his number and repeat it. You will still be able to remember your number every time. Moreover, you will be able to remember his number if he gives you yours. Or, if he still is not satisfied, construct your reply by adding a constant to his number. In either case, the situation is completely under control and you can handle an immense variety of stimuli without a single error. You do it by remembering a rule rather than by remembering what you actually said. If you tried to remember literally everything he said and every haphazard reply you made, the task would be overwhelmingly difficult.

If this example seems too artificial, then perhaps it can be transmuted into something more interesting by a series of easy steps. Suppose the psychologist utters not numbers, but words, and asks you for different words in reply. Again, you should adopt a rule. One of the simplest would be always to give the opposite of his word. If he says, "White," you say, "Black." If he says, "Boy," you reply, "Girl." To be sure, this rule will not always work. If he says, "Book," or "Chicago," you are stuck. Thus you may need an additional rule to the effect that when there is no opposite, you will use the commonest associate you can think of, or you will give a word that rhymes, and so on. Unlike the rules in the numerical example, the rule for words is not infallible. But it works far better than if you tried to remember each word-pair separately. You can probably give several hundred such replies and remember them with less than 5 percent error. And the beauty of it is that you merely make use of what you have already learned in order to avoid having to learn something new.

Suppose you did not do it this way. Suppose instead, you had a sound recorder in your head and could at any moment listen to every word you and the psychologist had said to each other. Even suppose you could turn the recorder on or off at will. And suppose you had no rule for giving replies, but gave them haphazardly because you relied upon this remarkable recording device. Then each time the psychologist said a new word to you, you would start your recorder playing at the beginning and listen to see if you had ever been given that word before, and, if so, what you had replied. The more words he gave, the longer it would take you to play the record through, and the slower your response would become. You would be quickly overloaded; you would remember so much that you could never find what you wanted when you needed it. Soon you would be almost as poorly off as if you remembered nothing. A verbatim recording of the stream of consciousness may indeed be preserved in the brain somewhere, but it is of very little use to us for most of the memory tasks we must constantly perform.

The truth is, your psychologist was too lenient. His tests left you free to choose replies according to your own strategy. He could make it much more difficult if he also told you what you were supposed to say in reply to his stimulus words. When he determines both members of the pair, it may take work to find a mnemonic rule. But your general strategy should be something like this. Look for a third word or image such that his stimulus word suggests it easily, and such that it in turn suggests the response you are supposed to give. For example he might give you the pair "Sugar-Lame." You must remember it well enough to be able, when he tests you later by saying, "Sugar," to reply, "Lame." If you discover the word "cane," it can serve as a mediator: "Sugar-cane" and "cane-Lame" are familiar associations that you have already learned before the experiment began. Given a good mediating word, therefore, you can perform the task easily. Very little of the time you would spend memorizing pairs of words would ordinarily go to engrave new associations into your brain tissue; most of it would be spent searching for some familiar association that satisfies a simple rule.

209

It should be remarked, incidentally, that it is not sufficient merely to know a mediator unless you actively think of it. The active arousal of the mediator seems to be an indispensable part of the process.

The usefulness of images and words to establish connections among apparently unrelated concepts is well known to authors of popular texts on *How to Improve Your Memory*, but it has not been studied extensively in the psychological laboratory. However, the effectiveness of this simple principle can be demonstrated in the following way.[6] A list of word pairs is presented, one pair at a time. For each pair the subject forms a clear visual image, the more bizarre the better. Ordinarily a person will spend about twenty-five seconds finding a satisfactory image and forming the association, but after some experience he can work accurately with about five seconds per pair. The list is not repeated. At the end of the presentation the subject is given one member of each pair and is asked to write down the other. In one study, lists of up to five hundred pairs were remembered about 99 percent correctly.

These examples indicate how useful rules and strategies can be to a person trying to remember something, and how they can have advantages not shared by a literal, photo-phono-graphic record. That is not to say that eidetic imagery—the so-called photographic mind—is not an extremely useful gift to have.[7] Rather, the point is that ordinary people can do extraordinarily well if they are permitted to use meaningful words and images as mediators. For some situations it is actually more efficient to remember a rule to generate X than to remember X itself.

If all this testing and searching and rule-making is supposed to go on while we are depositing new information in our memory bank, it seems likely that we must have at least two different kinds of storage. One, a long-term memory system; the other, a temporary memory that can hold information for a few seconds while we do whatever rehearsing or information-processing is necessary to transfer it into the long-term store. This model is derived from analogy to the computer.

One can isolate the temporary memory system and study its properties independently simply by crippling the rehearsal needed for making the transfer. Give a person three consonants—CHS or MXB, for instance—and then immediately have him count backwards by threes until you are ready to test his recall. The counting breaks up his normal processes of transfer from temporary to more permanent memory, so that twenty seconds later the string of consonants, which would ordinarily be perfectly recalled, is forgotten more than 90 percent of the time.[8] A curve showing the temporal course of this very rapid fading is plotted in Figure 13.1. If we do not process the information within a few seconds, it is lost.

210

FIGURE 13.1

When rehearsal is prevented, information drops very rapidly out of temporary memory. Subjects could not remember three consonants for more than a few seconds when they had to count backwards during the interval between the presentation and the test of recall.

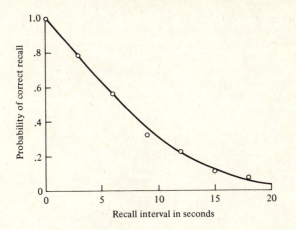

We are dealing here with a model of the memory system that is presumed by subjective behaviorists to be a functional description of what takes place in the brain. A representation of this hypothesized system can be seen in Figure 13.2, a scheme that a traditional behaviorist might find overly elaborate and not directly observable. Research on information processing models is a lively area with much disagreement among researchers over the fundamental findings. Even the basic findings on short-term memory have been challenged by Reitman on the basis of an experiment in which she used a signal detection task to try to "break" short-term memory by preventing rehearsal. In this experiment there was no noticeable forgetting; contrary to the usual finding Ms. Reitman concluded that forgetting is caused by entry into short-term storage of other similar information.[9]

The temporary (short-term or immediate) memory system seems to operate much the same way as sensory channels discussed in Chapter 5. Tests of temporary memory, such as a digit span test, require the person to listen to a string of numbers uttered once every second, after which he is asked to reproduce the series. Like the limitations on channel capacity described earlier, most people are able to reproduce only five to nine digits unless they are given the chance to rehearse or to employ mnemonic devices. The reaction of many citizens to the all digit dialing system for telephones (necessitated by an overload in the phone system) has often been the memorization of funny or meaningful letter sequences derived from decoding the numbers into some of the letters on the dial. In the San Francisco Bay

FIGURE 13.2

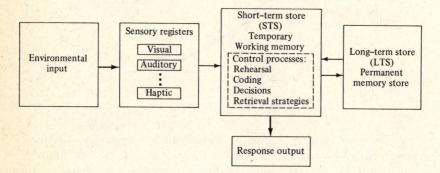

area, for example, one can dial for the exact time by dialing
POPCORN (in New York City you dial NERVOUS).

Perhaps the most compelling evidence for the existence of a
temporary memory system lies in the fact that short-term memory
appears to diminish markedly as a function of aging and senility,
becomes impaired by various diseases that seem to have no effect on
long-term memory, and seems to be affected by the use of intoxicants
such as alcohol or marihuana. Like the buffer storage mechanism
common to computers, the temporary memory system can be cleared
rapidly when attention shifts or when the topic is changed.

This rapid fading is important for many things we do. For
example, when we add a column of figures we must keep a subtotal in
mind just long enough to add a new number to it, then forget it. If the
memory of each subtotal did not fade, we would accumulate a great
deal of useless and distracting information. Similarly, the fading protects us from remembering all the apparent nonsense that goes on
while we are dreaming. It is possible, of course, to train oneself to
remember dreams; one learns to rehearse them immediately on awakening. And some dreams are so important to us that we wake up spontaneously thinking about them. But most of the time dreams are
forgotten because we cannot perform the necessary processes required

to fix them more permanently. Our ability to decide what we will try to remember and what we will permit to fade is one of our most powerful tools for selecting a personal world out of what William James called "the primordial chaos of sensation."

The particular associations that people exploit when they try to fix a memory permanently are apt to be somewhat personal and idiosyncratic, but the general strategy they follow is fairly clear. New experience is categorized in terms of familiar concepts shared by the culture and symbolized by the language; then the symbolically transformed experience is related to, and interwoven with, other things previously learned and remembered in terms of these categories and this language. In a new situation it is sometimes difficult to know how best to exploit previous learning, but after a little thought we can usually discover a rule that transforms the novel into the familiar.

But we must not assume that all our memories are so well behaved. The very personal memory that Proust revived with the madeleine is of a different character entirely. In an interesting comparison of Proust and Freud, Ernest Schachtel has called attention to the fact that these Proustian flashes characteristically revive some childhood scene, as though a psychological barrier separated the adult from his early experience. In order to become an adult, to adopt adult habits of thought, it is necessary to forget one's childhood. According to Schachtel

> The biologically, culturally, and socially influenced process of memory organization results in the formation of categories (schemata) of memory which are not suitable vehicles to receive and reproduce experiences of the quality and intensity typical of early childhood. The world of modern Western civilization has no use for this type of experience. In fact, it cannot permit itself to have any use for it, it cannot permit the memory of it, because such memory, if universal, would explode the restrictive social order of this civilization.[10]

These intimate memories of childhood are obviously of great concern to students of personality, many of whom believe that the adult personality sets like plaster after the first few years of life. Freud particularly emphasized the social necessity of repressing childish memories of sexual pleasure, in order to enable the adult to function effectively in Western culture. But Freud's observation does not explain why all our childhood memories, sexual and asexual alike, are so thoroughly forgotten. In the course of growing up there are several cognitive revolutions that completely reorganize a child's intellectual life. As new and more efficient cognitive systems emerge, the peculiarly intense memories of a child find no place in them. The child is not forgotten; it is simply isolated from the day-to-day experience of the normal adult, because the child existed before the categories of the adult mind had been achieved.

213

An attentive reader will not have overlooked the metaphorical basis of this discussion—the assumption that memory is a place where information can be stored, just as a warehouse is a place where merchandise can be stored. This seems to make memory a substantial thing that a person possesses in the same way he possesses a head and two hands. Although the metaphor may help us to organize and understand many phenomena of memory that are psychologically significant, it is difficult to suppress a certain uneasiness about this reification of the memory process. To avoid this metaphor, many psychologists prefer to speak of memory as something a person does, rather than something he has. This attitude leads to another set of questions about the effects of past experience on present behavior.

NOTES

1. Wilder Penfield, "Functional Localization in Temporal and Deep Sylvian Areas," in *The Brain and Human Behavior* (Baltimore: Williams & Wilkins, 1958), pp. 210–226.
2. H. Hydén, "Biochemical and Molecular Aspects of Learning and Memory," *Proceedings of the American Philosophical Society* 3, no. 6 (1967): 326–342.
3. *Worm Runners Digest*, a quarterly magazine published by the Planarian Press.
4. K. S. Lashley, "In Search of the Engram," in *Society of Experimental Biology Symposium No. 4: Physiological Mechanisms in Animal Behavior* (Cambridge: Cambridge University Press, 1950), pp. 454–482.
5. I. M. L. Hunter, *Memory: Facts and Fallacies* (London: Penguin, 1957).
6. Wallace H. Wallace, Stanley H. Turner, and Cornelius C. Perkins, *Preliminary Studies of Human Information Storage*, Signal Corps Project No. 132C (Institute for Cooperative Research, Philadelphia: University of Pennsylvania, December, 1957).
7. G. W. Allport, "Eidetic Imagery," *British Journal of Psychology* 15 (1924): 99–120; H. Kluver, "Eidetic Phenomena," *Psychological Bulletin* 29 (1932): 181–203. See also R. N. Haber, "Eidetic Imagery," in *Contemporary Psychology*, ed. R. C. Atkinson (San Francisco: Freeman, 1971), pp. 224–232.
8. L. R. Peterson and M. J. Peterson, "Short-term Retention of Individual Verbal Items," *Journal of Experimental Psychology* 58 (1959): 193–198.
9. J. S. Reitman, "Mechanisms of Forgetting in Short-term Memory," *Cognitive Psychology* 2 (1971): 185–195.
10. E. G. Schachtel, "On Memory and Childhood Amnesia," in *A Study of Interpersonal Relations*, ed. F. Mullahy (New York: Grove, 1949), pp. 3–49.

FOURTEEN
Ivan Petrovich Pavlov, Physiologist

"I propose to prove," said Claude Bernard in 1865, "that the science of vital phenomena must have the same foundations as the science of the phenomena of inorganic bodies, and that there is no difference in this respect between the principles of biological science and those of physico-chemical science."[1] This is *materialism*. At the time Bernard wrote, materialism was generally considered a necessary assumption for any scientific inquiry into living systems. When you study Bernard's book carefully, however, you discover that the great French physiologist was less concerned to reduce all vital phenomena to matter and energy than to show that they are, potentially, as intelligible as the more familiar physicochemical phenomena. No divine soul or free will capriciously altered his measurements, no supernatural or inexplicable forces intervened unpredictably to spoil his experiments. Bernard fully expected to see vital phenomena reduced to materialistic terms, but this meant less to him than the broader principle that scientific methods can be successfully applied to living organisms. Vital phenomena are governed by laws—laws true always and everywhere.

The positivistic faith (that science can be applied to man and all his affairs) and the materialistic faith (that the results will be expressed as physicochemical laws) are not always kept apart; they were never closer than when Bernard wrote. In Germany, for example, the science of physiology was controlled by four men: Hermann Ludwig von Helmholtz, Emil Du Bois-Reymond, Ernst Brücke, and Carl Ludwig. These four formed a private club in Berlin whose members were pledged to destroy vitalism, a pledge that one of them phrased so: "No other forces than the common physical-chemical ones are active within the organism. In those cases which cannot at the time be explained by these forces one has either to find the specific way or form of their action by means of the physical-mathematical method or assume new forces equal in dignity to the chemicalphysical forces inherent in matter, reducible to the force of attraction and repulsion."[2]

This pledge expresses materialism in a pure form, flatly denying that life might involve vital forces transcending "the force of attraction and repulsion." It is curious to see how easily

positivism, which began in violent opposition to any metaphysical dogma whatsoever, slips over into this kind of materialism—into the metaphysical dogma that true existence is reserved exclusively for physical and chemical objects. There is no way to know in advance what kinds of laws will prove necessary as science advances, yet a materialist feels comforted to think that the new laws will always look just like the old ones.

During the last half of the nineteenth century the Helmholtz school of medicine, brandishing its materialistic credo, completely dominated physiological and medical thinking. It was into this intellectual atmosphere that scientific psychology was born.

And it was in this intellectual atmosphere that the pioneer psychologists were educated. Freud was Brücke's student; Pavlov studied under Ludwig; Wundt was Du Bois-Reymond's student and Helmholtz's assistant. With physiology reduced to chemistry and physics, the next step was to reduce psychology to physiology. In that way the students were expected to carry on the work of their teachers. Freud to the end of his life talked about the mind in hydraulic, mechanical, electrical, and physical metaphors. Pavlov would never concede that his physiological interpretation of conditioning experiments was merely an elaborate figure of speech. And even Wundt, who tried to break with the positivistic tradition, founded his new psychology by writing a text, not on psychology, but on physiological psychology.

But the students were not always loyal to their teachers. Wundt deliberately defected, disagreeing with the materialist dogma, despite the evident hard-nosed proclivities of his many students. Helmholtz slipped up in one of his academic appointments at Berlin, bringing in Carl Stumpf because the two men shared a common love for the scientific study of music. Stumpf proved later to be an important catalyst to the gestalt psychologists—Koffka, Koehler, and Wertheimer—who radically changed psychology in Germany. Freud tried to remain loyal, but supplied the revolt with powerful ammunition. Of all the pioneer psychologists the one most faithful to the materialistic standards of nineteenth century science was Pavlov, probably because he never realized that he had become a psychologist.

When materialists try to defend the idea that living systems are nothing but machines, they generally begin with the most automatic and involuntary activities they can think of. Those are the reflexes and instincts. Exactly what an instinct is has been the focus of much argument. Some people use the term to mean all the driving desires and passions of the flesh; others mean any reactions an organism is born with and so does not need to learn; and still others take the position that an instinct is any highly automatic, involuntary, sequence of responses. The importance of instincts for a materialist conception of man has waxed and waned from one generation to the next. The reflex, however, has played a more constant role.

A reflex is an involuntary, unlearned, predictable response to a given stimulus (or class of stimuli), a response that is not influenced by any conscious thought or resolution, but that can usually be seen to have some clear purpose in protecting the organism or helping it to adjust to its environment. The study of reflex action has a long history.[3] Probably the first person to give a systematic discussion resembling our modern conception of the reflex was the French philosopher René Descartes. A mechanistic description of the body was a fundamental part of the Cartesian philosophy, which distinguished sharply between the mortal body, a machine, and the immortal soul that transcended space and time yet was somehow capable of controlling the material body. The automatic actions that the soul was unable to control voluntarily were what Descartes called reflexes. The seventeenth century's ideas about physiology were rather crude, however; Descartes spoke of animal spirits being reflected (hence the term reflex) into the muscles by an image in the pineal gland. Placing the soul in the pineal gland, Descartes provided a parallel model that separated mind and body, an important distinction for intellectuals who were experiencing resistance from ecclesiastical authority for daring to study human beings directly. The pineal gland was then (and to some extent still is) an organ about which little was known—an ideal location for the ever elusive soul. Finally, we should note that Decartes derived some of his ideas about animal spirits moving the muscles from the hydraulically operated statues and sprites found in the royal gardens, an early example of turning to technology to generalize to the human condition.

In the years that followed, a brilliant array of men—philosophers, physicians, natural scientists—contributed to the growing knowledge about the structure and function of the nervous system. The most significant step forward was probably the discovery, early in the nineteenth century, that the nerves attached to the spinal cord had a clear division of function. Sir Charles Bell in England and François Magendie in France were able to show that the nerves entering the back side of the spinal cord were important for sensory processes, and nerves entering the front side were important for muscular movements. Thus some of the neural pathways involved in reflex action were first revealed.

One of the most attractive figures in this story was the enthusiastic Scottish physician Marshall Hall, who had a rare gift for thinking clearly and simply in his experiments, his theories, and his writings. Hall's major argument was that reflexes are unconscious, an argument that struck at the well-established myth that all nervous activity is, or could be, conscious. Hall won his point so thoroughly that half a century later Wundt took it for granted that his new psychology could have nothing to do with reflexes. If they were unconscious, they were not accessible to introspection and so must be relegated to physiology. This convenient distinction between unconscious physiology and conscious psychology exploded, however, when Freud showed how much of our mental life is unconscious and when Pavlov adopted the reflexes as the fundamental building blocks for all behavior.

After Pavlov many psychologists, especially some American behaviorists, went to the opposite extreme from Wundt and based all psychology on reflexes. Their theories would have been nonsense, of course, if all the reflexes had to be inborn. Reflexes could not possibly play such an important role unless they could somehow be modified as the result of experience. But how can experience modify a reflex? This was the crucial question Pavlov tried to answer.

Ivan Petrovich Pavlov was born in 1849 in Ryazan, a provincial town in central Russia. He was the first of many children, most of whom died in infancy. His grandfather was a peasant and his father a priest; in nineteenth-century Russia that had a rather special meaning.

The social structure of Russia prior to the middle of the nineteenth century was exceedingly simple. There were effectively two social classes: the gentry, or aristocracy, which held all wealth and privilege, and the peasantry, which made up about 90 percent of the population. (The clergy served the peasantry and were close to them.) The Russian government was equally simple; it consisted of a military aristocracy that did little more than maintain order at home and wage war abroad. During the nineteenth century, however, a third, intermediate class, the intelligentsia, began to emerge from the educational system fostered by Alexander I. It consisted of members of the aristocracy who had fallen upon hard times and members of the peasantry whose talent and energy had lifted them above their class into an intellectual life centered around the universities. The intelligentsia was a uniquely Russian institution, a social class united solely by bonds of education and moral passion. Insofar as they filled a position intermediate between the gentry and the peasantry, the members of the intelligentsia might be compared with the middle-class bourgeoisie in the rest of Europe. But the comparison would be quite misleading. The Russian intelligentsia did not play any commercial role; its special dedication was to reform the Russian government.

As a son of a clergyman, Vanya was permitted to attend the local theological seminary, where his interest in science was encouraged, and in 1870 he was able to continue his studies at the University of St. Petersburg (now Leningrad). In that way he joined the socially intermediate class, too well-educated and too intelligent for the peas-

IVAN PETROVITCH PAVLOV

antry from which he came, but too common and too poor for the aristocracy into which he could never rise. These social conditions often produced an especially dedicated intellectual, one whose entire life was centered on the intellectual pursuits that justified his existence. And so it was with Pavlov, whose almost fanatic devotion to pure science and to experimental research was supported by the energy and simplicity of a Russian peasant. Those traits characterized the man and his work throughout his life.

In the theological seminary Pavlov was encouraged to follow his own intellectual inclinations, a freedom denied in most Russian schools at that time.[4] His early reading included Herbert Spencer, who became one of his favorite authors, and Charles Darwin, whose teachings and personality he idolized to the end of his days. While still a boy of fifteen he read a Russian translation of George Henry Lewes's *Physiology of Common Life* and became intrigued with a complicated drawing of the digestive system that Lewes had reproduced from Claude Bernard. Pavlov's interest in the physiology of digestion, which culminated in a Nobel prize forty years later, began when he looked at Bernard's drawing and asked himself how such a complicated system could work.

At the University of St. Petersburg the teacher who influenced him most was Ilya Cyon, the professor of physiology. Cyon was an artistic experimenter with exceptional skill in surgery; he wrote a first-rate text on experimental techniques in physiology; his lectures were both masterful and inspiring. "Never can such a teacher be forgotten," said Pavlov. It was Cyon who started Pavlov, then still an undergraduate, on his first physiological experiment. Upon graduation Pavlov was to have become a research assistant, but when Cyon was dismissed for political reasons, Pavlov resigned in protest.

Pavlov's determination to become an experimental physiologist seems never to have wavered. After one taste of research all the practical issues—his position, salary, living conditions, even the clothes he wore—became little more than unavoidable annoyances intruding upon the only part of life that really mattered. In the early years his single-mindedness protected him from the anxieties of poverty; later it protected him from the distractions of fame and administrative responsibility.

In 1881 he married Seraphima Karchevskaya, who devoted her life to protecting him from all mundane intrusions. She discovered her responsibilities rather suddenly when Ivan Petrovich turned up without the money to pay for their wedding or their return fares to St. Petersburg. So she paid their expenses out of her own savings, and the two of them arrived penniless in St. Petersburg. Pavlov's entire income was fifty rubles a month, but he refused to let Sara find a job. He borrowed two hundred rubles, and somehow they managed to exist. It was characteristic of him that Sara often had to remind him when it was time to go and collect his salary.

Only unwavering faith enabled his wife and friends to put up with him. His complete inability to manage his financial affairs was not his only peculiarity: he was equally difficult in other matters. For example, he liked to take long walks with his wife, but he set such a strenuous pace that she often had to run to keep up. During her first pregnancy this exertion caused Sara to miscarry. When he realized what had happened, of course, Pavlov was greatly dismayed. During her second pregnancy, therefore, he was determined to be more careful. So he swung over to the opposite extreme and even insisted on carrying her in his arms up to their fourth-floor apartment. In every way he was the tender, thoughtful husband, but when the child was born, he had no money to support it.

He once accepted an invitation for Sara and himself to attend a party at a professor's home. She was to go alone; he would join her there as soon as he could get away from a scientific meeting. It was a rare treat for her. She had a new dress, she was in excellent spirits, witty, animated, talkative. When Pavlov arrived later the host jokingly reproached him for having hidden so lovely a person from them all. Pavlov frowned. He had a headache. He was going home at once. Sara could stay if she liked. She left with him, told him everything she had said at the party and promised never to go anywhere again without him, but he sulked for two days. "This was so painful to me," she wrote later, "that I told myself that I would not take so much interest in dresses and that I would make a vow of silence. This attitude on my part brought extremely good results. Ivan Petrovich was spared sleepless nights and saved from unpleasant and painful thoughts."[5] In the words of James Thurber, a woman's place is in the wrong.

The Russian peasant custom of swaddling their babies for long periods, alternating with joyous episodes of play and affection, has been blamed for generating personalities that alternate between stolid, patient, self-restraint and explosive, emotional release.[6] Whether or not swaddling has anything to do with these extreme fluctuations is debatable, but certainly Pavlov's behavior often fell into this pattern. He would flare up at trivialities. If his surgery went badly, he might blame his assistant, waving his arms and swearing profusely. Once he hotheadedly whipped a dog whose whining bothered him, then admonished the assistant never to whip a dog because it might spoil his experiment. During the revolution he scolded one of his assistants for arriving ten minutes late for an experiment; shooting and fighting in the streets should not interfere when there was work to be done in the laboratory. Usually these outbursts were quickly forgotten. When a student discovered that no grudges were held, that no subtle meanings lurked behind the professor's words, he was usually grateful to know exactly where he stood and what he was expected to do. Pavlov was never reluctant to tell him.

His anger would become serious only when he thought his rigorous standards of pure science had been violated. If he suspected that a student had values he set above research, that an interest in night life, say, prevented him from arriving promptly at the laboratory, the student might never be forgiven. If someone defended a stupid experiment out of pity for the person who performed it or, worse yet, reported results that Pavlov could not confirm, he could be uncompromising in his opposition and his criticism. He himself was completely direct, completely honest, and he expected no less from others. He may not always have been considerate of the feelings of other people, but his honesty and integrity in research, in personal relations, in his political convictions, were beyond dispute.

During his entire career he worked on only three experimental problems. The first concerned the function of the nerves of the heart; he presented some of this work as his thesis for the degree of Doctor of Medicine, which he received in 1883. The second problem was the activity of the principal digestive glands; his brilliant experiments on digestion brought him world-wide recognition. The third was his study, from 1902 until his death in 1936, of the functions of the higher nervous centers in the brain. His use of conditioning as a way to attack this problem remains his greatest scientific accomplishment. His persistence, his energetic devotion to a few well-defined problems that he pushed as far as he could, was characteristic of him both as a scientist and as a personality.

His work on the digestive system followed two major lines: an analysis of the nervous control and regulation of the digestive glands and a study of the normal function of the glands under ordinary conditions. His remarkable success in these experiments was due in large measure to his use of chronic, rather than acute preparations. In an acute experiment the anesthetized animal is operated upon, and the experimental observations are made immediately while the organs are surgically exposed. But he had discovered that the surgery itself tended to inhibit the secretion he wanted to study. In order to eliminate any unnatural effects of the operation, therefore, he undertook the more difficult task of creating chronic preparations—animals whose digestive processes could be studied under normal living conditions. The purpose of the operation was to make the digestive process visible to the scientist; experimental observations were not begun until the operation was over and the wound had healed. These chronic animals—in Pavlov's laboratory they were always dogs—were available for prolonged and diverse experiments and, more important, they functioned in the natural manner that he was trying to understand.

The general approach he used in preparing his chronic animals was to divert the secretion of a particular gland through a tube to the outside of the animal's body where it could be collected and measured. Once the flow of the digestive juice could be directly observed and measured, it was possible to explore the conditions that affected it, that increased or decreased the rate of flow. Sometimes the operations were very difficult, because it was crucial that the nerves and blood supply not be injured. His ingenuity in solving these problems and his amazing skill in performing the necessary surgery became a legend among physiologists.

The results of these experiments, along with Pavlov's theoretical interpretation, were summarized in 1897 as *The Work of the Digestive Glands*. In that book he mentioned certain irregularities and interruptions in what seemed to be the normal functioning of the digestive glands, and he attributed them to psychic causes. For example, he noticed that sometimes the glands would start to work before the food was given to the dog; the dog began to secrete digestive juices as soon as it saw the man who customarily fed it. This observation, which could only have been made with chronic animals, led to Pavlov's discovery of the conditional reflex.[7] He debated with himself for several years whether or not these irregularities—he called them psychic secretions—should be studied by experimental methods. It was 1902 before he determined to track them to their source.

His first experiments were done simply by showing the dog some bread in his hand and then giving the bread to the dog to eat. Eventually the dog would begin to salivate as soon as it saw the bread. But if bread was repeatedly shown and withheld, the dog would gradually stop responding to the visual stimulus. The dog's salivation when bread was placed in its mouth was a natural reflex of the digestive system—what Pavlov called an inborn or unconditional reflex. Salivation at the sight of the bread, however, was not an inborn reflex, but was something the dog learned to do. Pavlov called the response at the sight of the food a conditional reflex because its occurrence was conditional upon a prior association between seeing the food and tasting it.

Pavlov thought of, and occasionally discussed, the difference between these two kinds of reflexes by analogy with a telephone system. For a reflex to occur when the appropriate stimulus is given, he believed, there must be a neural path connecting the receptor organ to the gland or muscle that makes the response. For the inborn reflex that path is already completed at birth and corresponds to a direct telephone line. The path of a conditional reflex, however, must be created by making a connection through the central switchboard, by creating an engram in the central nervous system.

He soon discovered that conditional reflexes are affected by everything that goes on around the animal. In order to eliminate as many haphazard influences as he could, he put the dog and the experimenter in separate rooms. The dog was loosely strapped into a test frame where, like a swaddled Russian baby, he remained patiently immobile for hours at a time. Pavlov devised elaborate systems of tubes for presenting the stimuli and observing the secretory response (usually salivation) from outside the animal's room. And he substituted arbitrary conditional stimuli—a bell or a light—in place of the sight of bread in his hand. He discovered that any stimulus whatever could be made the occasion for conditional salivation.

In this way he arrived at the experimental procedure known as conditioning: a bell (conditional stimulus) is repeatedly sounded just before food (unconditional stimulus) is placed in the mouth to produce salivation (unconditional response), until eventually the sound of the bell causes salivation (conditional response) before the food is presented. This was the weapon with which Pavlov attacked the terrible riddles of the central nervous system.

He took special pride in the fact that his method was completely objective. In 1903 in one of his first public descriptions of this research he emphatically rejected any of the subjective methods of psychology. "In our 'psychical' experiments on the salivary glands," he said, "at first we honestly endeavored to explain our results by fancying the subjective condition of the animal. But nothing came of it except unsuccessful controversies, and individual, personal, uncoordinated opinions. We had no alternative but to place the investigation on a purely objective basis."[8] For Pavlov, a single line separated physiology from psychology, objective from subjective, and science from metaphysics. But his own work helped to destroy this simple distinction by giving psychologists another way to study their subjective problems objectively.

Around 1907 Pavlov came into public conflict with Bechterev. Vladimir M. Bechterev provides an interesting contrast to Pavlov in several respects.[9] Bechterev, the son of a minor government official, was an idealist far more typical than Pavlov of the Russian intelligentsia of the time. Both men, like many young Russian scientists in those days, went abroad for advanced studies;[10] Pavlov took it as just another step in a direction he was already going, but Bechterev spent the remainder of his life working out ideas acquired during his year in Leipzig. Whereas Pavlov stayed entirely within a rather narrow part of experimental physiology, Bechterev ranged all over the intellectual map, using both experimental and clinical methods to study problems in neurology, physiology, psychiatry, psychology, even sociology. Bechterev cut a fine figure in academic gatherings, for he was picturesquely Russian in a dignified and eloquent fashion; Pavlov was totally oblivious of all appearances, not unlike Albert Einstein. One suspects that the battle between them was less caused than released by their scientific disagreement; the real animosity derived from their temperamental inability to understand one another.

Bechterev approached the conditioning experiment with different interests from Pavlov's. He was quick to appreciate the importance of Pavlov's discovery and to carry it over into psychological research; he saw it as the proper way to convert Wundt's physiological psychology into a truly objective science. As an experimental psychologist, however, he was less concerned to condition the digestive glands than the voluntary musculature. In that respect his interests closely paralleled those of American behaviorists. He trained dogs to raise a paw when a stimulus was presented, and he spoke of the result as an associative reflex. As a clinician, however, he was more interested in human patients than in dogs. In 1910 he published his ideas in a book, *Objective Psychology*, which went through several revisions; in subsequent editions the term psychology was eventually dropped and he wrote simply of *Reflexology*.

Bechterev's view of conscious phenomena was just as materialistic as Pavlov's. It was not on that score that their quarrel arose. The spark that set off the explosion was Pavlov's discovery that he could not duplicate an experimental result reported by one of Bechterev's students. The famous Pavlov could easily have ignored the circumstance, but that was not his way. He became convinced that Bechterev

226

was "debasing science," an offense he could never forgive. Pavlov attacked; Bechterev defended himself as best he could.

It had previously been discovered that stimulation of a particular point in the brain caused an animal to secrete saliva. The controversial claim from Bechterev's laboratory was that when this particular point in the brain was cut out, the conditional salivary reflex was abolished. In Pavlov's laboratory, however, it was not abolished. The argument dragged on for two years until finally Pavlov challenged Bechterev to demonstrate the claim experimentally. Bechterev accepted the challenge. Accordingly, the salivary centers in the brains of two dogs were taken out by surgical operation; Bechterev then publicly demonstrated the absence of a conditional salivary response by placing a glass jar containing lumps of sugar in front of the dogs, who did not salivate at the sight of the sugar. Bechterev seemed to be vindicated. But Pavlov and his followers were not impressed; they were not even sure the dogs really saw the sugar. Pavlov rose, took a flask of weak acid solution and splashed it several times into the dog's mouth. This simple procedure was sufficient to condition the dogs (acid, like food, naturally elicits the salivary reflex). After that, the mere sight, smell, or splash of the acid would arouse a conditional salivary response. The brain surgery had had no effect at all. On the spot and in the presence of a large audience, Pavlov had demonstrated his objection to Bechterev's work. In spite of the dramatic outcome, however, the argument dragged on; the role of higher brain centers in conditioning is still not well understood. No doubt it is true that many of Bechterev's experiments did not come up to the standards of experimental precision and control demanded by Pavlov, yet even today many psychologists, especially in America, feel that in the larger issues there is much to be said on Bechterev's side of the argument.

After 1917 the Bolsheviks had a chance to discover how difficult Pavlov could be to live with. He regarded the revolution as one of the greatest misfortunes sustained by Russia. He could not understand these new leaders who never acted from a sense of guilt. In a public speech he commented on the great social experiment that the Bolsheviks were conducting; for such an experiment, he said, he would not sacrifice a frog's hindleg. In 1922 he asked Lenin to transfer him somewhere abroad. But dialectic materialism needs a scientific base far more than most forms of government, and Pavlov's theories were recognized as a potential source of great educational reforms. Lenin wrote a considerate refusal and offered to increase his food rations. When a commissar phoned to say he should send for the chicken and eggs that he was allowed, Pavlov said, "No, I refuse. As long as you do not give them to every one of my collaborators, I will not take them"—a rare display of courage.

In 1927 when the sons of priests were expelled from the medical

227

schools, he resigned from his chair as Professor of Physiology, saying, "I am the son of a priest and if you expel the others, I will go, too." And when the so-called Red professors were forcibly admitted into the hitherto autonomous Academy of Science, Pavlov wrote strong letters of protest to Stalin and was the only Academician to vote against them. In order to demonstrate his disapproval of the Soviet regime he stayed away from Russian scientific meetings, even though the Congress of Physiologists regularly elected him honorary chairman *in absentia*. (In 1930, however, they passed him by and in his place elected the entire Political Bureau of the Communist Party.)

In 1930 the central theme of a popular play, *Fear*, by Afino-genov, dealt with an eminent professor of physiology who had unconsciously played into the hands of the enemies of the Soviet state by working out a theory that fear was the essential motive in the behavior of the Soviet people.[11] His theory was exposed in a public meeting by an old Bolshevik woman whose political experience compensated for her lack of formal education. She concluded her indictment of the professor with a cry to the audience to be merciless toward the real enemies of the state. The professor, converted, promised to give a public criticism of his malicious theory and to hand over all the keys to his research institute. Of course, nothing was said in the play about the Pavlov affair, but the parallel would have been hard to miss.

In 1933 apparently Pavlov had become convinced that the new government was going to survive, that it had in fact united the Russian people, and that the lavish support of science, which, in Pavlov's positivistic opinion, would in the long run resolve all social problems, meant that the government shared his own high regard for scientific truth and freedom. For the final three years of his life, therefore, Pavlov and Soviet Russia lived together in peace. Since his death in 1936 his research has been continued, his memory preserved, and his writings used to justify new scientific projects in physiology and psychology. When Russians talk about Pavlov today, the difficult interlude from 1917 to 1933 is no longer mentioned.

Why was the conditioning experiment so important? Because of its apparent simplicity, a tremendously important, voluminously discussed, little understood phenomenon, something that philosophers and psychologists had called association, was captured in simple, objective, experimental terms.

Ordinary human behavior is so enormously complicated that a scientist has great difficulty in knowing where to take hold of it. The first step is to find a satisfactory unit of analysis, a simple building block with which the complicated patterns of our daily conduct can be constructed. Presumably, complex behavior could be analyzed into unconditional and conditional reflexes. Pavlov's genius was to show

how those simple elements could be isolated, analyzed, and controlled in the laboratory.

But, if the conditional reflex is so simple, what was Pavlov doing between 1902 and 1936? The simplicity of this reflex unit has not prevented experimenters from finding many aspects of it worthy of careful study. Pavlov's experimental situation seems simple only by comparison with the overwhelming complexity of our uncontrolled behavior. Consider a few of the dimensions that must be explored.

First, there is the time dimension. How long should the experimenter wait between successive trials? If he varies the time at which the conditional and unconditional stimuli are turned on (or turned off), what happens? Is it possible to use an empty interval of time itself as a conditional stimulus? Many experiments had to be done on these questions of timing alone.

But that was only a start. There are several aspects of the unconditional stimulus that had to be investigated. What inborn reflexes are available for an experimenter to work with? Can a well-established conditional stimulus serve as an unconditional stimulus for a higher-order reflex? What happens when the amount of the unconditional stimulus is increased? What is the effect of withholding it repeatedly or according to some fixed or random schedule?

Similar questions can be posed about the conditional stimulus. What physical energies can be used as conditional stimuli? How sharp a distinction can an animal make between the conditional stimulus and all other stimuli?

The response also suggests several experimental questions. Is a conditional response exactly the same as an unconditional response? What aspects of a response—reaction time, probability, magnitude, variability, duration—should be recorded? What other responses normally accompany the unconditional response?

And some of the most important questions concern the animal. Does conditioning depend upon its state of deprivation—hunger, thirst, and the like? Or upon the time of day? Are some animals easier to condition than others? What are the effects of previous experience? Can conditional reflexes be abolished by destroying various parts of the nervous system? What would happen with a species of animal other than Pavlov's beloved dogs, with men, for example?

These questions suggest some of the variables that had to be studied. The simplicity of the conditioning situation is only relative. The important thing, however, is that all these questions can be answered—answered in objective terms. What is needed is patient experimentation, and that is exactly what Pavlov and his small army of students and assistants provided. After twenty years of research Pavlov was ready to report his preliminary answers to some of these questions, along with his theory as to why the answers came out as they did. In 1923 he published a collection of speeches, articles, and reports under the Russian title *Twenty Years of Objective Study of the Higher Nervous Activity (Behavior) in Animals;*[12] the anthology was ill-assorted, but Pavlov hoped it would to some extent foreshadow the book he was planing to write later. His more systematic report appeared in 1926 under the Russian title *Lectures on Conditional Reflexes.*[13] The delay between the time Pavlov began to study conditioning and the time he published these books was less the result of his advancing age—although he was near seventy-five—than of the great scope of the problem and his feelings of scientific responsibility for the validity of everything he published.

When a conditional salivary reflex is established by repeatedly pairing some arbitrary stimulus with food, there is characteristically a generalization from that particular conditional stimulus to others that resemble it. For instance, if a tone of 1000 Hz is established as a conditional stimulus, other tones spontaneously acquire similar properties. The ability of the other tones to evoke the conditional reflex diminishes in proportion to the intervals between these tones and 1000 Hz. Similarly, if touching a definite circumscribed area of skin is made into a conditional stimulus, touching other skin areas will also elicit some conditional reaction, the effect diminishing with increasing distance of these areas from the one for which the conditional reflex was originally established. This phenomenon, called stimulus generalization, is of great psychological significance; it illustrates how reactions acquired in one situation can be transferred to similar situations. If such transfer did not occur, animals, man included, would profit little from experience.

From an experimental point of view, the generalization experiment provides a way to measure how similar two situations are for the animal; the greater the similarity, the greater will be the stimulus generalization. Moreover, the experiment can be used to study how accurately the animal can perceive differences in its environment. Psychologists seized upon stimulus generalization as an especially clear instance of a very important psychological process (cf. Chapter 7).[14]

To Pavlov, however, stimulus generalization was a direct indicator of physiological processes taking place in the brain. He believed that there are two complementary processes, excitation and inhibition, perhaps corresponding to two different chemicals, that compete for control of the various parts of the brain. When a conditional reflex is formed, the conditional stimulus acquires excitatory powers; the differentiation of that particular stimulus from all others depends upon the development of inhibition for all nonreinforced stimuli.

Different stimuli affect different points on the surface of the brain. Stimulus similarity is, in Pavlovian theory, a matter of distance in the brain; the more alike two things are, the closer their neural representations will be and the greater the interaction between them. When a point is given excitatory (or inhibitory) properties by the conditioning procedure, stimulation of the point will produce a wave of excitation (or inhibition) radiating into the adjacent brain tissue, which thus lends its excitatory (or inhibitory) properties to similar stimuli. When a conditional discrimination is firmly established, only a small region of the brain corresponding to the conditional stimulus will produce a response. Inhibition lies over the rest of the brain like winter over the empty plains of central Russia, limiting all activity to the lonely stockades.

The excitation-inhibition paradigm was to be used later by von Békésy in his Nobel prize-winning work on audition and is a part of the lexicon of physiological researchers who propose that the hypothalamus is "tuned" by a balance of excitatory and inhibitory signals.

Just prior to the time Pavlov began his research on the higher nervous centers in the brain, interest in the activity of the lower nervous centers in the spinal cord had developed independently in England. C. S. Sherrington and his school carried out a brilliant analysis of the interactions among the various spinal reflexes; their results are today a generally accepted part of physiological knowledge.[15] It is interesting historically that Pavlov's work, similar in purpose and equally brilliant, has had almost no influence upon other branches of physiology. Pavlov's principal impact has been felt in psychology. The fact is a bit ironic, considering his low opinion of psychology as a science, but the reason is not difficult to find. Pavlov did not make any direct observations of the processes going on in the brain. He based his opinion of them entirely upon inferences from what the animals did in his experiments. What he looked at directly was not the animal's brain, but the animal's behavior. Consequently, all his statements about waves of excitation and inhibition that irradiate over the surface of the brain are little more than plausible fictions; if you opened up the skull you would not know how or where to look for them. His description of the animal's behavior in the conditioning experiment, however, is wonderfully acute. Since experimental psychologists, inspired in no small measure by Pavlov's success, have pursued the objective description and analysis of behavior, Pavlov's work has had its major effect on behavioristic psychology, rather than on physiology.

From a psychological point of view one of his most interesting discoveries was experimental neurosis. If a dog is forced to learn a very difficult discrimination between two stimuli, it may become extremely disturbed. The first systematic observations of this emotional reaction were made in 1914. A dog was trained to salivate when it saw a circle. Then an ellipse was presented without any reinforcement by food; the discrimination was easily established. On subsequent days the differ-

231

ence between the ellipse and the circle was reduced progressively. Finally the two were so much alike that discrimination failed. After three weeks of unsuccessful training the whole behavior of the dog changed abruptly.

> The hitherto quiet dog began to squeal in its stand, kept wriggling about, tore off with its teeth the apparatus for mechanical stimulation of the skin, and bit through the tubes connecting the animal's room with the observer, a behavior which never happened before. On being taken into the experimental room the dog now barked violently, which was also contrary to its usual custom; in short it presented all the symptoms of a condition of acute neurosis.[16]

Pavlov explained these symptoms as a conflict between the excitatory and inhibitory processes. Ordinarily the nervous system can establish an equilibrium between them, but when the sources of excitation and inhibition get very close together, the equilibrium breaks down and a generally excited or inhibited state appears.

The explanation is ingenious but somewhat unreal. Considering the amount of frustration normally involved in a conditioning experiment—the restraint in the test frame, the monotonous repetition of particular stimuli—the addition of a difficult discrimination seems but a small part of the animal's discomfort. If Pavlov's excitation and inhibition had been less metaphorical, it would have been easier to test his theory directly. But it is not a physiological theory at all; it is a psychological theory disguised in physiological language.

Pavlov's interest in experimental neurosis increased as he grew older; he devoted the last decade of his life largely to psychiatric problems.[17] When at last he began to think seriously about human behavior Pavlov recognized that the enormous complexities introduced by language required new explanations. To his earlier distinction between inborn and conditional reflexes, therefore, he added verbal symbols. The conditional reflexes that he had so long studied in animals comprised a "first signaling system." Men, he said, have evolved another, a "second signaling system" of verbal symbols. Although he was not able to develop this proposal himself, it has stimulated considerable speculation and research by subsequent generations of Russian psychologists.

The influence of Pavlov in contemporary Russian science is evident everywhere, from the research on "weak" versus "strong" nervous systems to some of the most ingenious experimental research on conditioning of the gastrointestinal system using cold water. The followers of the Pavlov tradition call themselves physiologists and look down on ordinary psychologists who apply many of the same concepts in education. One student of Bechterev, P. Anohkin, a pioneer in the extension of cybernetics into the theory of conditioning, resembles in style and ebullience, the flamboyant Bechterev. Soviet science today is still recovering from the more rigid Stalin era when bureaucrats dictated that every paper had to pay an often meaningless tribute to Pavlov and lesser officially recognized scientists.

Pavlov's contributions to science are everywhere known and admired, but their implications for social policy and their effects upon our conception of human nature are often deplored. Many people have been frightened by grim visions of a brave, new world where machines will condition every child into submissive uniformity. Such fears are fed by ignorance, but some fairly able spokesmen have given voice to them. George Bernard Shaw once called Pavlov a scoundrel and his teaching a crackle of blazing nonsense from beginning to end.[18] Similar applications have been expressed by many other humanists.

Pavlov has often been classed with Freud as a major source of antiintellectualism in the twentieth century. In their hands Sovereign Reason, benevolent ruler of the eighteenth-century mind, crumbled into unconscious reflexes and instincts, automatic processes that are the very antithesis of ratiocinative thought. Reason seemed to refute itself. Yet both men, Pavlov and Freud, were true children of the Enlightenment; both believed that the search for knowledge must never stop, that only knowledge allows reason to function, that only reason can make men free. Both were loyal to the highest values of their positivistic education. What they both attacked was not sovereign reason, but foolish optimism about the inevitability of human progress. To dismiss them as antiintellectuals is a dangerous oversimplification.

No doubt Pavlov himself would prefer to be classed with his hero Darwin, with the famous biologist rather than the famous psychologist. And there is reason to respect his wish. Where Darwin showed how living organisms can adapt to their environments by changing slowly from one generation to the next, Pavlov showed how a living organism can adapt by changing rapidly during its own lifetime. And, like Darwin, Pavlov angered the nonscientists whose preconceived notions were threatened by his discoveries. But such anger is the way we pay our greatest men. It is a special tribute reserved for those whose work is truly significant.

NOTES

1. C. Bernard, *An Introduction to the Study of Experimental Medicine,* trans. H. C. Greene (New York: Dover, 1957).
2. Quoted by Ernest Jones, *The Life and Work of Sigmund Freud* (New York: Basic Books, 1953), vol. 1, p. 40.
3. Franklin Fearing, *Reflex Action, A Study in the History of Physiological Psychology* (Baltimore: William & Wilkins, 1930).

4. B. P. Babkin, *Pavlov, A Biography* (Chicago: University of Chicago Press, 1949). See also the biographical sketch by W. H. Gantt at the beginning of his translation of I. P. Pavlov, *Lectures on Conditioned Reflexes* (New York: International, 1928).

5. Babkin, *Pavlov*, p. 48.

6. G. Gorer and J. Rickman, *The People of Great Russia* (London: Cresset Press, 1949).

7. The term "conditioned reflex," which has been in general use for many years, is an inaccurate translation of the Russian *ouslovny*. Since "conditional reflex" is closer to what Pavlov meant and is also more easily understood, it has been adopted here.

8. Gantt, *Lectures on Conditioned Reflexes*, p. 50.

9. P. I. Yakovlev, "Bechterev," in *The Central Nervous System and Behavior*, ed. M. A. B. Brazier, Transactions of the First Conference (New York: Josiah Macy, Jr., Foundation, 1959).

10. Pavlov spent a year with Heidenhain in Breslau and a year with Ludwig in Leipzig; Bechterev visited Charcot in Paris, Du Bois-Reymond in Berlin, but spent most of his time in Leipzig with Flechsig and with Wundt.

11. D. Joravsky, "Soviet Scientists and the Great Break," *Daedalus* 89 (1960): pp. 562–580.

12. I. P. Pavlov, *Lectures on Conditioned Reflexes*, trans. W. H. Gantt (New York: International, 1928).

13. I. P. Pavlov, *Conditioned Reflexes, trans.* G. V. Anrep (London: Oxford University Press, 1927).

14. E. R. Hilgard and D. G. Marquis, *Conditioning and Learning*, 2d ed., rev. G. A. Kimble (New York: Appleton-Century Crofts, 1961).

15. C. S. Sherrington, *The Integrative Action of the Nervous System* (New Haven: Yale University Press, 1906). See also J. Konorski, *Conditioned Reflexes and Neuron Organization* (Cambridge: Cambridge University Press, 1948).

16. Pavlov, *Conditioned Reflexes*, p. 291.

17. I. P. Pavlov, *Conditioned Reflexes and Psychiatry, Lectures on Conditioned Reflexes*, vol. 2, trans. H. W. Gantt (New York: International 1941).

18. G. B. Shaw, *Everybody's Political What's What* (1944), quoted by Babkin, *Pavlov*, p. 342.

FIFTEEN
The Search for Behavioral Atoms

"If I attempt to analyze a man's entire mind," said Edward Lee Thorndike, a psychologist who for forty years was an intellectual leader on the faculty of Columbia University's famed Teachers College, "I find connections of varying strength between (a) situations, elements of situations, and compounds of situations and (b) responses, readiness to respond, facilitations, inhibitions, and directions of responses. If all these could be completely inventoried, telling what the man would think and do and what would satisfy and annoy him, in every conceivable situation, it seems to me that nothing would be left out. . . . Learning is connecting. The mind is man's connection-system."[1]

Such was the associationist position in 1931. It was a linear descendant of an older associationism that began with John Locke and that inspired British empiricists for two centuries. But there was a crucial difference. Instead of connections between ideas, Thorndike talked about connections between situations and responses. In this way he accepted into his psychological theory a physiological frame of reference.

Thorndike stood in a proud tradition, and he spoke for a sizable constituency among America's academic psychologists during the 1920s and 1930s. If the mind is man's connection-system, then the program of research that lay ahead was clear. Isolate the elementary connection processes, and you will have under your control the very stuff that minds are made of. Pavlov had shown one way to study the formation of connections in animals. Similar analysis should be possible for human behavior, too.

Consider a person who deliberately and intentionally sets out to memorize certain verbal responses to a given set of verbal stimuli. To be definite, imagine an English-speaking student of the French language who undertakes to memorize a new section of French vocabulary. What he will try to do is to learn the meanings of French words; for a beginning student, learning the meanings involves learning what English words he should say, or think of, when he sees the French words. He will go over his list several times, each time looking at the French

235

stimulus, making his English response, and checking to see if he is right. Psychologists call this paired-associates learning.

The student will usually continue until he can give a correct English equivalent for every French word on his list. Attaining a criterion of one errorless recall of the entire list ordinarily satisfies him that he has mastered his lesson. He goes on about his other business until, perhaps, he is tested by his instructor. Then, alas, he discovers that he can no longer give the expected response to every French word. He recalls some words; others he has forgotten.

We normally think of this familiar situation as a build-up and then a slow decay, a strengthening followed by a weakening of the English-French connections, or associations. If there is no rehearsal, then the longer the interval between the building and the testing, of course, the more the associations will fade and the poorer recall will be.

Our description seems to give an adequate account of what happened to the student, but note that there is no mention in it of anything corresponding to a place where his memories of the French-English pairs must be stored. If one thinks of learning as a process of establishing connections between stimuli and responses, then the connection either exists or it does not exist. If it exists, it exists at a strength that waxes and wanes as a function of many different variables. But to know where it exists is not essential. Remembering, that is, making an appropriate response when a stimulus is repeated, is something we do, not something we have.

This approach has the great advantage of being related directly to observable events, to observable stimuli and responses and their co-occurrences. No reliance is placed upon hearsay evidence about

FIGURE 15.1

Schematic and highly idealized curves for learning and forgetting. During the initial study period the probability of a correct response increases to nearly 1.0; while the person is engaged in other activities, the probability slowly decays.

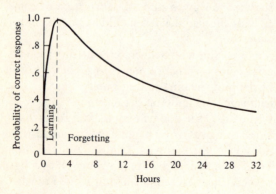

visual images or rules or mnemonic tricks. Because of the emphasis upon stimulus and response, this hardheaded approach is commonly referred to as the stimulus-response or S-R approach.

In written accounts of the philosophy of science, this approach is an example of the use of an operational definition of a process that is assumed to be taking place, and is properly called an inference from observable behavior. While the process can only be inferred from a change in behavior, the inference expands our descriptive vocabulary by applying a single word to a complex set of discrete observations of fact. Inferred variables are used in physics; for example, the concept of force is inferred from the acceleration of a mass, but is every bit as unobservable directly as is learning.

Psychologists have invented many different theories to account for our ability to profit from experience; it would be quite misleading to suggest that everyone would defend an S-R theory of learning. But many would, and do. S-R theory has long been a popular approach in America, and a kind of stereotype has developed around it. According to E. R. Hilgard, whose textbooks have for many years settled these matters for American students, S-R theories are characterized by (1) their emphasis upon peripheral muscular mechanisms—chained reflexes, movement-produced stimuli, anticipatory responses—rather than upon central brain processes as the source of behavioral integration, (2) their insistence that what we learn are not passive facts, but active responses, and (3) their faith that trial-and-error rather than insight is the basic mode of learning.[2] An S-R theorist has little use for quiet introspection; the organisms he studies are on the move, struggling, responding, changing constantly.

It is always dangerous to create an imaginary synthesis of the aims and accomplishments of many people, especially when they differ among themselves as violently as S-R theorists often do. But the convenience of the speculation can scarcely be resisted. We shall pretend, therefore, that the S-R stereotype represents something that many psychologists would agree with in spirit, if not in detail. But a cautious reader will remind himself that S-R theory is not really as one-sided as we shall make it seem.

The first self-conscious efforts to create a formal, mathematical theory along S-R lines were Clark L. Hull's *Mathematico-Deductive Theory of Rote Learning* (1940) and his *Principles of Behavior* (1943). Hull was a behaviorist, working in the tradition of Pavlov and Watson, with little respect for mentalistic concepts such as understanding or consciousness. His ambition was to specify rigorously a small number of mathematical variables inside the organism that would account for all of the observed correlations between stimulation and response.

The cornerstone of Hull's theory was the following idea:

whenever a response to some stimulus has the effect of reducing a biological drive, the strength of that stimulus-response association will be increased. The idea that we repeat actions that were successful before is, of course, quite ancient. The daring feature of this hypothesis is that, true to the behaviorist tradition, nothing is assumed about *understanding* the connection between the response and the satisfactions that follow it. If an organism is hungry in situation S, say, and if some response R is followed immediately by food, then the habit of responding R in situation S will be *automatically* reinforced. On closer inspection one recognizes that the situation is compounded of many different stimuli: of internal stimuli produced by hunger; of current environmental sights, sounds, and odors; of persisting traces of previous environmental stimuli; and of stimuli resulting directly from the organism's own movements. A description of a particular instance of learning must specify all the connections formed between each of these varieties of stimulation and the sequence of responses that leads to the goal. But the critical assumption is that all these S-R bonds are formed blindly and automatically, without intention or insight.

By making certain simple assumptions about the amount of the increase in habit strength produced by every successful experience, Hull was able to write mathematical expressions to describe the quantitative changes that measure the amount of learning. This mathematical formulation had at least one enormous advantage over theories stated in a purely verbal form: it could be proved wrong. If you cannot discover your mistakes, you cannot correct them. Hull showed the way toward greater rigor in psychological theory; the use of mathematical notation to describe the learning process has grown in popularity ever since.

In his conception of the psychological nature of man, however, Hull advanced little beyond what Herbert Spencer had said seventy years earlier. Hull's achievement was to bring Spencer's genetic philosophy into direct and meaningful connection with quantitative data from the experimental laboratory. Rather than criticize his theory, therefore, we should look at the kind of experimental data that the theory was intended to explain.

Hull wrote equations for the strength of S-R connections. Where does one find a typical S-R connection to study? And, having found it, how does one proceed to measure its strength?

Hull tested his equations in a series of elegant experiments with rats, as he and numerous followers labored in the 1930s and 1940s to test a growing set of postulates in the Hullian system. In any experiment of this genre, one can see the care taken by the researcher to define operationally every aspect of prediction equations which were growing larger and more complex. Habit strength was strictly defined in terms of the number of prior training trials at a task (usually bar-pressing); drive was defined as the number of hours of deprivation of food or water. But the equations, which came to include fatigue, aging, stimulus intensity, and quality of the food given as a reward, soon became unwieldy and still failed to fulfill the determinist's dream of knowing all relevant environmental causes in pursuit of perfect prediction. Even in the prosaic world of rat behavior a running battle ensued between Hullians, who stuck to the "empty-head" view of behavior, and other behaviorists, such as Tolman, who argued in favor of more complex cognitive and decision-making abilities in the rat which might explain some of the errors in Hull's prediction equations.

In the simpler forms of S-R theory little is said about the way we organize experience or discover rules that simplify a learning task. To any psychologist who defines learning in terms of the strength of an association between a stimulus and a response, remembering things according to rules is more appropriately classified as thinking or problem solving, not simple learning. What an S-R theorist asks is, "Where do the basic associations come from?" What is the origin of the already present associations that a person presumably exploits when he uses rules or images to facilitate new learning? Mnemonic tricks are merely ways to exploit old connections so as to save the trouble of making new ones. One would like to study the more basic, probably simpler kind of learning first. But how? How can a learner be forced to form new connections?

One strategy is to strip all meaningful associations away, to give the subject something so strange and unfamiliar that he cannot have any old associations to it and so is forced to form new ones. As early as 1885 the German psychologist Herman Ebbinghaus introduced the nonsense syllable as a way to obtain a large number of relatively homogeneous items for the person to learn; they are homogeneous because, being meaningless, they escape the learner's preestablished habits of thought.[3] There is an infinite variety of unfamiliar nonsense. The kind that psychologists have standardized, following Ebbinghaus, is a three-letter, consonant-vowel-consonant (CVC) "syllable." (CVC sequences that spell familiar words are frequently considered ineligible.)

In a typical experiment on serial rote memorization, for example, a subject may be presented with a list of ten or twelve nonsense syllables, one at a time. They appear at regular intervals, usually in the window of a mechanical device designed for this purpose. (In one simple version a cylindrical drum papered with the syllable list slowly rotates behind a covering hood arranged to expose the syllables in a window one at a time—see Figure 15.2.) As each syllable appears in the window, the memorizer is supposed to pronounce (or spell, since some syllables may be unpronounceable) the *next* syllable on the list. The first time around, of course, he will not anticipate any of the

FIGURE 15.2

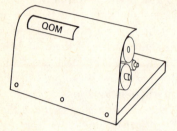

A teaching machine that presents nonsense syllables one at a time; this is commonly referred to as a memory drum.

syllables correctly, but gradually, after repeated trials, he will do better and better until eventually he will be able to anticipate each syllable before it appears.

Psychologists soon discovered that some nonsense syllables are more nonsensical than others. For example, "BAL," "BIZ," "DUL," "JAN," "TAL" have associations for almost everyone who speaks English, but "CEF," "GIW," "MEQ," "XAD," "ZOJ" do not often stir our memories. In order to eliminate mnemonic tricks, therefore, it is generally assumed that nonsense syllables having low association values should be used. A sample task consisting of twelve units might be the following.

YIC	XOL
QOM	HUQ
GEP	TEF
DUZ	ZIK
RIJ	VOB
NAW	PAH

At first glance it would appear that all previous training in the use of words and sentences has been rendered worthless and inoperative. Now, surely, any learner must start afresh and form new associations for us. But never underestimate a subject's cleverness. One person made up the following sentences in order to memorize the above list of syllables.

Why, I see	You need excellent
qom	hucksters
gets	t' have
duz,	sick
right?	vob.
Nah!	Pah!

True, it sounds like an argument between a lunatic and a misanthrope, but it is not difficult to remember; from it the original syllables can easily be reconstructed. The first time he memorizes such a list, a typical subject spends much of his time composing just such mnemonic crutches to guide his recitation. Syllables with low association values are more difficult to learn because it is harder, and takes longer, to construct the meaningful translation.

The junior author once constructed a list of paired nonsense syllables deliberately made exceedingly difficult by the repeated use of a small number of vowels and consonants, which created a great deal of similarity among the items in the list. After thirty-nine presentations on a memory drum, most people could correctly anticipate only three or four of the nonsense syllables. One day a young man learned every single item in a matter of six presentations, only then revealing that he was a native of Latvia where what is linguistically nonsensical to Americans makes perfect sense to the Latvians. Indeed, many three-letter syllables that were nonsense in 1930 (for example, VEL) have become easy to remember thanks to repeated presentations in commercials.

Even these Spartan measures, therefore, do not frustrate what has been called the learner's effort after meaning. A psychologist who is convinced that the real process of learning consists of lowering resistance to the flow of nerve impulses along certain pathways leading from the receptor that senses the stimulus to the muscles that make the response will look upon these verbal shenanigans as a pure nuisance. Of course, it is possible to ignore them, to deal only with an average number of correct responses on successive repetitions of the list. But if we want to examine a particular stimulus-response connection, averages do not tell us much. Some other approach is needed. If nonsense syllables do not eliminate the use of mnemonic tricks, then they are too complicated and something still simpler should be learned. Perhaps nonsense syllables are still too much like meaningful words. To get something completely nonverbal, the task has to be simplified. Perhaps the study of motor skills can furnish what is required.

Such skills, it must be admitted, are seldom learned without any taint of verbal guidance. Even if one ignores as obviously too verbal two such carefully analyzed skills as typewriting and radiotelegraphy, it remains that a verbal description of the general strategy a learner should pursue can be a tremendous aid. If you want to teach someone to hit targets that are under water, a verbal explanation of the principle of refraction can speed the learning considerably. Or if you tell a person who is learning to ride a bicycle that he should turn the front wheel in the same direction he is falling, you may shorten his learning time considerably. But verbal hints and helps are not easily discovered for every situation, and in any case it is always possible to withhold them, thus apparently forcing the learner to work without symbolic aids. Here, it would seem, is a place where the elementary connections can be studied. And, to a limited extent, this is true.

But the picture is still not as clean and neat as one might wish for the purposes of an analysis of stimuli and responses. A skilled motor performance usually runs on continuously in time, and it is not obvious where it should be dissected into discrete stimuli and responses. It is not only that both the stimulus and the response are continuous functions of time; the problem is further complicated by the fact that the consequences of the responses are fed back and modify the stimulus. Thus, one can no longer equate stimulus and response with antecedent and consequent, respectively.

The skill involved in steering a car along a winding road provides an obvious example. The road is a continuously varying stimulus that swerves left and right. The driver makes a continuously varying response as he moves the steering wheel left and right. But if he moves the wheel too far in one direction, the error shows up in the path of the car; the stimulus to turn back is correspondingly greater. The stimulus is not the road or the direction of the car; the stimulus is the discrepancy between the two. And the driver's response is to keep that stimulus as small as he can. The complete stimulus-response-feedback loop is closely analogous to what is called a servomechanism, and it is a good deal more complicated than the simple S-R atom we started looking for.[4] Apparently, the situation has still not been sufficiently simplified.

Research on psychomotor skills at one time occupied many psychologists, especially during World War II when hundreds of psychologists recruited for the war effort worked in a huge government laboratory in Texas. Focusing on simulated tasks that resembled the flying skills of pilots, they tested many of the Hullian and other theoretical concepts on motor skill learning. Much later, it became possible to program a large computer to sample the performance of a pilot flying a simulator and then reprogram the computer, so that it could produce, that is, predict, the performance of that pilot on the simulated display. This so-called "Manalog" was a mere complex equation which proved so accurate that, when the computer was actually in

FIGURE 15.3

Representation of an automobile and its driver as a servomechanism. The driver compares the direction of the road with the path of his car and adjusts the steering mechanism to reduce the discrepancy between them.

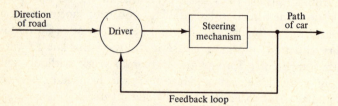

control of the simulator while the pilot was performing, the pilot never noticed that he was outside the loop of control.

Of course, knowledge of the equation helped psychologists to understand what the critical cues were in pilot or car-driver performance. It was found that people with extensive training do not, for example, merely judge the distance between them and the car in front when driving in traffic. Rather they pay more attention to the closing rate—a higher derivative of motion in the equation. One practical application of this finding has been in the spacing of cars going through tunnels. Instead of the seemingly logical way of spacing cars evenly, tests have shown that more cars go through faster if clusters of several cars are first delayed and then permitted to go into the tunnel as a kind of platoon. Several cars being driven together tend to maintain a higher speed and do not slow down as often because there are fewer separate cars making adjustments for changes in the rate of closure.

What is necessary is to strip the learning situation to its bare essentials. It is a typical story in science. To study gravity, one must ignore the falling leaves and the drifting clouds and the winged birds that fly upward—one must get to the naked essentials that are retained when a body falls freely through a vacuum. What the S-R theorist is trying to do is to find an experimental situation that, like bodies falling in a vacuum, will provide simple, quantitative laws for the basic, underlying processes in learning. Once the laws governing this fundamental S-R process are understood, complications can be added as they are required.

Consider the following simplification of the learning situation. A subject sits with one finger touching an electrode and a second electrode strapped to his wrist. When the experimenter closes a switch a painful electric shock results. The experimenter never closes the switch to deliver the shock, however, without first turning on a tone just a half second before. In the beginning the subject does not respond to the tone, but after a few trials in which the tone is followed by shock, he learns to straighten out his finger, thus lifting it from the electrode and avoiding the shock. So an association is established between the tonal stimulus and the response of straightening the finger.

This kind of learning is, of course, conditioning.[5] It resembles the general pattern of experimentation used by Pavlov, but a human subject has replaced Pavlov's dog. The electric shock is an unconditional stimulus; the withdrawal by straightening and lifting the finger to escape the shock is an unconditional response; the tone that comes on a half-second before the shock is a conditional stimulus; and the withdrawal by straightening and lifting the finger when the tone sounds and before the shock occurs—the response that avoids the shock—is a conditional response.

The principal difference between this procedure and Pavlov's is that here the unconditional stimulus is not given if the conditional response occurs soon enough to avoid it. The difference is important. The procedure just described above is often called *instrumental* conditioning (the response is instrumental in avoiding the shock), to distinguish it from the classical form of Pavlovian conditioning, where the unconditional stimulus is always presented on every training trial.

Here we have reached something basic. The instrumental conditioning experiment is extremely simple, it does not depend upon verbal instructions, and there is a close parallel between the results obtained from humans and animals. Some proponents of S-R theories assume that the conditioning experiment is the prototype of all learning. For more complex situations the theoretical task is to discover how the behavioral processes can be analyzed into these basic components. That analysis often requires considerable ingenuity, especially in the realm of verbal learning, but S-R theorists are confident it can be carried through successfully. "After all," they might say, "analysis into basic units is essential to all scientific progress: look at the analysis of matter into atoms, or the analysis of organisms into cells. Everywhere in science it is the same. We must find the proper elements and then discover the laws of their combination. That was, after all, what Wilhelm Wundt wanted to do; the trouble with Wundt was that he chose the idea instead of the S-R bond as his element."

But there are still problems that must be solved before one can accept this argument. For example, suppose in the finger-withdrawal experiment just described, one asks the subject after one or two hundred conditioning trials, to turn his hand over (as shown in Figure 15.4). Now, with his hand in this new position, if he straightens his finger it will still be touching the electrode and he will not avoid the shock. To avoid or escape the shock when his hand has been turned over the person must bend his finger, the exact opposite of the movement he had been conditioned to make. What will happen? Will he make the same *response* and extend his finger? Or will he perform the same *act* and flex his finger?

About seven out of every ten subjects flex the finger, even after

FIGURE 15.4

Arrangement used to demonstrate response generalization.

Train   Test

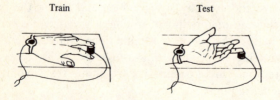

many long trials in which they have been conditioned to extend it.[6] Twenty-five percent do nothing at all, and about 5 percent persist in making the extensor movement. The subjects themselves can provide no explanation; they report later that the finger acted in the way it did more or less of its own accord. Moreover, there is no satisfactory way to discriminate in advance between people who will flex the finger and people who will continue to extend it. But the gross statistical fact can scarcely be avoided: for most subjects, the result of the conditioning procedure has been to condition the *act* of withdrawal, not the *response* of finger extension. This outcome can be called response generalization—the S-R bond has generalized from the extensor response to the flexor response—but whatever one calls it, it makes a conditional reflex in a human subject appear somewhat more complicated than before.

When you stop to think about it, this conditioning experiment is an unusual way to get a person to lift his finger at the sound of a tone. As R. S. Woodworth pointed out, an occasional subject will misunderstand the experiment and assume that the experimenter wants him to keep his finger on the electrode and take the shock. If his finger does withdraw before the shock, he feels silly and ashamed and increases his effort to keep it in place; and he does not develop a conditional response even after many sessions. Why does the experimenter let this misunderstanding persist? He could simply say to the subject, "I will give you strong shocks preceded by tones. I wish to discover how long it will take you to learn to avoid the shock by raising your finger when the tone comes on." But if he said that, his experiment would lose all point![7] Once again, verbal processes seem able to interfere with the basic process being studied. In an effort to escape the interfering effects of a human subject's symbolic habits the investigator has worked himself into the position of trying to fool the subject about what he is supposed to do.

To some investigators, this intransigence by people in conditioning experiments is an annoying source of measurement error, while others have found it to be a rich source of information on human behavior or a possibly devastating critique of S-R theory. In studies of conditioning the eye blink, Kimble has identified three "confounding factors": (1) the power of positive thinking, which includes willingness to be in experiments, approval of procedures, and a readiness to yield to those procedures; (2) emotional factors including anxiety and an aroused state of involvement, which is positively correlated with eye blink rate; (3) resistance, which includes hostility, suspicion, and fighting manipulation—contributing to lower eye blink rate.[8] If these factors sound familiar, we refer you back to our earlier discussion of attitudinal factors affecting sensory thresholds in signal detection work. In a closing statement in his classic book on conditioning,

Kimble said, ". . . phenomena associated with such conceptions as attitude, set, resistance to being manipulated, and even *volition* [italics added] may not be as unapproachable by the methods of objective psychology as most of us have thought."

Lest one becomes discouraged about conditioning human beings, however, a word of warning is needed. The fact that some experiments are not as simple as they look must not be interpreted to mean that human beings are invulnerable to Pavlov's procedures. All the evidence suggests that we can be conditioned, that we are being conditioned every day. We seem to be especially vulnerable when we are not actively aware of the conditional situation and when the response is made by our autonomic nervous system.

The autonomic nervous system controls the vegetative functions of our glands and smooth muscles, vital functions that involve few conscious decisions on our part, although recent research shows that they can all be brought under voluntary control. Pavlov, for example, worked with responses of the digestive glands; his Russian successors have extended his method to responses of other digestive glands, to stomach contractions and contractions of blood vessels, to heart rate and metabolic rate, and so on.[9] It seems plausible that many of the emotional symptoms of psychoneurosis are created by the pervasive action of the reflexes encompassed by Pavlov's laws on these autonomic processes of the body.

The finger-withdrawal experiment, however, involves a voluntary response of the striped musculature, which is under the control of the central nervous system. In man, the enormous central nervous system—brain and spinal cord—supports symbolic processes that introduce a whole new level of complexity into the control of our behavior. It is this very complexity that seems to thwart our efforts to find a pure example of an S-R connection.

Where can one find learning that is mediated by the central nervous system and yet is not impossibly complicated by all the verbal, pictorial, and formal symbol-systems that are such characteristic ornaments of the human mind? An obvious answer is, in the study of other animals. And, in fact, that is where many psychologists have turned.

The consequences have been rather curious. Animals provide fascinating problems for a psychologist. However, many psychologists who study animals have no profound interest in them except insofar as their behavior can be related to human psychology. Such psychologists would prefer to study the creation of new S-R connections in man, but in order to demonstrate the learning process in its raw and primitive form they are forced to use inarticulate subjects. Admittedly it is a dangerous business to argue by analogy from one species to another, yet many distinguished psychologists are convinced that the fundamental laws of learning are so simple and universal that they can be studied anywhere in the animal kingdom, or, at least, anywhere among the vertebrates. So, in this excellent company, let us descend one more step in our effort to simplify the study of the learning process.

One of the first attempts to use animals in a psychological study of learning was Thorndike's early (1898) experiment with cats in a puzzle box.[10] Thorndike put his cats into a rough wooden crate built of slats. The box had a door that was held shut by a button and a catch. If the cat could either turn the button or pull a loop that hung inside the box and that was connected directly to the catch, it could escape. The cats wanted out; they seemed to dislike the confinement. To reinforce this dislike, Thorndike deprived them of food prior to the tests and then fed them when they escaped.

On their first confinement in the box, the cats, particularly the young ones, scrambled around vigorously, attacked the bars, cracks, corners, and, eventually, the loop or the button until they accidentally worked the escape mechanism. There was no intelligent study of the situation, no insight, no plan: merely random, trial-and-error movements. But once the response that led to escape had been made, the cat could begin to strengthen the connection between its response and the escape mechanism, and to eliminate the responses that did not lead to escape. As the successful association grew stronger on repeated trials, the time it took for the cat to escape grew shorter, but the irregular nature of the function (see Figure 15.5) is eloquent testimony to the haphazard, trial-and-error nature of the learning process.

Here is a good example of experimental evidence that encourages S-R theorists to believe that learning is nothing but the formation of connections between stimuli and responses. Given that experimental paradigm, it is then possible to search for laws governing the rise and fall of associative strengths. Thorndike proposed two fundamental laws.

The Law of exercise. The more often a given situation is followed by a particular response, the stronger will be the associative

FIGURE 15.5

There were large variations from trial to trial in the length of time it took this cat to escape from Thorndike's puzzle box.

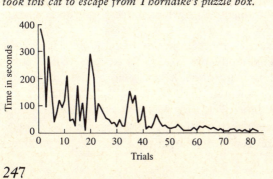

bond between them. Exercise—use, repetition, practice—makes perfect.

The Law of effect. If a response produces a good effect and leads to a satisfying state of affairs, it will tend to be repeated when the situation arises again. It is a variant of this law that Hull later adopted as the foundation of his S-R theory of learning.

Both of Thorndike's laws are excellent descriptive statements. Animals, including men, tend to repeat activities that are profitable or rewarding, and the more often they repeat them, the better they perform. There are exceptions, but on the whole these phenomena characterize much of the behavior we want to understand.

A large part of scientific psychology in America in the twentieth century has been based on, or directed at, these two laws. The conclusion seems to be that if they are interpreted literally as causal explanations, they are not true. Thorndike himself discredited the law of exercise by demonstrating that when a learner is denied information as to whether he succeeds or fails, all the exercise in the world cannot result in learning. On the other hand, the law of effect has had a more checkered career; it is not yet obvious that nothing will come of it. What is involved is a particular type of feedback loop; the satisfying effect of a response is fed back to strengthen it on future occasions. A major difficulty arises, however, in the attempt to define what is meant by a "satisfying state" of a response. Hull defined it as a reduction of a biological drive, but this additional assumption raises as many questions as it answers. (We will return to this problem in Chapter 19.)

A strong case can be made that the satisfying state of affairs does not determine what the animal will learn, but rather will determine what the animal will do. Edward C. Tolman has argued that animals will acquire information, will learn what to expect when certain signs occur, in situations where no apparent reward is offered.[11] The learning becomes evident only later when a reward is introduced that motivates the animal to use the information it has acquired. But the reward does not itself automatically stamp in the connection between a stimulus and a response. What happens is quite complex, and no simple generalization can adequately summarize the hundreds of experimental studies that have been directed toward the problem of rewards and punishments and their effects on both learning and performance.

Let us return to the cats in the puzzle box. Many years after Thorndike's original study the work was repeated with better equipment.[12] The box was arranged with a pole in the center. If the cat pushed against the pole and tilted it, an electric contact was made that released the door. Moreover, a camera was set to take a photograph of the cat at the instant the successful response occurred.

The pictures revealed a surprising thing: the cat's movements at

"For the creative and sustained pursuit of a theoretical integration of the multifaceted data of psychology, not just its more circumscribed and amenable aspects; for forcing theorizing out of the mechanical and peripheral into the center of psychology without the loss of objectivity and discipline; for returning man to psychology by insisting upon molar behaviorism purposely organized as the unit of analysis, most explicitly illustrated in his purposive-cognitive theory of learning.

EDWARD CHASE TOLMAN

the instant of escape were highly stereotyped for many trials in a row. For example, one of the cats, cat T, on the first trial happened to activate the mechanism by lying down, pausing, then rolling over until it hit the pole. The cat then repeated almost exactly the same elaborate pattern of actions on succeeding trials. Tracings from the photographic record are shown for the first eight escape trials in Figure 15.6. Other animals regularly brushed against the pole, or always chewed it, or always hit it with their tails, or always stepped on the base. A particular movement pattern would be repeated until by accident it failed to hit the post (or occasionally, the release mechanism in the box failed to work), and then the cat might discover another way to get out and would persist in using those movements for the next five or ten trials.

The regularity of these stereotyped movements has led to the suggestion that what the cats learned initially was an association between the stimuli provided by the box and a very specific pattern of movements, not an association between the stimuli and a purposeful act. The association seemed to be formed after a single successful pairing of stimulus with response. According to Edwin R. Guthrie, in

FIGURE 15.6

Escape behavior in cats is highly stereotyped. Here are tracings to show the position of cat T at the instant he activated the release mechanism on the first eight trials. (From E. R. Guthrie and G. P. Horton, Cats in a Puzzle Box *[New York: Rinehart, 1946].)*

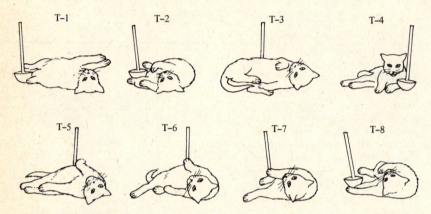

the course of many successive trials the animal built up several alternative movements that opened the door, and so appeared to be acquiring a specific skill. Thus, he argued, the act is slowly learned, yet the individual associations that comprise the act are each learned in a single trial.

Other psychologists have questioned Guthrie's conclusions, however. In maze learning, for example, one might suppose that an animal could learn a thoroughly stereotyped set of movements that would take it from the starting box through the maze to the goal box. But Karl Lashley showed that if rats which have acquired such a maze habit are operated upon, and their motor coordination is so disturbed by surgery that they are no longer capable of making the same movements, they will still be able to run the maze correctly. They may have to roll or somersault or drag paralyzed limbs, but they do not make mistakes. They have learned an act that takes them to a particular place; they have not learned a set of specific limb or muscle reactions.[13] The cats in the puzzle box are an exception to the general picture one gets from other research on this problem. Perhaps the cats cannot learn an act, but are forced to learn a response because the escape mechanism is so arbitrary, so impossible for them to understand. What alternative would they have but trial-and-error?

Many psychologists, even those who admire the hardheaded, quantitative posture of S-R theory, have come to a reluctant judgment that simple S-R connections are often more plausible than real. The apparently simple connection of a response to a stimulus situation has not been a convenient element to use in the general analysis of behavior. Faced with this dilemma, one must either broaden the meaning of stimuli and responses so as to include perceptions and acts, which is to retreat from the hardheaded objectivity of true behaviorism, or propose an alternative element that will be easier to define and study. Many psychologists have broadened their definitions of stimulus and response to include unobservable events and processes that play much the same role in their theories as perceptions, images, ideas, and intentions played in the older psychologies. That is, they have adopted a contradictory position which we call subjective behaviorism.

Subjective behaviorism is a term general enough to include the anti-Hullians, who, in a way, were trying to fit something between S and R which represented the organism's active role in interpreting the stimulus and in effect modifying S through his evaluation of the feedback resulting from responding. A theory embracing much of subjective behaviorism can be found in the book *Plans and the Structure of Behavior*, written by an experimental psychologist, a mathematical psychologist, and a physiological psychologist, each having a stake in the importance of cognitive behavior in man.[14] Basing their discussion on the historical development of the reflex as a useful fiction, the authors proposed the TOTE unit (see Figure 15.7), referring to Test, Operate, Test, Exit, as a more convenient functional unit of behavior which would incorporate our growing understanding of cybernetic mechanisms; "The TOTE asserts simply that the operations an organism performs are constantly guided by the outcome of various tests." If an initial test discloses a mismatch between the actual and the desired state of things, an operation (which might include further test-operate cycles) would be initiated to reduce the mismatch; if a subsequent test indicated that the operation had succeeded, control would be transferred to another TOTE. By incorporating a sense of purpose to behavior, the authors can speak of plans, comparison of plans to the environment, matching of feedback to plan, and decision to act or operate. Planning can be thought of as a bias level for a simple reflex (a neuron will fire all of its charge when a bias value is exceeded and none

FIGURE 15.7

The Tote unit.

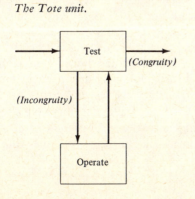

251

of its charge when that level is not reached), or it may be an hierarchical list of tests to be performed, which may number far more than the actions. To illustrate the TOTE, consider throwing a ball to second base while still running. Before you can act, you must have tested for distance, the position of the runner, the arrival of the receiver, and your own speed and have calculated a trajectory to boot. The feedback, especially if you miss, becomes a part of the plan that will be used in future tests, which are essentially comparisons for congruity between the "now" situation and the constantly revised plan. Physiological psychologists such as Pribram have made imaginative use of the TOTE in their experimental research on brain function,[15] but the accumulation of research findings bearing on the TOTE is presently much smaller than research based on the reflex.

The search for behavioral atoms has taken the subjective behaviorist to the electronic computer where research on various constructs can be done rapidly and models can be changed as research proceeds. The critics of this search, who condemn reductionism and the dehumanizing character of behavioristic models, argue for the wholistic study of living beings. B. F. Skinner would dismiss the subjective behaviorists for wasting time on inferred inner states, which he calls mentalisms. We will turn to these positions in later chapters.

Many learning experiments seem rather trivial, especially when isolated from their theoretical contexts. Indeed, it should probably be admitted that many of them would seem trivial in any context. But that must not mislead us. A most valuable strategy for the scientist is to take a plausible hypothesis and push it until it becomes ridiculous. Only in that way can he discover the range and power of his hypothesis, perhaps even find a better one. The ancient belief that learning is associative and that the mind is man's connection-system is a plausible hypothesis. But until it has been pushed as hard as possible one cannot tell how much truth there is in it.

Eventually this tedious pushing and testing may produce a valid scientific law, one whose importance could be literally overwhelming. Our entire way of life is predicated upon our ability to learn. Not only do we rely on learning to give us the basic skills with which we earn our daily bread, but also to educate our children for citizenship in a free society. It is a solid axiom of the great liberal tradition in England and America that education is the best tool for social progress. We believe that people learn their system of values, learn to love themselves and others, learn to channel their biological drives, even learn to be mentally ill. When we begin to analyze the learning process, therefore, we are probing the ultimate sources of our humanity. No one can now foresee what benefits or dangers may someday come from these fumbling efforts with caged animals and nonsense syllables—but we had better be prepared for success.

The Search for Behavioral Atoms

NOTES

1. E. L. Thorndike, *Human Learning* (New York: Appleton-Century-Crofts, 1931), p. 122. Unfortunately, Thorndike never asked whether such an inventory would be of finite length.

2. E. R. Hilgard, *Theories of Learning*, 2d ed. (New York: Appleton-Century-Crofts, 1956), pp. 9–11.

3. H. Ebbinghaus, *Memory: A Contribution to Experimental Psychology*, trans. H. A. Ruger and C. E. Bussenius (New York: Teachers College, Columbia University, 1913). A review of the field of research Ebbinghaus initiated can be found in J. A. McGeoch and A. L. Irion, *The Psychology of Human Learning*, rev. ed. (New York: Longmans, Green, 1952).

4. The idea that feedback loops (rather than reflex arcs) are the basic building blocks of the nervous system is the fundamental hypothesis of cybernetics. See, for example, N. Wiener, *Cybernetics* (New York: Wiley, 1948).

5. E. R. Hilgard and D. G. Marquis, *Conditioning and Learning*, rev. G. A. Kimble (New York: Appleton-Century-Crofts, 1961).

6. Delos D. Wickens, "The Transference of Conditioned Excitation and Conditioned Inhibition from One Muscle Group to the Antagonistic Muscle Group," *Journal of Experimental Psychology* 22 (1937): 101–123; also, D. D. Wickens, "The Simultaneous Transfer of Conditioned Excitation and Conditioned Inhibition," *Journal of Experimental Psychology* 24 (1939): 332–338.

7. R. S. Woodworth, *Experimental Psychology* (New York: Holt, 1938), p. 110.

8. G. Kimble, *Foundations of Conditioning and Learning* (New York: Appleton-Century-Crofts, 1967), p. 658.

9. K. Bykov, *The Cerebral Cortex and the Internal Organs* (New York: Chemical Publishing Co., 1957).

10. Edward L. Thorndike, *Animal Intelligence* (New York: Macmillan, 1898).

11. E. C. Tolman, *Purposive Behavior in Animals and Men* (New York: Century, 1932), p. 364.

12. Edwin R. Guthrie and G. P. Horton, *Cats in a Puzzle Box* (New York: Rinehart, 1946).

13. K. S. Lashley and D. A. McCarthy, "The Survival of the Maze Habit After Cerebellar Injuries," *Journal of Comparative Psychology* 6 (1926): 423–432.

14. G. A. Miller, E. Galanter, and K. H. Pribram, *Plans and the Structure of Behavior* (New York: Holt, 1960).

15. K. H. Pribram, *Languages of the Brain* (Englewood Cliffs, N.J.: Prentice-Hall, 1971).

SIXTEEN

B. F. Skinner: The Man, the Message, the Critique

I was taught to fear God, the
police, and what people will think.
—B. F. Skinner

B. F. Skinner is regarded as one of the most important and influential psychologists in the United States by professional psychologists and students, besides being a controversial figure in the eyes of the general public. Like other outstanding figures in the history of psychology before him, Skinner has reached out beyond the narrow confines of theorizing and research to tackle the larger issues of basic causality, how behavior can be controlled, and how behavioral science can be employed in the design of societies and cultures.

On one hand, he suffers the reputation of the scientific radical (in Kuhn's terms) who finds his work merely footnoted in the general textbooks as a departure from the mainstream of subjective behaviorism—a throwback to the early days of behaviorism which sometimes earns for Skinner the description from his critics as "one of the finest minds of the nineteenth century." On the other hand, Skinner's methodological and theoretical contributions have completely changed the way behavioral research is done, as a visit to any modern laboratory will testify. Further, he has a legion of followers organized under the Society for the Experimental Analysis of Behavior (a division of the American Psychological Association) who apply Skinnerian methods to research on a wide variety of problems, from animal behavior to the teaching of normal and retarded children. We shall also see that philosophers find Skinner a worthy enough target to attack, a tribute to his erudition and to his staunch advocacy of classic behaviorism as part of a fundamental statement on the nature of man. Skinner is also one of the few psychologists to engage in the philosophers' pastime of constructing a utopia.

Walden Two, Skinner's utopian vision of society, was published in 1948, producing a storm of criticism from many

intellectuals and journalists who were repelled by the plan of a society organized along the principles of determinism.[1] Skinner brought out *Beyond Freedom and Dignity*[2] with an accompanying barrage of publicity and television talk show appearances in 1971, producing even more national attention which was mixed but strong in tone.

> Monumental triviality![3]
>
> Intellectually bankrupt![4]
>
> Beginning with dogma and progressing through vague generalities and naive misinformation, it is hardly surprising that Skinner fails to make even the beginning of a credible case for his central thesis: that an effective, scientific "technology of behavior" is attainable.[5]
>
> . . . it is one of the strangest amalgams of compassion and misanthropy that has ever been my puzzlement to read.[6]
>
> . . . Dr. Skinner pays admirable attention to social problems at a time when psychology, as well as many other aspects of our society, seems ever more turned in upon itself.[7]
>
> Professor Skinner is a religionist and his religion is "Science." In the name of science he commits crucial errors of fact.[8]
>
> And from Vice President Spiro Agnew—"In this book Skinner attacks the very precepts on which our society is based saying that 'Life, Liberty and the pursuit of happiness' were once valid goals but have no place in 20th-century America or in the creation of a new culture such as he proposes."[9]

While many psychologists can take Skinner's writing with a grain of salt, it is obvious that the public does not. Thus, we should examine the life and scientific work of this remarkable and controversial man.

THE SHAPING OF B. F. SKINNER

Burrhus Fredric Skinner was born in Susquehana, Pennsylvania, March 20, 1904, beginning life in the embrace of a warm family in small-town America. Skinner writes of his own life in the series called *A History of Psychology in Autobiography*, revealing a kind of restrained sense of nostalgia one might not expect in a man thought to be the most hard-nosed of the behaviorists.

> Susquehana . . . was even then a rather dirty railroad town, but it is situated in a beautiful river valley. I roamed the hills for miles around. I picked arbutus and dogwood in early spring, chewed sassafras root . . . and found flint arrowheads. With another boy I built a shack in the hills alongside a creek, and I learned to swim in the pool we made by blocking the creek with a sod-and-stone dam. . . . I made slingshots, bows and arrows, blow guns and water pistols. . . . I worked for years on the design of a perpetual motion machine. (It did not

work.) I went through all twelve grades of school in a single building, and there were only eight students in my class when I graduated. I *liked* school.[10]

Skinner takes pains in his autobiography to point up the antecedent events or shaping forces in his early life that might account for his adult behavior. In his system, *operant behavior* is that behavior emitted by the unconstrained organism. Whether or not that behavior becomes a regular part of the organism's responses depends upon the environmental consequences or reinforcers which punish or reward the behavior. "Appropriate" behavior results from the scheduling of reinforcements which become more beneficial as the organism successively approximates the desired or expected behavior. Central to Skinner's thesis and to his evaluation of his own life is the argument that all behavior is controlled, including, of course, his own.

> My mother was quick to take alarm if I showed any deviation from what was "right." Her technique of control was to say "tut-tut" and to ask, "What will people think?" I can easily recall the consternation in my family when in second grade I brought home a report card on which, under "Deportment," the phrase "Annoys others" had been checked. . . . I was allowed to play in the cemetery next door, but it was not "right" to step on a grave. Recently in a Cathedral I found myself executing a series of smart right-angle detours to avoid the engraved stones on the floor. I was taught to respect books and it is only with a twinge that I can today crack the spine of a book to make it stay open. . . . My Grandmother Skinner made sure that I understood the concept of hell by showing me the glowing bed of coals in the parlor stove.

The story of Skinner's life is remarkable for its nonremarkableness. He appears to have been a bright youngster who read a great deal, who began an early and lasting acquaintance with the writings of Bacon, and who aspired (with much encouragement from his environment) to be a writer. The warmth of the academic embrace took over when he worked as a tutor for an intellectual family while attending Hamilton College, a small liberal arts college in New York. Skinner recalls fondly his progression to open revolt against the uninspiring faculty which took the form of elaborate pranks, editorial attacks, caricatures painted on the school walls, and disruption of the commencement exercises. One looks in vain for the direct environmental causes of this unseemly behavior.

Skinner worked for a while as a free-lance writer, making the obligatory tour of Greenwich Village and the Left Bank in Paris before going to Harvard to study psychology. He had been very excited by reading Pavlov in one of the Village bookstores. His literary

> *I had failed as a writer because I had nothing important to say, but I could not accept that explanation.*
>
> —*B. F. Skinner*

interests brought the intellectual magazine *The Dial* to his attention, and an article in it by Bertrand Russell opened a pathway to reading the man whom Skinner regarded as his most important influence— John B. Watson, the man who created and promoted behaviorism. At Harvard Skinner lived a spartan existence, concentrating on reading psychology and physiology to make up for lost study time. A self-propelled reader and thinker, Skinner did his thesis more or less on his own, submitting his papers to E. G. Boring, ignoring Boring's suggestions for revision, and finally winning approval of a committee from which Boring excused himself. The story of how his thesis evolved is described by Skinner in an article entitled "A Case History in Scientific Method," which perhaps gives the clearest insight into the man as a scientist.[11]

EVOLUTION OF A SCIENTIST

"So far as I can see, I began simply by looking for lawful processes in the behavior of the intact organism." Following up on work inspired by Sherrington's classic research on reflexes and the synapse, Skinner began developing apparatus to test his rats' behavior. In this work he

> *I had the clue from Pavlov: control your conditions and you will see order.*
>
> —*B. F. Skinner*

displayed great inventiveness in creating and dismantling gadgets and rat mazes in an almost chaotic flow of events, each of which built on the other in the manner of trial and error learning. Always one to attack the traditional view of learning as a logical, cumulative acquisition of habits, Skinner ended up with a research design he never contemplated at the beginning. The changes were not capricious; they were all concessions to the need for better control. In other words, Skinner would never settle for sloppy, deviant results without questioning his own manipulation of independent variables. Rather than rigidly following a preconceived hypothesis as one would do in formal empirical experimentation (or so published research would have us believe), Skinner would keep changing things until orderly behavior resulted. While many researchers use statistical combinations of data from the behavior of many rats to show averaged performance records, Skinner preferred to work with each individual case until the performance of each would be reliably produced by environmental manipulation.

Skinner's evolution as a scientist is a familiar enough story to anyone who has done laboratory research. Considering the charges raised later in his life about his advocacy of a dehumanizing amount of control in society, Skinner's unformalized principles of science are a familiar and quite human reminder of just how much art is involved in scientific research:

- *1.* When you run into something interesting, drop everything else and study it.
- *2.* Some ways of doing research are easier than others.
- *3.* Some people are lucky.
- *4.* Apparatuses sometimes break down.
- *5.* Welcome *serendipity*—the art of finding one thing while looking for something else.
- *6.* Any gain in rigor is more than matched by a loss in flexilibity.[12]

One fact that emerges from Skinner's account of his own scientific evolution is that he formulated his basic ideas very early and that he has not changed his thinking much since he earned his doctorate in 1931, except perhaps to become more sure of himself.

While doing his dissertation research, he invented the self-feeding mechanism for the rat, which became the basis for the operant conditioning scenario as distinguished from classical conditioning, the traditional S-R learning described previously. Skinner points to the crushing difficulties encountered in finding a stimulus for every response, as Pavlov's research seems to dictate. He proposed instead to distinguish two classes of responses, elicited and emitted.[13] Responses elicited by known stimuli are respondents; they can be studied by the traditional S-R approach. Operants are responses emitted without any known stimuli. Since there is no known stimulus for an operant response, it is logically impossible to talk about the strength of an S-R bond. As an alternative, therefore, Skinner proposed to measure the rate at which the operant is emitted and to explore all variables that can be shown to affect the rate of responding.

In his thesis research Skinner had developed an automatic feeder which fed the rat a single pellet whenever the bar was pressed. Normally, such events are recorded on an event recorder which consists of paper moving at a constant speed and a pen that is deflected with each event. The straight time line is similar to the abscissa of a graph. By having a string move the pen up one notch each time the bar was pressed, Skinner was able to produce a curved line that increased in slope as the rate of responding increased and flattened out when the animal ceased responding. This simple technique provided the ordinate of the graph and, as shown in Figure 16.1, gives a great deal more information about the time history of the response patterns of any organism. Since that time, the idea has been incorporated into the *cumulative recorder*, a standard behavioral instrument that has helped make the *rate of response* the fundamental unit of behavior for the Skinnerians.

In a typical experiment with operant conditioning, a hungry animal, usually a rat or a pigeon, is placed inside a small, soundproofed compartment (now known as a Skinner Box) and taught to make a simple response, to press a bar or peck a key, in order to obtain food. The grand convenience of this experimental situation derives from the fact that the relation between the animal's response and the presentation of food is completely arbitrary and at the disposal of the experimenter. Once an operant response is established, the rate at which it occurs can be influenced by a reinforcement that is itself contingent upon the response rate. Different reinforcement schedules can be invoked at various times or in the presence of different stimuli, depending upon the purpose of the experiment. Today, the scheduling of reinforcements and stimuli is facilitated by complex digital logic circuits and on-line digital computers whose use in research has been spurred greatly by the demands of the Skinnerians for more sophisticated control of behavior.

For example, when a key is illuminated by a red light, a pigeon

---

FIGURE 16.1

A typical cumulative record. Performance under variable-interval reinforcement for a pigeon (upper curve) and a chimpanzee (lower curve). (From Cumulative Record: A Selection of Papers, *Third Edition, by B. F. Skinner. Copyright © 1972 by Appleton-Century-Crofts, Educational Division, Meredith Corporation.)*

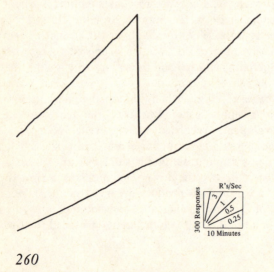

may be reinforced, say, after every fifth peck or haphazardly at a rate not faster than one per minute or at any preestablished rate. But when the light in the key changes color, turns green perhaps, no reinforcements are given pecking. The pecking response would soon come under the control of the red and green lights, which are called discriminative stimuli. In this way Skinner can bring an operant response under the control of a discriminative stimulus, a stimulus such as the red or green light that indicates when the response may be reinforced.

Several standard schedules which produce fairly stable rates of responding are commonly used.[14] The fixed ratio (FR) schedule involves the reinforcement of every nth response, and is often compared to the human experience of working for piece rate payment in a factory. The fixed interval (FI) schedule involves reinforcement given after a certain elapsed period of time. The FI schedule typically produces a cumulative record that looks scalloped, with an increase in rate of responding as the feeding time approaches, similar to the increased speed of the rented horse as he nears the stable. Variable interval and variable ratio schedules involve the sequencing together of varying time or number-of-response series which introduce the element of unpredictability of the reinforcement to the responding organism and usually lead to the highest rates of responding. Skinner's disciples like to point out the familiar human experience of playing the slot machines at Las Vegas casinos, which finds people responding at very high rates to a variable ratio reinforcement schedule built into each machine.

Skinner and his followers have developed a procedure that does reliably control animal behavior to such a degree that drug effects can be meaningfully studied by giving the drug to animals whose controlled behavior has been stabilized by operant conditioning. Increases or decreases in response rate are now cited as evidence in descriptions of new drugs which attest to their energizing or depressive qualities. Pigeons have been trained to discriminate visually between good and defective pills in an assembly line, although they have yet to replace quality control inspectors for practical reasons. In World War II Skinner worked on a secret project to train pigeons to discriminate target ships shown through a screen, as the first steps in using pigeons to guide an air-to-ground missile.[15] In the absence of an effective electronic guidance system, the idea was to have the pigeon peck at the ship image on the screen while attached to a complex rig that guided the missile. As long as the ship image was centered, the missile was on target, and the pigeon would be reinforced for his accuracy (until, of course, he got his final reinforcement). Skinner developed a simulator and conducted enough tests to prove that the pigeon was a reliable missile guidance system, but the project was canceled by an incredulous army brass who didn't doubt that the missile could be guided, but as Skinner reports, ". . . the spectacle of a living pigeon carrying out its assignment, no matter how beautifully, simply reminded the committee of how utterly fantastic our proposal was."

In a later episode Skinner again presented to the public a workable invention based on his ideas and met once again with skeptical and hostile reactions. In an article in the *Ladies Home Journal* he described how his daughter had been raised in a heated, efficient box instead of the conventional crib. He noted the efficiency of having the baby unencumbered by clothes, the reduced work involved in a roll-up sheet on the floor, the advantages of filtered air, his ability to control crying by slightly lowering the temperature, the protection granted to the family by soundproofing the box, and so forth.[16] The "baby box" article produced a predictable outcry, unfounded rumors about the mental health of his daughter, and no general use of the device. It produced in Skinner a certain testiness about the frivolous way in which the public avoids and dismisses workable improvements in technology as if they were arguing that nobility (dignity) results from doing things the hard way.

SKINNER VERSUS THE SUBJECTIVE BEHAVIORISTS

As an outspoken advocate of "radical behaviorism," Skinner has been involved in countless theoretical debates with subjective behaviorists, in spite of his feeling that theories are unnecessary. Just as Helmholtz and his followers attempted to stamp out vitalism, Skinner attacks mentalisms—those constructs invented by subjective behaviorists to intervene between S and R. According to Skinner, if we take determinism literally, such ideas as hunger, fatigue, guilt, anxiety, the self, mind, inner man, autonomous man, and free will are unnecessary explanatory fictions invented by observers who cannot observe them, by those who refuse to accept the argument that causality lies outside the organism, in the environment.[17] He sees the invention of inner states in man as the modern equivalent of the ancient idea that deviant behavior is the result of possession by an evil spirit ("The devil made me do it!" in Flip Wilson's terms). Skinner argues instead that the contingencies of reinforcement in the history of the organism can be examined to determine cause without appealing to hypothetical inner states or processes. Postulates such as those proposed by Clark Hull cannot become facts; they remain theories to the end. Observable behavior is, in Skinner's view, a subject worthy of study in and of itself, without taking flight to mathematical models, physiology, or economics because they seem more "scientific."

"The objection to inner states is not that they do not exist, but that they are not relevant to a functional analysis."[18] In this phrase

Skinner tries to soften the impact of some of his oft-repeated dismissals of hunger and other states inside the organism. These are called *intervening variables* by philosophers of science. One *infers* an intervening variable by observing behavior. The functional analysis Skinner speaks of is based on the attempt to predict and control the behavior of the individual organism. Behavior is the *dependent variable,* as most psychologists would agree. The *independent variables* are the external conditions manipulated by the environment or the scientist. The subjective behaviorists and many laymen would argue that the organism (in particular, a person) actively affects its behavior in accord with his internal states such as hunger, thirst, or state of awareness. Skinner argues that such words conceal references to independent variables, for example, "hunger" can be stated as the length of time for which the organism has been deprived of food. Subjective behaviorists and others retort that such a description leaves us with a view of organisms as empty boxes who are passive receivers of inputs, a picture that reduces the complexity of all organisms in general and the dignity of man in particular. This debate, which has raged on since the 1930s among psychologists, has now spilled out into the public arena.

SKINNER AND THE PROBLEMS OF SOCIETY

What we need is a technology of behavior. We could solve our problems quickly enough if we could adjust the growth of the world's population as precisely as we adjust the course of a spaceship. . . . One difficulty is that almost all of what we call behavioral science continues to trace behavior to states of mind, feelings, traits of character, human nature and so on. Physics and biology once followed similar practices and advanced only after discarding them.[19]

With this statement of faith in the natural, sciencelike application of the behavioral sciences, Skinner steps out as a futurist thinker in the book *Beyond Freedom and Dignity.* The title of this book means what Skinner says. In his view one of the main obstacles to a meaningful science of behavior is the view that man is free and that somehow his behavior is uncaused—the myth of an autonomous man. He sees the myth operating in many ways—in the literature of freedom, in the tendency to give credit to people for what the environment does, in the assignment of blame in the courts. Skinner quite clearly urges the abolishment of autonomous man as a false and unnecessary concept. He will probably be forever remembered for at least part of the following statement.

To man *qua* man we readily say good riddance. Only by disposing of autonomous man can we turn to the real causes of human behavior—from the inferred to the observed, from the miraculous to the natural, from the inaccessible to the manipulable.[20]

Skinner takes on his critics, the subjective behaviorists, soft thinkers, and the general public in extending his analysis of behavior as a function of reinforcement in all phases of life. Skinner argues that those who condemn his analysis simply can not face the facts, that they feel threatened by the idea that they can not really control themselves or the world through will power, that their objections are a display of wounded vanity because scientific facts have taken away reinforcers they are used to, resulting in a loss of dignity and worth. What follows is a summary of the nature of the American society as Skinner might view it.

Whether or not we are scientists or philosophers, whether or not we can accept the concept of determinism, whether or not we accept the implications of the main thrusts of behavioral science, we nonetheless dream occasionally about what a better, more orderly world might be like and think about the steps we might have to take to achieve that end. It may be true that western man develops in a democratic-humanistic tradition which tells him that man is free, is responsible for his actions, and is capable of making moral choices, but he seems to design his culture in ways that suggest that he has some

---

CITATION ACCOMPANYING THE DISTINGUISHED SCIENTIFIC
CONTRIBUTION AWARD PRESENTED BY THE AMERICAN PSYCHOLOGICAL
ASSOCIATION, 1958

"An imaginative and creative scientist, characterized by great objectivity in scientific matters and by warmth and enthusiasm in personal contacts. Choosing simple operant behavior as subject matter, he has challenged alternative analyses of behavior, insisting that description take precedence over hypotheses. By careful control of experimental conditions, he has produced data which are relatively free from fortuitous variation. Despite his antitheoretical position, he is considered an important systematist and has developed a self-consistent description of behavior which has greatly increased our ability to predict and control the behavior of organisms from rat to man. Few American psychologists have had so profound an impact on the development of psychology and on promising younger psychologists."

BURRHUS FREDRIC SKINNER

264

faith in determinism. The bureaucracies, organizations, and machines of a society indicate an acceptance of the belief that human behavior is caused by environmental influences, as experience with wage and price controls would suggest. But, contradictory to this belief stands the legal system and most organized religions which place responsibility for behavior in the individual, especially when the individual engages in deviant behavior. A cursory examination of any society will uncover the use of the law of effect to control behavior; but, as Skinner observes, emphasis is usually placed on punishment, suggesting that government be defined as the power to punish.

In the design of our American culture we have created more than just a system of punishments to fit crimes. Throughout our institutions we can find mechanisms that are built for the purpose of manipulating, channeling, or otherwise controlling behavior. The economy is a system of controlling behavior with rewards in the form of salaries, security, etc. The schools make no pretense about the fact that they are agencies to shape the behavior of our children through education. The threat of punishment, implicit in the power of legal and police institutions and in the heaven versus hell consequences of most religions, plays a role in controlling personal conduct. We reinforce certain types of conformity to group standards by manipulation of social reinforcements and punishments.

The priest has been replaced by the scientist who has gone to work for a technological society. Optimistic about how technology may contribute to the better life on earth, people turn to the scientist to lend his expertise and his tools; but invariably they forget to consider that a scientist comes with a set of values as well. Science and technology are founded on the regularity, predictability, and invariance of events. Most scientists preach determinism and faith in order. Future planning, so vital in our times, is said to be possible as long as we can control present events. If the behavior of man is uncontrolled, we sacrifice the possibility of controlling events. Yet, in Skinner's view, our societal practice of determinism is disturbed by our preaching of a philosophy of personal freedom—crediting accomplishments to heroes instead of the environment and embedding the concept of a free, responsible individual in our language and our literature. Arguing for more instead of less control, Skinner is highly critical of the literature of freedom because it may inspire "fanatical" opposition to control which may be "neurotic" or "psychotic." He sees signs of emotional instability in those who are deeply affected by the literature.

A scientific conception of human behavior dictates one practice, a philosophy of personal freedom another. Confusion in theory means confusion in practice. The present unhappy condition of the world may in large measure be traced to our vacillation. The principle issues in dispute between nations, both in peaceful assembly and on the battlefield, are intimately concerned with the problem of human freedom and control.[21]

The debate over the control of human behavior has been a continuing one, stimulating a great deal of writing among psychologists. In a now famous debate Skinner argued with Carl Rogers, a therapist and principal spokesman of the "soft" school of psychology.[22] Skinner first presented his familiar arguments in favor of control of behavior at the personal and governmental levels and his critique of the educational system, with its tendency to admire the student for knowledge he gains by "himself" while blaming him for ignorance. He feels that critics unfairly see "brainwashing" behind well-planned programs and that educators rationalize failure of the school systems while trying to deny that they are in the business of behavior control.

Rogers countered with a series of questions on who will control, who will be controlled, and toward what end will control be exercised. Fearful of turning the control of behavior over to scientists, Rogers argues that when an elite group of scientists (or any controllers) are the only ones free to make value choices of goals, ". . . the great majority are only slaves—no matter by what high-sounding name we call them." The choice of what to control is a value choice, a subjective choice made by a person. In Rogers's view we have a right to ask what values the controllers possess and to wonder just who will control the controllers.

Skinner, having the last word in the debate, said in response:

> Any list of values is a list of reinforcers. . . . People behave in [ethical] ways . . . because they are reinforced for doing so. . . . And whether we like it or not, survival is the ultimate criterion. . . . Do not ask me why I want mankind to survive. I can tell you why only in the sense in which a physiologist can tell you why I want to breathe. Once the relation between a given step and the survival of my group has been pointed out, I will take that step. And it is the business of science to point out just such relations.[23]

THE CRITIQUE

Skinner never knew what hit him. Few psychologists have generated as much critical writing as Skinner, but it is characteristic of the man that he seldom replied to or even read the criticism of his work. Stung by the widespread criticism of his vision of a behaviorally engineered utopian society (*Walden Two*), he lamented,

> One would scarcely guess that the authors are talking about a world in which there is food, clothing, and shelter for all, where everyone chooses his own work and works on the average of only four hours a day . . . where—in short—people are truly happy, secure, productive,

creative, and forward looking. What is wrong with it? Only one thing: someone planned it that way.[24]

Like Freud, Skinner sees little in the criticism of his ideas other than a naïve unwillingness to admit to the truth of his basic assumptions ("prescientific" thinking) or possibly poor behavioral programing in the life history of the critic. Skinner's critics, like Freud's, see a great deal of arrogance.

Critic Richard Sennett, reviewing *Beyond Freedom and Dignity,* noted that Skinner focused on the small group, villages, towns, and neighborhoods as the place where behavioral conditioning could operate morally, while stating that "control of the population as a whole must be delegated to specialists—to police, priests, owners, teachers, therapists, and so on." Suspecting that the advocate of neutral science applied to society's goals had made his own value judgment, Sennett summarized his reactions in a very searching way.

> The actual text of Skinner's new book reveals a man desperately in search of some way to preserve the old-fashioned virtues associated with 19th century individualism in a world where self-reliance no longer makes sense. . . . How in 1971 can a man equate industrial magnates with doctors of the soul? This is a child's view of society: there is no discrimination among controllers, everyone who has power is an authority. These beliefs . . . are the articles of faith in Nixonian America . . . [by one] who feels life has degenerated, has gotten beyond his control, and who thinks things will get better when other people learn how to behave. . . . Hoping to revive the morality of a less complicated age by invoking the certainties of an antiquated science, he appears to understand so little, indeed to care so little, about society itself that the reader comes totally to distrust him.[25]

Skinner's most persistent and strident critic is Noam Chomsky, who wrote a devastating review of *Beyond Freedom and Dignity.* In Skinner's boasting of the accomplishments of behavioral science and his assertions about what science must do, Chomsky finds that Skinner presents no evidence and that he displays dogmatism which is foreign to the nature of scientific inquiry. In this respect he sees Skinner stating that science must show that all behavior is determined by the environment, as is the case in other natural sciences. Why would any scientist insist on a particular conclusion stated in advance? Chomsky criticizes Skinner's dismissal of mentalisms and internal states.

> For Skinner's argument to have any force, he must show that people have wills, impulses, feelings, purposes and the like no more than rocks do. If people do differ from rocks in this respect, then a science of human behavior will have to take account of this fact.[26]

Chomsky is particularly bothered by the triviality of Skinner's basic assumptions, such as the great emphasis placed on how past ex-

267

perience determines behavior; "when we look for more specific predictions . . . we find virtually nothing." Instead, he finds a tendency to substitute jargon for commonly used words in his never-ending war on mentalisms. Skinner at one point retranslates an alienated young man's frustration into "extinction accompanied by emotional responses"; anxiety becomes "his behavior frequently has unavoidable aversive consequences which have emotional effects"; insecurity becomes "his behavior is weak and inappropriate." Even when Skinner describes a hobby as reinforcing, confusion results, as we wonder if he means that the behavior that leads to the hobby will be increased in probability of happening or whether he simply means that we enjoy the hobby. As Chomsky points out,

> A literal interpretation of such remarks yields gibberish and a metaphorical interpretation merely replaces an ordinary term by a technical term, with no gain in precision.[27]

Like many other critics, Chomsky senses some danger in accepting Skinner's image of man as entirely manipulatable, pointing out that "his approach could be as congenial to an anarchist as to a Nazi." He argues that the literature of freedom and dignity may be right in assuming that man has an intrinsic inclination toward free creative inquiry and productive work and that science at its best understands virtually nothing about human freedom and dignity.

> . . . it would be absurd to conclude merely from the fact that freedom is limited, that "autonomous man" is an illusion, or to overlook the distinction between a person who chooses to conform, in the face of threat or force or deprivation, and a person who "chooses" to obey. . . .[28]

How is a psychologist to react to Skinner? Few psychologists have chosen to attack his work in print, in part because they choose to ignore him and because there isn't much substance to attack. We are inclined to agree that Skinner's theory is a much oversimplified model, without much value to be generalized from pigeons to man. As pointed out in the introduction, many changes have taken place in all of the sciences, especially physics, causing us to question the limits of science. The basic model of determinism, so central to Skinner's faith, reveals itself to be a mentalism on close inspection. Laws governing matter turn out to have elements of unpredictability. Those many facts needed to predict and control behavior may be impractical to gather, and they can hardly be called unambiguous. In our opinion Skinner has failed to acknowledge or even to quote the many changes in the philosophy of science that have characterized twentieth-century science. By avoiding his critics and never fitting his ideas into the ideas of others, he stands very much alone. In pushing his model of man as a passive intermediary between the environment and behavior, Skinner has used his polished skills as a writer to lead a crusade.

No one can argue with the fact that behavior is controllable. Skinner's success with animal behavior and the success of his followers in shaping the behavior of mental retardates and prisoners will stand as useful social applications of the technology inspired by Skinner. But, in applying his principles and his values to all people in the whole of society, Skinner reveals this narrowness and dogmatism. Like many utopians, Skinner writes as if the Vietnam war never happened, as if social problems stemmed from minor defects in control mechanisms, and as if anger, oppression, violence, and other "mentalisms" could be legislated out of existence by a simple change in our language. Our point is that Skinner is tragically too late in urging society to control its culture scientifically.

The principles of determinism preceded Skinner by many thousands of years, as did the image of man as a passive robot. History is filled with the attempts of governments trying to arrange reinforcements, both positive and negative, to bring about control. Scientists

"DON'T LAUGH, HARKNESS—BUT EVERY TIME I START AN EXPERIMENT THESE DAYS, I WONDER WHETHER IT'S GOING TO BE THE ONE WHERE I END UP FINDING RELIGION."

(© *Punch, London.*)

(and their ancestors) who uncritically accepted the survival of the culture as the ultimate goal have been serving the controllers for centuries. In all of that time science and technology have been employed by controllers in the search for better mousetraps, and perhaps better Skinner Boxes as well. The mini-universe of the Skinner Box, like the totalitarian state, provides an illusory test of *any* theory of behavior. By definition, the exercise of choice is delimited or non-existent. In real life people may choose their own versions of Skinner Boxes, choosing to have their behavior controlled by an environment controlled by someone else. But, just as they choose to be controlled, they can and do choose *not* to be controlled—dropping out, tuning out, or rebelling for reasons that only the man himself can give accurate evidence on. It is this "semiautonomous" man that Skinner doesn't understand.

Skinner, science, technology, politicians, dictators, and liberals who value an efficiently programed society have been selling the basic ideas found in *Beyond Freedom and Dignity* since the beginning of organized cultures. The message is always the same—accept my views and my ways and I promise you the good life. But, the good life always turns out to be a function of the values of the controller, and in Skinner's case it looks suspiciously like his theory. Because his theory merely tells man that his inner self doesn't exist, the theory promises more than it can deliver. Whether fictional or real, people who live happily or unhappily with feelings, who plan their lives and make their choices on the basis of those feelings, tend to reject Skinner's theory and even his machines. Indeed, many people reject or run away from the good life, a behavioral fact that Skinner chooses to ignore.

Psychoanalysts are quick to argue that history, with its alternation between freedom and control, is a mirror of a "crucial struggle between man's impulse life and his capacity for intelligent and flexible self-control."[29] In effect, they argue that to freeze a culture into a design that takes into account only one side of man's dual nature (in this case, the rational) is to deny reality and to set the stage for revolutionary or catastrophic change.

In many ways Skinner's utopian visions force us all to face the logical consequences of continuing to move in the direction of an overcontrolled or overdetermined society. The absence of doubt in Skinner's writings stands as a symbol of the kind of dehumanization that could result from taking him, or any other controller with a simple answer, too seriously. We are living in a time of an ecological crisis which has proven that even the scientists who would control matter have limits on their knowledge which can lead to disastrous results when they experiment in the physical environment.

A child in today's world knows much more than his parents did at a similar age. But he doesn't know anything more than his parents did about the wisest ways to use what he knows. The psychologists have not speeded up the process of obtaining wisdom, only greatly increased the need for it. It becomes increasingly clear that our times are witness to the possibilities of terror. With their benign smiles, gentle manners, and blind minds, the psychologists would lead us straight for the sun.[30]

NOTES

1. B. F. Skinner, *Walden Two* (New York: Macmillan, 1948). Walden Two exists as an experimental community in Virginia (at this writing). A newsletter can be obtained at nominal cost from Twin Oaks Community, Louisa, Virginia 23093. Older newsletters have been collected in a book: *Experimenting with Walden Two: The Collected Leaves of Twin Oaks* (Louisa, Virginia: Twin Oaks Community, 1972), available from the same address.
2. B. F. Skinner, *Beyond Freedom and Dignity* (New York: Knopf, 1971).
3. A. Koestler, *The Ghost in the Machine* (New York: Macmillan, 1967).
4. *Time* Magazine, 20 September 1971, 47–53.
5. R. Claiborne, "Dr. Skinner's Game Plan for Human Society (Review of *Beyond Freedom and Dignity*)," *Book World*, 10 October 1971.
6. W. Arnold, "Review of *Beyond Freedom and Dignity*," *Saturday Review*, 9 October 1971, pp. 47–52.
7. Ibid.
8. M. Beldoch, "Science as Fiction (Review of *Beyond Freedom and Dignity*)," *Psychotherapy and Social Science Review* 6, no. 1 (1972): 12–18.
9. S. T. Agnew, "Farm Bureau Address," *Psychology Today* 5, no. 8 (1972): 4–87. For reactions by psychologists to *Beyond Freedom and Dignity*, see W. F. Day and O. Hobart Mowrer, "Beyond Bondage and Regimentation," *Contemporary Psychology* 17, no. 9 (1972): 465–472.
10. B. F. Skinner, "Autobiography," in *A History of Psychology in Autobiography*, ed. E. G. Boring and G. Lindzey (New York: Appleton-Century-Crofts, 1967), pp. 385–413.
11. B. F. Skinner, "A Case History in Scientific Method," in *Cumulative Record*, enlarged ed. (New York: Appleton-Century-Crofts, 1959), pp. 76–99.
12. Ibid. The quoted rules have been paraphrased.
13. B. F. Skinner, *The Behavior of Organisms* (New York: Appleton-Century-Crofts, 1938).
14. B. F. Skinner, *Contingencies of Reinforcement: A Theoretical Analysis* (New York: Appleton-Century-Crofts, 1969).
15. B. F. Skinner, "Pigeons in a Pelican," in *Cumulative Record*, enlarged ed. (New York: Appleton-Century-Crofts, 1959), pp. 426.01–426.18.
16. B. F. Skinner, "Baby in a Box," in *Cumulative Record*, enlarged ed., pp. 419–426.
17. Skinner, *Contingencies of Reinforcement*.
18. B. F. Skinner, *Science and Human Behavior* (New York: Macmillan, 1953), p. 35.

271

19. Skinner, *Beyond Freedom and Dignity*, p. 37.

20. Ibid., p. 78.

21. Skinner, *Science and Human Behavior*, p. 9.

22. C. R. Rogers and B. F. Skinner, "Some Issues Concerning the Control of Human Behavior," *Science* 124, no. 3231 (1956): 1057–1066.

23. Ibid., p. 1055.

24. Ibid., p. 1060.

25. R. Sennett, "Review of *Beyond Freedom and Dignity*," *New York Times Book Review*, 24 October 1971, pp. 1–18.

26. N. Chomsky, "The Case Against B. F. Skinner (Review of *Beyond Freedom and Dignity*)," *New York Review of Books*, 30 December 1971, p. 19.

27. Ibid., p. 22.

28. Ibid., p. 23.

29. M. Beldoch, "Science as Fiction."

30. Ibid., p. 18.

SEVENTEEN
Animal Behavior

Tony, the fox terrier, when he wants to go out into the road, puts his head under the latch of the gate, lifts it, and waits for the gate to swing open. Now an observer of the dog's intelligent action might well suppose that he clearly perceived how the end in view was to be gained, and the most appropriate means for effecting his purpose. The following chain of ideas might be supposed to pass through the dog's mind, not, indeed, in a clear-cut logical form, but at any rate in a rough and practically serviceable way: "Why does that gate remain shut? The latch holds it. I'll lift the latch. Now it is no longer held, therefore it swings open."

The English psychologist C. Lloyd Morgan doubted that any such thoughts ever entered his fox terrier's head; to prove it he described how the dog happened to learn the trick.

I was sitting at a window above the garden and heard the dog put out of door. I therefore watched him. He ran up and down the low wall, and put his head out between the iron bars, now here, now there, now elsewhere, anxiously gazing into the road. This he did for quite three or four minutes. At length it so happened that he put out his head beneath the latch, which is at a convenient height for his doing so, being about a foot above the level of the wall. The latch was thus lifted. He withdrew his head, and began to look out elsewhere, when he found that the gate was swinging open, and out he bolted. After that, whenever I took him out, I shut the gate in his face, and waited till he opened it for himself and joined me. I did not give him any assistance in any way, but just waited and watched, sometimes putting him back and making him open it again. Gradually he went, after fewer pokings of his head out in the wrong place, to the one opening at which the latch was lifted. But it was nearly three weeks from my first noticing his actions from the window before he went at once and with precision to the right place. . . .

Now what I am particularly anxious to enforce is that what we need is careful investigation in place of anecdotal reporting.[1]

This passage, an anecdotal refutation of the anecdotal method of studying animals, was written in 1894. Morgan's efforts to establish a true science of animal behavior were inspired by the theory of evolution. Charles Darwin had focused attention on the problems of adaptation—progressively improving adaptation—of the animal to its environment. Animals adapt to their environments through their *behavior;*

273

behavior thus becomes a central problem for all zoological sciences. At the time Morgan wrote, the future development of biology seemed to hinge upon the creation of a new science, a science of comparative behavior equal in scope and precision to the older science of comparative anatomy.

Earlier attempts to develop a comparative psychology, however, were more gossip than science. Animal trainers, zoo keepers, veterinarians, hunters, animal lovers generally, all had surprising yarns to spin of characteristically human achievements by animals. When these anecdotes had been carefully collected, classified, annotated, and published, the result was a welter of partly true, partly wishful, always interesting misinformation. Even the great Darwin treated such stories as if they were scientific evidence and used them to argue in favor of the evolution of man's mental powers.

Into this situation Morgan tried to introduce a scientific precept known as the law of parsimony. As he applied it to the study of animal behavior, the law decreed that, "In no case may we interpret an action as the outcome of the exercise of a higher psychical faculty, if it can be interpreted as the outcome of the exercise of one which stands lower in the psychological scale."[2]

Subsequent generations of psychologists have called this Lloyd Morgan's canon and have assumed that what he must have meant was that anthropomorphism—attribution of human characteristics to gods or, as in this case animals—is unscientific. A glance into Morgan's books, however, is enough to refute this assumption. Like all his contemporaries, Morgan took it for granted that since the only psychical faculties we can know anything about directly are our own, "introspection must inevitably be the basis and foundation of all comparative psychology."[3] Any human introspections would necessarily be anthropomorphic; all that Morgan hoped for were a few reasonable rules for playing the anthropomorphic game. The systematic, but probably impossible, effort to avoid projecting any human mental functions into animals did not really reach full strength until the advent of behaviorism. But that was at a later time and in another land.

Willingness to attribute human intelligence to animals is sometimes carried to fantastic extremes. Around the beginning of the century an eccentric German named von Osten decided that higher animals are as smart as men and took it as his mission to demonstrate the truth of his belief.[4] For the first pupil he chose a horse that for some reason had struck him as especially clever. He spent about two years educating it. In order to communicate, the horse shook its head appropriately to say yes or no; for all other answers it tapped on the ground with a foreleg. By the end of the second year the horse, known then as Clever Hans, could read and, by tapping, write; could under-

stand the four fundamental rules of arithmetic; could change common fractions into decimals and back again; and could give the day of the month. Moreover, Clever Hans could tell time and would even shake his head to indicate that an error had been made in playing a musical chord on the piano.

Many people were dubious. But Herr von Osten did not exploit his horse financially and was quite willing to let others ask the questions. A charlatan would hardly have dared to give such cooperation to his critics. Clever Hans seemed truly clever. Because this was obviously an important matter, a commission of eminent zoologists and psychologists was appointed to study the horse. The commission felt that in the course of its prolonged examination any possibility of trickery had been completely ruled out. Thus science put its awesome authority behind Herr von Osten's claims for the intelligence of higher mammals. Clever Hans's admirers were jubiliant. Aesop could scarcely have asked for more.

But there was trickery involved. Oskar Pfungst uncovered it only a few weeks after the distinguished commission gave its testimonial. Pfungst showed that when questions were written on cards and selected from a pile so that no one but Clever Hans knew what the question was, the horse could not answer anything at all. It would begin to tap and would continue indefinitely, looking intently at the questioner, as though waiting for some sign to stop. Pfungst discovered that the horse was looking for very small movements of the questioner's head. For the questioner to know whether the horse was giving the right answer, he first had to work the problem himself, then to count subvocally as the horse tapped out its answer. After the last of the expected taps the person would relax ever so slightly, thus inadvertently and unconsciously making a tiny movement. This was what

Clever Hans was waiting for. Once he had discovered this secret, Pfungst could get any answer he liked. It was not, to use Lloyd Morgan's terms, the higher psychical faculty of reasoning, but the lower psychical faculty of perception, that made Clever Hans so remarkable. Similar cueing of people by experimenters has been found.

We should not assume, however, that the turn of the century was a time of universal gullibility about the capacities of lower animals. Clever Hans got a great deal of notoriety from the newspapers, but simultaneously in less publicized quarters the real science of animal behavior was moving ahead at a remarkable pace. The cautious, insightful description of animal behavior was actually flourishing in one of its finest periods around the end of the nineteenth and beginning of the twentieth centuries. Nearly all the great biologists, both in Europe and America, were among the contributors. But then, just as the scientific study of animal behavior was beginning to prosper, the stream of research dried up, first in biology and later in psychology. The systematic description of natural behavior and the comparison of different species with one another and with man lost its impetus. After a brief period of advance, comparative psychology languished for more than a quarter of a century.

Why the sudden change in direction? Had Darwin's ideas been discredited? No, their value for dissolving old mistakes had never been more apparent. Had the work proved too difficult? No, the necessary methods had been slowly developing and progress was by and large encouraging. Had animals become uninteresting? Not at all. A topic that had fascinated men for centuries could scarcely lose its charm in a brief decade.

The true reason seems to have been that biologists were diverted into even more promising lines of research. The diversion arose from the rediscovery of the laws of heredity that Gregor Mendel had first described in 1865. In 1900 Mendel's laws were rediscovered independently by Correns in Germany, by DeVries in Holland, and by Tschermak in Austria. The true significance of the discovery could be recognized in 1900, and a science of genetics could be created to develop and extend the fundamental laws. Moreover, there already existed a relatively advanced science of the cell, cytology, that could be used to explore the actual mechanisms underlying the laws of heredity. It was around 1900 that cytologists formulated the correct hypothesis that the chromosome—a rod-shaped structure they had seen in the nucleus of the cell—plays an important genetic role. In 1902, independently of each other, the German Boveri and the American Sutton perceived the parallel between what a chromosome does under the microscope and what Mendelian genes do in breeding experiments. On the basis of this parallel, cytology and genetics were unified into a single body of knowledge. All this was profoundly exciting. Little wonder that biologists shifted from studies of animal behavior to the new opportunities in genetics.

For biologically oriented psychologists, a second diversion followed: Pavlov developed his objective method to investigate the conditioning of responses to new stimuli. The discovery of conditioning and the behavioral laws that grew out of the conditioning experiments had important consequences in at least two directions: in ecology, the part of biology that deals with processes outside the skin, and in physiology, the part of biology that deals with processes inside the skin.

The Russian discoveries introduced an analytic approach in place of the ecological study of animals in their natural habitats. The reflex became the basic unit of analysis. According to Pavlov, complex behaviors are built up automatically from simpler reactions by the process of conditioning. "It is obvious," he said, "that the different kinds of habits based on training, education and discipline of any sort are nothing but a long chain of conditional reflexes."[5] For example, Tony, the fox terrier, was simply acquiring a chain of conditional reflexes when he learned to lift the latch and open the gate; the fact that a detailed analysis of Tony's behavior into the component reflexes would obviously be a tedious task was beside the point. It seemed far wiser and simpler to study the basic atoms of behavior in a laboratory, where conditions could be properly controlled and precise measurements made, than to try to tease out all the unpredictable things that might be important in the animal's natural habitat.

In the United States it was John B. Watson who, more than anyone else, made Pavlov's work the basis for a new kind of psychological theory. Conditional reflexes gave him a technique to study association and learning without recourse to introspection. He undertook to demonstrate, for example, that emotional responses in babies are simply a form of conditional reflex.

Behaviorism corrected many of the worst tender-minded mistakes of the older psychologists. It imposed a rigorous discipline upon its adherents. To illustrate: When behaviorists applied Morgan's canon of interpretation to human beings, they reasoned that what a man does should not be explained in terms of higher mental processes until an explanation in terms of simpler processes—which often meant Pavlovian reflexes—had been shown to be inadequate. No longer would an introspective report be accepted as scientific evidence; all the older work had to be discarded to make way for a fresh start.

By the 1930s this revolution had led to a curious situation in American comparative psychology. Animals represented biological objectivity; a psychological law seemed truly basic only if it held for man and beast alike. In fact, however, behaviorists were still psychologists at heart and, like most psychologists, were interested more in people than in animals. Consequently, although they were willing to study animals, they did not really care what animals. They chose the rat, a creature as good as any for their purposes, and more convenient than most.

Robert Lockard has summarized the basic premises that he believes characterized the narrow, dogmatic position of comparative psychologists from the 1930s through the 1950s. These would apply to the hard-nosed Hullians as well as the more subjective behaviorists such as Tolman.

1. There is a phylogenetic scale, a sort of linear arrangement from simple to complex, from unintelligent to intelligent, from amoeba to man.
2. Convenient animals such as chickens, rats, cats, dogs, and monkeys can be arranged in order along the scale.
3. The comparative method is essentially a scaling problem of arranging animals of differing degrees of intelligence on the phylogenetic scale.
4. Because of the scale, animals lower in the scale are increasingly simpler but not different in kind. A white rat is a simple version of a human being.
5. Learning is the key to human behavior, because most behavior is acquired. Hunger, thirst, sex, respiration, and a thing or two more may be built in as original tendencies, but these few things are merely the unconditioned responses on which behavior is built.
6. Because so little is built into animals, genetics and evolution are irrelevant to psychology.
7. Most animals are pretty much alike. Species differences are few and probably accounted for by sensory differences and different experiences.
8. There are laws of behavior that are best formulated within the framework, "Such-and-such a treatment has such-and-such effect."
9. Animal behavior can be studied in the laboratory because of the controlled conditions. Laboratory conditions simplify behavior.
10. The best variables to study the effects of are physical variables.[6]

Thousands of behavioral experiments were done with rats; for decades the rest of the animal kingdom was largely forgotten. Thus behaviorism provoked the wisecrack that a psychologist differs from a magician because he pulls habits out of a rat. Indeed, some behaviorists claimed to pull the whole science of psychology out of a rat.

One rationalization for concentrating on a single species was that all behavior consists of reflexes; a reflex is much the same in one animal as in another. The important thing to study was how new reflexes are built out of old ones; this could be done as well with rats as with any other infrahuman vertebrate. In all this there remained only a hollow echo of an older, ecological concept of comparative psychology.

But just when comparative psychology seemed to have expired, it began to revive. The new ideas came largely from biologists. In Europe the revival took place under the name of ethology.[7] Without waiting to see whether conditional reflexes might be the atoms of all behavior, ethologists set out to discover what behavioral facts they had to explain. Whenever possible they preferred to study a species under its normal living conditions. It quickly became apparent that many of the tasks psychologists used were unnatural; the same animals that looked so stupid in a laboratory might behave most ingeniously when tested in their natural surroundings. In particular, social adaptation was discovered to be crucially important—yet animal society had been largely ignored in the psychological laboratories where animals were normally housed and tested in isolation. This revival of comparative studies had a salutary effect. A series of new and exciting discoveries about animal behavior and animal society have provided a broader and more realistic context for psychological research.

Since much of the interest in ethology has come from ornithologists and bird watchers (plus some repentant behaviorists), it is appropriate to introduce a bit of bird behavior as an example. For many years even the animal psychologists who did not like rats still tended to concentrate on mammals; psychological publications about the animal kingdom were mainly devoted to the small, mammalian duchy adjacent to *homo sapiens*. But mammals are very brainy beasts, and this concentration produced a distorted view of instinct, the nature and importance of which is clearest in lower animals. The study of birds has gone a long way toward correcting this false perspective.

Parental behavior in the ring dove (*Streptopelia risoria*) provides a particularly good example because it has been carefully analyzed and because so many different factors—instinct, social interaction, hormones, learning—can all be seen at work in the small and intimate universe of a dove's nest.

Doves and pigeons belong to the same order of birds; the little members are doves and the big ones pigeons, but the distinction has never been very sharp. The ring dove is a small, buff-colored bird with a black collar (hence the name) that normally lives in southeastern Europe and Asia. The male and the female are, to an untrained observer, indistinguishable. As in most birds, the breeding behavior of the ring dove goes through a succession of stages: courtship, mating, nest building, incubation, brooding over and feeding the young. If a pair is left together this cycle repeats about every five weeks. If the birds are kept in isolation, however, every trace of the cycle disappears; a female will not even lay an egg unless she has seen a male nearby. Apparently the appropriate visual stimulation is necessary before her pituitary gland can secrete the hormones required to start the cycle going.[8]

Ring doves normally lay two eggs in a clutch, and both parents share in the duties of incubating the eggs and brooding over the young. As soon as the eggs are laid the wonderful biochemical pacemaker that supplies the right hormones at the right time in the cycle now irritates the skin on the dove's breast. The cool, smooth surface of the eggs promises relief; the doves open out their feathers and settle down in comfort for the two-week period of incubation.

When the squabs hatch out they are fed in a manner that seems to be almost unique to pigeons and doves. Some birds, like ducks and geese, are able to pick up food as soon as they hatch. Others, like thrushes and blackbirds, hatch out naked, blind, and helpless, unable to do more than lift their heads and open their beaks so that the parents can drop food into them. Pigeons and doves are hatched in this helpless state, but the parent bird does not have to leave the nest to forage for food; another hormonal miracle anticipates the new conditions and fills the parent's crops with a secretion—the so-called cropmilk—that can be regurgitated to feed the young squabs. After the dove has been sitting on the eggs for about a week the walls of its crop begin to thicken as the cropmilk begins to form. The crop, a pouch in the walls of the esophagus where ordinarily food can be stored and prepared for entry into the true stomach, eventually fills up with milk and becomes so distended that the pouches on either side of the bird's throat can easily be felt with the fingers. Feeding behavior in the ring dove can occur only when those pouches are distended with cropmilk.

The problem is how to get the cropmilk out of the crops and into the squabs. It is solved by regurgitation, but the details are slightly complicated. Feeding can be initiated either by the parent or the squab. When the squab takes the initiative, the vomiting movements by the parent are triggered—released, the ethologists would say—by rapid head movements of the squab against the breast of the parent. The squab tries to raise its head, but its neck is so weak that the head wobbles back and forth unsteadily and eventually touches the skin over the distended crop. At this point the parent looks down, an act which brings its bill in contact with the rapidly moving head of the squab. When the bills meet, the parent grasps the bill of the squab, the squab thrusts its head deep into the parent's throat, and the regurgitation movements begin. Regurgitation movements consist of opening the bill as wide as possible, assuming a horizontal position with the neck rigid and slightly bowed, and making convulsive movements of the shoulders and nodding movements of the head and neck. The duration of this activity can range from one up to fifteen seconds.

Being touched on the full crop has an emetic effect on the ring dove, as the young squab can initiate the feeding activity by touching the parent's crop. It is also possible for the parent to initiate feeding. The parent can peck gently at the bill of the squab, thus arousing it to make the characteristic head movements that trigger the activity pattern. The parents often take the initiative in this way as the squabs grow older. When the squabs are four to eight days old the parents do not brood continuously; they may feed the squabs by coming to the nest and pecking the squabs' bills, which releases the feeding behavior. As the squabs grow older the parent's hormones continue their work and the crop glands begin to shrink, the crop gradually begins to hold less of the cropmilk and more of the grain that the bird is eating. In this way the squabs are gradually shifted to the adult diet. After ten or fifteen days, the feeding behavior stops entirely.

Here one sees an instinct at work. It is a fragile bit of machinery, at the mercy of hormonal changes and social interactions that must cooperate in exactly the right sequence if the young birds are to survive. A question that usually arises when one sees such a wondrous bit of biological engineering is the extent to which it can be modified by experience. Is it, in truth, rigid, preformed, predetermined by the way ring doves are built? Or is it, at least in part, a learned adjustment to the demands of the environment? In a very careful series of experiments the American psychologist D. S. Lehrman proved that learning does occur and that the normal pattern of parental behavior is, at least in part, the result of previous experience.[9]

What happens the first time a parent sees a newly hatched squab? After watching many new parents in this novel situation, Lehrman discovered that the feeding activity is always initiated by the squab; an inexperienced parent never tapped the squab to stimulate it to make the necessary head movements. This observation convinced him that the experienced parent learns how to arouse the squab at feeding time, that the instinctual act of feeding the young is normally modified by experience. In order to test his argument, Lehrman took two groups of ring doves, one with experience feeding the young, the other without experience. He injected both groups with prolactin, a pituitary hormone that stimulates secretion of cropmilk. After seven days of prolactin, all the doves had crops distended with cropmilk. They were then exposed to young squabs (borrowed from another family, of course). The experienced birds approached the squabs slowly, pecked at their bills gently to arouse the head movements, and so completed the feeding response. The inexperienced birds, however, did not know how to use the squabs to relieve the tension in their crops; since they were not broody and thus not in position to be touched by the squabs, none of the innocents showed the so-called instinctual pattern of regurgitation feeding. (Normally, an inexperienced parent will have secreted progesterone, the hormone that produces broodiness. A broody parent sits on the young and so is in position to receive tactual stimulation from the haphazard movements of the squab's head.)

In this particular instance, therefore, the instinct works by a peripheral mechanism—tension in the crop that must be relieved—and not through some inherited pattern laid down at birth in the bird's central nervous system. By comparison with higher mammals, the effects of learning are relatively slight, the effects of hormones are rather direct, and the stimuli that release the behavior are rather simple. But even here the instinct is not a blind, mechanical pattern that runs off mechanically without respect for environmental conditions.

Admittedly, it would be foolish to generalize from the parental behavior of a ring dove to any other species or to any other instinctual pattern. But a careful inspection of this relatively simple case should convey some impression of how difficult it is to distinguish between those two ancient, theoretical competitors, heredity and environment.

However, at least one by-product of the ethological revolution in animal behavior has been a return to consideration of the effects of heredity on behavior. Lockhard goes so far as to say, "Learning is not the key to animal behavior because most behavior is not acquired. The overwhelming majority of animals (96%) are invertebrates; of these, most are insects." From the almost poetic observations by early writers of the elaborate nest building of the digger wasp to the beautifully photographed sequences on the complex mating and social organizations of insects shown in the film *The Hellstrom Chronicles*, we find evidence of innate behavior sequences that are probably naturally selected learning mechanisms which respond to ecological demands. The field of behavior genetics or biopsychology has risen out of the integration of these observations and the breeding of behavioral tendencies into later generations of fruitflies and rats.

One very productive line of research on animal behavior has been labeled *imprinting*, a kind of learning that occurs in the earliest hours of the animal's existence. Unlike the association learning so revered by the behaviorists, imprinting deals with the first exposure of the animal to stimuli—an event that shapes the adult behavior for all time. The classic study by Konrad Lorenz involved exposing ducks to a decoy immediately after birth; the ducks would follow this object then and would prefer to follow the decoy when tested as adults.[10] In one wry variation of the study, Lorenz imprinted the ducks to follow *him*, posing, with appropriate quacking noises, as a surrogate mother duck.

The success of these experiments in social behavior has been extended to the imprinting of fear responses, sensory preferences, and food reinforcement. The theory of imprinting centers on an innate releasing mechanism in which instinctual behavior patterns can be observed only if the particular stimulus occurs during a critical period (which varies with species) shortly after birth. If the stimulus is experienced before or after the critical period, imprinting does not take place. Under ideal conditions, which include perfect timing and the expenditure of effort by the animal, imprinting leads to behavior patterns that are apparently irreversible.[11] Imprinting research, primarily with birds, has been done mainly in laboratories despite the focus on inherited behavior tendencies, as the need for precise control and a reductionist research strategy was evident from the start.

Turning our attention to research on mammals, let us consider how they discharge their parental duties. Mammals are more complicated than birds and take longer to develop. Part of the development is postponed until after birth, which is why the problem of parental care is particularly important for the survival of mammalian species.

A convenient example is the rat.[12] The rat's parental behavior is maternal behavior, since the female provides all the care for the young. (Baby rats are born during the night, an inconvenience that usually leads investigators who study them to keep their rats in a room where, by the modern miracle of electricity, the day-night cycle is reversed.) At the time of birth the mother rat is amazingly skillful at removing the foetal membranes, which she immediately eats, and at biting off the umbilical cord. This skill is just as apparent with the first litter as with all subsequent litters. The cleaning of each young pup is accomplished by much licking and cleaning, which is the mother's reaction to complex nutritional needs. For the young pups this mauling about is a necessary part of the birth process and serves to stimulate the circulation of blood.

At about the time of birth—a little before or a little after—the mother usually builds a nest out of whatever materials are available. Although it may vary greatly in its structural details, a rat's nest is a notoriously untidy thing. Some rats build no nest at all; others pile up all the straw or bits of paper they can find and so make a very large nest. A really eager builder may even pick up her own tail in her teeth and deposit that on the nest, too.

Nursing is not very complicated. The mother responds to the presence of young in the nest by simply crouching over them; most of the work is done by the pups. Young rats will try to crawl under any warm object, a kind of reaction known among ethologists as a taxis. Once under the mother, the pup finds a nipple by searching movements of the head. When a nipple is found the pup catches hold very strongly; if the mother is startled and leaves the nest, she will usually drag two or three youngsters along with her.

The part of this maternal behavior that has been studied most extensively, probably because it is easiest to see, is the mother's retrieving behavior. Whenever the pups are scattered the mother tries to collect them and put them back in the nest. This retrieving behavior is strongest at first. As the young rats become more and more active, the mother's efforts to keep them nursing in the nest become progressively less enthusiastic and eventually cease. During the time it is present, however, retrieving behavior presents a good opportunity to study instinctive behavior in a mammal.

A significant thing about mammalian instincts is the relative complexity of the stimuli that can release them.[13] With the feeding response of the ring dove the releaser was simply the squab touching the distended crop; with the retrieving response of the rat, things seem much more complicated. Consider the following evidence.

First, it is possible to cut the olfactory nerve in the female rat so that she cannot smell anything. When the nerve is cut, however, the retrieval responses remain unimpaired. This means that if there is some simple releasing stimulus, it is not an odor.

Next, one may take another group of mothers and try vision. The female can be blinded, but this does not interfere with retrieving either. Again, if there is a simple releasing stimulus, it is not something the rat sees.

Next, if one takes a group of mother rats and cuts the nerves to their mouths so that they cannot feel or taste the pups they are retrieving, once more there is no effect on the retrieving responses. If there is a simple releasing stimulus, it is not a touch or a taste.

If the releaser is not an odor, a taste, or a visual object, what is it? The answer is that all these aspects are involved. If one puts lavender on the pups to make them smell strange, or if they are dead and cold, or if their visual appearance is altered, the female will still retrieve them, but not as rapidly as she would normally. Since the instinctive behavior is triggered by a group of factors, taking away only one at a time does not stop the instinct from coming into play. This degree of complexity and redundancy, which is characteristic of mammalian instincts, may be related to the larger mammalian brain and to greater modifiability through experience.

There is no sense in which one can imagine this rodent behavior evolving out of the pattern described in the ring dove; nevertheless, the comparison between them is probably not unrepresentative of the picture one could gather from a broader sample of birds and mammals. A general rule of thumb is that mammals are more complex, more flexible, and more intelligent—all presumably correlated with the enlargement of the mammalian neocortex, which in turn probably evolved from different ecological factors.

There are, of course, astonishing differences in parental behavior even among the mammals. A rat is not especially typical of anything but rats. For comparison it is interesting to look at how our nearest relatives, the primates, take care of their young.[14] An infant monkey makes an especially good subject because it is enough like humans, perhaps, to enable psychologists or biologists to generalize what can be learned from observing it. On the other hand, unlike the completely helpless human infant, the baby monkey is active and ready to go the instant it is born. As soon as its shoulders and arms are free of the birth canal it reaches out and grabs anything it can reach—which is usually the hair on its mother's body. Since the monkey would normally be born in a tree, this grabbing reaction has obvious advantages.

As soon as the baby is born the mother carefully licks and cleans it; the source for this instinctive reaction is much the same as in the rat. Once clean, the baby is grasped somewhat haphazardly over one arm and must turn itself about until it discovers the nipple. Although an infant is strong enough to walk as soon as it is a few hours old, it normally spends its early days at its mother's breast. It is possible, however, to separate a newborn monkey from its mother and to raise it under experimental conditions in the laboratory. This has been done by Harry F. Harlow and his collaborators at the University of Wisconsin, with somewhat surprising results.[15]

Harry Harlow bridges the gap as an active researcher on animal behavior from the behaviorism of the 1930s to the controlled naturalistic observations of more recent times. A strong advocate of the importance of evolution, he had earlier based his thinking on phylogenetic differences in neuroanatomical structures as many investigators sought to compare the "intelligence" of one species with another. His

---

CITATION ACCOMPANYING THE DISTINGUISHED SCIENTIFIC
CONTRIBUTION AWARD PRESENTED BY THE AMERICAN PSYCHOLOGICAL
ASSOCIATION, 1960

"For his indefatigable curiosity which has opened up new areas of research in animal behavior and has helped greatly to keep comparative psychology near the center of the psychological stage. Throughout the years his vivid imagination has led to the analysis of many stimulus relationships, the exploratory and manipulatory motives, and the all-but-ubiquitous learning sets. Recently the age-old problem of love has been revitalized by his persistent concern for the facts of motivation. It is, indeed, his unswerving devotion to fact, observation, and experiment that has given his contribution an integrity of inestimable value to scientific psychology."

HARRY FREDERICK HARLOW

---

work with primates led to the development of many devices that are in current use for testing primate behavior. He invented the concept of "learning how to learn" which tested the rate at which animals learned to eliminate errors and profit from experience by determining the principle governing the presentation of reward in simple discrimination studies. Comparing the marmoset, a simple primate with a smooth cortex, and the chimpanzee, with a more complex, differentiated cortex, scientists have found that the simpler animal takes longer to learn how to learn. However, it is Harlow's more recent work with monkeys, characterized by a free-swinging research approach and a delightfully irreverent writing style, to which we will now turn.

Harlow constructed what he called surrogate mothers. A good surrogate mother was made of a block of wood covered by sponge rubber and sheathed in terrycloth. A bad one was made of wire hardware cloth. An infant monkey was then left free to go to either of the mothers it wished. For half of the infants the good mother gave milk; for the other half, the bad mother gave milk. In both cases, however, the infant monkey spent most of its time—as shown in Figure 17.1—clinging to the terrycloth mother. Those who were forced to do so would spend just enough time on the bad mother to nurse, but then would return to cling to the terrycloth mother. If something frightened the infant, it would run for comfort and protection to the mother that felt good, not to the wire mother that nourished it. Given a choice between a mother that fed it and a mother that provided comfortable tactual stimulation, the monkey clearly preferred tactual stimulation.

At the time these studies began it seemed curious but interesting that the attachment of a young monkey to its mother depended so much on a tactual element. The experiment was continued, however, until the young monkeys grew into adults, some singly, others in pairs, with their terrycloth mothers. In some respects a laboratory mother looked more satisfactory than a natural mother would have been; it was always available and it never cuffed or scolded. But as the youngsters grew up, it became increasingly apparent that they were all very unhappy, asocial, aggressive, maladjusted monkeys. The most significant biological handicap they suffered was that none of them, male or female, was able to copulate. They all looked interested, but they did not know what to do.[16] Inadvertently, the Wisconsin psychologists had deprived the infant monkeys of far more than they intended when they removed them from their mothers.

What is it that a reacting mother gives and an immobile mother does not? In a normal situation a baby monkey will begin to reach out for things when it is two or three weeks old. When it tries to grab food the mother usually seems annoyed and tries to discourage it, but this kind of maternal tuition does not begin in earnest until the baby starts to explore the world for itself. The mother teaches her baby to

FIGURE 17.1

Infant monkeys much prefer surrogate mothers that are covered with terrycloth. This monkey spends most of his time clinging to the cloth mother, even though his milk is provided by the wire mother. (From Wisconsin Regional Primate Center.)

hang tightly to her body with both hands and feet as she is moving about. And she teaches it not to wander too far away and not to approach strange objects. The method of teaching is quite simple; she cuffs the youngster whenever it is disobedient. All of this training the Wisconsin monkeys missed.

Ordinarily the babies will cling to and remain dependent on their mothers for some time, perhaps even until another baby is born. But during that period they gradually become independent of her and, most important, learn how to adapt their behavior appropriately to the other monkeys in the social group. The experience with the mother, the play and grooming with other young monkeys, the discipline by the older and stronger monkeys—this pattern of growing up is essential for the production of a normally curious, happy, well-adjusted monkey. Social relations among monkeys depend upon stable patterns of behavior—grooming, sexual presentation and mounting, threatening—that are released when the proper social cues are given by other monkeys. Monkeys whose social experience has been sharply restricted do not develop the usual social responses to those cues.

Harlow has unabashedly violated Morgan's canon by anthropomorphically talking about "love" in monkeys, although he sometimes uses more behavioristically acceptable language by calling love the "heterosexual affectional system" (presumably with tongue in cheek). By systematically degrading the more natural mother-child and peer to peer interactions in infancy, he has shown that socially deprived monkeys do not function well as adults and are, in fact, so clumsy that they do not even breed or show sexual prowess comparable to the normally raised monkeys. An example of his research and writing style can be seen in the following quote:

> . . . we gave the mother a face that was nothing but a round wooden ball, which displayed no trace of shame. To the baby monkey this featureless face became beautiful, and she frequently caressed it with hands and legs, beginning around 30–40 days of age. By the time the baby had reached 90 days of age we had constructed an appropriate ornamental cloth-mother face, and we proudly mounted it on the surrogate's body. The baby took one look and screamed. She fled to the back of the cage and cringed in autistic-type posturing. After some days of terror the infant solved the medusa-mother problem in a most ingenious manner. She revolved the face 180° so that she always faced a bare round ball! Furthermore, we could rotate the maternal face dozens of times and within an hour or so the infant would turn it around 180°. Within a week the baby resolved her unfaceable problem once and for all. She lifted the maternal head from the body, rolled it into the corner, and abandoned it. No one can blame the baby. She had lived with and loved a faceless mother, but she could not love a two-faced mother.[17]

Harlow's laboratory studies of monkeys has been augmented by some dedicated, long-term observations of gorillas, chimpanzees, and baboons in the natural setting.[18] Jane Goodall's observations of complex patterns of behavior among chimpanzees, including intimate relationships, tool using, and mutual grooming, suggest that the chimpanzees have established a primitive culture which is transmitted from generation to generation. Studies of the gorilla have shown that gorillas are markedly nonaggressive, a challenge to the concept of "King Kong" mentality which persists in popular understanding of the gorilla. Similar research on other animals has begun to destroy many familiar myths; it has been shown, for example, that lemmings do not commit mass suicide, that the swallows do not always go back to Capistrano on time, and that wolves are not dangerous to man.

Despite the efforts of many animal researchers to counter mythology with objective fact, there remains one pseudoscientific current that, in our opinion, panders to the ever-present desire for a simple explanation for the violent behavior of man. Even Lorenz has contributed to this dialogue with his book *On Aggression,* which, while it is a very charming and readable book, contains blatant anthropomorphism and a tendency to see aggression in animal facial expressions and other behavior.[19] Limited to animals these would be merely arguable, but Lorenz extrapolates all too easily from animals to man, arguing that man's irrational behavior is phylogenetically based and is "obviously impervious to experience and learning." Lorenz goes on to rest his case on the fragmentary archeological evidence of prehistoric man, where a few burned bones are seen as evidence of cremation by one observer and as proof of roasting one's enemy by others.

Perhaps the most farfetched of the writers committed to the theory of man's innate depravity is Robert Ardrey whose glibly written works include *The Territorial Imperative, African Genesis,* and *The Social Contract.*[20] The tone of his work and the hysterical protestations of his many critics seem to indicate that there is considerable acceptance of his views among those who are skeptical of social scientists and among journalists who may welcome a clearly written documentation of a position that they may secretly hold already: that man is basically and inherently an animal dressed with a thin veneer of civilization.

Ardrey specifies territoriality as a need state, innately determined, whose components are the more basic needs for identity, security, and stimulation. Besides the security of borders and the stimulation of border quarrels, territory provides identity which enables a living creature to assert that "This place is mine; I am of this place." Of course, most researchers would have no fault to find with territoriality as description of a behavior since examples can be cited in many (but not all) species. But Ardrey sees territoriality as "the chief mechanism of natural morality," representing a high degree of natural selection of behaviors directed toward the end of ensuring an adequate pool of male genes within a population. Cloaking himself in the robes of the antibehaviorists such as Lorenz, Ardrey decries the environmentalist bias in most of psychology and argues along the line of the Lamarck-Lysenko theory of evolution (belief in the inheritance of acquired behavior) which is generally discredited by the biological and behavioral establishments. A gifted phrase-maker, Ardrey can always provoke criticism with such lines as "I can discover no qualitative break between the moral nature of the animal and the moral nature of man." He goes on to see territoriality in the gang behavior of people and views war as one of the more successful social innovations for channeling aggression.

Ashley Montagu has written a brilliant critique of Ardrey, Lorenz, and other believers in man's depravity. Sorting out the anthropological evidence of early man, one can build a case for the natural selection of cooperation and nonviolence and the social process of hunting and food processing, if one uses that type of evolution theory. After cataloguing Ardrey's errors and inconsistencies, Montagu concludes with the following words, which stand as an environmentalist's answer to a popular hereditarian.

> The myth of early man's aggressiveness belongs in the same class as the myth of the "beast," . . . "wild" animals, . . . innate depravity and original sin. . . . What we are unwilling to acknowledge as essentially of our own making, the consequence of our own disordering in the man-made environment, we saddle upon "Nature." . . . What . . . such writers do, in addition to perpetrating their wholly erroneous interpretation of human nature, is to divert attention from the real sources of man's aggression and destructiveness, namely, the many false and contradictory values by which, in an overcrowded, highly competitive, threatening world, he so disoperatively attempts to live. It is not man's nature, but his nurture, in such a world that requires our attention.[21]

We must acknowledge that Ardrey has written some compelling and widely read accounts of the nature side of the controversy, which are today welcome as psychology comes to grip with basic issues and the so-called first causes of man's behavior. We just think that he is wrong. Perhaps all the effort that will go into mapping this vast domain will reward us with a better understanding of our own psychology. But in science such practical justifications of one goal in terms of another have a way of becoming irrelevant as the work progresses.

Why study animal psychology? Not to learn about man, even though we may. If we see ourselves mirrored there, it is good, but not necessary. The only true reason for studying animals is to learn about animals, about the lives and struggles of our fellow creatures.

NOTES

1. C. Lloyd Morgan, *An Introduction to Comparative Psychology* (London: Scott, 1894), pp. 287–291.

2. Ibid., p. 53.

3. Ibid., p. 37.

4. See D. Katz, *Animals and Men*, trans. H. Steinberg and A. Summerfield (London: Penguin, 1953).

5. I. P. Pavlov, *Conditioned Reflexes*, trans. G. V. Anrep (London: Oxford University Press, 1927), p. 395.

6. R. B. Lockard, "Reflections on the Fall of Comparative Psychology," *American Psychologist* 26, no. 2 (1971): 168–179.

7. N. Tinbergen, *The Study of Instinct* (London: Oxford University Press, 1951).

8. D. S. Lehrman, "Induction of Broodiness by Participation in Courtship and Nest-Building in the Ring Dove" (*Streptopelia risoria*), *Journal of Comparative and Physiological Psychology* 51 (1958): 32–36. Also D. S. Lehrman, "Effect of Female Sex Hormones on Incubation Behavior in the Ring Dove" (*Streptopelia risoria*), *Journal of Comparative and Physiological Psychology* 51 (1958): 142–145.

9. D. S. Lehrman, "The Physiological Basis of Parental Feeding Behavior in the Ring Dove" (*Streptopelia risoria*), *Behaviour* 7 (1955): 241–286.

10. K. Lorenz, *Evolution and Modification of Behavior* (Chicago: University of Chicago Press, 1965).

11. E. Hess, "Imprinting in Birds," *Science* 146 (1964): 1128–1138.

12. B. P. Wiesner and N. M. Sheard, *Maternal Behaviour in the Rat* (London: Oliver & Boyd, 1933).

13. F. A. Beach and J. Jaynes, "Studies of Maternal Retrieving in Rats, III." "Sensory Cues in the Lactating Female's Response to Her Young," *Behaviour* 10 (1957): 104–125.

14. C. R. Carpenter, "Societies of Monkeys and Apes," *Biological Symposium* 8 (1942): 177–204.

15. H. F. Harlow, "Love in Infant Monkeys," *Scientific American*, June 1959. See also H. F. Harlow, "The Heterosexual Affectional System in Monkeys," *American Psychologist* 17, no. 1 (1962): 1–9.

16. W. A. Mason, "The Effects of Social Restriction on the Behavior of Rhesus Monkeys: I. Free Social Behavior," *Journal of Comparative and Physiological Psychology* 53 (1960): 582–589.

17. H. F. Harlow, "Nature of Love Simplified," *American Psychologist* 23 (1968): 161–168.

18. J. Goodall, "My Life Among Wild Chimpanzees," *National Geographic* 124 (1963): 272–308.

19. K. Lorenz, *On Aggression* (New York: Harcourt, Brace & World, 1966).

20. References in the text come from R. Ardrey, *The Territorial Imperative* (New York: Atheneum, 1966).

21. M. F. Ashley Montagu, "The New Litany of 'Innate Depravity,' or Original Sin Revisited," in R. Buckhout, et al., eds., *Toward Social Change: A Handbook for Those Who Will* (New York: Harper & Row, 1971), pp. 139–143.

EIGHTEEN
Sigmund Freud, Psychoanalyst

THE UTILITARIAN CONCEPT OF MAN

It comes as something of a surprise that Freud—sensitive prober of dreams, outspoken defender of sexuality, patient interpreter of the neurotic and the insane—should have regarded his life's work as an inevitable extension of the positivistic tradition in which he was trained as a medical student. No one revolted more effectively or showed more clearly the narrowness of the mechanistic conceptions of man that dominated European thought in the nineteenth century. Yet throughout his life he considered himself faithful to the precepts of Helmholtz. He was a rebel, but he was a loyal one. In order to appreciate just how much of a rebel he was, it is necessary to resurrect an earlier conception of human nature.

Some historians say that modern intellectual history began sometime in the seventeenth century when, largely as a result of Descartes' teachings, mathematics replaced theology as the Queen of the Sciences.[1] Men became convinced that natural laws are always true everywhere and that the human mind is capable of understanding them. Faith in the powers of human reason persisted without effective scientific criticism for about two hundred years and provided the moving spirit of that great, optimistic period of modern history called the Enlightenment. Anyone who might have questioned sovereign reason was refuted immediately by examples from the natural sciences.

But what about man's own affairs? Can men live together rationally? If reason can comprehend the cosmos, does that mean it can serve equally well as a guide in social and economic matters? Can a society, having no mind of its own, be rational? It was generally assumed that either a rational God would do the necessary thinking for society or, in more positivistic quarters, that if every individual member of society did the most intelligent thing he could possibly do, given his personal circumstances, the cumulative effect of so much rationality would itself be rational. In other words, if every individual would make his decisions in a reasonable way so as to advance his own best interests, he would simultaneously advance the interests of society generally.

The whole matter was reduced to its crudest fundamentals by Jeremy Bentham near the close of the eighteenth century. Although Bentham was somewhat extreme, his arguments were only exaggerated versions of views widely held in his time. "Nature has placed mankind under the governance of two sovereign masters, pain and pleasure," said Bentham. "It is for them alone to point out what we ought to do, as well as to determine what we shall do."[2] In England and France Bentham's philosophy, called utilitarianism, was a close partner of positivism. Along with materialism, empiricism, and evolutionism—the nineteenth century bristles with isms—Bentham's utilitarianism was especially attractive to those who wished to discuss man in the language of the natural sciences.

The utilitarian philosophy consists of four simple propositions.

1. All that anybody wants is to be as happy as possible, to maximize his own happiness.

2. It is morally good for him to maximize his happiness as effectively, as intelligently, as he can.

3. Society must be organized so that maximizing his own happiness is always the most beneficial thing for his fellow men.

4. It is possible to calculate the quantities of pleasure and pain (by Bentham's "felicific calculus") expected from different kinds of behavior, and to arrange society so as to produce the greatest happiness for the greatest number.[3]

Bentham coupled these utilitarian propositions with a firm belief in empiricism and the laws of the association of ideas. It was central to his thinking that men should be simple machines whose choices and decisions could be anticipated perfectly and allowed for in a set of laws and social institutions that would automatically maximize the amount of happiness available for everyone.

It is not our task to criticize Bentham's ethical assumption that, because it is desired, happiness must be desirable. The fact remains that Bentham and his followers were remarkably influential in nineteenth-century England; utilitarianism was one of the intellectual foundations of British democratic thought and, by and large, its consequences were liberal and humanitarian. Each person was considered free to enter into any social contract that made him happy. Nevertheless, it was psychological nonsense; and it is remarkable that such an odd conception of man (as a felicity computer) captured the leading minds of the day. John Stuart Mill and Herbert Spencer both defended the "maximum happiness principle" and made it a part of their social philosophy. There were critics, but the utilitarians were able to remain in the ascendancy. In the hands of Jevons, Walras, Menger, Marshall, and others, utilitarianism later became the foundation for much of modern economic theory. Even those who questioned the ethical assumption that it is good to pursue happiness were inclined to accept the psychological assumption that each man automatically and inevitably pursues his own pleasure.

Psychological objections center around the fact that happiness depends far more upon what you expect than upon what you get. There is no absolute scale of happiness along which every possible event can be measured. The human ability to experience happiness is limited; it does not go on increasing indefinitely. There is no evidence that the rich are always happier than the poor. Indeed, there is not even any evidence that social progress promotes happiness, that Parisians are essentially happier than African Bushmen.

Not until the nineteenth century was drawing to a close did utilitarianism lose its iron grip on the scientific mind. One of the most effective attacks on it was initiated by a French sociologist, Emile Durkheim, who asked how such a theory could account for suicide.[4] Obviously, suicide is not motivated by happiness; it seems reasonable to suppose that a person who takes his own life is unhappy. If this is so, and if Bentham was right that unhappiness results from a loss of valuable possessions, then one should expect to find that the suicide rate increases during periods of economic depression. And this is in fact the case. But Durkheim turned up another fact that was more puzzling, namely, that suicide is frequently caused by sudden success during periods of unusual prosperity. This is difficult for a utilitarian to explain. Why should a man who is just beginning to prosper consider killing himself? Prosperity should make him happy.

Durkheim argued that happiness has little to do with it. Unexpected wealth can disorient a person with respect to all the social values that had previously governed his life; sudden wealth can weaken or destroy his former ties with a social group. The resulting loss of his goals and values, the resulting state of social disequilibrium—Durkheim termed it *anomie*—might in severe cases lead to suicide. And for the same reason a sudden loss of wealth is also dangerous; it weakens a person's ties with his social group. It is a loss of love, of sympathetic acceptance into the lives of other people, not a loss of material possessions, that can make a man take his own life. To strengthen his argument, Durkheim demonstrated that suicide is relatively rare among the perpetually poor, who are necessarily well integrated into their own social groups.

Durkheim considered himself a thorough positivist, carrying on the scientific traditions of the nineteenth century. He used empirical data on suicide rates and he analyzed them statistically with scientific precision; certainly there was nothing metaphysical in his method or his results. Yet his explanation in terms of loosening the sympathetic ties of the individual with his group has an almost spiritual character. How does one measure anomie in centimeters, grams, and seconds? If Durkheim was right, and his evidence was compelling, then somehow society has claims upon us far subtler and more complex than anyone in the eighteenth century would admit. To preserve a positivistic tradition, to make possible the continuation of the study of man and his affairs in scientific terms, the materialistic conception of science had to be enlarged.

Durkheim was one of several who, around the turn of the century, helped to expand our conception of science as it applies to human beings. Others included William James, Henri Bergson, Max Weber, Benedetto Croce, Vilfredo Pareto; beginning about 1890 a rebellious generation of genius completely reoriented European social thought.[5] And the most important of these young rebels was the Austrian Jew, Sigmund Freud.

THE PSYCHOANALYTIC DESCRIPTION OF THE HUMAN MIND

Freud was born at Freiberg, Moravia, in 1856. Except for the first three and the last two years of his life, however, he lived in, and was a part of, Vienna.[6] His father, a tall, kindly man who was said to resemble Garibaldi, was an unsuccessful wool merchant; when his business failed in Moravia he moved his growing family to Leipzig, then to Vienna. Their life was not easy, for anti-Semitism was rampant in Imperial Austria. Nevertheless, Jews had been granted citizenship and one who was willing to step into the gutter to let a Christian pass could earn a meager living.

At 17 Sigmund entered the University of Vienna, a somewhat reluctant medical student in negligent pursuit of anatomy, botany, chemistry, physics, physiology, and zoology. We get glimpses of him studying Aristotle's logic, engaging in violent arguments with fellow students, and obstinately refusing to apologize for his rudeness in philosophic debate. During this period he received a thorough grounding in the positivistic science of the nineteenth century. First he concentrated on biology, and as a research project dissected more than four hundred male eels in search of their testes. Next he moved on to physiology and the spinal cord of the fish; he spent countless hours hunched over a microscope in Ernest Brücke's laboratory. In 1881 he received his M.D. degree, but even that did not interrupt his devotions at the microscope. Finally Brücke explained to him that a penniless Jew could never become Professor of Neurology. It was a rude shock, but of course Brücke was right; the Vienna that was to give lessons to Adolf Hitler was a difficult place for a Jew, even one as brilliant as Freud.

Yet he must have known what was coming, for his decision to study medicine in the first place had been based on the assumption that he could, if necessary, practice for a living. So he left the scientific life of the university and hung out his shingle as a clinical neurologist. It was a difficult thing for him to do; even though he became famous for his neurological research, he was never greatly attracted to the practice of clinical neurology. Fortunately for him, however, most of the patients who went to see a neurologist were actually psychoneurotic.

In June, 1882, he became engaged to Martha Bernays, who was as penniless as he. Although he loved her passionately, it was necessary repeatedly to postpone their marriage until he could earn enough money to support her. For four intense, frustrated years he worked and saved and waited. There was hardly a moment in the long engagement when the first thought in his mind was not how soon he could convert it to marriage. Finally he could wait no longer; in September, 1886, they were married. The young couple managed to exist through their first months together by borrowing, by pawning their watches, until finally the tide began to turn. But the terrible poverty of those early years left a lasting impression on him.

It was during that difficult time that he became friendly with Joseph Breuer, who loaned him money and discussed interesting cases with him. Breuer had discovered a new way to use hypnosis in the treatment of hysteria. Hysteria is a form of neurosis in which there are bodily symptoms, paralysis and abnormal sensations, that cannot be attributed to any obvious abnormality of the nervous system. Actually the discovery was made by one of Breuer's patients, a stubborn young woman known to history only as Fräulein Anna O., who insisted that talking abut her problems while she was hypnotized would relieve her anxieties and temporarily cure her hysterical symptoms. Freud was very interested in Anna O. and tried to use Breuer's technique with other patients.

Although at this time Freud was publishing important work in neurology, his interests were steadily shifting toward his psychological studies with Breuer; in 1895 they published a book, *Studies on Hysteria*. By the time it appeared, however, Freud was already breaking off his personal friendship with Breuer and was well along toward replacing hypnosis by free association as a better method for treating hysteria. His adoption of free association was a critical step in the development of psychoanalysis.

In free association a person starts with some element of emotional significance and lets, or tries to let, his ideas flow spontaneously until, for one reason or another, they seem to break off. He then takes another item and repeats the process. Speaking freely of whatever enters one's head is not easy. Even without intending to, a person protects himself in certain matters. These points of resistance became the focus of Freud's inquiry and his basis for psychotherapy. The great advantage of free association over hypnosis is that these areas of resistance can be located and explored; the patient himself is forced to recognize consciously the nature of his problem.

Freud also discovered that a rich source of emotionally significant ideas, suitable to start the process of free association, can be found in a patient's dreams, which often contain valuable clues to the psychological problems underlying his sickness.

As a positivist, committed to the belief that everything has a cause, he knew that events in a dream cannot be as senseless as they seem. They must be the result of something going on in the person's mind, if not consciously, then unconsciously. He decided that there must be truth in the ancient theory that dream images are symbolic. They do not symbolize future events, of course; they refer to personal matters, things that can arouse strong emotions. It seemed to him that the purpose of a dream is to preserve sleep. (Recent research on the biological value of dreams as measured by REM indicates that preventing dreaming leads to periods of "catching up" in subsequent sleep periods.) If the emotionally charged images were to appear undisguised in the dream, they would be so disturbing that they would interrupt the sleeping state. So they appear only indirectly in a harmless, symbolic form. Instead of dreaming about a penis, the dreamer may substitute the image of a gun, a snake, a fountain pen, the number three, and so on. For masturbation the dream symbol may be climbing a tree or playing the piano. By recognizing these substitutions, therefore, it is possible to recover the true meaning of the dream.

It is a little hard, of course, to believe that a sleeping mind can perform all these complicated substitutions in its state of reduced activation. To Freud this meant that the unconscious is much cleverer than we usually give it credit for. It is possible to argue, however, that the symbols are not disguises at all, but are more like slang or figures of speech. C. S. Hall has pointed out that a dreamer may have a disguised dream of an incestuous relationship one night and a perfect barefaced dream of incest the next night.[7] If the symbol is hiding something obnoxious, why is it hidden one time and not another? But even though his hypothesis that symbols are protective disguises may be more imaginative than necessary, it remains that Freud discovered in dream analysis a very useful way to explore a person's emotional life.

Freud tried to get his neurotic patients to remember the events that had caused their symptoms; free association provided a method to probe their memories. The associations did not stop with a painful event, but often extended back into early childhood. Moreover, many of the most significant memories were of sexual experiences. Freud gradually became convinced that sexual disturbances are the essential causes of neurosis. In particular, he observed that his hysterical patients always reported a premature sexual experience during their childhood.

He was convinced of the validity of his method, and in all good faith he presented this observation publicly as his theory of hysteria. But then the truth dawned on him: most of the reported childhood seductions had never occurred. They were fantasies nourished by unconscious processes unrelated to ordinary reality. This realization was a severe jolt to his pride, but when he had time to ponder its implications he was not ashamed of his blunder. It had forced him to recognize the fundamental nature of infantile sexuality and so led him to one of his major contributions to psychological theory.

In the summer of 1897 Freud decided to apply his technique to himself. There were several reasons: his father's death had occurred a few months earlier and Freud wished to explore the emotions it had aroused; he was concerned by his increasing hostility toward an old friend; he wanted to be able to understand his patients better. He worked principally with his dreams, seeking to discover the unconscious processes that formed them. It was lonely work, but he slowly made progress. He recognized the truth about his father and separated it from ideas that he had projected into his image of his father. He remembered sexual feelings toward his mother and jealous rivalries with other children. And he rediscovered a nurse who had caused him most of his later troubles. The results were not magical, but he persisted and eventually mastered many of the problems that had disturbed him. For the rest of his life he spent the last half hour of each day in self-analysis.

In 1900 he published his major account of this work in *The Interpretation of Dreams*. It was written during the period of his self-analysis and is profusely illustrated with his own dreams. The book was received with thunderous indifference by both neurologists and psychologists; it took eight years to sell the first printing of 600 copies. Nevertheless, *The Interpretation of Dreams* is Freud's most important work. In particular, the seventh and last chapter contains the theory of mind that he was to amplify and develop in the period ahead.

For ten lonely but productive years he worked almost alone on his new ideas. In 1904 he wrote *The Psychopathology of Everyday Life* in which he described the now famous Freudian slip, and in the following year the *Three Essays on Sexuality*. But not until 1906 did he begin to attract colleagues and followers, and he did not gain international recognition until 1909, when he was invited to the United States, with Alfred Adler and C. G. Jung, to give a series of lectures at Clark University.

Those years were also filled with much bureaucratic activity centered around the founding of international societies and their journals. Freud tolerated no dissent from his emphasis on sexuality as the great motivating force behind all abnormal psychological processes; anyone who disagreed was excommunicated. In the second volume of his fine biography of Freud, Ernest Jones has sympathetically described these political struggles, with their attendant concern that psychoanalysis would be rejected by gentiles.

The psychoanalytic movement was launched much as a political party would be launched or as a new church might be founded. Thus when Freud broke with Adler in 1911 and with Jung in 1913 it was more than a scientific disagreement about the evidence and the conclusions that could be based on the evidence; it was also a personal quarrel, a political defection, and a religious heresy.

In 1914, pressed by fear that psychoanalysis would be discredited because its major proponents could not agree among themselves, Freud wrote a polemical *History of the Psychoanalytic Movement*. "Psychoanalysis is my creation," he said. "For ten years I was the only one occupied with it. . . . Nobody knows better than I what psychoanalysis is." One can sympathize with his attitude toward quarrelsome disciples, but the important distinction between a political movement and a scientific theory should never be forgotten; the success of one does not test the truth of the other.

Freud continued to live in Vienna, practicing as a psychoanalyst and writing many books of an increasingly speculative nature. In 1910 he wrote a psychoanalytic biography of Leonardo da Vinci. In 1913 he wrote *Totem and Taboo*, an imaginative anthropological adventure. He extended psychoanalysis further into the realm of social theory with *The Future of an Illusion* (1927) and *Civilization and Its Discontents* (1930). When the Nazis absorbed Austria in 1938, he escaped to London, carrying under his arm the manuscript of a book on *Moses and Monotheism*. The following year he died at the age of 83.

It is sometimes said that anybody who had as much interest in sex as Freud must have led a lusty and exciting life. As near as one can tell from published biographies this is simply not true; in his private life he appears to have been a complete puritan. He was so inhibited, in fact, that some writers have speculated that his sexual theories were rationalizations of his inability to love other people.[8] No insatiable lust inspired him; his mission was to save civilization. In his prime he dreamed of being a modern Leonardo, the creative genius; in his old age he saw himself as a modern Moses, the great lawgiver. He expected others to follow him and to sacrifice their independence and intellectual freedom for him. Certainly he must have been a difficult man to work with. He had his faults, for which his friends paid dearly, but lechery was not one of them. The sexual license that has so often been justified in terms of his theories must have been hateful to him, a sad mockery of his life and ideals.

Freud introduced a number of new terms for the theoretical constructs he used to describe the human mind.[9] He believed that the total personality is organized into three major systems: the *id*, which is concerned with the immediate discharge of energy or tension; the *ego*, which regulates the interactions of the person with his environment; and the *superego*, which represents the moral and judicial aspects of personality.[10] These three systems are in constant interaction.

In his early work Freud used a simpler twofold distinction between the conscious and the unconscious mind. Later, the unconscious became the id, the conscious the ego, and the superego was added to his theory as a new concept. This remarkable and imaginative man never shirked the burden of self-criticism and revision, and his theories grew and evolved continually for almost half a century. In describing psychoanalytic doctrine, therefore, it is always necessary to specify whether the ideas come from the early or the late Freud.

Dynamic aspects of personality depend upon a supply of instinctual energy from the id; Freud made the same distinction between the mind and its source of energy that an engineer would make between an engine and its fuel. Although he modified his theories several times, toward the end of his life he recognized two great groups of instincts that provide energy for the id. One group serves the purposes of life; their energy is called *libido*. The life instincts are a constant source of emotional tension, whose conscious impact is painful and unpleasant. One of Freud's first and most fundamental assumptions was that all activities of the mind are driven by the need to reduce or eliminate this tension. Because a conscious experience of pleasure was supposed to accompany all tension reduction, Freud called this fundamental assumption the *pleasure principle*, symbolized by *Eros*. The second group of instincts, symbolized by *Thanatos*, introduced later and never so well described, are in the service of death. These destructive instincts represent Freud's attempt to explain the sources of energy for aggression, for sadism and masochism, for suicide. That he toyed with so odd a conception as an instinct for death and destruction indicates how deeply he was impressed by the irrational hatred and violence he saw everywhere around him.

In a very young infant the functions of the id are purely automatic. But when reflex action fails, as eventually it must, frustration causes emotional tension to build up. The baby must then learn to form an image of the object that reduces its tensions. At first, this image, which is generated by the *primary process*, is offered as a kind of substitute satisfaction whenever frustration occurs. This use of imagery is pure wish-fulfillment. Freud believed that wish-fulfillments, or attempted wish-fulfillments, persist into adulthood; dreams were his prime example.

The ego is the executive branch of the personality. It operates according to a *reality principle*, rather than the pleasure principle. When reflex action and wish-fulfilling imagery have both failed, the child begins to develop a secondary process: the thinking, knowing, problem-solving processes necessary to produce the desired object itself. As a consequence of the secondary process, a plan of action is created and tested. The testing is called *reality testing*. Most of the psychological functions that had been studied prior to Freud's work—sensation, perception, learning, thinking, memory, action, will, and so on—are pure ego functions in Freudian terminology.

The ego has no energy of its own, so it steals energy from the id by a process known as *identification*. The theft is perpetrated as follows. The id invests its instinctual energy in the images that its primary process creates, but the id has no way to distinguish between its own wish-fulfilling imagination and the veridical images of perception. To achieve gratification the id's fomenting energy must be invested in an accurate image of a tension-reducing object; the imagination image that the id desires and the perceptual image of the goal object must be in good agreement. When the internal image corresponds closely to the perceptual object, the idea can be identified with the object, and the idea's psychic energy can be transferred to it. This identification process enables the energies of the id to be guided by an accurate representation of reality, and makes possible the further development of the ego.

The superego, which develops at a later age, is said to include two subsystems, an *ego-ideal* and a *conscience*. Both are assimilated by the child from examples and teachings provided by his parents. The ego-ideal is the child's conception of what his parents will approve; his conscience is the child's conception of what they will condemn as morally bad. The ego-ideal is learned through rewards, the conscience through punishments. The superego, in short, is the repository of social norms—Freud's way of dealing with the kinds of problems that Durkheim discovered in his studies of social action.

It should be noted that the superego was Freud's way of going beyond the felicity calculators that utilitarians had believed in. The id wants happiness and the ego does the calculating—that much of the older theory he preserved intact—but the superego is something more, something that holds the happiness-calculator within bounds set by society, something that introduces the social norms that are so necessary for our understanding of human society. Much that was most revolutionary in Freud's thinking had to do with how these social restraints become internalized to form the superego.

The process of investing instinctual energy is called *cathexis*. The id has only cathexes, but the ego and the superego can use the energy at their disposal in either of two ways, for cathexis or *anticathexis*. Anticathexis, which manifests itself in terms of self-frustration, is the way the ego and the superego keep the id in check. Perhaps the most important example of anticathexis has to do with memory. A person may fail to recall something, Freud would say, because the memory trace is not sufficiently charged with energy—it is too weakly

cathected. But sometimes his memory may fail because the cathexis
opposed by an even stronger anticathexis; in that case a memory is sai
to be *repressed*. The repressive mechanism is one way, a very commo
way, the ego protects itself against painful memories and the discon
fort or anxiety they would arouse.

Anxiety is a crucial concept in psychoanalytic theory, especiall
when the theory deals with neurosis and psychosis.[11] Freud distir
guished between objective, neurotic, and moral anxiety. Objectiv
anxiety is a painful emotion aroused by the recognition of a rea
objective danger. Neurotic anxiety is aroused by a recognition o
danger from instinctual forces—by fear that the anticathexes of th
ego will not be strong enough to prevent instinctual energy from bein
discharged in an impulsive action. When neurotic anxiety is focuse
upon a particular object or situation, it is called a *phobia;* when
person is unable to specify what is causing his discomfort, his anxiety i
called *free-floating*. Moral anxiety is aroused by the recognition o
danger from the conscience, and appears as feelings of guilt or o
shame at what one has done or, more often, what one is contemplating
doing. A virtuous person with a well-developed conscience alway
experiences more shame, more moral anxiety, than a less virtuou
person.

To protect itself from anxiety, the Freudian ego develop
various defensive methods or mechanisms.[12] We have already mentioned identification. When identification is used as a defense mechanism, the person identifies himself with someone who seems desirable
or admirable, with someone who would not be vulnerable to the danger
that is causing the subject anxiety. We have also mentioned repression,

(© *Jules Feiffer, Courtesy Publishers-Hall Syndicate.*)

which simply prevents an anxiety-arousing situation from becoming conscious. Other mechanisms include *sublimation* (a socially more acceptable goal is substituted for one that cannot be directly satisfied), *projection* (attributing the source of the anxiety to someone or something else external to the person), *reaction formation* (concealing a disturbing impulse by converting it into its opposite), *fixation* (refusing to take the next step in normal development because of anxiety aroused by fear of the new and the unknown), *regression* (retreating to an earlier stage of development when there was greater security, when this anxiety did not arise). A large part of the theoretical machinery developed by Freud and his followers is concerned with the various strategies whereby a person tries, usually irrationally and unsuccessfully, to escape from the intolerably unpleasant emotional experience of anxiety.

J. S. Bruner has aptly called this a dramatic theory of personality.

> Freud's is a theory or a proto-theory peopled with actors. The characters are from life: the blind, energetic, pleasure-seeking id; the priggish and punitive superego; the ego, battling for its being by diverting the energy of others to its own use. The drama has an economy and a terseness. The ego develops canny mechanisms for dealing with the threat of id impulses; denial, projection, and the rest. Balances are struck between the actors, and in the balance is character and neurosis. Freud was using the dramatic technique of decomposition, the play whose actors are parts of a single life.[13]

Because neurotic patients taught him that their troubles began in childhood, Freud developed an elaborate theory of how children grow up, how their sexual instincts develop and mature. The evidence for his theory of development came largely from retrospective accounts by adults; at first it had little support from actual observations of children. Even so, by placing his usual heavy emphasis on sexuality he forced child psychologists to recognize something that it had always been easier to ignore: Sweet, innocent, little children are just as sexual as anybody else. Sex does not spring suddenly into existence at puberty; it is there all along. Many people found psychoanalytic theory most shocking at this very point. One distinguished critic complained that in the study of infantile sexuality, "Freud went down deeper, stayed down longer, and came up dirtier than anyone else." But such complaints miss the point of Freud's insight. He was not talking of dirty habits in nasty little brats; he was telling the story of a force of nature.

Novelist William Golding tells such a story in his allegorical dystopia, *The Lord of the Flies*.[14] On one level of interpretation, Golding creates a microcosm, inhabited by displaced British choir boys, in which the main elements of Freudian theory are personified.

Stripped of the restraining forces of civilization, the boys regress to the status of a primitive tribe of hunters in which a leadership struggle takes place between the realistic, but vacillating Ralph (the ego) and the sadistic, impulsive Jack (the id). The vestigal superego is portrayed by a bookish, fat, asthmatic boy who is called "Piggy." Ralph assumes leadership by blowing on a phalliclike conch shell, directing the group to light a signal fire. As hope and direction fade and hunger grows, the boys indulge in the ritualistic killing of a pig, fantasize and fear a "beastie," and turn inexorably toward Jack, whose enthusiastic hunting becomes more satisfying than the adultlike advice of Ralph, who leans on Piggy for specific ideas. The adventure becomes an affirmation of the pessimistic view of man's instinctual aggressiveness as Piggy is killed and Jack leads the boys in a manhunt for Ralph. Consonant with Freud, Golding sees civilization as a thin veneer which covers the mixture of pleasure-seeking and evil characteristic of the unfettered id.

Freud was the first psychologist who took systematic account of the pleasures and problems every child has with the apertures of his body. He believed that a child's sexual gratifications come from different openings—different *erogenous zones*—at different ages. In unfortunate circumstances, a child can become fixated at an infantile stage and thus develop personality traits corresponding to that particular level.[15] According to Freud, the first erogenous zone is the mouth, where a baby first gets pleasure from sucking, then from biting. If any psychic energy becomes fixated on the *oral zone* during the ingestive, sucking stage, it will produce a dependent personality in the adult. If trouble arises later during the oral biting phase, the person will become aggressive in an oral sense: verbal scorn, sarcasm, cynicism are typical expressions of oral aggression. These problems can appear first when a child is being weaned, so the weaning practices of mothers have assumed great theoretical interest.

In the normal course of development, however, sexual gratification shifts from the mouth to the other end of the alimentary tract; the child will begin to experience pleasure in the *anal zone*. Again there are two modes of functioning: holding back and giving up. If there is important conflict during the period of toilet training, a person may grow up with an anal expulsive character—messy, dirty, wasteful, extravagant—or with an anal retentive character—neat, clean, compulsive, fastidious.

The next Freudian stage occurs when erotic impulses migrate to the sexual zone and the child enters the *phallic stage*. Masturbation and incestuous longings for the parents, who are a child's first love objects, must be brought under control; how that is achieved is one of the central features of Freudian theory and usually a central problem that has to be worked through and accepted by the patient during psychotherapy.

When a little boy begins to feel sexual impulses toward his

mother, Freud said, he becomes jealous of his rival, the father. Since this family crisis was discussed in terms of the Greek legend about Oedipus, who killed his father and married his mother, the boy's dilemma is generally referred to as an *Oedipus complex*. According to Freud, a boy normally becomes afraid that his father will castrate him as punishment for his incestuous desires; this *castration anxiety* eventually forces him to repress both his desire for his mother and his hostility toward his father. When the repression is complete, the Oedipus complex finally disappears. At this point he may identify with either the father or the mother, depending upon whether the masculine or the feminine components of his personality are dominant. In this process of identification the boy adopts the parental values and morality that will constitute his superego as an adult.

The little girl is not so thoroughly explained. She is supposed to develop *penis envy*, a female counterpart of the boy's castration anxiety, and she too may resolve her conflict by identifying with either parent. But many clinicians feel that Freud's theory is weakest in dealing with feminine psychology and that he disguised his well-developed contempt for women behind some scientifically specious biological assertions best captured in his phrase, "Anatomy is destiny." As the distinguished psychoanalyst Karen Horney and numerous feminist writers have indicated, Freud blamed the failure to resolve penis envy as the basis for passivity, dependence, sexual frigidity, incompetence, and a parasitic nature, all traits that characterize a woman as a sick man.[16] Such an interpretation is as convenient an explanation for a male-dominated culture as the concept of breast envy and womb envy would be for some of the more ardent feminists. Freud's limited experience with women—mostly neurotic, dependent middle-class patients—and his acceptance of the inferior status of women have earned him a place in the all-time pantheon of sexists. Indeed, the description of psychosexual stages following *him* from the oral through the phallic stages typifies most personality theories which are limited to generalizations about white males.

It is interesting to note that here, as elsewhere, Freud had an attitude characteristic of the nineteenth-century middle class, which was more concerned with having than with being. His deepest fears were always of losing something one has, a love object, a feeling, or the genital organs.[17] Thus castration anxiety and penis envy seemed to him the most powerful emotional forces that any child would have to cope with.

If, by a miracle, one manages to get through all these Freudian stages with some psychic energy left, he will, after a normal period of latency from about 5 to 12 years of age, pass into a final, adult phase of genital sexuality. People who negotiate the course successfully, however, seldom turn up in a psychoanalyst's office asking for help. Hence there is little psychoanalytic description of what the genital stage of adult sexuality is like.

Freud's theories often seem absurd, if not downright false, to readers who encounter them first in a brief summary such as this. It is an easy exercise for a detached outsider to be critical; Freud has little to say to someone who is not personally involved in psychoanalysis. Those who are involved, however, are usually less confident in their criticisms. Once the psychoanalytic expedition back into childhood begins, once the personal commitment to the therapeutic process is given, once one tries to look honestly at oneself, it is no longer so obvious what is reasonable and what is absurd. There is some merit to the claim that the criticism of psychoanalysis is best left to those who have experienced it. In this respect, at least, it is more like a way of life than like a scientific theory.

THE NEO-FREUDIANS

The powerful influence of Freud on the thinking of all social scientists can be seen in the legion of those who have adopted the psychoanalytic method or world view in their work, even though they usually operate by departing from the master on some crucial point of theory. Erik H. Erikson departed from Freud's preoccupation with how disturbed people cope with their instinctual urges, building instead a model of how the ego functions creatively in the development of "normal" personalities. In his classic book, *Childhood in Society*, Erikson identifies eight stages of psychosocial development, in which the individual copes with conflicts between orientations to himself and to other beings in the world.[18] In the first three stages, parallel to Freud's oral, anal, and phallic stages, Erikson describes (1) a period of *trust* versus *mistrust;* (2) the development of self-control, *autonomy* versus *doubt;* (3) the testing of self-control against adult standards, *initiative* versus *guilt.* In the fourth stage, *industry* versus *inferiority*, the child copes with the rules governing nature and outside society as in Freud's latency period. It is Erikson's description of the fifth stage, the adolescent period from 12 to 18 years of age characterized as *identity* versus *role confusion*, that begins to compel his many young readers to pay attention. To pass successfully through this stage the individual must develop his unique oneness as opposed to others if he is to avoid carrying these seemingly infantile hang-ups into adulthood.

In the sixth stage the young adult experiences conflict over personal relationships between the extremes of *intimacy* versus *isolation.* In the seventh and least studied stage of middle age Erikson sees people caught between *generativity* (a concern outside of himself and his family) versus *self-absorption.* The eighth stage, old age, at least in western society, can be seen as a battle to maintain *integrity* in the face of *despair,* as the individual contemplates the meaning and worthwhileness of his life in the face of imminent death.

Erikson has continued to reshape thinking about human behavior through the technique of psychohistory as applied to such men as Adolf Hitler, Martin Luther, and Mahatma Gandhi.[19] In his study of each, Erikson has highlighted an identity crisis that has meshed with history to produce radical turning points for mankind. Some of his students, notably Robert Jay Lifton, Robert Coles, and Kenneth Kenniston, have extended this technique to an analysis of the victims of Hiroshima, children caught in the civil rights crisis, and, most recently, alienated youth and young radicals who helped shape the antiwar movement of the 1960s.[20] One can contrast Kenniston's sympathetic study of the identity crisis of young men trying to bring about social change constructively with the more orthodox Freudian interpretation published by sociologist Lewis Feurer (*The Conflict of Generations*) which focuses on unresolved Oedipal conflicts as causal factors in the behavior of the young rebel.[21]

Carl G. Jung, a Swiss psychiatrist, is called a neo-Freudian by contemporary psychologists mainly because he broke away from Freud's psychoanalytic movement, but also because of the relatively recent translations of his work (a pattern of belated recognition by Americans of great foreign psychologists including Pavlov, Piaget, and Freud himself). The current popularity of Jung with young people in the United States appears to stem from a combination of Jung's eclectic interests in eastern mysticism and the supernatural as well as the fact that most psychology texts virtually ignore his contributions. Jung differed from Freud's positing of the pleasure principle as the principle motivating force behind man, arguing instead that man is continually trying to realize himself by achieving unity among the many elements of his nature. Besides the personal unconscious, man is influenced by a *collective unconscious* or racial memory, which is a storehouse of memories from man's ancestral past. These memories project themselves into man's behavior through what Jung called *archetypes.*

> The archetype is a tendency to form such representations of a motif . . . (e.g. an evil animal) . . . mental forms whose presence cannot be explained by anything in the individual's own life and which seem to be aboriginal, innate, and inherited shapes of the human mind. Just as the human body represents a whole museum of organs, each with a long evolutionary history behind it, so we should expect to find that the mind is organized in a similar way. . . . I am referring to the biological, prehistoric, and unconscious development of the mind in archaic man, whose psyche was still close to that of the animal.[22]

Jung drew complex pictures of the inner dynamics of man engaged in a never-ending struggle for unity.[23] The influence of

309

eastern philosophies can be seen in his positing of opposites such as the attitudes of *introversion*, orientation toward one's inner subjective world, and *extraversion*, orientation toward the outer objective world. Using the interpretation of dreams, Jung writes of a man's relationship to the unconscious symbolized in feminine form he calls *anima*, to a woman it appears in the masculine form he calls *animus*. "Every man carries a woman within himself"; this dual-gendered nature may be a source of trouble to the individual if one aspect is overdeveloped contrary to personal or societal expectations. The unity between these natures manifests itself in the ancient Taoist symbol of the Yin-Yang. Jung believed that the path to psychic heath lay in the process of *individuation* in which the energy of the collective unconscious is used consciously by a knowledgeable person, rather than surrendering to unconscious control. Like Freud, Jung's work came under criticism because of its emphasis on instincts, but in presenting a less pessimistic view of the nature of man, Jung was later to be appreciated by humanistic psychologists who value the idea that man can consciously channel even his most basic impulses.

FREUD AS A SOCIAL CRITIC

Freud's first and major contribution was his psychological theory of personality and neurosis, but he was also, particularly in the later years of his life, a social theorist of considerable importance. His first efforts in that direction were presented in *Totem and Taboo*, published in 1913. His point of departure was the family, the basic building block of all larger social groups, and a powerful influence on the psychosexual development of the child. His social argument—a modern version of the ancient doctrine of original sin—rested on a vast elaboration of the Oedipus complex, an elaboration that made the complex as important in the development of society as in the development of an individual personality. *Totem and Taboo* is an allegory about a "primal horde" and the banding together of the sons to slay their father and eat of his flesh. But Freud did not intend to be allegorical; he insisted that he was describing actual events that must have been repeated thousands of times before civilization could have been achieved.

It was Freud's idea that the uncivilized sons hated and feared their uncivilized father because he monopolized the women. After they killed him they felt remorse perhaps, but, more important, they recognized that they needed to replace him with a new moral authority or they would all perish in bloody strife of brother against brother. So they began to discipline themselves. Their first step was to impose a taboo on incest, outlawing the possibility of competition with the father for the mother and sisters. Only with an incest taboo is it possible for males to live together peacefully in a single family group.

This first and most fundamental prohibition was later followed by others, which became equally binding. These socially necessary restraints have never been completely accepted, however, so the battle has to be fought all over again in the development of every male child.

It is curious how culture-bound Freud was when he ventured into anthropology. Bronislaw Malinowski, who tried to use psychoanalytic concepts in his anthropological studies of the family, once commented that Freud, in a most attractive but fantastic hypothesis, equipped his primal horde with all the bias, maladjustments, and ill tempers of a middle-class European family let loose in a prehistoric jungle.

The implication of Freud's argument is that guilt (anxiety aroused by threats from the superego) is the motive force behind all social solidarity. Locke, Spencer, and the utilitarians explained social integration in terms of a social contract between individuals free to maximize their own happiness; Durkheim discussed the social facts that exist external to the actor yet somehow tie him to his group by providing norms and ideals; William James made habit the great flywheel of society that keeps us all within the bounds of ordinance; in place of these theories Freud proposed to substitute a vast burden of guilt shared by every civilized person.

The id impulses spring up in all of us; we want to destroy authority and enjoy our sensual pleasures. But in a civilized person the thought arouses guilt; self-indulgence is repressed to protect the ego. Thus social restraints are imposed by a superego that holds over us the unbearable threat of guilt, of moral anxiety. The more a social group imposes constraints upon the sexuality of an individual, the more powerful his superego must become and the greater must be the guilt he experiences. His feelings of guilt may increase beyond all tolerable bounds, until they usurp all his psychic energy and leave him helpless.

Is there some way to prevent this? Could we organize a society around love and reason, rather than around fear and guilt? On this question Freud was basically pessimistic. He had seen too much persecution of his own people, and he had listened to too many neurotic patients describe their inner thoughts ever to be lulled into thinking that men are gentle, friendly creatures who fight only when they are attacked. The great optimist Herbert Spencer could argue all he liked that the predatory habits of modern men were only vestigial survivals that would soon vanish in the upward sweep of evolution; Freud saw only the increasing burdens that modern society was placing on the ego, burdens that would create an ever-increasing measure of guilt and aggression.

When we compare his conception of man with the hopeful mood of the Enlightenment in the eighteenth century, it is obvious why he has so often been called the great anti-intellectual, the great destroyer of faith in rationality. Yet Freud never wavered in his faith that the search for truth must continue.

> We may insist as much as we like that the human intellect is weak in comparison with human instincts, and be right in doing so. But nevertheless there is something peculiar about this weakness. The voice of the intellect is a soft one, but it does not rest until it has gained a hearing. Ultimately, after endlessly repeated rebuffs, it succeeds.[24]

Norman O. Brown, a contemporary disciple of Freud, has carried the concept of repression into a causal analysis of culture which sees repression at the root not merely of individual neurosis but of social pathology as well.[25] Brown pays homage to the prophetic vision Freud expressed in *Civilization and Its Discontents*.

> Men have brought their powers of subduing nature to such a pitch that by using them they could now very easily exterminate one another to the last man. They know this—hence arises a great part of their current unrest, their dejection, their mood of apprehension. And now it may be expected that the other two of the "heavenly forces," eternal Eros, will put forth his strength so as to maintain himself along side of his equal immortal adversary.[26]

Freud struggled to see man as he is, not as he ought to be or as Freud would have liked to imagine him. As one trained in the Helmholtz school of medicine, he carried on this struggle in a positivistic spirit with what he felt were scientific methods of observation and analysis. He was convinced that all mental events are completely determined—even mistakes have a cause. And to the end of his life he used the mechanical, electrical, hydraulic terminology of his positivistic teachers. Thus we must classify him as loyal to the positivistic tradition. But in spite of his loyalty, he was a powerful and damaging critic. After he had completed his demonstration of the importance of unconscious, instinctual forces in human conduct, the old faith in the inevitability of human progress through man's constant growth of knowledge and understanding sounded like an innocent myth concocted to amuse little children. Few men have influenced us so deeply.

NOTES

1. J. B. Bury, *The Idea of Progress* (1920; reprinted ed., New York: Dover, 1955), chap. 3.
2. J. Bentham, *An Introduction to the Principles of Morals and Legislation* (1789).
3. O. H. Taylor, *A History of Economic Thought* (New York: McGraw-Hill, 1960), p 120.

4. E. Durkheim, *Suicide: A Study in Sociology* (Glencoe, Ill.: Free Press, 1951).
5. H. S. Hughes, *Consciousness and Society* (New York: Knopf, 1958).
6. Ernest Jones, *The Life and Work of Sigmund Freud* (New York: Basic Books, 1953).
7. C. S. Hall, "A Cognitive Theory of Dream Symbols," *Journal of General Psychology* 48 (1953): 169–186.
8. Erich Fromm, *Sigmund Freud's Mission* (New York: Harper, 1959).
9. There are several introductory books on psychoanalysis. Freud's own are the most authoritative: *Five Introductory Lectures on Psychoanalysis* (1910; London: Hogarth, 1947) and the supplementary *New Introductory Lectures on Psychoanalysis* (New York: Norton, 1933). A shorter introduction by Freud is *An Outline of Psychoanalysis*, trans. J. Strachey (New York: Norton, 1949). An excellent discussion that brings the ideas up to date is given by Ives Hendrick, *Facts and Theories of Psychoanalysis*, 3rd. ed. (New York: Knopf, 1958). A short and readable account for 95 cents is Calvin S. Hall, *A Primer of Freudian Psychology* (New York: Mentor, 1954).
10. S. Freud, *The Ego and the Id* (1923; London: Hogarth Press, 1927).
11. S. Freud, *The Problem of Anxiety* (1926; New York: Norton, 1936).
12. Anna Freud, *The Ego and the Mechanisms of Defense* (1936; New York: International, 1946).
13. J. S. Bruner, "Freud and the Image of Man," *Partisan Review*, Summer 1956, p. 343. Cf. Francis Bacon's "Idols of the Theatre" in the *Novum Organum*.
14. W. Golding, *Lord of the Flies* (New York: Capricorn Books, 1959).
15. S. Freud, *Three Essays on Sexuality* (1905; London: Hogarth, 1953).
16. B. Roszak and T. Roszak, *Masculine/Feminine* (New York: Harper Colophon, 1969). See also J. M. Bartwick, *Psychology of Women* (New York: Harper & Row, 1971).
17. Fromm, *Sigmund Freud's Mission*, p. 36.
18. E. H. Erikson, *Childhood in Society* (New York: Norton, 1950).
19. E. H. Erikson, *Gandhi's Truth* (New York: Norton, 1969).
20. K. Kenniston, *Young Radicals* (New York: Random House, 1968).
21. L. Feurer, *The Conflict of Generations* (New York: Basic Books, 1969).
22. C. J. Jung, ed., *Man and His Symbols* (New York: Dell, 1968), pp. 57–58.
23. C. J. Jung, *Analytical Psychology, Its Theory and Practice* (New York: Vintage, 1968).
24. S. Freud, *The Future of an Illusion* (1927; New York: Doubleday, 1957).
25. N. O. Brown, *Life Against Death* (New York: Vintage, 1959).
26. S. Freud, *Civilization and Its Discontents* (1930; New York: Norton, 1962).

NINETEEN
Goads and Guides

Emerson once said that every man is as lazy as he dares to be. It was the kind of mistake a New England Puritan might be expected to make. It is not that we don't dare, but that we don't care to be lazy. If we really set our minds to it, we could all be a lot lazier than we actually are.

How lazy can a man get? The absolute limits, of course, are imposed by his body. At the very least he must obtain and consume food and drink; he will occasionally have to move out of harm's way; he must deposit his wastes at some distance from his place of repose; he will have to cover himself when it gets too cold and move out of the sun when it gets too hot; and, while this is not vital in quite the same sense, he will one day surely advertise to attract the attentions of a mate. Yet in a friendly, nurturant environment these minimal demands of biology would fill only a fraction of his waking hours. From all we might learn in a textbook of physiology, a man could dare to be very lazy indeed.

In some idyllic lands blessed by natural advantages of food and safety, living may approach much closer to this biological minimum than it does in ours. But even at its simplest, human life boils at a temperature several degrees hotter than absolute lethargy. Trouble begins when we get mixed up with other people, all of whom take as much pleasure in laziness as we do. We have to compete with them for food and drink, we find they have already appropriated all the desirable clothing and shelter, and they insist that our wastes be deposited far from their places of repose, too. Moreover, they usually have strong opinions about proper ways to deal with these problems. What is dangerous, and requires real daring, is to be lazier than your neighbors think you should be. There are, in short, social as well as biological limits on just how lazy bone-lazy can be.

And, even when we have scrambled inside the bounds of social propriety, there are still other goads at work inside us. Something keeps us going: curiosity, play, humor, stories, boredom. The mind is a restless organ. Even Emerson would have admitted that the devil finds work for idle hands.

The study of motivation is the study of all those pushes and prods—biological, social, psychological—that defeat our lazi-

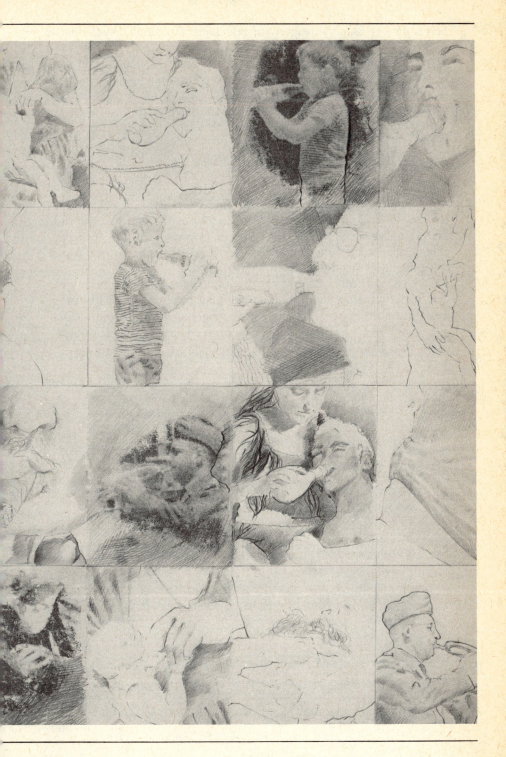

ness and move us, either eagerly or reluctantly, to action. Psychologists sometimes talk as though the study of motivation were their own private hunting ground, but it is a much larger, looser domain than that, extending from biochemistry on one end to sociology, economics, and anthropology on the other. A grand variety of mechanisms participates, and no single theory will ever account for them all.

This diversity has not always been apparent, however. The history of the subject has been a story of persistent search for a simple and sovereign principle to explain everything we do. Pleasure, instinct, mental faculties, volition, passion, reason—these are among the candidates put forward for the title.

Following Darwin, instinct became a favorite explanation. This conveniently vague notion said that men act as they do because they are born that way, because they cannot help themselves. When psychology first tried to become scientific, therefore, it was natural to try to catalogue all the instincts men were born with.

An especially enthusiastic cataloguer was William James. He held the unusual but interesting opinion that men are born with many, many instincts that remain active only long enough to establish necessary habits and then, if development proceeds naturally, fade quietly away. In 1890 his list mentioned the following:

Sucking	Walking	high places
Biting	Climbing	etc.
Chewing	Vocalizing	Hoarding
Licking	Imitating sounds	Constructing
Grimacing	Imitating gestures	Playing
Spitting	Rivalry	Curiosity
Clasping	Pugnacity	Sociability
Pointing	Anger	Shyness
Carrying to mouth	Resentment	Secretiveness
Crying	Sympathy	Cleanliness
Smiling	Hunting	Modesty
Turning head	Fear of	Shame
Holding head erect	noises	Love
Sitting up	strange men	Sex
Standing	strange animals	Jealousy
Creeping	black things	Parental love

All these and more were supposed to be transitory human instincts. With so many inherited reactions goading him on, a child would have little time to be lazy. "Repose," said James's close friend Justice Oliver Wendell Holmes, as if to correct Emerson, "is not the lot of man."

James's list was not the last word, of course. Every new author proposed his own version. In 1908 a particularly famous list by

William McDougall paired off seven human instincts with their corresponding primary emotions as follows:

Instinct		Emotion
flight	and	fear
repulsion	and	disgust
curiosity	and	wonder
pugnacity	and	anger
self-abasement	and	subjection
self-assertion	and	elation
parental care	and	tenderness[1]

In addition to these seven, McDougall believed there were other
instincts that did not arouse such specific and well-defined emotions:
reproduction, gregariousness, acquisition, and construction.

The full flavor of these discussions cannot be conveyed by mere
lists. One needs to read the detailed descriptions of each instinct and
the careful comparisons of one author's list with another's to appreciate how the various goads to action were supposed to be grouped
under these headings. The discussions contained many acute observations and much wise counsel, but they were lost in the loose and
shifting framework of the competing catalogues. And the lists continued to multiply. One careful survey found that by 1924 at least 849
separate instincts had been proposed by different writers on the
subject![2] No student could absorb all the subtleties of this vast and
tangled subject; it was easier to invent your own classification than to
try to understand the other fellow's.

By the 1920s American psychologists determined to dump these
overblown theories and start anew. Much behavior that was being
called instinctive was actually acquired through learning. And accounting for everything that happened in terms of its own specific instinct
dissolved the difficult art of explanation into an easy game of definitions. In order to fight their way back to scientific realities, therefore,
psychologists began to talk about physiological drives instead of inherited instincts. Instincts have since recovered some of their lost
respectability, especially for describing animal behavior—examples of a
new approach to instinct have already been displayed in Chapter 17—
but they will never again run quite as free as they did in the days of
James and McDougall.

While instincts were at their peak of popularity, the Viennese
shadow of Sigmund Freud was beginning to fall on American shores.
Freud is usually called an instinct theorist, but the accuracy of the
description is uncertain. The German word he used was *Trieb;* at the
time, "instinct" seemed a reasonable translation. When instincts lost
their monopoly, however, it became apparent that Freud had been
talking about something much closer to a sexual drive than to a sexual

FIGURE 19.1

A phrenological chart. Phrenologists not only constructed long lists of mental faculties, they located them on various parts of the skull. This attempted classification was a forerunner of the lists of instincts that psychologists later adopted.

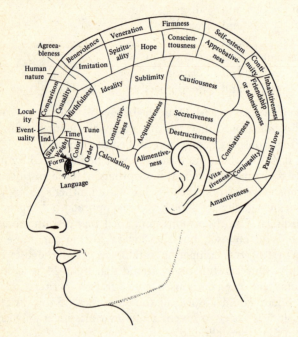

instinct. Nevertheless, the translation stuck and many Americans have ever since thought of Freud as a proponent of instinctive sexuality. Motivational terminology becomes confused so easily; it is almost as if we wanted to keep our terms vague and general enough to match our imperfect understanding of these very complex problems.

Freud's ideas about instincts were revised several times during his long career. Here is one of his final statements on the matter.

> It is possible to distinguish an indeterminate number of instincts and in common practice this is in fact done. For us, however, the important question arises whether we may not be able to derive all of these various instincts from a few fundamental ones. We have found that instincts can change their aim (by displacement) and also that they can replace one another—the energy of one instinct passing over to another. This latter process is still insufficiently understood. After long doubts and vacillations we have decided to assume the existence of only two basic instincts, *Eros* and *the destructive instinct*.[3]

This urge to derive the various instincts from a few simpler, basic processes was shared by Freudians and non-Freudians alike.

The aching void left in American psychology by the passing of the traditional theory of instincts was filled for many by Freudian explanations. Most hardheaded, laboratory-oriented psychologists, however, held out for something more tangible. For them the gap was filled by physiological theories, especially those of Walter B. Cannon and his associates at the Harvard Medical School.[4] But in many respects the two alternatives, Freud's and Cannon's, were much alike. Cannon's work on motivation seemed to provide a physiological foundation for those life-preserving instincts that Freud had lumped together under the general name of Eros.[5]

At the focus of Cannon's theory was the concept of *homeostasis*. The cells and organs of the body require very specific conditions of temperature, blood sugar, acidity, water balance, carbon dioxide, and so on. Mammals have evolved an almost endless variety of regulating mechanisms designed to maintain what Claude Bernard called the internal environment of the body. According to Cannon, when the internal environment begins to drift beyond tolerable limits, it acts as a stimulus for receptor organs located in specific parts of the body. These local irritations drive us into action until they are removed. As you get hungry, for example, your empty stomach begins to contract; these contractions are the source of stimuli for your hunger sensations. You eat, in short, to escape discomfort. When you go without water, your throat gets dry and produces a sensation of thirst. You drink to eliminate this unpleasant sensation.

These regulating mechanisms provided an objective basis for a theory of motivation; instead of postulating instincts for chewing and swallowing, psychologists began to look for homeostatic drives of hunger and thirst. And they tried to extend Cannon's ideas to account for other kinds of motivation; sexual behavior, for example, was represented as an attempt to relieve local irritation or pressure in the genitals.

Since Cannon's time scientists have learned how to talk about homeostatic drives in the language of servomechanisms. A servomechanism is a self-regulating system designed so that the difference between the actual and the intended state of the system is fed back as input, and the system becomes active, and remains so, until the difference is eliminated. Perhaps the most familiar example of a servomechanism is a thermostat that turns on a heater whenever the temperature falls below a predetermined level, then turns it off again as soon as the temperature rises above that level. The feedback loop that is involved is indicated in Figure 19.2. In a biological servomechanism, the organism becomes active whenever the sugar or the water is running low, and it stays active until food or drink reestablishes homeostatic equilibrium.

It soon became apparent, however, that the mechanisms of hunger and thirst are much more complicated than Cannon imagined.

FIGURE 19.2

The feedback loop that regulates room temperature.

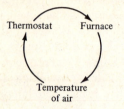

Hunger and thirst both activate very elaborate sensory and response systems that are under the control of neural and hormonal factors. Moreover, it takes a relatively long time before the ingestion of food and water can have any physiological effect, before eating and drinking can reduce the local irritations. For a simpler example of a homeostatic system that guides overt behavior it would be better to examine a temperature-regulating mechanism.

There are several servosystems that enable warm-blooded animals to keep their body temperatures at a constant level. Over a wide range of environmental temperatures these regulating systems do their work without conscious attention on our part. However, when it gets so hot or so cold that these autonomic systems are no longer adequate, we begin to search actively for a more temperate environment. The receptors that guide us in this search are located in the skin; we persist until they tell us that we are once again within a tolerable range of environmental temperatures.

This behavioral system for controlling body temperature can best be studied in the laboratory. Suppose rats are placed in a cold environment and permitted to press a lever to turn on a heat lamp for a few seconds. The feedback loop that is created in this way is indicated in Figure 19.3. There is little delay in this feedback. When it is turned on, radiant energy starts almost immediately to raise the skin temperature; when it is turned off, the skin temperature begins abruptly to fall

FIGURE 19.3

The feedback loop that is created when a cold animal learns to press a lever that temporarily activates a heat lamp.

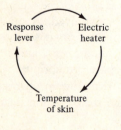

again. Rats will learn to push the lever under these conditions. Moreover, they push the lever at an average rate that keeps their skin temperature constant. That is to say, when they get only a little heat per press of the lever, they press at a rapid rate; when they get a lot of heat per press, their rate slows down.[6] If one thinks of the calories they absorb as a kind of reward, a payment for their work on the lever, then the more they are paid, the less they work! Clearly, the rats are not trying to hoard calories as a miser hoards gold; they are simply trying to keep their body temperatures in homeostatic equilibrium.

At the time Cannon put forward his speculations about homeostasis it was already a well-established fact, both inside and outside the laboratory, that behavior can be guided by giving or withholding particular kinds of stimulation: food and water, warmth, electric shock, and so on. Psychologists wanted to know why. Why do some stimuli control behavior when others do not? The concept of homeostatic drives seemed to provide an easy answer: stimuli are effective in controlling behavior to the degree that they serve to satisfy these drives and restore the organism to homeostatic equilibrium.[7]

In particular, Cannon's work seemed to provide a solid physiological basis for Thorndike's law of effect, which had become a pivotal issue in S-R theories of learning. Thorndike had said that we form only those stimulus-response connections that can lead to satisfying effects; many were willing to turn his law about and assume that effects are satisfying only if they can lead us to form stimulus-response connections. With this inversion it seemed possible to give an operational definition of motivation in terms of its reinforcing properties: a motive was anything that could be used to make an organism learn, that could reinforce a change in behavior. All that was missing was a theory to explain the mechanism of reinforcement, to explain why some effects are satisfying and others are not. And that is precisely what Cannon's drive theory seemed to offer. It is not surprising, therefore, that these ideas about homeostatic drives found an attentive audience among American psychologists and that research in this direction was quickly and vigorously pursued.[8]

Social psychologists in particular have adapted the homeostasis concept to talk about *psychological equilibrium* as a major explanatory model for the formation and changing of attitudes.[9] The normal state is defined in terms of a consistency or balance among attitude elements. Thus we would expect a racist not only to hate blacks, but to be in favor of segregation and against intermarriage. As long as these attitude elements are logically consistent with one another, the attitudinal equilibrium is maintained. However, when one element changes or a new, contradictory piece of information is accepted, disequilibrium results, setting up a tension or force toward the restoration of equilibrium. According to consistency and balance theories, the person is then motivated to change other attitude elements in order to restore the consistency.

In a classic experimental test of such models Rosenberg and Gardner measured the initial attitudes of a group of people, and then hypnotised them, and planted a posthypnotic suggestion that they had reversed their position on some strongly held attitude and would so publicly declare.[10] The investigators then repeated the overall attitude measure to see if the other positions changed to preserve balance among elements. The results confirmed the hypothesis. There was a general move on the part of the people to reorganize their beliefs around the new position and establish a new, but balanced position. There is also evidence from recent research that an imbalanced attitudinal state may be accompanied by increases in emotional activity such as blood sugar levels and heart rate, which are reduced when attitudinal balance is restored. But, the ways that imbalance is restored can be quite complicated.

Unfortunately for the cause of simplicity, evidence accumulated in research on homeostatic drives soon indicated that local irritation is only one of several goads to action. For example, a man whose stomach has been removed surgically cannot have stomach contractions, yet he can feel hunger. And persons born without salivary glands always have a dry throat, yet know when they are thirsty. Although the underlying concept of homeostasis seemed valid enough, Cannon's initial suggestions as to how these homeostatic systems guide behavior soon proved to be inadequate. Drives are not mere sources of irritating stimuli; neural and hormonal interactions of the most intricate design seem to be involved.

A variety of regulatory mechanisms may play a role over and above the local irritations that Cannon considered. Perhaps disequilibrium is signaled by variations in the pleasures of sensation, perhaps there is a direct effect on the central nervous system, perhaps there are hormonal changes in the blood stream, perhaps some connection is learned between a particular stimulus and an eventual change in homeostasis. Perhaps. Much research has been and is being done to evaluate these and other possible explanations. At present the consensus seems to be that most homeostatic drives arise through the internal environment acting on the central nervous system.[11] But it is difficult to be much more specific without going into great detail for each drive.

Let us focus on a simple behavioral fact: It is possible to train hungry animals to perform simple tricks by reinforcing their behavior with sweetened water. Why does sweetened water have this effect? Perhaps the sugar is absorbed into the blood stream, reduces the hunger drive, and thus relieves local irritation; the sweetened water is reinforcing because it removes a source of discomfort. The fact that so much time is required for digestion and absorption, however, makes this explanation dubious; for the reinforcement to occur promptly, as soon as the correct response is made, a neural process in the central nervous system—more rapid and symbolic—would have to be involved.

Some psychologists believe that reinforcement can be produced by the sheer pleasure of a sweet taste. In support of this belief they point out that animals appear to be as well reinforced by a saccharine solution, which has no nutritive value, as by a solution of glucose or sucrose. A sweet taste is rewarding whether or not it relieves the hunger drive. But why is it rewarding? Are animals born that way? Or do they learn to like sweetness because it is so often associated with the alleviation of hunger?

Questions such as these bring to mind the ancient doctrine of *hedonism,* the notion that we do the things that increase our pleasures and decrease our pains. At the root of this doctrine, no doubt, is an appreciation of the sensory pleasures aroused by genital stimulation, by the taste of sugar, by certain fragrant odors, and the like, and the sensory discomforts of heat, cold, shock, and so on. But no one who has argued for hedonism—Epicureans, Stoics, Utilitarians, Freudians—has ever argued for a purely sensory hedonism. It is rational, not sensory hedonism that has been defended. Rational hedonism assumes that an intelligent person will take the long view, will postpone small pleasures now in the hope of greater pleasures later. In Freudian language, the pleasure principle gives way to the reality principle. Certainly rational hedonism is the only form of this doctrine one can imagine applicable to man. But many of the experiments on the physiological bases of motivation are performed with lower animals whose ability to postpone their pleasures must be severely limited. Sensory hedonism may, therefore, be an important factor controlling the behavior of simpler organisms.

Hedonistic theories of motivation always seem to involve a semantic trick. A hedonist tells us, for example, that we do not really enjoy smoking; what we enjoy is the pleasure of smoking. With every pleasant activity the hedonist associates something called pleasure—or value or utility—which then becomes the real motive for the activity. "Don't spend your time smoking," he seems to say. "It is only a means to attain pleasure. Let it go and devote yourself directly to the true end, pure pleasure itself." As if you could experience the pleasure of smoking without smoking.

Yet divorcing the experience of pleasure from the pleasant experience may not be as ridiculous as it sounds. In 1954 two young psychologists, James Olds and Peter Milner, working together at McGill University in Montreal, stumbled across what seemed to be the pleasure center in a rat's brain.[12] They had pushed an electrode—two wires extending down into the brain from a plastic base mounted on the skull with jeweler's screws—into the limbic system, an old and vital region deep in the center of the brain. They were using the electrode to see what effects electric currents might have on the rat's behavior. Their happy innovation was to give the rat control of the electric stimulus; they let the animal press a lever that turned on the electrical stimulus to its own brain. The experimental arrangement is pictured schematically in Figure 19.4.

Under these conditions, and with exactly the right placement of the electrode, a rat will work hard to get the electric current, just as if it were a conventional reward. When the current is disconnected, the rat stops working. The electric stimulation can be powerfully attractive; a hungry rat may even refuse to eat if it is given a chance to stimulate itself instead. Exactly what goes on in this reinforcement center—if that is what it is—is not yet clear; this remains one of the most intriguing and, potentially, most important questions in the field of physiological psychology.

FIGURE 19.4

Diagram of circuit used in self-stimulation studies. When the rat presses the lever an electric current stimulates its hypothalamus. The response is simultaneously recorded via a separate wire. (From "Pleasure Center in the Brain" by James Olds, October 1956. Copyright © 1956 Scientific American, Inc. All rights reserved.)

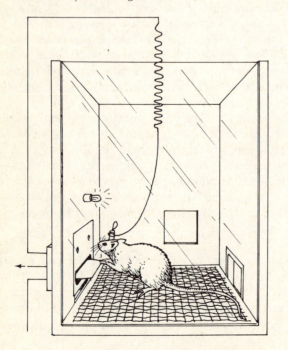

Detailed studies of all parts of the brain continue with remarkable success. Stimulation of some parts of the brain turn on and turn off fighting behavior, sexual behavior, thirst, etc. In one dramatic instance a bull was stopped during a charge by an electric current delivered to a part of the brain by means of a radio transmitter. Electrical brain stimulation has also been used on a limited basis for the study and treatment of mental patients.

Although there are many deep issues still unsettled, it appears that slow but steady progress is being made in the effort to understand the physiological drives.

But that is not enough. There is more to life than keeping one's blood chemistry in equilibrium.

Homeostatic drives play only the most general role in human conduct. They do not even account for all the motivated behavior observed in animals; manipulation, exploration, playfulness are motivated activities unrelated to homeostasis. Like the force of gravity, homeostatic drives are always around to trip us up if we become careless or unlucky. They goad us to action because they are part of being alive. But they are not the central focus for most of us most of the time.

The larger and more baffling problem is to understand what guides human action, what organizes it and assigns priorities. As a consequence of certain natural pleasures and many acquired tastes, we eventually come to make fairly predictable appraisals of the values of objects and activities in our daily lives. These are the values that guide us and channel our energies in one direction rather than another.

When one begins to ask about values one discovers that an old and elaborate theory of value already exists. The theory was not invented by psychologists, but by economists. Many psychologists have thought that it might be refitted for their purposes without too much trouble.

Beginning around 1870 a revolution in the classical science of economics led such men as W. Stanley Jevons and Alfred Marshall in England, Auguste Walras in Switzerland, and Karl Menger in Austria to try to analyze the psychological background of a consumer's motives, decisions, and actions. It was an abstract, mathematical kind of psychology that they adopted, based on the faith that men are rational and that rational men always try to maximize their happiness—or, as it was often called in honor of Jeremy Bentham, their utility.

A psychological assumption of crucial importance for these mathematical economists was that the satisfaction we get from any commodity—its value to us—grows more and more slowly as we acquire more and more of it. This situation is illustrated graphically in Figure 19.5. The first apple we get is the most satisfying; a man who already owns ten apples receives less satisfaction from his eleventh; and

FIGURE 19.5

*The economic principle of marginal utility. The increase in utility
(satisfaction) per unit of the commodity decreases progressively as the
amount of the commodity increases. A consumer will continue to buy
this commodity until he gets so much of it that his increase in satisfaction
per dollar becomes less than it would be for some other commodity.*

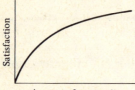

a man who has a thousand cares little for one more. For historical
reasons that would interest only an economist, this relation between
quantity and satisfaction is usually referred to as the theory of marginal utility. It was a crucial assumption to economists because they
could use it to explain why people wanted to exchange goods with one
another, which is, after all, the lifeblood of an economic system. If you
have too many apples and I have too many peaches, then according to
the principle of marginal utility we can both increase our satisfaction
by exchanging some of our fruit.

In many respects this economic theory was a mathematical
formulation of the pleasure principle, since behavior was explained in
terms of a single motive, namely, the increased satisfaction of the
individual. It was also a mathematical statement of the homeostatic
principle, because the principle of marginal utility plus the effort to
maximize satisfaction defines a point of equilibrium toward which a
person would gravitate. Only one detail seemed to keep economists
and psychologists apart: the economist's theory was normative, not
descriptive.

If your system of values is firmly established and you are trying
to maximize your satisfaction, economic theory is your best guide; if
you don't want to maximize your satisfactions, you should look elsewhere for guidance. By approaching the problem in this spirit, economists had the option of remaining indifferent to what people actually
did in economic contexts. The theory indicated what rational people
should do; what people actually did was their own foolish business.
Unfortunately, it was exactly that kind of foolish business that psychologists were most interested in. It was the economist's assumption
of rationality that most sharply distinguished his approach from that of
a psychologist who wanted to understand all choices, not only the
rational ones.

But perhaps a few minor modifications would enable psychologists to salvage a part of this elegant economic theory for their own use. What assumptions are involved? Theories fashioned along these lines generally begin with a person who is faced by a large, but well-defined set of alternative actions from which to choose. Moreover, this hypothetical person is able to decide, for any two of these alternatives, which one he would prefer; he has a preference ordering from the most valuable down to the least valuable alternative in the set. He knows, for example, that possessing five hundred apples and five hundred peaches is preferable to possessing one thousand apples and no peaches.

Assumptions of this kind are a glorious convenience for an economist, but they take for granted the very thing that a psychologist would like to explain. Consider the difficulties. In the first place, a flesh-and-blood consumer, unlike his theoretical counterpart, knows that large quantities of luck are needed to achieve economic success. Second, he almost never understands or tries to formulate explicitly all the alternatives that face him. Third, he seldom possesses either the ability or the patience to calculate his optimal course of action.

Certain of these objections are harder to meet than others. Perhaps the easiest is the one involving luck. Luck and uncertainty can be blended into an economic theory by using the mathematical theory of probability. As every gambler knows, the value of an outcome partly depends on the probability of attaining it. In the long run, a not-so-valuable outcome that is reliable may be worth more than a very valuable outcome that is highly improbable. To balance values against probabilities, economic theory introduces the concept of expected value. The expected value of a particular action is what one would receive on the average if one took that action again and again throughout a long sequence of choices. The expected (or mean) value of an action is obtained by listing all n of the possible outcomes, by assigning to each outcome $i = 1, 2, \ldots, n$, a value $v(i)$ and a probability $p(i)$, then averaging.

$$\text{Expected value} = p(1)v(1) + p(2)v(2) + \ldots + p(n)v(n)$$

By using expected values rather than absolute values, it is possible to preserve most of the economic theory intact. One merely assumes that people try to maximize their expected happiness, and all runs as smoothly as before. Uncertainty of success, therefore, is not the principal stumbling block in combining economic and psychological theories of choice.

Another obstacle that a psychologist must overcome if he hopes to adapt the economist's theory to his own ends is that the theory assumes people know things they don't know. For example, in introducing the notion of expected value, it is implicitly assumed that one knows the probabilities for every outcome that might result from one's actions. But often there is no possible way of knowing the true probabilities. All that the person usually knows is his subjective appraisal of the probabilities; he may in fact be far off the mark.

But all is not yet lost; the theory may still be adaptable to our psychological needs. Since the true probabilities are unknown, we must follow the next best course. Suppose, therefore, that subjective instead of true probabilities are used in the above equation. The result should then be closer to what the person subjectively expects; it will be wrong, but it may be more closely related to his choices than the true value. Because this is an attractively precise kind of theory, several experimental attempts have been made to test whether, under appropriate conditions, people really do try to maximize their subjective expected value.[13] But it is a difficult question, and the verdict is not yet in.

Whether or not a situation can be found in which people try to maximize their subjective expected value, there are clearly many situations in which they do not. For example, if people are paid for guessing correctly which of two lights is to flash next, then over a long string of trials their guesses will roughly match the probabilities. If one light comes on at random 80 percent of the time, people will guess it about 80 percent of the time.[14] If, however, they had wanted to maximize the amount they were being paid, they would have chosen that light at every trial. Unless there are important nonmonetary rewards involved, therefore, people do not naturally follow what most economists would consider an optimal strategy in this situation.

Even if one disregards the element of risk and the knowledge of probabilities there are other difficulties that the economic theory raises when it is used for descriptive purposes. Consider the assumption that a man has complete information about all the alternative courses of action that are open to him. In most practical situations this assumption is simply not true. A housewife does not learn the price of potatoes in every store in town before she makes her purchase. A real estate agent cannot know the price every potential customer would be willing to pay for a particular house before the agent makes the sale.

George Katona, a psychologist who looks at economic behavior through a magnifying glass called the University of Michigan Survey Research Center, has pointed out that what people do depends upon their level of aspiration.[15] They decide on a value that would be satisfactory and then accept the first offer that exceeds it. In experimental studies it has been shown that, if they are successful, people tend to raise their aspiration level next time; if they fail, they tend to lower the value they regard as satisfactory.[16] Herbert A. Simon, a behavioral scientist at the Carnegie Institute of Technology and a close student of administrative behavior, has suggested that this strategy of searching for something good enough—even though it may not be the best possible—should be called *satisficing*.[17] Satisficing does not always extract as large a return as maximizing would, but it is a much easier strategy to follow.

A person who has decided what will be good enough for him can then use this rude decision as a test. Each alternative that presents itself can be tested to see if it matches up to the standard. If it does, he accepts it. If not, he looks further. If a long search turns up nothing good enough, he may revise his level of aspiration.

The alternative choices available will depend partly upon what luck provides, partly upon the personal efforts of the satisficer. If he finds himself in an undesirable situation, he can take action to change or abandon the situation; he is not required to sit quietly until it goes away. This capacity to modify the environment develops progressively up the evolutionary scale, until in man it is so highly developed that the very operation of natural selection can be controlled. Let us consider briefly how the capacity operates.

Assume one is dealing with an organism complex enough to maintain an implicit image of the satisfactory states of its world—of itself and its environment. When the state that is perceived to exist does not fall within the bounds of satisfaction, the organism becomes active. If the activity changes the situation in a satisfactory way, it ceases and, presumably, the successful action is remembered for future reference. If the activity does not create a new situation more to the organism's liking, other actions may be initiated. If failures persist, it may be necessary to lower the level of aspiration, to revise the conception of what is desirable in order to bring it more in line with what is attainable. Such revisions, however, are often accompanied by strong emotions.

This description of the adjustment process is quite abstract. It describes the way we cope with our homeostatic drives as well as it describes the way we work toward any other valued objective. The underlying notion is that of a discrete servomechanism, with the one— very important—difference that the threshold for activation can vary as a function of success or failure. In very general terms, therefore, this description preserves the general philosophy of the early, biological accounts of motivation, but does so in terms of guidance and adjustment, rather than in terms of energy.

Leaving aside all the biological problems of energetics and focusing simply on the psychological problems of direction and control, it seems that several independent accounts of motivation—from physiology, from psychoanalysis, from economics—tend to converge. The organism struggles to reduce the mismatch between its own criteria and perceived reality. Of course, consensus is never a guarantee of validity. Even the most rapt admirer of this general picture has to admit that there are many blanks at critical points. How is value conferred or withheld as a result of experience? How do we decide what is good enough? How do we compromise between the claims of the present and our hopes for the future? How do we save, plan, and postpone?

When these questions are faced squarely, the picture begins to look very sketchy indeed—hardly more than an outline of a picture that may someday be drawn. Instinct, drive, reinforcement, pleasure, utility, level of aspiration—these will fit somewhere in the finished product, but exactly where is still an open question.

NOTES

1. W. McDougall, *An Introduction to Social Psychology* (New York: Barnes and Noble, 1960).
2. L. L. Bernard, *Instinct* (New York: Holt, 1924).
3. S. Freud, *An Outline of Psychoanalysis,* trans. J. Strachey (New York: Norton, 1949), p. 20.
4. W. B. Cannon, *The Wisdom of the Body* (New York: Norton, 1932).
5. I. Hendrick, *Facts and Theories of Psychoanalysis,* 3rd ed. (New York: Knopf, 1958), chap. 5.
6. B. Weiss and V. G. Laties, "Magnitude of Reinforcement as a Variable in Thermoregulatory Behavior," *Journal of Comparative and Physiological Psychology* 53 (1960): 603–608.
7. C. P. Richter, "A Behavioristic Study of the Activity of the Rat," *Comparative Psychology Monographs* 1, no. 2 (1922).
8. For a functionalist version, see H. A. Carr, *Psychology, A Study of Mental Activity* (New York: Longmans, Green, 1925). For a behavioristic version, see J. F. Dashiell, *Fundamentals of Objective Psychology* (Boston: Houghton Mifflin, 1928).
9. R. Brown, "Models of Attitude Change," in *New Directions in Psychology,* ed. R. Brown, E. Galanter, E. Hess, and G. Mandler (New York: Holt, Rinehart & Winston, 1962), pp. 1–85.
10. M. Rosenberg and C. W. Gardner, "Case Report: Some Dynamic Aspects of Posthypnotic Compliance," *Journal of Abnormal and Social Psychology* 57 (1958): 351–366.
11. C. T. Morgan, "Physiological Mechanisms of Motivation," in *Nebraska Symposium on Motivation 1957,* ed. M. R. Jones (Lincoln, Neb.: University of Nebraska Press, 1957), pp. 1–35.
12. J. Olds and P. Milner, "Positive Reinforcement Produced by Electrical Stimulation of Septal Area and Other Regions of Rat Brain," *Journal of Comparative and Physiological Psychology* 47 (1954): 419–427.
13. W. Edwards, "The Theory of Decision Making," *Psychological Bulletin* 51 (1954): 380–417.
14. L. G. Humphreys, "Acquisition and Extinction of Verbal Expectations in a Situation Analogous to Conditioning," *Journal of Experimental Psychology* 25 (1939): 294–301.

15. G. Katona, *Psychological Analysis of Economic Behavior* (New York: McGraw-Hill, 1951).
16. K. Lewin, T. Dembo, L. Festinger, and P. S. Sears, "Level of Aspiration," in *Personality and the Behavior Disorders,* ed. J. McV. Hunt (New York: Ronald, 1944), vol. 1, pp. 333–378.
17. H. A. Simon, *Models of Man* (New York: Wiley, 1957).

TWENTY
The Tyranny
of the Future

What do people want? As regards Americans in the second half of the twentieth century, what they want is all too familiar. Listen to Rosser Reeves, a high-powered salesman whose business it is to know what people want.

We know, for example, that we do not want to be fat. We do not want to smell bad. We want healthy children, and we want to be healthy ourselves. We want beautiful teeth. We want good clothes. We want people to like us. We do not want to be ugly. We seek love and affection. We want money. We like comfort. We yearn for more beautiful homes. We want honesty, self-respect, a place in the community. We want to own things in which we can take pride. We want to succeed in our jobs. We want to be secure in our old age.[1]

These are proven demands of the market place. Never mind whether it is good to want such things or whether we even have a right to want them. The point is that these are the things people in America work for, spend money on, devote their lives to. Surely here is where a psychologist should start to fashion his theory of human motivation.

This list, however, seems little better than our grandfathers' lists of instincts. If one is to make scientific sense out of these human desires, one will first have to discover the underlying dimensions of similarity among them.

Notice first of all that these American demands are all perfectly explicit, conscious, and socially acceptable. One may suspect that beneath these manifest desires is concealed a less admirable core, but this is a difficult issue.

Next, notice how typically American the list is. Imagine collecting a similar catalogue from Neanderthal men or the Tartar hordes. Americans find it difficult to believe that their own longings for particular things are learned, that the American conception of the good life is not universal and inevitable, that human nature has its own dimensions in India, Brazil, Nigeria.

Consider the salesman's list in a broader context. In many parts of the world obesity is judged beautiful. In extremely cold regions where clothes are seldom removed, body odors are simply ignored. Concepts of health and disease, of normal and

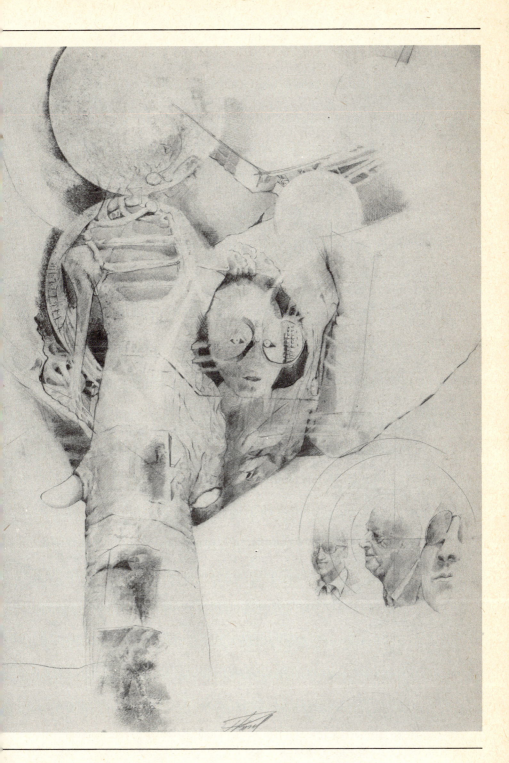

abnormal, vary widely from one culture to the next. Teeth we think beautiful do not look beautiful to everyone. And so on down the list. Each thing we think so desirable is desirable because we have learned to desire it. In another culture we would have learned to desire other things. Even within our own relatively homogeneous society different social groups have very different dreams of the future.

As a start, therefore, one asks how this learning takes place. Where and when in the life of a youngster does stern society sit him down and explain what to crave and what to despise?

One answer runs something like this. Homeostatic drives are primary, and all the environmental conditions that are consistently associated with the satisfaction of primary drives will thereby acquire a secondary power to satisfy us. Mother's smile becomes rewarding because it accompanies the satisfaction of so many of her child's primary motives. And by generalization the value of mother's smile extends to other smiles, to all smiles, to social approval in its broadest sense. Similarly, power over others becomes a social motive because it was first associated with the various biological satisfactions that others can provide. Avarice is a social motive because money is associated with the satisfaction of many other motives. And so on and on. It is apparently true that every social value can be traced back, in theory, at least, through some such hypothetical chain of associations, to primary, homeostatic drives. These biological primitives constitute, in theory, the latent core around which cluster these manifest desires that an advertiser can exploit.

There is little that is objectionable in such a theory until it is claimed that social action is *always* energized in this manner. No doubt it is true that some adult values are acquired by repeated association with eating, drinking, sexing. But many psychologists feel that the insistence—typified by orthodox Freudian theorists—that all human behavior, normal and abnormal alike, draws its energy either directly or indirectly from these life-preserving, species-preserving mechanisms imposes on us an unprofitable burden of explanation. According to this theory, the reasons for everything we do must somehow be traced back historically to our sex glands and to homeostatic changes in the chemistry of our blood.

It detracts little from the importance of homeostasis and the pleasure principle to argue that some important social motives are acquired and mediated by very different processes, symbolic processes that must take place in the central nervous system.

One objection to the borrowed-energy theory is that it encourages us to think of social motives as if they ran a course entirely parallel to homeostatic drives. For example, an organism works to reduce its primary drives, to bring its tensions to a balanced minimum, to return to homeostatic equilibrium. If social motives are learned by association with primary drives, it seems reasonable to assume that they will also manifest this self-terminating characteristic. When this pattern of tension-reduction is imposed on social motives, however, it leads to an odd distortion. The simple truth is that social action does not always reduce tensions. To imply that it must suggests that persistent diligence and hard work are symptoms of maladjustment, that exciting stories and martial music will never be popular, that sport, humor, and dancing are signs of insanity, in short, that nirvana is the only goal anyone could imagine in this life. But this is nonsense. Rarely would a person reduce all his motivation to a minimum. Emerson was wrong when he said that every man is as lazy as he dares to be. Instead—when homeostasis gives us a chance—we constantly seek out new tensions to keep us occupied and entertained.

If we slavishly follow an analogy to biological drives, we are likely to assume that social motives can be satiated, as hunger, thirst, and sex can be. And on that assumption we must be surprised to find that millionaires want to make money, that neurotics never seem to get all the love they desire, that famous people like to see their names in newspapers, and so on. Social motives grow by what they feed on; the more we succeed, the higher we set our level of aspiration.

The mistaken notion that social motives can be satiated has even confused some economists and led them to prophesy that when the market was saturated—when 80 percent of the American families owned refrigerators or 70 percent owned automobiles—the economy would slump to a level set by the rate of replacement. They failed to include the wages of optimism. Families with a refrigerator wanted a better one; families with one car wanted two cars; families with both a refrigerator and a car wanted their own house. One observer feels that this is a symptom of "the psychology of more," where people come to expect that their material goods will grow as the society grows around them.[2] Homeostasis follows an entirely different course.

The orthodox notion that we must have motives to energize our social actions—just as homeostatic drives energize our search for food, drink, and a mate—has been losing adherents for many years. Probably it would by now be abandoned, except that the defectors have been unable to agree among themselves on any single theory to replace the simple homeostatic analogy. When we desert it, therefore, we set out upon an uncertain journey of exploration; what follows here is only one of several directions that we might have chosen.

Suppose one asks, not where the energy for social action comes from, but where it is going. A psychologist can take the biological source of our vitality for granted; given that we are alive, metabolism provides our energy. The psychological problem is how we organize and guide a flow that must inevitably continue until our final tension-reduction in the grave. What determines how we will use our brief gift of time?

Most human endeavors are guided not by learned motives, but

by learned values.[3] There are important differences. Motives are a source of energy, values a form of knowledge. Motives like to push us from the past, values try to draw us into the future. Many psychologists feel that these differences are purely verbal, that motive and value are two sides of the coin. Perhaps this is true. There is as much of philosophy as of science in these distinctions. Here, however, we shall try to keep separate our energies and our concepts.

Let us turn, therefore, to the question of how we acquire and use our conception of the values and costs of things.

Along with every name and every skill a child learns he also absorbs an evaluation. Along with "What is it?" goes "Is it dangerous? Do you like it? What good is it? How much does it cost?" These evaluations are different in every society, and a person who does not know them cannot function in a manner acceptable to the members of that society. In short, costs and values constitute a kind of personal and cultural knowledge that we have all acquired through many years of experience.

In our society there are several different realms of value corresponding to different social functions. Within any single realm it may be possible to develop a consistent system of values, but the demands from separate areas may conflict in ways that seem impossible to reconcile. Value systems can be classified as theoretical, economic, esthetic, religious, social, political; men can be classified according to the ways they assign priorities to one or another of these six realms.[4]

Why do we have to learn these value systems? What purpose do they serve? The answer springs directly from the fact that we are constantly being put into situations where we must express a preference, must make a choice between two or more courses of action. If we believe in social motives, we say that we choose the course of action that mobilizes the greatest amount of energy. If we believe in values, we say that we choose the course of action that we expect will lead to the most valuable outcome. But whatever the explanation, the need to choose is inescapable.

The act of choice is often embedded in great conflict and uncertainty. We like to smoke; we value our good health; we are told the two are incompatible. What do we do? We have learned that freedom of speech is good, but we are convinced that someone is using it for evil ends. What do we do? We treasure all the human values that marriage represents, yet we chafe under its constraints and responsibilities. What do we do?

In these and in thousands of similar conflicts, what we must do is decide which values are greater, which are more important. And to facilitate the constantly recurring processes of choice, we try to organize our values into a coherent, usually hierarchical, system. It is a great help, of course, if the values involved are conscious, if we can make them explicit and talk about them. But even that is not enough to resolve all our problems, because our decisions are usually made in a complicated and idiosyncratic context of past achievements and future ambitions.

Since these comparisons must be made so frequently, it would be a wonderful simplification if we could always use a single, simple quantity as our measure of value. Money is the most obvious candidate, and we use it wherever we can. Indeed, Americans are often accused of putting too much faith in dollars and cents, of imposing a public rate of exchange where private opinion and personal conviction should be sovereign. Research on "economic man" or rational man has been conducted widely by social psychologists under the heading of social exchange theory. A person in a social setting is assumed to perform some kind of cost-benefits analysis when deciding to act. But even for Americans, money is not always a meaningful measure of value. Psychological value depends upon the situation we find ourselves in and the way we expect the situation to develop. It is not a price tag fixed once and for all, the same for every customer, every day. There are times when a man would offer his kingdom for a horse.

If one tries to analyze conflicts of value, one finds that the simplest involve a triadic system of relations.[5] There is the person himself and two other persons, things, or activities that are causing him trouble. If one represents the possible values as plus or minus, then the diagrams in Figure 20.1 help keep distinct the three simplest situations that lead to conflicts. Perhaps the easiest to sympathize with is a person who wants two things that are mutually exclusive; the child wants his dime, but he wants the candy, too. A bit more special, perhaps, is a person who must choose between two things that are both unpleasant for him; the student who dislikes studying, but also dislikes failing is caught in this dilemma. In the third case, a person likes one thing and dislikes another, but cannot separate them; the hostess who wants to invite a friend to a dinner party, but cannot tolerate her friend's husband, knows what kind of conflicting evaluations must be settled in this situation.

In all these simple conflicts the person is faced with two alternatives. The child is comparing his situation when he has a dime and no candy with the alternative situation when he will have the candy but no dime. The student is weighing the advantages of leisurely failure against stressful (and uncertain) achievement. The hostess contemplates her dinner party with both Jane and John, or without either of them. The choice is between two situations, and the situations differ in only the two respects, X and Y.

Most choices, however, are a good deal more complicated. They can involve several alternatives that differ from one another in many aspects, where each aspect has several intermediate shades of value

FIGURE 20.1

*Types of conflict. A person faced with a choice between two mutually
exclusive alternatives may have difficulty deciding which of two positive
values to accept (A is "approach-approach" conflict) or which of two
negative values to reject (B is "avoidance-avoidance" conflict). Or, if
the two things are inseparable, he may find it difficult to decide whether
the positive value of one overcomes the negative value of the other
(C is "approach-avoidance" conflict).*

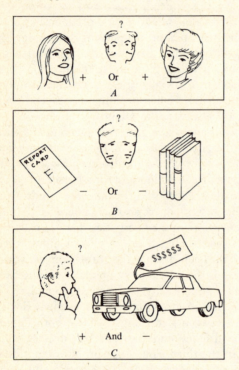

between all good and all bad, and where the choice may have consequences that will reverberate far into the unforeseeable future. Simply
keeping track of the various possibilities and all their distinguishing
features can be quite an intellectual feat; the additional task of deciding
how to reconcile conflicting values may completely overload one's
cognitive machinery. And on top of the cognitive problem, there may
be important values that we refuse to formulate explicitly—that are
banished into the limbo of unconsciousness.

It is scarcely surprising, therefore, that we adopt strategies for
cutting through this complexity, for reducing the cognitive strain of
making a rational decision. Probably the simplest strategy is to flip a
coin; the reasoning here is that if you really cannot decide, the coin at
least serves to get you back in action. A subtler variation on this
scheme is to flip the coin and notice carefully whether you are relieved

or disappointed by the way it falls; that bit of self-deception can sometimes help you to discover what you really want.

But random choices are too easy; they disregard all the relevant information. Less drastic is to disregard a part, but not all. A favorite strategy of this type is to ignore most of what one knows about the ways in which the alternatives differ from one another, to pretend that only one or two aspects of the situation are relevant. For example, when a group chooses a leader it should consider such values as power, ability, prestige, and the like; for each value the candidates may rank differently. But these several rankings are difficult to remember and think about. Instead of weighing Jane's skill against Barbara's influence against our personal friendship for Charlie, we lump these different value scales into a single figure of merit that covers everything. Instead of deciding which candidate would be the best leader in given situations, we convince ourselves that the one we favor is the best for every conceivable situation. This phenomenon has been called the *halo effect;* because we know that a person is good in one important aspect, we put a halo of goodness over his other aspects as well.[6] It makes the world a great deal simpler when the good guys are always smart, honest, beautiful, and brave, while the bad guys are always stupid, crooked, ugly cowards. We often see this in descriptions of the "enemy" in times of war.

Out of thousands of inner battles we try to evolve a workable hierarchy of our own. Repeatedly, day after day, we face conflicts and make decisions that force us to search for rules, for strategies, for a structure that will reduce the complexity and ease our burden of decision. Little wonder, therefore, that we prefer a single, simple ordering. We may even come to feel that there is a kind of inconsistency in multiple orderings, that all values *ought* to be measurable with a single yardstick.

The urge toward greater consistency among our various scales of value can itself assume the energizing properties of a social motive. When we find ourselves being inconsistent, it usually annoys us and we are likely to search for ways to eliminate the source of our inconsistency. As noted in Chapter 19, some psychologists have suggested that an effort toward consistency plays much the same role in our cognitive life that homeostasis plays in our biological drives.[7]

When a person feels himself caught in an evaluative inconsistency, there are usually several avenues of escape open to him. He can revise his evaluation of one or the other objects involved. He can modify or deny the incompatibility or the inseparability of the two objects. He can withdraw entirely. He can bring to bear additional factors that enrich or redefine the objects involved. Exactly what he will do in any particular situation cannot be predicted without an exact knowledge of his particular circumstances. Even then, we are not so sure that the assumption of rational man can be applied.

Examining the social psychology journals of the 1960s and 1970s might lead one to assume that the most important theory to emerge in social psychology was *cognitive dissonance* theory. It is a tribute to the imagination of Leon Festinger that he was able to take the basic ingredients of homeostasis and apply them to an understanding of attitude formation and change in more complex situations. He states his theory as follows.

> . . . [c]ognitive dissonance . . . centers around the idea that if a person knows various things that are not psychologically consistent with one another, he will, in a variety of ways, try to make them more consistent. . . . Cognitive dissonance is a motivating state of affairs. . . . dissonance impels a person to change his opinions or his behavior.[8]

We can better understand this theory by looking closely at an experiment on lying.

Imagine participating in an experiment that consisted of the boring job of placing spools on wooden pegs and removing them, only to be asked by the experimenter to help out by telling the next person how interesting and exciting the experiment was. This was the scenario for Festinger's experiment, with the added twist of paying each person

---

CITATION ACCOMPANYING THE DISTINGUISHED SCIENTIFIC
CONTRIBUTION AWARD PRESENTED BY THE AMERICAN PSYCHOLOGICAL
ASSOCIATION, 1959

"For fertile theorizing and ingenious experimentation in social psychology. He depicts social behavior as the responses of a thinking organism continually acting to bring order into his world, rather than as the blind impulses of a creature of emotion and habit. He and his students have devised laboratory techniques for reproducing under controlled conditions the subtle thought processes and motivations that regulate prejudice, communication of rumor, and social influence. He has been a leader in cooperative international experiments which test the validity of psychological generalization in various cultural settings. In his hands, psychological theory shows itself capable of explaining not only laboratory data, but complex social realities."

LEON FESTINGER

---

either $1 or $20 for lying to the next person. The dependent variable was the person's rating of what he really thought of the boring task, recorded after the person lied about the boring task to the next person. Festinger predicted from the cognitive dissonance analysis that people paid only $1 to lie, having less justification for their action, would have more dissonance and would change their private beliefs more to reduce the dissonance. The results shown in Figure 20.2 support the prediction; people paid $1 reported that they liked the task very much, in spite of their real initial feelings. A control group which just did the task without lying and then rated the task found it unfavorable. Festinger argues that the $20 group had sufficient justification for lying, experienced less dissonance, and thus did not feel impelled to change their private feelings about the boring task just because they had lied.

Festinger's interpretation of the experiment was that the change in attitude represents one example of how behavior does not conform to the law of effect, which would predict that the larger the reward, the greater the amount of change. He defends cognitive dissonance theory as one that allows the prediction of effects that are not obvious, where rational consistency acts in the way that people make their private beliefs accord with their publicly observed actions. In the thousands of experiments generated by cognitive dissonance theory, there has been no shortage of critics to this claim. Taking the experiment described, we can wonder if, in all of its clear-cut simplicity, it does not mask more subtle goings-on. We first wonder if people

---

FIGURE 20.2

> Consequences of lying are found to vary, depending on whether the justification for the lie is large or small. In this experiment students were persuaded to tell others that a boring experience was really fun. Those in one group were paid only $1 for their cooperation; in a second group, $20. The low-paid students, having least justification for lying, experienced most dissonance and reduced it by coming to regard the experience favorably. (From "Cognitive Dissonance" by Leon Festinger, October 1962. Copyright © 1962 by Scientific American, Inc. All rights reserved.)

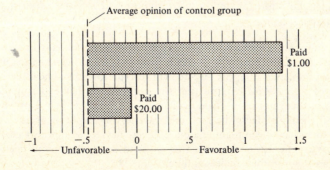

experienced any discomfort or dissonance; secondly, would dissonance be restricted to the $1 group? Is it possible that a person in the $20 group saw that amount of money symbolically as a bribe, cooperated with the experimenter, and told the truth at the end to resolve his discomfort at being seen as a willing liar by the experimenter? These and many other unanswered questions are typical of the ambiguities that can remain after any provocative experiment.

A group of social psychologists took on the task of sorting out these and many other ambiguities by first pointing out that dissonance theorists tend to take a limited and somewhat dehumanizing view of man in their research.[9] Too often, they argue, the "subject" in an experiment is seen as a "passive target of the clever manipulations of the experimenter." They also point out a well-known fact: that people seem to be able to tolerate a great deal of logical inconsistency among their private beliefs and in many instances prefer unbalanced relationships as long as the gains outweigh the expected losses. An experiment after all is a social relationship, which involves a person's balancing of his self-concept and the presentations he makes of his social role. If we agree that consistency is a much valued image in society, it is possible that a person in an experiment may be more concerned with appearing consistent than with actually being consistent. Tedeschi, Schlenher, and Bonama propose a theory of impression management in which a person manages the impression he wishes to leave with an experimenter after weighing the costs and gains. Thus the person in the $1 condition may be receiving unmistakable signals from the experimenter to make an impression of appropriate, consistent behavior due to the importance of being evaluated by an objective scientist in a project legitimized by the university. As has been pointed out in studies on experimenter bias, the $1 may be seen as unimportant while the social pressure may be to appear as one who saves face when he lies by squaring things with the experimenter. He tells the man what he wants to hear by saying he really enjoyed the boring task. The $20 person is presumably being signaled that the task was really boring, that a person who is true to himself would have to be highly compensated, and that there is no need to save face because the experimenter considered the lie important enough to give him $20. Same experiment, different interpretation.

> The impression management theory does not view subjects in experiments as passive targets. . . . Rather subjects have been the originators of influence attempts directed at the experimenter. The effectiveness of subjects in manipulating the impressions that experimenters have of them has been made evident by the fact that social-psychological theory reflects the lack of awareness by experimenters about how they have been manipulated. Subjects have been quite successful in leaving the impression that they are and have a profound need to be consistent in their beliefs and behaviors.[10]

Which is just what many experimenters want to believe—the experimenters act in a way to be consistent with their own dissonance theory.

Sometimes people acquire values so deeply at odds with everything else they believe that no simple resolution of their conflict seems possible. In that case they may actually deny their disturbing values, may refuse to formulate them explicitly as part of their conscious picture of themselves. It was Freud who explored the depths of our capacity to deceive ourselves about what we value and what we fear. When these unconscious systems become involved, a whole new dimension of complexity is added to our problem.

Consider an example. Suppose you are told that a certain man is a trained athlete, that he has won prizes in several sports, and that he places the highest value on physical fitness and stamina. Under most conditions you would probably assume he was a thoroughly masculine type of person. But suppose you ask further and discover that he is 35 years old, without heterosexual experience, living with his mother, and sponsoring boys' clubs. Then the very same athletic values may take on exactly the opposite appearance; you may begin to wonder whether the man has a homosexual component, strong but latent, in his personality. You may begin to suspect that his interest in athletics is what Freud called reaction formation: perhaps the athletic activity conceals, yet simultaneously indulges, some deeply disturbing impulses he does not dare to admit consciously. If you are correct, the athlete has a conflict that he cannot face squarely. His tragedy is too large to play on the same mental stage he uses for his ordinary decisions. A reconstruction project of considerable magnitude would be required before he could even recognize, much less resolve his dilemma.

In short, it is not always easy to discover what you want or to face what you discover. Only under the best possible conditions can you hope to resolve all claims in a reasonable and consistent way. Even if all your values can be stated explicitly, and even if you limit your attention to one decision at a time, the task is still formidable. But add the inescapable fact that each choice interacts with others now and in the future, that what you do presently determines the possibilities open to you later, and even the simplest decision will be seen to involve contingencies far too fine to contemplate. Who is wise enough to know what will be best for him in the long run? We can hope for little more than rude and abstract generalizations.

If we decide upon a particular course of action, it may be necessary to pursue it for long stretches of time—for days, months, even years. Some few decisions dedicate us to a particular path throughout an entire lifetime. Sticking to a long, elaborate program of activity is something we human beings can do—not as well as we would like perhaps, but far better than any other living organism. We manage it principally by using linguistic symbols to control our behavior, by constructing elaborate verbal plans that we remember and use to guide successive steps along the way.[11]

That is not to say that man is the only planful animal. Anyone who has worked around monkeys or apes has observed them constructing and executing simple plans. The chimpanzee that hears a visitor approaching, dashes quickly to the drinking fountain to fill its mouth with water, then runs back to its regular position where it waits patiently for an unsuspecting target to come within range has conceived and carried out a plan just as surely as any human bureaucrat ever did. Even in lower animals there seem to be plans, although they are usually rather inflexible and are probably better regarded as instincts. Organisms that live entirely in the present, uninfluenced by the past and unprepared for the future, are low on the evolutionary scale.

Many animals can follow simple plans, but man has carried planfulness to its most extreme form. Language is a critical element in this development, but language is not the sole reason for man's superiority.

When the gap between actuality and desirability grows so large that no simple reflex can repair it, we are forced to break up our task into a sequence of subtasks. In learning to perform such analysis man has been particularly favored, oddly enough, by his possession of an opposable thumb. The human hand is often praised as a marvelous tool and credited for much of man's success as an evolutionary experiment. Our ability to hold an object in front of our wonderful simian eyes, to

FIGURE 20.3

Hands: human and chimpanzee.

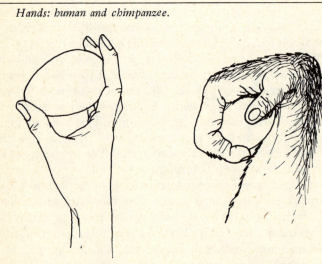

carry things with us, to feed ourselves, to grasp tools—the significance of these skills for the evolution of modern man is by now a familiar story. But the development of the hand also had great psychological significance. The hand is our basic tool. As a tool, it intervenes between the man and his task. Instead of moving directly to the desired object, he reaches out, grasps, and hauls in; a series of steps is substituted for the immediate response. The way we use our hands introduces a sequential character into our behavior. In order to exploit this marvelous new tool, the human brain came under selective evolutionary pressure to develop new ways to organize the sequential aspects of behavior. Here, then, was the beginning of our unique ability to analyze problems and to coordinate long sequences of actions, to subject ourselves to the guiding influence of long-term plans.

Most plans are hierarchically organized. We hold some image of the state we hope to achieve. By comparing this image with perceived reality we notice the major discrepancies, we analyze our task into several main parts, and we decide on an order for doing them. We then begin to execute the first part of our plan; other parts are relegated to the status of intentions. But each subpart in turn is usually too complex for a simple reflex; again we must analyze and postpone some parts while we start to work on others. Thus it sometimes happens that we find ourselves working at unpleasant tasks, doing things we dislike or disapprove of, because they fit into a larger, hierarchically organized plan whose eventual value will, we assume, justify all our temporary discomforts. It is this ability to postpone gratification that distinguishes rational from sensory hedonism, that justifies Freud's reality principle as a supplement to his pleasure principle. Our willingness to renounce the pleasures of the moment and to submit to the tyranny of the future is one of the best measures of our humanity.

The capacity to postpone rewards has been studied in some detail. In rats, for example, delays longer than a few seconds considerably reduce the effectiveness of the reward to reinforce the animal's behavior.[12] In children, the willingness to reject a small reward now on the promise of a larger reward later is known to develop with age; children are more likely to wait for a larger reward when parents are present than when they are absent; children who are socially responsible and reliable are more likely to postpone their rewards than are juvenile delinquents.[13] The acceptance of delayed gratification can also be studied by survey research;[14] many people plan far in advance for their large purchases—for houses, college education for their children, life insurance, cars, even for major appliances. Their plans and attitudes are often a more reliable indicator of future consumer buying than are such purely economic indicators as disposable personal income or savings.

There can be little doubt, therefore, of the psychological validity and importance of our expectations and the plans whereby we hope to achieve them, but they are so heterogeneous that only the most general and obvious comments can be made about them.

Suppose, for example, that we ask how much detail people include in their plans. There can be no universal answer, for this is one important way in which people differ. But one can point to variables that are probably involved. The amount of detail included in a plan will depend upon the importance of success, upon the amount of time available, upon the skill and competence of the person doing the planning. The first two are obvious enough, but the third merits further discussion.

There is little need to plan in detail an activity that you know you are competent to perform, that you have successfully performed many times before, that no longer holds any power to surprise you. If you are going to visit a friend, you need not decide in advance where to place your feet each step along the way. As one gets into more and more detail, the need for explicit planning declines correspondingly. Our most deliberate plans are constructed in terms of strategy, not tactics; in terms of molar acts, not molecular responses. One goes just far enough in elaborating a plan to reassure himself that he is competent to perform each subpart. Thus a person with considerable experience and competence in a particular area will not need to plan as carefully or in as much detail as would a novice. The old hand knows what he can do and how the parts must fit together; all of that must be painstakingly explored by the beginner.

A major component of our plans, therefore, must be our conception of our own competencies. As usual, the simplest example is an economic one. When we plan to buy something, the amount of money at our disposal sets a very clear, unambiguous limit on our ability to obtain the thing we want. Thus money serves as a kind of generalized competence, since it enables us to purchase the abilities of others and incorporate their extended competence into our own plans. People save money, often with no specific or immediate goal in view, but simply for a rainy day, for an emergency, for their old age, for any of a dozen vague reasons, but basically because it increases their potential competence to execute any of a variety of plans that they may someday formulate.

For most people there is a special kind of satisfaction and security associated with competence; in the absence of any very specific aim, they will work simply to increase their general level of skill and information. Reading, play, talking, going to school, traveling, hobbies, curiosity in general, all can contribute directly or indirectly to greater competence.

Professor R. W. White, the clinical psychologist, has referred to this urge for greater competence—the urge to be effective—as effectance motivation.

Of all living creatures, it is man who takes the longest strides toward autonomy. This is not because of any unusual tendency toward bodily expansion at the expense of the environment. It is rather that man, with his mobile hands and abundantly developed brain, attains an extremely high level of competence in his transactions with his surroundings. The building of houses, roads and bridges, the making of tools and instruments, the domestication of plants and animals, all qualify as planful changes made in the environment so that it comes more or less under control and serves our purposes rather than intruding upon them. We meet the fluctuations of outdoor temperature, for example, not only with our bodily homeostatic mechanisms, which alone would be painfully unequal to the task, but also with clothing, buildings, controlled fires, and such complicated devices as self-regulating central heating and air conditioning. Man as a species has developed a tremendous power of bringing the environment into his service, and each individual member of the species must attain what is really quite an impressive level of competence if he is to take part in the life around him.[15]

White's description emphasizes how very important the development of competence is for young children. He does not mean that a child at play is grimly storing up skills for the rainy days ahead; the child plays, masters, and enjoys the efficacy that mastery brings. An organism that depends as heavily as we do upon flexibility and adaptability needs to be born with the kind of hunger for competence that White describes.

But a teacher is all too prone to exaggerate the importance of competence. Room for individual differences in these matters is enormous. A feeling of effectiveness can be valuable and rewarding, but it is more valuable to some than to others. And it is only one aspect of the vast and intricate structure we blandly call human nature. In an adult the child's urge for competence can become a need for achievement, for power, for security; it may even atrophy and disappear.

NOTES

1. R. Reeves, *Reality in Advertising* (New York: Knopf, 1961), p. 73.
2. W. R. Looft, "The Psychology of More," *American Psychologist* 26 (1971): 561–565.
3. D. W. Taylor, "Toward an Information Processing Theory of Motivation," in *Nebraska Symposium on Motivation,* ed. M. R. Jones (Lincoln, Nebraska: University of Nebraska Press, 1960).
4. G. W. Allport, P. E. Vernon, and G. Lindzey, *Study of Values,* rev. ed. (Boston: Houghton Mifflin, 1951). See also C. Morris, *Varieties of Human Value* (Chicago: University of Chicago Press, 1956).
5. F. Heider, *The Psychology of Interpersonal Relations* (New York: Wiley, 1958).

6. C. B. De Soto, "The Predilection for Simple Orderings," *Journal of Abnormal and Social Psychology* 62 (1961): 16–23.
7. L. Festinger, *A Theory of Cognitive Dissonance* (Evanston, Ill.: Row, Peterson, 1957).
8. L. Festinger, "Cognitive Dissonance," in *Contemporary Psychology*, ed. R. C. Atkinson (San Francisco: Freeman, 1971), pp. 409–415.
9. J. T. Tedeschi, B. R. Schlenker, and T. V. Bonoma, "Cognitive Dissonance: Private Ratiocination or Public Spectacle," *American Psychologist* 26, no. 8 (1971): 685–694.
10. Ibid, p. 694.
11. G. A. Miller, E. Galanter, and K. Pribram, *Plans and the Structure of Behavior* (New York: Holt, 1960).
12. F. A. Logan, *Incentive* (New Haven: Yale University Press, 1960).
13. W. Mischel, "Preference for Delayed Reinforcement and Social Responsibility," *Journal of Abnormal and Social Psychology* 62 (1961): 1–7.
14. G. Katona, *Psychological Analysis of Economic Behavior* (New York: McGraw-Hill, 1951); *The Powerful Consumer* (New York: McGraw-Hill, 1960).
15. R. W. White, "Motivation Reconsidered: The Concept of Competence," *Psychological Review* 66 (1959): 297–333.

TWENTY-ONE
Jean Piaget and the Mind of a Child

MEASUREMENT OF MENTAL GROWTH

Imagine that you are given a number, somewhere between 0 and 1000, and are told that it represents a person's age in months. How much would you know about the person?

If the number is somewhere in the middle of the range—between 200 and 800, say—it would not tell you very much. Since you do not know the person's sex, education, native ability, or even the society in which he (she) lives, you could not form any clear picture of him (her). If the number gets large enough, of course, you have some feeling for the kind of constraints old age imposes. But you will extract the greatest amount of information from the number when it is small, and the smaller it gets the more accurate you can be.

Small numbers place the person in the time of life called the growth period, when successive phases unfold themselves in regular order. The predictable succession of changes in bodily size and structure, in motor skills, in mental competence and achievement, in social and emotional adjustment is generally familiar to everyone. For those who wish to know more—parents who wonder if their child is developing properly or educators trying to plan a school curriculum—many detailed facts have been collected and tabulated for ready reference, both in popular guides and in technical handbooks.[1]

A regular procession of structural changes is something we all take for granted. The emergence of motor skills is almost equally reliable. And cognitive development is only slightly more variable. Hundreds of studies, beginning even before Alfred Binet's experiments in the schools of Paris, have demonstrated convincingly that mental growth also pursues an orderly course, that measurable skills appear at predictable ages, that deviations above or below the average are not accidental. Binet calibrated a whole battery of tests, to which many subsequent workers have added, so that today we can sample quite different aspects of the unfolding process of mental growth. With those tests it has become possible to measure the growth of the mind.

But there are still many problems that remain unsettled.

Take, for example, that hotly debated subject, the constancy of the intelligence quotient. Adherents of hereditary theories of mental ability like to think of the IQ as if it were printed indelibly on the chromosomes at the moment of conception. Environmentalists, on the other hand, credit experience and education for all our mental accomplishments and recognize no other factors which might limit a child's IQ score. In the twentieth century this ancient argument has come to rest—or roost—on the question of whether or not an IQ score is indeed constant throughout life.

Consider what this constancy would imply. Suppose one thousand children of the same age are tested every year until they are adults. If the intelligence of every child is constant, their rank order from best to worst, from brightest to dullest, would never change, except, perhaps, for random errors inherent in the measuring instruments. The child who ranked 100 at the age of 1 year would still rank 100 at the age of 20 years.

When studies of this sort are actually done, however, it is found that the rank orderings can change markedly from year to year.[2] One child shows a sudden spurt in skill A while a second is developing skill B and a third seems to be standing still. In the first years of life the scores change considerably; after six or seven years they begin to settle down and our predictions get better and better.

It may be suggested, therefore, that the IQ is variable at birth, but becomes more stable as we get older. It is not apparent whether this finding favors either side of the heredity-environment battle. Perhaps one inherits one's constant IQ the way a man inherits his beard—it doesn't appear until the age is right. Or perhaps one needs time to decide what IQ will be necessary in one's social environment. Increasing stability of the IQ can be explained away by proponents of either theory. Nevertheless, it is fair to say that informed opinion in the United States is currently on the side of the environmentalist—if not completely, at least in spirit and emphasis. Within limits, Johnny can change his position in the rank ordering, although it becomes more and more difficult to do so as he grows older.

Psychologists who have puzzled over the instability of predictions based on the early years do not believe that it can be attributed to poor measurements—not entirely, anyhow. There is reason to think that even the most accurate tests during infancy have little power to predict adult intelligence.

Consider the following argument.[3] Suppose that mental growth is cumulative, so that the level a child attains by the age of 9 is simply the sum of all he has achieved in each of his preceding years. If this assumption were reasonable, it would mean that our prediction from age 9 to age 10 would be very good, since nine-tenths of the basis for the new measurement would be the same as for the old and only one-tenth would be attributable to new growth or experience during the tenth year. By the same argument, the prediction of the child's IQ score at age 2 on the basis of his score at age 1 would be based half on old achievements and half on novel achievements; hence the prediction would be less accurate. On a relative basis, therefore, more could happen to change the relative standings early in life than later on. Every baseball fan who has watched batting averages vary wildly during the early part of the season and then settle down as the players accumulate more turns at bat will understand this explanation of why the test scores should become more reliable as the children grow older.

For older children, at least, mental tests can give a valuable measure of mental age, one that can be usefully compared with chronological age. But there are still other problems we should recognize when we try to understand what an intelligence score means.

By combining all the individual tests in order to obtain a single number that represents a child's status, psychologists have encouraged uncritical people to imagine that mental growth is an undifferentiated process, to think that a child's mind grows like a potato. Even psychologists who should know better have been tempted to plot smooth curves of mental growth, forgetting that they were actually dealing with a composite of many separate curves for separate skills. The practical convenience of having a single number is, of course, too great to resist. But a scientist must look more closely.

As stated earlier, to measure a process is not necessarily to understand it. Mental tests may give a number—mental age—that is highly correlated with mental growth, but they do not contain within themselves any coherent explanation of that growth. One has to take the single number apart to see what it consists of. Why do certain skills emerge before others? Why are some tasks easy and others so difficult? What does a child actually do in the process of finding an answer to a test item? What manner of thing is the mind of a child that his abilities should multiply in this particular fashion? Binet's achievement cried out for support from a more comprehensive theory of mental growth.

A common assumption, already mentioned, is that mental growth is a cumulative affair, that new skills can be added steadily without modifying old skills in any significant way. An alternative assumption is that childhood is a series of abrupt transitions from one fairly stable stage to another which is equally stable but more advanced and (presumably) more complex. According to this view of development, the reason that early measures do not predict later measures of intelligence is that very different psychological processes are involved at different stages; a child might excel at one stage, yet be mediocre at another. These transitions supposedly have the character of sudden and radical reorganizations; they are not a simple summation of new and old. Different kinds of observations are relevant and necessary at different times in a child's life. The cumulative hypothesis is simpler, perhaps, but the hypothesis of distinct stages with critical transitions between them also has much to recommend it.

Undoubtedly the most dramatic illustration of a sudden transition is birth itself. The transition from the foetal stage to an independent and reactive stage of infancy may seem to be a sudden, mechanical process, but evidence indicates that the transition is neither brief nor simple. For months afterward constant stimulation and mothering are required in order to get an infant successfully through this transition.

The tragic effects of maternal neglect at this stage can be seen in very young babies who have lost their mothers. They commonly develop a regressive kind of reaction.[4] In the first stages of this reaction the orphaned infant may fall into a light stupor when given his bottle, so that strong stimulation is needed to keep the infant active and sucking. His muscles become flaccid and his skin begins to turn pale. As the condition gets more serious there may be vomiting and diarrhea, hiccups, and irregular breathing. Still later his skin may become gray and wrinkled. All the symptoms point to a regression by the baby to the prenatal mode of functioning, when breathing and circulation of the blood were the mother's responsibility. Poor breathing and poor circulation may interfere with the normal development of the nervous system, which in turn can have physiological and psychological consequences that persist throughout life. If nothing is done to prevent it, a baby may waste away and die, a fate that was once quite common in orphanages and hospitals. Today doctors know that the regression can be prevented by massage and stimulation and by vigorously exciting the sucking reflex. The prescription they usually give is TLC—a daily dose of Tender Loving Care. Even animal researchers find that handling is healthy for young animals.

The transition from foetus to infant is assumed to be merely the first of a long series of passages that the child must negotiate. Students of personality development generally concentrate on the important transitions involved in weaning, toilet training, sex training—on all the little tragedies and comedies that are required in order to develop competence in managing the orifices of the body.[5] Certainly these are the crises most apparent to a mother and probably to the child himself. The way they are handled is believed to have significant influences upon the way the child's personality develops, although opinions are easier to find than proof.[6]

Cognitive transitions are less immediately apparent, but are equally important for the growth of a normal, intelligent human being. By cognitive transitions are meant changes in the child's manner of knowing, knowing about himself and the world in which he lives.

Their subtle consequences often go unnoticed by the parent; the child does not notice them because his new way of knowing destroys the old. But the changes occur, nonetheless.

An adult deals with his world easily, almost automatically, in terms of certain concepts or systems of concepts involving space, time, number, quantity, causality, motion, velocity, and so on. These provide a frame of reference for all his other thoughts. Certain philosophers have assumed that, because these concepts are so important, they must be given immediately to all minds by a kind of a priori intuition. The fact is, however, that the concepts are acquired rather slowly during childhood and pass through several more-or-less predictable stages before attaining the obviously correct form familiar to all intelligent adults. The development of these fundamental concepts has been studied with particular care and ingenuity by Jean Piaget, Professor of Psychology at the Universities of Geneva and of Paris, and by his students and associates.

THE STAGES OF COGNITIVE DEVELOPMENT

Jean Piaget was born in Neuchatel, Switzerland, on August 9, 1896. Piaget is now considered to be one of the greatest psychologists of all time, but this was not always the case. Since the United States is the center of most psychology, it was to be a matter of decades before the early work of Piaget would be translated from French to English. Piaget, who was originally trained as a zoologist, began his study of children's spontaneous ideas about the physical world in 1922 while working in the laboratory school of Alfred Binet. While administering Binet's intelligence tests, he became interested in what lay behind children's correct and incorrect answers. With an investigatory style that is uniquely his own (a kind of interview that digs into the how as well as the what of a child's answer), Piaget found that "children not only reasoned differently from adults but also that they had quite different world-views."[7] This gentle Swiss psychologist, a father of three children, was to become, like Freud before him, a giant in the field of developmental psychology; but it wasn't until the 1950s that American psychology was ready for him. His inventions for testing and his basic ideas have profoundly changed the raising and teaching of children the world over. He was, in 1970, director of the Center for Genetic Epistemology in Geneva, Switzerland, a mecca for visiting biologists, philosophers, mathematicians, linguists, and psychologists.

If Piaget's observations are correct, even so simple an idea as that of an object—a relatively permanent, enduring thing that continues to exist regardless of whether you are looking at it—is one that must be slowly and patiently learned during the first two years of life. An adult considers space and substance to be very different things, but

JEAN PIAGET

to an infant who has no concept of an object, this difference between space and substance is literally inconceivable.

Consider some of the necessary steps along the path from birth to the final development of an object concept.

What does a baby do when the perceptual image of an object disappears from view? This question is relevant from the first week of life. What does the baby do when the mother's breast escapes his lips? At first his response is undirected, but after the second week a nursling is able to find the nipple and differentiate it from other objects. Now we ask the following question: Can it be assumed that a baby recognizes the nipple or has any conception that the nipple just recovered at this instant is identical with the nipple that escaped a few seconds ago?

Or, to choose other examples, when mother's face disappears from view and then reappears, does baby recognize it as the same face? Where does a baby think the face goes when it disappears?

At first, of course, the baby cannot think about such matters at all, for he does not have the concepts available to think with. Nevertheless, it is possible, as Piaget has demonstrated, to infer something of the nature of the child's world from his behavior. As soon as the child is old enough to follow a moving image with his eyes, we can watch him search for vanished objects and thus learn at least a little about his conception of the things he is looking for.

Few objects are more interesting to a baby than his bottle. Piaget always had a cooperative collaborator when the object that appeared and disappeared in the various tests was a bottle of milk. Piaget describes an experiment with his child whom he had studied most carefully.

> At six months and nineteen days Laurent immediately began to cry from hunger and impatience on seeing his bottle (he was already whimpering, as he does quite regularly at mealtime). But at the very moment when I make the bottle disappear behind my hand or under the table—he follows me with his eyes—he stops crying. As soon as the object reappears, a new outburst of desire; then flat calm after it disappears. I repeat the experiment four more times; the result is constant until poor Laurent, beginning to think the joke bad, becomes violently angry.[8]

At this age—around 6 months—when the bottle disappears from view, it ceases to exist.

A very young child seems to behave as if an object were merely a visual image that enters and leaves the field of view capriciously, appearing for no particular reason and disappearing into the void just as unpredictably as it came. A toy that falls from the child's hand vanishes instantly from the universe. But before the same child is 6 months old he will begin to coordinate his visual and tactual worlds. He begins to reach toward and grasp things in his visual field. Then a series of skills are learned in quick succession. This learning does not seem to require any biological satisfactions to reinforce it; the child seems to regard competence as its own reward. He learns to move his eyes slightly in advance of an object; hence a rapidly moving object that vanishes briefly and reappears is correctly followed. He begins to practice at making images enter or leave his visual field at will. He learns to reconstruct the whole object when only a part is visible. He learns to pull or push aside things that block his view of an object he is searching for. Each step represents a separate triumph of infantile persistence. But even at this stage the child does not yet seem to dissociate his own actions from the objects themselves.

By the time a child is 9 or 10 months old he will ordinarily have achieved a rather stable concept of an object. Human beings provide the child the best instances. But even at this late age it is possible to uncover surprising reactions if one looks carefully. For example, the child watches while a toy that he has often played with is put under a cloth. The situation is pictured at the top of Figure 21.1. After a little

FIGURE 21.1

A child sees a toy placed under a cloth and learns to find it there. When it is placed under a second cloth, he looks again under the first. (Figure 1, of Chapter 1, "The Equality of Angles of Incidence and Reflection and the Operations of Reciprocal Implication" in The Growth of Logical Thinking *by Barbel Inhelder and Jean Piaget. Copyright © 1958 by Basic Books, Inc., Publishers, New York.)*

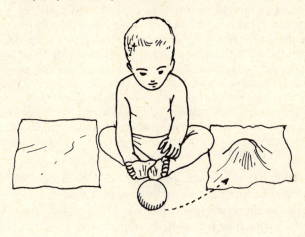

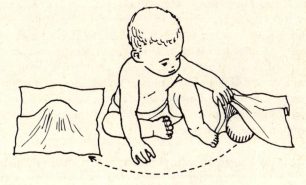

experience the child learns to pull the cloth aside and find the toy. But now the same toy is put under another coverlet at a slightly different place. The child is baffled, looks under the original cloth, then stops searching! As shown at the bottom of Figure 21.1, he does not look where he saw the object last, but where he found it before.

Piaget describes another example in the following passage.

> Gerard, at 13 months, knows how to walk, and is playing ball in a large room. He throws the ball, or rather lets it drop in front of him and, either on his feet or on all fours, hurries to pick it up. At a given moment the ball rolls under an armchair. Gerard sees it and, not without some difficulty, takes it out in order to resume the game. Then the ball rolls under a sofa at the other end of the room. Gerard has seen it pass under the fringe of the sofa; he bends down to recover it. But as the sofa is deeper than the armchair and the fringe does prevent a clear view, Gerard gives up after a moment; he gets up, crosses the room, goes right under the armchair and carefully explores the place where the ball was before.[9]

How should we account for such odd behavior? Should we shrug and say that children are naturally unpredictable?

Perhaps the simplest explanation would be to say that the child has learned an association between the object and the first place he recovered it. This object-place connection has been practiced and reinforced by success. According to this view, the connection between the object and a new location is much weaker, so it is quickly extinguished, and the child is left with the prior, but strong and irrational association. Indeed, such experiences are not confined to children. A man gets a necktie out of his closet, puts it where he can reach it; but when he is ready to put it on he goes back to the closet to look for it. We all do such foolish things every day. Perhaps the child has merely suffered a common lapse of memory.

But no.

According to Piaget, the difference is that a man is capable of remembering but has momentarily forgotten, whereas the child is incapable of remembering—he does not know he is dealing with a single object. For the child, ball-under-the-armchair is one thing and ball-under-the-sofa is another. Having lost the ball-under-the-sofa, he decides to play with the other ball instead. The association between object and place that the child has established is complete; he does not yet have a clear enough conception of an object to realize that the same ball might be associated with two different places. The child has not forgotten anything. Instead, he is remembering something different from what an adult would remember. In an adult, object-place associations are much more flexible than they are for the child; the same object can be recalled as being in any of several different places. Thus the child's apparently poor memory and his deficient conception of physical objects are simply two different aspects of the same psychological process. The child has established the various appearances of the ball as forming a class of equivalent objects, but he has not yet thoroughly mastered the concept of a single, identical object.

Recognition that a variety of sensory images can be generated by an identical, individual, physical object is learned so young that we cannot remember how we did it or what life was like without the concept. We can try to imagine a preobjective state of consciousness by observing carefully what happens when, for example, we enter a new visual world through a telescope or under a microscope. But comparisons of this experience with a child's perceptual world can be little more than a suggestive fantasy.

The first two years of life, called the *sensory motor* period by Piaget, are devoted to the acquisition of many perceptual-motor coordinations. Out of them the child develops a concept of permanent objects—objects existing in a spatial framework defined by his own bodily orientation.

Next the child is ready to develop symbols associated with these sensory-motor objects. As his language begins to develop, he is launched into a new domain of learning, into completely new ways of coping with his environment. From 2 to 7 years is called the preoperational stage.

An average child is capable of imitating speech sounds and forming simple words during his second year of life, but not until he is about 2 years old does he seem capable of sustaining true symbolic processes. This ability can be observed in his play activities as well as in his vocalizations. For a very young child, play is merely a kind of exercise. But as he develops he becomes able to carry out actions that would be appropriate in a situation not actually experienced—for example, pretending to sleep or pretending that the teddy bear is asleep. Such activities are a form of symbolic play. Once the child has achieved the symbolic processes necessary for enjoying this kind of play, he has developed all that is needed to begin using spoken noises to signify an (possibly but not necessarily) absent thing or situation.

It is at about this stage, when language is first beginning to play an important role, that most children develop a kind of willfulness. They begin to assert their own opinions and to make some of their own decisions. The development of volition and of language must be closely related, since voluntary actions are so often responses to verbal commands generated internally and subvocally. But talking to yourself about what you must do is a very complicated skill, one that children develop only slowly over several years.

It is possible to study the way in which words come to control behavior; Russian psychologists have found this especially interesting. Imagine two different pictures. One shows a bright red circle on a pale yellow background, the other a bright green circle on a gray background. The child is told something like this: "When I show you the picture with the pale-yellow background, I want you to raise your *right* hand. When I show you the picture with the gray background, I want you to raise your *left* hand." This is a simple task and young children have little trouble performing it correctly.

Now notice what has been done with the verbal instructions. The child's attention has been directed to the part of the picture that is the least impressive, that has the least attention value. We tell him to ignore the strong red and green colors and to pay attention instead to the pale background colors. He may not learn the task exactly the way we described it, however. It is more natural to look at the bright colors. For a child to be able to follow the instructions, he must control his attention by the use of words, by internal commands.

It is easy to test the child and to see which way he has solved the problem. One merely reverses the circles and their backgrounds. If the red circle was at first on a pale yellow background, one now puts a red circle on a gray background and shows this new picture to the child. Will he respond to the bright red circle which is the natural thing to do) or will he respond to the pale background (which is what we told him to do)? If the child raises his right hand, we know he was paying attention to the dominant red circle; if he raises his left hand, we know he was paying attention to the weaker background color.

Russian psychologists have found that children 3 years old do not follow the verbal command; they pay attention to the impressive color of the circle instead. At 4 years they seem confused, now doing one thing, now the other. Not until the child is 5 will a verbal command produce a stable reorganization of this perceptual field.

Experiments of this sort illustrate the fact that long after a child has mastered the basic skills needed for social communication, there are still important changes going on in the way these linguistic skills modify and control other aspects of his cognitive life.

The reorganization of thought in terms of verbal symbols has a number of advantages in terms of easier communication, more abstract kinds of thinking, greater speed and efficiency in processing information, and so on. One of the most important advantages, however, is that after the psychological processes have been brought under the control of verbal symbols, it becomes possible for the child to control himself with his own words. Eventually, the child can give himself the orders that he has heard so often from his parents—parental control can be internalized. Then he can begin to explore the realm of self-control, the realm of independent, voluntary behavior that is so important for psychological maturity.

By the time a child is 4 years old his skill with language will have progressed to a point where one can talk with him and ask indirect questions about his concepts. If the questions are artfully posed, surprising results may turn up. Consider the following example:

> Two small glasses, A and A_2, of identical shape and size, are each filled with an equal number of beads, and this equality is acknowledged by the child, who has filled the glasses himself, e.g., by placing a bead in A with one hand every time he places a bead in A_2 with the other hand. Next, A_2 is emptied into a differently shaped glass B, while A is left as a standard. Children of 4–5 years then conclude that the quantity of beads has changed, even though they are sure none has been removed or added. If the glass B is tall and thin they will say that there are "more beads than before" because "it is higher," or that there are fewer because "it is thinner," but they agree on the non-conservation of the whole.[10]

Children who give this response are following the maxim that seeing is believing, that the world is the way it appears to be. When the beads are poured into B there appear to be more of them; therefore, there are more of them!

If the same experiment is tried with a child 7 or older, the question will surprise him. He may look around on the floor to see if any beads were spilled. Or he may think the experimenter is joking. Of course, he says, the two are the same. Pouring them from one glass to another does not create or destroy beads. The 7-year-old responds as would an adult.

Suppose, however, that we question him. Our (imaginary) conversation might sound like this:

"How do you know that they are the same?" we ask.

"Because I put the same number of beads in both glasses," he replies.

The 4-year-old interrupts. "I knew *that*," he says.

We ask the 7-year-old, "Is that the only reason you said they were equal?"

"You didn't spill any, did you?"

"No," we admit, "we didn't spill any."

We turn to the younger child. "Did you know that we didn't spill any?" we ask him.

"Sure, I knew that."

We press the 7-year-old again. "Is that the only way you knew?"

He considers a moment. "Well . . . if you pour them back into the first glass again, it will come to the same level."

We turn again to the younger child. "Did you know that?" we ask.

"Yes," he replies, "I knew that."

What facts, what evidence, what new data does the older child have to guide him so easily to the correct answer? Surely there must

FIGURE 21.2

A child of 5 years agrees that beaker A and beaker A_2 contain the same amount of juice. He then pours the contents of A_2 into another beaker, B, of a different shape. When asked, he judges that A and B do not contain the same amount of juice. At 7 years, however, the child knows that A must equal B.

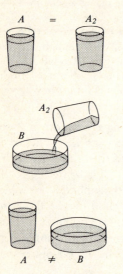

be some crucial fact that the older child observed but the younger child missed. But what can it be? We insist, "What other reasons do you have?"

"The new glass," says the 7-year-old, "is tall and thin, so the level is higher and maybe it looks like there are more. But the amount it is higher is just equal to the amount it is narrower, so there really isn't any change."

We turn back once more to the 4-year-old. "Did you know that the new glass made the beads look both taller and also thinner?"

"Yes," he replies, "I could see that."

Try as we may, we cannot discover any objective fact about the beads that the older child knew and the younger child did not know. Both possessed the same information. Both understood the question. Yet they responded in different ways. Why?

According to Piaget, somewhere between the age of 4 and 7 a cognitive revolution takes place. Instead of dealing with appearances as if they were the true reality, an older child believes in a theory. This theory, which says that physical quantities are invariant under simple changes in shape or location, seems more fundamental to him than the way the world looks. Indeed, it will actually change the way things look. When he knows they are the same, he may find it very difficult to see them as different. But the important point is that the universe of the 7-year-old is not merely the same old universe he lived in at the age of 4 with a simple addition of certain new facts. His world is organized—seen, remembered, imagined, thought about, behaved in—in a new and better way. Moreover, it is difficult for him to remember how the world appeared to him before he organized it in this new way. Memories stored in terms of the old concepts become almost inaccessible after such revolutions; therein lies the source of much of our childhood amnesia, our inability to recall our earliest experiences.

A 7-year-old child cannot state explicitly in so many words the nature of the theory he has adopted; that must come at a still later stage of intellectual development. And at first his theory may be somewhat limited in its range of applications; it must be discovered all over again in a new context. Piaget refers to the years from 7 to 11 as the stage of *concrete operations*.

For example, suppose he is given two balls of modeling clay which he recognizes as equal. Then one of the two balls is mashed flat. Which contains the more clay? The young child takes this question seriously. If he is impressed by the density per unit area as he holds the ball in the palm of his hand, he may say the ball has more clay. If he is impressed by the visual extent of the clay pancake, he may nominate it as having more clay. As he grows older, however, the day will arrive when he says they must be equal. Yet, on that very day, if we ask him which one weighs the most (which we can do in the course of playing with a balance), the same child will usually be surprised to find they weigh the same. Moreover, even after both quantity and weight are known to be conserved in spite of the mashing, he may expect the pancake to displace more water from a full glass than would the ball. Conservation of volume is the last to appear; that may not happen until the eleventh or twelfth year.

Boys and girls 5 years old have many curious ideas about their world. They are not clear about the difference between some and all. Their notions of contradiction, even of negation, are not the adult notions. Time, movement, and speed are mutually confounded in a world where the distance traveled is more important than the time elapsed. Space is plastic, bearing only a crude, topological resemblance to what an adult means by space. It is rather marvelous that such intuitive thinkers manage to survive long enough to grow up and join the ruling majority.

Of course, Piaget does not say that children are incapable of forming the more sophisticated concepts before they are 7 years old. He says merely that in the normal Swiss environment they do not develop these concepts until about the age they start to school. What they might be able to do, given appropriate coaching, is still unknown.[11] But this exciting possibility has not yet been carefully explored. Piaget cautions us to remember that rushing children through stages may be harmful.

Dependence upon the perceptual field, with little capacity for going beyond or behind it, characterizes a young child's orientation toward space as well as toward quantity. Consider this example. Three cardboard mountains are constructed on top of a square table. A child is brought in and walked around the table, inspecting the mountains from every angle. Then he sits down and watches while a doll is moved around the table. His task is to select out of a set of pictures the one that corresponds to the way the mountains might look to the doll. Now, even though the child understands the task perfectly well, if he is under 7 or 8 he will select a picture that shows how the mountains look to him and he seems to believe that this is also how the mountains must look to the doll. His own perception is the only reality.

Another way to study a child's orientation in space is to ask which way is up. Under normal conditions this is an easy question to answer, but psychologists know how to make it difficult. The child sits in a chair that can be tilted to the left or right. He looks at a visual display, a room with clear indications of vertical and horizontal. As shown in Figure 21.3, the room can also be tilted.

FIGURE 21.3

The girl who is seated in a tilted chair, looking at a tilted room, has been challenged to adjust her chair to the upright. Younger children are more affected by visual cues and tend to adjust the chair off the true upright in the direction suggested visually by the tilted room.

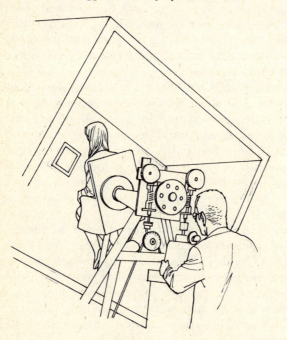

The child's problem is to adjust the tilt of his chair to zero, that is to say, to bring himself to a normal sitting position while he is looking at the room. When asked, "Is this the way you sit when you eat your dinner?" the child who has adjusted his chair properly should say, "Yes," without any hesitation.

In this situation some people align themselves fairly accurately with the true vertical, that is to say, with the vertical determined by gravitation. But many do not feel they are vertical until their bodies line up with the visual directions they see in the slanted room. When they are looking at a very tilted visual field they may have to tilt themselves as much as 35 degrees before they feel upright. The instant they shut their eyes, of course, they know they are tilted.

Children at the age of 8 will be strongly dominated by the visual field. They will accept as up whatever *looks* up. But between the ages of 8 and about 13 there is marked learning, so that older children are better able to ignore the visual appearance and to judge on the basis of internal clues.[12]

The final phase of intellectual development, the *formal operations* stage, begins when the child starts to describe or explain the principles and operations that he has previously learned in a tacit, unverbalized way. From about 8 to 12 years the child's knowledge is largely organized in terms of concrete operations to be performed on concrete objects. In many situations the child obviously knows the rules for performing a task, since he can be consistently successful, yet at the same time he does not know them, since he cannot communicate them. A boy who is quite expert at catching a ball will be completely unable to explain anything about its trajectory; a girl who rides her bicycle with great skill will have nothing to say about balance or the center of gravity. Their situation can be rudely described by saying that they know a great deal more than they understand. Adolescence, famous for its social crises and its emotional tempests, is also the period during which the tacit becomes explicit, when what is known becomes understood.

The process of converting tacit into explicit knowledge may continue throughout life as a part of the never-ending education of those who try to stay intellectually alive. Probably there will never come a time when everything will be explicit, when everything that can be known can be written down on paper. But the adolescent is beginning to move in this direction; he is beginning to codify his knowledge, to extend it in ways that only formal, abstract thought can support.

What advantages are there in making tacit knowledge explicit? An obvious advantage is that the knowledge thereby becomes communicable. Science is a prime example of the enormous benefits that can result.

But there are personal consequences as well. When facts are well expressed in terms of a symbol system, it becomes clear that certain relations between propositions are necessary. When this symbol system is imposed upon reality a similar kind of necessity is attached to the physical events. Where, before, a relation may have seemed arbitrary or accidental, it now inherits requiredness from its symbolic representation.

Still another important advantage of symbolic knowledge is that it can be broadly generalized. Quite different situations can, when summarized symbolically, be seen as variations on a single theme. Behind apparent diversity one discovers a formal core, a single scheme, that can be expressed and manipulated symbolically. Once this is seen, knowledge gained in one situation can be transferred immediately to all other situations fitting the same schema. As in the child's earlier intellectual revolutions, this one also extends his ability to see behind and beyond the surface of things. Whereas at first he went beyond sensations to discover perceptual objects, and then went beyond perception to discover physical objects and operations, now he goes beyond physical things to discover the conceptual symbols and transformations of language and logic. Each stage of development carries with it new rewards in terms of greater power, subtlety, and economy of thought.

An example may make these claims more intelligible.[13] A group of children are asked to play a kind of billiard game. Balls are launched with a tubular spring device that can be pivoted around a fixed point and aimed in various directions. The ball is shot against one wall of the billiard table. The wall, like all billiard tables, has a rubber cushion. The ball rebounds out onto the table. The nature of this game should be clear from Figure 21.4. A target is placed at successively different points on the table and the children are asked to make the ball hit it. Afterwards, they report what they observed.

The psychological question is not how accurately they manage to aim the ball at the target, but how they cope with a simple principle, namely, that the angles of incidence and reflection are equal.

Young children are concerned only with success or failure. They often manage to hit the target, but when asked about it they will usually describe the path of the ball as a smooth curve. They may ignore the angle of rebound entirely. They may realize that moving the plunger changes the direction the ball will go, but they do not explore the matter in a systematic way.

At age 8 or so, however, most children attain complete mastery of the concrete operations involved in hitting the target. They clearly recognize the rectilinear trajectory and rebound, and will even make such spontaneous comments as, "The more I move the plunger this way, the more the ball will go that way." These children see the

FIGURE 21.4

The equality of angles of incidence and reflection is demonstrated for children on this billiard table. (The dotted line shows the path of the ball.) Targets are placed on the circles and balls are shot out of the plunger, which can be pivoted and aimed by the child. (After B. Inhelder and J. Piaget, The Growth of Logical Thinking *[New York, Basic Books, 1958].)*

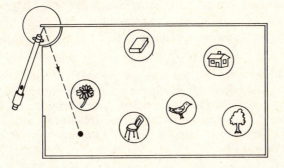

relation between plunger position and trajectory quite clearly. But they do not attempt to go beyond this observation, which is sufficient for hitting the targets consistently.

Boys and girls do not discover that the angles are equal until they are somewhere between 11 and 14. At first the equality seems to them a curious fact, interesting perhaps, but little more. Finally, there is a recognition that the equality of the angles is necessary. The recognition usually follows a comment about lines that are perpendicular to the wall of the table at the point of impact. Suddenly they are convinced that the equality is not accidental. The angles *must* be equal. The necessity of the principle becomes clear to them once they recognize that the ball returns to its starting point when the plunger is perpendicular to the wall. With this insight, they can break up the total angle into component parts and recognize the symmetry around an imaginary perpendicular line. At this point the children have achieved a formal principle that is not restricted to this particular game of billiards. Their new comprehension can now be transferred easily to any new situation that involves reflection.

It is a long and tenuous path that leads from the cradle to symbolic knowledge. The wonderful thing is how often the path is pursued successfully to its conclusion, how seldom any one of a thousand components fails to make its contribution in the right place at the right time. The growth of human understanding in a young child is one of the most intricate, amazing, and beautiful phenomena in nature.

Piaget, like many of the world's leading scientists, is able to express his ideas in simple, elegant prose. He had written, as of 1970, thirty books and over a hundred articles. In a conversation he was once asked how adults misunderstand children.

> It's just that no adult ever had the idea of asking children about conservation. It was so obvious that if you change the shape of an object, the quantity will be conserved. Why ask a child? The novelty lay in asking the question.[14]

While he has made effective use of experiments and did his research early in the history of psychology, Piaget remains a subjective behaviorist who gives the person much more credit for his behavior than would the strict behaviorist.

> Biologists have shown that the organism constantly interacts with its environment; the view that it submits passively to the environment has become untenable. How then can man be simply a recorder of outside events? When he transforms his environment by acting upon it he gains a deeper knowledge of the world than any copy of reality ever could provide.[15]

STAGES OF MORAL DEVELOPMENT

> In Europe, a woman was near death from a very bad disease, a special kind of cancer. There was one drug that the doctors thought might save her. It was a form of a radium that a druggist in the same town had recently discovered. The drug was expensive to make, but the druggist was charging ten times what the drug cost him to make. He paid $200 for the radium and charged $2,000 for a small dose of the drug. The sick woman's husband, Heinz, went to everyone he knew to borrow the money, but he could only get together about $1000 which is half what it cost. He told the druggist that his wife was dying, and asked him to sell it cheaper or let him pay later. But the druggist said, "No, I discovered the drug and I'm going to make money from it." Heinz got desperate and broke into the man's store to steal the drug for his wife.[16]

Was it objectively right or wrong to steal the drug?

This is the kind of moral dilemma posed by Lawrence Kohlberg who has been inspired by the work of Jean Piaget to do research on the stages of moral development. Using cases like the one described above, Kohlberg studies the motives given for following rules; that is, he studies the moral reasoning as well as a person's direct answer to questions such as whether it was right to steal the drug. He evaluates these responses against a system of six stages of moral development. According to Kohlberg these stages are an invariant developmental sequence, always coming in the same order, similar to Piaget's developmental sequence in the acquisition of skills.[17]

Kohlberg's six stages of moral development fall into three groups and can be summarized as follows.

Preconventional

> *Stage 1.* Orientation toward punishment and unquestioning deference to superior power (Might makes right).
> *Stage 2.* Right action consists of action that instrumentally satisfies one's own needs and occasionally the needs of others (You scratch my back and I'll scratch yours).

Conventional

> *Stage 3.* Good boy–good girl orientation; where good behavior is what pleases or helps others and is approved by them (She means well).
> *Stage 4.* Orientation toward authority, fixed rules and the maintenance of the social order (I'm just following orders).

Postconventional

> *Stage 5.* A social contract orientation, generally with legalistic and utilitarian overtones (The Constitution implies the greatest good for the greatest number).
> *Stage 6.* Orientation toward the decisions of conscience and toward self-chosen *ethical principles* appealing to logical comprehensiveness, universality and consistency.[18]

In the winter I'm a Buddhist, in the summer I'm a nudist.

—*Joe Gould*

Kohlberg has an elaborate way of scoring responses to moral dilemmas which evaluates the moral responses as they relate to each level of his scale. What results is a level score that can describe an individual, group, or culture. "A good citizen would not steal the drug because it is against the law," is a response that would be scored somewhere in the conventional range of morality. A response that would be scored in the sixth stage would be, "I would steal the drug regardless of the consequences because I place the value of a human life above any other consideration."

When this question was asked in a representative national survey conducted by a polling organization, 75 percent of those responding thought that it was wrong to steal, while most of them said they might steal the drug anyway.[19] In a blistering criticism of modern education, Kohlberg argues that such answers reflect a moral relativism; in trying to avoid conflict with any values held by the society in general, the schools fail to teach any moral values at all. The result, in Kohlberg's opinion, is a confusion that denies the existence of universal human values. To him, certain values—empathy (concern for the welfare of others) and justice (concern for equality and reciprocity)—are universal moral ideals which are not relative to the individual or the culture.

Every child believes it is bad to kill because regard for the lives of others or pain at death is a natural empathic response, though it is not necessarily universally and consistently maintained.[20]

Moral development then is the restructuring by stages of these universal human tendencies into more adequate forms. Kohlberg has done extensive cross-cultural testing of moral levels in other countries (as shown in Figure 21.5). He has found that the same basic moral concepts are used in every culture and that the stages of development are the same. He argues that the role of the teacher is to facilitate the child's development through the sequence that is natural for him.[21] In order to progress from one stage to the next, a person must recognize the conflict and inadequacy of his behavior in the stage that he is in.

Kohlberg is critical of the socialization approach to education which may so often lead to rather limited development of moral values in a culture.

> [The] definition of morality as the internalization of the standards of the group [is] a definition which denotes nothing worthwhile. While

FIGURE 21.5

Middle-class urban boys in the U.S., Taiwan, and Mexico. At age 10 the stages are used according to difficulty. At age 13 Stage 3 is most used by all three groups. At age 16 U.S. boys have reversed the order of age 10 stages (with the exception of 6). In Taiwan and Mexico, conventional (3-4) stages prevail at age 16, with Stage 5 also little used. (Reprinted from Psychology Today *Magazine, September 1968, © Communications/ Research/Machines, Inc.)*

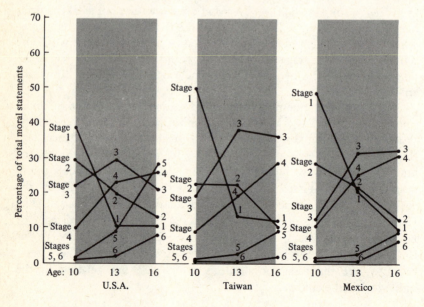

370

in a democratic or just society moral internalization may culminate in just action, in a Nazi society it will culminate in genocide.[22]

Kohlberg generously acknowledges his intellectual debt to the pioneer efforts of Piaget by noting the *developmental-philosophic* strategy for relating the study of human development to educational aims from the beginning. The initial concept of what cognitive and moral development *are* has direct implications for what cognitive and moral development *ought* to be. This frank admission of Kohlberg's aims and his obvious belief in development aimed at greater moral adequacy impress us as a refreshing alternative to the patently false claim by many psychological researchers that their work is value-free. We also admit to sharing Kohlberg's and Piaget's values.

NOTES

1. L. Carmichael, ed., *Manual of Child Psychology*, rev. ed. (New York: Wiley, 1954).

2. N. Bayley, "On the Growth of Intelligence," *The American Psychologist* 10 (1955): 805–818.

3. J. E. Anderson, "The Prediction of Terminal Intelligence from Infant and Preschool Tests," in *39th Yearbook, National Society for the Study of Education* (1940), part 1, pp. 385–403.

4. M. A. Ribble, "Infantile Experience in Relation to Personality Development," in *Personality and the Behavior Disorders*, ed. J. McV. Hunt (New York: Ronald, 1944), vol. 2.

5. R. W. White, "Competence and the Psychological Stages of Development," in *Nebraska Symposium on Motivation, 1960*, ed. M. R. Jones (Lincoln Neb.: University of Nebraska Press, 1960), pp. 97–141.

6. J. W. M. Whiting and I. L. Child, *Child Training and Personality: A Cross-Cultural Study* (New Haven: Yale University Press, 1953).

7. D. Elkind, "Giant in the Nursery," *New York Times Sunday Magazine*.

8. J. Piaget, *The Construction of Reality in the Child*, trans. M. Cook (New York: Basic Books, 1954), p. 30.

9. Ibid., p. 59.

10. J. Piaget, *The Psychology of Intelligence*, trans. M. Piercy and D. E. Berlyne (London: Routledge & Kegan Paul, 1950).

11. J. S. Bruner, *The Process of Education* (Cambridge: Harvard University Press, 1960).

12. H. A. Witkin, "The Perception of the Upright," *Scientific American*, February, 1959.

13. B. Inhelder and J. Piaget, *The Growth of Logical Thinking from Childhood to Adolescence*, trans. A. Parsons and S. Milgram (New York: Basic Books, 1958), pp. 3–15.

14. E. Hall, "A Conversation with Jean Piaget and Bärbel Inhelder," *Psychology Today* 3, no. 12 (1970): 27.

15. Ibid., p. 32.

16. L. Kohlberg, "The Contribution of Developmental Psychology to Education—Examples from Moral Education" (Address to the American Psychological Association, Washington, D.C., September 7, 1971), p. 17.
17. L. Kohlberg, "The Child as a Moral Philosopher," in *Readings in Psychology Today* (Del Mar, Calif.: CRM Books, 1972), pp. 248–254.
18. Ibid., p. 250.
19. Kohlberg, "The Contribution of Developmental Psychology."
20. Ibid., p. 20.
21. Ibid., p. 22.
22. Ibid., p. 25.

TWENTY-TWO
Clinical or Statistical; Science or Profession?

For several years there has been a running battle between the clinical heirs of Sigmund Freud and the statistical heirs of Sir Francis Galton. The Freudians learn about people by talking to them; the Galtonians give tests and compute statistics. When both groups are not both busy doing this, they like to spend their time criticizing each other.

Galton, you will recall, did not set out to understand people. His more modest goal was to measure certain basic capacities that he assumed were important components of intelligence. He devised and standardized simple tests to measure these capacities in large groups of people, and he developed statistical tools to evaluate the correlations among the resulting scores.

Freud, on the other hand, tried to cope with a whole person, not with one of his isolated aspects. He measured nothing. Instead, he dealt with his patients one at a time, and approached each individual, not with a comparative, but with an historical orientation. He developed a procedure to explore his patient's past and provided an extensive, though perhaps overly dramatic theory to interpret what the patient said and did.

Freud and Galton were worlds apart in methods and in philosophy. Yet both scored notable successes, and both attracted vocal and energetic followers. Feuding between two such incompatible views of psychology was almost inevitable.

In 1954 Paul Meehl, a professor of psychology at the University of Minnesota, wrote a small book surveying the battleground, evaluating the opposing forces, and estimating the chances for an armistice.[1] By way of introduction Meehl classified the various epithets that are hurled in both directions; this classification is summarized in Table 22.1. He listed all these terms at the outset "for cathartic purposes so that we may proceed to our analysis unencumbered by the need to say them," which is an academic way of asking the gunmen to check their weapons at the door. The real issues are difficult

FIGURE 22.1

The engraved aluminum plate carried aboard Pioneer 10. It contains information on the position, epoch, and nature of the spacecraft.

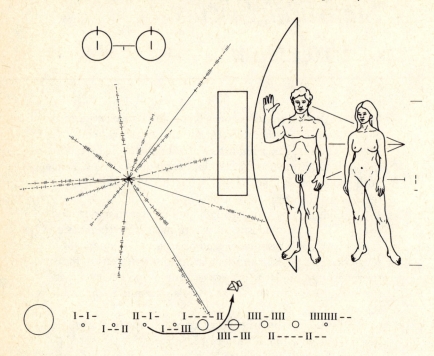

enough without the emotional intensification that name-calling can provoke.

Think of this argument in terms of the mental health problem. It comes up elsewhere, but it is usually found in purest form among the members on the staff of a psychological or psychiatric clinic. Many decisions must be made about a patient who is disturbed mentally or emotionally. What kind of person is he? What kind of illness does he have? How serious is it? Is he dangerous? Should he be hospitalized? What kind of therapy is indicated? What are the chances that he will cooperate with the therapist? What are the chances that he will recover? How long will it take? Is he getting better? Can he be discharged? Does he need vocational training? Should his family be visited by a social worker? Some of these are questions of diagnosis and classification; others are questions of prediction, questions about the future. They must be asked and somehow answered for every individual who requests treatment. They are usually asked and answered in an atmosphere of ever-growing urgency, as the number of patients and the cost of medical care continue to grow.

In these pages we have persistently skirted around the practical

TABLE 22.1

Table of Compliments

	That the clinical method is:	That the statistical method is:
Clinicians say:	Dynamic, global, meaningful, holistic, subtle, sympathetic, configural, patterned, organized, rich, deep, genuine, sensitive, real, sophisticated, living, concrete, natural, true to life, understanding	Mechanical, atomistic, additive, cut-and-dried, artificial, arbitrary, unreal, incomplete, dead, pedantic, fractionated, trivial, forced, static, superficial, rigid, sterile, academic, oversimplified, pseudoscientific, blind
Statisticians say:	Mystical, transcendent, metaphysical, supermundane, vague, hazy, subjective, unscientific, unreliable, crude, private, unverifiable, qualitative, primitive, prescientific, sloppy, uncontrolled, careless, verbalistic, intuitive, muddleheaded	Operational, communicable, verifiable, public, objective, reliable, behavioral, testable, rigorous, scientific, precise, careful, trustworthy, experimental, quantitative, down-to-earth, hardheaded, empirical, mathematical, sound

After P. E. Meehl, *Clinical vs. Statistical Prediction* (Minneapolis: University of Minnesota Press, 1954).

applications of psychology and have focused instead on scientific issues. We will not try here to discuss the many pressing problems of clinical psychology; we mention them only to indicate one context in which the clinical-statistical argument can arise. This is not a mere tempest in an academic teapot; the way the argument is resolved can affect the health and happiness of hundreds of thousands of people.

In Meehl's opinion there are at least two different arguments involved. First, there are disagreements about the kinds of data that a psychologist should collect when he is asked to diagnose or predict a person's behavior. On one side, faith rests in the objective, psychometric test: a standardized situation in which a person's responses can be objectively recorded, scored, and compared with statistical norms preestablished on large samples of other people. For example, a long list of opinionated statements may be presented and the person asked to indicate which ones he endorses; he can then be classified according to the degree of agreement between his responses and the responses of the criterion groups on which the test was standardized. On the other side, enthusiasm feeds on nonpsychometric data: information gathered from interviews, social histories, police records, ratings by physicians or teachers, marital status, history of employment, and especially from subjective impressions based on appearance, mannerisms, expressed opinions, and so on.

The disagreement does not end there. After the evidence is collected there is a second focus for controversy about what to do with the evidence. One camp likes to base predictions on some perfectly mechanical procedure, such as an equation or an actuarial table; no weighing, judging, or inferring is done by any trained clinician. The other camp insists that someone with clinical experience, intelligence, and sensitivity must personally look at the data, comprehend it, and come to a considered opinion about it before a meaningful prediction can be made.

By combining these two disagreements, one gets four different positions that have to be distinguished: (1) mechanical predictions based on psychometric tests, (2) personal predictions based on psychometric tests, (3) mechanical predictions based on nonpsychometric data, (4) personal predictions based on nonpsychometric data. And, in addition, there are various other combinations of these four alternatives that can be defended for one purpose or another. The question, "Which is better, a clinical or a statistical procedure?" is not nearly as simple as it sounds when you first hear it, for in practice one often shades off gradually into the other. In order to sharpen the issues involved, therefore, we shall concentrate here on the opposition between the first and last, between the extreme positions of a pure statistician and a pure clinician.

In the realm of intelligence testing, of course, some believe that predictions can follow more or less mechanically from test data. There the Galtonians (with considerable help from a French clinician named Binet) have carried the day. The present feud, however, is concerned with something even more complex and elusive than the measurement of intelligence; the feud is concerned with questions of personality, of mental health, of future behavior, so it seems plausible that purely mechanical methods would lack the sensitivity and power necessary to do the job.

Certainly that is how clinicians feel about it. Any clinician worth his salt soon acquires confidence in his ability to help people, an ability that he feels must rest on his special and superior power for understanding them. And anybody on the receiving end of these investigations will surely feel more comfortable in the tender, understanding hands of a sympathetic clinician than in the electronic grasp of a computer.

In spite of all this confidence in a clinician's good judgment, however, a number of empirical checks have been run that should make us more cautious and humble in our claims. In several careful studies it has been found that a stubbornly statistical approach—objective tests and mechanical predictions—is a great deal more accurate and dependable than it has any right to be. Often an unskilled clerk does even better than the best-trained clinicians. And so the battle rages.

The statistician argues, with good reason, that a clinician can not hold in mind at one time all the diverse knowledge he has acquired about his patient; by fixing upon one or another item of information as specially significant he distorts the larger picture. Only an actuarial table or a regression equation can incorporate all the data and weigh them appropriately. Moreover, the fact that this chore can be done mechanically by a mere clerk is an unexpected, but highly welcome bonus that leaves the clinician free to do what no test can ever do—to administer therapy. The clinician's objection that statistical equations will never be able to comprehend a patient's inner essence seems completely irrelevant to a statistician.

In the eyes of a statistician, the problem to be solved is the old and familiar one of inductive inference, of arguing logically from observations to conclusions. Because of the vast complexity of the clinical problem and the black depths of our ignorance, the inference must necessarily be tentative and fallible. The problem is even worse when clinical evidence is used to predict future events; such predictions are necessarily vulnerable to all the uncertain and unforeseeable developments that the future may hold. In this situation the mathematical machinery of probability theory would seem to be indispensable. The psychologist must not pretend that he owns a crystal ball. The most that he can do is to classify this patient as similar to others seen previously and to assume that his case will probably develop as most of the others did. The result is a statement of this form: "On the basis of my information about Mr. X, I must classify him in category Y, which has in the past done Z with a probability p."

But probability statements are easily misunderstood. To say that "On the basis of his test performance, the probability is 0.2 that Mr. X will commit suicide sometime within the year," is to invite confusion.

"Nonsense," snorts the clinician, "either he will or he won't. Nobody can commit suicide once in every five lives."

It is possible that part of the conflict could be resolved if clinicians as a group had a better understanding of the logic of probability and of statistical inference. But it is hard to believe that the real source of disagreement does not run much deeper than that.

If a clinician had nothing to do but make predictions, it would undoubtedly follow that he could do it better by using statistical tools. That is exactly the kind of job that the science of statistics is designed to handle and, where data are available for statistical analysis, a clinician's hunches are bound to come off second best. He has about as little chance of beating the equations as he would have of persuading a bank to respect his subjective impression of his cash balance.

Since clinicians are intelligent people, the power of statistical analysis must be apparent to them. Yet they persist in their objections to statistical procedures. Could their stubbornness mean that they are trying to do something more than to predict?

Obviously they are. It is far less important to a clinician to make

377

an accurate, terminal prediction than it is to understand his patient on a moment-to-moment basis and to help him get well again. In this larger, vaguer task of understanding people the objective tests and equations simply get in the way and obscure his view.

Moreover, he is not deeply impressed by a statistician's predictions; even though they are right, he is convinced they are right for the wrong reasons. The tests may work, but no one understands why. If you are going to be effective as a clinician, you must somehow probe behind the observed correlation to find the underlying process that produced it.

Certainly the clinician is right when he says that one can make accurate predictions before one can explain why they work. For example, in our society it would probably be possible to predict a child's success in school from a knowledge of the number of electric motors in his home. But this is obviously not a cause-and-effect kind of relation. No one would expect to raise his child's grades by purchasing more electric motors. Scholastic success and electric motors are both tied to socioeconomic status in a very complicated matrix of relations, a social matrix that we understand quite imperfectly. In spite of our ignorance, however, we could, if we had to, use the grades-motors correlation for predictive purposes. Nevertheless, the job of untangling the network of other variables in which this correlation occurs must still remain the central scientific problem. Clinicians like to feel that many of the predictive relations used so successfully by statistically inclined colleagues smell of just this kind of superficiality. You cannot in truth understand a person by asking him to check which of five hundred opinions he agrees with; if such procedures work, it can only be a lucky coincidence. They are of little assistance, clinicians say, in the other, more important departments of this work.

If the clinician and the statistical clerk are doing different jobs, how do they differ? Is it possible to say more explicitly what other things a clinician does? Meehl offers the following formulation: between observations and prediction there must always be an hypothesis. This hypothesis is not itself a formal consequence of the facts that support it.

> When the hypothesis has been stated, the original data are seen as entailed *by* it, in conjunction with the general laws and the rules of inference. But someone has to state the hypothesis in the first place. It is in the initial *formulation* of the hypothesis that there occurs a genuine creative act with which the logician, as such, has no concern. There is a stage at which someone must have thought up a hypothesis which, in the context of discovery, was, to be sure, suggested by the facts, but is not a formal consequence of them.[2]

For those who adopt the statistical approach, the hypothesis has been formulated and standardized long in advance. In clinical experience, however, the situation is more difficult. The unexpected is the rule rather than the exception, every patient is unique, and well-formulated hypotheses simply do not exist for most of the bizarre and pathetic episodes in which a clinician must participate. His indispensable contribution, therefore, is to formulate hypotheses that can tame the raw designs of madness and capture them in a form to which science might conceivably apply. The basis for his hypothesis is often exceedingly subtle. By a slip of the tongue and an indescribable change in the tone of voice, the patient betrays a sudden anger; from the context the clinician guesses that his patient has a reaction formation against feelings of dependency. (In a different context, of course, the same behavioral evidence might have suggested an entirely different hypothesis.) In the course of an interview the clinician may entertain dozens of such hypotheses that he tries to fit together into his developing concept of this patient.

Formulating appropriate hypotheses as to how a patient's behavior can be classified and what it really means is a clinician's central business; he knows that it is something no clerk can ever do for him, unless, of course, the clerk also becomes a skilled clinician. However, once the hypothesis has been invented, it must be subjected to the usual canons of inference and tested by the usual scientific criteria of evidence and probability. The clinical context of discovery may be unique, but the context of justification is not.

In principle, perhaps, all the enormously diverse and imaginative sources of a clinician's hypotheses might be spelled out in sufficient detail so that the entire job, both discovery and justification, could be done automatically. It is at least conceivable. The development of modern computers has put powerful clerical help at our disposal, and clearly we should try to think creatively about how to use it. But such a detailed explication of the clinician's role would be an extravagant undertaking, even if all the appropriate probabilities were known. One major obstacle is that existing descriptions of how a clinician creates his hypotheses are far too vague to program for any computer. Freud once commented that he let his unconscious hover over the unconscious of his patient; others say they learn to read between the lines or to listen with a third ear. Such metaphors are suggestive, but they are little help in generating the hypotheses and formulas that a clerk—either human or mechanical—would require in order to replace the clinician. For the present, therefore, the clinician can relax, secure in his knowledge that automation is not much of a threat; and at the same time the statistician can feel vindicated that automation of the clinic is at least conceivable, even if only in principle. Indeed, considerable research has been done using computers to score and interpret tests done before and after therapy. But, the high expense of procedures such as screening interview content with a computer program to diagnose makes such applications somewhat impractical. One development in medical circles involves the use of a sophisticated check-list program which asks a person detailed questions about his medical history and interprets the answers for the doctor. However, what worries the clinical psychologist is not the medium but the message.

Many clinical psychologists believe there is something intrinsically valuable about the experience of understanding another person, a very different person, in great and intimate detail. Those values are lost when objective tests are substituted for interviews and impersonal equations replace personal comprehension. Until recently, however, most statisticians have felt that their freedom from conceptual luggage of this kind was more of an asset than a liability. But freedom is not to be confused with irresponsibility, and increasing criticism of the extreme empiricism of many psychometricians has been emanating in recent years, not only from the psychological clinic, but from other sources as well.

In order to convey a sense of the immediacy of the problem, this controversy has been described in a context of mental health, for it is there that the issues have been most sharply framed. However, personality tests are widely used outside the clinic—in research, in vocational counseling, in all kinds of personnel selection, in schools—and have come in for heavy criticism in those spheres, too.

Many critics accuse psychologists of pretending that the tests can perform feats that, on the face of it, are impossible. For instance, there is a famous physicist who, whenever personality tests are mentioned, likes to ask whether the felony-proneness test has yet been perfected. As soon as it is, he points out, we can wipe out crime by throwing all felony-prone children into jail for life. (Remember the bad gene theory?) It is a crude joke, but it makes a blunt point that enthusiastic psychometricians often forget to mention. There are very real limits on what any personality test can tell us, even if it is the best personality test imaginable.

In 1956 William H. Whyte, Jr., included in his best-selling book, *The Organization Man,* a scathing denunciation of the use of objective personality tests in personnel selection. In Whyte's opinion the psychometric instruments are being used by The Organization as a kind of loyalty test. Since the tests force a man to bear witness against himself, they are basically immoral. Whyte advises his readers to cheat and gives explicit instructions how to do it. Research shows that most personality tests can be faked.

In order to get a good score—one that will earn you a new job or a big promotion—Whyte's advice is to give the most conventional, pedestrian, run-of-the-mill answers possible. When in doubt, repeat to yourself: "I loved my father and my mother, but my father a little bit more. I like things pretty much the way they are. I never worry much about anything. I don't care for books or music much. I love my wife and children. I don't let them get in the way of company work."[3] If you take the tests in this frame of mind, The Organization will discover unsuspected depths of normalcy in you, and you can look forward to a substantial promotion. You should have no qualms about cheating. Since you are really not that kind of person at all, you may do very well on your new job. This theme is continued in more recent books[4] and in some well-founded fears of the amount of control over private lives that is being achieved by computer-aided investigative and government agencies. Alienation—not anti-intellectualism—seems to be at the root of public dismay with tests.

Whyte's tirade is aimed about equally at the psychometricians who create, and at The Organizations who use, the personality tests. Since his argument sounds so plausible and was so widely publicized, one might think that by now the tests would have been abandoned. At the very least, one would expect the tests to begin losing their discriminating power as everyone suddenly adopted the same disguise. In fact, the evidence indicates that people were already way ahead of Whyte. The desire to look good, to endorse what is socially acceptable, has always been a major factor at work in most of these objective tests.

In 1953 Allen Edwards presented clear evidence that the more socially desirable a statement is, the better are the chances that it will be endorsed on a personality test.[5] And even earlier, psychologists had suspected that such attitudes might be biasing the results they were getting.[6] It is possible, of course, to avoid this bias. You can word the questions so that social desirability does not affect the personality trait you are trying to measure. If, for example, you want to measure ambition, you can make half the symptoms of ambition sound socially acceptable and half sound socially reprehensible. Or, if that is impossible, you can include dummy items on the test specifically aimed at measuring a person's defensiveness, then correct his test score accordingly. By using such devices it is easy enough to cancel out the effects of social desirability.

Although not all test-makers have guarded against faking, most of the better-known tests were protected against it long before Whyte even thought about the problem. Few psychologists are so gullible as to accept what people say about themselves without at least a twinge of doubt.

The new twist that Edwards and others have added in recent years is that the bias toward giving the socially acceptable answer may be something more than a nuisance. It may, in fact, be measuring something important about the person. Instead of eliminating the effects of social desirability, therefore, a current tendency is to regard the desire for social approval as one of the more important and unbiquitous attributes that an objective test can measure.

One variation of Edwards's approach is the Marlowe-Crowne Need for Social Approval Scale, reproduced in Table 22.2.[7] This test is similar to those used in clinical practice but was developed for research

TABLE 22.2

Marlowe-Crowne Need for Social Approval Scale.

Listed below are a number of statements concerning personal attitudes and traits. Please read each item and decide whether the statement is *true* or *false* as it pertains to you personally. (Base this on your opinion of yourself.) If, when applied to you the statement is true, or mostly true, check "T" before the question. If false, or not usually true, check "F".*

T F 1. Before voting I thoroughly investigate the qualifications of all candidates.

T F 2. I never hesitate to go out of my way to help someone in trouble.

T F 3. It is sometimes hard for me to go on with my work if I am not encouraged.

T F 4. I never intensely disliked anyone.

T F 5. On occasions I have had doubts about my ability to succeed in life.

T F 6. I sometimes feel resentful when I don't get my way.

T F 7. I am always careful about my manner of dress.

T F 8. My table manners at home are as good as when I eat out in a restaurant.

T F 9. If I could get into a movie without paying and be sure I was not seen, I would probably do it.

T F 10. On a few occasions I have given up doing something because I thought too little of my ability.

T F 11. I like to gossip at times.

T F 12. There have been times when I felt like rebelling against people in authority even when I knew they were right.

T F 13. No matter who I am talking to I am always a good listener.

T F 14. I can remember playing sick to get out of something.

T F 15. There have been occasions when I took advantage of someone.

T F 16. I'm always willing to admit when I make a mistake.

T F 17. I always try to practice what I preach.

T F 18. I don't find it particularly difficult to get along with loud-mouthed, obnoxious people.

T F 19. I sometimes try to get even rather than try to forgive and forget.

T F 20. When I don't know something I don't at all mind admitting it.

T F 21. I am always courteous, even to people who are disagreeable.

T F 22. At times I have really insisted on having things my own way.

T F 23. There have been occasions when I felt like smashing things.

T F 24. I would never think of letting someone else be punished for my wrongdoings.

T F 25. I never resent being asked to return a favor.

* To score yourself, check for the "correct" answer: 1. T, 2. T, 3. F, 4. T, 5. F, 6. F, 7. T, 8. T, 9. F, 10. F, 11. F, 12. F, 13. T, 14. F, 15. F, 16. T, 17. F, 18. T, 19. F, 20. T, 21. T, 22. F, 23. F, 24. T, 25. T, 26. T, 27. T, 28. F, 29. T, 30. F, 31. T, 32. F, 33. T. The total number correct is the score. The higher the score, the higher the need for social approval.

T F *26.* I have never been timid when people expressed ideas very different from my own.
T F *27.* I never make a long trip without checking the safety of my car.
T F *28.* There have been times when I was quite jealous of the good fortune of others.
T F *29.* I have almost never felt the urge to tell someone off.
T F *30.* I am sometimes irritated by people who ask favors of me.
T F *31.* I have never felt that I was punished without cause.
T F *32.* I sometimes think when people have a misfortune that they only got what they deserved.
T F *33.* I have never deliberately said something that hurt someone's feelings.

as a measure of a person's need to be accepted in his peer group and his conformity to group pressure. In essence, it contains a large number of platitudes which the person marks as true or false. In numerous studies using the scale high scorers have been shown to be more likely to conform, to change their attitudes, and to yield to consensus judgments. In one study it was found that high need for social approval scores were prevalent among jurors who had served in trials, a fact that fits the courtroom situation in which a juror is lavished with praise for performing his duty and is expected to be passive in his role and to be compliant to the law as interpreted for him by the judge.[8]

Attempts to isolate a social desirability variable, however, have repeatedly been confused by the effects of another personality variable that also reflects the style of the person taking the test. Apparently some people like to say yes, no matter what you ask them, and other people like to say no. If you try, for example, to measure anxiety by an objective test, and if you happen to phrase your questions so that "yes" means high anxiety and "no" means low anxiety, you will discover that your measure of anxiety is colored by this tendency to acquiesce to or to negate anything. All the yea-sayers will look anxious; all the nay-sayers calm and collected. Here again it is a simple matter to eliminate the effect by phrasing the questions properly. Many of the older tests, however, were strongly contaminated by an acquiescence variable.

These two stylistic variables—social desirability and acquiescence—account for many of the individual differences that turn up on personality inventories and questionnaires.[9] To the extent that Whyte's jibes were directed at tests that disregarded response biases of this sort, they performed a valuable service. Fortunately, there are corrective measures available; the objective tests are not quite as vulnerable to cheating as Whyte made them seem.

Response bias is something a psychometrician can make allowances for. But other criticisms are not so easily met. How, for instance, does one answer the indignant gentleman who charges that the whole test movement is a form of pseudoscience, based on spurious and misleading correlations dressed up in quantitative language to swindle the yokels? It is unfortunate that these wild and frequent accusations sound so simple when an honest answer must be so complicated, often too complicated for a busy reader to study carefully. It is easy to raise suspicions that something improper is going on; so much smoke must mean at least a small fire somewhere.

Personality tests are not perfect and they are not always wisely used. But it is foolish to say they are undermining our national character. To form an intelligent opinion of their value it is necessary to know something about the tests, and particularly how they are constructed.

Here in rough outline are the steps usually involved in putting together an objective personality test. First, we assemble a large group of people known to possess trait A and another group known to lack it. (Trait A, which is called the criterion, may be anything from gallstones to schizophrenia. Our eventual goal is to predict the occurrence of trait A in other people about whom nothing is known, simply on the basis of their responses to our test.) Next, we make up a pool of questions, using whatever theory, experience, or intuition we can muster to guide our selection. (This is where theory could play an explicit role, but in practice it is usually easier to include everything, even the kitchen sink. The idea is to collect a basketful of different but similar test items—there is always safety in large numbers.) Then we ask our two groups all the questions, often by printing the questions in booklets and having people check the answers they prefer. (As we have already seen, there is quite an art to phrasing the questions. Presenting them is a tricky business, too, particularly if the tests are to be scored with a computing machine.) We then break out the statistical techniques and pore over the results to see which questions were discriminating—that is, which questions were answered differently by the two groups. (Here is where we get rid of the kitchen sink, unless, of course, it happens to discriminate.) If we find enough questions that seem to predict the criterion, we can announce that we have developed a new psychometric test. Dozens of shiny new tests are manufactured this way every year.[10]

Notice that inclusion of an item on the test depends entirely on whether or not it works. Why it works is, in most instances, an academic question. We do not need to know why it works to use it for predicting, often very accurately, who will have trait A and who will not.

This who-gives-a-damn-why-it-works attitude—called the criterion method of test construction—has bothered many people, including some who are themselves in the psychometric business. It frequently happens that a test originally constructed to predict trait A also turns out to be equally useful in predicting trait B. If traits A and B are intuitively very different psychological variables, we will be somewhat embarrassed to say exactly what it is that our test tests. But embarrassments of success are easily borne, and for many years nobody worried much about the logic of this situation.

What is lacking is a psychological theory that dictates explicitly which items should be included on the test. Then the criterion would be used, not to validate the test, but to validate the theory on which the test was based. Such an explicit theory—if it were true—would resolve all doubts as to whether or not the test actually measured what it was intended to measure. Questions of validity would be transferred to the larger domain of psychological theory in general, and the tests would become an instrument of research comparable in power and dignity to experiments conducted in the laboratory.

As experience with these tests has accumulated and as new uses for them have been discovered, the need for a theoretical integration and explanation of all the relations among the different tests has become increasingly apparent. One trend, therefore, is toward the explicit use of psychological theory in constructing new tests.[11] With this changed emphasis the psychometric problem enters a new phase, less technological and more scientific. And as the fundamental concepts of various psychological theories are introduced into the objective tests in this more direct and intimate fashion, the gap between the statisticians and the clinicians—between the statisticians and all other psychologists—will surely narrow. The psychometricians have developed a marvelous research tool, but we are only beginning to understand how to use it properly to test our psychological theories. The battle over using tests as practical tools in the real world sets the stage for a debate of profound significance to the future of psychology.

Looking more closely at what Meehl was describing, we see more at issue than a choice of working models for the clinical psychologist. There is a basic clash of value systems, a choice of life styles for the psychologist and a basic decision by academic departments of psychology on where they are going to direct their energies to train future psychologists. For many years, psychologists have realized that pursuit of psychology as a science meant one thing, while helping people—the art of applying psychological knowledge to the service of society—was "another country."

During the 1960s the training of clinical psychologists reached high levels, accounting for a third of all doctoral degrees in psychology. This growth was spurred by fairly lavish government financing from agencies whose goal is to deliver expanded mental health services to more people. But the model for training psychologists was based on the idea of a *scientist-practitioner*, a kind of paragon who would combine the values of a scientist, who publishes regularly and teaches, with the values of a healer, who spends time treating the mentally ill. As the decade of the 1970s opened, this model was under severe attack from the practitioners and from psychology students who had come into the discipline to answer the call to service.

In an analysis, which sounds like the beginnings of the civil rights movement, the critics of the scientist-practitioner model argue that the separate-but-equal doctrine has not worked; that psychology departments never met the challenge of teaching people how to help people, that jobs and promotions went only to those who published frequently, and that to succeed, the scientist-practitioner had to make so many compromises that he frequently became a marginal scientist and a half-baked, tired clinician. Indeed, surveys reveal that the publication rate of those identified as practitioners is much lower than for the pure scientists. Because academic departments have refused to set up meaningful training clinics that provide training and service, clinical psychologists most often train in psychiatric settings, which are owned by the medical profession with its own set of values. In the opinion of George Albee, former president of the American Psychological Association, the result has been that psychologists have been exposed to a very narrow range of human problems encompassing hospitalized and poor schizophrenics and walk-in wealthy neurotics, all precategorized by the medical profession as "sick."[12]

Albee feels that clinical psychologists have to define their own area of expertise and not depend on the scientific reputation of academic departments of psychology or the training facilities of a different and, to him, alien training environment provided by the medical profession. To Albee, the sources of "sickness" lie less in hypothesized mental states in the individual and more in the societal institutions that control behavior and limit the options of free men.

> Racist attitudes and behavior, which can be found in a great many places throughout our social and economic institutions, including our state and federal governments, are far more *dangerous to others* than schizophrenia. . . . [W]e could forget "psychiatric patients" for a century and turn our attention to the psychological causes of racism, sexism, and of the profit motive as sources of danger to the human centered life.[13]

Feeling that professional psychology has no place in an academic department, Albee points out that if a professional psychologist is forced to play the game of science, he must open up his theories and methods to critical public scrutiny, a course that is inhibiting because of the intuitive nature of the development of therapy approaches, the time it takes to search out causes of mental problems which may have their roots in childhood, and the messier, hard to control research conditions of real life.

I feel that all these basic incompatibilities between the *science* of psychology and the *profession* of psychology may be so serious as to soon require a separation or divorce.[14]

The separation papers have already been filed, as schools designed exclusively to train professional (usually clinical) psychologists begin to open. Albee recommends making alliances with social work and education professionals, who already have a value commitment to service and have the training facilities that clinical psychology is lacking. However, he concludes with a conciliatory note with which we agree.

> Finding the roles of scientist and of professional incompatible when existing *within the same individual* does not mean that scientists and professionals do not need each other. The two groups must exist in a mutually rewarding and symbiotic relationship. I feel that both science and the profession will benefit from the impending division, and psychology can truly move forward in both areas as a means of promoting human welfare.[15]

NOTES

1. P. E. Meehl, *Clinical vs. Statistical Prediction* (Minneapolis: University of Minnesota Press, 1954).
2. Ibid., p. 57.
3. W. H. Whyte, *The Organization Man* (New York: Simon and Schuster, 1956), pp. 197, 405–410. For a sober rebuttal, see S. Stark, "Executive Personality and Psychological Testing," *University of Illinois Bulletin* 55 (1958): 15–32.
4. See, for example, M. L. Gross, *The Brainwatchers* (New York: Random House, 1962).
5. A. L. Edwards, *The Social Desirability Variable in Personality Assessment and Research* (New York: Dryden, 1957).
6. L. J. Cronbach, "Response Sets and Test Validity," *Educational and Psychological Measurement* 6 (1946): 616–623.
7. D. P. Crowne and D. Marlowe, *The Approval Motive* (New York: Wiley, 1964).
8. R. Buckhout et al., "A Jury Without Peers" (Paper presented to the Western Psychological Association, Portland, Ore., 1972).
9. D. N. Jackson and S. J. Messick, "Content and Style in Personality Assessment," *Psychological Bulletin* 55 (1958): 243, 252; S. J. Messick and D. N. Jackson, "Acquiescence and the Factorial Interpretation of the MMPI," *Psychological Bulletin* 58 (1961): 299–304.
10. O. K. Buros, ed., *The Fifth Mental Measurements Yearbook* (Highland Park, N.J.: Gryphon, 1959).
11. H. Peak, "Problems of Objective Observation," in *Research Methods in the Behavioral Sciences*, ed. L. Festinger and D. Katz (New York: Dryden, 1953); L. J. Cronbach and P. E. Meehl, "Construct Validity in

Psychological Tests," *Psychological Bulletin* 52 (1955): 281–302; J. Loevinger, "Objective Tests as Instruments of Psychological Theory," *Psychological Reports,* Monograph Supplement 9, 3 (1957): 635–694.

12. G. W. Albee, "The Uncertain Future of Clinical Psychology," *American Psychologist* 25, no. 12 (1970): 1071–1080.
13. Ibid., p. 1074.
14. Ibid., p. 1078.
15. Ibid., p. 1080. For a more thorough understanding of psychology as a profession see Appendix B: A Career in Psychology.

TWENTY-THREE
Communication and Persuasion

Social psychology inherits from philosophy the ancient query, "What is the social nature of man?"

A question so profound obligates the social psychologist to learn a great deal about human societies. He must know and work with facts and theories drawn from art, history, economics, sociology, anthropology, political science, and all the other social and behavioral sciences. It is an ambitious project, yet those who trust science to resolve the central dilemmas of human existence find social psychology one of the most exciting intellectual endeavors of our time. It is a large and explosively expanding field whose boundaries fade hazily into a dozen neighboring disciplines.

To give a flavor of social psychology in a few brief pages, we shall focus on the social process of communication— a process indispensable for any kind of social interaction. A social group affects an individual by communicating with him; the study of human communication is a particularly important section of social psychology. What we will try to do here is to illustrate how a scientific psychologist can use his methods and techniques to study this critically important process.

Let us look at some of the pioneering experiments on persuasive communication. Go back to early 1945. Germany, after losing the Battle of the Bulge, had few resources left; it was clear to everyone that the European war was rapidly drawing to a close. Allied commanders were beginning to think more immediately about the war in the Pacific. Eventual victory in that theater also seemed assured, but long months would pass before sufficient strength could be assembled to mount a full-scale invasion of the Japanese homeland. Once the Allies could concentrate their strength on a single front the outcome would be inevitable, but the time required to shift troops from Europe to the Pacific would enable the Japanese to postpone their eventual defeat for months, even years. The troops in Europe were in no mood to face another war on top of the one they were just finishing. They had done their job, they were fed up with war, they expected to be sent home directly. The effect on morale was bad; the U.S. Army issued

a directive to impress upon enlisted men the seriousness of the job remaining to be done. Military experts knew they must plan for a long and expensive war; the common soldiers hoped that in a few weeks it would all be over. The debate quickly caught everyone's attention.

In this situation a group of psychologists in the Army's information and education branch saw an opportunity to study an old and controversial issue in the art of persuasive communication.[1] As part of the general campaign to persuade enlisted men that they had a tough job ahead, that the war with Japan would be long and difficult, the psychologists decided they would try to compare two different techniques of radio presentation. In one radio program they would present the story that the Army was trying to tell; just that and no more. In the other they would add something to the Army's argument; they would add some of the counterarguments that they knew were simmering in the men's own talk among themselves. The aim of the experiment was to see whether a one-sided or a two-sided presentation is more persuasive. Is there an advantage in trying to give an impression of fairness or is it a disadvantage to publicize the other side's case?

Two radio scripts were written and transcribed for broadcast. Program I presented only the reasons for expecting a long war; the vast distances in the Pacific, the large Japanese stockpiles, the quality of the Japanese troops not yet met in battle, the determination of the Japanese people. Program II presented all these reasons in exactly the same way, but it also spent a small amount of time considering arguments on the opposite side: our naval victories, our previous progress even in a two-front war, our ability to concentrate on Japan after victory in Europe, Japan's inferior industrial strength, our increasingly effective air warfare. These additional points were woven into the context of the rest of the program.

Before the programs were presented to any troops, two groups of men were selected and their opinions were determined in a preliminary survey. Once that had been done each group heard one of the programs, after which their opinions were sampled again to see if any changes had occurred.

Since events were moving rapidly, it seemed possible that changes could result from external factors other than the radio programs. It was necessary, therefore, to use a third group of men—the control group—whose opinions would also be measured twice, but who would not hear either of the radio programs. Having a control group would make it possible to say whether the observed changes were attributable to the radio programs or to some other events occurring at the same time.

Throughout these tests and measurements extreme precautions

IF YOU WANT TO FIGHT!

JOIN THE MARINES

were taken to prevent the men from suspecting that they were being experimented upon.

During the first week of April (while Allied armies were crossing the Rhine) the preliminary questionnaire was administered. A week later (while American troops were mopping up Japanese resistance in the Philippines) the two programs were presented, each to a different group of men during their regular orientation meetings.

Immediately after hearing the programs the men answered the second questionnaire.

Both questionnaires contained the item, "What is your guess as to how long it will take us to beat Japan after Germany's defeat?" Before they had heard the program about 37 percent of the men estimated it would take more than eighteen months. On the second questionnaire, 34 percent of the men in the control group gave the same answer. It seemed reasonable to assume, therefore, that little change could be attributed to sources other than the radio programs. In the experimental groups, on the other hand, those who, after they had heard the one-sided program, estimated more than eighteen months, increased to 59 percent. Those who estimated more than eighteen months after hearing the two-sided program also increased—also to 59 percent.

The increases were significant; both programs were effective in changing the men's opinions. But from an experimental point of view the results were indecisive. Apparently it does not matter whether one side or both sides of an argument are given. In order to understand why this should be the case the experimenters carried their analysis a step further.

When the groups of men were broken down according to educational level, a difference in the persuasiveness of the two programs became apparent. As indicated in Figure 23.1, it was found that the two-sided presentation was more effective with the better educated men; the one-sided presentation was more effective with the less

FIGURE 23.1

Two-sided presentations are more persuasive with well-educated audiences, less persuasive with people who have not graduated from high school. The length of the horizontal bars represents the net proportion of men in each of the four classifications who revised their estimates in the desired direction after hearing the radio programs.

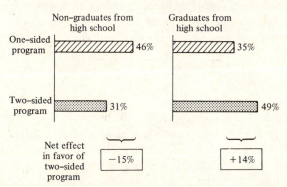

educated men. Habits of thought acquired in high school and college tended to make the educated listeners resist a one-sided presentation, whereas their less critical, less educated friends were impressed by the one-sided program and were not challenged to think of possible objections to it.

As is often the case in mass communications, however, there was a boomerang effect. It turned up in the form of an apparent contradiction in the data. One of the questions that had been asked about the radio programs concerned the adequacy with which they presented the facts on the Pacific War; men who heard the one-sided presentation replied more often that it did a good job than did the men who heard the two-sided presentation. How could such a contradictory result have occurred? Why did so many men who had just heard a two-sided program feel it was not fair?

When the experimenters poked into this unexpected outcome, they discovered that the source of trouble was their failure to mention the possibility of Russian aid. Apparently, when no counterarguments at all were presented, Russian aid was not missed. But when the program tried to give an appearance of fairness and objectivity, omission of Russian aid became glaringly obvious. And it was especially obvious to those men who considered Russian aid a major factor in shortening the war with Japan; when their best counterargument was not included, they resisted the communication more than if no counterarguments had been mentioned at all.

Similar boomerang effects have been observed in dozens of different studies of mass communications; avoiding them is one of the principal reasons for pretesting a message on a small group of people before broadcasting it to thousands or millions of listeners.

With the rapid growth of the communication sciences since World War II experiments of this sort have become commonplace for both the practical and the theoretical study of mass communications. One of the scientists involved in this particular experiment, Dr. Carl I. Hovland, continued the work after he returned to his regular duties at Yale University. The significant thing about his approach was not that it was aimed at mass media of communication; that had been tried many times before. The novel element was the introduction of experimental techniques, techniques that had been developed first in the psychological laboratory.

The fact that research on attitude change dominates the social psychology journals to this day can probably be credited to Hovland, who had formerly made basic contributions in the area of classical conditioning. Working at Yale University, Hovland trained many attitude researchers who are leading figures in social psychology today. The Yale Communication series of books emerged under his editorship as highly influential guides to all the many separate subdisciplines of the communication field. William J. McGuire, a leading chronicler of trends in social psychology, points out that the Hovland "school" focuses primarily on the dependent variables in attitude change, as opposed to the concentration on independent conditions that produce change, which one might find in experiments inspired by the work of Leon Festinger (see Chapters 19 and 20).[2] The Hovland school has been closely identified with the development of consistency theory, showing a preference for more complex experimental designs and elaborate models of the communication process.

Models are guides (not necessarily complete) to the research and understanding of complex processes. Figure 23.2 presents a model of the social ecology of communication. The term ecology is important because the process must be seen as a dynamic whole with inter-related parts; we cannot manipulate just one part without considering other parts. The model contains the familiar communication model that engineers use in analyzing the telephone system: the message, source, channel, receiver, and destination. In McGuire's review of the literature on attitude change, he identifies variables under each of the headings which have been studied extensively.

FIGURE 23.2

The social ecology of communication, showing how the engineering model of the communication process fits into an overall context which is always changing.

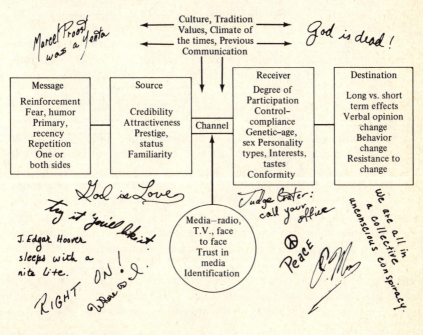

By source variables, we mean the attributes of the perceived source of the message, for example, his trustworthiness, his perceived intent to persuade, or his similiarity to the receiver. Message factors include the content and structure of what is said, for example, the kind of appeal used, whether the conclusion is made explicit or not, how opposition arguments are dealt with, or the order in which material is presented. Channel factors have to do with the media, the modality (for example, auditory vs. visual) through which the message is presented, etc. Examples of receiver factors include the characteristics of the person receiving the message, for example, his personality and ability, or the extent of his active participation in the communication process. Under destination factors, we include variables having to do with the exact target of the message, for example, the type of issue at which the persuasive induction is aimed, long- vs. short-term effects, or verbal opinion change vs. gross action changes.[3]

To this basic model we have added an overlying *context*, the *zeitgeist* or climate of the times which reflects the culture, traditions, current values, and prevailing ideologies which constitute a collective awareness or background within which all communication takes place. Jung's collective unconscious comes closest of the theories to describing this, especially with his emphasis on symbols. We include it because so often attitude and communication theorists have used the more explicit engineering communication model as if communication were taking place in some sort of a vacuum.

What are the advantages of an experimental approach? The answer to this question becomes obvious when we compare experimental with correlational methods for studying the same problem. Consider an example drawn from studies of race prejudice.

Attempts to discover who listens to communication aimed at countering racial antagonisms often take the form of survey questionnaires administered to carefully randomized samples of people drawn from the general population. The interviews may or may not be conducted in connection with some particular radio or television program. One regular finding in every case has been that the amount of information people have about a minority group and the extent to which they approve of that group and its aims tend to be positively correlated. For example, people who listen to propaganda deploring anti-Semitism and who know the most about the Jews are usually those who approve most of Jews and Jewish aims. The correlation agrees nicely with common sense. "To know them is to love them," we say, or, "To understand is to forgive." Consequently, the correlation is often carelessly interpreted to mean that education eliminates race prejudice. Because information and approval are correlated, it would seem to mean that we need only provide more information to create more approval.

When we look at the correlations closely, however, we discover that the facts are misleading. Too often it turns out that the people who know most about black people and who approve most of blacks *are* blacks.

A spurious correlation can be a dangerous weapon in the hands of a person who does not suspect it, who does not stop to think through the correlation to the underlying causes that produced it. In order to test the suggested relation between information and approval, we must perform an experiment. We must experimentally manipulate one variable (increase the amount of information about an ethnic group) and see if the other variable (approval of that ethnic group) is affected. This has been done and the results are negative. So far, the experimental results indicate that prejudice can seldom be attributed to ignorance. Yet the stereotype of the ignorant bigot persists, notably in entertainment, where in 1971 millions laughed at the blatant racist Archie Bunker on the television program *All in the Family*.

When they are applicable, experimental methods enable us to test a correlation to see if it is basic or derivative in nature. Thus the introduction of experimental methods into the study of mass communication has been an important contribution to the social sciences.

To understand how experiments can be pursued until they turn into programs of research and lead to new theories, consider a question that arises directly out of the problem of two-sided presentations.

Imagine that both sides of an issue must be presented in a single discussion, but you are in favor of one over the other. In which order should you present the two arguments? Should you get your side in first, while your listeners are fresh and receptive? Or should you present it last, so that no counterarguments can follow and interfere with a listener's memory of it? The advantage of the first position produces a primacy effect in persuasion. The terminal position has a recency effect. The question is, "Which effect is bigger?" This is a problem we can approach by experimental methods.

Take the following episode.

Jim left the house to get some stationery. He walked out into the sun-filled street with two of his friends, basking in the sun as he walked. Jim entered the stationery store which was full of people. Jim talked with an acquaintance while he waited for the clerk to catch his eye. On his way out, he stopped to chat with a school friend who was just coming into the store. Leaving the store, he walked toward school. On his way out he met the girl to whom he had been introduced the night before. They talked for a short while, and then Jim left for school. After school Jim left the classroom alone. Leaving the school, he started on his long walk home. The street was brilliantly filled with sunshine. Jim walked down the street on the shady side. Coming down the street toward him, he saw the pretty girl whom he had met on the previous evening. Jim crossed the street and entered a candy store. The store was crowded with students, and he noticed a few familiar faces. Jim waited quietly until the counterman caught his eye and then gave his order. Taking his drink, he sat down at a side table. When he had finished his drink he went home.[4]

With no more information than that, would you say Jim is friendly or unfriendly? Shy or forward? Social or unsocial? Aggressive or passive? A group of students who read this description of Jim's behavior decided that he was friendly, forward, social, and aggressive; you probably agree with them.

You have a right to be suspicious, however. After all, Jim turned up in a psychology book as part of a discussion on two-sided communications. Perhaps you were cautious and studied the passage closely. If so, you probably noticed a striking change in Jim's personality after he got out of school and headed home. Before school he seemed extroverted; afterwards he had suddenly become an introvert. Although a sizable fraction of the students did not notice it, the account was written with a deliberate intent to be contradictory. Half of the students saw it in the form given above. The other half saw it in the opposite order, with the episode in the candy store preceding the episode in the stationery store. For this second group there appeared to be a remarkable blossoming in Jim's character as the story ends. This second group, which learned about Jim initially as an introvert, judged him to be unfriendly, shy, unsocial, and passive. The two groups had read exactly the same words. The only difference between them was the order in which the two episodes were presented.

The experiment just described gave relatively clear evidence of a primacy effect. The first impression we get of a person or a topic is likely to be the one that prevails.

But how much travel can we expect from this one study? Even when this kind of experimental evidence is available, most people are reluctant to jump to conclusions, to generalize the results to all situations, or to believe in any universal law of primacy in persuasion.

The difficulties are all too plain. We have observed a primacy effect for personality judgments by students. Does that tell us what would happen if different materials were presented, if different media of communication were used, if different people received the message, if the two sides were presented by different people, and so on? Before we generalize to the many situations in which an order effect might occur, we should conduct a program of experiments to explore some of the conditions that might alter any conclusion based on this single study of Jim's hypothetical personality. That program is part of the research that the Yale workers undertook.

As a result of a program of experimental research, therefore, we now know that the most important factor is whether the opposing messages originate from the same source or from different sources. When the two sides come from two different persons, there is usually a recency effect; the second debater has a slight advantage over the first. If the two sides are presented by a single source, most people try to perceive a coherent message; contradictory information introduced later is merely confusing, not persuasive.

But why, we might ask, should there be any effect at all? Given that two arguments are, in an absolute sense, equally persuasive, why should the second be either more or less effective than the first? Suppose we phrase the puzzle this way. Imagine possible opinions represented along a continuum ranging from very unfavorable opinions on the left to very favorable on the right. A person's initial opinion can be represented by a point along that line. He gets the first message; it moves him in one direction or the other. He gets the second message, which is equally persuasive; it moves him right back to wherever he was at the start. Two equal and opposite persuasions should cancel each other out, regardless of the order in which they occurred.

One clue that things are not so simple comes from the observation that the size of the change you will produce in an attitude is usually proportional to the amount of change you try to produce. That is to say, if you are trying to move people in a given direction, you should advocate a position more extreme than the one you actually hold. The bigger the difference between your argument and the listener's initial position, the larger the change you are likely to produce. That effect is itself open to further study and confirmation, but for the moment let us assume a proportionality effect does occur. What consequences would it have for an order effect?

At this point we must keep track of several things simultaneously; mathematical notation becomes very helpful. Let X represent values along the opinion scale. Let X_a represent the particular position that is being advocated by the argument a that is presented, and let X_0 represent a recipient's initial position. Then $X_a - X_0$ represents the magnitude of the change that the argument is attempting to produce in the recipient's opinion. The opinion that he will hold after hearing the argument will be given by

$$X_1 = X_0 + d$$

where d indicates the difference actually produced by the message. This definition of d is represented graphically in Figure 23.3.

Now we are able to state precisely our hypothesis of proportionality: the change d produced by argument a will be proportional to the difference $(X_a - X_0)$ between the opinion that the argument advocates and the opinion that the listener holds. Therefore,

$$d = k(X_a - X_0)$$

where k is a constant of proportionality depending upon the persuasiveness of the message, the credibility of the source, and other variables not directly related to our interest in the order of presentation. Presumably, k will usually be a number between 0 and 1. If k is between 0 and 1, then our assumption means that we should advocate a

FIGURE 23.3

A person holding opinion X_0 hears an argument advocating X_a and as a result he revises his opinion from X_0 to X_1.

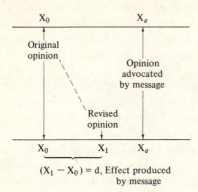

$(X_1 - X_0) = d$, Effect produced by message

larger change than we really want to produce. Negative values of k would represent a boomerang effect; the listener would change in a direction opposite to the one advocated. Values of k greater than 1 would mean that the argument produced an even greater change than we intended.

When we combine the two equations we obtain

$$X_1 = X_0 + k(X_a - X_0)$$

as our prediction of the opinion that the person will hold after hearing argument *a*, on the assumption that the change produced will be proportional to the change attempted. (Alternatively, we could rewrite the relation as

$$k = \frac{X_1 - X_0}{X_a - X_0}$$

and use this equation to define a coefficient of persuasiveness k as the ratio of the shift produced to the shift advocated.)

Now let us apply this simple equation to the situation that arises when two different points of view, pro and con, are argued in some particular order. Let X_c represent the position advocated in the con argument and X_p the position advocated in the pro argument, and assume for the sake of simplicity that both arguments are equally persuasive, so that k has the same value in both cases. Then, for instance, if the two are presented in the order con-pro, the result will be:

initially X_0
after con $X_1 = X_0 + k(X_c - X_0)$
after pro $X_2 = X_1 + k(X_p - X_1)$

This doubt shift is represented graphically in Figure 23.4.

400

FIGURE 23.4

The recency effect. A person holding opinion X_0 first hears an argument X_c against an issue and so revises his opinion to X_1. He then hears an argument X_p in favor of it and revises his opinion again now to X_2. If the arguments are equally persuasive (in this case $k = 0.75$), the net effect will be in favor of the argument heard most recently.

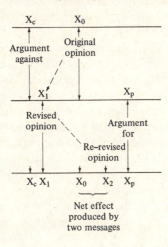

To get an intuitive glimpse of what these equations mean, consider what happens when $k = 1$, that is to say, when both arguments are completely persuasive. In that case, X_2 will equal X_p simply because the pro argument was the last one to be presented. If k is unity, therefore, we have a dramatic recency effect. On the other hand, consider what happens when $k = 0$, that is to say, when neither argument carries any weight. In that case, obviously, $X_2 = X_1 = X_0$, that is, there will be no change in opinion at all and, consequently, neither a primacy nor a recency effect. With values of k between 0 and 1, there is always some recency effect, the magnitude increasing as the persuasiveness of the argument increases.

Thus we see that we can tie together two apparently unrelated phenomena, the recency effect and the proportionality effect. From such modest beginnings we might hope that a matrix of further connections will eventually develop.

The fact that a theory is clear and explicit, however, does not mean that it is true. One very suspicious feature of this theory is its prediction that the person who is most strongly opposed to something will be the most persuaded by an argument in its favor. It may apply only to neutral or undecided listeners who are still willing to consider both sides of the question. But these speculations cannot settle the matter. What we need is some evidence. To test the theory we must turn to observations and experiments. What results do we know that might either support or contradict this particular fragment of theory?

There are several studies that might be cited as relevant to the ideas just presented; the following serves to illustrate the kind of data that have been obtained.[5] The communication materials for the study were taken from an actual law case tried early in the nineteenth century, the case of Thomas Hoag, who was indicted for making a bigamous marriage with Catherine Secor. For the purpose of the experiment, the evidence was organized into seventeen sections. The first one of these was the indictment itself, the next twelve sections were the summarized testimony of twelve different witnesses (reworded slightly if necessary to make them all approximately 175 words long), and finally two pieces of court procedure (two prosecution arguments followed by a two-section revelation of innocence) brought the case to a close. Each one of these seventeen sections was reproduced on a separate page; the pages that presented the twelve witnesses could be bound together in different orders in the test booklets. As the experimental juror read each page of his booklet, he encountered at the bottom of the page a numbered line running from 0 to 10. Unlike a trial, where the jurors would decide guilty or innocent at the close, the experimental jury was asked to give its opinion after every witness. The jurors marked the scale at 0 if they believed completely in the defendant's innocence, at 10 if they believed completely in his guilt. A neutral judgment was marked at 5.

The experimental manipulations had to do with the order in which the twelve witnesses, six for the prosecution and six for the defense, were presented in the booklets. When two witnesses from one side were given, followed by two witnesses from the other side, the experimental jurors wound up favoring the side that the most recent witnesses represented. The results supported the theory just outlined, whether the order-effect was introduced early or late in the case. Moreover, as Figure 23.5 indicates, a substantial recency effect was also observed when all six witnesses from one side were presented, then all six from the other side.

In the course of reading the evidence from the several witnesses, however, the jurors seemed to reach a point beyond which they were no longer susceptible to persuasion. The order effect, although real and measurable, was only a preliminary phenomenon. At first the arguments added and subtracted much as the equations predicted, but behind these local fluctuations there was a more fundamental process of opinion formation going on, a process not described by the equations. Perhaps if one could present the best evidence at the critical instant, when judge and jury were ripe for decision, one would have a far more telling effect than could be produced with the same evidence presented either earlier or later. But what this more basic process consists of remains a question for further research.

A great amount of work is going on aimed squarely at this question. We can do little more than sample it here.

FIGURE 23.5

Experimental demonstration of the recency effect. One group of experimental jurors (open circles) heard six prosecution witnesses followed by six defense witnesses; the other group (filled circles) heard the defense first, then the prosecution. The groups tended to favor the side they had heard most recently. (After N. H. Anderson, "Test of a Model for Opinion Change," Journal of Abnormal and Social Psychology *59 [1959]: 371–381.)*

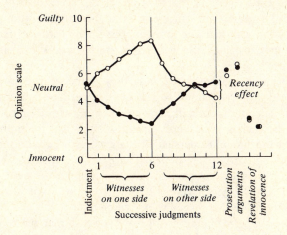

For many years psychologists have known that active participation in the learning process produces faster learning and better retention. Every teacher knows that the best way to learn something is to teach it to others. Suppose we try to generalize this observation. Does active participation by the receiver also produce conviction? To remember an argument does not mean that we must believe it—yet the two may be more closely related than we think. We are accustomed to say that a person expresses a particular opinion because he believes it; perhaps he believes it because he expresses it.

Suppose you could force a person to make your argument for you. Would the fact that he himself had actively expressed it make him tend to believe what he had said? A man who is promoted into an executive position may find that he is required to say things and to support opinions and policies that are really not his own; does he come eventually to believe what he is saying? Does a preacher persuade anyone as much as he persuades himself?

In order to put the matter to an experimental test, the Yale workers performed an experiment in role playing.[6] Young men, college students, were given an "oral speaking test." Each speaker was assigned the task of defending an extreme position on some topic of current interest. At the end of a session all the students answered a series of questions, ostensibly to help in the evaluation of the different speakers, but actually to measure the extent to which their own opinions had been modified. In most cases the students who had actively argued for a particular side showed a larger change in their opinions on that question than did the students who merely listened. They had convinced their listeners to a certain extent, but they had done an even better job of convincing themselves.

Of course, there were exceptions. Some speakers did not show the effect. The experimenters noted that these were usually the speakers who had shown little imagination in elaborating the arguments they had been assigned and who expressed the least satisfaction with their own performance. So a further study was aimed at the questions they posed.

The experiment was repeated, but now some of the students were asked to read a passage aloud to the class, whereas other student speakers saw the script of the talk, but were not permitted to read aloud from it. The results were clear. Speakers who had to improvise their arguments were far more persuaded than were those who merely read the script aloud. Moreover, personal satisfaction with the effectiveness of the performance seemed to have nothing to do with it. It was the amount that a person contributed from his own store of information and anecdote that served to convince him.

One of the slippery characteristics of words is that we tend to believe them, especially when they are our own. In this simple experiment we see at work the kind of process that enables us to adopt our social roles wholeheartedly, complete with all the values and opinions that go with them. Attitudes and behavior initially prescribed by some external authority come to be genuinely accepted and adhered to even in the absence of surveillance. If it were not so, civilized society as we know it could scarcely exist.

Why does a public declaration, especially if it seems to come from us personally, have this persuasive effect? One suggestion is that the declaration forces us into an incongruous position and that the change in attitude is simply an attempt to reduce the inconsistency. Previously, in Chapter 19, we noted how strong and pervasive is the human urge to make things look simple and consistent.

This high value people set on being consistent in their opinions gives us excellent leverage for persuading them to change their opinions. The recipe runs something like this. If you want someone to revise his considered opinion A, first find another opinion of his, B, and convince him that A and B are inconsistent. Since you now have the tendency to eliminate inconsistencies working in your favor, offer him a simple resolution of the problem that involves changing A. Of course, this strategy will work only on reasonable people. But most people are willing to be reasonable, at least some of the time, about all but a few things.

If you are going to persuade somebody by pitting one of his opinions against another, you will have to know your victim rather well. The argument that traps Jones into feeling inconsistent may not work at all with Smith. When we take this tack, therefore, we are beginning to look at the fine grain, the microstructure of public opinion. If we want techniques that are more effective than mass appeals via mass media of communication, we must learn how to analyze in considerable detail the cognitive structures of the men and women we want to influence.

Thus social psychology comes back once more to a familiar question. If you want to change a person's mind, you must know how his mind was made up to begin with. And that is, after all, the central question for any science of psychology.

The experimental study of attitude change has produced a wealth of useful data, put into practice by advertisers, propagandists, public speakers, journalists, the mass media, and the ordinary person interested in producing a change in attitude or behavior. A number of books are available that list methods to be employed in political campaigns which have been demonstrated as effective in laboratory studies.[7] A sampling of some of these findings follows.

One of the most stable findings is that *repetition of messages produces change and sales increases.* Successes of television advertising suggest that the principle applies even to matters that are not seen as terribly important by the receiver. The same technique has been applied with some success in the creative, repetitious use of "commercials" interpreting the alphabet and number concepts on television's "Sesame Street" program for children.

Numerous experiments have explored the use of fear content, especially in trying to modify behavior affecting health. The classic experiment by Janis and Feshbach used a graded set of materials from no fear to high fear (color slides of mouth diseases) to encourage children to brush their teeth.[8] Minimal fear arousal was more effective than high fear arousal, with high fear provoking a sense of disbelief in the children. This apparent contradiction to the law of effect does not always occur since some studies show that there is a positive relation between fear and attitude change, but the relation is quite complex. High fear causes smokers to cut down on cigarettes, but the fear is also generalized so as to inhibit their willingness to take a chest X-ray for diagnostic purposes. Thus they fear finding out the consequences, and continue to smoke . . . and to quit . . . and to smoke. As McGuire

---

If we are seeking to describe a pretzel-shaped reality we must be allowed to use pretzel-shaped hypotheses.

—*William McGuire*

---

points out, *high fear seems to be most effective if the simplicity and clarity of the message and the opportunity to take action is present.*[9] The facts are that fear seems to be more effective in producing attitude change (for example, telling your mother you'll never touch the hot stove again) than in ensuring behavior change.

Many studies have demonstrated that the believability of the source of a message can be a crucial factor. *High credibility sources produce more attitude change than low credibility sources.* Despite the appearance of sports figures, astronauts, and well-endowed actresses pushing deodorants on television, credibility is not exclusively dependent on high status or attractiveness in the communicator. Research indicates that the grapevine and rumors are effective in changing attitudes partly because the source appears to have nothing to gain from passing on a message. Overheard conversations seem to be especially effective. These sources have in common the fact that they cannot be checked directly. In the past radio was shown to be an effective source and channel for producing changes, being trusted to such a degree that people would plan their lives according to radio messages. In 1938 a radio broadcast by Orson Welles, simulating a fast-breaking news story of a Martian invasion of earth, caused widespread panic.[10] When a similar reaction to the same broadcast started to occur in 1960 in Ecuador, people checked and found out it was hoax. The people then burned down the radio station.

The personality of the receiver affects his susceptibility to persuasion. This is a rather obvious finding, which has long been used by speakers and propagandists in "tuning" their presentations according to their analysis of their receivers, but the particular personality trait and the particular situation interact in ways that often defy straightforward common sense. In a study of white people's attitudes toward black people, the investigator used a test to identify authoritarians, that is, those people who have unquestioned respect for people in authority.[11] The main finding was that high authoritarian people were swayed more by high authority figures than by the content of the message, that is, whether the message was anti- or pro-black. In a more recent study of mock jurors, high authoritarian jurors tended to give stiffer penalties than low authoritarians, who tended toward leniency, in response to the same persuasive evidence.[12] Similar results have been found with the need-for-social-approval scale described in Chapter 20; people having a high need for social approval are found to be more susceptible to persuasion accompanied by social platitudes.

We could catalogue more ideas for how to influence people (if not win friends), but one must treat them with all the caution necessary in applying any laboratory findings to the real world. It should be obvious that each firm finding about one element of the communication model carries with it implicit assumptions about the state of all other elements. We can tell you how effective humor was in persuading people under some conditions, but cannot predict its effect on all people in all conditions. Persuasive communication may be a science, an art, or both. In the real world we may never be able to control or even know the condition of all elements of the model. Further, very little research has been done on the social ecological context in which all communication takes place. Far from being a vacuum, this ever-changing context, comprising the culture, traditions, group consciousness, and immediate experiences of all people, affects the persuader as well as the persuadee.

Imagine writing a television commercial aimed at persuading people to have fewer children in the face of the population explosion. People in the United States have experienced millions of commercials, many of which subtly persuade people to have and enjoy children—in order to purchase more detergents, more diapers, etc. This prior experience is a part of the context. So, too, are existing attitudes about human fulfillment, passing on the family name, love of children, and religious values. One cannot deny that in this pronatalist context the advocate of zero-population growth (ZPG) has a formidable assignment as a *social change agent*, not merely as a pitchman for another product. Moreover, he usually does not have the budget to capitalize on techniques of persuasion in the mass media and cannot compete with the advertising expenditures of large corporations. The corporate structure pushes a psychology of "more," while our ZPG advocate pushes a psychology of *enough!*[13]

If he looks to our catalogue of research findings for help he may be disappointed. Most persuasion research has been directed toward changing attitudes rather than behavior, the persuasive techniques seem to produce minor changes in the preferred direction rather than large-scale shifts of value. Furthermore, it is difficult to assess the effectiveness of any particular technique because of the tendency of well-financed campaigners to try the whole bag of tricks. In election campaigns, for example, both sides may use television, billboards, direct mail, and face-to-face contact, with messages employing fear, humor, selective relevance to ethnic groups, appeals to get on the bandwagon, and so forth. A political campaign takes on a dynamic of its own with so much overloading of the persuasion channels that even the winner may have no idea which part of his communication strategy worked. Still, inevitably, observers will try to pin the success on one cause. Like scientists, they seek simple answers to complex questions.

We make life more difficult when we see a problem like overpopulation as merely the result of uninformed, nonresponsible behavior by people whose attitudes *must* be changed, by any gimmick necessary. People are then viewed as objects who are somehow re-

FIGURE 23.6

Family planning symbols; six countries with national programs. An elephant carries a family planning banner in India. (From "Communication in Family Planning," Reports on Population/Family Planning, *April 1971, pp. 10, 11.*)

Kenya	Pakistan	India
Singapore	Jamaica	Korea

moved from the benevolent control of more rational minds or sensible masters. The social ecology of the situation reveals an interdependence between people's attitudes and the maintenance of those attitudes. In the case of having large families there has never been a group of manipulators in the United States who consciously urged people to have more children. To have more children was a logical and presumably happy decision by millions of people who were being urged convincingly that the United States was growing and would continue to grow. To change a person's logically held attitude and behavior would seem to require a change in the whole context in which those attitudes and behaviors play a part. Why should a person show restraint in having children while the rest of the society pursues a policy of unlimited growth?[14]

Our point here is that we might find some short-term success in using the persuader's skills—in the form of attitude changes that please the ZPG advocate. But the real test—behavior change in having fewer children—takes time to evaluate. A person who declares he will have fewer children, but sees growth everywhere else—including the size of his neighbor's family—may just decide "to hell with it." If, as has happened in Japan, the government policy is changed to encourage *more* children to offset a too-rapid population decline, then our convert to ZPG may find himself labeled as a deviant. The social context can change as dramatically as the attitudes of an individual.

Psychologists have yet to face the challenge of dealing with communication as a total problem. Like the natural scientists who successfully changed some parts of the environment only to find a disaster resulting somewhere else, psychologists must begin to discover ecological relationships in society, which approach the complexity of ecological relationships in nature. By applying heavy control and using good coercive strategy we can get people to appear to agree to anything. But when they walk away from the speaker or the television tube and open their eyes to the rest of the context, they may "boomerang," tune out, or rebel against the entire context—which they know includes the persuader.

A Non-slanderous Political Smear Speech:
A Message for All Seasons

I ask you, my fellow Americans: is this the kind of person we want in public office to set an example for our youth?

Of course, it's not surprising that he should have such a typically pristine background—no, not when you consider the other members of his family:

His female relatives put on a constant pose of purity and innocence, and claim they are inscrutable, yet every one of them has taken part in hortatory activities.

The *men in the family are likewise completely amenable to moral suasion.*

My opponent's second cousin is a Mormon.

His uncle was a flagrant heterosexual.

His sister, who has always been obsessed by sects, once worked as a proselyte outside a church.

His father was secretly chagrined at least a dozen times by matters of a pecuniary nature.

His youngest brother wrote an essay extolling the virtues of being a homo sapiens.

His great-aunt expired from a degenerative disease.

His nephew subscribes to a phonographic magazine.

His wife was a thespian before their marriage and even performed the act in front of paying customers.

And his own mother had to resign from a woman's organization in her later years because she was an admitted sexagenarian.

Now what shall we say of the man himself?

I can tell you in solemn truth that he is the very antithesis of political radicalism, economic irresponsibility and personal depravity. His own record proves that he has frequently discountenanced treasonable, un-American philosophies and has perpetrated many overt acts as well.

He perambulated his infant son on the street.

He practiced nepotism with his uncle and first cousin.

He attempted to interest a 13-year-old girl in philately.

He participated in a seance at a private residence where, among other odd goings-on, there was incense.

He has declared himself in favor of more homogeneity on college campuses.

He has advocated social intercourse in mixed company—and has taken part in such gatherings himself.

He has been deliberately averse to crime in our city streets.

He has urged our Protestant and Jewish citizens to develop more catholic tastes.

Last summer he committed a piscatorial act on a boat that was flying the American flag.

Finally, at a time when we must be on our guard against all foreign isms, he has coolly announced his belief in altruism—and his fervent hope that some day this entire nation will be altruistic!

I beg you, my friends, to oppose this man whose life and work and ideas are so openly and avowedly compatible with our American way of life. A vote for him would be a vote for the perpetuation of everything we hold dear.

The facts are clear; the record speaks for itself.

Do your duty.

—*From* Mad Comics

NOTES

1. C. I. Hovland, A. A. Lumsdaine, and F. D. Sheffield, *Experiments in Mass Communication* (Princeton: Princeton University Press, 1949).
2. W. J. McGuire, "The Nature of Attitudes and Attitude Change," in *Handbook of Social Psychology*, 2d ed., ed. G. Lindzey and E. Aronson (Reading, Mass.: Addison-Wesley, 1969), vol. 3, pp. 136–314.
3. Ibid., p. 172.
4. Carl I. Hovland et al., *The Order of Presentation in Persuasion* (New Haven: Yale University Press, 1957).
5. N. A. Anderson, "Test of a Model for Opinion Change," *Journal of Abnormal and Social Psychology* 59 (1959): 371–381.
6. Carl I. Hovland, I. L. Janis, and H. H. Kelley, *Communication and Persuasion* (New Haven: Yale University Press, 1953). For a review of the concept of role in social psychology see T. R. Sarbin, "Role Theory," in *Handbook of Social Psychology*, ed. G. Lindzey (Cambridge: Addison-Wesley, 1954), pp. 223–258.
7. R. P. Abelson and P. G. Zimbardo, *Canvassing for Peace: A Manual for Volunteers* (Ann Arbor, Mich.: Society for the Psychological Study of Social Issues, 1970).
8. I. L. Janis and S. Feshbach, "Effects of Fear-Arousing Communications," *Journal of Abnormal and Social Psychology* 48 (1953): 78–92.
9. McGuire, "The Nature of Attitudes and Attitude Change."
10. Ibid.
11. H. B. Linton, "Dependence on External Influence: Correlates in Perception, Attitudes and Judgment," *Journal of Abnormal and Social Psychology* 51 (1955): 502–507.
12. Virginia Boehm, "Mr. Prejudice, Miss Sympathy and the Authoritarian Personality. An Application of Psychological Measuring Techniques to the Problem of Jury Bias," *Wisconsin Law Review* (1968): 734–747.
13. W. R. Looft, "The Psychology of More," *American Psychologist* 26 (1971): 561–565.
14. R. Buckhout, "Toward a Two-Child Norm," *American Psychologist* 27, no. 1 (1972): 16–26.

411

TWENTY-FOUR
The Third Force

So far we have presented the contributions of the hard-nosed and subjective behaviorist schools of psychology in considerable detail. This is no accident, nor does it reflect a bias. It reflects the facts of life in the psychology establishment where even the leading spokesmen of the "softer" theories have been socialized in the behaviorist tradition through learning an agreed upon core of scientific knowledge accumulated over many years. This came first. The "third force" is the self-proclaimed label of the humanistic psychologists, a label that is often applied to any psychologists who question the dominant natural science model in psychology.

Either their commitment is to science, and thus meeting the criteria of science becomes the privileged position; or they are committed to man, with special emphasis on the essentially human characteristics of man, and they thus render to a secondary place the concern for meeting the standards of science understood as a natural science.[1]

Despite the dominance of the natural science model, dissenters from that model have coexisted within the establishment. During the 1960s they moved from the fringes of the establishment to a more central position, clearly denying any image of psychology as a unified discipline. The emergence of this third force has been facilitated by the success of the subjective behaviorists' research in memory, perception, social psychology, and clinical psychology. In addition, the movement owes much of its increased influence to the vision and persistence of some remarkable men and women who pioneered in new approaches to the study of people. Although contemporary humanistic psychologists may trace their origins back to Kant and other phenomenologists of the nineteenth century, we will focus first on the work of Kurt Lewin (1890–1947), who lived through a critical transitional period.

KURT LEWIN, PSYCHOLOGIST

Kurt Lewin was born in Mogilno, Poland (then in a Prussion sector of Germany) on September 9, 1890.[2] His parents were middle-class Jewish residents of a small town, who suffered the publicly approved discrimination against all Jews. His practical parents, faced with the fact of limited opportunities, moved to Berlin where the young Kurt would flourish as a student. Like many of the other psychologists we have studied, Lewin began the study of medicine only to give it up for biology and later philosophy. Fascinated by the theory of science, Lewin worked for his doctorate at the University of Berlin, where the Psychological Institute was directed by Carl Stumpf.

Carl Stumpf was the man Helmholtz mistakenly brought to Berlin for the hard-nosed scientific study of behavior (see Chapter 14). Stumpf was a wide-ranging thinker whose interests spanned perception, philosophy, music, and child development as well as experimental psychology. Lewin, clearly repelled by Wundt's imperious nature, chose Stumpf as his thesis advisor, bringing him closer to Stumpf's faculty team—Wertheimer, Koffka, and Köhler, the founders of gestalt psychology.

Early in his academic career Lewin showed signs of unconventionality and genius. He was a popular student; at this time he became involved with groups of students who sought to democratize German society. His group organized evening classes for worker-adults and even preached the liberation of women (but apparently didn't practice it). Lewin tended to be a critic of conventional theories and to take his own original thinking quite seriously, foreshadowing his later reputation as a leader in breaking taboos about the limits of science.

Lewin served as a soldier in World War I, earning a field commission and the Iron Cross. His experience in the war had a profound influence on his thought. His observation of that now familiar phenomenon of how barbaric acts can become accepted as commonplace and correct in the context of war led him to speculate on how the individual's perception of his physical environment is changed by and dependent on his needs. Returning to the economic and political chaos of postwar Germany, he resumed his work in the sanctuary of the University of Berlin. There the gestaltists were developing their ideas, stimulating Lewin with their vision of *wholistic* psychology (the whole is different from the sum of the parts).

As a *dozent* (a lecturer for fees), Lewin was an exciting giver of ideas, if not a great lecturer. He would invent ideas on his feet, which often confused his students, but was consistent with his argument that science means change. He was his own man—independent in his own ideas, but exceptionally tolerant if his students wished to follow their own. So thoroughly involved was he in psychology that he would work and converse with students until the late hours at dinner or at the local tavern. His students formed a group (the Quasselstrippe) which met weekly at a Berlin cafe to discuss psychology with the effervescent Lewin. Clearly he was the most gregarious of all of the psychologists we have discussed so far.

During this period of the 1920s Lewin developed the essential

elements of his *field theory*, his own version of a concept generally accepted by thinkers in the gestalt tradition. For Lewin, the field is psychological; it is a *life space* that consists of a person and the environment as a single constellation of interdependent factors. Some observers have credited Lewin with changing the focus of psychology; after Lewin it became "meaningless to speak of behavior without reference to both the person and his environment."[3] Behavior for Lewin is a function of the life space, and the life space is the result of interaction between the person and his environment.

Lewin represented the life space by geometric diagrams that varied in complexity depending on the degree of differentiation of the person and the number and strength of environmental influences the person was aware of. The self became more complex with age, responding in a more differentiated way than the wholistic responses of childhood. In Figure 24.1 the child (c) is in a conflict-bungle versus disliked food. An object in the life space is said to have a *valence*, that is, it can attract or repel the individual. A rich set of dynamics is possible and predictable if all of the elements are understood. The valences of various objects add up to forces affecting the position of the person in his life space. Lewin hoped to develop a mathematical model to quantify such predictions, but he was more successful in inspiring research than in making his field theory very systematic. Central to his theory were his stress on the *whole* of a given setting and his focus on the "now" as well as past events, the influence of the knowledge of future events, and the changes in behavior produced by the testing methods themselves. The life space can include group climate (vibes), dreams, fantasies; elements which are "unreal," as well as "real" (when reality is narrowly defined as elements that other observers could agree were present). But, whatever constitutes the life space, it is unique to the individual.

FIGURE 24.1

A positive central field of forces corresponding to a positive valance. "The Representation of the Person," from Principles of Topological Psychology *by K. Lewin [New York: McGraw-Hill, 1936], as it was reproduced and adapted in* The Handbook of Social Psychology, *ed. Lindzey and Aronson, vol. 1. [Reading, Mass.: Addison-Wesley, 1954), p. 424.)*

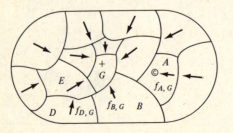

The appeal of Lewin's models rests on their dynamic quality and their derivation from and for the human condition. It was fascinating to his students to apply these models—to explain such behavior as prejudice, for example, as being related to different life spaces. In Lewin's terms the man who hates chicano people might have a kind of life space very different from that of a more tolerant person. Milton Rokeach was later to describe the prejudiced person as having a closed belief system, characterized by less differentiation of self and more dependence on outside authorities.[4] The more tolerant person is described as having an open internal belief system which is well differentiated and more independent.

One obvious criticism raised by behaviorists is that Lewin's models are so complex that they are not easily expressed as psychological laws governing behavior in general. There seems to be a different science for each person. But this was Lewin's intent: "What is the value of general concepts if they do not permit prediction for the individual case?"[5] This point brought his thinking in direct conflict with the model of man that underlies behaviorism, the model that focuses on manipulative external causes and a relatively passive responding organism. Lewin's field theory brings the internal makeup of the person into interaction with the more familiar source of influence, the environment. He and his students were among the first to apply the concept of *ecology* to behavior, looking at the effects of naturally

---

Psychology is surely one of the few sciences that has little more knowledge than laymen about the occurrence in nature of many of its phenomena: of talk, of fear . . . of laughter, of frustration, of of being disciplined. . . .

—Roger Barker

---

occurring environmental factors that influence behavior, but that cannot be effectively changed by the investigator. Much of the present-day interest in "field research" and criticism of the relevance of laboratory experiments can be traced to this early influence.

Much of this early work was done by Lewin while he was still in Germany. However, by the 1930s it was no longer possible to be a Jew and somewhat prominent in Germany. Germany was polarized by the Nazis and Communists and paralyzed by an economic depression; Jews like Lewin became targets for displaced frustration. Nazi riots broke out at the University over demands to oust Jewish students and faculty and later Lewin saw some of his own family murdered by the Nazis. As his biographer Alfred Marrow notes, Lewin ". . . foresaw that no Jew and no man concerned with the spirit of free inquiry could live in Nazi Germany." He made arrangements to leave Germany in 1933, and was followed later by Koffka, Köhler, and Wertheimer. Thus did the four brightest names in gestalt psychology come to the United States—part of a pattern of intellectual emigration that eventually revolutionized science and technology in this country.[6]

Although Lewin's work had begun to be noticed in the United States, partly as a result of his infectious enthusiasm when he lectured to visiting American students, his first job here hardly matched his stature. He received a two-year appointment as a lecturer in the School of Home Economics at Cornell, financed by an emergency committee to help refugees. But Lewin began following his own path, which was to lead him further away from gestalt psychology and into the application of his unique ideas to practical and social problems in the United States. His next base of operations was on the distinguished faculty of the University of Iowa. As always, Lewin attracted a large number of talented, dedicated colleagues and students who did research with him and who each week met informally with him. Lewin's influence as a stimulating teacher left deep impressions. Many of these students were to become the leaders of modern social psychology in later decades.

SOCIAL ACTION RESEARCH AND GROUP DYNAMICS

In the late 1930s the United States was slowly recovering from the depression while history moved forward inexorably toward World War II. Lewin's research interests shifted naturally to social problems, spurred by his highly personal identification with the plight of fellow Jews caught in the struggle against anti-Semitism. While he could easily understand the growth of anti-Semitism in Germany, he was surprised to find obvious prejudice and restrictions against Jews in the United States. Extending his theory of the life space, Lewin was to argue that a major component of the life space was the group to which one belongs. Uncertainty of identity, characteristic of a minority group trying to fit in, was seen as a major cause of conflict, confusion, and overreaction by the individual.[7] Considering the history of racial and religious discrimination in the United States, he opted for a strengthening of the separate group identity, rather than pressuring each person to assimilate the majority culture.

We look on Lewin's work as part of the beginning of relevant research on social problems, with the stamp of a determinist who

---

The American cultural ideal of the "self-made man," of everyone "standing on his own feet," was as tragic as the initiative-destroying dependence on a benevolent despot. We all need continuous help from each other. This type of interdependence is the greatest challenge to the maturity of individual and group functioning.

—Kurt Lewin

always felt that "there is nothing as practical as a good theory." When World War II broke out, Lewin and his colleagues turned to the application of psychological research to the war effort. This service orientation promised both to help society and to give the psychologist access to basic social processes he would not ordinarily come in contact with. The team did research and advisory work on military leadership, psychological warfare, training for human relations in the office and factory, selection and training of spies, persuasion of people to consume more available but unfamiliar food, and other problems that received definition by the war situation.

Lewin started so many projects of great significance that a complete accounting would be impractical here. Perhaps the most influential of the experiments to be done by his team was the Lewin, Lippit, White study of leadership styles.[8] The idea was to compare autocratic and democratic leadership of children's groups and to measure group atmosphere and productivity. Observations of the "whole" setting were made by hidden observers and cameras. Under the surface was an ideological question: Can democracy be as efficient as a more authoritarian type of political organization? The autocrat initiated all orders and activities and was severely critical of the group's work. It was observed that under autocratic leadership the children quarreled more, picked on scapegoats, and were generally less friendly than under democratic leadership. The democratic approach to leadership was, however, not without drawbacks; a laissez-faire atmosphere resulted in less work and discussion and a sense of frustration over the lack of rules—a familiar result of some present-day experiments in unstructured education. Lewin felt that these studies demonstrated that the cause of the observed behavior was the overall climate, not the personalities of the participants. Most of the children preferred the democratic leadership and the observers concluded that the group atmosphere was more beneficial and productivity was higher under democratic leadership. Subsequent action projects by Lewin's students involved changing the usual autocratic styles of organizations to more democratic ones. In terms of values, Lewin was decidedly committed to the promotion of cooperation and interdependence as a means of achieving group cohesiveness. This "bias" characterized most of his research methods as well as the findings—resulting in many well-organized, interdisciplinary research teams.

The famous food habits study, as described by Marrow,[9] was a blend of the Lewin penchant for action research and his affinity for interdisciplinary cooperation, which in this study brought him into collaboration with the distinguished anthropologist, Margaret Mead. The research centered around how people's food preferences could be changed, so people would eat less popular but more available foods (for example, turnips) in order to maintain nutrition levels in spite of wartime food shortages. Margaret Mead's brilliance in doing careful field research to determine what people in America actually eat blended with Lewin's use of the laboratory to test experimentally ways of changing food habits. Mead identified the wife and mother as the ultimate arbiter of what the family eats (regardless of the husband's veto power), while Lewin's researchers ran a test of communication strategies on groups of housewives. They discovered that the use of a high-prestige expert to push the use of turnips was less effective than "group decision" in bringing about change. The group decision saw the participants cooperatively sharing the information on turnips and mutually deciding to try them.

Lewinian contributions to the theory, to the practice, and even to the language of social science can be partially appreciated by the following capsule review.

The Zeigarnik effect. We recall uncompleted tasks more readily than those we complete. The effect was named for Lewin's student Bluma Zeigarnik, who theorized that the interruption prevented the natural release of tension.

Level of aspiration. The degree of difficulty of the goal toward which the person is striving varies. When progress toward a goal is partial, level of aspiration is raised. Hence revolutions often start after slight progress has begun.

Psychic satiation. Repetitions of the same activity (even one that is valued) can cause a person to refuse to continue, especially if the activity involves the whole undifferentiated person.

Insight into frustration. Barker, Dembo, and Lewin showed that frustration produces a change in the constructive activity of children, causing them to regress (or reduce differentiation).

Effects of integrated housing. In a study of white attitudes toward black neighbors, Lewin's colleagues found antiblack prejudice to be lower in integrated than in segregated housing, apparently due to a relaxation of tension from getting to know one another.

In summing up the impact of Lewin on psychology in the United States, we can best point to prominent students and colleagues such as Leon Festinger, Stanley Schacter, Morton Deutsch, Karl Deutsch, Al Pepitone, Fritz Heider, Dorwin Cartwright, Ronald Lippit, Roger Barker, Stuart Cook, Harold H. Kelley, Rensis Likert, John W. Thibaut, J. P. French, Alvin Zinder, and others who have shaped and led the field of social psychology. Many of these men worked with Lewin when he opened the M.I.T. Research Center for Group Dynamics, one of the most productive research groups ever assembled. It later moved to the University of Michigan and became one of the main centers of the social psychology establishment. After Lewin's death in 1948 this establishment headed toward experimental social psychology with great fervor. For our story of the third force in psychology, we point to two of Lewin's fringe area contributions which helped to revolutionize psychology.

The first was his founding of the Society for the Psychological Study of Social Issues (SPSSI) in 1942. SPSSI, more than any other group, has kept alive the tradition of research oriented toward social problems. Its *Journal of Social Issues* provides the space for publication of lengthy, descriptive treatments of research and theory of social change. The Kurt Lewin Memorial Award is given annually by the society for outstanding work in at least one of the fields Lewin created. The society continues to support research on the controversial social problems of our times.

In 1946 Lewin directed an experiment that began what we now call sensitivity training by creating the National Training Laboratories. It was designed to help people deal more effectively with complex human relations and to develop ways of changing people's attitudes. Lewin put into practice the democratic-cooperative model of group decision-making his research had helped create. After the first day the researchers shared their own data gathered on the group with group members—feedback was helpful. It made the members more sensitive to their own conduct. The test of the effectiveness came in follow-up studies which showed that the participants in the training group (T-group) were greatly improved in their dealings with people. The National Training Laboratories became a permanent and leading force in the encounter group movement. This was a long way from Esalen Institute and the human potential boom, but it began with Lewin.

We can only guess how Lewin might feel today about the developments he inspired. He was a complex but complete man who enthusiastically did too many things. He is remembered less for his publications than for his personal impact as a teacher and as a creative innovator of enduring programs. He was one of the first psychologists to really grasp the meaning of the uncertainty principle as it applies to the scientific study of human behavior. We think that he might be somewhat disturbed by those of his successors who have overexploited the development of laboratory techniques in social psychology to the point where some methods have become ends in themselves. We have a hunch that he might be a little amused by the growth of the human potential movement, but pleased by the growing importance of making psychology relevant to the betterment of human life.

Warren G. Bennis perhaps best captures the spirit of this remarkable man in the following passage.

> I was never a student of Lewin's. . . . I was always surprised when I actually read his work. Always a significant question, innocently explored with diagrams out of St. Exupery, and restlessly leading to such subjects as friendship, cultural differences in child-rearing, leadership and its consequences, social change, and the origins of the

philosophy of science. I thought that, like most charismatic men, his spirit would predominate rather than his mind. Only recently have I changed my mind about that. . . . I rediscovered the extent to which I internalized his ideas and some of his methods. Several of the sections dealt with change and resistance to change: their intellectual forefather was Lewin. Several other sections cover subjects like power, authority, and social influence. Here, also the intellectual legacy is Lewin. . . . I used to think that Kurt Lewin was a giant metaphor with terrific influence on the family but with no or little substantive grasp over the activities of his inheritors. Now I have come to believe that we have so carefully disguised our identification to ourselves that we forget we are all Lewinians.[10]

THE POST-LEWIN PERIOD

Kurt Lewin, of course, did not dominate the times in which he lived. Psychology in the United States then (as now) was too big; until World War II American psychology was dominated by the behaviorists. As we have noted in earlier chapters, subjective behaviorists came into prominence as they found errors in the older predictive models and new, more sophisticated tools which helped them to clarify not only the behavioral effects but the sources of errors as well. Most of Lewin's followers made effective use of Lewin's concept of the whole situation to do more complex laboratory research with individuals and groups in the laboratory. But some were following another pathway, which was to lead to the foundation of humanistic psychology.

The creation of the new experimental social psychology was to some extent based on an image of man as a complex but still manipulatable creature, with the search for cause still focused on the environment or on states of mind created by the experimenter through his clever techniques. Two of the most popular models are an economic model (social exchange theory) and homeostasis consistency seeking. If there were two major parts to the man Lewin they might be called scientist and humanistic practitioner, similar to the opposites we previously noted in clinical psychology in Chapter 22. In a blistering criticism of the dominant trends in social psychology, Kenneth Ring sees too much emphasis on a scientifically oriented social psychology—science for science's sake. Ring also sees an even more disturbing trend toward "fun and games" research, "a game of 'can you top this?' . . . Whoever can conduct the most contrived, flamboyant and mirthproducing experiments receives the highest scores . . ."[11]

This last point speaks to the truth of what has been called "the politics of pure science." Laboratory research in normal times is the acceptable thing to do in the psychological establishment, contrary to Lewin's feeling that we should be testing good theories in the natural environment. But more important, perhaps, is Ring's criticism of the

423

frivolous values displayed by those who publish quick but clever studies based on fads, more impressive in style than in substance, which are irrelevant to and a perversion of what Lewin had in mind.[12] William McGuire gave a mild rejoinder to Ring's paper, arguing that the manipulational experiment is too efficient to drop.[13] He calls for trying to maintain the best of both worlds.

But there are not that many Lewins around who can maintain the balanced approach. Many social psychologists and clinical psychologists have become so alienated by the trends Ring describes that they have left the mainstream to pursue research and practice that bears directly on human affairs; the kind of humanistic action-oriented social psychology that was one of Lewin's legacies. The contemporary world of the "third force" is made up of these people plus some other men who began marching to a different drummer much earlier.

A NEW IMAGE OF MAN

Man is basically _____ ? What is the nature of man as seen through the eyes of the humanistic psychologist, a confirmed member of the "soft" tradition in psychology? The encounter group, the search for a guru, sensitivity training, and other currently popular movements have become associated with humanistic psychology, but its underlying assumptions go much deeper. Humanistic psychology, as a would-be scientific revolution, is founded on an image of man as *becoming* rather than reacting. While the behaviorist sees man as motivated to reduce tension from unmet biological needs, the humanistic psychologist speaks of higher needs—the need to grow, to self-actualize, to love, and to be loved. The reasons for a man's behavior are to be found inside as well as outside the person. As Abraham Maslow expresses it, "Human beings seem to be far more autonomous and self-governed than modern psychological theory allows for."[14]

Maslow was a major philosophical force in humanistic psychology, despite his early training as a behavioristic psychologist. He was Harry Harlow's first PhD student (see Chapter 17), but his education in a new vision began while he was a professor of psychology at Brooklyn College, as he read or came face to face with the ideas of Freud, Adler, Jung, Fromm, and the gestalt psychologists.[15] "I had

---

The ultimate happiness for man is the realization of pure beauty and pure truth.

—Abraham Maslow

---

the best teachers . . . of any person who ever lived . . . just because of the historical accident of being in New York City when the very cream of European intellect was migrating away from Hitler."

When World War II broke out Maslow vowed to seek a comprehensive theory of human behavior, one that would "prove that human beings are capable of something grander than war, prejudice and hatred." Placing this value at the center of his scientific work seemed to lead Maslow inevitably to criticizing both the mechanistic views of the behaviorists and the pessimistic views of the Freudians. He felt that the positive aspects of human behavior were being ignored by psychologists. Thus began a long study of good, happy people whom Maslow referred to as *self-actualizing*.

Self-actualization for Maslow meant "the full use of talent, capacities, potentialities," the best possible human, a representative of the "growing tip" of the population.

> All the growth for the human species takes place in the growing tip, among that one percent of the population. The growing tip is made up of pioneers, the beginners. That's where the action is. . . .[16]

One can deplore the elitism here, but the uniqueness of Maslow's research was that he wanted to understand life from the perspective of those people who were happily fulfilled as human beings. He chose public figures (for example, Eleanor Roosevelt), historical figures (Jefferson, Lincoln, Einstein), and outstanding students.

We arrive at self-actualization in our later years, around 60, when we can identify the self. Maslow's subjects proved to be capable of seeing life clearly—to be objective about the present and accurate in predicting the future; they had humility and the dedication to work on a task that they considered important. Creativity was evident in all, combined with perseverance in the face of unpopularity, willingness to face the unknown, low self-conflict, a need for privacy, harmonious personality, independence, and a psychological freedom that aided decision-making. Maslow describes the self-actualizers as healthy in contrast to the person who is motivated by deficiencies in basic needs, who is absorbed in coping rather than becoming. Self-actualizing people enjoy life, unlike the neurotic who experiences a failure of personal growth, doubts about the goals of life, loss of meaning, and despair—a psychological sickness founded on a failure to achieve good human relations.

Unlike Freud, Maslow saw these positive needs as weak instincts (instinctoid traits), while he felt that aggression was culturally based rather than genetic. A sick person who has no love identification with

---

The demonstration that wonderful people can *and do exist—even though in very short supply . . . is enough to give us courage, hope, strength to fight on, faith in ourselves and in our own possibilities for growth.*

—Abraham Maslow

---

other people—due to early deprivation of love—can kill or injure easily without emotion. Reality therapy, as Maslow calls his technique, places responsibility for behavior directly on the individual.

Like Lewin, Maslow believed in wholistic research and an image of man as an integrated, organized whole. Maslow's theory of motivation (illustrated in Figure 24.2) assumes that man has a hierarchy of needs, basic biological needs and then growth needs aimed at self-actualization. The basic physiological needs have powerful effects on behavior, as long as they are not fulfilled. Man is always desiring something. When physiological and safety needs are met, the need for love, affection, and belongingness begins to emerge. Maslow is critical of Freud's description of love as a derivative of sex and the pleasure principle. Love hunger was seen by Maslow as a deficiency disease. At

FIGURE 24.2

Abraham Maslow's Hierarchy of Needs. (*From* The Third Force *by F. G. Goble. Copyright © 1970 by Thomas Jefferson Research Center. Reprinted by permission of Grossman Publishers.*)

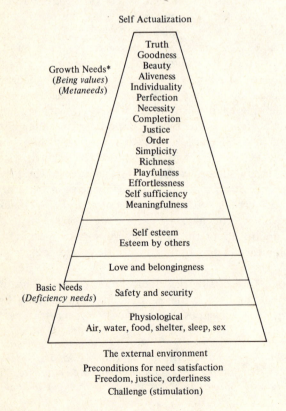

*Growth needs are all of equal importance (not hierarchical)

the top of the hierarchy is self-actualization—a goal that is attained late in life because it cannot be reached until the other needs are satisfied. The higher needs are not vital to survival, hence are less urgent, weaker. Contrasting Maslow's hierarchy of needs to Freud's suggests that both are statements of faith, but Freud's is founded on a pessimistic view of innately depraved man held in check by the super-ego, while Maslow's is founded on an optimistic view of an innately beautiful creature who turns to base behavior because its higher needs are not satisfied.

We are responsible for our own evolution.
—Abraham Maslow

In Maslow's last writings, just before his death in 1970, he attacked the pessimists and the behaviorists in what could be taken as a manifesto for humanistic psychology, or what he calls the "unnoticed revolution."

> The new humanistic Weltanschaung seems to be a new and more hopeful and encouraging way of conceiving any and every area of human knowledge. . . . This subculture of despair, this more corrosive than thou attitude, this counter-morality in which predation and hopelessness are real and good will is not, is flatly contradicted by humanistic psychologies. . . . It is already possible to reject firmly the despairing belief that human nature is ultimately depraved and evil. . . . It can now be maintained only by a determined blindness and ignorance, by a refusal to consider the facts. . . . Holism is obviously true—after all, the cosmos is one and interrelated. . . . The atomistic way of thinking is a form of mild psychopathology, or is at least one aspect of the syndrome of cognitive immaturity. . . . Human life will never be understood unless its highest aspirations are taken into account. Growth, self-actualization, the striving toward health, the quest for identity and autonomy, the yearning for excellence . . . must be accepted beyond question as a widespread and perhaps universal human tendency.[17]

This somewhat dogmatic statement was part of Maslow's criticism of "value-free science," which he argued led to a stress on the techniques

Science was not, is not and cannot be completely objective . . . independent of human values.

—Abraham Maslow

of science rather than its goals. The tendency in psychology and other social sciences to borrow the techniques and models of the natural sciences and to look down on new techniques turns the psychologist ". . . into a technician and expert rather than a venturesome truth seeker, into one who *knows* rather than one who is *puzzled*."

Maslow felt that science should be seen as based on human values, seen as a value system justifiable only by the merits of its goals. It is only one means of access to knowledge. This is a point we have been arguing since the first chapter. While Maslow shows some of the same dogmatism in his faith as such men as Helmholtz, Freud, and Watson, he differs markedly in his image of man. As Kuhn would predict, the followers of Maslow, feeling convinced of the correctness of Maslow's paradigm, are busily attacking the older establishment, while the establishment questions the mental health of the humanistic psychologists. The break has led to the holding of separate professional meetings and the explosive growth of what has been called the human potential movement.

CHANGE AND GROWTH

The humanistic psychologists are everywhere (except in first-rate jobs in academic departments), spreading a message and doing research aimed at a fundamental change in the way we relate as human beings. Experience in an encounter group or sensitivity training is now widespread, bringing psychology directly into more people's lives than any other application, even psychoanalysis. The informal structure of the encounter group strips away the need for elaborate offices, couches, professional staff, degrees, and the high fees characteristic of individual therapy. Whereas the offshoot of Lewin's original organization, the National Training Laboratories, requires more structure and a postgraduate degree for trainers, a larger number of "growth centers" have spread all over the United States under the leadership of untrained people as well as alienated professionals. Neither the psychology nor psychiatry professions have taken a clear stand on what to do about encounter groups, except to hope that they stay outside of the establishment. But, the movement has grown anyway, "without benefit of clergy," just as psychotherapy grew at one time despite the reluctance of the psychology establishment.

What is an encounter group? The key word is *experience* in an atmosphere of trust and honest communication.[18] The individual is expected to experience himself—his body, his emotional feelings in the here and now—and to share experiences with his fellow group members. He is instructed to focus on feelings rather than ideas, striving to reach and touch people, releasing and receiving energy while fully responsible for his actions and their results. The common relaxation of taboos and inhibitions in encounter groups has stirred rumors about anarchy and orgies, but over the years the more serious practitioners have developed the art of leadership to the point where encountering is merely a very different sort of group dynamics with its own rules.

The opportunity to achieve a level of intimacy with trusted and trusting people is apparently filling some deep-seated cultural need that is not being met by other societal institutions. A person who wants to may open up to the group more than he might dare to on the job or to his wife or family. As one spokesman puts it,

> In our culture, it's extremely difficult to find experiences with other people which provide a degree of freedom and intimacy and a real opportunity to deal with persons at a fairly intense level. A lot of that has led to the growth in sensitivity training.[19]

One model which expresses the role of the individual in a group is shown in Figure 24.3. The Johari Window is used to evaluate the degree of openness of interpersonal communication, aiming to enlarge the "open" area.[20] The hidden area looms large in most group settings, as does the unknown. The goal in encounter groups is to reduce individual blindness through group communication. (You will note that this model is similar to the signal detection model described in Chapter 7.) Democracy, in Lewin's system, also would show up with a larger "open" area. But in research on various business groups it has been found that most show no naturally occurring affect or interpersonal feelings.[21] When these groups were retrained or sensitized, the immediate results were positive—more affect and personal feelings—but follow-up studies showed that the changes were short-lived. The most pessimistic observers wonder if democracy or openness in communication are really desired by the American people!

The encounter group enthusiasts have argued that the concept should be extended to all areas of society, so that it is experienced not as a rare peak on a rushed weekend, but as a fundamental way of functioning in school, work, politics, and in one's family. They point

FIGURE 24.3

The Johari window. (Reprinted from Group Processes: An Introduction to Group Dynamics *by J. Luft by permission of National Press Books.)*

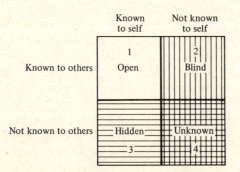

to Douglas MacGregor's Theory X Management[22] as the most common form of management, and one that serves all too often as a model for all social relationships. Theory X is the authoritarian idea of management which assumes that people dislike work and must be controlled or coerced with the threat of punishment to get the job done. In contrast, Theory Y Management—capturing the spirit of both Lewin and Maslow—assumes the following:

1. Work and play are natural, sometimes rewarding and sometimes punishing.
2. "Man will exercise self-direction and self-control in the service of objectives to which he is committed."
3. Ego and self-actualization needs can be satisfied in meeting organizational objectives.
4. "The average human being learns under proper conditions, not only to accept but to seek responsibility."
5. Imagination, ingenuity, and creativity are widely, not narrowly, distributed in the population.
6. "Under the conditions of modern industrial life, the intellectual potentialities of the average human being are only partly utilized."

These ideas are quoted by every person who sells human relations training to industry or who leads encounter groups for the citizen. Government agencies, industries, church groups, and the police have used the approach. Who could knock Theory Y? Moreover, if human relations training results in higher productivity (as it seems to), who could fault such a double benefit? Encounter groups have been convened to bring together warring groups (blacks versus whites, police versus citizens) in successful attempts to cool down community crises. But solid empirical research on the benefits of encounter groups has been rare and rather primitive—as it has been in the case of virtually all methods of effecting change in people.

One problem with all of the encounter group work and the exposure of people to the higher potentials of their being is that such efforts may, like religion, be seen as nice diversions, but as dangerous opiates, pacifying feelings while the baser motives of men keep business going on as usual. After having a peak experience in an encounter group on a lovely weekend at the beach, a person must still return to the cold, cruel world which doesn't react too kindly to the person who weeps and reveals all. The problem with Theory X is its persistence. Black people in the United States have been skeptical of police-community encounter groups, suspecting that when the city brings in an encounter group leader it is motivated by the desire to pacify people who have legitimate, but militantly expressed demands. The encounter group movement, as the leading edge of the third force, offers an exciting and fulfilling image of a freer and happier man. However, if it is seen only as a means to blow off steam, it may simply serve as another means of preserving the status quo, draining off energy that might better be directed toward change. A group is still a group; creativity is one possible result of the dynamic interaction that takes place, but so is conformity.

What then is the future of the third force in psychology? We think that it is a healthy revolution and the sign of a basically healthy profession, despite the obvious disunity that has resulted from such a fundamental clash over images of the nature of man. A fruitful type of controversy is taking place, which gets down to the basic definition of what science is as well as what man is. While some form of behaviorism dominates the academic scene in psychology, the demands of society for a more relevant, responsive psychology are beginning to affect the profession to its roots. Even hard-nosed experimental psychologists are questioning how relevant to the human condition their work is. Third force figures such as Carl Rogers have been raising these fundamental questions for years, often as lone voices pitted

---

CITATION ACCOMPANYING THE DISTINGUISHED SCIENTIFIC CONTRIBUTION AWARD PRESENTED BY THE AMERICAN PSYCHOLOGICAL ASSOCIATION, 1956

"For developing an original method to objectify the description and analysis of the psychotherapeutic process, for formulating a testable theory of psychotherapy and its effects on personality and behavior, and for extensive systematic research to exhibit the value of the method and explore and test the implications of the theory. His imagination, persistence, and flexible adaptation of scientific method in his attack on the formidable problems involved in the understanding and modification of the individual person have moved this area of psychological interest within the boundaries of scientific psychology."

CARL R. ROGERS

---

against the "center" of the establishment (see the Rogers-Skinner Debate in Appendix A). Today Rogers is a principle advocate and an innovative user of encounter group techniques in quest of his psychology of the person. The public is now witness to the debate between the followers of Rogers, Maslow, and Lewin and the determinists such as B. F. Skinner.

Our feeling is that the problems faced by society need all three major forces in psychology. It seems clear that the behaviorists in power must give a little room to the third force in the academic world, lest they see the very popular third force adopted by everybody on the outside with possibly bad consequences for the more basic researchers on the inside. The third force, with its image of man and its commitment to promoting human welfare, seems bound to find a place somewhere in society. Its roots are in the scientific study of human behavior, and it would be tragic if the third force, with all of its unorthodox elements, were forced to abandon its roots.

The schism between the competing forces in psychology is real, but good sense emerges from time to time from all parties concerned. From Edward Walker comes a challenge to experimental psychologists.

> . . . in judging the merit of basic research, colleagues have an obligation to evaluate the research in terms of relevance and social need in the broadest sense. . . . [U]ltimate human usefulness is the primary criterion on which the social support of psychological research should be based.[23]

And from Abraham Maslow, a few words for those who might expect too much from a revolutionary idea.

> . . . if for instance we could teach our young people to give up their unreal perfectionism, their demands for perfect human beings, a perfect society, perfect teachers, perfect parents . . . none of which can exist—that is, except for transient moments of peak experience. . . . Such expectations . . . are illusions, and therefore must inevitably and inexorably breed disillusionment along with attendant disgust, rage. . . . The demand for Nirvana *Now* is itself a major source of evil, I am finding. If you demand a perfect leader or a perfect society, you thereby give up choosing between better and worse. If the imperfect is defined as evil, then everything becomes evil, since everything is imperfect.[24]

NOTES

1. A. Giorgi, *Psychology as a Human Science* (New York: Harper & Row, 1970).
2. A. J. Marrow, *The Practical Theorist: The Life and Work of Kurt Lewin* (New York: Basic Books, 1969).
3. M. Deutsch, "Field Theory in Social Psychology," in *The Handbook of Social Psychology*, 2d ed., ed. G. Lindzey and E. Aronson (Reading, Mass.: Addison-Wesley, 1968), vol. 1, pp. 412–487.
4. Ibid.
5. K. Lewin, *Field Theory in Social Science* (New York: Harper & Row, 1951), p. 61.
6. Marrow, *The Practical Theorist.*
7. K. Lewin, "Psycho-sociological Problems of a Minority Group," *Character and Personality* 3 (1935): 175–187.
8. R. Lippit and R. White, *Autocracy and Democracy: An Experimental Inquiry* (New York: Harper & Row, 1960).
9. Marrow, *The Practical Theorist*, pp. 128–131.
10. Ibid., pp. 233–234.
11. K. Ring, "Experimental Social Psychology: Some Sober Questions and Some Frivolous Values," *Journal of Experimental Social Psychology* 3 (1967): 113–123.
12. We can acknowledge Ring's accuracy by counting the thousands of cognitive dissonance studies published as one-shot articles by young social psychologists until the fad died out. Festinger himself is now in an en-

tirely unrelated field while a smattering of cognitive dissonance studies continues to appear in the literature.

13. W. J. McGuire, "Some Impending Reorientations in Social Psychology: Some Thoughts Provoked by Kenneth Ring," *Journal of Experimental Social Psychology* 3 (1967): 124–139.

14. A. H. Maslow, *Motivation and Personality*, 2d ed. (New York: Harper & Row, 1970).

15. F. G. Goble, *The Third Force* (New York: Grossman, 1970); M. H. Hall, "A Conversation with Abraham Maslow," *Psychology Today* 2, no. 2 (1968): 35–57.

16. Ibid., p. 56.

17. Maslow, *Motivation and Personality*, pp. x–xii.

18. W. C. Schutz, *Here Comes Everybody* (New York: Harper & Row, 1971).

19. S. Fantus, R. R. Harmon, S. Kallerup, and C. Sutton, "The Encounter Group Boom," in *Toward Social Change: A Handbook for Those Who Will*, ed. R. Buckhout et al. (New York: Harper & Row, 1971), pp. 309–344.

20. J. Luft, *Group Processes* (Palo Alto, Calif.: National Press Books, 1971).

21. C. Argyris, "The Incompleteness of Social Psychological Theory: Examples from Small Group, Cognitive and Attribution Research," *American Psychologist* 24 (1969): 893–908.

22. D. MacGregor, *The Human Side of Enterprise* (New York: McGraw-Hill, 1960).

23. E. L. Walker, "Experimental Psychology and Social Responsibility," *American Psychologist* 24 (1969): 862–868.

24. Maslow, *Motivation and Personality*, p. xxii.

TWENTY-FIVE
Conclusion

In taking a historical perspective in the presentation of the psychology of man, we have provided a personal selection of the work of a number of revolutionaries whose thinking made a difference. In most cases these men found themselves in direct conflict with an established paradigm and dared to challenge it with ideas that were later to be targets for challenges by other revolutionaries. With the rise and fall of each major theory about the psychology of man comes the hope that the accumulated wisdom will permit a more intelligent search for answers by carefully building on the past. However, in our opinion, such a hope represents wishful thinking.

The view that knowledge automatically accumulates with added information and revised thinking presupposes that each new generation reads and incorporates the knowledge and wisdom of the past. But, as the sheer bulk of information expands, men do not necessarily have or take the time to synthesize and use it. In the debate over whether history is made by events or by men, we could make a case for both. Scientists, including psychologists, are only men, and they demonstrate in their lives the ability to pursue a singular personal vision, only to shift at times to total attention to pressing events. Atomic scientists who synthesized the knowledge to create nuclear weapons have been known in recent times to stop and argue the ethical merits of pursuing knowledge for knowledge's sake. The disastrous social consequences of their inventions have led many of the more sensitive atomic scientists to be active in trying to bring the arms race to an end. More is not necessarily better. More is not even necessarily necessary, as evidenced by the many areas of physics and chemistry that are so mined out by researchers that further research would be regarded as an extravagant waste of money and effort.

Psychologists, too, are facing up to the practical and social limits of scientific research in their domain of interest. Until a century ago psychology was a branch of philosophy; the great thinkers somehow knew intuitively what was true (with some fifty thousand years of direct observation of human behavior to help them) and spent their days inventing clever arguments designed to prove it. Then, beginning with Fechner and Wundt and some of their contemporaries, they began to

buttress arguments with observations and experiments; at that point the shift into scientific modes of thinking began. But it was still a philosophical kind of psychology, concerned primarily with the source and nature of man's conscious knowledge.

In the background, however, a tremendous development was taking place in the biological sciences. At the first sign of trouble with the introspective analysis of mental life, therefore, the philosophical preoccupation with Man as Knower was swept away and replaced with the newer vision of Man as Animal. The new focus was not knowledge, but adaptation, not thought, but behavior. The mental life that psychology now began to study was not something to be experienced, but something inferred from action. For some thinkers, highly influenced by the growth of sophisticated technology, the appeal of Man as Machine was irresistible. With the development of computers it became possible to simulate some behavioral processes inferred from action. Isidor Chein, a social psychologist who criticizes the concept of man as a robot, points out that such a view carries with it the implication of "Man as an impotent reactor, with his responses completely determined by two distinct and separate, albeit interacting factors: (1) the forces impinging on him and (2) his constitution. . . ."[1]

Eventually, however, problems inherent in a purely behavioral conception of psychology also began to appear. So the vision of man was once more revised and extended, this time emphasizing Man as Social Animal, buffeted as much by the strange whims of his fellow men and women as by the stern demands of physiology and the environment. Developments in the social sciences, in anthropology and sociology, enabled psychologists to recognize the extent to which all mental life is conditioned by cultural traditions, by personal participation in the social process. The adaptation that man struggled to achieve was now seen to be largely a social adaptation, the knowledge he accumulated to be largely symbolic knowledge, encoded in whatever language his culture provided. And this concern with socially significant symbols led back once more to a renewed concern with Man as Knower, but now in a vastly expanded context of new methods and new theories. At the root of the humanistic psychology of the late 1960s was the image of man as an active, responsible agent, one who *can* act reflexively to the environment, but who can also choose to transcend and will his own actions.

The now huge enterprise called psychology embraces adherents of all of the aforementioned images of man among its scientists and practitioners. The dominance of the Man as Machine image, which seemed so conveniently matched to the interests of an emerging technological culture, seems to have been broken by the pressure of events and the revolutions that are changing the culture itself. The poverty of this model has been demonstrated in the unfortunate laboratory of the battlefield—in Vietnam, where the predictions of social scientists as well as presidents lie buried in a shameful disaster that has almost destroyed the United States. The control of behavior, which logically seems so achievable by applying the law of effect, must now be evaluated again in a world where man may no longer be needed by his technology to the degree that rewards can be used to induce production. Assuming the success of the dream of providing for all of man's material needs, would the dominant image of man change to something like that proposed by Maslow?

Perhaps. But the dream of a better society also seems related to a radical restructuring of society, as Maslow's idea of the self-actualized person is related to revolutions in thinking. We will risk a little predicting on our own about possible radical changes in thinking in our chosen profession of psychology.

The rising underground. The underground of psychology—which has at times included Freud, Jung, humanistic psychologists, prophets, ESP believers, mystics, the religious—appears to be infiltrating the psychological literature and the universities and gaining a more open-minded, respectful hearing by the establishment. Always popular among laymen, this body of thought which exists outside the establishment is an important part of the culture that psychology is supposed to help understand, rather than label as metaphysical or misguided. We believe that anything that brings the people to psychology is healthy.

Experience. The phenomenological experiences of people are being studied with more care as valid and important data, a trend we feel will continue. R. D. Laing and his followers are making revolutionary waves in the mental health field by questioning the borderlines between sane and insane.[2] By living with his patients, Laing avoids the usual diagnostic classifications and sees "individual madness as the distorted reflection of a pervasive social and political madness, of which psychiatry was itself a part." His work, and the work of the more responsible people in the encounter group field, may well revolutionize the treatment of people who have previously been stigmatized as ill, a concept borrowed from the medical model which assumes a fixed, external cause of disease.

Personality. Much of personality theory in psychology is related to the personality of the white male. As minority group psychologists and women rise to prominence in the field, we expect a restructuring of much of the knowledge which women and minority group members find so irrelevant. Like the one-dimensional definition of intelligence which has discriminated against the black man in the United States, the notion of a universal definition of a normal personality is a perverse distortion of the very different socialization experiences which shaped the middle-class white male, women in different strata, and minority group members.

Social responsibility. In the shocked reactions of many psychologists to overly manipulative experiments in social psychology, we see the start of some preplanning of the ethical and social importance of psychological research before it begins. In the past the professional scientist with his own image of man and little accountability to anyone would occasionally abuse the general public's sense of value and even exploit their willingness to support science with some experiments of questionable relevance or even dangerous consequences for the subjects. The angry response of the public and the government for more accountability could be dangerous to free inquiry in science, but a happier outcome would be for the psychologists to screen their own behavior. Much of what psychology does is paid for by public funds, a resource with finite limits which should be respected. Science is, in fact, quite political, purposive and full of value judgments. As many psychologists turn their work toward the solving of the problems of society, we can foresee a fruitful sharing of those value judgments between the public and the psychologists. Psychology is too important to be left to the experts.

Giving psychology away. This means first giving psychologists away. The move of psychologists into the community where the social problems are is a trend that needs to be accelerated. We believe that psychology has much to offer to society, but the academic institutions are, for the most part, still clinging to a traditional method of educating people to perpetuate the older basic research ideas, resulting in an overabundance of people who are simply incapable of bringing psychological knowledge to bear on society's problems. Those problems are wholistic, complex, and quite practical. A new breed of researchers with a broad perspective plus large numbers of psychological technologists who can apply knowledge directly are desperately needed.[3]

We are optimistic about the future role of psychology in helping to restructure society by putting a top priority on the promotion of human welfare. The history of psychology has been marked by revolutions. Before we see one take place in the society at large, we dedicate this book to the next revolution in psychology.

"To begin with," he said heavily, "you've got to understand that a seagull is an unlimited idea of freedom, an image of the Great Gull, and your whole body, from wingtip to wingtip, is nothing more than your thought itself."

—*Richard Bach,* Jonathan Livingston Seagull

NOTES

1. I. Chein, *The Science of Behavior and the Image of Man* (New York: Basic Books, 1972), p. 6.
2. R. D. Laing, *The Politics of Experience* (New York: Ballantine, 1967).
3. G. A. Miller, "Psychology As a Means of Promoting Human Welfare," *American Psychologist* 24, no. 12 (1969): 1063–1075. See Appendix C.

APPENDIX A

Some Issues Concerning the Control of Human Behavior

A Symposium

CARL R. ROGERS AND B. F. SKINNER

1 [SKINNER]

Science is steadily increasing our power to influence, change, mold—in a word, control—human behavior. It has extended our "understanding" (whatever that may be) so that we deal more successfully with people in nonscientific ways, but it has also identified conditions or variables which can be used to predict and control behavior in a new, and increasingly rigorous, technology. The broad disciplines of government and economics offer examples of this, but there is special cogency in those contributions of anthropology, sociology, and psychology which deal with individual behavior. Carl Rogers has listed some of the achievements to date in a recent paper.[1] Those of his examples which show or imply the control of the single organism are primarily due, as we should expect, to psychology. It is the experimental study of behavior which carries us beyond awkward or inaccessible "principles," "factors," and so on, to variables which can be directly manipulated.

It is also, and for more or less the same reasons, the conception of human behavior emerging from an experimental analysis which most directly challenges traditional views. Psychologists themselves often do not seem to be aware of how far they have moved in this direction. But the change is not passing unnoticed by others. Until only recently it was customary to deny the possibility of a rigorous science of human behavior by arguing, either that a lawful science was impossible because man was a free agent, or that merely statistical predictions would always leave room for personal freedom. But those who used to take this line have become more vociferous in expressing their alarm at the way these obstacles are being surmounted.

Reprinted from *Science* 124, no. 3231 (30 November 1956), pp. 1057–1066.

Now, the control of human behavior has always been unpopular. Any undisguised effort to control usually arouses emotional reactions. We hesitate to admit, even to ourselves, that we are engaged in control, and we may refuse to control, even when this would be helpful, for fear of criticism. Those who have explicitly avowed an interest in control have been roughly treated by history. Machiavelli is the great prototype. As Macaulay said of him, "Out of his surname they coined an epithet for a knave and out of his Christian name a synonym for the devil." There were obvious reasons. The control that Machiavelli analyzed and recommended, like most political control, used techniques that were aversive to the controllee. The threats and punishments of the bully, like those of the government operating on the same plan, are not designed—whatever their success—to endear themselves to those who are controlled. Even when the techniques themselves are not aversive, control is usually exercised for the selfish purposes of the controller and, hence, has indirectly punishing effects upon others.

Man's natural inclination to revolt against selfish control has been exploited to good purpose in what we call the philosophy and literature of democracy. The doctrine of the rights of man has been effective in arousing individuals to concerted action against governmental and religious tyranny. The literature which has had this effect has greatly extended the number of terms in our language which express reactions to the control of men. But the ubiquity and ease of expression of this attitude spells trouble for any science which may give birth to a powerful technology of behavior. Intelligent men and women, dominated by the humanistic philosophy of the past two centuries, cannot view with equanimity what Andrew Hacker has called "the specter of predictable man."[2] Even the statistical or actuarial prediction of human events, such as the number of fatalities to be expected on a holiday weekend, strikes many people as uncanny and evil, while the prediction and control of individual behavior is regarded as little less than the work of the devil. I am not so much concerned here with the political or economic consequences for psychology, although research following certain channels may well suffer harmful effects. We ourselves, as intelligent men and women, and as exponents of Western thought, share these attitudes. They have already interfered with the free exercise of a scientific analysis, and their influence threatens to assume more serious proportions.

Three broad areas of human behavior supply good examples. The first of these—*personal control*—may be taken to include person-to-person relationships in the family, among friends, in social and work groups, and in counseling and psychotherapy. Other fields are *education* and *government*. A few examples from each will show how nonscientific preconceptions are affecting our current thinking about human behavior.

Personal Control

People living together in groups come to control one another with a technique which is not inappropriately called "ethical." When an individual behaves in a fashion acceptable to the group, he receives admiration, approval, affection, and many other reinforcements which increase the likelihood that he will continue to behave in that fashion. When his behavior is not acceptable, he is criticized, censured, blamed, or otherwise punished. In the first case the group calls him "good"; in the second, "bad." This practice is so thoroughly ingrained in our culture that we often fail to see that it is a technique of control. Yet we are almost always engaged in such control, even though the reinforcements and punishments are often subtle.

The practice of admiration is an important part of a culture, because behavior which is otherwise inclined to be weak can be set up and maintained with its help. The individual is especially likely to be praised, admired, or loved when he acts for the group in the face of great danger, for example, or sacrifices himself or his possessions, or submits to prolonged hardship, or suffers martyrdom. These actions are not admirable in any absolute sense, but they require admiration if they are to be strong. Similarly, we admire people who behave in original or exceptional ways, not because such behavior is itself admirable, but because we do not know how to encourage original or exceptional behavior in any other way. The group acclaims independent, unaided behavior in part because it is easier to reinforce than to help.

As long as this technique of control is misunderstood, we cannot judge correctly an environment in which there is less need for heroism, hardship, or independent action. We are likely to argue that such an environment is itself less admirable or produces less admirable people. In the old days, for example, young scholars often lived in undesirable quarters, ate unappetizing or inadequate food, performed unprofitable tasks for a living or to pay for necessary books and materials or publication. Older scholars and other members of the group offered compensating reinforcement in the form of approval and admiration for these sacrifices. When the modern graduate student receives a generous scholarship, enjoys good living conditions, and has his research and publication subsidized, the grounds for evaluation seem to be pulled from under us. Such a student no longer *needs* admiration to carry him over a series of obstacles (no matter how much he may need it for other reasons), and, in missing certain familiar objects of admiration, we are likely to conclude that such *conditions* are less admirable. Obstacles to scholarly work may serve as a useful measure of motivation—and we may go wrong unless some substitute is found—but we can scarcely defend a deliberate harassment of the student for this purpose. The productivity of any set of conditions can be evaluated only when we have freed ourselves of the attitudes which have been generated in us as members of an ethical group.

A similar difficulty arises from our use of punishment in the form of censure or blame. The concept of responsibility and the related concepts of foreknowledge and choice are used to justify techniques of control using punishment. Was So-and-So aware of the probable consequences of his action, and was the action deliberate? If so, we are justified in punishing him. But what does this mean? It appears to be a question concerning the efficacy of the contingent relations between behavior and punishing consequences. We punish behavior because it is objectionable to us or the group, but in a minor refinement of rather recent origin we have come to withhold punishment when it cannot be expected to have any effect. If the objectionable consequences of an act were accidental and not likely to occur again, there is no point in punishing. We say that the individual was not "aware of the consequences of his action" or that the consequences were not "intentional." If the action could not have been avoided—if the individual "had no choice"—punishment is also withheld, as it is if the individual is incapable of being changed by punishment because he is of "unsound mind." In all these cases—different as they are—the individual is held "not responsible" and goes unpunished.

Just as we say that it is "not fair" to punish a man for something he could not help doing, so we call it "unfair" when one is rewarded beyond his due or for something he could not help doing. In other words, we also object to wasting *reinforcers* where they are not needed or will do no good. We make the same point with the words *just* and *right*. Thus we have no right to punish the irresponsible, and a man has no right to reinforcers he does not earn or deserve. But concepts of choice, responsibility, justice, and so on, provide a most inadequate analysis of efficient reinforcing and punishing contingencies because they carry a heavy semantic cargo of a quite different sort, which obscures any attempt to clarify controlling practices or to improve techniques. In particular, they fail to prepare us for techniques based on other than aversive techniques of control. Most people would object to forcing prisoners to serve as subjects of dangerous medical experiments, but few object when they are induced to serve by the offer of return privileges—even when the reinforcing effect of these privileges has been created by forcible deprivation. In the traditional scheme the right to refuse guarantees the individual against coercion or an unfair bargain. But to what extent *can* a prisoner refuse under such circumstances?

We need not go so far afield to make the point. We can observe our own attitude toward personal freedom in the way we resent any interference with what we want to do. Suppose we want to buy a car of a particular sort. Then we may object, for example, if our wife urges us to buy a less expensive model and to put the difference into a new refrigerator. Or we may resent it if our neighbor questions our need for such a car or our ability to pay for it. We would certainly resent it if it were illegal to buy such a car (remember Prohibition); and if we find we cannot actually afford it, we may resent governmental control of the price through tariffs and taxes. We resent it if we discover that we cannot get the car because the manufacturer is holding the model in deliberately short supply in order to push a model we do not want. In all this we assert our democratic right to buy the car of our choice. We are well prepared to do so and to resent any restriction on our freedom.

But why do we not ask *why* it is the car of our choice and resent the forces which made it so? Perhaps our favorite toy as a child was a car, of a very different model, but nevertheless bearing the name of the car we now want. Perhaps our favorite TV program is sponsored by the manufacturer of that car. Perhaps we have seen pictures of many beautiful or prestigeful persons driving it—in pleasant or glamorous places. Perhaps the car has been designed with respect to our motivational patterns: the device on the hood is a phallic symbol; or the horsepower has been stepped up to please our competitive spirit in enabling us to pass other cars swiftly (or, as the advertisements say, "safely"). The concept of freedom that has emerged as part of the cultural practice of our group makes little or no provision for recognizing or dealing with these kinds of control. Concepts like "responsibility" and "rights" are scarcely applicable. We are prepared to deal with coercive measures, but we have no traditional recourse with respect to other measures which in the long run (and especially with the help of science) may be much more powerful and dangerous.

Education

The techniques of education were once frankly aversive. The teacher was usually older and stronger than his pupils and was able to "make them learn." This meant that they were not actually taught but were surrounded by a threatening world from which they could escape only by learning. Usually they were left to their own resources in discovering how to do so. Claude Coleman has published a grimly amusing reminder of these older practices.[3] He tells of a schoolteacher who published a careful account of his services during 51 years of teaching, during which he administered: ". . . 911,527 blows with a cane; 124,010 with a rod; 20,989 with a ruler; 136,715 with the hand; 10,295 over the mouth; 7,905 boxes on the ear; [and] 1,115,800 slaps on the head. . . ."

Progressive education was a humanitarian effort to substitute positive reinforcement for such aversive measures, but in the search for useful human values in the classroom it has never fully replaced the variables it abandoned. Viewed as a branch of behavioral technology, education remains relatively inefficient. We supplement it, and rationalize it, by admiring the pupil who learns *for himself;* and we often attribute the learning process, or knowledge itself, to something *inside* the individual. We admire behavior which seems to have inner sources. Thus we admire one who *recites* a poem more than one who simply *reads* it. We admire one who *knows* the answer more than one who *knows where to look it up.* We admire the *writer* rather than the *reader.* We admire the arithmetician who can do a problem in his head rather than with a slide rule or calculating machine, or in "original" ways rather than by a strict application of rules. In general we feel that any aid or "crutch"—except those aids to which we are now thoroughly accustomed—reduces the credit due. In Plato's *Phaedus,* Thamus, the king, attacks the invention of the alphabet on similar grounds! He is afraid "it will produce forgetfulness in the minds of those who learn to use it, because they will not practice their memories. . . ." In other words, he holds it more admirable to remember than to use a memorandum. He also objects that pupils "will read many things without instruction . . . [and] will therefore seem to know many things when they are for the most part ignorant." In the same vein we are today sometimes contemptuous of book learning, but, as educators, we can scarcely afford to adopt this view without reservation.

By admiring the student for knowledge and blaming him for ignorance, we escape some of the responsibility of teaching him. We resist any analysis of the educational process which threatens the notion of inner wisdom or questions the contention that the fault of ignorance lies with the student. More powerful techniques which bring about the same changes in behavior by manipulating *external* variables are decried as brainwashing or thought control. We are quite unprepared to judge *effective* educational measures. As long as only a few pupils learn much of what is taught, we do not worry about uniformity or regimentation. We do not fear the feeble technique; but we should view with dismay a system under which every student learned everything listed in a syllabus—although such a condition is far from unthinkable. Similarly, we do not fear a system which is so defective that the student must *work* for an education; but we are loath to give credit for anything learned without effort—although this could well be taken as an ideal result—and we flatly refuse to give credit if the student already knows what a school teaches.

A world in which people are wise and good without trying, without "having to be," without "choosing to be," could conceivably be a far better world for everyone. In such a world we should not have to "give anyone credit"—we should not need to admire anyone—for being wise and good. From our present point of view we cannot believe that such a world would be admirable. We do not even permit ourselves to imagine what it would be like.

Government

Government has always been the special field of aversive control. The state is frequently defined in terms of the power to punish, and jurisprudence leans heavily upon the associated notion of personal responsibility. Yet it is becoming increasingly difficult to reconcile current practice and theory with these earlier views. In criminology, for example, there is a strong tendency to drop the notion of responsibility in favor of some such alternative as capacity or controllability. But no matter how strongly the facts, or even practical expedience, support such a change, it is difficult to make the change in a legal system designed on a different plan. When governments resort to other techniques (for example, positive reinforcement), the concept of responsibility is no longer relevant and the theory of government is no longer applicable.

The conflict is illustrated by two decisions of the Supreme Court in the 1930's which dealt with, and disagreed on, the definition of control or coercion.[4] The Agricultural Adjustment Act proposed that the Secretary of Agriculture make "rental or benefit payments" to those farmers who agreed to reduce production. The government agreed that the Act would be unconstitutional if the farmer had been *compelled* to reduce production but was not, since he was merely *invited* to do so. Justice Roberts expressed the contrary majority view of the court that "The power to confer or withhold unlimited benefits is the power to coerce or destroy." This recognition of positive reinforcement was withdrawn a few years later in another case in which Justice Cardozo wrote "To hold that motive or temptation is equivalent to coercion is to plunge the law in endless difficulties."[5] We may agree with him, without implying that the proposition is therefore wrong. Sooner or later the law must be prepared to deal with all possible techniques of governmental control.

The uneasiness with which we view government (in the broadest possible sense) when it does not use punishment is shown by the reception of my utopian novel, *Walden Two*.[6] This was essentially a proposal to apply a behavioral technology to the construction of a workable, effective, and productive pattern of government. It was greeted with wrathful violence. *Life* magazine called it "a travesty on the good life," and "a menace . . . a triumph of mortmain or the dead hand not envisaged since the days of Sparta . . . a slur upon a name, a corruption of an impulse." Joseph Wood Krutch devoted a substantial part of his book, *The Measure of Man*,[7] to attacking my views and those of the protagonist, Frazier, in the same vein, and Morris Viteles has recently criticized the book in a similar manner in *Science*.[8] Perhaps the reaction is best expressed in a quotation from *The Quest for Utopia* by Negley and Patrick:

"Halfway through this contemporary utopia, the reader may feel sure, as we did, that this is a beautifully ironic satire on what has been called 'behavioral engineering.' The longer one stays in this better world of the psychologist, however, the plainer it becomes that the inspiration is not satiric, but messianic. This is indeed the behaviorally engineered society, and while it was to be expected that sooner or later the principle of psychological conditioning would be made the basis of a serious construction of utopia—Brown anticipated it in *Limanora*—yet not even the effective satire of Huxley is adequate preparation for the shocking horror of the idea when positively presented. Of all the dictatorships espoused by utopists, this is the most profound, and incipient dictators might well find in this utopia a guidebook of political practice."[9]

One would scarcely guess that the authors are talking about a world in which there is food, clothing, and shelter for all, where everyone chooses his own work and works on the average only 4 hours a day, where music and the arts flourish, where personal relationships develop under the most favorable circumstances, where education prepares every child for the social and intellectual life which lies before him, where—in short—people are truly happy, secure, productive, creative, and forward-looking. What is wrong with it? Only one thing: someone "planned it that way." If these critics had come upon a society in some remote corner of the world which boasted similar advantages, they would undoubtedly have hailed it as providing a pattern we all might well follow—provided that it was clearly the result of a natural process of cultural evolution. Any evidence that intelligence had been used in arriving at this version of the good life would, in their eyes, be a serious flaw. No matter if the planner of *Walden Two* diverts none of the proceeds of the community to his own use, no matter if he has no current control or is, indeed, unknown to most of the other members of the community (he planned that, too), somewhere back of it all he occupies the position of prime mover. And this, to the child of the democratic tradition, spoils it all.

The dangers inherent in the control of human behavior are very real. The possibility of the misuse of scientific knowledge must always be faced. We cannot escape by denying the power of a science of behavior or arresting its development. It is no help to cling to familiar philosophies of human behavior simply because they are more reassuring. As I have pointed out elsewhere,[10] the new techniques emerging from a science of behavior must be subject to the explicit countercontrol which has already been applied to earlier and cruder forms. Brute force and deception, for example, are now fairly generally suppressed by ethical practices and by explicit governmental and religious agencies. A similar countercontrol of scientific knowledge in the interests of the group is a feasible and promising possibility. Although we cannot say how devious the course of its evolution may be, a cultural pattern of control and countercontrol will presumably emerge which will be most widely supported because it is most widely reinforcing.

If we cannot foresee all the details of this (as we obviously cannot), it is important to remember that this is true of the critics of science as well. The dire consequences of new techniques of control, the hidden menace in original cultural designs—these need some proof. It is only another example of my present point that the need for proof is so often overlooked. Man has got himself into some pretty fixes, and it is easy to believe that he will do so again. But there is a more optimistic possibility. The slow growth of the methods of science, now for the first time being applied to human affairs, *may* mean a new and exciting phase of human life to which historical analogies will not apply and in which earlier political slogans will not be appropriate. If we are to use the knowledge that a science of behavior is now making available with any hope of success, we must look at human nature as it is brought into focus through the methods of science rather than as it has been presented to us in a series of historical accidents.

If the advent of a powerful science of behavior causes trouble, it will not be because science itself is inimical to human welfare but because older conceptions have not yielded easily or gracefully. We expect resistance to new techniques of control from those who have heavy investments in the old, but we have no reason to help them preserve a series of principles that are not ends in themselves but rather outmoded means to an end. What is needed is a new conception of human behavior which is compatible with the implications of a scientific analysis. All men control and are controlled. The question of government in the broadest possible sense is not how freedom is to be preserved but what kinds of control are to be used and to what ends. Control must be analyzed and considered in its proper proportions. No one, I am sure, wishes to develop new master-slave relationships or bend the will of the people to despotic rulers in new ways. These are patterns of control appropriate to a world without science. They may well be the first to go when the experimental analysis of behavior comes into its own in the design of cultural practices.

II [ROGERS]

There are, I believe, a number of matters in connection with this important topic on which the authors of this article, and probably a large majority of psychologists, are in agreement. These matters then are not issues as far as we are concerned, and I should like to mention them briefly in order to put them to one side.

Points of Agreement

I am sure we agree that men—as individuals and as societies—have always endeavored to understand, predict, influence, and control human behavior—their own behavior and that of others.

I believe we agree that the behavioral sciences are making and will continue to make increasingly rapid progress in the understanding of behavior, and that as a consequence the capacity to predict and to control behavior is developing with equal rapidity.

I believe we agree that to deny these advances, or to claim that man's behavior cannot be a field of science, is unrealistic. Even though this is not an issue for us, we should recognize that many intelligent men still hold strongly to the view that the actions of men are free in some sense such that scientific knowledge of man's behavior is impossible. Thus Reinhold Niebuhr, the noted theologian, heaps scorn on the concept of psychology as a science of man's behavior and even says, "In any event, no scientific investigation of past behavior can become the basis of predictions of future behavior."[11] So, while this is not an issue for psychologists, we should at least notice in passing that it is an issue for many people.

I believe we are in agreement that the tremendous potential power of a science which permits the prediction and control of behavior may be misused, and that the possibility of such misuse constitutes a serious threat.

Consequently Skinner and I are in agreement that the whole question of the scientific control of human behavior is a matter with which psychologists and the general public should concern themselves. As Robert Oppenheimer told the American Psychological Association last year the problems that psychologists will pose for society by their growing ability to control behavior will be much more grave than the problems posed by the ability of physicists to control the reactions of matter.[12] I am not sure whether psychologists generally recognize this. My impression is that by and large they hold a laissez-faire attitude. Obviously Skinner and I do not hold this laissez-faire view, or we would not have written this article.

Points at Issue

With these several points of basic and important agreement, are there then any issues that remain on which there are differences? I believe there are. They can be stated very briefly: Who will be controlled? Who will exercise control? What type of control will be exercised? Most important of all, toward what end or what purpose, or in the pursuit of what value, will control be exercised?

452

It is on questions of this sort that there exist ambiguities, misunderstandings, and probably deep differences. These differences exist among psychologists, among members of the general public in this country, and among various world cultures. Without any hope of achieving a final resolution of these questions, we can, I believe, put these issues in clearer form.

Some Meanings

To avoid ambiguity and faulty communication, I would like to clarify the meanings of some of the terms we are using.

Behavioral science is a term that might be defined from several angles but in the context of this discussion it refers primarily to knowledge that the existence of certain describable conditions in the human being and/or in his environment is followed by certain describable consequences in his actions.

Prediction means the prior identification of behaviors which then occur. Because it is important in some things I wish to say later, I would point out that one may predict a highly specific behavior, such as an eye blink, or one may predict a class of behaviors. One might correctly predict "avoidant behavior," for example, without being able to specify whether the individual will run away or simply close his eyes.

The word *control* is a very slippery one, which can be used with any one of several meanings. I would like to specify three that seem most important for our present purposes. *Control* may mean: (i) The setting of conditions by B for A, A having no voice in the matter, such that certain predictable behaviors then occur in A. I refer to this as external control. (ii) The setting of conditions by B for A, A giving some degree of consent to these conditions, such that certain predictable behaviors then occur in A. I refer to this as the influence of B on A. (iii) The setting of conditions by A such that certain predictable behaviors then occur in himself. I refer to this as internal control. It will be noted that Skinner lumps together the first two meanings, external control and influence, under the concept of control. I find this confusing.

Usual Concept of Control of Human Behavior

With the underbrush thus cleared away (I hope), let us review very briefly the various elements that are involved in the usual concept of the control of human behavior as mediated by the behavioral sciences. I am drawing here on the previous writings of Skinner, on his present statements, on the writings of others who have considered in either friendly or antagonistic fashion the meanings that would be involved in such control. I have not excluded the science fiction writers, as reported recently by Vandenberg,[13] since they often show an awareness of the issues involved, even though the methods described are as yet fictional. These then are the elements that seem common to these different concepts of the application of science to human behavior.

1) There must first be some sort of decision about goals. Usually desirable goals are assumed, but sometimes, as in George Orwell's book *1984*, the goal that is selected is an aggrandizement of individual power with which most of us would disagree. In a recent paper Skinner suggests that one possible set of goals to be assigned to the behavioral technology is this: "Let men be happy, informed, skillful, well-behaved and productive."[14] In the first draft of his part of this article, which he was kind enough to show me, he did not mention such definite goals as these, but desired "improved" educational practices, "wiser" use of knowledge in government, and the like. In the final version of his article he avoids even these value-laden terms, and his implicit goal is the very general one that scientific control of behavior is desirable, because it would perhaps bring "a far better world for everyone."

Thus the first step in thinking about the control of human behavior is the choice of goals, whether specific or general. It is necessary to come to terms in some way with the issue, "For what purpose?"

2) A second element is that, whether the end selected is highly specific or is a very general one such as wanting "a better world," we proceed by the methods of science to discover the means to these ends. We continue through further experimentation and investigation to discover more effective means. The method of science is self-correcting in thus arriving at increasingly effective ways of achieving the purpose we have in mind.

3) The third aspect of such control is that as the conditions or methods are discovered by which to reach the goal, some person or some group establishes these conditions and uses these methods having in one way or another obtained the power to do so.

4) The fourth element is the exposure of individuals to the prescribed conditions, and this leads, with a high degree of probability, to behavior which is in line with the goals desired. Individuals are now happy, if that has been the goal, or well-behaved, or submissive, or whatever it has been decided to make them.

5) The fifth element is that if the process I have described is put in motion then there is a continuing social organization which will continue to produce the types of behavior that have been valued.

Some Flaws

Are there any flaws in this way of viewing the control of human behavior? I believe there are. In fact the only element in this description with which I find myself in agreement is the second. It seems to me quite incontrovertibly true that the scientific method is an excellent way to discover the means by which to achieve our goals. Beyond that, I feel many sharp differences, which I will try to spell out.

I believe that in Skinner's presentation here and in his previous writings, there is a serious underestimation of the problem of power. To hope that the power which is being made available by the behavioral sciences will be exercised by the scientists, or by a benevolent group, seems to me a hope little supported by either recent or distant history. It seems far more likely that behavioral scientists, holding their present attitudes, will be in the position of the German rocket scientists specializing in guided missiles. First they worked devotedly for Hitler to destroy the U.S.S.R. and the United States. Now, depending on who captured them, they work devotedly for the U.S.S.R. in the interest of destroying the United States, or devotedly for the United States in the interest of destroying the U.S.S.R. If behavioral scientists are concerned solely with advancing their science, it seems most probable that they will serve the purposes of whatever individual or group has the power.

But the major flaw I see in this review of what is involved in the scientific control of human behavior is the denial, misunderstanding, or gross underestimation of the place of ends, goals or values in their relationship to science. This error (as it seems to me) has so many implications that I would like to devote some space to it.

Ends and Values in Relation to Science

In sharp contradiction to some views that have been advanced, I would like to propose a two-pronged thesis: (i) In any scientific endeavor—whether "pure" or applied science—there is a prior subjective choice of the purpose or value which that scientific work is perceived as serving. (ii) This subjective value choice which brings the scientific endeavor into being must always lie outside of that endeavor and can never became a part of the science involved in that endeavor.

Let me illustrate the first point from Skinner himself. It is clear that in his earlier writing[15] it is recognized that a prior value choice is necessary, and it is specified as the goal that men are to become happy, well-behaved, productive, and so on. I am pleased that Skinner has retreated from the goals he then chose, because to me they seem to be stultifying values. I can only feel that he was choosing these goals for others, not for himself. I would hate to see Skinner become "well-behaved," as that term would be defined for him by behavioral scientists. His recent article in the *American Psychologist*[16] shows that he certainly does not want to be "productive" as that value is defined by most psychologists. And the most awful fate I can imagine for him would be to have him constantly "happy." It is the fact that he is very unhappy about many things which makes me prize him.

In the first draft of his part of this article, he also included such prior value choices, saying for example, "We must decide how we are to use the knowledge which a science of human behavior is now making available." Now he has dropped all mention of such choices, and if I understand him correctly, he believes that science can proceed without them. He has suggested this view in another recent paper, stating that "We must continue to experiment in cultural design . . . testing the consequences as we go. Eventually the practices which make for the greatest biological and psychological strength of the group will presumably survive."[17]

I would point out, however, that to choose to experiment is a value choice. Even to move in the direction of perfectly random experimentation is a value choice. To test the consequences of an experiment is possible only if we have first made a subjective choice of a criterion value. And implicit in his statement is a valuing of biological and psychological strength. So even when trying to avoid such choice, it seems inescapable that a prior subjective value choice is necessary for any scientific endeavor, or for any application of scientific knowledge.

I wish to make it clear that I am not saying that values cannot be included as a subject of science. It is not true that science deals only with certain classes of "facts" and that these classes do not include values. It is a bit more complex than that, as a simple illustration or two may make clear.

If I value knowledge of the "three R's" as a goal of education, the methods of science can give me increasingly accurate information on how this goal may be achieved. If I value problem-solving ability as a goal of education, the scientific method can give me the same kind of help.

Now, if I wish to determine whether problem-solving ability is "better" than knowledge of the three R's, then scientific method can also study those two values but *only*—and this is very important—in terms of some other value which I have subjectively chosen. I may value college success. Then I can determine whether problem-solving ability or knowledge of the three R's is most closely associated with that value. I may value personal integration or vocational success or responsible citizenship. I can determine whether problem-solving ability or knowledge of the three R's is "better" for achieving any one of these values. But the value or purpose that gives meaning to a particular scientific endeavor must always lie outside of that endeavor.

Although our concern in this symposium is largely with applied science, what I have been saying seems equally true of so-called "pure" science. In pure science the usual prior subjective value choice is the discovery of truth. But this is a subjective choice, and science can never say whether it is the best choice, save in the light of some other value. Geneticists in the U.S.S.R., for example, had to make a subjective choice of whether it was better to pursue truth or to discover facts which upheld a governmental dogma. Which choice is "better"? We could make a scientific investigation of those alternatives but only in the light of some other subjectively chosen value. If, for example, we value the survival of a culture, then we could begin to investigate with the methods of science the question of whether pursuit of truth or support of governmental dogma is most closely associated with cultural survival.

My point then is that any endeavor in science, pure or applied, is carried on in the pursuit of a purpose or value that is subjectively chosen by persons. It is important that this choice be made explicit, since the particular value which is being sought can never be tested or evaluated, confirmed or denied, by the scientific endeavor to which it gives birth. The initial purpose or value always and necessarily lies outside the scope of the scientific effort which it sets in motion.

Among other things this means that if we choose some particular goal or series of goals for human beings and then set out on a large scale to control human behavior to the end of achieving those goals, we are locked in the rigidity of our initial choice, because such a scientific endeavor can never transcend itself to select new goals. Only subjective human persons can do that. Thus if we chose as our goal the state of happiness for human beings (a goal deservedly ridiculed by Aldous Huxley in *Brave New World*), and if we involved all of society in a successful scientific program by which people became happy, we would be locked in a colossal rigidity in which no one would be free to question this goal, because our scientific operations could not transcend themselves to question their guiding purposes. And without laboring this point, I would remark that colossal rigidity, whether in dinosaurs or dictatorships, has a very poor record of evolutionary survival.

If, however, a part of our scheme is to set free some "planners" who do not have to be happy, who are not controlled, and who are therefore free to choose other values, this has several meanings. It means that the purpose we have chosen as our goal is not a sufficient and a satisfying one for human beings but must be supplemented. It also means that if it is necessary to set up an elite group which is free, then this shows all too clearly that the great majority are only the slaves—no matter by what high-sounding name we call them—of those who select the goals.

Perhaps, however, the thought is that a continuing scientific endeavor will evolve its own goals; that the initial findings will alter the directions, and subsequent findings will alter them still further, and that science somehow develops its own purpose. Although he does not clearly say so, this appears to be the pattern Skinner has in mind. It is

457

surely a reasonable description, but it overlooks one element in this continuing development, which is that subjective personal choice enters in at every point at which the direction changes. The findings of a science, the results of an experiment, do not and never can tell us what next scientific purpose to pursue. Even in the purest of science, the scientist must decide what the findings mean and must subjectively choose what next step will be most profitable in the pursuit of his purpose. And if we are speaking of the application of scientific knowledge, then it is distressingly clear that the increasing scientific knowledge of the structure of the atom carries with it no necessary choice as to the purpose to which this knowledge will be put. This is a subjective personal choice which must be made by many individuals.

Thus I return to the proposition with which I began this section of my remarks—and which I now repeat in different words. Science has its meaning as the objective pursuit of a purpose which has been subjectively chosen by a person or persons. This purpose or value can never be investigated by the particular scientific experiment or investigation to which it has given birth and meaning. Consequently, any discussion of the control of human beings by the behavioral sciences must first and most deeply concern itself with the subjectively chosen purposes which such an application of science is intended to implement.

Is the Situation Hopeless?

The thoughtful reader may recognize that, although my remarks up to this point have introduced some modifications in the conception of the processes by which human behavior will be controlled, these remarks may have made such control seem, if anything, even more inevitable. We might sum it up this way: Behavioral science is clearly moving forward; the increasing power for control which it gives will be held by someone or some group; such an individual or group will surely choose the values or goals to be achieved; and most of us will then be increasingly controlled by means so subtle that we will not even be aware of them as controls. Thus, whether a council of wise psychologists (if this is not a contradiction in terms), or a Stalin, or a Big Brother has the power, and whether the goal is happiness, or productivity, or resolution of the Oedipus complex, or submission, or love of Big Brother, we will inevitably find ourselves moving toward the chosen goal and probably thinking that we ourselves desire it. Thus, if this line of reasoning is correct, it appears that some form of *Walden Two* or of *1984* (and at a deep philosophic level they seem indistinguishable) is coming. The fact that it would surely arrive piecemeal, rather than all at once, does not greatly change the fundamental issues. In any event, as Skinner has indicated in his writings, we would then look back upon the concepts of human freedom, the capacity for choice, the responsibility for choice, and the worth of the human individual as historical curiosities which once existed by cultural accident as values in a prescientific civilization.

I believe that any person observant of trends must regard something like the foregoing sequence as a real possibility. It is not simply a fantasy. Something of that sort may even be the most likely future. But is it an inevitable future? I want to devote the remainder of my remarks to an alternative possibility.

Alternative Set of Values

Suppose we start with a set of ends, values, purposes, quite different from the type of goals we have been considering. Suppose we do this quite openly, setting them forth as a possible value choice to be accepted or rejected. Suppose we select a set of values that focuses on fluid elements of process rather than static attributes. We might then value: man as a process of becoming, as a process of achieving worth and dignity through the development of his potentialities; the individual human being as a self-actualizing process, moving on to more challenging and enriching experiences, the process by which the individual creatively adapts to an ever-new and changing world; the process by which knowledge transcends itself, as, for example, the theory of relativity transcended Newtonian physics, itself to be transcended in some future day by a new perception.

If we select values such as these we turn to our science and technology of behavior with a very different set of questions. We will want to know such things as these: Can science aid in the discovery of new modes of richly rewarding living? more meaningful and satisfying modes of interpersonal relationships? Can science inform us on how the human race can become a more intelligent participant in its own evolution—its physical, psychological and social evolution? Can science inform us on ways of releasing the creative capacity of individuals, which seem so necessary if we are to survive in this fantastically expanding atomic age? Oppenheimer has pointed out[18] that knowledge, which used to double in millennia or centuries, now doubles in a generation or a decade. It appears that we must discover the utmost in release of creativity if we are to be able to adapt effectively. In short, can science discover the methods by which man can most readily become a continually developing and self-transcending process, in his behavior, his thinking, his knowledge? Can science predict and release an essentially "unpredictable" freedom?

It is one of the virtues of science as a method that it is as able to advance and implement goals and purposes of this sort as it is to serve static values, such as states of being well-informed, happy, obedient. Indeed we have some evidence of this.

459

Small Example

I will perhaps be forgiven if I document some of the possibilities along this line by turning to psychotherapy, the field I know best.

Psychotherapy, as Meerloo[19] and others have pointed out, can be one of the most subtle tools for the control of *A* by *B*. The therapist can subtly mold individuals in imitation of himself. He can cause an individual to become a submissive and conforming being. When certain therapeutic principles are used in extreme fashion, we call it brainwashing, an instance of the disintegration of the personality and a reformulation of the person along lines desired by the controlling individual. So the principles of therapy can be used as an effective means of external control of human personality and behavior. Can psychotherapy be anything else?

Here I find the developments going on in client-centered psychotherapy[20] an exciting hint of what a behavioral science can do in achieving the kinds of values I have stated. Quite aside from being a somewhat new orientation in psychotherapy, this development has important implications regarding the relation of a behavioral science to the control of human behavior. Let me describe our experience as it relates to the issues of this discussion.

In client-centered therapy, we are deeply engaged in the prediction and influencing of behavior, or even the control of behavior. As therapists, we institute certain attitudinal conditions, and the client has relatively little voice in the establishment of these conditions. We predict that if these conditions are instituted, certain behavioral consequences will ensue in the client. Up to this point this is largely external control, no different from what Skinner has described, and no different from what I have discussed in the preceding sections of this article. But here any similarity ceases.

The conditions we have chosen to establish predict such behavioral consequences as these: that the client will become self-directing, less rigid, more open to the evidence of his senses, better organized and integrated, more similar to the ideal which he has chosen for himself. In other words, we have established by external control conditions which we predict will be followed by internal control by the individual, in pursuit of internally chosen goals. We have set the conditions which predict various classes of behaviors—self-directing behaviors, sensitivity to realities within and without, flexible adaptiveness—which are by their very nature unpredictable in their specifics. Our recent research[21] indicates that our predictions are to a significant degree corroborated, and our commitment to the scientific method causes us to believe that more effective means of achieving these goals may be realized.

Research exists in other fields—industry, education, group dynamics—which seems to support our own findings. I believe it may be conservatively stated that scientific progress has been made in identifying those conditions in an interpersonal relationship which, if they exist in *B*, are followed in *A* by greater maturity in behavior, less dependence on others, an increase in expressiveness as a person, an increase in variability, flexibility and effectiveness of adaptation, an increase in self-responsibility and self-direction. And, quite in contrast to the concern expressed by some, we do not find that the creatively adaptive behavior which results from such self-directed variability of expression is a "happy accident" which occurs in "chaos." Rather, the individual who is open to his experience, and self-directing, is harmonious not chaotic, ingenious rather than random, as he orders his responses imaginatively toward the achievement of his own purposes. His creative actions are no more a "happy accident" than was Einstein's development of the theory of relativity.

Thus we find ourselves in fundamental agreement with John Dewey's statement: "Science has made its way by releasing, not by suppressing, the elements of variation, of invention and innovation, of novel creation in individuals."[22] Progress in personal life and in group living is, we believe, made in the same way.

Possible Concept of the Control of Human Behavior

It is quite clear that the point of view I am expressing is in sharp contrast to the usual conception of the relationship of the behavioral sciences to the control of human behavior. In order to make this contrast even more blunt, I will state this possibility in paragraphs parallel to those used before.

1) It is possible for us to choose to value man as a self-actualizing process of becoming; to value creativity, and the process by which knowledge becomes self-transcending.

2) We can proceed, by the methods of science, to discover the conditions which necessarily precede these processes and, through continuing experimentation, to discover better means of achieving these purposes.

3) It is possible for individuals or groups to set these conditions, with a minimum of power or control. According to present knowledge, the only authority necessary is the authority to establish certain qualities of interpersonal relationship.

4) Exposed to these conditions, present knowledge suggests that individuals become more self-responsible, make progress in self-actualization, become more flexible, and become more creatively adaptive.

5) Thus such an initial choice would inaugurate the beginnings of a social system or subsystem in which values, knowledge, adaptive

skills, and even the concept of science would be continually changing and self-transcending. The emphasis would be upon man as a process of becoming.

I believe it is clear that such a view as I have been describing does not lead to any definable utopia. It would be impossible to predict its final outcome. It involves a step-by-step development, based on a continuing subjective choice of purposes, which are implemented by the behavioral sciences. It is in the direction of the "open society," as that term has been defined by Popper,[23] where individuals carry responsibility for personal decisions. It is at the opposite pole from his concept of the closed society, of which *Walden Two* would be an example.

I trust it is also evident that the whole emphasis is on process, not on end-states of being. I am suggesting that it is by choosing to value certain qualitative elements of the process of becoming that we can find a pathway toward the open society.

The Choice

It is my hope that we have helped to clarify the range of choice which will lie before us and our children in regard to the behavioral sciences. We can choose to use our growing knowledge to enslave people in ways never dreamed of before, depersonalizing them, controlling them by means so carefully selected that they will perhaps never be aware of their loss of personhood. We can choose to utilize our scientific knowledge to make men happy, well-behaved, and productive, as Skinner earlier suggested. Or we can insure that each person learns all the syllabus which we select and set before him, as Skinner now suggests. Or at the other end of the spectrum of choice we can choose to use the behavioral sciences in ways which will free, not control; which will bring about constructive variability, not conformity; which will develop creativity, not contentment; which will facilitate each person in his self-directed process of becoming; which will aid individuals, groups, and even the concept of science to become self-transcending in freshly adaptive ways of meeting life and its problems. The choice is up to us, and, the human race being what it is, we are likely to stumble about, making at times some nearly disastrous value choices and at other times highly constructive ones.

I am aware that to some, this setting forth of a choice is unrealistic, because a choice of values is regarded as not possible. Skinner has stated: "Man's vaunted creative powers . . . his capacity to choose and our right to hold him responsible for his choice—none of these is conspicuous in this new self-portrait (provided by science). Man, we once believed, was free to express himself in art, music, and literature, to inquire into nature, to seek salvation in his own way. He could initiate action and make spontaneous and capricious changes of course.

. . . But science insists that action is initiated by forces impinging upon the individual, and that caprice is only another name for behavior for which we have not yet found a cause."[24]

I can understand this point of view, and I believe that it avoids looking at the great paradox of behavioral science. Behavior, when it is examined scientifically is surely best understood as determined by prior causation. This is one great fact of science. But responsible personal choice, which is the most essential element in being a person, which is the core experience in psychotherapy, which exists prior to any scientific endeavor, is an equally prominent fact in our lives. To deny the experience of responsible choice is, to me, as restricted a view as to deny the possibility of a behavioral science. That these two important elements of our experience appear to be in contradiction has perhaps the same significance as the contradiction between the wave theory and the corpuscular theory of light, both of which can be shown to be true, even though incompatible. We cannot profitably deny our subjective life, any more than we can deny the objective description of that life.

In conclusion then, it is my contention that science cannot come into being without a personal choice of the values we wish to achieve. And these values we choose to implement will forever lie outside of the science which implements them; the goals we select, the purposes we wish to follow, must always be outside of the science which achieves them. To me this has the encouraging meaning that the human person, with his capacity of subjective choice, can and will always exist, separate from and prior to any of his scientific undertakings. Unless as individuals and groups we choose to relinquish our capacity of subjective choice, we will always remain persons, not simply pawns of a self-created science.

III [SKINNER]

I cannot quite agree that the practice of science *requires* a prior decision about goals or a prior choice of values. The metallurgist can study the properties of steel and the engineer can design a bridge without raising the question of whether a bridge is to be built. But such questions are certainly frequently raised and tentatively answered. Rogers wants to call the answers "subjective choices of values." To me, such an expression suggests that we have had to abandon more rigorous scientific practices in order to talk about our own behavior. In the experimental analysis of other organisms I would use other terms, and I shall try to do so here. Any list of values is a list of reinforcers—conditioned or otherwise. We are so constituted that under certain circumstances food, water, sexual contact, and so on, will make any behavior which produces them more likely to occur again.

463

Other things may acquire this power. We do not need to say that an organism chooses to eat rather than to starve. If you answer that it is a very different thing when a man chooses to starve, I am only too happy to agree. If it were not so, we should have cleared up the question of choice long ago. An organism can be reinforced by—can be made to "choose"—almost any given state of affairs.

Rogers is concerned with choices that involve multiple and usually conflicting consequences. I have dealt with some of these elsewhere[25] in an analysis of self-control. Shall I eat these delicious strawberries today if I will then suffer an annoying rash tomorrow? The decision I am to make used to be assigned to the province of ethics. But we are now studying similar combinations of positive and negative consequences, as well as collateral conditions which affect the result, in the laboratory. Even a pigeon can be taught some measure of self-control! And this work helps us to understand the operation of certain formulas—among them value judgments—which folk-wisdom, religion, and psychotherapy have advanced in the interests of self-discipline. The observable effect of any statement of value is to alter the relative effectiveness of reinforcers. We may no longer enjoy the strawberries for thinking about the rash. If rashes are made sufficiently shameful, illegal, sinful, maladjusted, or unwise, we may glow with satisfaction as we push the strawberries aside in a grandiose avoidance response which would bring a smile to the lips of Murray Sidman.

People behave in ways which, as we say, conform to ethical, governmental, or religious patterns because they are reinforced for doing so. The resulting behavior may have far-reaching consequences for the survival of the pattern to which it conforms. And whether we like it or not, survival is the ultimate criterion. This is where, it seems to me, science can help—not in choosing a goal, but in enabling us to predict the survival value of cultural practices. Man has too long tried to get the kind of world he wants by glorifying some brand of immediate reinforcement. As science points up more and more of the remoter consequences, he may begin to work to strengthen behavior, not in a slavish devotion to a chosen value, but with respect to the ultimate survival of mankind. Do not ask me why I want mankind to survive. I can tell you why only in the sense in which the physiologist can tell you why I want to breathe. Once the relation between a given step and the survival of my group has been pointed out. I will take that step. And it is the business of science to point out just such relations.

The values I have occasionally recommended (and Rogers has not led me to recant) are transitional. Other things being equal, I am betting on the group whose practices make for healthy, happy, secure, productive, and creative people. And I insist that the values recommended by Rogers are transitional, too, for I can ask him the same kind of question. Man as a process of becoming—*what?* Self-actualization—for what? Inner control is no more a goal than external.

What Rogers seems to me to be proposing, both here and elsewhere,[26] is this: Let us use our increasing power of control to create individuals who will not need and perhaps will no longer respond to control. Let us solve the problem of our power by renouncing it. At first blush this seems as implausible as a benevolent despot. Yet power has occasionally been foresworn. A nation has burned its Reichstag, rich men have given away their wealth, beautiful women have become ugly hermits in the desert, and psychotherapists have become nondirective. When this happens, I look to other possible reinforcements for a plausible explanation. A people relinquish democratic power when a tyrant promises them the earth. Rich men give away wealth to escape the accusing finger of their fellowmen. A woman destroys her beauty in the hope of salvation. And a psychotherapist relinquishes control because he can thus help his client more effectively.

The solution that Rogers is suggesting is thus understandable. But is he correctly interpreting the result? What evidence is there that a client ever becomes truly *self*-directing? What evidence is there that he ever makes a truly *inner* choice of ideal or goal? Even though the therapist does not do the choosing, even though he encourages "self-actualization"—he is not out of control as long as he holds himself ready to step in when occasion demands—when, for example, the client chooses the goal of becoming a more accomplished liar or murdering his boss. But supposing the therapist does withdraw completely or is no longer necessary—what about all the other forces acting upon the client? Is the self-chosen goal independent of his early ethical and religious training? of the folk-wisdom of his group? of the opinions and attitudes of others who are important to him? Surely not. The therapeutic situation is only a small part of the world of the client. From the therapist's point of view it may appear to be possible to relinquish control. But the control passes, not to a "self," but to forces in other parts of the client's world. The solution of the therapist's problem of power cannot be *our* solution, for we must consider *all* the forces acting upon the individual.

The child who must be prodded and nagged is something less than a fully developed human being. We want to see him hurrying to his appointment, not because each step is taken in response to verbal reminders from his mother, but because certain temporal contingencies, in which dawdling has been punished and hurrying reinforced, have worked a change in his behavior. Call this a state of better organization, a greater sensitivity to reality, or what you will. The plain fact is that the child passes from a temporary verbal control exercised by his parents to control by certain inexorable features of the environment. I should suppose that something of the same sort happens in successful psychotherapy. Rogers seems to me to be saying this: Let us put an end, as quickly as possible, to any pattern of master-and-slave, to any direct obedience to command, to the submissive following of suggestions. Let the individual be free to adjust himself to more rewarding features of the world about him. In the end, let his teachers and counselors "wither away," like the Marxist state. I not only agree with this as a useful ideal, I have constructed a fanciful world to demonstrate its advantages. It saddens me to hear Rogers say that "at a deep philosophic level" *Walden Two* and George Orwell's *1984* "seem indistinguishable." They could scarcely be more unlike—at any level. The book *1984* is a picture of immediate aversive control for vicious selfish purposes. The founder of *Walden Two*, on the other hand, has built a community in which neither he nor any other person exerts any *current* control. His achievement lay in his original *plan*, and when he boasts of this ("It is enough to satisfy the thirstiest tyrant") we do not fear him but only pity him for his weakness.

Another critic of *Walden Two*, Andrew Hacker,[27] has discussed this point in considering the bearing of mass conditioning upon the liberal notion of autonomous man. In drawing certain parallels between the Grand Inquisition passage in Dostoevsky's *Brothers Karamazov*, Huxley's *Brave New World*, and *Walden Two*, he attempts to set up a distinction to be drawn in any society between conditioners and conditioned. He assumes that "the conditioner can be said to be autonomous in the traditional liberal sense." But then he notes: "Of course the conditioner has been conditioned. But he has not been conditioned by the conscious manipulation of another *person*." But how does this affect the resulting behavior? Can we not soon forget the origins of the "artificial" diamond which is identical with the real thing? Whether it is an "accidental" cultural pattern, such as is said to have produced the founder of *Walden Two*, or the engineered environment which is about to produce his successors, we are dealing with sets of conditions generating human behavior which will ultimately be measured by their contribution to the strength of the group. We look to the future, not the past, for the test of "goodness" or acceptability.

If we are worthy of our democratic heritage we shall, of course, be ready to resist any tyrannical use of science for immediate or selfish purposes. But if we value the achievements and goals of democracy we must not refuse to apply science to the design and construction of cultural patterns, even though we may then find ourselves in some sense in the position of controllers. Fear of control, generalized beyond any warrant, has led to a misinterpretation of valid practices and the blind rejection of intelligent planning for a better way of life. In terms which I trust Rogers will approve, in conquering this fear we shall become more mature and better organized and shall, thus, more fully actualize ourselves as human beings.

NOTES

1. C. R. Rogers, *Teachers College Record* 57 (1956): 316.
2. A. Hacker, *Antioch Review* 14 (1954): 195.
3. C. Coleman, *Bulletin of American Association of University Professors* 39 (1953): 457.
4. P. A. Freund et al., *Constitutional Law: Cases and Other Problems* (Boston: Little, Brown, 1954), vol. 1, p. 233.
5. Ibid., p. 244.
6. B. F. Skinner, *Walden Two* (New York: Macmillan, 1948).
7. J. W. Krutch, *The Measure of Man* (Indianapolis: Bobbs-Merrill, 1953).
8. M. Viteles, *Science* 122 (1955): 1167.
9. G. Negley and J. M. Patrick, *The Quest for Utopia* (New York: Schuman, 1952).
10. B. F. Skinner, *Transactions of the New York Academy of Science* 17 (1955): 547.
11. R. Niebuhr, *The Self and the Dramas of History* (New York: Scribner, 1955), p. 47.
12. R. Oppenheimer, *American Psychologist* 11 (1956): 127.
13. S. G. Vandenberg, *American Psychologist* 11 (1956): 339.
14. B. F. Skinner, *American Scholar* 25 (1955–1956): 47.
15. Ibid.
16. B. F. Skinner, *American Psychologist* 11 (1956): 221.
17. B. F. Skinner, *Transactions*, p. 549.
18. R. Oppenheimer, *Roosevelt University Occasional Papers* 2 (1956).
19. J. A. M. Meerloo, *Journal of Nervous Mental Disease* 122 (1955): 353.
20. C. R. Rogers, *Client-Centered Therapy* (Boston: Houghton Mifflin, 1951).
21. C. R. Rogers and R. Dymond, eds., *Psychotherapy and Personality Change* (Chicago: University of Chicago Press, 1954).
22. J. Ratner, ed., *Intelligence in the Modern World: John Dewey's Philosophy* (New York: Modern Library, 1939), p. 359.
23. K. R. Popper, *The Open Society and Its Enemies* (London: Routledge and Kegan Paul, 1945).
24. B. F. Skinner, *American Scholar*, pp. 52–53.
25. B. F. Skinner, *Science and Human Behavior* (New York: Macmillan, 1953).
26. Rogers, *Teachers College Record*.
27. A. Hacker, *Journal of Politics* 17 (1955): 590.

APPENDIX B
A Career in Psychology

This booklet was prepared by C. Alan Boneau, Stuart E. Golann, and Margaret M. Johnson, with the assistance of the following persons: George W. Albee and students at Case Western Reserve University, Anne Anastasi, Nancy S. Anderson and students at the University of Maryland, Jack I. Bardon, Brent Baxter, John E. Bell, William Bevan, Nea Carroll and students at Gordon Junior High School, Judith Cates, Tena Cummings, Leah Gold Fein, John Feldhusen, Charles Gersoni, Melvin A. Gravitz, Leslie Hicks, Jane Hildreth, Ernest R. Hilgard, Barbara A. Kirk, Herschel W. Leibowitz, Robert F. Lockman, Estelle Mallinoff, William McClelland, William McGehee, Wilbert McKeachie, John McMillan, Jesse Orlansky, Robert Perloff, Wilbert S. Ray, Vin Rosenthal, Alan O. Ross, Sherman Ross, William Schofield, Julius Segal, Max Siegel, Gary Simpkins, William L. Simmons, M. Brewster Smith, Fay H. Starr, John A. Stern, Ernestine Thomas, Harold Van Cott, Alfred Wellner, and Robert L. Williams.

WHAT IS PSYCHOLOGY
Major Facets

Psychology is at one time a scholarly discipline, a scientific field, and a professional activity. Its overall focus is on the study of both animal and human behavior and related mental and physiological processes.

As a *scholarly discipline*, psychology represents a major field of study in academic settings, with emphasis on the communication and explanation of principles and theories of behavior.

As a *science*, it is a focus of research through which investigators collect, quantify, analyze, and interpret data describing animal and human behavior, thus shedding light on the causes and dynamics of behavior patterns.

As a *profession*, psychology involves the practical application of knowledge, skills, and techniques for the solution or prevention of individual or social problems; the professional role also provides an opportunity for the psychologist to develop further his understanding of human behavior and thus to contribute to the science of psychology.

Subject-Matter Areas

Like any field, psychology is organized into subject-matter areas, each with its own methods of study and focus of concerns:

EXPERIMENTAL PSYCHOLOGY refers to a method by which a number of behavioral processes are studied, particularly learning, perception, motivation, emotion, language, and thinking. The term is used in relation to subject-matter areas of psychology in which experimental methods are emphasized. *Mathematical psychology*, a branch of experimental psychology, is concerned with the development, application, and evaluation of mathematical descriptions and explanations of psychological processes.

COMPARATIVE PSYCHOLOGY focuses on comparisons of the behavior of different organisms; its scope encompasses the study of evolutionary and genetic determinants of behavior, thus giving it a close identity with the biological sciences.

PHYSIOLOGICAL PSYCHOLOGY probes the relationship between behavior and the biological and physiological processes of the body—for example, between emotion and the function of the brain and nervous system.

SOCIAL PSYCHOLOGY, concerned with human interaction in the social environment, examines such phenomena as attitude development and change, social pressures, leadership, and mass movements; group dynamics, with its increasingly broad and important social applications, is another emphasis of the area.

DEVELOPMENTAL PSYCHOLOGY focuses on the development of the organism from its prenatal origins through old age. The important subarea of *child psychology* studies how, for example, the infant's growing repertoire of behavior and feeling is related to biological growth patterns of the body or how the processes of social learning and socialization contribute to an infant's development into a socialized person.

PSYCHOLOGY OF PERSONALITY is concerned with the processes by which a person becomes a unique individual; many of the best known theoretical statements about human behavior—for example, those of Sigmund Freud—are part of its substance. *Psychopathology*, or abnormal psychology, is an important branch of this area; it is concerned with those factors that contribute to deviant and maladjusted behavior and the processes or techniques by which such behavior may be modified; the exceptional, creative, and highly effective personality is a subject of interest along with the disordered personality.

PSYCHOMETRICS deals with the development and application of procedures—for example, psychological tests—for measuring the many psychological variables which underlie and affect human behavior; the area emerged from observations of differences in behavior among individuals and has developed into a highly technical area relevant to all subject-matter areas.

EDUCATIONAL PSYCHOLOGY encompasses the study of such phenomena as individual differences, learning, motivation, group behavior, and personality, all in the context of education; its principal focus is on the interaction of the child with his educational environment, but it also includes the selection and training of teachers.

WHAT DO PSYCHOLOGISTS DO?

Because psychology tends to be confused with psychiatry, a medical specialty, many people erroneously assume that psychologists concern themselves primarily with psychopathology and deviant behavior. Although some psychologists do, of course, deal with abnormal persons and phenomena, the concerns of psychology are considerably more diverse.

Psychology began in the classroom as a philosophical approach to understanding behavior and in the laboratory as a scientific approach toward the same goal. Its association with both the classroom and the laboratory has changed dramatically, however, over the last 50 years. Many psychologists now work in various social, institutional, and industrial settings such as schools, community agencies, mental health clinics, and private industries. Indeed, psychologists today rarely are exclusively scholars, scientists, or professionals; most combine these roles. Thus, a psychologist may be primarily a teacher, but he may also conduct research and provide services as part of his regular activities.

Specialty Areas

Whereas basic subject-matter areas define the substance of psychology, its specialty areas reflect how psychologists work with that substance. Each specialty is built on a base of knowledge in one or more of the subject-matter areas. Psychologists who function primarily as scientists or scholars will usually concentrate their research or study on a single subject-matter area such as experimental psychology, or on an even more circumscribed topic such as human learning. On the other hand, psychologists who function primarily as professionals outside academic or research settings are usually knowledgeable in a cluster of relevant subject-matter areas which they apply in their work.

Following are sketches of those specialty areas in which psychologists apply various combinations of subject matter to specific kinds of problems in unique settings.

CLINICAL PSYCHOLOGY. The clinical psychologist specializes in the assessment and therapeutic treatment of persons suffering emotional or adjustment problems. Typically, he is knowledgeable in the psychology of personality, psychopathology, and psychometrics, and he is also trained in the application of diagnostic and psychotherapeutic techniques; other skills and techniques may be acquired as he assumes new responsibilities—for example, mental health consultation with community agencies.

Like most psychologists, the clinician is also trained in the skills and methods of scientific inquiry. Thus, in addition to or instead of his applied professional activities, he may conduct research—for example, to determine the characteristics of a psychotherapist which are related to patient improvement or the conditions under which young children develop a sense of responsibility.

PSYCHOLOGIST IN COMMUNITY MENTAL HEALTH CLINIC

Peter Newman, PhD, clinical psychologist . . . Conducts individual and group psychotherapy . . . Meets in 50-minute sessions with several adults . . . Is cotherapist with two graduate students from a local university in group therapy sessions, one with adolescent boys, the other with three sets of parents . . . Confers with other psychologists and with psychiatrists and social workers on planning and evaluation of community programs . . . Maintains contact with representatives of school, correctional, and welfare systems . . . Collaborates with a psychiatrist in providing consultation to a prison system . . . Is a member of community committees evaluating preschool enrichment programs and studying riot prevention.

COUNSELING PSYCHOLOGY. In contrast to clinical psychologists, who deal with maladaptive behavior, counseling psychologists place greater emphasis on facilitating normal development and on helping people cope with important problems of everyday living—for example, the choice of a career or the improvement of interpersonal relationships. Many counseling psychologists help persons by measuring their abilities, interests, and temperament; this service is especially important in *rehabilitation psychology*, a specialty in which human disability is often a consideration. The subject-matter areas typically utilized by counseling and rehabilitation psychologists are developmental psychology, psychopathology, psychology of personality, educational psychology, and psychometrics.

Like the clinician, the counseling psychologist may also use his scientific training—for example, in standardizing tests of vocational interests. In another role, he may consult with business executives on the selection of personnel for various jobs or on the development of programs to maximize job satisfaction and performance.

SCHOOL PSYCHOLOGY. Psychologists working in this specialty area are concerned with increasing the effectiveness of educational institutions to facilitate the intellectual, social, and emotional development of children. They may function in various roles within the school system —for example, as research specialists in the development of programs to implement and evaluate special educational projects; as leaders of inservice training programs for teachers and as their consultants regarding specific teaching or classroom behavior problems; or as clinicians treating the interrelated psychological and educational problems

---

PSYCHOLOGIST IN UNIVERSITY COUNSELING CENTER

Robert Franklin, PhD, counseling psychologist . . . Interviews and tests students to assess ability, motivation, and interests . . . Works intensively with students who are having serious difficulty adjusting to college or are experiencing emotional problems which hamper their college work . . . Conducts group meetings in reading and study skills . . . Supervises three interns enrolled in the university's doctoral program in counseling psychology . . . Teaches undergraduate courses in child psychology, psychology of personality, and tests and measurements . . . Is faculty adviser to a group of student volunteers in mental hospitals.

PSYCHOLOGIST IN PUBLIC SCHOOL SYSTEM

Frank Wright, PhD, school psychologist . . . Employed by an urban school system of 6 high schools, 14 junior high schools, and 45 elementary schools . . . Supervises two psychologists who administer and interpret individual tests and conduct a standardized testing program for entire system . . . Plans and conducts frequent workshops for teachers on such skills and techniques as effective classroom management, diagnosis of learning problems, and role playing . . . Acts as consultant to system-wide committee planning preschool programs for inner-city children . . . Currently experimenting with computer-assisted instruction in one elementary school and advising two graduate students on related thesis research.

---

of children. Many school psychologists also have responsibility for administering and interpreting the results of standardized tests.

INDUSTRIAL PSYCHOLOGY. The industrial psychologist focuses his scientific research on and applies his professional skills to problems that people encounter at work. He may function in several capacities

472

within an organization: He may study the way work is organized, making changes to improve productivity, the quality of services, and consumer satisfaction; he may consult with management in the development of employee training programs to maximize employee potential; or he may use scientific techniques to measure employee morale, analyzing the data in terms of their implications for job definitions, training programs, and the organization of work. *Personnel psychology* focuses more specifically on the selection and assignment of personnel to enhance job satisfaction and productivity. Both industrial and personnel psychologists work with the subject matter of experimental, developmental, and social psychology, and psychometrics.

ENGINEERING PSYCHOLOGY. The engineering psychologist is concerned with the development and improvement of man-machine systems. He advises on the design of equipment intended to maximize human performance—for example, the control systems of spacecraft. His expertise finds applications in such fields as communications, transportation, and commercial and industrial production. Knowledge of sensory processes, perception, motor skills, and psychometrics is essential to the work of the engineering psychologist.

PSYCHOLOGIST IN INDUSTRIAL PLANT

> *Judith Simmons, PhD, industrial psychologist . . . Consults on selection and placement of employees and training of employment interviewers and personnel specialists . . . Is conducting a study to evaluate new interview techniques . . . Confers with department heads, union representatives, and foremen on criteria for performance evaluation . . . Advises management on questions of employee morale . . . Supervises applied research program to reduce accidents and worker fatigue . . . Is developing a special training program for workers from disadvantaged backgrounds.*

CONSUMER PSYCHOLOGY. This specialty area involves the study of psychological factors that determine an individual's behavior as a consumer of goods and services. The consumer psychologist is interested in learning, for example, why people buy certain kinds of toothpaste or automobiles or what strategies might be used to help an individual reduce his rate of consumption. He attempts also to improve the acceptability and safety of products offered to the consumer and to enhance the consumer's capacity for decision making, such as in the selection of newly available public health services.

An Overview

Table B.1 describes the proportions of psychologists engaged in various specialty areas, and Table B.2 reveals the percentages employed by various institutions and agencies. Clinical psychologists are shown to

473

TABLE B.1

Subfields of Psychology

Specialty area	Percent of psychologists involved
Clinical	29
Educational and school	19
Experimental, comparative, physiological, developmental	14
Counseling	10
Industrial and personnel psychology and psychometrics	10
Social and personality	5
General, engineering, and other	13

Figures taken from 1968 National Register of Scientific and Technical Personnel.

TABLE B.2

Employers of Psychologists

Employers	Percent of psychologists employed
Colleges and universities	40
Schools	12
Clinics, hospitals, medical schools	11
State and local government and other government agencies	8
Federal government civil service	6
Private industry and business	6
Self-employed	6
USPHS and military service	1
Other	6
No report	4

Figures taken from 1968 National Register of Scientific and Technical Personnel.

constitute the largest specialty area, while the largest number of psychologists are employed by academic institutions. This apparent contradiction is explained by the fact that, for the large majority of psychologists, the primary identification is with a college or university. It is in this environment that the three roles—scientist, scholar, and professional—may be combined most conveniently. Here, a psychologist in any of the specialties normally has access to the institution's research facilities, to its counseling centers, and to a variety of other facilities. Here, too, a psychologist, whatever his specialty, may teach undergraduate students the general principles and methods of psychology, or he may guide the studies of graduate students in his own or a related specialty area.

Because of their knowledge of a particular subject matter, psychologists are frequently called upon to solve practical problems. For example, social psychologists may act as consultants to community action projects, or experimental psychologists may help in the designing of teaching devices.

Alan Stuart, PhD, social psychologist . . . Employed by a large state university as an associate professor of psychology . . . Teaches two courses each semester, from repertoire that includes psychology, introduction to social psychology, group dynamics, and specialized topics of social psychology . . . Chairs departmental committees on undergraduate curriculum and graduate examinations . . . Sits on university committee on institutional goals . . . Is conducting research program on group reactions to the introduction of deviant members and supervising related thesis research of two master's degrees students . . . Is member of dissertation committees of several doctoral candidates . . . Is consulting editor for the Journal of Personality and Social Psychology.

One Career May Equal Many

The work that an individual psychologist actually does is determined by a number of factors: the subject-matter emphasis of his training, his level of education, the setting in which he works, and the specific day-to-day demands confronting him. In addition, the psychologist is free to follow his own inclinations. He may choose among the rigors and excitement of science, the challenge of understanding and helping individuals, the rewards of promoting social change, the demands of teaching, or the satisfaction of enhancing an institution's effectiveness.

The psychologist's level of education is often a major factor in shaping his career. Because most doctoral level psychologists have been exposed to a large and diversified body of knowledge and techniques in psychology, those who hold the doctoral degree enjoy the widest range of work choices and the most responsible positions. A clinical psychologist with a doctoral degree may thus be qualified to function in a school setting, or a rehabilitation setting, or even an industrial setting where, among other responsibilities, he might deal with the adjustment problems of executives. In contrast the psychologist with master's level training usually finds a more limited range of opportunities open to him, partly because of the position qualifications prescribed by potential employers and partly because he must limit his responsibilities only to those for which his background has prepared him.

Traditionally, a bachelor's level education has not been considered sufficient for a career in psychology. Bachelor's degree programs have not covered in depth either the subject matter or scientific method of psychology, nor have they provided professional training for dispensing psychological services. However, several recent developments have emphasized the importance of reexamining psychological training and the uses of manpower. These include the rapid growth in the number of programs designed to meet the educational and mental health needs of society, the concomitant need for more manpower to provide the psychological services involved in these programs, and changing conceptions of the psychologist's role. An outgrowth of these developments may be more numerous and more diversified careers in psychology than presently exist and more opportunities at different levels of training. The new programs in community colleges for training mental health technicians suggest at least one of many possibilities for diversification in psychological careers.

Looking Ahead

With the continuing impetus provided by social change and development, psychology will make important advances in the 1970s. Three examples are illustrative.

In the field of education, psychology has only begun to realize its potential contribution. The schools are natural laboratories for research-minded psychologists who study such processes as learning, motivation, and thinking. The schools are also natural work settings for psychologists with professional knowledge, skills, and techniques that can be utilized in planning for educational change and reform. Psychologists will play important roles in the 1970s as they grapple with such basic educational issues as measurable effects of student protest, design of optimum curricula, and effective methods for teaching children and training teachers.

In the field of health, the programs of Medicare and Medicaid may evolve in the 1970s into a national health care program, challenging psychology and other health-related professions to respond adequately to public needs. In the field of mental health, a recently initiated federal program of community-based mental health centers has made psychological services accessible and economical for many thousands of citizens. This program and the growing emphasis on preventive mental health are creating new demands on psychology and other mental health fields in terms of manpower and diversification of services. Already, a new specialty area, community psychology, has emerged from clinical and social psychology to cope with this and other broad challenges posed by social change.

HOW DO YOU BECOME A PSYCHOLOGIST?
Education

In a time of change and progress—as the decade ahead promises to be—educational requirements for a career in any field will be changing to keep pace with the demands of new jobs and new demands on established jobs. Thus, at any given time, the best source of information about educational requirements for careers in psychology, will be the institutions that offer training programs for such careers. What follows is general guidance only.

Preparation for a career in psychology at the master's or doctoral level begins with enrollment in a graduate program for advanced study in psychology. Receipt of the master's degree will generally involve completion of one or two years of course work beyond the bachelor's degree and the completion of additional requirements such as practical experience in an applied setting and/or a thesis based on a research project. Doctoral training requires a minimum of three years beyond the bachelor's degree and ordinarily consumes four or more years. Earning the doctorate demands a high level of academic achievement and may require a research project that makes an original contribution to the field of psychology. Doctoral students in many professional specialties may complete an internship either prior to or immediately after receiving their degrees; such internships normally involve at least an additional year of formal training.

Admission to graduate programs is highly competitive. Since graduate work in psychology requires close supervision, enrollment is limited in order to insure high quality in the preparation of students. Even with such constraints, there are approximately 2,000 doctoral and 5,000 master's degree recipients emerging from psychology graduate programs each year, with many of the latter going on to earn the doctorate. Approximately 25,000 bachelor's degrees are awarded to psychology majors each year.

Specific information about opportunities for graduate study in psychology and possible financial support is contained in an annual publication of the American Psychological Association, *Graduate Study in Psychology*, available from the Educational Affairs Office of the APA.

A career choice should, of course, be based on a thorough exploration of various alternatives so that one's interests, abilities, and values are most suitably matched with one's lifework. There are various other careers in which psychological knowledge, techniques, and skills are applied, but which differ substantially from psychology itself. Among these are psychiatry, psychiatric nursing, social work, work as a mental health technician, and certain aspects of student personnel work such as guidance counseling.

Accreditation and Certification

To insure that psychologists who perform public service functions are adequately trained, the American Psychological Association evaluates doctoral programs in clinical and counseling psychology and accredits those programs that meet minimum standards. Following is a list of universities with APA-approved doctoral programs in clinical and counseling psychology for 1969–70. (For a more current listing, write to the Educational Affairs Office of the APA.)

Clinical Psychology

Adelphi University
Alabama, University of
Arizona State University
Arizona, University of
Arkansas, University of
Boston University
California, University of Berkeley)
California, University of (Los Angeles)
Case Western Reserve University
Catholic University of America
Chicago, University of, Committee on Human Development
Chicago, University of, Department of Psychology
Cincinnati, University of
Clark University
Colorado, University of
Connecticut, University of
Denver, University of
Duke University
Florida State University
Florida, University of
Fordham University
George Peabody College for Teachers
Georgia, University of
Harvard University, Department of Social Relations
Houston, University of
Illinois, University of
Indiana University
Iowa, University of
Kansas, University of
Louisiana State University
Loyola University (Chicago)
Maryland, University of
Massachusetts, University of
Miami, University of
Michigan State University
Michigan, University of
Minnesota, University of
Missouri, University of
Nebraska, University of
New York, State University of (Buffalo)

New York University, Graduate School of Arts and Sciences
North Carolina, University of
Northwestern University
Ohio State University
Oklahoma, University of
Oregon, University of
Pennsylvania State University
Pennsylvania, University of
Pittsburgh, University of
Purdue University
Rochester, University of
Rutgers—The State University
Southern California, University of
Southern Illinois University
St. Louis University
Syracuse University
Teachers College, Columbia University
Temple University
Tennessee, University of
Texas, University of
Utah, University of
Vanderbilt University
Washington State University
Washington, University of
Washington University (St. Louis)
Wayne State University
West Virginia University
Wisconsin, University of
Yale University
Yeshiva University

Counseling Psychology

Boston University
Catholic University of America
Florida, University of
George Peabody College for Teachers
Illinois, University of
Iowa, University of
Maryland, University of
Michigan, University of
Minnesota, University of, Department of Psychology, College of Liberal Arts

Minnesota, University of, Department of Educational Psychology, College of Education

Missouri, University of, Department of Psychology and Counseling and Personnel Service

Nebraska, University of, Department of Educational Psychology and Measurements

New York, State University of (Buffalo)

Ohio State University

Oregon, University of, School of Education

Purdue University

Southern Illinois University

Teachers College, Columbia University

Temple University

Texas Technological College

Texas, University of, Department of Education and of Psychology

Utah, University of, Departments of Educational Psychology and of Psychology

Newly Approved Programs

All newly approved university programs are listed on a provisional status for two years.

Clinical Psychology

Emory University—Approved 1968

Kent State University—Approved 1969

McGill University, Montreal, Canada—Approved 1968

New York, City University of (City College)—Approved 1969

Ohio University—Approved 1968

Although the APA presently accredits only doctoral programs in the two specialties noted previously, plans are under way to broaden the accrediting authority to apply to all professional programs in psychology offered by universities and colleges.

In most states, the use of the title "psychologist" by those who have a private practice is restricted to persons with adequate training as defined by law. Standards set by the profession itself and by most state laws define a qualified professional psychologist as one with a doctoral degree in psychology and at least one year and preferably two years of supervised experience in the practice of psychology. Many psychologists work in institutional settings that are governed by state or federal regulations, and, almost universally, these regulations require at least a master's degree for a position as a psychologist.

The American Board of Professional Psychology offers diplomate status to individual practitioners of clinical, counseling, industrial, and school psychology who meet certain standards of excellence.

ABOUT THE AMERICAN PSYCHOLOGICAL ASSOCIATION

The APA is a scientific and professional society organized to advance psychology as a science and as a means of promoting the public welfare. Its membership in 1970 was approximately 30,000. The Association publishes scientific journals in the various subject-matter areas and specialties of psychology and holds an annual convention to facilitate and encourage communication and exchange of new knowledge among psychologists. It also sponsors various other meetings and activities which deal with the professional concerns and scientific interests of psychologists. Regional, state, and local associations also facilitate exchange of information and the pursuit of mutual interests among psychologists. The addresses of these associations may be obtained by writing to the Professional Affairs Office of the APA, 1200 Seventeenth St., N.W., Washington, D.C. 20036.

Divisions of the APA

The numerous interests and activities of psychologists are currently represented in the APA by 31 divisions.

1. General Psychology
2. Teaching of Psychology
3. Experimental Psychology
5. Evaluation and Measurement
6. Physiological and Comparative Psychology
7. Developmental Psychology
8. Personality and Social Psychology
9. The Society for the Psychological Study of Social Issues— A Division of the APA
10. Psychology and the Arts
12. Clinical Psychology
13. Consulting Psychology
14. Industrial and Organizational Psychology
15. Educational Psychology
16. School Psychology
17. Counseling Psychology
18. Psychologists in Public Service
19. Military Psychology
20. Adult Development and Aging
21. The Society of Engineering Psychologists—A Division of the APA
22. Psychological Aspects of Disability
23. Consumer Psychology
24. Philosophical Psychology
25. Experimental Analysis of Behavior
26. History of Psychology
27. Community Psychology
28. Psychopharmacology
29. Psychotherapy
30. Hypnosis
31. State Psychological Association Affairs

32. Humanistic Psychology

33. Mental Retardation

Publications

The APA publishes 14 psychological journals:

American Psychologist. Official papers of the Association; articles on psychology.

Contemporary Psychology. Critical reviews of books, films, and research material in the field of psychology.

Journal of Abnormal Psychology. Theoretical and research contributions in behavior pathology.

Journal of Applied Psychology. Applications of psychology to business and industry.

Journal of Comparative and Physiological Psychology. Original contributions in the field of comparative and physiological psychology.

Journal of Consulting and Clinical Psychology. Research in clinical psychology: psychological diagnoses, psychotherapy, personality, psychopathology.

Journal of Counseling Psychology. Research on counseling theory and practice.

Journal of Educational Psychology. Studies of learning and teaching: measurement of psychological development, psychology of school subjects, methods of instruction, school adjustment.

Journal of Experimental Psychology. Original contributions of an experimental character.

Journal of Personality and Social Psychology. Theoretical and research papers on personality dynamics, group process, and the psychological aspects of social structure.

Psychological Abstracts. Noncritical abstracts of the world's literature in psychology and related subjects.

Psychological Bulletin. Evaluative reviews of research literature, discussions of research methodology in psychology.

Psychological Review. Original contributions of a theoretical nature.

Developmental Psychology. Studies on growth and development and their major associated variables.

(Journal subscriptions are on a calendar year basis.)

Employment Bulletin. Notices of vacancies and situations wanted.

APA Directory. Biographical, geographical, and divisional listings of APA Associates, Members, and Fellows.

APA Monitor. News about APA, behavioral science legislation, and general happenings in psychology.

Special Groups of Interest to Students

Black Students Psychological Association. A central source of information on educational opportunities and financial assistance in psychology for black and other minority group students. Address: 1200 Seventeenth Street, N.W., Washington, D.C. 20036.

Psi Chi. The national college honor society in psychology. Address: 1200 Seventeenth Street, N.W., Washington, D.C. 20036.

Students in Psychology. Undergraduate or graduate students taking courses in psychology are eligible for participation as Student in Psychology subscribers to APA journals. They must be endorsed by a member of the Association, preferably by a faculty member of the university or college where the student is registered. Subscriptions to the Association's journals are available to them at the special rates charged to members.

Recent Groups. American Women in Psychology, Psychologists for La Razza, etc.

Additional Sources of Information

BOOKS AND BOOKLETS

American Psychological Association. *Ethical standards of psychologists.* Washington, D.C.: Author, 1963.

American Psychological Association. *Casebook on ethical standards.* Washington, D.C.: Author, 1967.

American Psychological Association. *Psychology as a profession.* Washington, D.C.: Author, 1968.

American Psychological Association. *The psychologist and voluntary health insurance.* (Rev. ed.) Washington, D.C.: Author, 1968.

American Psychological Association. *Graduate study in psychology: 1970–71.* (Rev. annually) Washington, D.C.: Author, 1969.

Cass, J. & Birnbaum, M. *Comparative guide to American colleges.* New York: Harper & Row, 1969.

Guilford, J. P. (Ed.) *Fields of psychology.* (3rd ed.) New York: Van Nostrand, 1966.

Hawes, G. R. *The new American guide to colleges.* New York: Columbia University Press, 1966.

Hoch, E. L., Ross, A. O., & Winder, C. L. *Professional preparation of clinical psychologists.* Washington, D.C.: American Psychological Association, 1966.

National Commission on Mental Health Manpower. *Careers in psychiatry.* New York: Macmillan, 1968.

National Commission on Mental Health Manpower. *Recruiting for mental health.* New York: Mental Health Materials Center, 1969. (Address: 419 Park Avenue South, New York, New York 10019)

Smith, M. B., & Hobbs, N. *The community and the community mental health center.* Washington, D.C.: American Psychological Association, 1966.

Super, D. E. *Opportunities in psychology careers.* New York: Universal, 1968.

Umbarger, C. C., Dalsimer, J. S., Morrison, A. P., & Breggin, P. R. *College students in a mental hospital: An account of organized social contacts between college volunteers and mental patients in a hospital community.* New York: Grune & Stratton, 1962.

Webb, W. B. (Ed.) *The Profession of psychology.* New York: Holt, Rinehart & Winston, 1962.

PAMPHLETS

American Psychological Association, Division of Counseling Psychology. *The counseling psychologist.* New York: Teachers College Press, undated. (Address: Teachers College, Columbia University, New York, New York 10027)

American Psychological Association, Division of Industrial Psychology. *A career in industrial psychology.* Washington, D.C.: Author, undated.

American Psychological Association, Division of School Psychology. *The school psychologist.* Highland Park, N.J.: Division of School Psychology, undated. (Address: 39 North Fifth Avenue, Highland Park, New Jersey 08904)

College Entrance Examination Board. *Financial planning for study in the United States: A guide for students from other countries.* New York: Author, 1969. (Address: 475 Riverside Drive, New York, New York 10027)

Hawes, G. R. *Entering higher education in the United States: A guide for students from other countries.* New York: College Entrance Examination Board, 1969. (Address: 475 Riverside Drive, New York, New York 10027)

National Academy of Sciences, National Research Council. *A selected list of major fellowship opportunities and aids to advanced education for foreign nationals.* Washington, D.C.: Author, 1969. (Address: 2101 Constitution Avenue, N.W., Washington, D.C. 20418)

National Academy of Sciences, National Research Council. *A selected list of major fellowship opportunities and aids to advanced education for United States citizens.* Washington, D.C.: Author, 1969. (Address: 2101 Constitution Avenue, N.W., Washington, D.C. 20418)

National Association for Mental Health. *A guide to scholarships, fellowships, and loans in the mental health field.* New York: Author, undated. (Address: 10 Columbus Circle, New York, New York 10019)

National Science Foundation. *Information on science scholarships and student loans.* Washington, D.C.: United States Government Printing Office, 1960.

Ogg, E. *Mental health jobs today and tomorrow.* (Public Affairs Pamphlet No. 384) New York: Public Affairs Committee, 1966. (Address: 381 Park Avenue South, New York, New York 10016)

Powledge, F. *New careers, real jobs and opportunities for the disadvantaged.* (Public Affairs Pamphlet No. 427) New York: Public Affairs Committee, 1968. (Address: 381 Park Avenue South, New York, New York 10016)

United States Department of Health, Education, and Welfare, Office of Education. *Aids to students.* Washington, D.C.: United States Government Printing Office, 1966.

United States Department of Labor, Bureau of Labor Statistics. *Employment outlook for psychologists.* (Occupational Outlook Report Series) Washington, D.C.: United States Government Printing Office, 1968–69.

United States Department of Labor, Bureau of Labor Statistics. *Employment outlook: Psychologists.* (Occupational Outlook Reprint Series) Washington, D.C.: United States Government Printing Office, 1970.

PROFESSIONAL ASSOCIATIONS AND ORGANIZATIONS

American Medical Association
535 North Dearborn Street, Chicago, Illinois 60610

American Psychiatric Association
1700 Eighteenth Street, N.W., Washington, D.C. 20009

National Association for Mental Health
10 Columbus Circle, New York, New York 10019

National Association of Social Workers
2 Park Avenue, New York, New York 10016

Scientific Manpower Commission
2101 Constitution Avenue, N.W., Washington, D.C. 20418

APPENDIX C

Psychology as a Means of Promoting Human Welfare*

GEORGE A. MILLER
Rockefeller University

The most urgent problems of our world today are the problems
we have made for ourselves. They have not been caused by
some heedless or malicious inanimate Nature, nor have they
been imposed on us as punishment by the will of God. They are
human problems whose solutions will require us to change our
behavior and our social institutions.

As a science directly concerned with behavioral and
social processes, psychology might be expected to provide
intellectual leadership in the search for new and better personal
and social arrangements. In fact, however, we psychologists
have contributed relatively little of real importance—even less
than our rather modest understanding of behavior might justify.
We should have contributed more; although our scientific base
for valid contributions is far from comprehensive, certainly
more is known than has been used intelligently.

This is the social challenge that psychologists face. In
the years immediately ahead we must not only extend and
deepen our understanding of mental and behavioral phenomena,
but we must somehow incorporate our hard-won knowledge
more effectively into the vast social changes that we all know

* Presidential Address to the American Psychological Association in
Washington, D.C., September 1969. It is customary on this occasion to
summarize one's own research. Although that would be a more comfortable role, I have decided instead to take this opportunity to express
some personal opinions about the current state of our discipline and its
potential role in meeting the human problems of our society. This
departure from tradition is intended to honor the theme of the 1969
Convention, "Psychology and the Problems of Society." I am indebted to
several friends, and especially to J. A. Varela, for critical comments on
earlier drafts.

Reprinted from *American Psychologist* 24, no. 12 (December 1969):
1063–1075. Copyright 1969 by the American Psychological Association
and reproduced by permission.

are coming. It is both important and appropriate for us, on occasions such as this, to consider how best to meet this social challenge.

In opening such a discussion, however, we should keep clearly in mind that society has not commissioned us to cure its ills; a challenge is not a mandate. Moreover, there is nothing in the definition of psychology that dedicates our science to the solution of social problems. Our inability to solve the pressing problems of the day cannot be interpreted as an indictment of the scientific validity of our psychological theories. As scientists we are obliged to communicate what we know, but we have no special obligation to solve social problems.

Our obligations as citizens, however, are considerably broader than our obligations as scientists. When psychological issues are raised in this broader context, we cannot evade them by complaining that they are unscientific. If we have something of practical value to contribute, we should make every effort to insure that it is implemented.

I believe that the majority of American psychologists have accepted this broader interpretation of our responsibilities and have been eager—perhaps, sometimes, overly eager—to apply our science to social problems. We have not been aloof or insensitive; the bulk of our profession works full time on exactly such problems. And I do not wish to discount the many and often successful efforts toward application that we have made already. Yet I cannot escape the impression that we have been less effective than we might have been. "Why" and "what more might be done" are questions that have troubled me increasingly in recent years.

First, however, I would like to raise a somewhat parochial question.

ROLE OF THE AMERICAN PSYCHOLOGICAL ASSOCIATION

If we accept this challenge to use psychology to solve social problems, what role should we expect the American Psychological Association to play? I raise this question because my experience as an officer of APA has taught me that many of our members look to their national organization for leadership in insuring that our scientific and professional activities have greater social relevance.

Psychologists have been well represented among those who sign petitions of political protest,[1] and they have not failed to make their opinions heard in their own national headquarters. Scarcely a meeting of the Board of Directors in recent years has not featured one or more petitions from concerned members, committees, boards, divisions, or state associations requesting some action related to public affairs. These matters range all the way from the proper use of psychological tests, where APA usually has something to say, to the endorsement of particular political candidates, where APA usually does not.

These demands have imposed considerable strain on the Association, which was not created to be an instrument for social action and which responds hesitantly to any suggestion that it should become something more than a scientific and professional organization. But it does respond. I was surprised to discover how seriously APA regards any legitimate request from its membership, and how sensitive it is to the social implications of its actions, policies, and communications. Some members wish APA would do more, some less. On balance, I think APA has reflected reasonably accurately the general consensus of its members with respect to its role in public affairs.

It is not my intention to raise here any of the specific issues of public policy that have concerned the Board of Directors and the Council of Representatives, or even to offer a general formula for deciding what the public role of the APA should be. Procedurally, I am willing to stand on the thoughtful recommendations of the ad hoc Committee on Public Affairs.[2]

A point of general interest, however, and one that relates more directly to the theme I wish to discuss, is the frequently heard argument that APA should take some action or other because the first article of our Bylaws states that the Association shall have as its object to promote human welfare, a goal that is echoed in our statement of the *Ethical Standards of Psychologists*.

This argument is usually made by those who recommend that APA should publicly advocate some particular social reform. When these recommendations are appropriate, the action is adopted—the necessary letters are written, public statements are released to the press, etc. But not every recommendation is acceptable. It has been my impression that the less related the issue is to the scientific and professional interests of our membership, the greater is the likelihood that the promotion of human welfare will be invoked in the course of the discussion.

In most cases this argument has not persuaded me; I have traced my skepticism to two sources.

First, even the most cursory study of welfare economics will show that human welfare has never been operationally defined as a social concept. If there is such a thing as human welfare in the general sense, it must be some kind of weighted average. In difficult cases, where disagreement is most probable, something that advances the welfare of one group may disadvantage another group. The problem is to decide whose welfare we wish to promote. The APA is committed to advancing the welfare of psychologists, of course, but we dare not assume blindly that whatever is good for psychology must always be good for humanity.

Vague appeals to human welfare seldom answer specific questions because we seldom have sufficient information to decide which actions will have the desired result. And even when we do have sufficient wisdom to know in advance which actions will promote human welfare most effectively, we still face the ethical question of whether such actions are morally permissible.

My first reason for distrusting appeals to human welfare, therefore, is that they do little to clarify the logical, informational, or ethical bases for making difficult decisions. Something more is required than a sincere declaration that our heart is in the right place.

My second reason has to do with the fact that the phrase is usually quoted out of context. At the risk of losing your attention, therefore, I would like to state Article I of our Bylaws in full:

> The objects of the American Psychological Association shall be to advance psychology as a science and as a means of promoting human welfare by the encouragement of psychology in all its branches in the broadest and most liberal manner; by the promotion of research in psychology and the improvement of research methods and conditions; by the improvement of the qualifications and usefulness of psychologists through high standards of professional ethics, conduct, education, and achievement; by the increase and diffusion of psychological knowledge through meetings, professional contacts, reports, papers discussions, and publications; thereby to advance scientific interests and inquiry, and the application of research findings to the promotion of the public welfare.[3]

As I understand Article I, our corporate aim is to promote psychology. We justify that aim by our belief that psychology can be used for the public good. I do not understand Article I as a general license to endorse social actions or positions, however meritorious on other grounds, that do not advance psychology as a science and as a means of promoting human welfare. The APA is our own creature, of course; we can change our Bylaws any way we like. As presently conceived, however, APA does not have a charter to intervene on behalf of every good cause that comes along.

There are many things of social value that APA can do, and many that it has already done. If your officers have not always seemed hungry for innovation, eager to reshape APA to meet every new social issue, they have certainly been open to constructive change within the scope of our charter. I believe they have reflected the wishes of the bulk of the membership, and I feel no need to apologize for what has been accomplished. The APA has been doing what its membership wanted to do, and doing it rather well.

Of course, the membership has been far from unanimous in these matters. For example, there has been a running debate in recent years concerning the proper role for individual psychologists to play in the initiation of social reforms. We have been divided as to whether psychologists should remain expert advisers or should take a more active, participatory responsibility for determining public policy. An adviser is expected to summarize the arguments pro and con, but to leave the policy decisions to others; a participant wants to make the policy decisions himself.

Those who favor more active participation by individual psychologists tend to argue that APA should also become directly involved in advocating particular social policies. This whole debate seems to presuppose, however, that social reforms can occur only as a result of policy decisions by government or industry. This presupposition should not go unchallenged. Perhaps our options for promoting human welfare are broader than this debate would suggest.

It was E. G. Boring who first impressed on me the importance of a clear distinction between Psychology with a capital P and psychology with a small p. Capital-P Psychology refers to our associations, departments, laboratories, and the like. Small-p psychology refers to the discipline itself. Capital-P Psychology can do little to promote human welfare, outside of its faithful promotion of small-p psychology. We should not, through impatience or bad judgment, try to use capital-P Psychology where only small-p psychology could succeed. Let us by all means do everything we can to promote human welfare, but let us not forget that our real strength in that cause will come from our scientific knowledge, not from our national Association.

In my opinion, our Association can never play more than a supporting role in the promotion of social change. I do not conclude from this that APA has become irrelevant or useless, or, even worse, that it has tacitly endorsed a political bureaucracy that presides over the inequitable distribution of health, wealth, and wisdom in our society. The fact that APA has not reformed society does not mean that it approves the status quo; it means simply that there is relatively little such an association can do. When one considers the magnitude and urgency of the problems mankind faces, the question of what positions APA takes is, after all, a minor matter.

The important question, to my mind, is not what APA is doing, but what psychologists are doing. What Psychology can do as an association depends directly on the base provided by psychology as a science. It is our science that provides our real means for promoting human welfare.

So let me turn now to broader aspects of my topic.

REVOLUTIONARY POTENTIAL OF PSYCHOLOGY

I will begin by stating publicly something that I think psychologists all feel, seldom talk about. In my opinion, scientific psychology is potentially one of the most revolutionary intellectual enterprises ever conceived by the mind of man. If we were ever to achieve substantial progress toward our stated aim—toward the understanding, prediction, and control of mental and behavioral phenomena—the implications for every aspect of society would make brave men tremble.

Responsible spokesmen for psychology seldom emphasize this revolutionary possibility. One reason is that the general public is all too ready to believe it, and public resistance to psychology would be all too easy to mobilize. Faced with the possibility that revolutionary pronouncements might easily do more harm than good, a prudent spokesman finds other drums to march to.

Regardless of whether we agree that prudence is always the best policy, I believe there is another reason for our public modesty. Anyone who claims that psychology is a revolutionary enterprise will face a demand from his scientific colleagues to put up or shut up. Nothing that psychology has done so far, they will say, is very revolutionary. They will admit that psychometric tests, psychoanalysis, conditioned reflexes, sensory thresholds, implanted electrodes, and factor analysis are all quite admirable, but they can scarcely be compared to gunpowder, the steam engine, organic chemistry, radio-telephony, computers, atom bombs, or genetic surgery in their revolutionary consequences for society. Our enthusiastic spokesman would have to retire in confused embarrassment.

Since I know that rash statements about the revolutionary potential of psychology may lead to public rejection and scientific ridicule, why do I take such risks on this occasion? My reason is that I do not believe the psychological revolution is still pie in the sky. It has already begun.

One reason the psychological revolution is not more obvious may be that we have been looking for it in the wrong place. We have assumed that psychology should provide new technological options, and that a psychological revolution will not occur until someone in authority exercises those options to attain socially desirable goals. One reason for this assumption, perhaps, is that it follows the model we have inherited from previous applications of science to practical problems. An applied scientist is supposed to provide instrumentalities for modifying the environment—instrumentalities that can then, under public regulation, be used by wealthy and powerful interests to achieve certain goals. The psychological revolution, when it comes, may follow a very different course, at least in its initial stages.

Davis has explained the difference between applied social science and applied natural science in the following way:

> Applied science, by definition, is instrumental. When the human goal is given, it seeks a solution by finding what effective means can be manipulated in the required way. Its function is to satisfy human desires and wants; otherwise nobody would bother. But when the sci-

ence is concerned with human beings—not just as organisms but as goal-seeking individuals and members of groups—then it cannot be instrumental in this way, because the object of observation has a say in what is going on and, above all, is not willing to be treated as a pure instrumentality. Most so-called social problems are problems because people want certain things or because there is a conflict of desires or interests.[4]

Davis goes on to argue that once conflicts of interest have developed, applied social science is helpless; that it is only when people are agreed on their goals that our information can be usefully applied.

Although I agree with Davis that behavioral and social sciences cannot be applied to people and institutions in the same way physical and biological sciences are applied to objects and organisms, I do not agree with his view that we must remain impotent in the face of conflict. We know a great deal about the prevention and resolution of conflicts, and that information could certainly be put to better use than it has been. Indeed, sometimes what is needed is not to resolve conflict but to foster it, as when entrenched interests threaten segments of the public that have no organizational identity. And there, in turn, we know a great deal about the creation of appropriate constituencies to defend their common interests. Behavioral and social scientists are far from helpless in such situations.

More important, however, I believe that the real impact of psychology will be felt, not through the technological products it places in the hands of powerful men, but through its effects on the public at large, through a new and different public conception of what is humanly possible and what is humanly desirable.

I believe that any broad and successful application of psychological knowledge to human problems will necessarily entail a change in our conception of ourselves and of how we live and love and work together. Instead of inventing some new technique for modifying the environment, or some new product for society to adapt itself to however it can, we are proposing to tamper with the adaptive process itself. Such an innovation is quite different from a "technological fix." I see little reason to believe that the traditional model for scientific revolutions should be appropriate.

Consider, for example, the effect that Freudian psychology has already had on Western society. It is obvious that its effects, though limited to certain segments of society, have been profound, yet I do not believe that one can argue that those effects were achieved by providing new instrumentalities for achieving goals socially agreed upon. As a method of therapy, psychoanalysis has had limited success even for those who can afford it. It has been more successful as a method of investigation, perhaps, but even there it has been only one of several available methods. The impact of Freud's thought has been due far less to the instrumentalities he provided than to the changed conception of ourselves that he inspired. The wider range of psychological problems that Freud opened up for professional psychologists is only part of his contribution. More important in the scale of history has been his effect on the broader intellectual community and, through it, on the public at large. Today we are much more aware of the irrational components of human nature and much better able to accept the reality of our unconscious impulses. The importance of Freudian psychology derives far less from its scientific validity than from the effects it has had on our shared image of man himself.

I realize that one might argue that changes in man's conception of himself under the impact of advances in scientific knowledge are neither novel nor revolutionary. For example, Darwin's theory changed our conception of ourselves, but not until the past decade has it been possible to mount a truly scientific revolution based on biological science. One might argue that we are now only at the Darwinian stage in psychology, and that the real psychological revolution is still a century or more in the future. I do not find this analogy appropriate, however.

To discover that we are not at the center of the universe, or that our remote ancestors lived in a tree, does indeed change our conception of man and society, but such new conceptions can have little effect on the way we behave in our daily affairs and in our institutional contexts. A new conception of man based on psychology, however, would have immediate implications for the most intimate details of our social and personal lives. This fact is unprecedented in any earlier stage of the Industrial Revolution.

The heart of the psychological revolution will be a new and scientifically based conception of man as an individual and as a social creature. When I say that the psychological revolution is already upon us, what I mean is that we have already begun to change man's self-conception. If we want to further that revolution, not only must we strengthen its scientific base, but we must also try to communicate it to our students and to the public. It is not the industrialist or the politician who should exploit it, but Everyman, every day.

The enrichment of public psychology by scientific psychology constitutes the most direct and important application of our science to the promotion of human welfare. Instead of trying to foresee new psychological products that might disrupt our existing social arrangements, therefore, we should be self-consciously analyzing the general effect that our scientific psychology may have on popular psychology. As I try to perform this analysis for myself, I must confess that I am not altogether pleased with the results.

I would like now to consider briefly some of the effects we are having and where, in my view, our influence is leading at the present time. Let me begin with a thumbnail sketch of one major message that many scientific psychologists are trying to communicate to the public.

CONTROL OF BEHAVIOR

One of the most admired truisms of modern psychology is that some stimuli can serve to reinforce the behavior that produces them. The practical significance of this familiar principle arises from the implication that if you can control the occurrence of these reinforcing stimuli, then you can control the occurrence of adaptive behavior intended to achieve or avoid them. This contingency between behavior and its consequences has been demonstrated in many studies of animal behavior, where environmental conditions can be controlled, or at least specified, and where the results can be measured with some precision.

Something similar holds for the human animal, of course, although it is complicated by man's symbolic proclivities and by the fact that the disparity between experimenter and subject changes when the subject is also a man. Between men, reinforcement is usually a mutual relation and each person controls the other to some extent. This relation of mutual reinforcement, which man's genius for symbols has generalized in terms of money or the promise of money, provides the psychological basis for our economic system of exchange. Psychologists did not create this economic system for controlling behavior, of course. What we have tried to do is to describe its psychological basis and its limits in terms sufficiently general to hold across different species, and to suggest how the technique might be extended to educational, rehabilitative, therapeutic, or even political situations in which economic rewards and punishments would not normally be appropriate. Once a problem of behavior control has been phrased in these terms, we may then try to discover the most effective schedule of reinforcements.

My present concern has nothing to do with the validity of these ideas. I am concerned with their effect on the public at large, for it is there, if I am right, that we are most likely to achieve a psychological revolution.

In the public view, I suspect, all this talk about controlling behavior comes across as unpleasant, if not actually threatening. Freud has already established in the public mind a general belief that all behavior is motivated. The current message says that psychologists now know how to use this motivation to control what people will do. When they hear this, of course, our scientific colleagues are likely to accuse us of pseudoscientific claims; less scientific segments of the public are likely to resent what they perceive as a threat to their personal freedom. Neither reaction is completely just, but neither is completely unjustifiable.

I believe these critics see an important truth, one that a myopic concentration on techniques of behavior control may cause us to overlook. At best, control is but one component in any program for personal improvement or social reform. Changing behavior is pointless in the absence of any coherent plan for how it should be changed. It is our plan for using control that the public wants to know about. Too often, I fear, psychologists have implied that acceptable uses for behavior control are either self-evident or can be safely left to the wisdom and benevolence of powerful men. Psychologists must not surrender the planning function so easily. Humane applications of behavior control must be based on intelligent diagnosis of the personal and social problems we are trying to solve. Psychology has at least as much, probably more, to contribute to the diagnosis of personal and social problems as it has to the control of behavior.

Regardless of whether we have actually achieved new scientific techniques of behavior control that are effective with human beings, and regardless of whether control is of any value in the absence of diagnosis and planning for its use, the simple fact that so many psychologists keep talking about control is having an effect on public psychology. The average citizen is predisposed to believe it. Control has been the practical payoff from the other sciences. Control must be what psychologists are after, too. Moreover, since science is notoriously successful, behavior control must be inevitable. Thus the layman forms an impression that control is the name of the road we are traveling, and that the experts are simply quibbling about how far down that road we have managed to go.

Closely related to this emphasis on control is the frequently repeated claim that living organisms are nothing but machines. A scientist recognizes, of course, that this claim says far more about our rapidly evolving conception of machines than it says about living organisms, but this interpretation is usually lost when the message reaches public ears. The public idea of a machine is something like an automobile, a mechanical device controlled by its operator. If people are machines, they can be driven like automobiles. The analogy is absurd, of course, but it illustrates the kind of distortion that can occur.

If the assumption that behavior control is feasible in some precise scientific sense becomes firmly rooted in public psychology, it could have unfortunate consequences, particularly if it is coupled with an assumption that control should be exercised by an industrial or bureaucratic elite. Psychologists must always respect and advocate the principle of *habeas mentem*—the right of a man to his own mind.[5] If we really did have a new scientific way to control human behavior, it would be highly immoral to let it fall into the hands of some small group of men, even if they were psychologists.

Perhaps a historical analogy would be appropriate. When the

evolution of species was a new and exciting idea in biology, various social theorists took it up and interpreted it to mean that capitalistic competition, like the competition between species, was the source of all progress, so the great wealth of the new industrialists was a scientifically necessary consequence of the law of the survival of the fittest. This argument, called "social Darwinism," had unfortunate consequences, both for social science and for society generally.[6]

If the notion should now be accepted that it is a scientifically necessary consequence of the law of reinforcement that industrialists or bureaucrats must be allowed the same control over people that an experimenter has over his laboratory animals, I fear that a similar period of intolerable exploitation might ensue—if, indeed, it has not already begun.

The dangers that accompany a science of behavior control have been pointed out many times. Psychologists who study motivation scientifically are usually puzzled by this widespread apprehension that they might be successful. Control is not something invented by psychologists. Everyone is "controlled" all the time by something or other. All we want is to discover how the controls work. Once we understand that, society can use the knowledge in whatever manner seems socially advantageous. Our critics, on the other hand, want to know who will diagnose our problems, who will set our social goals, and who will administer the rewards and punishments.

All that I have tried to add to this familiar dialogue is the observation that the social dangers involved need not await the success of the scientific enterprise. Behavior control could easily become a self-fulfilling prophecy. If people generally should come to believe in the scientific control of behavior, proponents of coercive social programs would surely exploit that belief by dressing their proposals in scientific costumes. If our new public conception of human nature is that man's behavior can be scientifically controlled by those in positions of power, governments will quickly conform to that conception. Thus, when I try to discern what direction our psychological revolution has been taking, some aspects of it disturb me deeply and lead me to question whether in the long run these developments will really promote human welfare.

This is a serious charge. If there is any truth to it, we should ask whether any other approaches are open to us.

Personally, I believe there is a better way to advertise psychology and to relate it to social problems. Reinforcement is only one of many important ideas that we have to offer. Instead of repeating constantly that reinforcement leads to control, I would prefer to emphasize that reinforcement can lead to satisfaction and competence. And I would prefer to speak of understanding and prediction as our major scientific goals.

In the space remaining, therefore, I want to try to make the case that understanding and prediction are better goals for psychology than is control—better both for psychology and for the promotion of human welfare—because they lead us to think, not in terms of coercion by a powerful elite, but in terms of the diagnosis of problems and the development of programs that can enrich the lives of every citizen.

PUBLIC PSYCHOLOGY: TWO PARADIGMS

It should be obvious by now that I have somewhere in the back of my mind two alternative images of what the popular conception of human nature might become under the impact of scientific advances in psychology. One of these images is unfortunate, even threatening; the other is vaguer, but full of promise. Let me try to make these ideas more concrete.

The first image is the one I have been describing. It has great appeal to an authoritarian mind, and fits well with our traditional competitive ideology based on coercion, punishment, and retribution. The fact that it represents a serious distortion of scientific psychology is exactly my point. In my opinion, we have made a mistake by trying to apply our ideas to social problems and to gain acceptance for our science within the framework of this ideology.

The second image rests on the same psychological foundation, but reflects it more accurately; it allows no compromise with our traditional social ideology. It is assumed, vaguely but optimistically, that this ideology can be modified so as to be more receptive to a truer conception of human nature. How this modification can be achieved is one of the problems we face; I believe it will not be achieved if we continue to advertise the control of behavior through reinforcement as our major contribution to the solution of social problems. I would not wish to give anyone the impression that I have formulated a well-defined social alternative, but I would at least like to open a discussion and make some suggestions.

My two images are not very different from what McGregor once called Theory X and Theory Y.[7] Theory X is the traditional theory which holds that because people dislike work, they must be coerced, controlled, directed, and threatened with punishment before they will do it. People tolerate being directed, and many even prefer it, because they have little ambition and want to avoid responsibility. McGregor's alternative Theory Y, based on social science, holds that work is as natural as play or rest. External control and threats are not the only means for inspiring people to work. People will exercise self-direction and self-control in the service of objectives to which they are committed; their commitment is a function of the rewards associated with the achievement of their objectives. People can learn not only to accept but to seek responsibility. Imagination, ingenuity, and creativity are widely distributed in the population, although these intellectual

496

potentialities are poorly utilized under the conditions of modern industrial life.

McGregor's Theory X and Theory Y evolved in the context of his studies of industrial management. They are rival theories held by industrial managers about how best to achieve their institutional goals. A somewhat broader view is needed if we are to talk about public psychology generally, and not merely the managerial manifestations of public psychology. So let me amplify McGregor's distinction by referring to the ideas of Varela, a very remarkable engineer in Montevideo, Uruguay, who uses scientific psychology in the solution of a wide range of personal and social problems.

Varela contrasts two conceptions of the social nature of man.[8] Following Kuhn's discussion of scientific revolutions,[9] he refers to these two conceptions as "paradigms." The first paradigm is a set of assumptions on which our social institutions are presently based. The second is a contrasting paradigm based on psychological research. Let me outline them for you very briefly.

Our current social paradigm is characterized as follows: All man are created equal. Most behavior is motivated by economic competition, and conflict is inevitable. One truth underlies all controversy, and unreasonableness is best countered by facts and logic. When something goes wrong, someone is to blame, and every effort must be made to establish his guilt so that he can be punished. The guilty person is responsible for his own misbehavior and for his own rehabilitation. His teachers and supervisors are too busy to become experts in social science; their role is to devise solutions and see to it that their students or subordinates do what they are told.

For comparison, Varela offers a paradigm based on psychological research: There are large individual differences among people, both in ability and personality. Human motivation is complex and no one ever acts as he does for any single reason, but, in general, positive incentives are more effective than threats or punishments. Conflict is no more inevitable than disease and can be resolved or, still better, prevented. Time and resources for resolving social problems are strictly limited. When something goes wrong, how a person perceives the situation is more important to him than the "true facts," and he cannot reason about the situation until his irrational feelings have been toned down. Social problems are solved by correcting causes, not symptoms, and this can be done more effectively in groups than individually. Teachers and supervisors must be experts in social science because they are responsible for the cooperation and individual improvement of their students or subordinates.

No doubt other psychologists would draw the picture somewhat differently. Without reviewing the psychological evidence on which such generalizations are based, of course, I cannot argue their validity. But I think most of you will recognize the lines of research on which McGregor's Theory Y and Varela's second paradigm are based. Moreover, these psychologically based paradigms are incompatible in several respects with the prevailing ideology of our society.

Here, then, is the real challenge: How can we foster a social climate in which some such new public conception of man based on psychology can take root and flourish? In my opinion, this is the proper translation of our more familiar question about how psychology might contribute to the promotion of human welfare.

I cannot pretend to have an answer to this question, even in its translated form, but I believe that part of the answer is that psychology must be practiced by nonpsychologists. We are not physicians; the secrets of our trade need not be reserved for highly trained specialists. Psychological facts should be passed out freely to all who need and can use them. And from successful applications of psychological principles the public may gain a better appreciation for the power of the new conception of man that is emerging from our science.

If we take seriously the idea of a peaceful revolution based on a new conception of human nature, our scientific results will have to be instilled in the public consciousness in a practical and usable form so that what we know can be applied by ordinary people. There simply are not enough psychologists, even including nonprofessionals, to meet every need for psychological services. The people at large will have to be their own psychologists, and make their own applications of the principles that we establish.

Of course, everyone practices psychology, just as everyone who cooks is a chemist, everyone who reads a clock is an astronomer, everyone who drives a car is an engineer. I am not suggesting any radical departure when I say that nonpsychologists must practice psychology. I am simply proposing that we should teach them to practice it better, to make use self-consciously of what we believe to be scientifically valid principles.

Our responsibility is less to assume the role of experts and try to apply psychology ourselves than to give it away to the people who really need it—and that includes everyone. The practice of valid psychology by nonpsychologists will inevitably change people's conception of themselves and what they can do. When we have accomplished that, we will really have caused a psychological revolution.

HOW TO GIVE PSYCHOLOGY AWAY

I am keenly aware that giving psychology away will be no simple task. In our society there are depths of resistance to psychological innovations that have to be experienced to be believed.[10]

Solving social problems is generally considered to be more

difficult than solving scientific problems. A social problem usually involves many more independent variables, and it cannot be finally solved until society has been persuaded to adopt the solution. Many who have tried to introduce sound psychological practices into schools, clinics, hospitals, prisons, or industries have been forced to retreat in dismay. They complain, and with good reason, that they were unable to buck the "System," and often their reactions are more violent than sensible. The System, they say, refuses to change even when it does not work.

This experience has been so common that in my pessimistic moments I have been led to wonder whether anything less than complete reform is possible.

Deutsch has made an interesting case that competitive and cooperative social relationships tend to be mutually exclusive. He summarizes the result of considerable research in the following terms:

> The strategy of power and the tactics of coercion, threat, and deception result from and also result in a competitive relationship. Similarly, the strategy of mutual problem solving and the tactics of persuasion, openness, and mutual enhancement elicit and also are elicited by a cooperative orientation.[11]

Each orientation has its own internal consistency; elements of one are not easily injected into the other.

Perhaps a similar pressure toward internal coherence lies at the root of public resistance to many of our innovative suggestions. It often seems that any one of our ideas taken alone is inadequate. Injected into the existing social paradigm it is either a foreign body, incompatible with the other presuppositions that shape our social institutions, or it is distorted and trivialized to fit the preexisting paradigm.

One of the most basic ideas in all the social sciences is the concept of culture. Social anthropologists have developed a conception of culture as an organic whole, in which each particular value, practice, or assumption must be understood in the context of the total system. They tell terrible tales about the consequences of introducing Western reforms into aboriginal cultures without understanding the social equilibria that would be upset.

Perhaps cultural integrity is not limited to primitive cultures, but applies also to our own society here and now. If so, then our attempts at piecemeal innovation may be doomed either to fail or to be rejected outright.

I label these thoughts pessimistic because they imply a need for drastic changes throughout the whole system, changes that could only be imposed by someone with dangerous power over the lives of others.

And that, I have argued, is not the way our psychological revolution should proceed.

In my more optimistic moments, however, I recognize that you do not need complete authority over a social organization in order to reform it. The important thing is not to control the system, but to understand it. Someone who has a valid conception of the system as a whole can often introduce relatively minor changes that have extensive consequences throughout the entire organization. Lacking such a conception, worthwhile innovations may be total failures.

For example, if you institute a schedule of rewards and punishments in the psychiatric ward of a Veterans Hospital, you should not be indignant when the American Legion objects on the grounds that you cannot withhold food and clothing from veterans. If you had had a more adequate understanding of the hospital as a social system, you would have included the interests and influence of the American Legion in your diagnosis of the problem, and you would have formulated a plan to gain their endorsement as part of your task as a social engineer. You should not demand inordinate power just because you made an inadequate diagnosis of the problem. Understanding must come first.

In my optimistic moments I am able to convince myself that understanding is attainable and that social science is already at a stage where successful applications are possible. Careful diagnosis and astute planning based on what we already know can often resolve problems that at first glance seemed insurmountable. Many social, clinical, and industrial psychologists have already demonstrated the power of diagnosis and planning based on sound psychological principles.

Varela has illustrated such applications by his work in Uruguay. Diagnosis involves not only a detailed analysis of the social organization and of the perceptions and goals of all the people caught up in the problem, but also the description of their abilities and personalities. Planning involves the explicit formulation of a series of steps that will lead these people to consider the problem together and will help them to discover a solution that respects everyone's hopes and aspirations. If, in the course of this plan, it becomes necessary to persuade someone, this is not to be accomplished by coercion or by marshaling facts, but by a gradual, step-by-step process that enables him to reduce his reactance little by little as he convinces himself of the virtues of the alternative view and broadens his conception of the range of acceptable solutions.[12] This is not the place and I am not the person to describe the ingenuity with which Varela has constructed such plans and carried them out, but such applications give me some reason for optimism.

Diagnosing practical problems and developing detailed plans to deal with them may or may not be more difficult than solving scientific problems, but it is certainly different. Many psychologists, trained in an empiricist, experimental tradition, have tried to serve two masters at once. That is to say, they have tried to solve practical problems and simultaneously to collect data of scientific value on the effects of their interventions. Other fields, however, maintain a more equitable division of labor between scientist and engineer. Scientists are responsible for the validity of the principles; engineers accept them and try to use them to solve practical problems.

Although I recognize the importance of evaluating an engineer's product, in this domain it is no easy thing to do. Assessing social innovations is a whole art in itself, one that we are only beginning to develop. Economic considerations are relevant, of course, but we must also learn to evaluate the subtler psychological and social implications of our new solutions.[13] Technological assessment in this sense will not be achieved by insisting that every reform should resemble a well-designed experiment. In particular, the need for assessment should not be allowed to discourage those who enjoy and have a talent for social engineering.

We are in serious need of many more psychological technologists who can apply our science to the personal and social problems of the general public, for it is through them that the public will eventually discover the new paradigm that psychologists are developing. That is to say, it is through the success of such practical applications that we have our best hope for revolutionizing public psychology.

Obviously, we must avoid the evils of superficiality; we must continue as scientists to refine, clarify, and integrate our new paradigm. Most importantly, we must self-consciously recognize that it *is* a new and revolutionary conception that we are working toward, so that isolated discoveries can be related to and evaluated in terms of that larger context. But all that would be futile, of course, if the general public did not accept it, or if public psychology were not altered by it.

There is no possibility of legislating the changes I have in mind. Passing laws that people must change their conceptions of themselves and others is precisely the opposite of what we need. Education would seem to be our only possibility. I do not mean only education in the schoolroom, although that is probably the best communication channel presently at our disposal. I have in mind a more ambitious program of educating the general public.

It is critically important to shape this education to fit the perceived needs of the people who receive it. Lectures suitable for graduate seminars are seldom suitable for laymen, and for a layman facing a concrete problem they are usually worse than useless. In order to get a factory supervisor or a ghetto mother involved, we must give them something they can use. Abstract theories, however elegant, or sensitivity training, however insightful, are too remote from the

501

specific troubles they face. In order to get started, we must begin with people where they are, not assume we know where they should be. If a supervisor is having trouble with his men, perhaps we should teach him how to write a job description and how to evaluate the abilities and personalities of those who fill the job; perhaps we should teach him the art of persuasion, or the time and place for positive reinforcement. If a ghetto mother is not giving her children sufficient intellectual challenge, perhaps we should teach her how to encourage their motor, perceptual, and linguistic skills. The techniques involved are not some esoteric branch of witchcraft that must be reserved for those with PhD degrees in psychology. When the ideas are made sufficiently concrete and explicit, the scientific foundations of psychology can be grasped by sixth-grade children.

There are many obvious and useful suggestions that we could make and that nonpsychologists could exploit. Not every psychological problem in human engineering has to be solved by a professional psychologist; engineers can rapidly assimilate psychological facts and theories that are relevant to their own work. Not every teaching program has to be written by a learning theorist; principles governing the design and evaluation of programmed materials can be learned by content specialists. Not every personnel decision has to be made by a psychometrician; not every interview has to be conducted by a clinical psychologist; not every problem has to be solved by a cognitive psychologist; not every reinforcement has to be supervised by a student of conditioning. Psychological principles and techniques can be usefully applied by everyone. If our suggestions actually work, people should be eager to learn more. If they do not work, we should improve them. But we should not try to give people something whose value they cannot recognize, then complain when they do not return for a second meeting.

Consider the teaching of reading, for example. Here is an obviously appropriate area for the application of psychological principles. So what do we do? We assemble experts who decide what words children know, and in what order they should learn to read them; then we write stories with those words and teachers make the children read them, or we use them in programmed instruction that exploits the principles of reinforcement. But all too often the children fail to recognize the value of learning these carefully constructed lessons.

Personally, I have been much impressed with the approach of Ashton-Warner,[14] who begins by asking a child what words he wants. Mummy, daddy, kiss, frightened, ghost, their own names—these are the words children ask for, words that are bound up with their own loves and fears. She writes each child's word on a large, tough card and gives it to him. If a child wants words like police, butcher, knife, kill, jail, and bomb, he gets them. And he learns to read them almost immediately. It is *his* word, and each morning he retrieves his own words from the pile collected each night by the teacher. These are not dead words of an expert's choosing, but words that live in a child's own experience. Given this start, children begin to write, using their own words, and from there the teaching of reading follows naturally. Under this regimen, a word is not an imposed task to be learned with reinforcements borrowed from some external source of motivation. Learning the word is itself reinforcing; it gives the child something he wants, a new way to cope with a desire or fear. Each child decides where he wants to start, and each child receives something whose value he can recognize.

Could we generalize this technique discovered by an inspired teacher in a small New Zealand school? In my own thinking I have linked it with something that White has called competence motivation.[15] In order to tap this motivational system we must use psychology to give people skills that will satisfy their urge to feel more effective. Feeling effective is a very personal thing, for it must be a feeling of effectiveness in coping with personal problems in one's own life. From that beginning some might want to learn more about the science that helped them increase their competence, and then perhaps we could afford to be more abstract. But in the beginning we must try to diagnose and solve the problems people think they have, not the problems we experts think they ought to have, and we must learn to understand those problems in the social and institutional contexts that define them. With this approach we might do something practical for nurses, policemen, prison guards, salesmen—for people in many different walks of life. That, I believe, is what we should mean when we talk about applying psychology to the promotion of human welfare.

If you tell me that such a program is too ambitious or too foreign to our conception of ourselves as scientists and practitioners, I must agree that I do not know where to place our fulcrum to move the world. My goal is to persuade you that this is the problem we face, and that we dare not leave it for bureaucrats or businessmen to solve. We will have to cope with it however we can, and I hope that someone has better ideas than I about how to do it.

I can see some promise for innovations in particular subcultures. If we apply our new paradigm in particular institutions—in schools, hospitals, prisons, industries—we can perhaps test its validity and demonstrate its superiority. Many such social experiments are already in progress, of course. And much of the recent surge of interest in community psychology[16] has been stimulated by the realization that we really do have something to contribute to community life. Perhaps all this work will eventually have a cumulative effect.

One trouble, of course, is that we are trying to reverse the natural direction of influence. Ordinarily, an institution or a community models its own subculture more or less automatically after the larger culture in which it is embedded, and new members require little indoctrination in order to understand the tacit assumptions on which the institution is based. Whether the new paradigm will be powerful enough to reverse this direction is, I suppose, a matter for pure speculation at the present time. It seems unlikely that we will succeed, however, if each application of the new paradigm is viewed as unrelated to every other, and no attempt is made to integrate these experiments into a paradigm for society as a whole.

It is possible, however, that our society may not be quite as resistant as we anticipate. The demand for social relevance that we have been voicing as psychologists is only one aspect of a general dissatisfaction with the current state of our society. On every hand we hear complaints about the old paradigm. People are growing increasingly alienated from a society in which a few wise men behind closed doors decide what is good for everyone. Our system of justice based on punishment and retribution is not working. Even those most blessed by economic rewards are asking for something more satisfying to fill their lives. We desperately need techniques for resolving conflicts, and for preventing them from becoming public confrontations from which reasonable retreat is impossible. Anyone who reads the newspapers must realize that vast social changes are in the making, that they must occur if civilized society is to survive.

Vested interests will oppose these changes, of course, but as someone once said, vested interests, however powerful, cannot withstand the gradual encroachment of new ideas. If we psychologists are ready for it, we may be able to contribute a coherent and workable philosophy, based on the science of psychology, that will make this general agitation less negative, that will make it a positive search for something new.

I recognize that many of you will note these ambitions as little more than empty rhetoric. Psychologists will never be up to it, you will say. We should stay in our laboratories and do our own thing. The public will work out its own paradigms without us. Perhaps such skepticism is justified.

On the other hand, difficulty is no excuse for surrender. There is a sense in which the unattainable is the best goal to pursue. So let us continue our struggle to advance psychology as a means of promoting human welfare, each in our own way. For myself, however, I can imagine nothing we could do that would be more relevant to human welfare, and nothing that could pose a greater challenge to the next generation of psychologists, than to discover how best to give psychology away.

504

NOTES

1. E. C. Ladd, Jr., "Professors and Political Petitions," *Science* 163 (1969): 1425–1430.
2. L. Tyler, "An Approach to Public Affairs: Report of the Ad Hoc Committee on Public Affairs," *American Psychologist* 24 (1969): 1–4.
3. American Psychological Association, "Bylaws of the American Psychological Association," *1968 Directory* (Washington, D.C.: Author, 1968).
4. K. Davis, "The Perilous Promise of Behavioral Science," in *Research in the Service of Man: Biomedical Knowledge, Development, and Use,* a Conference Sponsored by the Subcommittee on Government Research and the Frontiers of Science Foundation of Oklahoma for the Committee on Government, Operations of the U.S. Senate, October 1966 (Washington, D.C.: U.S. Government Printing Office, 1967).
5. F. H. Sanford, "Creative Health and the Principle of *Habeas Mentem*," *American Psychologist* 10 (1955): 829–835.
6. R. Hofstadter, *Social Darwinism in American Thought* (Philadelphia: University of Pennsylvania Press, 1944).
7. D. McGregor, *The Human Side of Enterprise* (New York: McGraw-Hill, 1960).
8. J. A. Varela, *Psychological Solutions to Social Problems* (New York: Academic Press, 1971).
9. T. Kuhn, *The Structure of Scientific Revolutions* (Chicago: University of Chicago Press, 1962).
10. A. M. Graziano, "Clinical Innovation and the Mental Health Power Structure: A Social Case History," *American Psychologist* 24 (1969): 10–18.
11. M. Deutsch, "Reflections on Some Experimental Studies of Interpersonal Conflict" (Presidential Address to the Eastern Psychological Association, New York, April 11, 1969), p. 4.
12. P. Zimbardo and E. Ebbeson, *Influencing Attitudes and Changing Behavior* (Reading, Mass.: Addison-Wesley, 1969).
13. R. A. Bauer, ed., *Social Indicators* (Cambridge: M.I.T. Press, 1966).
14. S. Ashton-Warner, *Teacher* (New York: Simon & Schuster, 1963).
15. R. W. White, "Motivation Reconsidered: The Concept of Competence," *Psychological Review* 66 (1959): 297–333.
16. C. C. Bennett, *Community Psychology*, Report of Boston Conference on the Education of Psychologists, for Community Mental Health (Boston: Boston University, 1966).

APPENDIX D

Introduction to Statistical Methods in Psychology

FOSTER LLOYD BROWN

The purpose of this appendix is to help you learn how to prescribe, compute, and interpret a few of the more commonly used statistical tools. The same data will be used throughout both to cut your learning time and to help you discover relationships between the techniques.

Sample problems are given throughout the text. The correct answers are supplied following each problem. Cover the answers until you have responded, and then see how you did.

DESCRIPTIVE AND INFERENTIAL STATISTICS

Statistical methods are divided into two groups: descriptive statistics, which are used to describe a situation, and inferential statistics, which are used to draw conclusions from research data. Descriptive statistical methods seldom give psychology students much difficulty and will be treated here only briefly.

Describing Distributions

While many kinds of graphs are used in psychology, two are particularly common, frequency diagrams and scatter diagrams. For an example of a frequency diagram see Figure 1 and also Figures 10.1 and 10.3 in the text. An example of a scatter diagram is given in Figure 2 (see also Figure 10.2).

In scatter diagrams the prior or possibly causative variable (called the independent or X variable) is plotted along the horizontal (X) axis. The later occurring or possibly caused variable (called the dependent or Y variable) is plotted on the vertical (Y) axis.

In the scatter diagram shown, Joy received a perception (X in this case) score of _____ and a reading (Y) score of _____ .

6
4

FIGURE 1

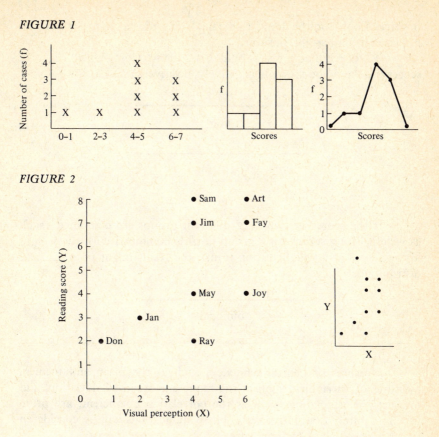

FIGURE 2

Some commonly encountered distributions are illustrated in Figure 3. It is easy to remember which skew is negative and which is

FIGURE 3

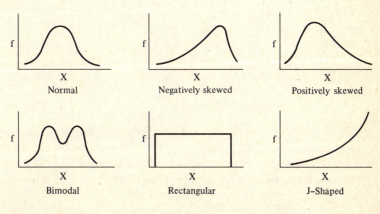

positive. Look for the long, thin tail. If it's to the left, the skew is negative; if to the right, positive.

A very difficult test would have many (low, high) _____ scores and would be skewed (negatively, positively) _____.

---

low

---

positively

If the scores of two very different groups are combined (such as weight lifting scores for a group of girls combined with the weight lifting scores of a weight lifting team), the result might be a _____ distribution.

---

bimodal

Measures of central tendency, such as the mean and median, measures of variability, such as the range and standard deviation, and measures of association, such as the correlation coefficient, are often used in a purely descriptive way. These applications will be considered under the heading of each measure.

Random Sample

Assume a set of scores for a test on visual perception given to a random sample of nine children from a large first grade:

	Scores
Don	0
Ray	4
Jan	2
May	4
Joy	6
Jim	4
Sam	4
Fay	6
Art	6

By random sample is meant that each of the first graders had an equal chance of being included in the sample. A *sample* is chosen perhaps because it is too expensive or there is not enough time to test the entire class, but the group that we really wish to know about, called the *population*, is the entire first grade.

It is often this way in the real world; the entire population about which we wish to know—all voters in a national election, all children in Headstart, all white rats, the students in a particular college, heroin addicts being maintained on methadone, cigarette smokers—is not readily measured and so a sample is studied from which one can make *inferences* about the population.

COMPUTING THE MEAN AND THE MEDIAN

Given data such as the above, one might wish to find a number that represents the best estimate of the *central tendency* the visual perception scores would have shown if the entire class had taken the test. There are two major indices of central tendency: the mean (commonly called the average) and the median. A third index, the mode (most frequent score), is seldom used in psychology.

The *mean* of a set of scores is simply the sum of all the scores divided by the number of scores. This section on the mean is not so much to teach you how to compute a mean (which you can probably already do), but to introduce some symbols and a way of learning how to do more complex computations.

Using the notes and example problem, solve the practice problem.

	Example problem		
Notes		*scores* (X)	*Practice problem*
Sum up the scores and	Don	0	Ima	0
label the sum as ΣX.	Ray	4	Lil	2
Σ (the capital Greek	Jan	2	Dot	2
letter sigma) may be	May	4	Hal	3
read as "sum of." X	Joy	6	Sue	8
stands for scores.	Jim	4		
	Sam	4		
	Fay	6		
	Art	6		
	ΣX = 36		__ = __

$$\Sigma X \qquad 15$$

N symbolizes the number of scores. $N = 9$ $N = \_\_\_$

$$5$$

The mean, symbolized
by M, is the
ΣX divided by N.

$$M = \Sigma X/N$$
$$= 36/9$$
$$= 4$$

$$M = \underline{\hspace{1cm}}$$

3

When a few extreme scores lie at one end of a distribution
(called a skewed distribution), the mean may not meaningfully reflect
the central tendency of the distribution. For example, consider a
hypothetical set of yearly salaries (in thousands) for a small company,
the last figure being the salary of the owner.

10, 9, 9, 10, 12, 8, 12, 50

The mean salary is 15,000, but that figure would hardly communicate the real situation, say to a prospective employee. In a case
like this it is generally better to use the *median*, which is computed by
lining up the scores from low to high thus:

8, 9, 9, 10, 10, 12, 12, 50

and simply noting the middle score (or mean of the two middle scores
in the case of even-numbered distributions).

The median for the above salaries is _____.

10

The mean, median, and mode are also used as descriptive statistics. When used to describe an existing set of scores (as contrasted to
making inferences about a population), the computations are performed
in just the same way as outlined above.

VARIABILITY

One common way of expressing variability is the *range*. It is computed
by the formula: Range = Highest score − Lowest score. The range
for the example problem on page 508 is 6 − 0 = 6. The primary
advantage of the range is the ease with which it is computed and understood. However, it is unstable because the range can be changed greatly
by one extreme score. Another problem is that it tends to get bigger
as the sample size gets bigger since a large sample is more likely to
contain any extreme scores that may be in the population. Samples

thus tend to yield estimates of the range that are *biased* in the direction of being too small.

A more useful estimate of variability is called the *standard deviation*. It is a more stable and sensitive measure than the range since it reflects the variability of every score and not just the two extreme scores at each end. Using the formula to be taught later, sample scores can be used to figure an *unbiased* estimate of a population standard deviation, that is, the estimates, over the long run, would not average too low (as with the range) or too high.

As an example to help clarify the nature of the standard deviation, assume that 100 students were to take a test that had a mean of 50 and a standard deviation of 10. Assuming these scores to be distributed in the most usual way, they might line up about as in Figure 4.

FIGURE 4

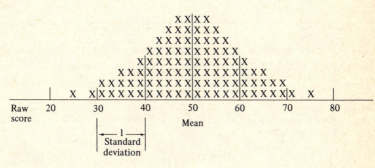

If the standard deviation were 5 instead of 10, the 100 students would be distributed more as in Figure 5. Notice the piling up of cases about the mean and the thinning out toward the tails. In its purest form the type of bell-shaped distribution in Figures 4 and 5 is called a *normal distribution*. When a distribution is normal or near normal the proportion of the total cases in any particular segment of the curve is

FIGURE 5

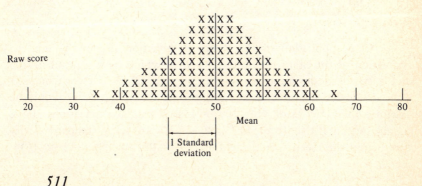

rather predictable. About 68 percent of the cases lie between 1 standard deviation below the mean (called a z score of −1) and 1 standard deviation above the mean (z of +1).

Because there are 100 cases in Figures 4 and 5, each figure counts as 1 percent. One can see that the percent of cases lying above a z score of +1 is about _____ percent.

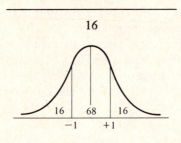

16

| 16 | 68 | 16 |
| −1 | | +1 |

Figure 6 offers a rather explicit view of the relationship between some types of scores and the normal distribution.

TABLE 1

The Proportion of Cases Equalling or Exceeding
Certain z Scores

z	Proportion
0.674	.2500
1.000	.1587
1.282	.1000
1.645	.0500
1.960	.0250
2.000	.0228
2.054	.0200
2.326	.0100
2.576	.0050
3.000	.0013
3.090	.0010
3.291	.0005
3.719	.0001
4.265	.00001

One application of the standard deviation lies in the modern derivation of the Stanford Binet IQ scores which have a mean of 100 and a standard deviation of 16 (see Figure 6). A person who is 1 standard deviation above his age group on the raw test score would be assigned an IQ score of 116 (100 + 16), 2 standard deviations above would get an IQ score of 132 [100 + (2 × 16)], ½ standard deviation below the mean would yield an IQ of 92 [100 + (−.5 × 16)], etc.

FIGURE 6

Normal distribution. A crowd of 1000 persons viewed from an airplane might look like this if each person lined up behind a sign giving his standard score on some text. Caution: Each type of standard score is in reference to the persons who took that particular test, so that one type of score can not be compared directly to another. For example, an IQ score gives one's standing compared with the entire population, while an SAT score gives one's standing compared with only those who took the SAT test.

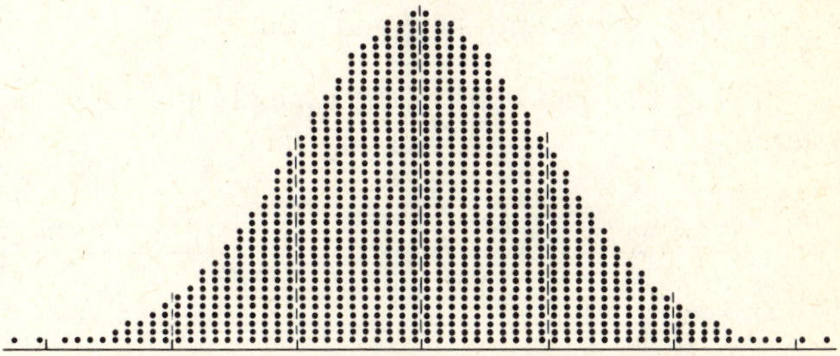

Standard deviations from mean	−3s	−2s	−1s	0	+1s	+2s	+3s
Percentile ranks		1	5 10 20 30 40 50 60 70	80 90 95	99		
Standard scores z scores	−3	−2	−1	0	+1	+2	+3
t scores and PSAT scores	20	30	40	50	60	70	80
CEEB (SAT) scores	200	300	400	500	600	700	800
Stanford Binet IQ	52	68	84	100	116	132	148
Wechsler IQ	55	70	85	100	115	130	145

How many standard deviations above the mean of his age group is a person with an IQ of 124? _____

1.5

Similarly, the mean for College Board (CEEB) scores (SAT) is arbitrarily set at 500 and the standard deviation at 100 (see Figure 6). An SAT score of 400 indicates that a person is 1 standard deviation below the mean.

An SAT score of 700 would indicate that a person had a raw score _____ standard deviations _____ the mean.

2

---

above

As a prelude to computing the standard deviation, we shall compute a statistic that, while of little utility in itself, is an important module of each of the major techniques to follow. This statistic is the *sum of squares* (symbolized SS).

The fundamental (but in practice the slowest) formula for computing the SS is:

$$SS = \Sigma (X - M)^2$$

= the sum of the squared differences between each of the scores and the grand mean

For the data used in the example and practice problems on the means (p. 509), the computations run:

Example problem				*Practice problem*			
X − M	(X − M)	(X − M)²		X	M	X − M	(X − M)²
0 − 4 =	−4	16		0 − 3 =	――	――	
4 − 4 =	0	0					
2 − 4 =	−2	4		2 − ― =	――	――	
4 − 4 =	0	0					
6 − 4 =	2	4		2 − ― =	――	――	
4 − 4 =	0	0					
4 − 4 =	0	0		3 − ― =	――	――	
6 − 4 =	2	4					
6 − 4 =	2	4		8 − ― =	――	――	
		SS = 32				SS =	――

	−3	9
3	−1	1
3	−1	1
3	0	0
3	5	25
		36

This direct computation of the SS seems simple and fast. The rub comes with natural data where the mean is not rigged to come out as a whole number. As illustration, compute SS for the following distribution: 0, 2, 4, 6, 6, 8. The mean of these six scores is 4.33.

X	M		X − M	(X − M)²
0 −	4.33	=	――	――
2 −	4.33	=	――	――
4 −	4.33	=	――	――
6 −	4.33	=	――	――
6 −	4.33	=	――	――
8 −	4.33	=	――	――
			SS =	――

−4.33	18.75
−2.33	5.43
−0.33	.11
1.67	2.79
1.67	2.79
3.67	13.47
	43.34

Not only does this squaring of decimal values become tedious when N is large, but the process involves two passes with a calculator or computer; the first to determine the mean, the second to compute and square differences and sum those squares. It is all a bit awkward. There is, fortunately, an algebraically equivalent formula that, while it appears more foreboding at first, is much faster and more convenient in actual practice.

This formula, to be explained shortly, for SS is:

$$SS = \Sigma X^2 - \frac{(\Sigma X)^2}{N}$$

Notes		Example problem			Practice problem	
		X	X²		X	X²
Compute ΣX as	Don	0	0	Ima	0	——
before, but in	Ray	4	16	Lil	2	——
addition square	Jan	2	4	Dot	2	——
each score (X²)	May	4	16	Hal	3	——
and sum up the	Joy	6	36	Sue	8	——
squares (ΣX²).	Jim	4	16			
	Sam	4	16			
	Fay	6	36			
	Art	6	36			
		ΣX = 36			ΣX = ——	
			ΣX² = 176			ΣX² = ——

	0
	4
	4
	9
	64
15	81

Square the ΣX. Note that $(\Sigma X)^2$ is the symbol. Do not confuse this with ΣX^2. For ΣX^2 we square first and then sum; for $(\Sigma X)^2$ we sum first and then square.

$$(\Sigma X)^2 = 36^2$$
$$= 1296$$

$$(\Sigma X)^2 = (\underline{\quad})^2$$
$$= \underline{\quad}$$

15
225

Divide $(\Sigma X)^2$ by N. The result is called the correction factor (CF).

$$CF = (\Sigma X)^2/N$$
$$= 36^2/9$$
$$= 1296/9$$
$$= 144 \quad CF = \underline{\quad}/\underline{\quad}$$
$$= \underline{\quad}$$

225/5   45

Subtract CF from ΣX^2. The result is the corrected sum of squares (SS).

$$SS = \Sigma X^2 - CF$$
$$= 176 - 144$$
$$= 32 \quad SS = \underline{\quad} - \underline{\quad}$$
$$= \underline{\quad}$$

---

81 − 45
36

The "correction" the CF makes is to compensate for using raw scores rather than deviation scores (i.e., $X - M$). When deviation scores are used, since their mean and sum would equal 0.0, the CF drops out.

Computing Estimates of the Population
Variance and Standard Deviation

With the SS computed, computing estimates of population variance and population standard deviation is easy.

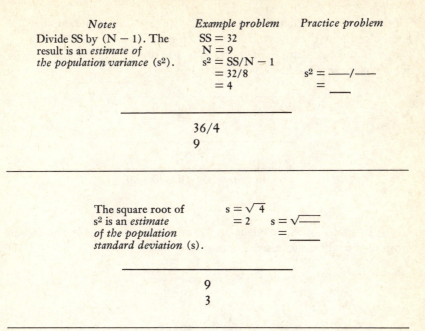

Notes	*Example problem*	*Practice problem*
Divide SS by (N − 1). The result is an *estimate of the population variance* (s²).	SS = 32 N = 9 s² = SS/N − 1 = 32/8 = 4	s² = ——/—— = ——

36/4
9

The square root of s² is an *estimate of the population standard deviation* (s).	s = √ 4 = 2	s = √—— = ——

9
3

The standard deviation is also used as a descriptive statistic for an existing set of scores. In such a case the scores on hand actually comprise the population. The symbol for the population standard deviation is σ (lower case Greek sigma). The computation differs from that for s in that the SS is divided by N instead of by N − 1.

For the example problem, $\sigma = \sqrt{32/9}$; for the practice problem, $\sigma = \sqrt{36/\_\_}$

5

CONFIDENCE INTERVALS

Up to this point inferential methods have been used to give the best estimate of some population value. There is a class of statistical methods directed to giving an interval within which we could feel rather confident the population value lay.

If we wished to know the mean SAT for a college and had the resources to test a random sample of students, we could determine not only that the best estimate was 525 (for example), but also that there was a 95 percent chance that the population mean was in the interval from 514 to 536 (for example).

To get some insight into this approach, consider the cases in

Figure 4 as a population. Let us now take a random sample of 4 scores, compute their mean, and plot it on the X axis.

If the first sample of scores was 40, 50, 70, and 80, place an X where its mean would be on the line below:

```
 20  30  40  50  60  70  80
```

```
                  X
 20  30  40  50  60  70  80
```

In similar manner, place an X on the line below for the means from each of these successive samples:

Sample number	Hypothetical values	Mean
1st	40, 50, 70, 80	60
2nd	40, 50, 55, 55	—
3rd	30, 35, 35, 80	—
4th	45, 45, 50, 60	—
5th	30, 35, 40, 55	—

```
                  X
 20  30  40  50  60  70  80
```

```
               60
               50
               45
               50
               40
               X
            X X   X
 20  30  40  50  60  70  80
```

Since extreme values would tend to cancel out, the distribution of means should be (less, more) _____ variable than the original distribution of single scores.

less

The standard deviation of these means, called the *standard error of the mean* (symbolized s_m), is easily estimated from the formula

$$s_m = \frac{s}{\sqrt{N}}$$

where s is the estimated standard deviation and N is the sample size. This relationship pops up in so many formulas and concepts that it may be to the behavioral scientist what $E = mc^2$ is to the physicists.

In the present example, if s = 10 and N = 4,

$$s_m = s/\sqrt{N} = \underline{\hspace{1em}}/\sqrt{\underline{\hspace{1em}}} = \underline{\hspace{1em}}$$

$$10/\sqrt{4} = 5$$

Compute s_m for the visual perception scores given earlier on p. 509.

Recall that these 9 scores had an s of 2.

$$s_m = s/\sqrt{N} = 2/\sqrt{9} = 2/3 = .67$$

DISTRIBUTION OF MEANS

No matter what the shape of the original distribution (skewed, bimodal, rectangular, normal, etc.), a wondrous event occurs with the distribution of the means. It approaches the normal distribution. Since the mean of all the means would naturally approach the population mean, the theoretical distribution of means can be completely described.

With sample sizes equal to 4, the population mean equal to 50, and the population standard deviation equal to 10, the standard error of the means would equal _____, the mean of the means would equal _____, and the distribution would be close to _____.

5

50

---

normal

In short, the means would be distributed about as in Figure 5. From the section on the normal distribution, it follows that 95 percent of the means would be within 2 standard errors of the population mean.

The experimenter does not, of course, have a large number of means. He has only his sample mean, and his need is not so much to know how sample means distribute, but how to use the values he has (M, s, and N) to get an idea of how far away the population mean is likely to be from his particular sample mean.

The following medieval spy story may help illustrate the logic behind how this is done. There was once a walled village named Gaussburg. In the very center of the village was a famous mint. Figure 7 is

FIGURE 7

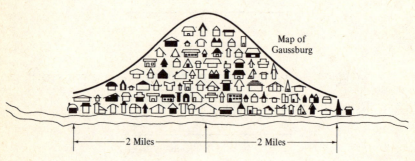

Map of
Gaussburg

|← 2 Miles →|← 2 Miles →|

a map of the village and its 100 houses. The large building marked M is the mint. Notice that about 2½ percent of the houses are beyond 2 miles upstream from the mint and about 2½ percent are beyond 2 miles downstream.

A roving band of numismatists from Würm wished to position a spy within 2 miles of the mint. Their problem was to determine how likely it was that the mint would be within 2 miles of any house chosen at random from the classified shouts of the town crier.

The map shows that 95 percent of the houses were within 2 miles of the mint.

The entire band was puzzled about how to use this information until it was realized that, conversely, the mint itself must be within 2 miles of _____ percent of the houses.

95

Feeling 95 percent confident now that the mint would be within 2 miles of any house they might randomly acquire, the numismatists finally had peace of mind. This period later came to be known as the "peace of the Würm mint spy."

In other words, 95 percent of sample means (given that the sample size is moderately large) will fall within about 2 standard errors of the population mean.

You may feel 95 percent confident that, for any particular sample mean you might gather, the population mean is not more than _____ standard errors away.

——————————— ———

2

With small samples (below 20 or so) s (and thus s_m) starts to become erratic, so one has to cast the net somewhat further than $2s_m$ on each side of the sample mean in order to have some particular surety (as 95 percent) of capturing the population mean.

In this circumstance one computes s_m just as before, but, instead of multiplying by 2, the s_m is multiplied by a special value (t) which depends on the sample size and the probability with which one wishes to be sure of catching the population mean. For example, if one wishes to set boundaries that have a 95 percent chance of including the population mean, he could use the t table (Table 2).

TABLE 2

.05 Points for the Distribution of t	
$N - 1$	t
1	12.71
2	4.30
3	3.18
4	2.78
6	2.45
8	2.31
12	2.18
20	2.09
30	2.04
60	2.00
120	1.98
∞	1.96

In the case of the visual perception scores, since $N = 9$, the t value is 2.31 (i.e., using Table 2, $N - 1 = 9 - 1 = 8$, and the t value for df $= 8$ is 2.31). Multiplying the standard error of the mean (.67) by t (2.31) yields 1.55. The mean of the population has a 95 percent probability of being within 1.55 of the sample mean. Since the sample mean is 4, the population mean has a 95 percent probability of being between 2.45 ($4 - 1.55$) and 5.55 ($4 + 1.55$). This interval from 2.45 to 5.55 is called the 95 percent confidence interval (see Figure 8).

FIGURE 8

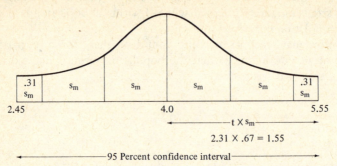

If for a sample of N = 64 the s is 16 and the mean 10, an estimate of the standard error of the mean would be _____ and the nearest t for the 95 percent would be _____. Their product is _____. The confidence interval thus extends from a lower confidence limit of 10 − _____ = _____ to an upper confidence limit of 10 + _____ = _____.

———————————————

2
2.0
4
10 − 4 = 6
10 + 4 = 14

TESTING STATISTICAL HYPOTHESES

It is common in the literature of psychology to see a phrase such as, "The difference was found to be significant, at the .05 level." Significant, as used this way, does not mean important or noteworthy, but rather it means probably not due to luck and thus trustworthy. The .05 level refers to the maximum probability that the difference does not really exist in the population. In other words, if the difference between the effect of two treatments is found to be significant at the .05 level, the probability is at least .95 (19 chances out of 20) that there really is a difference in the population values and this is not just a lucky event.

Fortunately, from the standpoint of studying behavior, chance events frequently form predictable patterns. If a particular event falls outside the pattern, it can then be ascribed to nonchance.

For example, suppose that an ESP experiment is conducted in which the tester tosses a coin and concentrates on the result. A subject in the next room tries to read the mind of the experimenter. If the subject were to call 69 out of 100 tosses correctly, it would be true that he could have just been lucky. It is possible to calculate how likely this number of "hits" could occur by luck. The probability is just about (actually a little less than) 1 in 10,000 of doing this well or better when only luck is involved. If we had made a bet that only luck would be involved (such a bet is called the *null hypothesis*), the odds would be:

Probability that the null hypothesis could be correct and that only chance is involved	about 1 in 10,000 (actually c. 00009)
Probability that the null hypothesis is incorrect and should be rejected	about 9,999 in 10,000 (actually c. 99991)

It is obvious in this case that the best bet is with rejecting the null hypothesis. If the subject got 59 correct, the odds would be:

Probability null hypothesis could be correct	about 1 in 20 (actually c. 04431)
Probability null hypothesis is incorrect	about 19 in 20 (actually c. 95569)

In most research it would still be appropriate to reject the null hypothesis if the odds for it are smaller than 1 in 20 (.95), but it is customary not to reject the null hypothesis if the odds for it are greater than 1 in 20. When the kind of error where one incorrectly rejects a null hypothesis seems particularly worth avoiding, 1 chance in 100 may be used as the cutoff point. Results would then be said to be significant at the .01 level. Researchers thus lean over backward to let chance remain as the explanation for results and reject it only when the odds against it become overwhelming.

If one were using the .01 significance level and the probability that the null hypothesis could be correct was only as rare as .02, the appropriate decision would be to (fail to reject, reject) _____ the null hypothesis.

---

fail to reject

ANALYSIS OF VARIANCE

A psychologist might want to find out if different treatments make any difference in means. Assume that two different investigators were studying a chemical that was supposed to stimulate growth. The results of their experiments are illustrated in Figure 9. The mean gain in the

FIGURE 9

groups receiving the chemical was the same for both experiments.

The experiment having the greatest variability within groups is that of Dr. _____. The most convincing experiment that the drug would make a difference in the population is that of Dr. _____.

Aikes

Paines

When it is judged that a difference showing up in an experiment probably reflects a difference that would show up in the population, the experimental difference is said to be *significant*.

The difference noted in Dr. Paines experiment appears more likely to be _____.

---

significant

If we know the variability within groups, the relative amount of variability that means between groups will show by chance may be found from tables. We thus can make a hypothesis (the null hypothesis) that chance alone is the cause of any variability in means.

If the means do not behave within the bounds expected by chance, the hypothesis that chance alone is causing any variability in means (i.e., the _____) can then be (rejected, not rejected) _____.

_____

null hypothesis

_____

rejected

_____

When the null hypothesis is rejected, the difference(s) among means can then be declared _____.

_____

significant

_____

High variability *between* groups tends toward (rejecting, not rejecting) _____ the _____.

_____

rejecting

_____

null hypothesis

_____

High variability *within* groups tends toward (rejecting, not rejecting) _____ the _____.

_____

not rejecting

_____

null hypothesis

_____

Which of the following combinations is most likely to result in a significant difference being found among the means?

525

	Estimate of variability between groups	*Estimate of variability within groups*
A	Low	Low
B	High	Low
C	Low	High
D	High	High

B

Based on the information we have just derived in the preceding problems, we can formulate an equations for the ratio between estimates of variability between groups and within groups.

$$F = \frac{\text{Estimate of variation between}}{\text{Estimate of variation within}}$$

In order to declare differences to be significant, a researcher would find the F ratio to be (high, low) _____.

high

The measure of variability to be used in studying F ratios is called the *variance*. Since the decisions are based on estimates of variance between and estimates of variance within, the method is appropriately called Analysis of _____.

Variance

Analysis of Variance (abbreviated ANOVA), while based on ratios of estimates of variance, is actually a tool for deciding the statistical significance of differences between _____.

means

Suppose that the visual perception tests (see p. 509) had been given under different conditions to different children, the matching of child to condition being random. The psychologist might now ask if it is probable that any difference in means would appear between different segments of the population if they were to be given different treatments or, equivalently, whether the different treatments caused any difference between groups in the test scores other than the fluctuation that one would expect to occur by chance or, even more simply, whether the treatments really made a difference.

The assignment of treatments might have run something like: Don and Ray were warned of dire consequences should they do badly on the test; Jan, May, and Joy comprise a sample that received neither warning nor encouragement; Jim, Sam, Fay, and Art were told only that they would probably do very well.

The visual perception data, grouped by treatment, would now look like this.

Warned		Neutral		Encouraged	
Subjects	*Scores*	*Subjects*	*Scores*	*Subjects*	*Scores*
Don	0	Jan	2	Jim	4
Ray	4	May	4	Sam	4
		Joy	6	Fay	6
				Art	6

Even though it is generally desirable to have the number of subjects in each treatment group be as near to equal as is convenient, notice that equality is not necessary.

For the practice problem assume that Ima and Lil receive one treatment, while Dot, Hal, and Sue received the other. The breakdown would now be:

Treatment A		Treatment B	
Ima	0	Dot	2
Lil	2	Hal	3
		Sue	8

Don't try to fill in the answers for the next problem now. As you compute values in the next several pages, come back and fill in the blanks.

Notes	*Example problem*				*Practice problem*			
		SS	df MS	F	SS	df	MS	F
As each value is calculated, fill in	TOTAL	32	8		—	—		
the blanks of the practice problem	BETWEEN	12 / 2 = 6.0		= 1.8	_ / _ = _		= _	
table. Correct	WITHIN	20 / 6 = 3.3			_ / _ = _			
entries will be given when the necessary calculations have been completed.								

Recall that the SS for the entire practice problem on p. 515 (TOTAL SS) was:

$$\text{Total SS} = \Sigma X^2 - \frac{(\Sigma X)^2}{N}$$

$$= 0^2 + 2^2 + 2^2 + 3^2 + 8^2 - \frac{(0 + 2 + 2 + 3 + 8)^2}{5}$$

$$= 0 + 4 + 4 + 9 + 64 - \frac{15^2}{5}$$

$$= 81 - 45 = 36$$

Notes	Example problem	Practice problem
Calculate the SS for the entire sample as before (total SS). The degrees of freedom (df) for TOTAL = N − 1.	TOTAL SS $= \Sigma X^2 - \dfrac{(\Sigma X)^2}{N}$ $= 176 - \dfrac{36^2}{9} = 32$ TOTAL df $= N - 1 = 8$	TOTAL SS = ——— TOTAL df = ———

36

4

The total SS is composed of the SS between groups and the SS within groups. Since the total SS has been calculated, it is only necessary to calculate the SS between groups. The SS within groups can then be obtained by subtraction.

Notes	Example problem	Practice problem
Sum up all scores in a cell, square this total, and divide by the number of scores in the cell. Total up this value for all cells and then subtract CF. The result is the SS between groups (SS_{bg}).	$SS_{bg} = \dfrac{(\Sigma X_1)^2}{n_1} + \dfrac{(\Sigma X_2)^2}{n_2} + \ldots - CF$ $\dfrac{(\Sigma X_1)^2}{n_1} = \dfrac{(0+4)^2}{2} = \dfrac{16}{2} = 8$ $\dfrac{(\Sigma X_2)^2}{n_2} = \dfrac{(2+4+6)^2}{3} = \dfrac{144}{3} = 48$ $\dfrac{(\Sigma X_3)^2}{n_3} = \dfrac{(4+4+6+6)^2}{4} = \dfrac{400}{4} = 100$ $SS_{bg} = 8 + 48 + 100 - 144$ $= 12$	$SS_{bg} = $ ———

13.33

With k equal to the number of groups, the df between groups (df_{bg}) is equal to $k-1$.

$$df_{bg} = k - 1$$
$$= 3 - 1$$
$$= 2$$

$$df_{bg} = \underline{\qquad}$$

1

The SS within groups (SS_{wg}) is equal to the total SS (SS_{Tot}) minus the SS between groups (SS_{bg}).

$$SS_{wg} = SS_{Tot} - SS_{bg}$$
$$= 32 - 12$$
$$= 20$$

$$SS_{wg} = \underline{\qquad} - \underline{\qquad}$$
$$= \underline{\qquad}$$

$$36 - 13.33$$
$$22.67$$

Similarly, the degrees of freedom within groups (df_{wg}) is equal to the total df (df_{Tot}) minus the df between groups (df_{bg}).

$$df_{wg} = df_{Tot} - df_{bg}$$
$$= 8 - 2$$
$$= 6$$

$$df_{wg} = \underline{\qquad}$$

3

For each of the components of the total variance, the estimate of variance or *mean square* (MS) is equal to the SS divided by the df.

Notes	*Example problem*	*Practice problem*
For MS_{bg} divide SS_{bg} by df_{bg}.	$MS_{bg} = SS_{bg}/df_{bg}$ $= 12/2$ $= 6$	$MS_{bg} = \underline{\qquad}/\underline{\qquad}$ $= \underline{\qquad}$

$$13.33/1$$
$$13.33$$

For MS_{wg} divide SS_{wg} by df_{wg}.	$MS_{wg} = SS_{wg}/df_{wg}$ $= 20/6$ $= 3.33$	$MS_{wg} = \underline{\qquad}/\underline{\qquad}$ $= \underline{\qquad}$

$$22.67/3$$
$$7.56$$

For F divide MS_{bg} by MS_{wg}.

$$F = MS_{bg}/MS_{wg}$$
$$= 6/3.33$$
$$= 1.80$$

$$F = \underline{\hspace{1cm}} / \underline{\hspace{1cm}}$$
$$= \underline{\hspace{1cm}}$$

$$13.33/7.56$$
$$1.76$$

The completed ANOVA table for the practice problem should now look like:

	SS	df	MS	F
TOTAL	36.00	4		
BETWEEN	13.33	1	13.33	1.76
WITHIN	22.67	3	7.56	

The calculated F can now be compared with the values in a table showing F values that cut off the most extreme 5 percent of the chance distribution (see Table 3). To use this table merely follow across the top until the column for the df between groups is reached. For the example problem, $df_{bg} = 2$. Then follow the left hand column down to the df within groups. For the example problem, $df_{wg} = 6$. The table value is 5.14.

TABLE 3

.05 Points for the Distribution of F

Degrees of freedom within groups	Degrees of freedom between groups		
	1	2	3
1	161.4	199.5	215.7
2	18.51	19.00	19.16
3	10.13	9.55	9.28
4	7.71	6.94	6.59
6	5.99	5.14	4.76
8	5.32	4.46	4.07
12	4.75	3.88	3.49
20	4.35	3.49	3.10
30	4.17	3.32	2.92
60	4.00	3.15	2.76
120	3.92	3.07	2.68
∞	3.84	2.99	2.60

In order for us to reject the null hypothesis (that no differences exist among the means) our calculated F would have to equal or exceed (meet or beat) this table value. Since our 1.80 does not meet or beat 5.14, we cannot reject the null hypothesis. We would report, "No significant difference (.05 level) was detected among the means."

For the practice problem, our calculated F was _____, the df_{bg} was _____, df_{wg} was _____. The critical F would be _____.

1.76
1
3
10.13

Since our calculated F (fails to, does) _____ meet or beat the table F, our decision follows that we (do not have evidence to, may) _____ reject the null hypothesis and conclude that (no evidence was found to suggest, it is most probable) _____ that the treatments make a difference in the population.

---

fails to
do not have evidence to
no evidence was found to suggest

When only two means were being compared, a technique called the t test has been much used. It involves just a bit more computation than analysis of variance and offers little in the way of advantages. If computation of a t between two independent means is called for, just compute F and take its square root. When only two groups are being compared, $t = \sqrt{F}$. The same t table (Table 2) used in setting a confidence interval is used in the t test.

Compare the t value from Table 2 for $N - 1 = 60$ which is _____ with the F value from Table 3 for 1 df between (since there are two groups) and 60 df within which is _____.

2.00

4.00

CORRELATION COEFFICIENT

We may want to find out how well variables relate to each other. Assume that in addition to the set of scores for a test on visual perception we analyzed previously there is a second set for a test on reading skill given to the same children after three months of reading instruction. The data might be:

	Visual perception scores	Reading scores
Don	0	2
Ray	4	2
Jan	2	3
May	4	4
Joy	6	4
Jim	4	7
Sam	4	8
Fay	6	7
Art	6	8

See Figure 2 for a scatter diagram of these scores.

A psychologist might be curious about the degree of relationship between how well an individual does on the visual perception test and how well he does later on the reading test. This relating together is called correlation. In order to correlate scores they must be paired. For example, in the data above the 0 that Don received on the visual perception test is paired with his score of 2 on the reading test. The members of the pair of scores were linked because the same person made both scores. This is probably the most common reason for pairing, but the correlation can also be studied between scores made by identical twins, husbands and wives, and so forth.

There does seem to be a tendency for those who do well on the visual perception test to also do well on the reading test. This suggests a positive correlation. Later on we will show how the degree of correlation can be expressed numerically.

If one of two paired variables can be considered the prior, causative, or more independent variable of the two, it is given the symbol X. The variable which follows the other in time or tends to be dependent on the other is symbolized as Y. However, even a high correlation does not prove a cause-effect relationship. You could predict days of high ice cream sales by measuring the softness of asphalt roads. Obviously, the soft roads do not stimulate ice cream sales and ice cream sales do not soften roads. They are apparently both dependent upon a third variable. Even when there is a cause-effect relationship, it is frequently not clear which is the cause and which is the effect. The assigning of X and Y labels is thus more a matter of convenience than of philosophical position.

532

In the example above, visual perception scores would be symbolized by ——— and reading scores by ———.

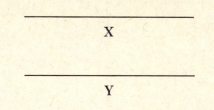

The most important measure of degree of straight-line or linear correlation is the *product moment correlation coefficient* (symbolized "r"). Values for r go all the way from +1 meaning perfect positive linear correlation (that is, if you know the value of one variable for a person, you could accurately predict that the value of the other variable for him would be the same) to −1 which signifies a perfect negative linear correlation. Values in nature usually fall somewhere between −1 and +1. A correlation of 0.0 indicates that knowing the value of one variable sheds no light at all on the value of the second.

The scatter diagrams in Figure 10 may help give a feel for the shape of various sized correlations (see also Figure 10.2).

FIGURE 10

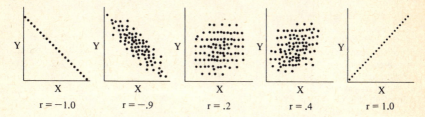

In computing the correlation coefficient, a value similar to the SS must be found; it is the sum of products (SP). The SP involves a merger of the two variables and, just as an estimate of variance resulted when the SS was divided by $N-1$, the SP yields a covariance when divided by $N-1$ (the number of pairs minus 1).

The formula for the SP, to be explained below, is:

$$SP = \Sigma XY - \frac{(\Sigma X)\,(\Sigma Y)}{N}$$

Notes	Example problem			Practice problem		
	X	Y	XY	X	Y	XY
X represents the scores on the visual percep-tion test. Y is the score on the reading test. Each Y score is multiplied by its corresponding X score. The products are then summed (ΣXY).	$0 \times 2 =$		0	0	3	——
	$4 \times 2 =$		8			
	$2 \times 3 =$		6	2	1	——
	$4 \times 4 =$		16			
	$6 \times 4 =$		24	2	2	——
	$4 \times 7 =$		28			
	$4 \times 8 =$		32	3	3	——
	$6 \times 7 =$		42			
	$6 \times 8 =$		48	8	1	——

$\Sigma X = 36$ $\Sigma X = $ ——

$\Sigma Y = 45$ $\Sigma Y = $ ——

$\Sigma XY = 204$ $\Sigma XY = $ ——

```
                        0
                        2
                        4
                        9
                        8
                       ──
        15    10       23
```

Notes	Example problem	Practice problem
Note the similarity of the formula for SP to that for SS. With SS it was the sum of all the X times X (i.e., itself) and then (ΣX) times (ΣX). With SP it is the sum of all the X times their respective Y and then (ΣX) times (ΣY).	$SP = \Sigma XY - (\Sigma X)(\Sigma Y)/N$ $= 204 - (36)(45)/9$ $= 204 - 180 = 24$	$SP = $ —— $-$ —— $/$ —— $= $ ——

$$23 - (15)(10)/5$$
$$-7$$

	Y	Y²	Y	Y²
The SS for Y (SS_y)	2	4	3	___
will be needed and	2	4		
is computed in the	3	9	1	___
same way as SS_x.	4	16		
	4	16	2	___
	7	49		
	8	64	3	___
	7	49		
	8	64	1	___
	45	275		___

$$SS_y = \Sigma Y^2 - (\Sigma Y)^2/N$$
$$= 275 - 45^2/9$$
$$= 50$$

$$SS_y = \underline{\quad} - \underline{\quad} / \underline{\quad}$$
$$= \underline{\quad}$$

9
1
4
9
1
———
24
$24 - 10^2/5$
4

The formula for r is:

$$r = \frac{SP}{\sqrt{SS_x SS_y}}$$

Notes	Example problem	Practice problem
Collecting the	$SP = 24$	$SP = $ ___ (see p. 534)
needed statistics	$SS_x = 32$	$SS_x = $ ___ (see p. 516)
from previous	$SS_y = 50$	$SS_y = $ ___ (see above)
calculations.		

−7
36
4

$$r = SP/\sqrt{SS_x SS_y}$$
$$= 24/\sqrt{(32)\,(50)} \qquad = \underline{\quad}/\sqrt{(\quad)\,(\quad)}$$
$$= 24/\sqrt{1600} \qquad\quad = \underline{\quad}/\sqrt{\underline{\quad}}$$
$$= 24/40 \qquad\qquad = \underline{\quad}/\underline{\quad}$$
$$= .60 \qquad\qquad\quad = \underline{\quad}$$

$$-7/\sqrt{(36)\,(4)}$$
$$-7/\sqrt{144}$$
$$-7/12$$
$$-.58$$

The r is also used as a descriptive statistic. In such a case, the computations are performed exactly as above.

You may wish to know if a correlation from some sample is significant. It's easy. Just enter Table 4 with the number of pairs minus 2 (N−2) and, in order to reject the null hypothesis of no relationship in the population, your r has to be as large or larger than the table value (either in a positive or negative direction).

TABLE 4

.05 Point for the Distribution of r	
N − 2 (Degrees of freedom)	r
1	.997
2	.950
3	.878
4	.811
6	.707
8	.632
12	.532
20	.423
30	.349
60	.250
120	.179

In the earlier calculations of r, a sample of 9 pairs of scores was found to have an r of .60. Would this indicate a probable positive correlation in the population? _____

No. With df $= 9 - 2 = 7$ the r needed would be somewhere between .632 and .707. With our computed r of only .60 we cannot reject luck as the explanation for the correlation in the sample.

FINDING OUT IF FREQUENCIES ARE DIFFERENT THAN EXPECTED (CHI SQUARE)

Analysis of variance deals with means, but sometimes a psychologist wishes to study frequencies. As an example, assume a six room house where only men were allowed in one side and only women in the other. Different drinks were served in each set of rooms so that the house plan would look like Figure 11.

FIGURE 11

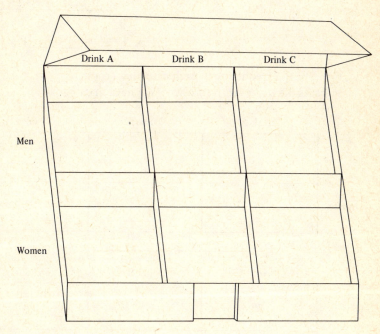

A large party is now held in the house and when it gets going well, we gently lift the roof off the house and, peering inside, we see what is illustrated in Figure 12.

FIGURE 12

Observe the frequency in each category (room).
What is the *observed frequency* (O) in each category?

	Drink A	Drink B	Drink C
Men	_____	_____	_____
Women	_____	_____	_____

	Drink A	Drink B	Drink C
Men	10	5	15
Women	5	10	5

And now to find out if there is some relationship between sex and drink preferred? It looks like women might tend toward drink B and men toward drink C, but chance could cause some effect in our sample even if there was no relationship in the population.

It's the null hypothesis approach again. We first hypothesize that there is no relationship between sex and drink preferred.

If there were no relationship, given that 30 out of the 50 people are men (60 percent), what percent of those preferring drink C would you *expect* to be men? _____

---

60 percent

Since 20 persons preferred drink C and you would expect 60 percent to be men, what would be the expected frequency (E) for men preferring drink C? _____

---

60 percent of 20 = 12

We can summarize the separate effects by totaling around the margins. These totals are called *marginals*.

Complete the marginals for this table.

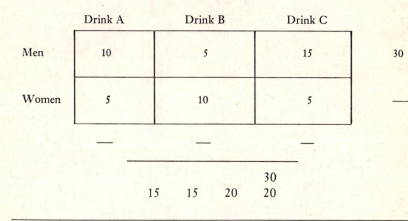

	Drink A	Drink B	Drink C	
Men	10	5	15	30
Women	5	10	5	___
	___	___	___	30
	15	15	20	20

The sum of the expected frequencies in one column (or line) also equals the marginal.

Since 20 persons prefer drink C and the E for men is 12, the E for women for drink C must be _____.

---

20 − 12 = 8

In case this intuitive approach to getting E's isn't clear to you, alternate formula may help.

$$E \text{ for any square} = \frac{(\text{Column marginal})(\text{Row marginal})}{\text{Grand total for all squares}}$$

For the present example,

$$E \text{ men, drink B} = \frac{15 \quad \times \quad 30}{50} = \frac{450}{50} = 9$$

Compute the E for the remaining cells and complete this table.

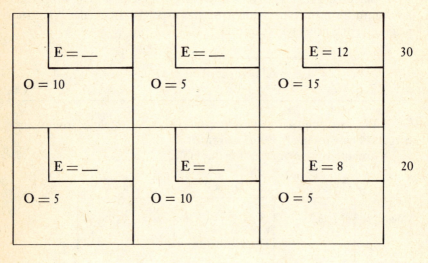

E = ___ O = 10	E = ___ O = 5	E = 12 O = 15	30
E = ___ O = 5	E = ___ O = 10	E = 8 O = 5	20
15	15	20	

9	9	12
6	6	8

With O and E for each cell in hand, the final calculations are easy.

For each separate cell, compute $(E = O)^2/E$.

$(E - O)^2/E = (9 - 10)^2/9$ $= -1^2/9$ $= 0.111$ _____	_____	_____
_____	_____	_____

_____

	Drink A	Drink B	Drink C
Men	0.111	1.778	0.750
Women	0.167	2.667	1.125

The sum of $(E - O)^2/E$ for all of these cells is called *chi square*. For the present problem chi square (X^2) = 0.111 + 1.778 + 0.750 + 0.167 + _____ + _____ = _____.

_____

2.667
1.125
6.598

If the observed frequencies were quite different from the expected, we would find each $(E - O)^2$ and thus $\Sigma(E - O)^2/E$ to be relatively (small, large) _____.

_____

Large

A relatively large chi square should indicate that the E's differed more from the O's than is likely by chance. As to how large a value for chi square is needed to reject the null hypothesis of no difference in the population, we again consult a table (Table 5). To enter the table, find the degrees of freedom by multiplying the number of rows minus 1 by the number of columns minus 1. In this case it is $(3 - 1) \times (2 - 1) = 2$.

TABLE 5

.05 Points for the Distribution of Chi Square

Degrees of freedom	Chi square
1	3.84
2	5.99
3	7.81
4	9.49
6	12.59
8	15.51
12	21.03
20	31.41
30	43.77
60	79.08
120	146.57

In the present problem, what value of chi square would we have to meet or beat in order to declare a significant (.05 level) relationship between sex and preferred drink? _____

5.99

Since our computed X^2 of 6.598 beats the critical value of 5.99, at the .05 level, we may now (reject, fail to reject) the null hypothesis of no relationship.

reject

Two precautions and an extension: chi square should not be used unless at least 80 percent of the E's are greater than 5. If there is only 1 degree of freedom, an adjustment is necessary. There are other applications for chi square such as testing to see if a population distribution could possibly be some particular shape. For expansion on these topics, see the texts cited at the end of this appendix or, indeed, just about any elementary statistics text.

SOME RELATIONSHIPS

The comparisons to be made only hint at the order and elegance to be found in the study of statistics.

From Table 1 on the normal distribution, the z value that would cut off .025 (i.e., 2½ percent) of one tail and thus a total of .05 in both tails is _____. In the t distribution (Table 2), the .05 value for ∞ df is _____.

1.96

1.96

What is this value squared? _____. From Table 3, what is the value of F for 1 df between and ∞ df within? _____ From Table 5, what is the value of chi square for 1 df? _____

3.84

3.84

3.84

Critical r values can be calculated from the formula:

$$r = \sqrt{\frac{t^2}{(N-2) + t^2}}$$

From Table 4, the critical r for N = 62 (i.e., df = 60) is _____. The 60 df value for t^2 = _____, so if the number of pairs is 62, the critical r = _____.

$r = \sqrt{t^2/(N-2) + t^2}$
$ = \sqrt{4/(62-2) + 4}$
$ = \sqrt{4/64}$
$ = \sqrt{1/16}$
$ = 1/4 = $ _____

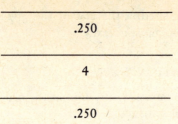

$$.250$$

$$4$$

$$.250$$

FURTHER READING

This introduction has been necessarily brief. For further exploration into using statistical methods in psychology you may find the following useful:

Amos, J. R., F. L. Brown, and O. G. Mink. *Statistical Concepts: A Basic Program.* New York: Harper & Row, 1965. A clear, brief programed text.

Downie, N. M., and R. W. Heath. *Basic Statistical Methods.* New York: Harper & Row, 1970. A popular introductory text.

Dubois, P. H. *An Introduction to Psychological Statistics.* New York: Harper & Row, 1965. Particularly thorough on correlational analysis.

Roscoe, J. T. *Fundamental Research Statistics.* New York: Holt, Rinehart and Winston, 1969. Particularly strong at illustrating relationships between different techniques.

Glossary

Acquired characteristic. A structural or functional modification that occurs as a result of an organism's own activities or through the influence of its environment. Contrasts with an inherited characteristic.

Adaptation. In general, an adaptive process is one appropriate for maintaining an organism's vital processes in a given situation. In discussions of sensation and perception, however, adaptation usually refers to some reduction in sensitivity as a result of steady stimulation.

Amnesia. A partial or complete inability to remember.

Anthropomorphism. Man's tendency to shape the description of animal behavior according to the tastes, biases, and hunches of the human observer. Man might see jealousy, for example, in the behavior of two cats, reaching a conclusion that cannot be verified.

Anxiety. An unpleasant, apprehensive emotion aroused by the recognition of danger. Anxiety is considered to be neurotic if it grows out of all proportion to its realistic justification.

Associationism. A psychological theory, dating from Aristotle, that explains our complicated mental experiences as the product of combinations of simpler mental elements.

Attention. The active selection of certain stimuli or certain aspects of experience, with consequent inhibition of all others.

Auditory nerve. That part of the VIII cranial nerve that transmits neural activity from the auditory receptors in the ear to the central nervous system.

Autonomic nervous system. That part of the nervous system that innervates glands and smooth muscles. It is involved in the regulation of vital homeostatic processes and in the physiological changes that accompany emotions.

Behavior. An extremely complex pattern of responses that may have special meanings for the organism is often called, somewhat loosely, behavior.

Behaviorism. A psychological theory that emphasizes objective, publicly observable events (usually called stimuli and responses), rather than private consciousness, as the subject matter of scientific psychology.

Biofeedback. A recently coined word that describes information about bodily responses after they occur; the information being usable in order to adjust or "tune" further responses. The source may be sensory organs or external signals arranged through electronic means to signal changes in physiological functions which the person is usually unaware of.

Brain waves. Electrical activity of the brain, as recorded in an electroencephalogram.

Cathexis. Psychoanalytic term denoting the investment or concentration of
instinctual energy in some object or idea.

Central nervous system. The brain and spinal cord.

Cognitive. Pertaining to the various psychological processes involved in
knowing.

Cognitive dissonance, theory of. A theory developed by Leon Festinger that
people are motivated to achieved consistency between their attitudes
and their behavior.

Collective unconscious. A concept in Jung's theory that states that there is
psychic material that is inherited and shared with other members of
the species.

Conditioning. A training procedure, usually associated with the name of
I. P. Pavolov, whereby a response is brought under the control of
(made conditional upon the occurrence of) a new stimulus.

Discrimination. An organism is said to be capable of discriminating between
two different stimuli if it can respond differently to them.

Drive. Urge. A condition that impels the organism to become active until
the drive can be reduced. Sometimes used with special emphasis on
the physiological needs of the body, as contrasted with social motives.

Ego. The individual's conception of himself. In the psychoanalytic concept
of personality structure, the term is used to refer to that part of the
mind that controls conscious experience and regulates the interactions
of the person with his environment.

Ego-ideal. Psychoanalytic term denoting one's image of self-perfection.

Electroencephalogram. A record of electrical potentials from the brain, obtained by amplifying and recording the electrical activity picked up
by electrodes applied to the scalp. Popularly called "brain waves."

Emotion. Any experience of strong feeling, usually accompanied by bodily
changes in circulation, breathing, sweating, etc., and often accompanied by tense and impulsive actions. The opposite of calm relaxation.

Empiricism. The empirical method refers to the pursuit of knowledge by
observation and experiment. In psychology, the empiricist theory
emphasizes the importance of perception and learning in the growth
of the mind.

Engram. A modification that is assumed to occur somewhere in the nervous
system as a result of learning and that therefore provides the physiological basis for memory in higher organisms.

Erogenous zones. Areas of the body where stimulation can produce pleasure
and, under appropriate conditions, can arouse sexual reactions.

Evolutionism. Any theory that regards the present state of the world as the
cumulative result of a long series of small steps. The biological version, usually associated with the name of Charles Darwin, holds that
maladaptive variations in the members of a given species will die out
and that advantageous variations will be propagated so the species
will slowly change over the course of many generations.

Fechner's law. A formulation of the relation between stimulus-intensity and sensory magnitude proposed by G. T. Fechner as an extension of Weber's Law: the subjective magnitude of a sensation is measured by the logarithm of the physical magnitude of its stimulus.

Field theory. A contribution of gestalt psychologists that describes a person's behavior as determined by forces in an environment perceived by him in conjunction with characteristics possessed by the person. The whole prediction cannot be created by summing all the parts of the field.

Fixation. Focusing the eyes in such a way that a particular point falls on the fovea. In psychoanalytic theory, fixation refers to the persistence of an unconscious wish for some infantile mode of gratification.

Free association. The spontaneous association of ideas in the absence of any specific purpose or instruction. Insofar as they are able, patients undergoing psychoanalytic therapy are encouraged to associate freely; a block in their revery may signal an emotionally disturbing topic.

Freudian slip. An accident that is not wholly accidental, but that seems to be determined, at least in part, by personal causes unknown to the person who commits it.

Functionalism. In general, any doctrine that emphasizes function, use, adaptation. As a psychological theory, functionalism holds that all mental processes serve an adaptive function for the organism. Often contrasted with structuralism.

Gestalt. A German word, sometimes translated as structure or configuration. As a theory, gestalt psychology emphasizes that organized units, both in perception and in behavior, have characteristic properties that cannot be reduced to the properties of their component parts.

Habit. A response pattern, acquired by learning, that is relatively stable, easily elicited, and hard to get rid of. Most habits are motor acts, but sometimes the term is used more broadly to refer as well to habits of thought.

Hallucinogenic. A family of drugs (also called psychedelic) that produces altered states of consciousness—especially cognitive and perceptual effects—of an unusual nature.

Halo effect. A common source of error in judging people. Because we rate the person high (low) on some particular trait—or hold a favorable (unfavorable) impression of him in general—we are likely to overrate (underrate) him on other traits.

Homeostasis. Steady state. A term introduced by W. B. Cannon, who wrote, "The co-ordinated physiological processes which maintain most of the steady states in the organism are so complex and so peculiar to living beings—involving, as they may, the brain and nerves, the heart, lungs, kidneys, and spleen, all working cooperatively—that I have suggested a special designation for these states, *homeostasis*."

Hypnosis. An induced state of heightened suggestibility.

Hysteria. A psychoneurosis, in which (according to psychoanalytic theory) unacceptable impulses are repressed and unconscious, yet presumably find outlet through bodily symptoms—abnormal sensations, paralysis —that occur without any apparent injury to the nervous system.

Id. In the psychoanalytic concept of personality structure, the id is the deepest, unconscious part of the mind, devoted entirely to pleasure and driven by blind, instinctual impulses.

Identification. An unconscious mental process whereby we can, according to the psychoanalysts, invest our instinctual energies in particular images by adopting them as our own, by identifying ourselves with them.

Imprinting. In ethology, a learning mechanism in which birds form attachments to other organisms or objects. Imprinting occurs early in life during a species' specific critical period; known to be resistant to later modification.

Information theory. A mathematical theory developed by Claude Shannon and Norbert Wiener that enables engineers to measure the average amount of information (in bits/sec) that a communication channel can transmit.

Inhibition. A term broadly used to denote any suppressive interaction between two or more processes, whether in the physiological, behavioral, mental, or social realm.

Ink-blot test. A projective test. The person taking the test describes all of the scenes he recognizes in an ink blot.

Instinct. An organized and often complicated pattern of behavior, characteristic of a given species, that is adaptive in certain environmental situations, but that seems to arise with a relatively small amount of experience and learning.

Instrumentalism. A form of pragmatic philosophy, often associated with the name of John Dewey, that holds ideas to be instruments of action whose usefulness determines their truth. In psychology this doctrine gave rise to functionalism.

Intelligence quotient (IQ). Originally computed as mental age (measured by some suitable intelligence test) divided by chronological age (where, usually, everyone over some given chronological age—say, 16—is considered to be exactly that age), the quotient then being multiplied by 100. IQ is now regarded as a standard score with a mean of 100 and a standard deviation of 16 (or 15 in some tests).

Interval scale of measurement. The type of measurement that is possible when there exist empirical operations for determining whether two intervals along the scale are equal.

Just noticeable difference (jnd). Difference threshold. The smallest difference between two stimuli that can be reliably detected.

Kinesthesia. Sensitivity to movements by parts of the body.

Law of effect. The hypothesis that responses leading to rewards are learned, while those that do not are extinguished.

Learning. Adaptive change in thought or behavior.

Libido. Psychoanalytic term for sexual energy.

Limen. Threshold.

Materialism. The faith that everything in the universe will eventually be explicable in terms of the existence and the properties of matter. In psychology, this faith usually leads to an emphasis on the importance of the body, and especially the nervous system, as the basis for all mental processes.

Memory. The retention of acquired skills or information.

Mentalism. The principle that mental processes are distinct from physiological processes. Derived from introspection; the proper area for psychological analysis according to its adherents. Denounced by behaviorists such as B. F. Skinner.

Mind. A four-letter Anglo Saxon word.

Motivation. Conditions determining persistent and goal-directed activity. Sometimes used with special reference to social goals and incentives, as contrasted with biological drives.

Motor skill. A capacity for proficient performance—prompt, smooth, accurate—of some practiced pattern of movements: walking, talking, driving a car, playing tennis, chipping flints, etc.

Neurology. The branch of biology that studies the nervous system.

Neuron. A nerve cell.

Neurophysiology. The branch of physiology that deals with the functions of the nervous system.

Neurosis. A common abbreviation for psychoneurosis.

Nominal scale of measurement. The type of measurement that is possible when the only empirical operations available are those for determining whether two objects are identical. The "values" assigned are simply names, letters, serial numbers, etc.

Objective. That which exists independent of any conscious experience or personal judgment. Contrasts with subjective.

Operant. A term introduced into discussions of conditioning by B. F. Skinner. It denotes a response that at first may seem to occur spontaneously, but that can, through conditioning, be brought under the control of discriminative stimuli.

Operationism. The doctrine that the meaning of any concept derives from the operations by which it is observed.

Optic nerve. The II cranial nerve that transmits neural activity from the light-sensitive receptors in the retina of the eye to the central nervous system.

Ordinal scale of measurement. The type of measurement that is possible when there exist empirical operations for determining the rank order to be assigned to the measured objects.

Paradigm. A conceptual model or system describing some aspect of reality from which one draws conclusions about how to proceed in doing research.

Perception. The process of becoming aware of objects and relations in the world around us, insofar as that awareness depends on sensory processes.

Perceptual defense. A process by which the nervous system blocks recognition of stimuli that are painful or threatening. A much disputed theory offered to explain low recognition of taboo words.

549

Perceptual-motor. Pertaining to the coordination of skilled movements, guided by previous experience and corrected by perceptual feedback as to their effects.

Personality tests. Any psychological test—there are numerous varieties—that endeavors to provide a basis for classifying people into various personality types.

Phenomenology. The study of objects and events as they are experienced rather than from the view of objectively described reality.

Phobia. A psychoneurotic dread of some particular object or situation.

Phylogenetic scale. A scale showing the development and evolution of biological characteristics specific to a species or group; derived from Darwin's theory of evolution.

Physiological psychology. The branch of psychology that deals with the relation between physiological and psychological processes.

Physiology. That branch of biology that investigates the processes and functions of the living cells, tissues, organs, and organ systems of the body—as distinguished from anatomy, which studies their structure.

Pleasure principle. A psychoanalytic name for the hypothesis that all pleasure results from the satisfaction of instinctual drives: The id is assumed to be dominated by the pleasure principle. Contrasts with reality principle.

Positivistic. An adjective used rather loosely in the nineteenth century to describe any discussion of human beings in the language of natural science. According to Ambrose Bierce, "Its longest exponent is Comte, its broadest Mill, and its thickest Spencer."

Posthypnotic suggestion. A specific order, given during hypnosis, to be obeyed after the hypnotic state has ended.

Power law. A general law of psychophysics (credited to S. S. Stevens) which states that the subjective magnitude of sensation, Ψ, is proportional to the physical magnitude of a stimulus, S, raised to a power, n. $\Psi = \kappa S^n$

Pragmatism. Defined by William James as "the doctrine that the whole *meaning* of a conception expresses itself in its practical consequences." This doctrine became the basis for a highly influential school of American philosophy.

Preconscious. The latent ideas and feelings that are potentially conscious, even though the person may not be aware of them at the moment.

Primacy effect. The name used to refer to a situation in which earlier items of a series are remembered better than later items. Contrasts with recency effect.

Projection. A term used in several loosely related contexts. In discussions of perception, it generally refers to the localization of a perceived object at a distance outside of the body. In social psychology, it is the tendency to asume that other people experience the same ideas and feelings that we do. In psychoanalytic theory, projection is one of several ways the ego can defend itself from anxiety—by attributing a repressed idea to someone else.

Projective test. A personality test, so-called because the person unwittingly projects his own feelings, attitudes, preoccupations, etc., into his perception of some ambiguous picture or situation.

Psychiatry. That branch of medicine dealing with the treatment of psychological disorders and abnormalities.

Psychoanalysis. A system of psychological hypotheses orginated and developed by Sigmund Freud as the basis of his technique for the psychiatric treatment of personality defects, nervous and mental disorders.

Psychogenic disorders. Disorders having their origin in psychological problems or conflicts. Contrasts with somatogenic disorders.

Psychology. The science of mental life, based on evidence obtained through the observation and analysis of one's own behavior and the behavior of others.

Psychometric. Any quantitative technique of scientific psychology, but especially those used in mental testing.

Psychoneurosis. A psychological or physiological disturbance, less severe than psychosis but severe enough to limit the patient's social adjustment and ability to work, usually attributed to some unconscious emotional conflict. Commonly abbreviated as "neurosis."

Psychopathic. A type of personality characterized by an inability to restrain immoral and antisocial impulses.

Psychopathology. The study of psychological disorders and abnormalities.

Psychophysics. In its narrow and traditional sense, which stems from the work of G. T. Fechner, psychophysics in the name for the several methods that are used to measure thresholds. Recently there have been attempts to apply the term more generally to any study of the relations between psychological phenomena and the physical properties of stimuli.

Psychosis. Insanity. A mental illness characterized by cognitive disorders so severe (often including delusions or hallucinations) that social adjustment becomes impossible and the patient must be placed under medical supervision.

Psychotherapy. The treatment of disease by psychological methods.

Ratio scale of measurement. The type of measurement that is possible when there exist empirical operations for determining the natural zero value and for determining whether two ratios of the measured attribute are equal. Ratio scales are more common in physics than in psychology.

Reaction formation. In psychoanalytic theory, reaction formation refers to an unconscious mental process that converts a personality trait or disposition into its exact opposite.

Reality principle. A psychoanalytic term used to describe the functions of the ego in controlling the pleasure-seeking id impulses by postponing their gratification until external difficulties and constraints can be avoided. Contrasts with pleasure principle.

Recency effect. The name used to refer to a situation in which later items of a series are remembered better than earlier items. Contrasts with primacy effect.

Receptor. A specialized cell that is very sensitive to one kind of stimulation and that, when stimulated, initiates neural activity in a sensory nerve.

Recall. In discussions of remembering, recall denotes the arousal of a memory trace. Recall of verbal materials can be tested by asking a person to name or recite the items he has learned earlier.

Recognition. In discussions of remembering, recognition denotes perception accompanied by a feeling of familiarity. Can be tested by asking a person to identify the familiar objects when they are scattered haphazardly among similar but novel objects.

Regression. In statistics, regression is a general term, originated by Francis Galton, to describe the relation between two correlated variables. In psychoanalytic theory, regression is the return to younger stages of personality development.

Reinforcement. Strengthening. In discussions of conditioning, a reinforcement is any outcome of an act that tends to increase the likelihood of that act under similar circumstances in the future.

Repression. In psychoanalytic theory, repression is the involuntary rejection of any conscious awareness of a sexual or hostile impulse.

Reproduction. In discussions of remembering, reproduction denotes a particular method of testing memory by asking the person to duplicate, orally or graphically, some previously learned pattern of behavior.

Response. Any pattern of glandular secretions and muscular contractions resulting from activity that arises in the nervous system as a result of a stimulus.

Self-actualization. The process of fulfilling one's potentials; or the state resulting from that fulfillment. An idea put forth by Abraham Maslow. Self-actualization results from the satisfaction of higher needs.

Sensation. The process of sensing, considered abstractly without concern for the stimulus object responsible for the experience.

Sign. A stimulus that can stand for or suggest something that is not itself present as a stimulus.

Signal. A sign that is not a symbol.

Signal detection theory. An alternative theory of the sensory threshold that argues that perception results from the sensitivity of the receptor mechanism and the attitude or motivation of the observer. Using two separate measures (sensitivity and attitude) the theory specifies that the observer chooses a criterion to test a hypothesis, that a low energy signal is present or not present.

Situation. An extremely complex stimulus object that may have special meanings for the organism is often called, somewhat loosely, a situation.

Smooth muscles. Found in the walls of the internal organs and blood vessels, and innervated by the automatic nervous system; so-called because, in contrast to skeletal muscles, they have a smooth, unstriped appearance.

Social desirability variable. On personality questionnaires, the tendency some people have to give those answers that seem socially most acceptable and commendable.

Social psychology. That branch of psychology that treats of the relation between the individual and his social environment.

Somatogenic disorders. Disorders having their origin in physiological (bodily) abnormalities. Contrasted with psychogenic disorders.

Somesthesia. Bodily sensations, both external (touch) and internal.

Stimulus. Any change in energy that causes an excitation of the nervous system leading to a response.

Stimulus generalization. In discussions of conditioning, stimulus generalization is said to occur when a response that has been conditioned to one particular stimulus is also observed in the presence of different (but usually similar) stimuli.

Stimulus object. Any object that is the source of a stimulus. Often referred to loosely as if it were the stimulus itself.

Stimulus-response (S-R) theory. The theory that all psychological phenomena can be described in terms of stimuli and responses and the correlations between them.

Structuralism. In general, any doctrine that emphasizes structure, form, composition, rather than function. As a psychological theory, structuralism tries to describe the anatomy of conscious experience, to identify mental elements and to state the laws governing their integration. Often contrasted with functionalism.

Subjective. That which exists only by virtue of conscious experience. Contrasts with objective.

Sublimation. In psychoanalytic theory, sublimation is an unconscious process whereby a sexual desire is desexualized and used to motivate art, work, play.

Subliminal. Below the threshold.

Superego. In the psychoanalytic concept of personality structure, the superego includes those prohibitions and ideals—largely unconscious—that comprise the moral and judicial aspects of personality.

Supraliminal. Above the threshold.

Symbol. A meaningful sign, one of a system of related signs whose uses are governed by rules.

Symbolic knowledge. Knowledge that can be expressed in symbols and communicated to other people.

Synapse. The region of contact between neurons in chain.

Tachistoscope. An instrument to present visual stimuli for very short periods of time, usually so short that their appearance and disappearance seem instantaneous.

Territoriality. A hypothesized need state, describing an animal's need for territory based on the observation of territorial battles in the wild among some animals.

Threshold. A statistically determined boundary point on a stimulus scale, where one variety of experience changes into another. The absolute threshold is the boundary separating what we can perceive from what we cannot. The difference threshold is the smallest stimulus change that produces a noticeable difference in perception.

Unconscious. An adjective applied to any mental process whose operation can be inferred from a person's behavior, but of which the person himself remains unaware and which he is unable to report or discuss. "The unconscious," according to Sigmund Freud, "is the true psychical reality; in its innermost nature it is as much unknown to us as the reality of the external world, and it is as incompletely presented by the data of consciousness as is the external world by the communications of our sense organs."

Visual field. The more-or-less oval-shaped scene that we can experience visually when our eyes are immobile and fixed on some given point; correlated roughly with the momentary pattern of stimulation on the retina. Sometimes contrasted with the visual world, which is not bounded and which remains stable even when eye or head movements cause the visual field to change.

Weber's law. According to H. C. Warren, *Dictionary of Psychology* (Boston: Houghton Mifflin, 1934), Weber's Law is a formulation of the relation between changes in stimulus-intensity and perception, devised by E. H. Weber, and expressed as follows: "The just perceptible difference of sensation occurs when the stimulus is increased (or decreased) by a certain proportion of itself, that proportion being constant for any given sense." Further experimentation has indicated that the law is only approximately true. The name was suggested by G. T. Fechner; cf. Fechner's Law.

Index

73 74 75 76 77 9 8 7 6 5 4 3 2 1